Praise for
The Last Empire

Sunday Telegraph **Best History Books 2014**

Evening Standard **Bestseller (UK)**

BBC History Magazine **Best History Books of 2014**

"Using recently released documents, Plokhy traces in fascinating detail the complex events that led to the Soviet Union's implosion."—*Foreign Affairs*

"A fine-grained, closely reported, highly readable account of the upheavals of 1991."—*Financial Times*

"What elevates *The Last Empire* from solid history to the must-read shelf is its relevance to the current crisis."—**Wall Street Journal**

"Serhii Plokhy's extraordinarily well-timed new book…makes a convincing case that contrary to the triumphalist American narrative of Cold War victory, or the more recent paranoid Russian narrative of Cold War defeat, the U.S. never anticipated the breakup of the Soviet Union—in fact, the U.S. tried to use what little influence it had over the situation to prevent it. . . Plokhy makes a convincing case that the misplaced triumphalism of the senior Bush's administration led to the disastrous hubris of his son's."—*Slate*

"A fascinating and readable deep dive into the final half-year of the Soviet Union." — *Sunday Telegraph* (UK)

"A superb work of scholarship, vividly written, that challenges tired old assumptions with fresh material from East and West, as well as revealing interviews with many major players."—*Spectator* (UK)

"An incisive account of the five months leading up to the Union's dissolution. . . . His vibrant, fast-paced narrative style captures the story superbly."—*Sunday Times* (UK)

"Our memories of the upheavals of 1989-91 blur into one picture, with the Soviet collapse indistinguishable from the fall of the Berlin Wall, the death of communism and the end of the Cold War. Now along comes Serhii Plohky…to bring

part of that historical blur into focus in a day-by-day account of the Soviet empire's final five months. . . . Plokhy's account of the coup is a riveting thriller."
—*Mail on Sunday* (UK)

"Almost a day-by-day, blow-by-blow account of the actions and reactions of the main figures. . . . Very relevant to today's Ukrainian crisis…very well recounted."—*Literary Review* (UK)

"Serhii Plokhy's great achievement in this wonderfully well-written account is to show that much of the triumphalist transatlantic view of the Soviet collapse is historiographical manure."—*Times of London* (UK)

"Plokhy does a good job of debunking much of the conventional wisdom, especially prevalent in the United States, about the American role in the break-up of the Soviet Union…. His setting the record straight is also of more than historiographical significance."—*Times Literary Supplement*

"Especially provocative given current affairs, this book doesn't dismiss U.S. Cold War policy's contributions but contends the USSR fell mainly because of its imperial nature, ethnic mix and political structure, with the inability of Russia and Ukraine, the biggest Soviet republics, to agree on continuing unity as the straw that broke the Soviet camel's back."—*Pittsburg Tribune-Review*

"A meticulously documented chronicle of the evil empire's demise…. [Plokhy] is the voice Ukrainians have been yearning for."—*Ukrainian Weekly*

"Serhii Plokhy…has written the best account yet of the Soviet collapse. Focusing on the fateful months from July to December 1991, Plokhy's narrative challenges several prevailing interpretations about the U.S.S.R.'s demise. *The Last Empire* places events in Ukraine and other republics at the center of the drama. Plokhy's study is a must-read and at times a gripping page-turner, particularly when describing the August coup attempt against Gorbachev and the December events that brought an end to Soviet communism."—*The Moscow Times*

"Tragedy or not, the process of the Soviet collapse is meticulously chronicled by Serhii Plokhy…in a work that develops new interpretations and challenges some conventional thinking. Plokhy has written a challenging revisionist narrative that attributes the demise of the Soviet Union to its political structure, rather than to American policy."—*Winnipeg Free Press*

"The story of the USSR's final months, from the failed coup in August 1991 by Soviet hardliners to Gorbachev's resignation on Christmas Day 1991, has been told before, but never so vividly or with such trenchant analysis as in *The Last Empire*…. Although this book was written before the Ukrainian crisis of recent months, it must be required reading for anyone wishing to understand its historical roots and its potential impact both on Ukraine and on Russia itself." —*Times Higher Education*

"With Crimea annexed and eastern Ukraine starting to break away to Russia, *The Last Empire* may be the most timely book of the year." —*National Review*

"In his magisterial book, *The Last Empire: The Final Days of the Soviet Union*, published earlier this year, Professor Serhii Plokhy of Harvard University has documented a surprising facet of US policy. Contrary to the gung-ho, 'we won the Cold War' proclamations that emanated after the red flag was lowered for the last time in the Kremlin on December 25, 1991, the reality was that the George Bush administration tried quite hard to preserve the Soviet Union in the face of the pro-independence impulses of the Soviet Republics, notably Russia, Ukraine and Belarus." —*The Asian Age* (India)

"Plokhy's cleanly written narrative presents a clear view of the complex events and numerous parties involved in the Soviet Union's demise as well as the reasons that the Soviet government could not ultimately rein in Ukrainian and Russian national movements. VERDICT: Plokhy's fine scholarship should be set alongside such great works as David Remnick's *Lenin's Tomb* and Vladislav M. Zubok's *A Failed Empire*. An excellent text for historians, students of current events, and anyone fascinated with political intrigue." —*Library Journal*, **Starred Review**

"One of a rare breed: a well-balanced, unbiased book written on the fall of Soviet Union that emphasizes expert research and analysis." —*Publishers Weekly*

"[Plokhy] provides fascinating details (especially concerning Ukraine) about this fraught, historic time." —*Kirkus*

"Serhii Plokhy's fine book combines a colorful, fast-paced narrative with trenchant analysis of key players in the Soviet collapse: Gorbachev and Yeltsin battling each other to the bitter end; President George H. W. Bush encouraging the former 'evil empire' to stay together, while unintentionally facilitating its demise; Ukrainians' all-out push for independence turning out to be the coup de grace. By far our best account yet of the death spiral of the USSR." —**William Taubman, Pulitzer Prize-winning author of *Khrushchev: The Man and His Era***

"At last, a definitive account of the breakup of the USSR: for the first time, Serhii Plokhy tells the story not just from the point of view of Moscow, and not from Washington, but also from Kiev and the other republics where many of the most important decisions were actually made. If you don't understand what really happened in 1991, and if you don't remember the roles played by the former

Soviet republics, then you'll find it impossible to understand the politics of the region today. This book usefully eviscerates some of the remaining mythology about the end of the Cold War, and is an indispensable guide to the tensions and rivalries of the present."—**Anne Applebaum, Pulitzer Prize-winning author of** *Gulag: A History*

"Serhii Plokhy's dramatic account of the high politics behind the collapse of the Soviet Union could not be more timely. Serhii Plokhy examines the choices, fears, personal conflicts and geopolitical delusions of the principal actors in the drama in the US and across the republics of the disintegrating USSR. While the world was spared a nuclear apocalypse, the seeds of new tragedies were sown. As Serhii Plokhy sees it, the mistaken belief that the US had 'won the Cold War' led directly to the hubris of the Iraq invasion of 2003. Now, in the context of what many see as a new Cold War between Russia and the West, it is crucial that we understand what really happened in 1991. *The Last Empire* is a brilliant work of political narrative: vivid, original, urgent and, above all, wise."—**Rachel Polonsky, author of** *Molotov's Magic Lantern: Travels in Russian History*

"Serhii Plokhy's masterful book provocatively places Ukrainian independence as the central factor in the Soviet Union's collapse. Gripping reading, full of surprises and revelations for everyone, especially on the American role in this revolutionary event."—**Vladislav Zubok, Professor at the London School of Economics**

"'In this highly original reanalysis, drawing on rarely used sources scattered from Texas to Ukraine, Serhii Plokhy gives us a whole new perspective on the Fall of the Soviet Union. Did the USA really 'win' the Cold War, he asks—or did democracy undo the Soviet Empire from the inside?"—**Ian Morris, Professor of History at Stanford University and author of** *Why the West Rules— For Now*

"Gripping, vivid and incisive—essential reading for anyone wanting to counter modern Russian myth-making about the Soviet collapse."—**Edward Lucas, senior editor at the** *Economist and author of The New Cold War*

"A masterful account of the end of the Soviet Union. The narrative tale alone, enriched by reams of new evidence, makes it well worth reading for anyone interested in the making of the contemporary world. But *The Last Empire* is equally notable for its penetrating analysis. It is particularly revealing on the contradictions built into US policy and on the contributions to the outcome of the many nations of the USSR, including the Ukrainians, whose pivotal role has often been neglected in previous studies."—**Timothy Colton, Professor of Government at Harvard University and author of** *Yeltsin: A Life*

THE LAST EMPIRE

THE LAST
EMPIRE

The Final Days
of the Soviet Union

SERHII PLOKHY

BASIC BOOKS
A MEMBER OF THE PERSEUS BOOKS GROUP
New York

Published by Basic Books,
A Member of the Perseus Books Group
First paperback edition published in 2015 by Basic Books

Books published by Basic Books are available at special discounts for bulk
purchases in the United States by corporations, institutions, and other
organizations. For more information, please contact the Special Markets
Department at the Perseus Books Group, 2300 Chestnut Street, Suite 200,
Philadelphia, PA 19103, or call (800) 810-4145, ext. 5000, or e-mail special
.markets@perseusbooks.com.

Book design by Cynthia Young

A CIP catalog record for this book is available from the Library of Congress.
ISBN: 978-0-465-05696-5 (hardcover)
ISBN: 978-0-465-04671-3 (paperback)
ISBN: 978-0-465-06199-0 (e-book)

Printing 3, 2021

*To the children
of empires who set
themselves free*

Contents

"Empire Strikes Back":
A Foreword to the Paperback Edition

THE LAST EMPIRE, released in May 2014, hit the bookshelves at the height of what is now considered the worst international crisis since the end of the Cold War—a conflict between two post-Soviet states, Russia and Ukraine, which has had major global consequences. As the book received its first reviews, the crisis kept growing, spreading from the Crimea to the Donbas region of eastern Ukraine and claiming not only thousands of lives of local civilians but also close to three hundred innocent lives of the passengers and crew of Malaysia Airlines Flight MH 17, shot down by pro-Russian rebels on its way from Amsterdam to Kuala Lumpur on July 17, 2014. Why and how that could happen, and what had given rise to the Russo-Ukrainian crisis, were the questions on the minds of those who picked up *The Last Empire* in bookstores in the summer of 2014 and those who reviewed it for media outlets in the United States, Britain, and the Netherlands. (The title of this foreword comes from a reviewer's suggestion in the British *Mail on Sunday*). The book, written as a work of history, was often treated as a guide to events unfolding in Eastern Europe. Indeed, what the world watched in the Crimea and eastern Ukraine in the spring and summer of 2014 was a sequel to the dramatic disintegration of the Soviet Union twenty-three years earlier.

In 2014, the old Soviet empire that had disappeared from the map of the world struck back as the Russian leadership decided to use its newly acquired economic and military might to rewrite the history of the Soviet collapse. Vladimir Putin, who has never concealed his regret and even bitterness about the fall of the Soviet Union, referred specifically to the Soviet collapse in a speech delivered on the occasion of the Russian annexation of the Crimea in March 2014. "The Soviet Union fell apart. Things developed so swiftly that few people realized how truly dramatic those events and their consequences would be," said Putin, recalling the events of 1991. "It was only when the Crimea ended up as part of a different country that Russia realized that it had not only been robbed but plundered." He continued: "And what about the Russian state? What about Russia? It humbly accepted the situation. This country was going through such hard times then that, realistically, it was incapable of defending its interests." Putin's speech was meant to remove all doubt that the "hard times" were over and that Russia was back, prepared to undo the "injustice" inflicted on it by the disintegration of the USSR.

What exactly that would mean, and how far Russia was prepared to go in order to undo perceived injustice, was the question on the minds of many world leaders. After a telephone conversation with Putin, Chancellor Angela Merkel of Germany said in apparent disbelief that he was living "in another world." The former American president, Bill Clinton, provided clarification of what world that was, suggesting that Putin wanted to reestablish Russian greatness in nineteenth-century terms. Prime Minister Arsenii Yatseniuk of Ukraine repeatedly accused Putin of wanting to restore the Soviet Union. The Russian president denied the charges, stating that he was not trying to bring back either the empire or the USSR. Technically, he was right. During the past decade, Russia has been waging open and hybrid wars, annexing territories, and using its virtual monopoly on energy supplies to the countries of Eastern Europe as a weapon, the object being to establish a much less costly and more flexible system of political control over post-Soviet space than was available either to the Russian Empire or to the Soviet Union. Yet many policies of the present-day Russian leadership have their origins in the last years and months of the existence of the USSR.

By far the most important of those policies has been the Russian leadership's early decision to maintain Moscow's political, economic, and military control over the "near abroad," as the Russian political elite and media dubbed the former Soviet republics. As early as the fall of 1991, advisers to Boris Yeltsin envisioned Russia gathering in the republics on its borders within the subsequent twenty years. Like many other former imperial powers, Russia opted out of the empire because it lacked the resources to keep the costly imperial project going. Unlike most of its counterparts, however, it took along the rich oil and gas resources of the empire—most of the Soviet oil and gas reserves were located in Russian Siberia. Thus Russia had more to gain economically than to lose from the collapse of the USSR. Russian control over oil and gas resources made the divorce with the empire in 1991 easier in economic terms and prevented armed conflict between Russia and the republics that declared independence. We now know that such conflict was not eliminated but merely postponed. Over the last decade, rising oil and gas prices have made it possible for Russia to rebuild its economic potential and military might, allowing it to reopen the question of disputed borders and territories, and step up its efforts to gather back the Soviet republics more than twenty years after the Soviet collapse.

Ukraine, the second-largest post-Soviet republic, has played a crucial role in preventing successive Russian attempts to reintegrate the "near abroad" in economic, military, and political terms. Back in 1991, Russo-Ukrainian relations were the key factor in deciding the future of the Soviet Union. In August 1991, once the Ukrainian parliament declared the republic's independence, the Russian government of Boris Yeltsin threatened Kyiv with partitioning of its territory. Fingers were pointed specifically at the Crimea and the Donbas, which became a battleground twenty-three years later. Despite threats from Moscow, Ukraine pushed forward with its quest for independence, and in December 1991 the Soviet Union was replaced by the Commonwealth of Independent States, which was the result of a Russo-Ukrainian compromise. In his speech on the annexation of the Crimea, Putin claimed that many in Russia regarded the Commonwealth as a new form of statehood. But that was not the position of the Ukrainian leadership, which took its own independence and that of the other Soviet republics with the utmost seriousness.

In the 1990s, Ukraine turned the Commonwealth into an instrument for a "civilized divorce"—a term coined in Kyiv—as opposed to one for Russian control over the "near abroad." Ukraine worked hard to ensure recognition of its borders by Russia. In 1994, Kyiv gave up its nuclear arsenal in exchange for "assurances" of territorial integrity and independence given by Russia, the United States, and Great

Britain. In 1997, the Ukrainian government agreed to lease the naval base in Sevastopol to the Russian fleet in exchange for a treaty that recognized the inviolability of Ukrainian borders. It took the Russian parliament two years to ratify the treaty that formally recognized the Crimea and Sevastopol as integral parts of Ukrainian territory. It seemed that the two countries had finally resolved all outstanding issues in their relations resulting from the Soviet collapse.

The next decade demonstrated the limits of the Russo-Ukrainian understanding and the degree to which Russia was prepared to recognize Ukraine as an independent state. In the late 1990s, Ukraine began its drift toward the West, declaring integration into the European Union as the goal of its foreign policy and refusing to join Russia-led economic, military, and political institutions. Domestically, Ukraine managed to remain a much more pluralistic society than Russia, with a strong parliament, competitive politics, and an influential opposition. In 2004, Ukrainian civil society refused to accept the results of a rigged election and endorse the Russian-backed candidate, Viktor Yanukovych, as the country's new president. After a long and peaceful protest that became known as the Orange Revolution, the outgoing president of Ukraine agreed to a new round of elections that brought to power a pro-Western candidate, Viktor Yushchenko. From that time on, Moscow treated Kyiv's orientation on the West not only as a growing external danger but also as a threat to its own increasingly authoritarian regime. As far as the Kremlin was concerned, Ukraine's rejection of rigged elections and resistance to a corrupt regime was setting an example to Russia's own struggling civil society and had to be stopped at all costs.

The current crisis in Russo-Ukrainian relations began on the night of November 21, 2013 with a Facebook post by a Ukrainian journalist of Afghan descent, Mustafa Nayem. He was disturbed by news that the government of Viktor Yanukovych, who had come to power in 2010, had refused to sign a long-awaited association agreement with the European Union. "Fine," wrote Nayem in his Facebook account, "Let's be serious. Who is ready to show up on the Maidan by midnight tonight? Curses will be ignored. Only comments on this post with the words 'I'm ready.'" There were six hundred "I'm ready" responses. At 9:30 p.m., Nayem typed another post: "Dress warmly, bring umbrellas, tea, coffee, a good mood, and friends." Shortly after 10:00 p.m., he was on Kyiv's central square, known in Ukrainian as the Maidan, where the Orange Revolution had begun ten years earlier. About thirty people had gathered by the time he arrived. By midnight, there were more than a thousand young, educated urbanites. For them, the expected association agreement with the EU was the last hope that Ukraine might finally embark on a European course of development, overcome corruption, modernize its economy, and provide a decent standard of living for its people. Now, those hopes were being crushed. Nayem and his friends could not remain silent.

The protest began like a festival, with singing and dancing to brave the cold weather of late November. It soon became known as the Euromaidan—the largest pro-European rally in history. President Yanukovych, for his part, had learned from the Orange Revolution of 2004 that the sooner one got rid of protesters, the better. Thus, in the early hours of November 30, riot police were ordered to attack the students camping on the Maidan. They did so with the utmost brutality under the pretext of clearing the square to allow the construction of a huge Christmas tree in preparation for New Year celebrations that were still one month away. Once images of police beating unarmed students were posted on the Internet, dormant Ukrainian civil society reacted sharply. The next day was Sunday, and more than half a million people showed up in downtown Kyiv to protest police brutality. The Euromaidan, which had begun with protests against the postponement of the signing of the EU association agreement, turned into what became known as the Revolution of Dignity. Hundreds of thousands of people would join the protests that continued through December 2013 into January and February 2014.

With the United States and EU countries applying pressure on President Yanukovych for a peaceful resolution of the crisis, Yanukovych turned to Russia. Ever since his election in 2010, the Kremlin had wanted him to stop Ukraine's drift toward the West, refuse to sign the association agreement with the EU, and join the Russia-led customs union whose members included Belarus and Kazakhstan. Yanukovych was at first reluctant to do so, but the Kremlin raised the stakes by starting a trade war with Ukraine in the summer of 2013. In November, Yanukovych gave up. He refused to sign the agreement with the EU and went to Russia instead to negotiate a US $15 billion loan needed to keep his kleptocratic government afloat until the next presidential elections, which were scheduled for 2015. The Russian government granted the loan and delivered the first installment. The task now was to keep Yanukovych in power, and the Kremlin thought it could best be done by suppressing the Maidan protests—an option advocated publicly by Putin's adviser Sergei Glazev. In January 2014, as protests continued, Yanukovych forced laws through parliament allowing him to do just that. But the new laws, condemned by the opposition as draconian, only brought more people onto the streets.

Clashes between protesters and police began in late January, reaching their peak on February 18, 2014, when dozens of protesters and policemen were killed by gunfire. The Ukrainian government would subsequently claim that the fire was opened by the Russian snipers, who were coordinated by one of the aids to the Russian president. Those killed by the snipers, and hired thugs became known as the "heavenly hundred." The European Union imposed sanctions, including travel bans and asset freezes, on members of the Ukrainian government responsible for the use of force against the protesters. The Ukrainian parliament, dominated by big-business oligarchs who did not want to lose access to money stashed in Western banks, passed a resolution prohibiting the government from using force against citizens. That was the end of the Yanukovych regime, which could not survive without reliance on brute force. On February 21, 2014, EU delegates led by the Polish minister of foreign affairs, Radosław Sikorski, negotiated a deal between Yanukovych and the leaders of the opposition. One of its conditions was a new presidential election before the end of the year. But Yanukovych, who had no illusions about its outcome, fled his mansion near Kyiv the same night, taking reportedly hundreds of millions of dollars and leaving behind a private zoo and a fleet of vintage cars. Next day the parliament voted to remove him from office. He drove with his bodyguards to the Crimea, and made way to the Russian Federation, where he was granted citizenship.

The Russian government was extremely displeased with the turn of events in Kyiv. On February 21, the Russian representative at the negotiations conducted by Sikorski refused to sign the agreement on behalf of his state, but after Yanukovych fled Kyiv, Moscow accused the West and the Ukrainian opposition of not honoring the agreement. It declared the Kyiv events a coup and branded the new Ukrainian government unconstitutional. As the world watched the closing ceremonies of the Sochi winter Olympic games on February 23, 2014, the corridors of European foreign ministries were rife with speculation about what Russia might do once the games were over. The answer came on February 27, four days after the end of the Olympics. That day Yanukovych, now safe on Russian territory, issued a statement claiming to be the legitimate president of Ukraine, and a detachment of "polite green men"—heavily armed special-forces personnel in unmarked uniforms—seized the buildings of the Supreme Council and government of the Crimea and flew Russian flags atop both centers of power.

On the same day, with the "green men" firmly in control, the Crimean parliament held a closed session that lacked a quorum, according to numerous reports, and dissolved the Crimean government. As the new prime minister, it appointed Sergei Aksenov, the leader of the Russian Unity Party, which had obtained only 4 percent of the vote in the Crimean parliamentary elections. On March 1, Aksenov appealed to Vladimir Putin to help ensure "peace and order" on the peninsula. The next day, Russian military units moved out of their barracks in Sevastopol and, with the support of troops brought from Russia, seized control of the Crimea. They were assisted by specially trained groups of Russian Cossacks and mercenaries from Russia, as well as local militias. Vladimir Putin and the members of his government, who had originally denied allegations of Russian military intervention in the Crimea, eventually admitted the participation of the Russian military in its takeover.

The Russian annexation of the Crimea was given a veneer of legitimacy by a referendum hastily organized on March 16, 2014. Officials declared that more than 83 percent of eligible voters had taken part in the referendum, with close to 97 percent voting in favor of joining Russia. Unofficial reports, including those from the Human Rights Council subordinate to the Russian president, cut both numbers almost in half, estimating the turnout at under 40 percent and the vote for joining Russia at under 60 percent. Those figures find support in a poll conducted in the Crimea in February 2014, when not many more than 40 percent of those polled were in favor of joining Russia. But the new authorities clearly did not want to take any risks and went for outright falsification. In the city of Sevastopol, they reported a turnout that amounted to 123 percent of registered voters. The referendum was boycotted by the 250,000-strong Crimean Tatar community and declared illegal by the government of Ukraine. Its results were not recognized by the international community. But on March 18, Russia officially annexed the peninsula. In his speech on the occasion, Vladimir Putin claimed that the Crimean referendum had been held "in full compliance with democratic procedures and international norms."

It turned out that the annexation of the Crimea was just the beginning of Russian aggression against Ukraine. In April, veterans of the Crimean campaign from the ranks of the Russian Cossacks, nationalist activists, and undercover intelligence officers moved from the Crimea to the cities and towns of southern and eastern Ukraine. Their targets were government administration buildings, as well as headquarters of police and security services in the cities of Kharkiv, Luhansk, Donetsk, Mykolaiv, and Odesa, as well as in the smaller towns of southeastern Ukraine. The goal, many believe, was to proclaim a number of separatist republics that would then unite as one Russia-backed state of Novorossiia, or New Russia—the name originally used for one of the imperial provinces in southern Ukraine after the Russian annexation of the Crimea in the late eighteenth century. Participants in anti-government rallies were often bussed across the border from Russia and the Russian-controlled Transnistria region of Moldova.

The new revolutionary government in Kyiv was completely unprepared to deal with the Russian annexation of the Crimea and the hybrid war that the Kremlin had begun in the eastern Ukrainian Donbas (Donets Basin). For months, the leaders of the new government had led the opposition in its street war against the police and now could not rely on its support in dealing with the foreign-inspired insurgency. In fact, many policemen joined the Russian mercenaries and the local rebels. The Ukrainian army was virtually non-existent. It was in transition from a conscript army to a professional one, severely underfunded, with no combat experience. The Russians had been fighting their war in Chechnia since 1991, and the Ukrainians were no match for the well-trained Russian regular troops and special forces. It soon turned out they had major problems in dealing even with Russian-trained local militias. The troops originally could not bring themselves to shoot at paramilitaries who were firing on them and taking over their barracks and equipment.

Kyiv began to put its act together only in mid-April. It was then that one of the leaders of the Maidan protests and the new minister of the interior, Arsen Avakov, managed to reclaim the regional administration building in his native Kharkiv, and Igor Kolomoisky, a Ukrainian oligarch, returned from de facto exile in Switzerland to lead the government of his native Dnipropetrovsk region. Avakov, an ethnic Armenian, and Kolomoisky, an ethnic Jew, emerged as the "saviors" of Ukraine from the Russian hybrid-war offensive, dispelling the myth of the nationalist or even fascist leanings of the new government in Kyiv and its supporters disseminated by Russian propaganda. By mid-May, it was clear that the Russian attempt to raise a revolt throughout southeastern Ukraine and create Novorossiia, a state that would divide Ukraine in half and provide the Russian government with land access to the Crimea and Transnistria, had failed.

The Russian strategists of the hybrid war were much more successful in the Donbas industrial region on Ukraine's eastern border with Russia, where Russian-backed separatists declared the formation of the Luhansk and Donetsk People's Republics. On April 12, armed men led by Igor Girkin (nom de guerre Strelkov), a former colonel in the Russian Federal Security Service and a veteran of the Yugoslav wars of the 1990s, seized the government and police headquarters in the city of Sloviansk in the northeastern Donbas. By the end of the month, militias led by the former Russian intelligence officers and reinforced by Cossacks, volunteers, and Chechen fighters brought in from Russia and funded with Russian money had seized administrative buildings in most cities and towns of the region, including its two major centers, the cities of Luhansk and Donetsk. They also seized radio and television stations, cutting off Ukrainian channels and bombarding listeners and viewers with misinformation about the new Kyiv government, which was called a "fascist junta," and its plans, which allegedly included the desire to ban the Russian language in the region. Viewers and listeners were promised Russian salaries and pensions, which were significantly higher than those in Ukraine, and citizenship either in Russia or in the new state of Novorossiia, which would include a good half of Ukraine.

The propaganda was effective: significant numbers of unemployed and semi- employed youth joined the rebel militias, where they were paid for their services. The resistance of the pro-Kyiv activists was crushed, and some of them were kidnapped and killed, while help from Kyiv failed to arrive. There were several reasons why the covert Russian invasion met little resistance in the Donbas. A major industrial powerhouse in Soviet times, it had become an economically depressed area with the switch from a command economy to the market after 1991. Like cities in rust belts throughout the world, Donetsk became a criminal capital. Many of its new elites had criminal backgrounds or connections, with the region's best-known politician, Viktor Yanukovych, having served two prison sentences in his youth. While dependent on subsidies from Kyiv, the region had a strong sense of local pride and identity. Its ethnic composition differed from that of neighboring regions of Ukraine, as ethnic Russians constituted pluralities in Donetsk and some other towns of the area. In 2001, only 24 percent of the inhabitants of Donetsk oblast and 30 percent of those in Luhansk oblast gave Ukrainian as their native language, as compared with 67 percent in neighboring Dnipropetrovsk oblast. Although ethnic Ukrainians made up 47 percent of the population of Donetsk, only 27 percent of the city's children received their education in Ukrainian. Russian was the dominant language on the streets of the Donbas, and the local elites exploited that fact to mobilize their electorate, claiming that the new Kyiv government was a threat to the Russian language.

Despite their strong sense of local identity, in early April 2014 85 percent of Donetsk residents were opposed to the seizure of government buildings and installations by militias, and more than 60 percent favored the arrest of separatist activists. But the local political and business elites refused to act against the Russia-led insurgents. They either remained neutral or even tacitly supported the protests in the hope that the new government in Kyiv would be more willing to make a deal with them if the region was in turmoil. It was a short-sighted tactic. They would soon lose control over the rapidly developing crisis. As the leaders of the Russian-inspired and funded insurgency took a page from the local elite's playbook and used the theme of protecting the allegedly threatened Russian language and culture, the region's political and business elites decided to go with the flow. In the local referendum that took place on May 11, 2014 and was not recognized by Kyiv, voters were asked whether they supported the *samostoiatel'nost'* of the republic—a term that could mean either autonomy or independence. The leaders of the Donetsk republic declared that 89 percent of voters favored independence, and the corresponding figure in Luhansk was 96 percent, but these figures were as fraudulent as the ones released in the Crimean referendum, and many of those who voted later claimed that they wanted broad autonomy, not independence. The referendum took place without the presence of international observers and was not recognized by the international community.

The Ukrainian government launched a counteroffensive against the separatist takeover of the Donbas in mid-April, without apparent success until after the presidential election of May 25. It brought to power one of the leaders of the Euromaidan protests, Ukrainian business tycoon Petro Poroshenko, who won more than half the vote in the first round. On May 26, the Ukrainian army recaptured the Donetsk international airport; on June 13, it took control of the port city of Mariupol on the Azov Sea; and on July 5, it took the city of Sloviansk, forcing the units of Colonel Igor Girkin, who by then had declared himself defence minister of the Donetsk People's Republic, to retreat to Donetsk. With the Ukrainian forces on the offensive, Russia increased its support for the separatist insurgents, now led by two Russian citizens with close links to the Russian government and security services—Colonel Girkin and the self-proclaimed prime minister of the Donetsk People's Republic, Aleksandr Borodai. In the second half of June, the Ukrainian government claimed and NATO intelligence confirmed the continuing influx from Russia to Ukraine not only of trained militants but also of heavy military equipment, including tanks and multiple rocket launchers.

On July 17, 2014, the war in eastern Ukraine became truly international as Russia-backed separatists shot down Malaysian Airlines Flight MH 17, killing all 298 people on board. The destruction of a civilian airliner produced a flood of protests throughout the world, forcing US and EU leaders to step up sanctions against Russian political and business elites associated with the undeclared war against Ukraine. But sanctions, which have an impact over time, had no immediate effect on Russian behaviour. If anything, Russia increased its involvement in Ukraine. In July, Russian artillery and missiles began bombarding Ukrainian territory from the Russian side of the border, and in August regular units of the Russian army crossed the border not just to reinforce Russian mercenaries and local militias but also to take the lead in fighting the Ukrainian armed forces and volunteer battalions. Thousands of Russian regular troops took part in the offensive launched by the separatists during the last week of August 2014. Some of them were captured by the Ukrainian military and paraded before television cameras as proof of Russia's invasion of Ukraine. By sending regular troops into a battle previously fought under the command of Russian military officers and with Russian equipment, Moscow stopped the Ukrainian advance and saved the self-proclaimed Luhansk and Donetsk republics from imminent defeat. In early September 2014, with the participation of Russia and the Organization for Security and Cooperation in Europe (OSCE), the two sides signed an agreement that resulted in a shaky ceasefire, which was violated more than once and saw the Russia-backed rebels seizing more territories from the Ukrainian government.

What should be expected next? The Russian Empire, the Soviet Union, and then post-Soviet Russia all associated international power and security with control over territories along their borders. If they could not control such territories completely, they would partition them and control what they could. This was the rationale behind the partitions of Poland in the second half of the eighteenth century and the division of Germany after World War II. The "New Russia" project launched by the Russian government in 2014 had as its primary goal the partitioning of Ukraine and the creation of a Russian-controlled state in the southern and eastern parts of the country. That project failed, as Russia managed to destabilize and control only a small part of the projected state of New Russia. While the Crimea was annexed right away, the Russian invasion of the Donbas created conditions for the establishment of another enclave of "frozen conflict" unrecognized by the rest of the world, not unlike Transnistria on the territory of Moldova and Southern Ossetia and Abkhazia on the territory of Georgia. These enclaves are used to apply pressure to Western-leaning republics. Chances are that this will be the primary function of the new frozen-conflict area in eastern Ukraine.

Many in Russia and around the world believe that the crisis is far from over, mainly because Vladimir Putin did not achieve most of what he wanted when he began his invasion of Ukraine. "Putin wanted to tie Ukraine to Russia, to encourage its entry into the Customs Union. He got the exact opposite," wrote the Russian opposition leader Boris Nemtsov who was gunned down by an assassin not far from Kremlin in February 2015. "He wanted Ukraine to maintain a neutral status. He failed miserably.... He wanted to win the respect of the Ukrainian people. He created a long-term enemy.... Putin wanted a 'Novorossiia' stretching from Donetsk to Odesa. He got a small section of the Donetsk and Luhansk oblasts.... [H]e wanted a corridor to the Crimea via Mariupol. He raised awareness and resistance among the locals and spurred Russians residents in Mariupol to dig trenches around the city.... He wanted to seize land without firing a single shot, as in the Crimea. He got 4,000 people killed on both sides.... Putin wanted to be recognized as a strong leader in world politics. He became an outcast."

Indeed, in the wake of the Russian invasion of Ukraine, Vladimir Putin's (and, by extension, Russia's) stock in the West fell to an unprecedented low. Relatives of those who perished in the shooting down of Malaysian Airlines Flight MH 17 held him responsible for the deaths of their loved ones. Many began speaking of a return of cold-war relations between Russia and the West. Some American politicians, including Hillary Clinton, compared Russia's readiness to use the rhetoric of protecting Russian-speakers abroad as a pretext for the invasion and annexation of foreign territories with the policies of Nazi Germany on the eve of World War II. The Russian invasion of Ukraine and annexation of the Crimea was indeed the first case of forcible takeover by a major world power of territory in Europe since the end of World War II. Parallels were also drawn between the actions of Slobodan Milošević in Yugoslavia in the 1990s and Vladimir Putin in 2014—both had used the national minorities card as a pretext for war.

Back in 1991, President George H. W. Bush and the Western leaders pooled their resources and coordinated their policies to prevent the Soviet Union from turning into what was then called "Yugoslavia with nukes." They achieved their goal and were able to ensure the relatively peaceful demise of the Soviet empire. Western unity is as important today as it was in 1991. The Russian invasion of Ukraine and the current crisis in Russia's relations with the West reveal with unprecedented clarity that the drama of the disintegration of Europe's last empire is far from over. To understand its driving forces and take an informed look into the future, one would be well advised to start where it all began, with the unexpected Soviet collapse of 1991.

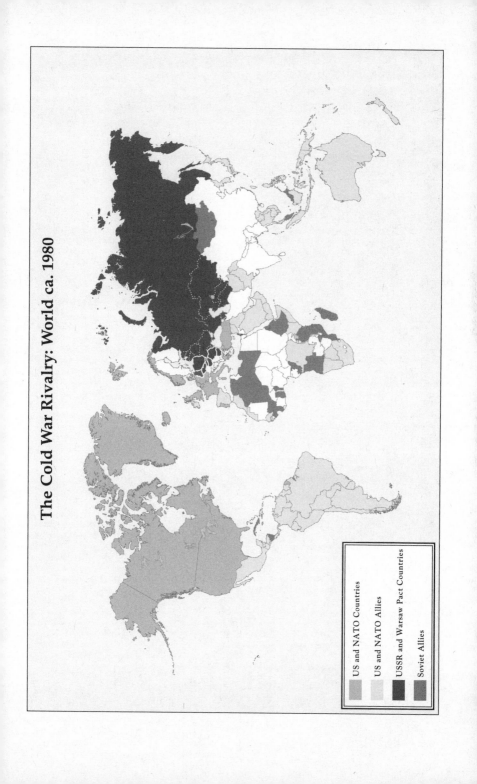

The Cold War Rivalry: World ca. 1980

US and NATO Countries
US and NATO Allies
USSR and Warsaw Pact Countries
Soviet Allies

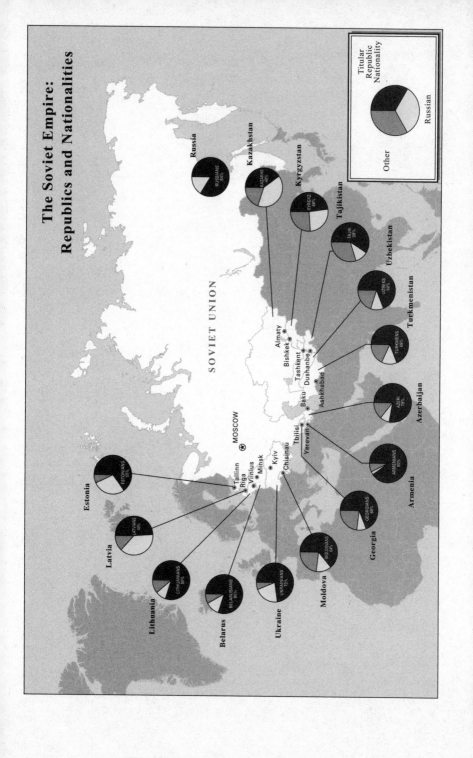

The Soviet Empire:
Republics and Nationalities

Introduction

IT WAS A CHRISTMAS GIFT that few expected to receive. Against the dark evening sky, over the heads of tourists on Red Square in Moscow, above the rifles of the honor guard marching toward Lenin's mausoleum, and behind the brick walls of the Kremlin, the red banner of the Soviet Union was run down the flagpole of the Senate Building, the seat of the Soviet government and until recently the symbol of world communism. Tens of millions of television viewers all around the world who watched the scene on Christmas Day 1991 could hardly believe their eyes. On the same day, CNN presented a live broadcast of the resignation speech of the first and last Soviet president, Mikhail Gorbachev. The Soviet Union was no more.

What had just happened? The first to give an answer to that question was the president of the United States, George H. W. Bush. On the evening of December 25, soon after CNN and other networks broadcast Gorbachev's speech and the image of the red banner being lowered at the Kremlin, Bush went on television to explain to his compatriots the meaning of the picture they had seen, the news they had heard, and the gift they had received. He interpreted Mikhail Gorbachev's resignation and the lowering of the Soviet flag as a victory in the war that America had fought against communism for more than forty years. Furthermore, Bush associated the collapse of communism with the end of the Cold War and congratulated the American people on the victory of their values. He used the word "victory" three times in three consecutive sentences. A few weeks later, in his State of the Union address, Bush referred to the implosion of the Soviet Union in a year that had seen "changes of almost biblical proportions," declared that "by the grace of God, America won the Cold War," and announced the dawning of a new world order. "A world once divided into two armed camps," Bush told the joint session of the US Senate and House of Representatives, "now recognizes one sole and preeminent power, the United States of America." The audience exploded in applause.[1]

For more than forty years, the United States and the Soviet Union had indeed been locked in a global struggle that by sheer chance did not end in a nuclear holocaust. Generations of Americans were born into a world that seemed permanently divided into two warring camps, one symbolized by the red banner atop the Kremlin and the other by the Stars and Stripes over the Capitol. Those who went to school in the 1950s still remembered the nuclear alarm drills and the advice to hide under their desks in case of a nuclear explosion. Hundreds of thousands of Americans fought and tens of thousands died in wars that were supposed to stop the advance of communism, first in the mountains of Korea and then in the jungles of Vietnam. Generations of intellectuals were divided over the issue of whether Alger Hiss spied for the Soviets, and Hollywood remained traumatized for decades by the witch hunt for communists unleashed by Senator Joseph McCarthy. Only a few years before the Soviet collapse, the streets of New York and other major American cities were rocked by demonstrations staged by proponents of nuclear disarmament that divided fathers and sons, pitting the young political activist Ron Reagan against his father, President Ronald Reagan. Americans and their Western allies fought numerous battles at home and abroad in a war that seemed to have no end. Now an adversary armed to the teeth, never having lost a single battle, lowered its flag and disintegrated into a dozen smaller states without so much as a shot being fired.

There was good reason to celebrate, but there was also something confusing, if not disturbing, about the president's readiness to claim victory in the Cold War on the day when Mikhail Gorbachev, Bush's and Ronald Reagan's principal ally in ending that war, submitted his resignation. Gorbachev's action put a symbolic if not legal end to the USSR (it had been formally dissolved by its constituent members four days earlier, on December 21), but the Cold War was never about the dismemberment of the USSR. Besides, President Bush's speech to the nation on December 25, 1991, and his State of the Union address in January 1992 contradicted the administration's earlier statements about the Cold War having ended not in confrontation with Gorbachev but in cooperation with him. The earliest such pronouncement was made at the summit of the two leaders on Malta in December 1989. The most recent one was the statement released by the White House a few hours before Bush's Christmas speech. It praised Gorbachev's cooperation: "Working with President Reagan, myself, and other allied leaders, President Gorbachev acted boldly and decisively to end the bitter divisions of the Cold War and contributed to the remaking of a Europe whole and free."[2]

Bush's Christmas address was a major departure from the way in which the president himself and the members of his administration had treated their erstwhile Soviet partner and assessed their ability to affect developments in the Soviet Union. Whereas Bush and his national security adviser, General Brent Scowcroft, had insisted publicly for most of 1991 that their influence was limited, they were now suddenly taking credit for the most dramatic development in Soviet domestic politics. This new interpretation, born in the midst of Bush's reelection campaign, gave rise to an influential, if not dominant, public narrative of the end of the Cold War and the emergence of the United States as the sole world superpower. That largely mythical narrative closely linked the end of the Cold War with the collapse of communism and the disintegration of the Soviet Union. More important, it treated those developments as direct outcomes of US policies and, indeed, as major American victories.[3]

This book challenges the triumphalist interpretation of the Soviet collapse as an American victory in the Cold War. It does so in part on the basis of recently declassified documents from the George Bush Presidential Library, including memoranda from his advisers and formerly secret transcripts of the president's telephone conversations with world leaders. These newly available documents show with unprecedented clarity that the president himself and many of his White House advisers did much to prolong the life of the Soviet Union, worried about the rise of the future Russian president Boris Yeltsin and the drives for independence by leaders of other Soviet republics, and, once the Soviet Union was gone, wanted Russia to become the sole owner of the Soviet nuclear arsenals and maintain its influence in the post-Soviet space, especially in the Central Asian republics.

Why did the leadership of a country allegedly locked in combat with a Cold War adversary adopt such a policy? The White House documents, combined with other types of sources, provide answers to this and many other relevant questions posed in this book. They show how Cold War–era political rhetoric clashed with realpolitik as the White House tried to save Gorbachev, whom it regarded as its main partner on the world stage. The White House was prepared to tolerate the continued existence of the Communist Party and the Soviet empire in order to achieve that goal. Its main concern was not victory in the Cold War, which was already effectively over, but the possibility of civil war in the Soviet Union. That would have threatened to turn the former tsarist empire into a "Yugoslavia with nukes," to use a term coined by newspaper reporters at the time. The nuclear age had changed the nature of great-power rivalry and the definition of victory and defeat, but not the rhetoric of the warrior's ethos or the thinking of the masses. The Bush administration had to square the circle by reconciling the language and thinking of the Cold War era with the geopolitical realities of its immediate aftermath. It did its best in that regard, but its actions far outshone its inconsistent rhetoric.

It is easy to understand (and sympathize with) the excitement of those involved in the events of late 1991 as they saw the red banner going down the Kremlin flagpole and recalled the sacrifices associated with American participation in the global rivalry with the Soviet Union. But it is no less important today, almost a quarter of a century after those events, to take a more dispassionate look at what actually happened. The declaration of the fall of the USSR as an American victory in the Cold War helped create an exaggerated perception of the extent of American global power at the time when such perception mattered most, during the decade leading up to the 9/11 attacks and the start of the nine-year-long Iraq War. Inflated accounts of the American role in the collapse of the Soviet Union feed present-day Russian nationalist conspiracy theories, which present the collapse of the Soviet Union as the outcome of a CIA plot. Such interpretations not only appear in extremist Internet publications but also are voiced on major Russian television channels.[4]

My narrative provides a much more complex and potentially controversial picture of what actually occurred in the months leading up to the Soviet collapse than the popular image that exists today on both sides of the former Cold War divide. It also claims that the American world, which replaced the Cold War–era division of the globe into two rival camps, came into existence as much by chance as by design. It is important to revisit the origins of that world and the perceptions and actions of its creators, both deliberate and inadvertent, on both sides of the Atlantic if we are to understand what has gone wrong with it over the last decade and a half.

THIS BOOK LIFTS THE CURTAIN OF TIME on the dramatic events leading up to the lowering of the Soviet flag and the collapse of the Soviet Union. The concept of empire, which I include in the title of this book, is vital to my interpretation of the dramatic events of 1991. I join those political scientists and historians who argue that while the lost arms race, economic decline, democratic resurgence, and bankruptcy of communist ideals all contributed to the Soviet implosion, they did not predetermine the disintegration of the Soviet Union. That was caused by the imperial foundations, multiethnic composition, and pseudofederal structure of the Soviet state, features whose importance was fully recognized neither by American policy makers in Washington nor by Gorbachev's advisers in Moscow.

Although the Soviet Union was often called "Russia," it was in fact a conglomerate of nationalities that Moscow secured through a combination of brute force and cultural concessions and ruled with an iron fist for most of the Soviet period. The Russians were de jure in charge of the largest republic by far, the Russian Federation, but there were fourteen others. Numbering close to 150 million, the Russians constituted only 51 percent of the total Soviet population. The Ukrainians were the second-largest group, with more than 50 million people, accounting for close to 20 percent of the country's population.

The victory of the Bolsheviks in the Russian Revolution allowed them to salvage the Russian Empire by turning it into a quasi-federal polity, at least with regard to its constitutional structure. This expedient prolonged the imperial history of Russia but did not allow it to escape the fate of other empires in the long run. By 1990 most of the Soviet republics had their own presidents, foreign ministers, and more or less democratically elected parliaments. Not until 1991 did the world finally comprehend that the Soviet Union was not Russia.[5]

I put the collapse of the USSR into the same category as the twentieth-century collapse of the world's major empires, including the Austro-Hungarian, Ottoman, British, French, and Portuguese. I call the Soviet Union the last empire not because I believe that there will be no empires in the future but because it was the last state that carried on the legacies of the "classical" European and Eurasian empires of the modern era. I approach the history of the Soviet collapse with the basic premise that imperial rule is incompatible with electoral democracy and that the conflict between them led to the fall of the world's last empire. Once Gorbachev introduced elements of electoral democracy into Soviet politics in 1989, the newly elected politicians in Russia were suddenly empowered to say whether they were willing to continue bearing the burdens of empire, while the politicians in the non-Russian republics faced the question of whether they wanted to remain under imperial rule. Eventually, both groups answered in the negative.

The first to use the opportunity to say no were politicians in the Baltic states and western Ukraine, the parts of the Soviet Union forcibly incorporated into the USSR on the basis of the Molotov-Ribbentrop Pact of 1939. The next were their counterparts in Russia and eastern Ukraine, which had belonged to the USSR before World War II. In the Baltics, Georgia, and Armenia, new democratic leaders pushed for independence. In the rest of the republics, the old elites hung to power, but with Gorbachev withdrawing the center's support from its regional viceroys and making their political survival dependent on democratic election, they began making deals with rising democratic forces—a development that eventually led to the disintegration of the Soviet Union along the borders established for its fifteen republics.[6]

My narrative focuses on five months—late July to late December of 1991—that literally changed the world as critical decisions were made on the fate of the USSR. It was in late July, a few days before George H. W. Bush's visit to Moscow to sign a historic arms reduction treaty with Gorbachev, that the Soviet president reached a fateful agreement with Boris Yeltsin on reforming the Soviet Union—an agreement that would trigger the August coup of 1991. In late December, Gorbachev's resignation as president made the Soviet collapse final. While many academic and nonacademic writers have covered the history of the Soviet collapse, they have all but ignored the crucial period between the August coup and Gorbachev's resignation in December. Some of these authors subscribe, consciously or implicitly, to the proposition that the elimination of the Communist Party after the coup automatically meant the end of the Soviet Union—a misleading assumption, as I show in this book. By the time of the August coup, the party could hold nothing together, including itself. The Soviet Union was wounded during the coup and its aftermath but continued to exist for another four months. It is the period analyzed in this book—the fall and early winter of 1991—that determined what would happen to its constituent parts and, no less important, to its nuclear arsenals.[7]

In his insightful studies of the Soviet collapse and the end of communist rule in Eastern Europe, Stephen Kotkin focuses attention on "uncivil society"—the communist elites that ruled the inner and outer Soviet empires before deciding to abandon the communist experiment. It has been argued that the Soviet Union, like the Romanov empire before it, collapsed from the top and that the disintegration of the Soviet state was initiated and carried out by the elites, both in the center and in the regions. Indeed, there were no angry crowds in the streets demanding the dissolution of the USSR. The collapse of the former superpower also turned out to be surprisingly peaceful, especially in the four nuclear republics— Russia, Ukraine, Belarus (Belorussia), and Kazakhstan—which played a decisive role in the disintegration of the USSR. The fate of the USSR was decided, in the last analysis, in high offices. It was decided in the midst of a political struggle that involved major political figures in both East and West—a battle of nerves and a test of diplomatic skills. The stakes were enormous, involving the political and, in some cases, even physical survival of those involved.[8]

At the center of the events of 1991 were several individuals whom I consider most responsible for that dramatic but also peaceful turn in the history of the world. My narrative is not unipolar, as the world became after 1991, or even bipolar, as it was during the Cold War, but rather multipolar, as the world has been for most of its history and is probably becoming again, with the rise of China and the development of political and economic problems in the United States. I take note of decisions made not only in Washington and Moscow but also in Kyiv, Almaty (previously Alma-Ata, renamed in 1993), and capitals of other Soviet republics that would soon become independent. My main characters are four political leaders who arguably had the greatest impact on what happened to the Soviet Union and, following its collapse, on the world at large.

I tell my story by following the actions and trying to uncover the motivations of President George H. W. Bush of the United States, the cautious and often humble leader of the Western world, whose backing of Soviet president Mikhail Gorbachev and insistence on the security of the nuclear arsenals prolonged the existence of the empire but also ensured its peaceful demise; Boris Yeltsin, the boorish and rebellious leader of Russia, who almost singlehandedly defeated the coup and then refused to take the Serbian president Slobodan Milošević's route of saving the crumbling empire or revising existing Russian borders; Leonid Kravchuk, the shrewd leader of Ukraine, whose insistence on his country's independence doomed the Union; and, last but not least, Mikhail Gorbachev, the man at the center of events who had the most to gain or lose from the way they turned out. He lost it all—prestige, power, and country. Gorbachev's personal drama—the story of a leader who dragged his country out of its totalitarian past, opened it to the world, introduced democratic procedures, and initiated economic reform, changing his homeland and the world around him to such an extent that there was no place left for him—is at the center of my narrative.

My main argument is closley linked to the idea that the fate of the Soviet Union was decided in the last four months of its existence, between the coup that began on August 19 and the meeting of the leaders of the Soviet republics in Almaty on December 21, 1991. I argue that the most important factor in deciding the future of the last world empire was not the policy of the United States, the conflict between the Union center and Russia (respectively represented by Gorbachev and Yeltsin), or tensions between the Union center and other republics, but rather the relationship between the two largest Soviet republics, Russia and Ukraine. It was the unwillingness of their political elites to find a modus vivendi within one state structure that drove the final nail into the coffin of the Soviet Union.

On December 8, in a hunting lodge in the Belarusian forest of Belavezha, having failed to reach agreement on the basis of Gorbachev's proposed template for the creation of a new Union,

Yeltsin and Kravchuk decided to dissolve the USSR and opt instead for the creation of a Commonwealth of Independent States. The Belarusian leaders who played host to the two presidents in Belavezha did not imagine the Union without Russia. Neither did the presidents of the Central Asian republics, who had no choice but to follow suit. A Gorbachev-led Union without Russia or Ukraine did not appeal to anyone. George H. W. Bush contributed to the dissolution of the world's last empire mainly by helping to ensure that the process occurred without major conflict or proliferation of nuclear arms.

In the two decades that have passed since the fall of the Soviet Union, many of the principals in my story have published their memoirs. These include books by George H. W. Bush, Mikhail Gorbachev, Boris Yeltsin, and Leonid Kravchuk, as well as the recollections of their advisers and other participants. While the stories told by eyewitnesses and participants in the events contain a wealth of information and some make for interesting reading, they often fail to present the bigger picture and explain the full meaning of the events they describe. Journalistic accounts, while indispensable for grasping the mood of the time and the feelings of the main actors and people in the street, appeared at a time when confidential documents were still unavailable to the public and participants at the highest levels were reluctant to talk. I have overcome these limitations of many of my predecessors by supplementing their accounts with material drawn from interviews with participants in the events and, most important, with archival documents, which have become available only recently.

As noted above, this book takes advantage of recently declassified American documents made available to scholars through the George Bush Presidential Library. These include National Security Council files, the correspondence of White House officials responsible for the president's travel abroad, and transcripts of meetings and telephone conversations conducted by President Bush, some of which I acquired through Freedom of Information Act (FOIA) requests. Combined with other primary sources from the National Archives in Washington, the James A. Baker Papers at Princeton, and the Gorbachev Foundation in Moscow, these new materials allow me to tell the story of the Soviet collapse with a degree of detail unmatched by earlier writers. I was fortunate enough to interview some of the individuals involved personally, including Leonid Kravchuk of Ukraine and Stanisłaŭ Shushkevich of Belarus.

The historical sources that I consulted in writing this book helped answer many "how" questions and quite a few "why" questions. My answers to the second set of queries generally began with an attempt to grasp the ideological, cultural, and personal motives of the leaders at the center of my narrative and learn the information that informed their decisions. I hope that my discussion of both sets of questions will not only shed light on the reasons for the collapse of the Soviet Union but also help explain the chronic difficulties of the two principal stakeholders in the Union, Russia and Ukraine, in finding a modus vivendi after 1991. I also hope that this book will prove useful to readers trying to understand the involvement of the United States in the Soviet collapse and the role that America should play in a world still largely shaped by decisions made back in 1991. Misunderstanding the reasons for the fall of a rival empire may very well result not only in imperial hubris but also in the decline of one's own empire, whether it uses that name as a self-description or not.

I.

THE LAST SUMMIT

1

MEETING IN MOSCOW

A SUMMIT IS THE TOP OF A MOUNTAIN. The word has also been used to denote a supreme achievement, but it was not until 1953 that it entered the vocabulary of diplomacy. That year, as two brave mountain climbers finally conquered Everest, Winston Churchill spoke in the British parliament of a will to peace "at the summit of the nations." Two years later, when the word was applied to the meeting of Soviet and Western leaders in Geneva, it gained popularity. The world of international politics badly needed a new term for diplomatic meetings at the highest level, which had become an important feature of international relations since the 1930s. "Summit" fit the bill. Although rulers had met to discuss mutual relations since time immemorial, such meetings were quite rare before the age of air travel. The airplane not only revolutionized warfare but also had the same effect on diplomacy, which aimed to prevent war. And so diplomacy took to the skies.

Modern summitry was born in September 1938, when Prime Minister Neville Chamberlain of Britain flew to Germany to try to convince Adolf Hitler not to attack Czechoslovakia. In the course of World War II, Winston Churchill, Franklin D. Roosevelt, and Joseph Stalin gave a new boost to the practice of personal diplomacy, which did not yet have a proper name. Summitry reached its peak during the Cold War, as meetings between Nikita Khrushchev and John F. Kennedy, and then Leonid Brezhnev and Richard Nixon, captured the attention of the world media, but it was not until the very end of the conflict that the Soviets adopted the Western term for their own use. In the summer of 1991, in a dramatic shift symptomatic of larger political and ideological changes in Moscow and around the world, Soviet newspapers dropped their preferred term, "a meeting at the highest level," and replaced it with the English "summit." This was a pyrrhic victory for a term that would virtually disappear from international relations within the next decade.[1]

The "meeting at the highest level" for which the Soviets had changed their diplomatic terminology was scheduled to take place on July 30 and 31, 1991, between the forty-first president of the United States, George Herbert Walker Bush, and the first president of the Soviet Union, Mikhail Sergeevich Gorbachev. The summit was long in preparation, but its final date was decided a few short weeks before the event. Until the very end, Soviet and American experts found it difficult to iron out every last detail of the historic treaty that the two presidents were going to sign in Moscow. Bush wanted to do so as soon as possible. No one knew how long Gorbachev would remain in the Kremlin and how long the opportunity to reach agreement would last.

The Bush-Gorbachev meeting in Moscow was presented by the White House to the media as the first post–Cold War summit. What George H. W. Bush was going to sign with Mikhail Gorbachev was a treaty that was supposed to launch the two superpowers into a new era of mutual trust and cooperation, starting with issues as sensitive as nuclear weapons. START I, or the Strategic Arms Reduction Treaty, which was finally ready for signature after nine years of negotiations, called for the reduction of overall nuclear arsenals by roughly 30 percent and of Soviet intercontinental missiles, largely aimed at the United States, by up to 50 percent. In the forty-seven-page treaty, accompanied by seven hundred pages of protocols, the two presidents would agree not just to curb the arms race but also to begin reversing it.[2]

The confrontation between the world's two most powerful countries, which began soon after World War II and had brought the planet to the brink of nuclear Armageddon, was now all but over. With the fall of the Berlin Wall in November 1989, German reunification under way, and Mikhail Gorbachev adopting the "Sinatra doctrine," which allowed Moscow's East European clients to "do it their way" and eventually leave the Kremlin's embrace, the conflict at the core of the Cold War was resolved. Soviet troops began to leave East Germany and other countries of the region. But the nuclear arsenals were virtually unaffected by these changes in the political climate. The famous Russian playwright Anton Chekhov once remarked that if there was a gun onstage in the first act of a play, it would be fired in the next. The two superpowers had placed plenty of nuclear arms on the world stage. Sooner or later there would be a second act involving different actors who might want to fire them.

Nuclear arms were an integral element of the Cold War, responsible both for its most dangerous turns and for the fact that the two superpowers, the first to possess atomic weapons, never entered into a direct, open conflict—the risk of nuclear annihilation was too great. With a divided Germany at the center of the Cold War geopolitical contest, the United States, which acquired the atomic bomb in the summer of 1945, felt safe in the face of the overwhelming preponderance of Soviet conventional forces in Central and Eastern Europe, occupied and then subjected to communist rule by Joseph Stalin. But if the Americans felt safe, the Soviets did not. They intensified their efforts to acquire an atomic bomb, and in 1949, with the help of technological secrets stolen from the United States, they succeeded in producing their own nuclear weapon.

The world now had two nuclear powers, and, if the Korean War was an indication of things to come, they were on a collision course. They tried to outdo each other by developing a new generation of nuclear arms. In the 1950s both countries acquired the hydrogen bomb, far more powerful and much more difficult to control than the atomic bomb. When the Soviets put Sputnik into orbit in the fall of 1957, demonstrating that they had missiles capable of delivering bombs to the United States, the world entered a new and significantly more dangerous stage of rivalry between the two superpowers. After Stalin's death in 1953, his successors were more open to the possibility of dialogue with the West, but, riding high on recent Soviet successes in missile technology (they were the first to put an unmanned satellite and then a manned one into orbit), they were often unpredictable and thus even more dangerous than their predecessor.

Under Khrushchev and Kennedy, the two powers found themselves on the brink of nuclear war over the deployment of Soviet missiles in Cuba in October 1962. By that time, Soviet-American competition extended around the globe. It had begun over the fate of Eastern Europe, captured and never released by the Soviets, and spread to Asia when China went communist in 1949 and Korea was permanently divided a few years later. The crumbling of the British and French empires in the 1950s opened the rest of Asia and Africa to great-power competition, and once Cuba under Fidel Castro turned to the Soviet Union for military assistance and ideological inspiration, Latin America also became a battleground.

The Cuban crisis of October 1962 was resolved by compromise—the Soviets agreed to remove their missiles from Cuba and the Americans theirs from Turkey—but both Kennedy and Khrushchev were shaken by the experience. Something had to be done to reduce tensions and the danger of nuclear war. In 1963 the two leaders signed the first accord to bring the nuclear arms race under control—the Limited Nuclear Test-Ban Treaty. It had taken eight years to negotiate such a document, and the beginning was modest indeed, but it was a step in the right direction. From then on, while continuing to compete globally and fighting proxy wars throughout the world, from Vietnam to Angola, the two superpowers kept negotiating to reduce their nuclear arsenals, finding solace in the doctrine of mutual assured destruction (MAD), according to which both countries had enough weapons to wipe each other off the face of the earth and were thus obliged to negotiate in order to survive.

Nixon flew to Moscow in May 1972 to sign SALT I—the Strategic Arms Limitation Treaty—with Brezhnev, and President Jimmy Carter flew to Vienna in 1979 to sign SALT II with the same leader. Both treaties placed caps on the production of nuclear weapons. But SALT II was quickly followed by the Soviet invasion of Afghanistan in 1979 and the American boycott of the Moscow Summer Olympic Games a year later. The next American president, Ronald Reagan, wanted to restore the spirits and international standing of the United States after the Vietnam debacle. In the Soviet Union, the death of Leonid Brezhnev in 1982 unleashed a succession crisis in the Kremlin. International tensions rose, threatening for the first time since the early 1960s to turn the Cold War into a hot one.[3]

On September 1, 1983, near Sakhalin Island, the Soviets shot down a South Korean airliner with 269 people aboard, including a sitting member of the US Congress. They then awaited American retaliation.

Later that month, Lieutenant Colonel Stanislav Petrov of the Soviet Air Defense Forces Command near Moscow saw a blip on his radar screen indicating a missile headed toward the USSR. Then he saw what appeared to be four more missiles headed in the same direction. Suspecting a computer malfunction, he did not report the image to his superiors. Had he done so, nuclear war between the two powers might well have become a reality. It turned out that a rare alignment of sunlight and clouds had caused a glitch in the Soviet early-warning system. Petrov was later celebrated as a hero. However, what impelled him to help save the world from nuclear war was not a belief that the Americans would not strike first but his conviction that an American assault would start with hundreds of missiles, not one or four. After what became known as the Petrov incident, the Soviets continued to await an American attack.[4]

In November of the same year, the Soviets mistook the Able Archer NATO exercises in Europe for preparations leading up to nuclear war. All their spy stations abroad were placed on high alert to detect signs of the coming Armageddon. That same month, 100 million Americans watched the premiere of *The Day After,* a made-for-TV film in which the inhabitants of Lawrence, Kansas, coped with a nuclear attack. Many credited the film with changing the tone of President Reagan's rhetoric toward the Soviet Union. Whereas in March 1983 he had referred to the USSR as an "evil empire," in January 1984 he made his famous "Ivan and Anya" speech, talking about the desire of the Soviet and American peoples to live in peace. "Just suppose with me for a moment," Reagan told a surprised nation in January 1984, "that an Ivan and an Anya could find themselves, say, in a waiting room, or sharing a shelter from the rain or a storm with a Jim and Sally, and there was no language barrier to keep them from getting acquainted. Would they then debate the differences between their respective governments? Or would they find themselves comparing notes about their children and what each other did for a living?"[5]

IT TOOK MORE THAN A CHANGE OF RHETORIC to switch the focus of Soviet-American relations from the interests of the superpowers to those of ordinary people. George H. W. Bush knew that better than anyone else. For a good part of the Cold War he had helped make American policy toward the Soviet Union, often holding positions of the utmost responsibility. Born in June 1924 to the family of a US senator in the American Northeast, the young Bush joined the US Navy on hearing the news about Pearl Harbor, postponing his studies at Yale. At the age of nineteen, he became the youngest naval aviator in the American forces and flew fifty-eight combat missions in the course of the war. In January 1945, while on leave from his duties in the Pacific, he married the nineteen-year-old Barbara Pierce, who became the mother of his six children. Their first child, the future US president George Walker Bush, was born in 1946, while George senior was studying economics at Yale. After completing the four-year program in two and a half years, the elder Bush, unexpectedly for a man of his origins and upbringing, moved his family to Texas to start a career in the oil business. By the time he turned to politics in the mid-1960s, he was already the millionaire president of an oil company specializing in offshore drilling.

George Bush's international career began at the dawn of détente in Soviet-American relations. In 1971, President Nixon appointed the forty-five-year-old former Republican congressman from Houston to serve as US representative to the United Nations. With his patron out of office in the wake of the Watergate scandal, Bush found himself in the role of chief architect of the US-Chinese rapprochement initiated by Nixon. He spent fourteen months as head of the US liaison office in Beijing, helping to build an alliance then aimed primarily against the USSR. In 1976, Bush returned to Washington to head the Central Intelligence Agency, where he presided over US covert operations in Angola directed against the Cuban-backed government of Angola's first president, Agostinho Neto. As director of the Council on Foreign Relations between 1977 and 1979, Bush witnessed from the front row the deterioration of Soviet-American relations during the last years of Jimmy Carter's administration.

In 1981, George H. W. Bush became the forty-third vice president of his country. The man at the top of his ticket, Ronald Reagan, dramatically raised the level of anti-Soviet rhetoric in Washington. He built up American military capability and boosted the nation's morale in the wake of the Vietnam debacle and the economic crisis of the late 1970s. But Reagan was also looking for a Soviet leader with whom he could negotiate the reduction of both sides' nuclear arsenals. It was a frustrating search, as the Soviet leaders kept dying on him. Soon after

Reagan came up with his START initiative, Leonid Brezhnev died in November 1982. His successor, the former KGB chief Yurii Andropov, followed suit in February 1984. Finally, Andropov's successor, Konstantin Chernenko, passed away in March 1985. Representing his country at the funerals of the Soviet leaders, George Bush became a frequent guest in Moscow in the 1980s. At home he became known as a man with a motto: "You die, I fly." It was at Chernenko's funeral, in March 1985, that Bush first met and greeted a new Soviet leader, the fifty-four-year-old Mikhail Gorbachev.[6]

In July 1991 Bush came to Moscow as chief executive for the first time—he had won the presidency in 1988. He came not to attend another funeral but to negotiate with a vital and energetic Soviet counterpart. Much had changed in the USSR in the intervening period. "Since my last visit in 1985, we've witnessed the opening of Europe and the end of a world polarized by suspicion," read a speech prepared by the president's staff for the signing of a new treaty to reduce nuclear arsenals. "That year, Mikhail Gorbachev assumed leadership of the Soviet Union, put many monumental changes into motion. He began instituting reforms that basically changed the world. And in the United States, everyone now knows at least two Russian words: glasnost and perestroika. And here everyone appreciates the English word: democracy."[7]

George Bush was accompanied on his trip to Moscow by his wife, Barbara, a sixty-six-year-old with silver-gray hair, and members of his staff. As is always the case with eastward transatlantic flights, passengers lose both sleep and time: Moscow time is eight hours ahead of Washington. On the flight over, Bush tried to catch up on time if not sleep by reading the papers his staff had prepared for him in the days leading up to the summit. Landing at Sheremetevo International airport on the warm Moscow evening of July 29, George and Barbara Bush were greeted by Mikhail Gorbachev's newly appointed vice president, Gennadii Yanaev. This was Bush and Yanaev's first meeting, and in the course of his brief three-day visit to the USSR, the president grew to like his modest and unpretentious host, whose performance of ceremonial duties and exclusion from policy making probably reminded Bush of his lonely years as the number two man in the Reagan White House. By the time the president's motorcade approached Moscow, darkness was falling. "A few people waved, and we turned on the parade lights of the car (which illuminate the interior and let people see clearly who is inside)," recalled Bush. "It was hard to see out and we waved at lampposts a few times, giving us a good laugh."[8]

The procession through the dark streets of Moscow was a perfect metaphor for the upcoming summit. The bright parade lights of American foreign policy were turned on, and expectations were high, but it was difficult to see clearly in the twilight of the Soviet Union's existence. After a period of wavering and hesitation, Gorbachev appeared to be solidly on the side of continuing reform and Soviet-American cooperation. He seemed increasingly persistent about requesting American financial assistance. Some of Gorbachev's closest advisers, including Prime Minister Valentin Pavlov and the head of the KGB, Vladimir Kriuchkov, were opposed to asking for American help and clearly tending toward authoritarian rule, away from the democratic achievements of Gorbachev's reforms. Then there was the military, which believed that Gorbachev was going too far in reducing Soviet military might in return for little or nothing from the American side.

Finally, there were the increasingly self-confident leaders of the Soviet republics—the constituent parts of the USSR. One of them, the flamboyant leader of Russia, Boris Yeltsin, would meet with Bush in Moscow. The US president would then fly to Kyiv to see another rising star, the leader of Ukraine, the second-largest Soviet republic. Soviet power was no longer concentrated in the hands of one person and was not wielded in Moscow alone. It was becoming increasingly dispersed, and the program of the summit, which included meetings with republican leaders, underlined that reality. Bush would have to try to look past the Potemkin villages of the new Soviet political edifice to see the future. The president had had many opportunities to discuss these questions with his advisers. It was now time to judge the new Soviet reality for himself. His immediate question was how to help Gorbachev stay in power and continue the honeymoon in Soviet-American relations.

MIKHAIL GORBACHEV HAD HIGH HOPES for the Moscow summit. This would be his third meeting with Bush in slightly more than a year. In late May and early June 1990 he had visited the American president in Washington, and in mid-July 1991 they negotiated at the meeting of the Group of Seven (G-7), the world's richest nations, in London. Each time, Gorbachev asked Bush for American economic assistance. But it was not only money that interested the Soviet leader. He badly needed a boost to his flagging popularity at home, and the only place he could get one was in the international arena. The summit was supposed to remind Soviet citizens of Gorbachev's role as a world leader.

Born in March 1931 and thus seven years younger than Bush, Mikhail Gorbachev was the first Soviet leader to be born and raised after the Bolshevik Revolution of 1917. Like Bush, Gorbachev was a "southerner"—he came from the Stavropol region of the USSR, next to the volatile North Caucasus. Like Bush, he received an elite education, obtaining a law degree from the prestigious Moscow University, and made his initial career outside the capital. But there the parallels ended. Bush came from the ranks of the American political aristocracy, whereas Gorbachev was born to a peasant family of settlers from Russia and Ukraine. He never mastered proper Russian pronunciation, speaking a heavily accented southern Russian dialect strongly influenced by Ukrainian—a characteristic that allowed his critics in the Moscow intellectual elite to dismiss him as a provincial upstart. In Moscow the young Mikhail married Raisa Titarenko, a fellow student and another product of the Soviet-promoted friendship of peoples: her father was a railway worker from Ukraine and her mother a Russian peasant from Siberia, where Raisa was born and grew up. Unlike the Bushes, who had six children, the Gorbachevs had one daughter, Irina.

After graduating from Moscow University, Gorbachev returned to his native Stavropol region, where he made a spectacular career in the Communist Party apparatus. According to a concise biography of Gorbachev included in Bush's Moscow briefing book, "Gorbachev's early career included Komsomol [[Young Communist League]] and party posts in Stavropol. He became first secretary of the Stavropol regional party committee in 1970, when only 39, and held this post till his appointment to the CPSU Secretariat." In Stavropol Gorbachev attracted the attention and made allies of two powerful members of Brezhnev's ruling elite who had direct links with Stavropol. One of them was the Soviet ideological watchdog Mikhail Suslov, while the other was the KGB chief and future general secretary of the party,

Yurii Andropov. The two allies made possible Gorbachev's move to Moscow in the waning years of the Brezhnev regime.[9]

Until his arrival in Moscow in 1979 as Central Committee secretary in charge of agriculture, Gorbachev had had little exposure to foreign relations of any kind, aside from infrequent travel abroad in low- and mid-level party delegations. However, once he received a more prominent government position during Andropov's brief tenure and then was elected to the country's highest office, general secretary of the Communist Party Central Committee, in March 1985, he turned out to be a quick learner. Liberal policy advisers in Moscow finally found in him a man at the top prepared to listen and take risks in an effort to change the status quo both at home and abroad. Many of them longed for the relatively liberal times of Nikita Khrushchev and the détente-era policies of the early Brezhnev years. They were also secret admirers of the Prague Spring of 1968—the attempt of Czech communists (crushed by Soviet military force) to create socialism "with a human face." Gorbachev, who was influenced by Khrushchev's denunciation of Stalin's terror in the mid-1950s (both of his grandfathers had been arrested by Stalin's police), and who shared a room at Moscow University with Zdeněk Mlynář, one of the architects of the Prague Spring, was a good listener and, more important, a doer.

In domestic policy Gorbachev initiated perestroika (literally, "restructuring"), which loosened party control over the centralized economy and introduced elements of the market. He also began the policy of glasnost (openness), a term borrowed from the arsenal of the Soviet dissidents, which reduced party control over the media and made some allowance for ideological pluralism. Abroad, Gorbachev returned to ideas reminiscent of Brezhnev's détente policy while eventually abandoning the "Brezhnev Doctrine" of political and military intervention in Eastern Europe. In Gorbachev, Reagan and Bush had finally found a Soviet leader who not only would not die on them but also would be prepared to talk nuclear disarmament. Less than a month after taking office, Gorbachev suspended the deployment of Soviet medium-range missiles in Eastern Europe; a few months later, he invited the United States to cut the Soviet and American strategic nuclear arsenals in half.

In November 1986, at a summit in Reykjavik, Iceland, Reagan and Gorbachev all but agreed—to the horror of their advisers—to liquidate nuclear arms entirely. What stood in the way of the deal was Reagan's insistence on continuing to develop his Strategic Defense Initiative (SDI), a missile defense program. Gorbachev believed that SDI, if ever implemented by the Americans, would put the Soviets at a disadvantage. The summit ended in a deadlock, and the world seemed to be returning to the darkest days of the Cold War. But the dialogue was eventually resumed. Andrei Sakharov, the father of the Soviet hydrogen bomb and a prominent political dissident, helped convince Gorbachev that SDI was little more than a figment of Reagan's imagination. The Soviet leader flew to Washington in 1987 to sign an agreement limiting the US and Soviet nuclear arsenals and dismantling intermediate-range nuclear weapons in Europe. Now, in July 1991, Gorbachev and Bush were about to use pens made from "Euromissiles" to sign a new treaty cutting the number of long-range nuclear weapons that targeted Washington, New York, and Boston on one side of the Atlantic and Moscow, Leningrad, and Kyiv on the other.[10]

In the months leading up to the Moscow summit, the Soviet leader had been struggling for his political survival. While the Soviet president and his advisers and well-wishers at home and abroad firmly believed that reform of the Soviet system was impossible without a democratic transformation of society, in practice economic reform and democracy did not work very well together. Perestroika broke up the old economic structure before market mechanisms could be put in place and produce results. Glasnost angered the party apparatus by ending its monopoly control of the media and unleashing public criticism for the first time since 1917. As economic difficulties increased and living conditions declined drastically, Gorbachev came under attack both from the party apparatchiks and from the reformers who called for radical transformation of the economy and society on the model of Poland and other former East European satellites of the Soviet Union.

The advance report for Western journalists arriving in Moscow for the Bush-Gorbachev summit, prepared by Gene Gibbons of Reuters, pointed to a growing gap between the Kremlin and the people on the Moscow streets. "Fort Apache, says a sign over an entranceway of the U.S. Embassy in Moscow, aptly capturing the flavor of a Soviet capital in the throes of economic disintegration," read the report. "As

George Bush motorcades through this city of 8.8 million, he will see long shopping lines, empty store windows, broken-down cars along the roadsides and dozens of idle construction cranes. At the Kremlin he will see the other extreme—glittering gold and crystal chandeliers, fabulous paintings, exquisite inlaid wood floors and enough marble to build thousands of monuments."[11]

Deteriorating living standards for average Soviet citizens—they were increasingly unhappy not only with their own situation but also with the privileges of the ruling elite—were making Gorbachev unpopular among the people he wanted to set free. Reporting from Moscow during the summit, Peter Jennings, one of America's "big three" news anchors, told ABC network viewers that Gorbachev's approval rating had dropped to a precarious 20 percent (Bush's approval rating at that time, soon after the American victory in the Gulf War, was in excess of 70 percent). Talking to Western correspondents, however, Gorbachev showed optimism and humor. Pointing to the friendly crowds at the Kremlin, he told Jennings, "See, some people like me." He added, "I am the man who began all this. If anyone's writing off Gorbachev, this is a superficial judgment." For the first time in months, Gorbachev felt that he was finally getting the situation under control by reining in the conservative opposition, and he was eager to use the summit to secure international support for his domestic agenda.[12]

THE FIRST OFFICIAL MEETING of the Moscow summit took place at noon on July 30, 1991, in St. Catherine's Hall of the Grand Kremlin Palace. "Gorbachev was marvelous," wrote George Bush, recalling his impressions of the first summit session, "and how he could stand up to all the pressures against him I simply did not know." The Soviet leader was in a very tight spot indeed, and the composition of the delegation he brought along to meet Bush indicated his diminished stature in Soviet politics. Gorbachev was accompanied to the meeting by one of the republican leaders, Nursultan Nazarbayev of Kazakhstan. Another republican leader, Boris Yeltsin of Russia, was invited but refused to attend—he was expecting Bush to come to his office later that day. Finally, the minister of defense, Marshal Dmitrii Yazov, was also absent, having sent his deputy to represent him.[13]

Gorbachev's road to the summit was anything but easy. What he saw as a moment of triumph for his new foreign policy was regarded by some of the most powerful members of the ruling elite as a sellout of Soviet interests. While the Soviet military brass had always grumbled about budget reductions, Gorbachev was more out of tune with his military-industrial complex than any of his predecessors, including Nikita Khrushchev, who was still remembered with hatred by the military for his huge reduction of conventional forces in the early 1960s. But it was not only the Soviet military who believed that the Americans had gotten their way on almost every major issue pertaining to the nuclear arms treaty. The same sentiment was expressed by Strobe Talbott, one of the leading American commentators on foreign affairs and, in the second half of the 1990s, the principal architect of State Department policy toward Russia.

In a signed article that appeared in *Time* magazine immediately after the Moscow summit, Talbott wrote, "On almost every major question in START, the U.S. demanded, and got, its own way. . . . In the START treaty Gorbachev is tacitly accepting a position of overall inferiority, at least in the near term, since he is giving up right away much of the U.S.S.R.'s principal strength, which is in land-based ballistic missiles, while allowing the U.S. to keep its own advantages in bombers, cruise missiles and submarine weapons." Talbott had called a spade a spade. But why was Gorbachev prepared to sign a treaty so unbalanced as to not only upset his minister of defense but also raise questions among American political commentators? Talbott offered an answer: "The U.S.S.R. has conceded so much and the U.S. reciprocated so little for a simple reason: the Gorbachev revolution is history's greatest fire sale. In such transactions, prices are always very low."[14]

Gorbachev had charged his defense minister with the difficult if not impossible task of convincing the General Staff and the military-industrial complex to accept treaty conditions that cut the number of missiles on both sides but excluded aviation, giving the Americans clear superiority in means of delivering nuclear warheads—they indeed had a preponderance of heavy bombers. The Soviet military eventually gave its consent.[15]

The last sticky issue of the treaty was resolved less than two weeks before the start of the Moscow summit. It concerned the American right to monitor a flight test of the Soviet SS-25 missile. The first Soviet mobile intercontinental ballistic missile, the SS-25, known to the Soviets as "Poplar" and to the Americans as "Sickle," was the latest addition to the Soviet nuclear arsenals. Its firing tests were fully completed in December 1987, and by July 1991 the Soviet Union had 288 Poplars deployed against the United States, which lacked comparable mobile ballistic missiles. The Poplars were "sausages" 1.7 meters wide and 20.5 meters long, mounted on fourteen-wheel transporter-launchers that gave them unique mobility and chances of avoiding detection compared with other weapons in their class. The three-stage rocket was armed with a nuclear warhead up to 1,000 kilograms in size with a blast yield of 550 kilotons, approximately equivalent to forty Hiroshima-size bombs.

A post–Cold War study assessing the possible impact of a 550-kiloton blast on New York City claimed that it would result in more than 5 million deaths, burying half the population of midtown Manhattan under the debris of collapsing buildings and exposing the rest to fatal doses of radiation. Massive fires would devastate everything within a four-mile radius of ground zero, and the fallout plume would extend across Long Island. The American negotiators were not daunted by the SS-25 or its devastating power, since they had more than enough weapons in their arsenal to match it. Their main concern was that the Poplars were powerful enough to carry more than one warhead, which would dramatically change all calculations. To find out whether the Poplars had such a capability, National Security Adviser Brent Scowcroft—who characteristically focused on capabilities rather than intentions—and his team wanted the right to monitor a test firing of the Poplar at a range of eleven thousand kilometers. The Soviets found the request unacceptable, given the American preponderance in other types of nuclear weapons. Eventually they agreed to the test range of ten thousand kilometers used for other ballistic missiles but refused to "walk" the extra thousand kilometers.[16]

Gorbachev had wanted all disagreements between American and Soviet negotiators to be resolved before his departure for the G-7 meeting in London on July 16, 1991. On the following day he was planning to meet with President Bush and the leaders of the G-7 to make an indirect appeal for financial aid to the cash-strapped Soviet Union. On July 17, 1991, a few hours before Gorbachev's planned meeting with Bush, Marshal Yazov had reluctantly signed the document that accepted the American demand. The road to the Moscow summit was finally open. Gorbachev officially invited Bush to Moscow, and the president agreed to visit as soon as possible, specifying the end of July, before his planned vacation in Maine.[17]

During his first meeting with Bush in Moscow on July 30, Gorbachev urged his guest to speed up the Soviet Union's admission to the International Monetary Fund (IMF), which could provide a financial lifeline for the Soviet economy. In London, Gorbachev had refused to link the signing of the START agreement with his request for Soviet membership in the IMF and American financial assistance, trying to avoid the impression that he was selling out his country's strategic interests for American cash. But in Moscow he was less shy about his financial expectations. "I ask once again in the presence of the delegation that the President instruct them to consider membership [[for the USSR]] in the IMF," said Gorbachev. "I have big problems in the next 1–2 years. Call us what you like—associate members, half associate members. It is important for us to *use* that fund." Bush was reluctant to commit himself to full membership and thus full financial support, as he had been at the London meeting of the G-7 earlier in the month. "We're talking about exactly what you want, without the burden of full membership," he replied.[18]

After lunch, Gorbachev invited his American guest of honor to take a stroll on the Kremlin grounds. They were immediately surrounded by dozens of reporters. "The KGB agents had to bowl people over to keep our group moving," recalled Bush. "There were a few incidents, with staff members and press photographers pushed down, and a camera broken—but the 'tank' rolled forward and Gorbachev himself told the shoving press people to get out of the way." Thousands of correspondents had descended on Moscow to cover the eagerly anticipated top-level encounter, and they were all anxious to catch a glimpse and snap a picture or two of the world's most powerful leaders.

To some, the scene brought a sense of déjà vu. Three years earlier, Ronald Reagan had visited Moscow for the formal ratification of the intermediate-forces treaty, signed the previous year in Washington. Back then, Reagan and Gorbachev had also talked to ordinary Soviet citizens on Red Square. There was more symbolism than content in Reagan's visit to Moscow. Bush's visit now was all about content—he and Gorbachev were going to sign a new treaty, not just ratify an old one. But according to David Remnick, the future editor of the *New Yorker* and then Moscow correspondent for the *Washington Post*, the Moscow "all-business" summit was nothing like Ronald Reagan's visit, which had been full of drama and excitement. Remnick wrote in his dispatch from the Soviet capital, "Bush worked the crowd as if he were at a Yale mixer. 'So,' he said to a small clutch of Russian tourists, 'are you all from Siberia?'" The hoped-for glamour was missing.[19]

One reason for the perceived lack of glamour was the personality of George Bush himself. A competent administrator and a cautious, responsible statesman, he was no match for his predecessor when it came to charisma. His Soviet host also outshone him in that regard. "Gorby," as the outspoken Soviet leader had become known in the Western media since December 1987, when he won the hearts of the American people during his visit to the United States, was the center of attention. The solid but unspectacular Bush could not hold a candle to the animated general secretary. "In the image wars," wrote Walter Goodman of the *New York Times*, "Mikhail S. Gorbachev, even in translation, effortlessly demolishes George Bush." And yet, while Gorbachev was clearly the more engaging of the two grave diggers of the Cold War, it was generally acknowledged that Bush carried more political weight. According to Goodman, the Moscow summit "shattered the first rule of television, the one that says image defeats reality."[20]

WHILE THE TWO LEADERS were busy discussing Soviet membership in the International Monetary Fund, their wives, Barbara Bush and Raisa Gorbacheva, seized the opportunity presented by the summit to promote not only a new image of Soviet-American relations but also the personal political agendas of their husbands. Barbara Bush, in particular, took advantage of the media's focus on the summit to appear on a number of American morning talk shows, laying to rest speculation that she did not want her husband to run for a second term on health grounds. Indeed, she virtually initiated his reelection campaign by claiming that he should run for the sake of his country. The success of the Moscow summit created the right atmosphere to kick off the campaign, and George Bush would make his own announcement to that effect immediately upon his return to Washington.

Despite differences of age and upbringing (Raisa was approximately seven years younger than her American counterpart), the two first ladies got along extremely well. It was a major change from the tense relationship between Raisa and Nancy Reagan, who had publicly taken issue with Raisa's comment that the White House was more an official building and a museum than a place to live. Like many who knew Raisa, Nancy Reagan claimed that she preferred lecturing to conversation. The spirit of Nancy Reagan must have been hovering in the Moscow air in late July 1991 when Raisa Gorbacheva, responding to a journalist's question about what she was currently whispering in her husband's ear, remarked, "It was not I who spoke about whispering in my husband's ear. Maybe it was someone else." The reference was to an earlier comment of Nancy Reagan's that Raisa had whispered the word "peace" to her husband. Raisa killed two birds with one stone, patronizing Nancy Reagan and deflecting accusations by her Soviet critics to the effect that she was unduly influencing her husband on matters of policy and official appointments.[21]

Raisa Gorbacheva and Barbara Bush had established good personal relations during the Gorbachevs' visit to Washington in June 1990. While their husbands negotiated trade issues, Raisa had accompanied Barbara Bush to a commencement ceremony at Wellesley College, a women's institution in Massachusetts. Originally Barbara had been scheduled to deliver a commencement address on her own, but 150 students signed a petition of protest against a keynote speaker who had dropped out of college after a year in order to marry and spend her life as a homemaker. The college administration changed the mood by inviting Raisa Gorbacheva to speak as well. Not only was she a career university teacher with a doctorate in sociology, but she was also extremely popular in the United States thanks to her husband's policies. The fact that Raisa had studied Marxist-Leninist philosophy and technically held a degree in scientific communism was conveniently overlooked (her biography in the Moscow briefing book claimed that she had studied and taught philosophy). Given the controversy at Wellesley, the Soviets were originally reluctant to agree to that visit, but the Americans insisted. Raisa enjoyed the opportunity to meet with American students. She later claimed that their questions prompted her to write her autobiographical book *I Hope,* which promoted her husband's policies at home and abroad.[22]

On the opening day of the Moscow summit, the first ladies toured Kremlin churches and museums and then took part in the unveiling of a sculptural composition donated to the city of Moscow in the name of Barbara Bush. It was a replica of "Make Way for Ducklings," showing a mother duck leading eight ducklings, inspired by a popular 1941 children's book by Robert McCloskey and installed in the Boston Public Garden, where the action of the book takes place. "There's something magical about the thought of American children loving and playing with ducks in Boston while children in Moscow are doing the same," said Barbara Bush at the ceremony. The Moscow donation was a way of continuing her domestic crusade for children's literacy. But although the ducklings sculpture was intended to bridge cultural and ideological differences, it actually became a symbol of the difficulties encountered by the Moscow-Washington dialogue after the Cold War: American cultural and ideological imports, enthusiastically welcomed at first, did not thrive on local ground. While Muscovites and their children loved the ducklings, most of them had no knowledge of the story behind them. McCloskey's *Make Way for Ducklings* was not available in Russian translation.[23]

ON JULY 31, 1991, THE SECOND DAY of the summit, soon after the clock on the Kremlin tower struck half past three, George Bush and Mikhail Gorbachev entered the Winter Garden of the Grand Kremlin Palace. Their brief encounter there was part of the elaborate Kremlin protocol that accompanied the signing of important international treaties. The two presidents proceeded down the ornamented stairs of the former tsarist palace to St. Vladimir Hall, a rectangular room decorated with pink marble panels, one of five reception halls named after the chivalric orders of the Russian Empire. The palace itself had been built by Tsar Nicholas I in the mid-nineteenth century to celebrate Russian military might and glory. After the Revolution of 1917, the communists had turned the palace into a venue for party and state functions, as well as for official receptions of foreign dignitaries.[24]

The nuclear arms reduction treaty was ready to be signed. It looked like the dawn of a new era, a triumph of reason over the madness that had kept the world in thrall far too long. "I really did feel emotionally involved at the ceremony," recalled President Bush later. "For me this was more than a ritual; it offered hope for young people all around the world that idealism was not dead." Mikhail Gorbachev was no less moved than his guest of honor. When Bush mentioned in his speech half a century of growing military arsenals, Gorbachev remarked, "Thank God, as we say in Russian, that we stopped this." He called the treaty "an event of global significance, for we are imparting to the dismantling of the infrastructure of fear that has ruled the world a momentum which is so powerful that it will be hard to stop."[25]

By signing the START agreement, the two leaders solemnly agreed not to deploy more than six thousand nuclear warheads against each other and limited each side's number of intercontinental missiles capable of carrying the warheads to sixteen hundred. Bush and Gorbachev also managed to go beyond the arms control and arms reduction agenda that had dominated Soviet-American relations for most of the previous thirty years. In a sign that the ideological confrontation of the Cold War era was also nearing its end, Bush pledged to ask Congress to grant the Soviet Union most-favored-nation trade status—a privilege heretofore withheld from the USSR on grounds of its violation of human rights and denial of exit visas to its Jewish citizens.

There were also signs of growing cooperation in the international arena. The two presidents issued a joint communiqué on the Middle East, promising to work together to summon an international conference on regional security and cooperation. The Soviets would strive to bring the Palestinians to the table, and the Americans would do likewise with the Israelis. Both presidents would send their foreign secretaries to Israel, where the US secretary of state, James Baker, would discuss the proposed conference while his Soviet counterpart, Aleksandr Bessmertnykh, negotiated the opening of full diplomatic relations between Israel and the USSR. Some newspapers claimed that the Middle East announcement almost overshadowed the signing of the START agreement. Finally, there was a basic understanding on Cuba: in order to accommodate American demands, the Soviets promised to curtail their economic support of Fidel Castro's regime. There seemed to be no bilateral or international issue that the leaders of the two formerly hostile superpowers could not deal with and eventually resolve.[26]

Bush and Gorbachev had come to the signing ceremony at the Grand Kremlin Palace from the Soviet president's country residence in Novo-Ogarevo, near Moscow. There they had spent five hours discussing world affairs with no preset agenda and tried to delineate a new world order to follow the abolition of the balance of nuclear terror. Gorbachev later called those informal talks a "moment of glory" for his foreign policy approach, which he dubbed "the new thinking." For him, they marked a turning point in the formulation of "a *joint* policy of powers that had until only recently considered themselves mortal enemies and had in their enmity been prepared to push the entire world towards catastrophe." If it were up to Gorbachev, the world would have become a Soviet-American condominium in which the two countries would not only live in peace but also resolve all international problems to their mutual satisfaction.[27]

Sitting on an open porch overlooking the Moskva River, Gorbachev presented his vision of a new world order to the American president. Gorbachev's interpreter, Pavel Palazhchenko, later recalled the gist of his boss's argument: "The world is getting increasingly diverse and multipolar, but in this world there needs to be a kind of axis, which our two countries could provide." The Soviet leader did not use the axis metaphor in his own memoirs, but there is little doubt that it well reflected the essence of his thinking. Gorbachev was prepared to discuss a broad range of issues. He wanted a joint US-Soviet policy on the European Union, which appeared to be gaining not only political and economic power but also military strength. He also wanted a common front in dealing with Japan, India and China, with their 2 billion people, were on the rise; there was also the ever-troublesome Middle East and the undetermined role of Africa in the world balance of power.

Bush was receptive but, as always, cautious. Privately, he must have been more than skeptical. In his memoirs, Bush wrote, "Gorbachev began with a lengthy monologue, during which I barely managed to squeeze in a comment." The Soviets, however, believed that this was no mere monologue. "Bush agreed," recalled Palazhchenko, "not in so many words, but in the way he was willing to discuss with Gorbachev in cooperative mode matters the United States would not have allowed the Soviet Union even to touch before." Bush assured his host that despite pressures from both the right and left of the American political spectrum, he was committed to the success of Gorbachev's reforms in the Soviet Union. While the Right wanted to take advantage of Soviet weakness to destroy its Cold War rival and the Left lamented continuing violations of human rights in the USSR, Bush was against taking advantage of Soviet vulnerabilities.

The Soviets felt that they had been heard. They were euphoric. Gorbachev later remembered nostalgically that "we were living for the future." Gorbachev's foreign policy adviser, Anatolii Cherniaev, one of the few Soviet officials who participated in the informal brainstorming session at Novo-Ogarevo, recorded these thoughts in his diary a few days later: "Our relations are closer than those with our 'friends' in the socialist countries used to be. There is no pharisaism or hypocrisy; no paternalism, backslapping, and subordination."[28]

The conversations that so greatly impressed the Soviets, who were desperate for support and hungry for recognition as equals by their new American partner, barely registered on the American radar. Brent Scowcroft, experienced and no less cautious than Bush, later recalled his feelings after the summit: "It had been a satisfactory set of talks. We finally had put START I to bed, a large step on the road to rationalizing strategic nuclear forces in a new era."[29] In his memoirs, recalling the Novo-Ogarevo conversations, Bush made no mention of any Soviet overtures concerning a joint Soviet-American policy. The Soviets knew that he was listening, but did he hear them?

An episode at the press conference following the signing of the START agreement became a metaphor for the Bush-Gorbachev dialogue about a special relationship. When Gorbachev began his preliminary remarks, praising the spirit and results of the summit, Bush, who was using an earpiece for simultaneous translation, turned to his host and said with a smile, "I have not heard a word you said." There was a problem with the equipment. "Do you hear me now? Do you hear me now?" asked the worried Gorbachev. Bush heard him clearly in Russian but did not understand a word. The confusion lasted a few more minutes until finally the system was fixed. "I understand you are almost in complete agreement with me?" asked Gorbachev after the mini-crisis was over. Bush got the translated message and responded in his trademark way: "What I heard, I liked."

Judging by Bush's memoirs, Gorbachev's overtures to him at Novo-Ogarevo regarding the creation of a joint Soviet-American world order were lost in translation. Gorbachev was daydreaming.[30]

2

THE PARTY CRASHER

ON THE EVENING OF JULY 31, 1991, George and Barbara Bush hosted a reception for their Soviet guests at Spaso House, the official residence of the American ambassador in downtown Moscow. Next morning they would leave for Kyiv. The guests, apart from Mikhail and Raisa Gorbachev, included republican leaders, the most prominent among them being the newly elected president of Russia, Boris Yeltsin. There were also members of Gorbachev's government, including the minister of defense, Marshal Dmitrii Yazov, and KGB chief Vladimir Kriuchkov. They were treated to a dinner of watercress soup with sesame seeds, roast tenderloin of beef with truffle sauce, and roasted potatoes. The waiters served 1970 Beaulieu Vineyards Georges de Latour cabernet sauvignon, 1987 Iron Horse Brut Summit Cuvée, and 1990 Cuvaison chardonnay. Coffee, tea, and sweets rounded out the menu.[1]

In his welcoming remarks at the reception, George Bush went out of his way to praise his Soviet counterpart. He knew what difficulties lay ahead for Gorbachev and what serious opposition he was facing in his own government. Bush declared, "I believe the signing of that treaty offers hope beyond the borders of the Soviet Union, beyond the borders of the United States of America, all across the world. I really believe that from the bottom of my heart." He raised his glass in a toast to his guests, especially Mikhail Gorbachev, whom he called a man "that I respect and admire, a man whose deeds during the past 6 years have given hope to those who believe, as I do, that one individual can change the world for the better." Bush continued, "I salute President Gorbachev, then, and I say that we leave confident, more confident than when I came here, that we can, together, build a lasting peace and, with it, a brighter tomorrow for our children."[2]

Bush's praise for Gorbachev clearly failed to convince the latter's conservative ministers. Bush's national security adviser, Brent Scowcroft, sat at the same table as Gorbachev's minister of defense, Marshal Yazov. Over dinner they exchanged opinions on the START treaty. Yazov, whom the US delegation briefing book characterized as someone who wanted "to shield the military against a decline in its influence and prestige," had very little to say in favor of it or of his president's foreign policy in general. "He was in a morose mood," commented Scowcroft, recalling his conversation with Yazov at Spaso House, "complaining that everything was going our way while the Soviet military was deteriorating daily. No new equipment was coming in . . . young men were not responding to the draft, there was no housing for troops returning from Europe, and so on. I asked him why he was concerned anymore about Soviet military readiness. What was the threat? He responded that NATO was the threat." Scowcroft showed little understanding of his interlocutor's concerns. He eventually prevailed upon the clearly unhappy Yazov to join him in a toast to NATO. Whatever the wine they drank of those available at dinner, the aftertaste could not have been pleasing to Yazov.[3]

At the Spaso House dinner, one could sense opposition to Gorbachev not only from conservatives but also from reformers. The latter were represented by Boris Yeltsin, recently elected to the brand-new office of president of Russia. Clearly unhappy about not being seated at the head table, he rose from his seat in the middle of dinner, walked over to George Bush's table in the company of Nursultan Nazarbayev of Kazakhstan, and loudly assured the American president that he would do everything in his power to ensure the success of democracy. "Those seated at the tables observed all this not only with curiosity but above all with amazement, and the natural question as to what it all might mean," wrote Gorbachev later. He clearly felt embarrassed. In his memoirs he described that episode along with another one that had taken place the previous evening at the reception in Bush's honor.[4]

The reception took place on July 30, the first day of the summit, in the Chamber of Facets in the Grand Kremlin Palace. Mikhail and Raisa Gorbachev and George and Barbara Bush were standing in the receiving line, welcoming guests. Suddenly the Gorbachevs noticed a couple who did not seem to belong together: the mayor of Moscow, Gavriil Popov, was accompanying Naina Yeltsina, the wife of the newly elected president of Russia. The president himself was not in evidence. But when the greetings were over, he suddenly came into view and approached the hosts with a broad smile. "Why did you entrust Popov with your wife?" joked Gorbachev with some unease. "He is no longer a danger," answered Yeltsin, making a joke at the expense of his close ally.

Yeltsin had called Gorbachev the previous evening and asked whether he could enter the dining hall together with him and Bush. Gorbachev had refused. Now it appeared that, having been snubbed, Yeltsin felt entitled to do as he pleased. He unexpectedly approached Barbara Bush and, playing the host, invited her to proceed to the dining hall. She was shocked and asked, "Is that really all right?" before making a maneuver that placed Raisa Gorbacheva between herself and Yeltsin. The journalists who witnessed the scene were not sure what exactly was going on. "During all this, Bush and Gorbachev were looking the other way and were engaged in a long and detailed conversation that seemed to be about the elaborate chandelier hanging above their heads," wrote a correspondent for the *Wall Street Journal* who witnessed the scene. The guests, many of whom were members of the Gorbachev administration, were put off by Yeltsin's domineering behavior. So were the Americans.

George Bush apparently told his entourage that Yeltsin was a "real pain," trying to use him in order to upstage the Soviet leader. He recalled the episode in his memoirs, noting that Yeltsin escorting Barbara to the dinner "would have been quite embarrassing to Gorbachev." Scowcroft, who had taken a dislike to Yeltsin on the latter's first visit to the White House a few years earlier, was furious: "That guy's got to be told we're not going to let him use us in his petty games." Jack Matlock, the American ambassador in Moscow, was instructed to deliver a message in this vein to Yeltsin's minister of foreign affairs, Andrei Kozyrev. Matlock later wrote, "Yeltsin's behavior was both boorish and childish, designed to draw attention to himself and make both Gorbachev and Bush uncomfortable."[5]

Despite their displeasure with Yeltsin, Bush, Scowcroft, and other members of the American delegation knew that they had no choice but to deal with the newly elected Russian leader. With Gorbachev's political star on the wane, Yeltsin was putting himself forward as the great new hope for the American government in its dealings with the Soviets. He was everything Gorbachev was not: a popularly elected leader who openly denounced communist ideology and was determined to conduct a radical reform of Moscow's policies at home and abroad. But could one really work with Yeltsin, given his eccentricities? And how should one handle him without undermining Gorbachev? These were major puzzles for President Bush and his advisers.

BORIS YELTSIN WAS THE SAME AGE as Gorbachev and from a somewhat similar background. Born in the Urals in 1931 to a family of blue-collar workers, Yeltsin was a self-made man who attained the highest levels of power thanks to, among other things, his boundless energy. An engineer by education, he first made a name for himself in the construction industry, arguably the toughest sector of the Soviet economy. Always underfunded and understaffed, unlike the military-industrial complex, construction companies fulfilled their five-year plans by relying on the work of recent convicts and riffraff sent to building sites by party officials. Much depended on the individual construction chief's sheer strength of personality, of which Yeltsin had no shortage. He began his career in 1955 as a foreman in the city of Sverdlovsk in the Urals and bulldozed his way to the top by showing better-than-average results. In 1976 he was elected first secretary of the Sverdlovsk regional committee of the Communist Party. At the age of forty-five he became de facto ruler of a huge industrial region that was much more important in the Soviet hierarchy of regions than Gorbachev's Stavropol *krai*.

Whereas Gorbachev rose through the ranks by growing grain and entertaining Moscow party bosses who came to relax at the mineral-spring spas in his region, Yeltsin did so by fulfilling industrial production and construction quotas. In Sverdlovsk Yeltsin became known not only for what he built (his many completed projects

included the operetta theater, which the young party secretary loved
to attend) but also for what he destroyed. In 1977, on orders from
Moscow, Sverdlovsk officials demolished the house in which the
Bolsheviks had executed Tsar Nicholas II and members of his family
in the summer of 1918. The party bosses worried that the house might
turn into an object of veneration and pilgrimage. Yeltsin destroyed
as quickly as he built—the last refuge of the tsar, which had seen the
demise of the old Russia, was demolished in a single night. The party
could celebrate the sixtieth anniversary of the Great October Socialist
Revolution with no physical reminder of the crime committed by the
founding fathers of the socialist state.

Boris Yeltsin was always at home speaking to ordinary Soviet
citizens and loved public adulation, but his rise as a democratic leader
began only in the era of perestroika and glasnost, when Gorbachev
invited the human dynamo from Sverdlovsk to come to Moscow. He
soon took over the city administration, paralyzed by the metastasis of
Brezhnev-era corruption. Yeltsin got rid of the old cadres and opened
his office to city journalists, who adored the energetic, innovative first
secretary of the Moscow party committee. But Yeltsin soon found
that he was no longer his own master, as he had been in faraway
Sverdlovsk. In Moscow, the powerful new city secretary had to deal
with the even more powerful all-Union Politburo, of which he was a
candidate member. His colleagues soon noticed that Yeltsin's bouts of
feverish activity were followed by periods of depression.

Yeltsin clashed over the pace of reforms in Moscow with his former
patron Yegor Ligachev, a former party secretary from Siberia who
represented the conservative wing of Gorbachev's Politburo. In the fall
of 1987 Yeltsin lashed out not only against Ligachev but also against
Gorbachev himself, pointing out problems with the implementation
of reforms and accusing Politburo members of adulating their boss.
Gorbachev struck back, removing Yeltsin from his position at the
helm of the Moscow party organization and revoking his status as
a candidate member of the Politburo. Yeltsin's party career was now
over. He pleaded with Gorbachev and his colleagues for forgiveness,
but to no avail. His life seemed to have come full circle: he was sent
back to supervise construction sites in a country that was still putting
up buildings but was now beset with doubts about the "restructuring"
of socialism. Yeltsin's expulsion from the Politburo was a defeat for

the liberal elements in Gorbachev's perestroika camp and a victory for party conservatives. A year later, the victorious Ligachev publicly lectured Yeltsin: "Boris, you are wrong."[6]

But if the Politburo lost one of its radical voices, the emerging democratic movement in Russia unexpectedly found a leader in Yeltsin. The situation in the country as a whole was changing in Yeltsin's favor. Always mindful of the power of the party apparatus to interfere with his reform policies and unable to bring it fully under his control, Gorbachev had skillfully begun to maneuver it out of power. In 1989, the year after Yeltsin's expulsion from the Politburo, Gorbachev allowed the renewal of political activity outside the party, ending its monopoly of more than sixty years in the political sphere. The new electoral system introduced competitive elections for the first time in Soviet history, and party secretaries were told that they could stay in power only by being elected—not only to their party offices but also as heads of local soviets (councils). Real power was being transferred from the offices of party secretaries to those of the regional soviets and republican parliaments.

The party secretaries complained but did not rebel. They all got a chance to take part in the transition, and the most skillful of them succeeded in using the party machine and its broader influence to gain election to the increasingly powerful local soviets. Change at the local level was directed and encouraged from the top. In March 1990 the Congress of People's Deputies removed from the Soviet constitution an article granting the party special status in the Soviet state and society; it also elected Gorbachev to the newly created position of president of the Soviet Union. Gorbachev retained his post of general secretary of the party's Central Committee but almost immediately began to move his advisers and the most important elements of the party apparatus from the Central Committee to the newly created presidential administration.

Few former party bosses benefited from the sweeping changes introduced by Gorbachev more than Yeltsin, now his archenemy. When the first semi-free Soviet elections were held in the Soviet Union in the spring of 1989, Yeltsin embarked on a career path unavailable to any of the disgruntled Soviet politicians who had preceded him. He seized the opportunity with all his vigor and energy. "His anti-establishment bent appeals to common people," read the bio of Yeltsin included in

President Bush's briefing book for the Moscow summit, "and his call to speed the pace of reform finds favor with the liberal intelligentsia." If Yeltsin would not play the games of the apparatus, he was brilliant at playing the crowd. And there were plenty of crowds willing to listen at a time when perestroika was failing but glasnost was flourishing.[7]

Gorbachev's attempt to reform Stalin's centralized system of economic management had accelerated the speed of its collapse. Given the failure of perestroika's economic reforms, increasing shortages of goods, and growing scope for criticism of party policies, past and present, the Communist Party was losing the race with its opponents. The opposition organized itself politically at the First Congress of People's Deputies of the Soviet Union, which took place in May and June 1989. There, reform-minded deputies from Moscow, Leningrad, and other major urban centers allied themselves with fellow reformers from the Baltic republics, who were pushing for wider autonomy and, eventually, independence for their nations. The alliance was directed against the party apparatus.

YELTSIN EMERGED AS the unquestioned leader of the Russian opposition to the regime. Ordinary Russians were tired of Gorbachev's endless speeches, which produced few tangible results. The failure of Gorbachev's policies, which left store shelves empty and people dissatisfied, contributed as much to Yeltsin's popularity as did his striking political instincts and ability to rally liberal proponents of perestroika and the leaders of the Russian labor movement—all this under the national banner of the rebirth of Russia. In March 1989, against the Kremlin's wishes, the citizens of Moscow elected Yeltsin to the Congress of People's Deputies. In the following year, his native Sverdlovsk sent him to the parliament of the Russian Federation, where he was elected Speaker after defeating two Kremlin candidates. He then quit the Communist Party.

Yeltsin cut his ties with the party in the most public fashion imaginable—in front of the deputies to the party's last congress in July 1990. After the rejection of his proposed new name for the party—the Party of Democratic Socialism—the former party boss from Sverdlovsk delivered a speech announcing his resignation. He cited the need for transition to a multiparty democracy and declared that, as head of the presidium of the Russian parliament, he could not take orders from any party. This was not an act that came easily to Yeltsin; nor did he take it lightly. He worked endlessly on the text of his resignation speech and grew very anxious as the day approached for its delivery. Late on the eve of that day, Yeltsin shared his concerns and doubts with Gennadii Burbulis, also a native of Sverdlovsk and his closest adviser at the time. "This was a man who not only agonized over his impending appearance," recalled Burbulis. "He was most deeply concerned about what he was being called upon to do. . . . And he did not hide it: he said, 'But that is what raised me!'"[8]

Gorbachev believed that leaving the party meant the end of Yeltsin's career, a "logical end," as he told his liberal adviser Anatolii Cherniaev. In reality, Yeltsin's public resignation from the party signaled the end of its preeminent role in society, unleashing a wave of desertions from the party. They were generally undemonstrative: party members simply stopped paying dues, attending meetings, and carrying out party assignments. As the party lost members, its power diminished. In 1990, the year of Yeltsin's exit, it lost 2.7 million members, dropping from a total of 19.2 million to 16.5 million. Direct losses from resignations amounted to 1.8 million. Gorbachev later recalled that in the eighteen months before July 1, 1991, more than 4 million members, or close to a quarter of the total, either left the party or were expelled from its ranks for taking antiparty positions or refusing to follow party orders and pay party dues.[9]

The exodus left party bureaucrats flummoxed. In January 1991 a Central Committee secretary, Oleg Shenin, warned the secretaries of the republican and oblast committees that many of those who had left the party in 1990 were workers and peasants—a worrisome signal to a party that prided itself on just such members. Even worse was the mass exodus of the intelligentsia. While workers were always reluctant to join a party that offered few if any benefits to its rank and file, many members of the intelligentsia had been eager to join it in order to advance their careers and gain entry into the managerial class and, eventually, the *nomenklatura*—the top echelon of the party and state bureaucracy, which consisted almost exclusively of party members. Not only managerial positions but also those in institutions of higher learning and the vast and well-funded research sector were all directly linked to membership in the party.[10]

In the fall of 1990 cracks began to appear even in the walls of the most prestigious bastion of Soviet privilege—the diplomatic service and the corps of Soviet experts allowed to work in the West. Party membership was an important prerequisite for positions that allowed one to live in the "capitalist paradise" and collect salaries unimaginable by Soviet standards. Even though many Soviets traveling abroad had long been disillusioned with the system, they had hidden their subversive thoughts for some time behind a façade of loyalty to the regime and the party that embodied it. But the informal arrangement between the party apparatus and the Soviet intelligentsia, whereby the party agreed to accept formal declarations of loyalty at face value and the intelligentsia agreed to offer such declarations in return for the perquisites of working abroad, reached its limit in 1990.

Yeltsin's resignation from the party without losing his post as Speaker of the Russian parliament showed the elite that party membership was no longer a prerequisite for a professional career. In the last four months of 1990, fourteen Soviet officials working at international organizations in Geneva resigned from the party. The Geneva situation was discussed in a memo submitted to the Central Committee leadership by its Organizational Department. The authors of the memo fully recognized the ideological reasons behind the new phenomenon. The main culprit, they believed, was in Moscow. Some Soviet citizens in Geneva, the Central Committee was informed, maintained close ties with Yeltsin's circle and opposition newspapers in Moscow and were even planning to form a Geneva branch of the oppositional Russian Republican Party.

The revolt was not limited to Geneva. The Central Committee was informed that the tendency to jump the Soviet ship, which had become so prominent in Geneva, was also apparent in Soviet diplomatic missions and communities in New York, Vienna, Paris, and Nairobi. Demands for the depoliticization of the foreign service were also coming from the central apparatus of the Ministry of Foreign Affairs in Moscow. The Central Committee apparatchiks were prepared to blame the revolt on the greed of privileged members of the Soviet intelligentsia. According to the Central Committee memo, the former communists were simply refusing to pay party dues in hard currency, which they regarded as an additional tax on their earnings. There was some substance to this claim, as Soviet international bureaucrats were indeed generally dissatisfied with the confiscation of the lion's share of salaries paid to them by international organizations. They were under orders to turn over their hard-currency earnings to the financial departments of Soviet representations abroad. Many refused.

Some did not want to go back home at all. In 1989–1990, claimed the memo, seven Soviet officials working in Geneva had refused to go back to the USSR after their state-negotiated and party-approved contracts expired. They signed contracts on their own instead, continuing their employment abroad. These "defectors" refused to stay in touch with the Soviet diplomatic mission in Geneva or take orders from its management. The revolt in the Soviet Foreign Service and among Soviet citizens working in international organizations was indicative of the party's failure to keep its ideologically disillusioned managerial class in line. Once people in a position to obtain real benefits ceased applying for membership and began to leave the party, the writing was on the wall.[11]

YELTSIN'S ABANDONMENT of the party did not mean any loss of privilege. By the time he made that move, he was already head of the Russian parliament, with a good salary, a large office, and a chauffeured limousine assigned to him. He was not in fact the first former party official to become an official in the new democratic institutions. The first to do so were party officials in the Caucasus and the Baltic republics, which were in de facto revolt against the center by the summer of 1990.

The first steps taken by Gorbachev and his allies toward the democratization of the authoritarian system did little to mobilize public support for his effort to reform the USSR from the center. Instead, they gave the Soviet nationalities an opportunity to assert themselves and threaten the integrity of the union into which they had been brought by force. Gorbachev and his backers and opponents both in the USSR and abroad all believed that the national question had been resolved in the Soviet Union. Unlike the masters of the collapsed British, French, and, most recently, Portuguese empires, the Soviet leaders had managed to keep the non-Russian nationalities together for an astonishingly long time without maintaining the external trappings of an empire. It all came to an end in the late 1980s.

The ethnic clashes that began in early 1988 between Azeris and Armenians in Nagornyo-Karabakh, an Armenian enclave in Azerbaijan, caught believers in the success of the Soviet internationalist experiment by surprise. In the fall of that year up to 2 million people participated every month in demonstrations organized by national leaders, mostly in the Baltics and in the Caucasus. The central authorities often resorted to force to stop ethnic clashes and restore order. The main threat to the Union came, however, not from the Caucasus but from the Baltic provinces, which had been occupied in 1940 and fully reintegrated into the empire after World War II. On August 23, 1989, activists of Baltic pro-independence organizations demonstrated their strength by organizing the Baltic Way, a human chain stretching from Tallinn (Estonia) to Riga (Latvia) and Vilnius (Lithuania). This was done to mark the fiftieth anniversary of the Molotov-Ribbentrop Pact, which had led to Soviet annexation of the region—a seizure of territory never formally recognized by the United States.

In late 1989 the Lithuanian Communist Party declared its independence from the Central Committee in Moscow. Not only was the party losing power, but the party state that Gorbachev and others served and were proud of was coming down all around them. The protests, especially numerous that year in the Baltic states and the Transcaucasian republics of the USSR, were sparked mainly by proposed amendments to the Soviet constitution that would have given the all-Union parliament the right to override republican laws it found incompatible with those of the Union and unilaterally decide issues of secession from the Union. In March 1990, the newly elected parliament of Lithuania declared the republic's independence from the Soviet Union. By the summer of 1990 most of the Soviet republics, including Russia under Yeltsin's leadership, had declared sovereignty, which meant that republican laws took precedence over those of the Soviet Union. The outer forms of empire, disguised as a voluntary union, were still intact, but the drama of its disintegration had begun to unfold before the frightened and confused government officials in Moscow.[12]

Russian national mobilization began in earnest in early 1989 not in the Russian Federation but beyond its borders as a reaction to the rising tide of local nationalism in the Baltics, Moldova (Moldavia), and other non-Russian republics of the Soviet Union. It soon spread to Russia proper, but in a most unexpected way. Russian liberals, whose power bases were Moscow and Leningrad, began to move toward a political alliance with the Baltic republics, which had declared their sovereignty. The leaders of the Russian democratic movement shared their Baltic colleagues' liberal economic views and now decided to copy their political strategy in order to promote the sovereignty of their own republic. In the spring of 1990, campaigning for a seat in the Russian parliament, Yeltsin embraced the idea of Russian sovereignty—a notion that under the circumstances meant shifting more political and economic power to the republics. It was a brilliant political move that helped expand Yeltsin's appeal beyond the Moscow and Leningrad intelligentsia.

Before Gorbachev's perestroika, few Russians, including Yeltsin himself, had associated themselves with the Russian Federation, the largest Soviet republic, which nevertheless lacked its own Communist Party or Academy of Sciences. Why bother, if the Communist Party of the USSR and the all-Union Academy of Sciences had their headquarters in Moscow and were not only run by Russians but also dominated by them? Yeltsin admitted his original lack of strong attachment to Soviet Russian institutions in an interview that he gave in late 1990: "I recognized myself as a citizen of the country [[the Soviet Union]] and not of Russia. Well, I also considered myself to be a patriot of Sverdlovsk, inasmuch as I had worked there. But the concept of 'Russia' was so relative to me that while serving as first secretary of the Sverdlovsk party obkom I had not turned to the Russian departments on most questions. I would first turn to the Central Committee of the CPSU, and then to the Union government."[13]

Yeltsin was not the only politician now playing the Russian card. His conservative opponents did so as well, rallying around the idea of creating a Communist Party of the Russian Federation on the model of party branches in the non-Russian republics. The idea gained momentum in the first months of 1990, in reaction to the formation in late 1989 of the Democratic Platform within the CPSU, led by Yeltsin and other supporters of radical reform. Members of the all-Union Politburo did not know how to react to the new developments. Gorbachev himself was on both sides of the issue. "If there is an RCP [[Russian Communist Party]]," he told his colleagues at a Politburo meeting on May 3, 1990, "then it will press harder on the communist parties of other republics, and they will say: why do we need the CPSU at all?" A few minutes later he rebuked a secretary of the Central Committee who had voiced his opposition to the creation of a Russian Communist Party: "If we refuse [[concerning the RCP]], the Russians will say: we gathered them (the non-Russians) for a thousand years. And now they're telling us what to do! Get out of Russia, as far as possible!"

Gorbachev did not want the creation of a separate Russian party organization, as it might well strengthen chauvinistic tendencies in Russia and nationalism in the non-Russian republics; moreover, it could turn into an organizational platform of conservative opposition to his reforms. But neither could he say no. As Nikolai Ryzhkov, the head of the Soviet government, remarked at the same Politburo meeting, "If we go against the formation of the RCP, our place within it will be taken by the Yeltsins." Gorbachev wanted to stay in control, no matter what happened in the Russian party. He offered to resolve the issue at the forthcoming twenty-eighth party congress in June 1990. That month a separate Communist Party of the Russian Federation was born. As expected, it became a bastion of ultraconservative anti-Gorbachev opposition within the all-Union Communist Party.[14]

For Gorbachev and his associates, the rise of Russia either in democratic garb, represented by Yeltsin, or in communist trappings, embodied by his conservative opponents, was a nightmare coming true. The growing assertiveness of the Russians had the potential to forge a distinct identity that would not fully overlap with the Soviet one and would break the Russian attachment to empire—past, present, and future—that kept the Union together. The threat of Russian sovereignty had been discussed in the Politburo as early as the summer of 1989. Vadim Medvedev, the leading party ideologue at the time, spoke out against giving Russia sovereign rights already conceded to other republics: "If we fashion it like the other republics, then the transformation of the USSR into a confederation is inevitable. The RSFSR [[Russian Soviet Federative Socialist Republic]] is the core of the Union."

Gorbachev was in full agreement: "Yes to restoring the authority of Russia. But not in such a way as to make it sovereign. That would mean removing the core of the Union." It was not clear how Russia's "authority" could be enhanced while denying it what republics had successfully claimed. The decision was postponed, but the problem was not resolved: if anything, it became more acute. The Soviet prime minister, Ryzhkov, told a Politburo meeting in November 1989, "We should not fear the Baltic[[s]], but Russia and Ukraine. This would smell like total disintegration. And then we would need another government, another leadership for the country, and already another country." Few could foresee in the fall of 1989 how prophetic Ryzhkov's comment would prove only a few months later.[15]

In May 1990 Yeltsin was elected Speaker of the Russian parliament on the third ballot by a rather slim margin: 535 deputies voted for him, 467 against. But the declaration of Russian political sovereignty that he proposed a few months later gained the support of two-thirds of the deputies. "The center is for Russia today the cruel exploiter, the miserly benefactor and the favorite who doesn't think about the future. We must put an end to the injustice of these relations. Today it is not the center but Russia that must think about which functions to transfer to the center, and which to keep to itself," Yeltsin told the deputies. The new champion of Russia was born. In the summer of 1990 the Yeltsin-led Russian parliament declared Russia sovereign, giving its laws priority over those of the Union. In the fall of that year, Ryzhkov told the Politburo that none of his orders were being followed. He was soon dismissed by Gorbachev as part of a cabinet reshuffle intended to crush what became known as the "parade of sovereignties."[16]

WHEN MOST OF THE SOVIET REPUBLICS declared sovereignty, there was no formula in place to define the new relationships between them and the central government. The constitution provided an all-Union façade for the heavily centralized state and even guaranteed republics the right to leave the Union, but it offered no tools for managing relations between the center and the republics. In effect, according to established procedures, either a republic was in the Union and wholly under Moscow's control, or it was out. Lithuania wanted out, whereas Russia, Ukraine, and some other republics wanted a new deal. Gorbachev did his best to stop Lithuania from leaving and the Russian parliament from electing Yeltsin and declaring sovereignty. He failed on both counts. The Soviet political and economic space was disintegrating, worsening the economic crisis and threatening the very existence of the central authorities.

The solution that Gorbachev was offered by the conservative members of his entourage in the summer of 1990 was to impose the supremacy of all-Union laws over republican ones by force. This could be achieved only by the introduction of a state of emergency. Gorbachev gave his blessing for the preparation of contingency plans. He also declared sweeping reforms: the Presidential Council and the Council of Ministers were to be abolished and replaced by a Security Council and Cabinet of Ministers under the direct control of the president. But he kept resisting pressure to introduce a state of emergency. In December 1990, with the Congress of People's Deputies in session, close to four hundred members of the legislature voted to place the question of Gorbachev's resignation on the agenda. They did not get a majority. Instead, Gorbachev's close liberal ally Eduard Shevardnadze, the minister of foreign affairs, resigned after being attacked by the conservatives for selling out Soviet national interests abroad. Gorbachev, with his own career on the line, did not try to stop him. Shevardnadze warned the congress delegates of an imminent coup d'état. In a letter to his American counterpart and personal friend, James Baker, Shevardnadze stated that he had acted according to his conscience.[17]

A coup had indeed taken place, as Shevardnadze predicted. At the congress, the conservatives had recaptured the initiative, and Gorbachev, instead of stepping down, decided to lead the parade himself. In January 1991, without formally declaring a state of emergency, he gave carte blanche to head of the KGB Vladimir Kriuchkov, Minister of Defense Dmitrii Yazov, and the new minister of the interior, Boris Pugo, to take any measures necessary to stop the movement of Soviet republics toward sovereignty and independence. On January 5, Yazov ordered paratroopers into the Baltic republics, allegedly to facilitate the conscription of new recruits into the Soviet army. On January 11, the central media announced the formation of a pro-Moscow Committee of National Salvation in Vilnius, Lithuania. Three days later, special units of the Ministry of Internal Affairs and KGB commandos stormed the Vilnius television tower, which was defended by proponents of Lithuanian independence. Fifteen people died in the attack. On January 20 Interior Ministry troops opened fire in Riga, the capital of the Latvian republic, killing four. Five days later Soviet newspapers published a decree on the joint patrolling of cities by troops of the Interior Ministry and the Soviet army. The decree provided a legal rationale for the presence of military units on the streets of Soviet cities.

In March, Gorbachev formed a Security Council, his main advisory body, which consisted almost exclusively of hard-liners. That month he also managed to secure a 76 percent vote in favor of preserving the Union in a referendum that was ignored by the newly elected authorities in the Baltics and in the Caucasus but still emboldened the Soviet president and his advisers. On March 28 he ordered troops in Moscow to prevent demonstrations in support of Boris Yeltsin. That day hard-liners in the Russian parliament were supposed to orchestrate a vote removing Yeltsin as Speaker of parliament. The attempt failed. Demonstrations in Moscow went ahead despite government prohibitions. Troops were not used to disperse them. Whereas elite Russian and Slavic units did not hesitate to fire on non-Russians and non-Slavs in the Baltics and the Caucasus, they were much less inclined to fire on fellow Slavs. Besides, Gorbachev balked at the prospect of large-scale bloodshed. He ordered the troops back into their barracks—a move welcomed by the democratic opposition (Yeltsin ceased his direct attacks on the president for a while) but condemned by the party hard-liners. Gorbachev had fooled them again by refusing to go all the way. From their point of view, he was now an obstacle to be removed.

Many in the party apparatus tried to free themselves from the party leader who had gone astray. Unlike Yeltsin, Gorbachev could not imagine leaving the party of his own free will, not only because of his oft-declared adherence to socialist ideals and belief in his ability to reform the party but also for tactical reasons: he did not want the party machine, which still possessed enormous power in the country, to turn against him. A few days before Yeltsin's resignation from the party, Cherniaev had recorded in his diary a conversation he had had that day with Gorbachev: "They are concerned only with their own interests. They need nothing but the trough and power," said Gorbachev about the party secretaries he had met earlier in the day. "He swore, using foul language," continued Cherniaev. "I said to him: 'Abandon them. You are the president; you see what sort of party this is, and in fact you remain its hostage, its whipping boy.'" Gorbachev was not convinced. "Don't you think I see that? I see it," he told Cherniaev.

"But I can't let that mangy dog off its leash. If I do that, the whole machine will come down upon me."[18]

The decisive showdown was supposed to take place at a meeting of the Central Committee scheduled for April 24, 1991. Party committees all over the country were demanding Gorbachev's resignation as general secretary of the party. But Gorbachev once again outmaneuvered his opponents. Those attending the meeting were surprised to learn from the morning newspapers that the previous day he had made a deal with his archenemy, Boris Yeltsin, and the leaders of the republics, who were pushing for more sovereignty. At a meeting in Gorbachev's compound in Novo-Ogarevo, they agreed to work on the text of a new union treaty.

Gorbachev had finally found an alternative to a state of emergency: instead of going back to the status quo ante and relying on force to restore the power of the center, he would go forward and find a formula to balance the interests of the center and the republics. That expedient would free him from the dictates of the party leaders and hard-liners in his entourage. On April 24, responding to a brutal critique of his actions at the Central Committee meeting, Gorbachev declared that he was prepared to resign. The party leaders backed down: without Gorbachev, their party would be doomed. At that moment he was their only protection against Yeltsin and his democratic entourage. The attempted party coup had failed and Gorbachev survived, but the hard-liners did not give up.[19]

In June 1991 Yeltsin won the Russian presidency on a promise to enhance Russian sovereignty. In the oath that Yeltsin took at his inauguration on July 10, he promised to defend the sovereignty of Russia. The empire was crumbling. The "nation-builders," as the Harvard historian Roman Szporluk called the proponents of Russian national assertiveness, were emerging victorious in the struggle with the "empire-savers." On the day of the Russian presidential election, Gorbachev's adviser Anatolii Cherniaev recorded in his diary, "M[[ikhail]] S[[ergeevich]] showed himself less perspicacious than Yeltsin with his animal instinct. M.S. feared that the Russian people would never forgive him for renouncing the empire. But it turned out that the Russian people could not care less." Cherniaev realized the hopelessness of any imperial project without Russia. "After all, there will be nothing without Russia," wrote Gorbachev's adviser in his diary. "There will be no Union. And in real terms the president can rely only on it, and by no means on Turkmenia with Nazarbayev!"[20]

Gorbachev had to accept the results of the first presidential elections in Russia—his former protégé, now his opponent, became the first president of the Russian Federation thanks to a popular mandate that Gorbachev himself lacked. Gorbachev had become president of the Soviet Union on the basis of ballots cast by members of the Soviet parliament. He now found himself obliged to deal with Yeltsin.

On the eve of President Bush's visit to Moscow, Gorbachev, Yeltsin, and the leader of Kazakhstan, Nursultan Nazarbayev, finally agreed on the conditions of the new union treaty. It was a major victory for the republics. They would be declared sole owners of natural resources on their territories and would reserve for themselves the right to decide what contributions, in what amounts, they would make to the Union budget. The Union government was to maintain control over the military and national security, but not foreign policy, which was to be decided in consultation with the republics. Gorbachev, Yeltsin, and Nazarbayev also agreed on changes in government: the hard-liners brought in by Gorbachev were to go, and Nazarbayev would form and lead the new cabinet. The new union treaty was to be signed on August 20, 1991.[21]

BORIS YELTSIN, WHO HAD EMBARRASSED Gorbachev at his own party and then at the Spaso House reception hosted by Bush, was not just the popularly elected leader of the Union's largest republic; he was also about to take control of most of the Union's oil and gas resources. The state of the Union's coffers and, possibly, the salary of Mikhail Gorbachev himself would depend on Yeltsin's goodwill. No matter how embarrassed and annoyed Gorbachev was by Yeltsin's bizarre behavior, he had no choice but to tolerate it. The same seemed to apply to the president of the United States. The gift prepared by Bush's staffers for Yeltsin—a Tiffany sterling silver bowl priced at $490—was more expensive than those for the other members of the Soviet leadership, including Gorbachev. The Soviet president received a copy of the first American edition of Leo Tolstoy's *Anna Karenina*, which appeared on the gift list without a price. The White House still put most of its geopolitical eggs in Gorbachev's basket. His gift was priceless.[22]

President Bush first met Yeltsin during his initial visit to the United States in September 1989. In the course of that trip Yeltsin, then a deputy to the Soviet parliament, visited eleven cities, gave numerous lectures on American campuses, appeared on *Good Morning America*, visited the Johnson Space Center and the Mayo Clinic, and met with American business leaders and politicians all over the United States, including Texas and Florida. Yeltsin called the trip the realization of a lifelong dream. After circling the Statue of Liberty twice on a helicopter, Yeltsin told one of his associates that he had become "doubly free." Nor did he hide his feelings in public. If anything, he was eager to outdo Gorbachev and charm the American public away from him.

"All my impressions of capitalism, of the United States, of Americans that have been pounded into me over the years, including by the *Short History of the Communist Party*—all of them have changed 180 degrees in the day and a half I have been here," he told the press. But his strongest impression, like that of almost every Soviet citizen visiting the United States for the first time, occurred in a supermarket. The abundance and diversity of products he encountered in a Houston emporium contrasted sharply with the empty shelves of Soviet stores. It was during this trip, according to one of his advisers, that "the last drop of Yeltsin's Bolshevik consciousness decomposed."[23]

Yeltsin's visit to the United States included a short stopover at the White House, where he met with George Bush. The visit left a bitter aftertaste among the presidential advisers who had arranged the meeting. While Bush wanted to see Yeltsin and learn his opinion of developments in the Soviet Union, he wanted to do so in a way that would not offend Gorbachev, who by the fall of 1989 considered Yeltsin his archenemy. Yeltsin was invited to the White House, but his official appointment was with Brent Scowcroft, not with the president, and that created problems. "He had been told," recalled Robert M. Gates, the future head of the CIA and secretary of defense, who was then serving as deputy national security adviser, "that he probably would see the President, but because we wanted as low key a visit as possible he was not given absolute assurances." When Condoleezza Rice, the Soviet Union expert on the National Security Council, brought Yeltsin into the White House through the basement entrance of the West Wing, he asked whether that was an entrance used by visitors to the president and refused to go any farther unless he was assured that he would see Bush. Rice told Yeltsin that if he was not going to see Scowcroft, he could leave the White House and go back to his hotel.

Yeltsin finally dropped his objections and went to see Scowcroft, to whom he presented his vision of how the United States could help the Soviet economy. Scowcroft was not interested and, according to Gates, almost fell asleep. Everything changed when Bush dropped by Scowcroft's office. "Chameleonlike, Yeltsin was transformed," recalled Gates. "He came alive, was enthusiastic, interesting. Plainly, in his view someone had arrived worth talking to—someone powerful." Bush confirmed his support for Gorbachev, but Yeltsin had achieved his goal of meeting with the president of the United States. As soon as he left the White House, he approached the reporters waiting on the lawn and gave an account of his meeting to the world. "It was not the quiet, uneventful conclusion to the visit we had hoped," remembered Scowcroft, "but no harm was done."[24]

Boris Yeltsin made a positive impression on Bush, but Scowcroft found the future Russian president devious, and judging by his memoirs, he never fully shed that impression. Yeltsin's early advocates in the administration, including Rice and Gates, were appalled by his uncouth and unpredictable behavior. Recalling the visit, Gates wrote in his memoirs, "He apparently drank too much, gave a poor account of himself in a speech at Johns Hopkins University, and was generally boorish." Nevertheless, the people around Bush could not help noting the shift of power in Moscow in the spring of 1990, after the first semi-free elections to the republican parliaments. Although Gorbachev was the choice of Western politicians and the favorite of the Western public, there was no denying that the mercurial Yeltsin was on the rise.

In June 1990, a week after Yeltsin's election as chairman of the Russian parliament, Gates sent a memo to George Bush saying that Yeltsin "has proved himself remarkably adept at using the new rules of the system to reemerge as a political leader. He appears to be an effective and popular politician, however erratic." Gates recommended avoiding any negative comments about Yeltsin: "We may someday find ourselves across the table from him." Bush was in agreement. Yeltsin's next visit to the United States took place in June

1991, soon after his election to the Russian presidency. It was a huge success that improved his standing with the American administration. Bush and Yeltsin placed a joint call to Gorbachev in Moscow, warning him about a possible coup attempt by hard-liners—the information came through American diplomatic channels from a Yeltsin ally in Moscow. Yeltsin's relations with the Bush administration, which had begun with a faux pas in the fall of 1989, were now back on track, or so it seemed for a time.[25]

Bush's official visit to Moscow in July 1991 included a meeting with the Russian president. Bush met him in the late morning of July 30. Gorbachev, who wanted to prevent Bush from meeting Yeltsin without him, invited Yeltsin and Nazarbayev to a luncheon with the American president. They were supposed to join Bush's and Gorbachev's advisers, who were also invited to the event. The meeting with the American president, which Yeltsin and Nazarbayev were eager to have, would take place, but under Gorbachev's control and supervision. Nazarbayev accepted and took the opportunity to lobby the US president for investments in Kazakhstan's natural resources sector, but Yeltsin refused to play the role assigned to him by the Soviet leader and take part in what he called a "faceless mass audience." Instead of coming to the luncheon, he invited Bush to visit him in his new Kremlin office. Bush accepted the invitation.[26]

The Bush-Yeltsin meeting lasted approximately forty minutes and dealt largely with the problems of the new union treaty initiated by Gorbachev and supported by Yeltsin. The meeting itself was a sign of the special status accorded to Yeltsin by the White House. Judging by Bush's talking points, his main task was to assure Yeltsin of American support for the policy of reform, both his and Gorbachev's, while forestalling any possible initiative on Yeltsin's part either to open a Russian representation in the United States or to sign an official agreement on cooperation with the United States. "As you know, we cannot establish diplomatic relations with your republic, which we recognize to be a constituent part of the USSR," Bush was supposed to tell Yeltsin. He held to that line at the meeting. When Yeltsin asked him, "Do I understand that you support my idea of formalizing the basics of our relationship?" Bush responded, not very diplomatically, "Which relationship? Do you mean the U.S. and Russia or yours with the center? I am unclear about what you are asking." Secretary of State James Baker, who was present, "translated" Bush's answer to the disappointed Yeltsin: "President Yeltsin, the answer will depend on what the Union treaty says about the authority of the republics to enter into agreements with other countries. We will have to see this new Union treaty."[27]

If by inviting Bush to visit him in his new Kremlin office Yeltsin was seeking to build up his image as an independent world leader in the eyes of his domestic audience, he certainly succeeded. If he wanted to poke Gorbachev in the eye, he succeeded as well. Gorbachev recalled the episode with bitterness in his memoirs. But if Yeltsin wanted to improve his relations with the American president, he failed completely. Bush was furious with Yeltsin for being almost ten minutes late. "How long are we supposed to wait for His Highness?" complained Scowcroft. The originally planned fifteen-minute courtesy call was then extended to forty minutes, with Yeltsin repeating the points he had made to Bush during their private meeting to a group of Russian and American advisers who joined the two presidents afterward. Yeltsin then sprang another surprise when he attempted to hold an impromptu press conference with journalists who had been brought to the Kremlin without Bush's consent. He told them that the two sides had already prepared a draft agreement on Russian-American cooperation, for which he was grateful to President Bush. Bush swallowed the bitter pill, but as Yeltsin was getting ready to answer the journalists' questions, the president told him that he was already late and had to leave. Getting into his car, Bush told Scowcroft that he had been ambushed by the "grandstanding" Yeltsin.[28]

What happened at the Moscow summit reminded Bush and Scowcroft of the erratic politician they had first met in September 1989. But however boorish, childish, and unpredictable Yeltsin's behavior turned out to be, Bush was increasingly finding more common ground with him than with Gorbachev. In the summer of 1991, one of the most important questions on Bush's Soviet agenda was the independence of the Baltic republics of Estonia, Latvia, and Lithuania—a cause supported by many members of the US Senate and Congress. Bush was gently pushing Gorbachev toward recognition of Lithuanian and Latvian independence, declared in 1990. If Gorbachev was indecisive, Yeltsin was not. On behalf of Russia, Yeltsin had condemned the actions of the center during the crackdown of early

1991 and supported the Baltic drive for independence. Now, standing next to Bush, he restated his support for that cause. He told the reporters he had gathered without Bush's consent that Russia and the United States had a joint position on the Baltics: the three republics should be allowed to leave. It was a position that Gorbachev did not dare to take.[29]

George Bush would leave Moscow the next day as concerned about the threat to Gorbachev from his own military as about the challenges posed by the republican leaders. Yeltsin was the most outspoken of them, but he was not the only one who wanted a weaker center and more freedom for his homeland.

3

CHICKEN KIEV

SHORTLY BEFORE NOON ON AUGUST 1, 1991, George Bush's Air Force One took off from Sheremetevo International Airport near Moscow and headed for Kyiv, the capital of Ukraine and the third-largest urban center in the Soviet Union. In early 1991, approximately forty US nuclear warheads were aimed at the city known in Russian as Kiev. In case of a nuclear exchange, multiple nuclear blasts would have turned the city into rubble and killed all of its more than 2 million citizens. The signing of the START agreement meant that the city would be the object of fewer nuclear blasts in the event of war. If it came to the worst, some of its citizens might actually survive. But delivering this dubious good news was not the goal of George Bush's visit. The American president was coming to deliver a message of a different nature.[1]

The visit was supposed to be just a five-hour stopover, but it was not the number of hours that mattered. Rather, it was the simple fact that Bush believed negotiations in Moscow were not enough: one had to go to the republics and talk to their leaders as well. This was a new development in the history of Soviet-American relations and a sign of rapidly changing political conditions in the USSR. The White House wanted to signal its readiness to work with the republics while warning their leaders against using violence to achieve their goals. No one in the Bush administration could then have predicted the rapid disintegration of the Soviet Union or foreseen the crucial role that Ukraine would play in that process a few months later. Kyiv was chosen as the place to announce the new American policy on the Soviet republics because its top leadership did not favor complete independence. Ukraine's anti-Moscow forces were strong but not violent, and its audiences might be receptive to the new message from Washington.

But Gorbachev was by no means happy with the idea of the American president visiting Ukraine, the second most populous Soviet republic, whose leadership was more than reluctant to sign the new union treaty that he had been promoting aggressively since April. Unlike Bush, he fully understood the importance of Ukraine to the future of the Union and was afraid that the US president's visit could give a boost to anti-Union forces in the republic. The Soviet president had done his best to block the visit. On Monday, July 21, slightly more than a week before Bush's arrival in Moscow, US Ambassador Matlock received an unexpected call from Ed Hewett, President Bush's special adviser on Soviet affairs. A Soviet chargé d'affaires had come to Hewett's White House office to deliver an urgent message from the Kremlin, which wanted the Kyiv leg of the visit to be canceled. Matlock was taken aback by this request. The Soviets cited unspecified tensions, but Kyiv appeared quite calm. Moreover, preparations for the visit, which Matlock had begun with the approval of the Soviet Foreign Ministry, were already well under way. They involved not only Americans but also their Ukrainian counterparts, and canceling the visit at this point would be a major embarrassment to the American side.

Bush was caught by surprise by the Soviet request. The news reached him on board Air Force One en route to Turkey. Together with Brent Scowcroft, the president drafted a response to the effect that if the Soviets did not want him to go to Kyiv, he would cancel the visit, but, given the advanced state of preparations and the involvement of the Ukrainian side, Moscow would have to take responsibility for the cancellation. Matlock called the State Department on an open line and, knowing that the KGB was probably listening, described the possible negative consequences of the cancellation—not for Washington but for Moscow and its relations with Ukraine. The following day he repeated the same message to the Soviet foreign minister, Aleksandr Bessmertnykh. The alarmed Bessmertnykh contacted Gorbachev, who allegedly told him, "Just forget about it. Tell the Americans not to worry and to go ahead with their plans. If the president wants to go to Kiev, I am sure he will be welcome there." The crisis was resolved. Gorbachev had to accept the new rules of the game.[2]

During Bush's meeting with Gorbachev on July 30, the American president tried to convince his counterpart that he had nothing to fear from Bush's upcoming visit to Kyiv. He told the Soviet president, "I want to assure you that during my trip to Kyiv neither I nor any of those accompanying me will do anything that might complicate existing problems or interfere in the question of when Ukraine might sign the Union treaty." Gorbachev hinted at the source of his original concern: "As for Ukraine, perhaps the following fact played a role: it has become known that not long before your visit the Heritage Foundation prepared a report in which it recommended that the president make use of his visit to Ukraine to stimulate separatist attitudes there, as that is strategically important." Bush denied any knowledge of it: "I do not know about that report. But I hope you were informed that I stressed the need for the utmost tact in preparing the itinerary of the visit. I would be prepared not to visit Kyiv but Leningrad, for example. I would very much like to visit one of your cities. But I am not about to support separatism in any instance. Kyiv was included in the itinerary of the visit only after your minister of foreign affairs informed us that it was perfectly acceptable to you."[3]

If it had been for Gorbachev to decide, Bush never would have gone to Kyiv. Moreover, Boris Yeltsin shared Gorbachev's stand on Ukraine. Both believed that the second-largest Soviet republic could not be allowed to go its own way. If Gorbachev, in his conversations with Bush, raised the possibility of civil strife and even war involving Ukraine and other Soviet republics, Yeltsin was calmer but no less determined. "Ukraine must not leave the Soviet Union," he told the American president during their meeting in Yeltsin's Kremlin office. Without Ukraine, Yeltsin argued, the Soviet Union would be dominated by the non-Slavic republics. His "attachment" to Ukraine reflected the attitude of the Russian population in general. According to a poll sponsored by the United States Information Agency in February and March 1991, only 22 percent of Russians favored Ukrainian independence, while almost 60 percent were opposed. The Russian public's attitude toward the Baltics was strikingly different:

41 percent of those polled were in favor of Lithuanian independence, with 40 percent against.[4]

In late June 1991, the CIA prepared an intelligence estimate for the president and his advisers, laying out possible scenarios for developments in the USSR. Only one of them, violent fragmentation, included the possibility of Ukrainian independence. Two other options were further "muddling through" and a coup by hard-liners, with the Soviet Union remaining intact. The last option, called "System Change," foresaw independence for the Baltics, the three North Caucasus republics, and Moldova, with Ukraine entering a Russia-dominated Slavic–Central Asian union. Yeltsin wanted Ukraine to be part of that union, while Gorbachev feared "violent fragmentation." It appeared that the CIA, Gorbachev, and Yeltsin were all agreed on one thing: if the United States wanted a peaceful transformation of the Soviet regime, which was now abiding by the START agreements to cut its nuclear arsenals, it should make certain that Ukraine stayed in the Union.[5]

Bush was reminded of the importance of the Soviet nationality question during his talks with Gorbachev at Novo-Ogarevo. Gorbachev's monologue on the future of the Soviet-American world order was interrupted by a message for Bush. Nicholas Burns, a thirty-five-year-old staffer on the National Security Council and the White House liaison to Baltic Americans, had received a call from one of his Baltic acquaintances with the news that unidentified gunmen had attacked a recently established customs post on the Lithuanian border with Belarus and killed six Lithuanian customs agents in execution style. Burns passed the news to President Bush and his party in Novo-Ogarevo. Gorbachev was at once humiliated and infuriated; according to Bush, he visibly paled. The American president had heard of a shooting on Soviet territory before the country's own chief executive! Gorbachev sent advisers to find out what was going on. The US embassy believed that it was the work of the OMON, a special unit of the Interior Ministry forces. The Americans suspected that hard-liners in Moscow had arranged the incident to embarrass Gorbachev. If that was the case, they achieved their goal. Gorbachev's presentation of his vision of a new world order was cut short. "A pall fell over the meeting," remembered Bush. "We resumed the discussions but the ebullient spirit was gone."

As far as Gorbachev was concerned, the tragic events in Lithuania had given new urgency to the problem of self-determination, raising the specter of civil war in the USSR. He took the opportunity to switch his discussion with Bush to problems of national self-determination and requested American assistance with regard to Soviet policy in Yugoslavia, where Moscow wanted to prevent the disintegration of another Slavic-Muslim state. He also wanted support vis-à-vis the Soviet republics. "There are an enormous number of real and imaginary international and inter-ethnic problems," Bush told Gorbachev. "Carving up states along these lines means provoking utter chaos. If I were to start listing the potential territorial problems, I wouldn't have enough fingers, not just on my own hands but on everyone's here. For example, here is the Soviet Union, 70% of inter-republic borders have not been definitely drawn. Before, no one cared about that, and everything was decided pragmatically, virtually at the district soviet level." If news of the killings on the newly established Lithuanian border embarrassed Gorbachev before Bush, it also legitimized his fears about the possibility of Yugoslav-type chaos in the Soviet Union. From Gorbachev's perspective, the news came at a most opportune time—on the eve of Bush's "unsupervised" visit to Ukraine.[6]

SOON AFTER 1:00 P.M. ON AUGUST 1, 1991, the leaders of the Ukrainian Soviet Socialist Republic gathered at Boryspil airport near Kyiv to welcome their guests of honor. It was the second time that an American president was visiting the city. The first visit occurred in late May 1972, when Bush's onetime patron, Richard Nixon, came to the Ukrainian capital after signing the Strategic Arms Limitation Treaty (SALT I) and the Anti-Ballistic Missile Treaty with Leonid Brezhnev. He flew to Kyiv from Moscow on a Soviet plane that had to be changed at the last minute because of a technical problem detected on the ground in Moscow. George Bush flew to Kyiv on the newly built Air Force One, a Boeing 747 jet that had replaced the Boeing 707 used by American presidents from Nixon to Reagan. Back in 1972, Nixon had found the interior of the Soviet plane that took him to Kyiv quite impressive—as he remembered later, "in some ways more impressive even than ours."[7]

Now George Bush was proud to show off the interior of his own brand-new plane, designed in American Southwest style at the suggestion of Nancy Reagan, to Gennadii Yanaev, the Soviet vice president. Yanaev had greeted the Bushes on their arrival in Moscow, and Gorbachev had asked Bush to take him along to Kyiv. Some Americans believed that Gorbachev's motive was to underscore Ukraine's membership in the USSR, while others thought Yanaev was being assigned to keep an eye on the American president. As Air Force One took off, Bush led Yanaev on a tour of the airplane, including the presidential command center. Yanaev, whom Bush later identified as the most senior Soviet official to fly on Air Force One, responded with polite comments. Bush later told his aides that the Soviet vice president was a "friendly sort of guy" but "not a heavy hitter."[8]

While Bush entertained his Soviet guest on the flight to Kyiv, the members of his staff became involved in a linguistic debate with major political implications. Jack Matlock, who was shown the text of the speech that Bush was scheduled to deliver later that day in the Ukrainian parliament, protested to one of the speechwriters against the use of the definite article with "Ukraine." The ambassador told his interlocutor, "Make sure the president leaves out the article. He should just say 'Ukraine.' Ukrainian Americans think the article makes it sound like a geographic area rather than a country." The speechwriter protested, "But we say 'the United States,' don't we?" But Matlock eventually prevailed. His argument was not linguistic but political: "If the president says 'the Ukraine,' the White House will be getting thousands of letters and telegrams in protest next week."

The United States had close to 750,000 citizens of Ukrainian descent. Canada had another million. It was not a huge community by North American standards, but it was well organized, politically active, and persistent. Throughout the Cold War, leaders of the Ukrainian American diaspora had successfully urged their followers to vote Republican. Bush was aware of this, and on hearing Matlock's political argument, he endorsed it. Dropping the article would appease his voters at home without hurting Gorbachev: the Russian language has neither definite nor indefinite articles. The version of the speech now on the website of the George Bush Presidential Library and Museum in College Station, Texas, includes a few passages where the definite article before "Ukraine" was overlooked and not stricken from the text—a sign of the confusion prevailing on the issue among the president's advisers during their flight to Kyiv. Matlock also tried to strike passages from Bush's speech that lent support to Gorbachev and the new union treaty, as he considered them inappropriate in Kyiv, but it was too late—the text of the speech had already been distributed to journalists.[9]

"In Kiev, capital of the Ukraine on the Dnieper River 515 miles south of Moscow, Bush will see a different face of the Soviet Union," read the advance pool report for the members of American media. "The city is neat and clean with broad, tree-lined avenues and will make for a colorful, moving finale of the trip." The author of the report joked that the real reason for the president's visit was to launch the campaign of the deputy White House news secretary, an ethnic Ukrainian named Roman Popadiuk, for the Ukrainian presidency. "His campaign slogan: I have nothing for you on that," quipped the author of the report.

Kyiv was welcoming Bush not as the "mother of Russian cities," as Richard Nixon had referred to it nineteen years earlier, but as the capital of a sovereign if not yet independent state. A sign at the terminal read, "Mr. Bush, welcome to Ukraine!" Besides the Soviet and American anthems, the band played the anthem of Ukraine. The degree of Ukraine's allegiance to Moscow was an open question. Jack Matlock, who had accompanied Nixon on his 1972 visit, noticed other differences as well. The speeches were now given in English and Ukrainian, not in English and Russian, as had been the case in 1972.[10]

These were different times. Nixon had flown to Kyiv ten days after Brezhnev replaced the nationally minded party boss of Ukraine, Petro Shelest, with his own loyalist, Volodymyr Shcherbytsky. Brezhnev's protégé crushed the national revival then under way in Ukraine, turning it into an exemplary Soviet republic and a bulwark of Moscow's rule in the USSR. A native of the same Dnipropetrovsk region of Ukraine as Brezhnev, Shcherbytsky was a key figure in the Dnipropetrovsk clan, a group of Brezhnev loyalists who effectively ruled the Soviet Union until the death of their boss in November 1982. Shcherbytsky created a pyramid of party officials in Ukraine personally loyal to him, and it took four long years for Gorbachev to become powerful enough to remove him from office in the fall of 1989.

Since the 1950s, the Ukrainian party elite had not only governed its own republic but also become a junior partner in running the Soviet Union. The "second Soviet republic," as Ukraine became known to political scientists in the West, had entered into an informal power-sharing agreement with its Russian counterpart in the 1950s, when the Ukrainian establishment helped propel its former boss, the longtime first secretary of the Communist Party of Ukraine, Nikita Khrushchev, to power in Moscow. Given that the Russians did not have their own communist party and ran the all-Union party instead, the Ukrainian party cadres emerged as the largest voting bloc at party congresses in Moscow. They used their voting power well. Khrushchev brought dozens of his Ukrainian backers to Moscow and appointed them to positions of power there. If anything, his ouster from power in the Kremlin coup of 1964 enhanced the status of the Ukrainian cadres.

Khrushchev's replacement at the helm of the party was Leonid Brezhnev, an ethnic Russian from Ukraine who had given "Ukrainian" as his nationality on his party registration card in the 1930s. Nikolai Podgorny (Ukrainian: Mykola Pidhorny), another native of Ukraine, became the chairman of the Supreme Soviet, the formal head of the Soviet state. The post of head of government went to an ethnic Russian, Aleksei Kosygin, but when he died in the late 1970s, his replacement was another former Ukrainian functionary, Nikolai Tikhonov. The minister of internal affairs and two deputy heads of the KGB were members of the Brezhnev clan and products of the Ukrainian party machine. The rule of the Dnipropetrovsk clan was supposed to continue even after Brezhnev's demise: the ailing leader saw Volodymyr Shcherbytsky as his successor.

But after Brezhnev's death in 1982, the KGB under Yurii Andropov took control of the Kremlin. Andropov brought to prominence Gorbachev, who, although half Ukrainian, had no links to the party machine in Ukraine or to Ukrainians in the capital. Furthermore, Gorbachev removed Shcherbytsky from his post in Ukraine and blocked the pipeline that was bringing Ukrainian functionaries to Moscow and making them influential there. With no prospect of furthering their careers in the center and under attack at home, the Ukrainian party elite felt betrayed by Moscow. The deal they had had with the Union since the time of Khrushchev—loyalty in exchange for unlimited rule at home and power sharing in the center—was no longer in effect, and they were not the ones who had abrogated it.

Resentment in the party elite had begun soon after the Chernobyl nuclear catastrophe in April 1986. The power station was entirely under Moscow's control, but it was the Ukrainian authorities who were left to deal with the long-term consequences of the disaster and take care of those resettled from the contaminated areas. Besides, Moscow pushed for a May Day parade even as the radioactive cloud reached Kyiv. The party elite believed that Gorbachev had forced Shcherbytsky to hold the parade, threatening him with expulsion from the party if he did not comply. Chernobyl unleashed a mass protest movement against the authorities, and again it was the party elite in Ukraine that had to deal with the situation. On top of that, the center was now encouraging democratic movements in the republic, which would further undermine the authorities' power. The Ukrainian party elite felt betrayed, abandoned, and angry. The center was now bringing them nothing but trouble.[11]

On their arrival in Kyiv, George and Barbara Bush were greeted by the fifty-seven-year-old Speaker of the Ukrainian parliament, Leonid Kravchuk. A pool report characterized Kravchuk as "a dynamic-looking, silver-maned, tanned guy who looks a little like John Gotti; he is obviously a natural politician, maybe the Newt Gingrich of the Ukraine." Kravchuk's background could not have been more different from those of the notorious New York Mafia boss or the rising star of the Republican Party. A former party apparatchik, now into his second year in the Speaker's office, Kravchuk performed a difficult balancing act, maintaining a veneer of loyalty to the center while aggressively advancing the interests of his homeland in relations with the weakened Gorbachev and the increasingly powerful republican leaders. He also emerged as the only figure capable of reconciling the interests of the Shcherbytsky-era party machine with the agendas of the rising pro-independence and democratic movements in Ukraine.[12]

A member of the same generation as Gorbachev and Yeltsin (Kravchuk was born in 1934), the Ukrainian leader had a background different from that of his Moscow counterparts. Born in the western Ukrainian province of Volhynia, which was then part of Joseph Pilsudski's Poland, Kravchuk experienced firsthand the brutality of World War II, which brought not only opposing German and Soviet armies but also the Holocaust, ethnic cleansing, and a struggle between Ukrainian and Polish nationalist guerillas to his home region. His father was killed fighting the Germans as a Red Army soldier, and the young Kravchuk learned survival skills early. As he later recalled, his grandfather's philosophy was not to stick out one's neck.

Having witnessed the secret police persecution of surviving members of the Ukrainian national movement in the late 1940s and early 1950s, Kravchuk had no need of Khrushchev's secret speech of 1956 to show him the political bias of the Soviet judicial system in the era of Stalin's "cult of personality." Still, not unlike Gorbachev and Yeltsin, whose relatives had been persecuted during the Great Terror, Kravchuk apparently had no qualms about serving the Communist Party. After graduating from Kyiv University with a diploma in political economy, he made a spectacular career for himself. Whereas Gorbachev and Yeltsin were party bosses entrusted with running huge regions of the Soviet Union, Kravchuk was an apparatchik, or party bureaucrat, par excellence.

By the 1980s, Kravchuk, a former Polish subject, had risen through the ranks to head the Communist Party propaganda apparatus in Ukraine. Given that he did not come from the industrial Donbas in eastern Ukraine or belong to the Dnipropetrovsk clan, this was probably the highest position to which he could aspire in Brezhnev's USSR. But then came Gorbachev's perestroika and glasnost, the first semi-free elections, and the party's need for people who could speak to the masses and hold their own in debates with political opponents. Kravchuk turned out to be a master of this trade and was promoted to secretary of the Ukrainian Central Committee in charge of ideology after Shcherbytsky, who never trusted the Volhynian propaganda genius, was forced to retire in the fall of 1989.

In the summer of 1990 Kravchuk became Speaker of the Ukrainian parliament, replacing Volodymyr Ivashko, a party boss whom Gorbachev summoned to Moscow to serve as his second in command in the party apparatus in an attempt to restore the shaken Russo-Ukrainian partnership at the center. Kravchuk found himself at the helm of a legislative body in which roughly one-third of the deputies advocated independence, while two-thirds were bent on enhancing their autonomy in the USSR. "As chairman of the Ukrainian Supreme Soviet," read Kravchuk's biography in Bush's briefing book, "Kravchuk must carefully balance the demands of the Communist majority in the legislature with those of independent-minded deputies."

Indeed, he skillfully maneuvered between the two factions, finding common ground in a policy of endowing the declaration of Ukrainian sovereignty adopted by the parliament that summer with political and economic substance. David Remnick, reporting on Bush's visit to Kyiv for the *Washington Post,* quoted Kravchuk as saying that he saw an opportunity to create a full-blooded Ukrainian state and was not going to miss the chance.[13]

Kravchuk was happy to welcome his prominent American guest in Kyiv, although the visit itself came as a surprise to him. As he recalled later, Moscow allowed him no part in preparing the visit, and at the last moment he was recalled from vacation to greet the American president. He flew from the Crimea directly to Boryspil airport—the press noticed his suntan—with no time to go into the city. Kravchuk began his address by welcoming George and Barbara Bush on "Ukrainian soil," pointedly referring to Ukraine rather than the Soviet Union but avoiding any reference to it as a country or a republic. Like the president's advisers who were concerned about the use of the definite article with "Ukraine," Kravchuk had his own linguistic conundrum to solve. For a year, Ukraine had been an officially sovereign but not independent state. What was the difference? No one but Gorbachev seemed to know, and Kravchuk did his best to equate the two terms. "The American Nation knows only [[too]] well the price of genuine sovereignty, and the Declaration of Independence was one of the first to proclaim to the whole world the ideals of freedom, equality, and brotherhood," he told his American guests.

George Bush was not prepared to endorse Kravchuk's equation of sovereignty with independence (he would draw a distinction between freedom and independence a few hours later). In his response to the Speaker's greetings, Bush began with less controversial matters. He noted that Ukraine was the ancestral homeland (he used the Soviet-friendly term "motherland") of hundreds of thousands of Americans. He quoted Ukraine's national poet, Taras Shevchenko, and welcomed the return to Ukraine from the West of Christian church leaders once banned by Moscow and the beginning of the spiritual revival of other religious groups. On Washington's relations with the republics, he was as cautious as he had been in his talks with Yeltsin. "We want to retain the strongest possible official relationship with the Gorbachev government," declared Bush, "but we also appreciate the importance of more extensive ties with Ukraine and other Republics, with all the peoples of the Soviet Union." Apparently he managed to deliver his first brief address on Ukrainian soil without ever using the definite article before "Ukraine."[14]

From the airport, Bush's motorcade proceeded to downtown Kyiv. "Large numbers of people were gathered in the square in front of the terminal with the yellow-and-blue flags of the Ukrainian independence movement," wrote Jack Matlock in his memoirs. "The motorcade route was lined with thousands of Ukrainians," read a media pool report. "Many waved, nearly all seemed friendly to Bush; several women held bouquets of home-grown flowers; some people held up babies; and one man carried a large loaf of bread and a bag of salt, in the traditional welcome." This was nothing like the modest public reception that Bush had received in Moscow, where he was a guest of the increasingly unpopular Gorbachev. Kyiv differed not only in its level of enthusiasm but also in appearance. Gorbachev's aide Anatolii Cherniaev, who had accompanied his boss to a meeting with Chancellor Helmut Kohl of Germany in Kyiv in early July, recorded his positive impressions of the visit in his diary: "It felt as if we were in some large West European city, more precisely, a German one: an air of the nineteenth century, avenues, greenery, neat, clean, well looked after . . . and generally sated. As compared with Moscow."

The mood of the demonstrators in August was the same as in July, when Cherniaev had noticed slogans such as "Kohl yes! Gorbachev no!" The crowds were profoundly anti-Gorbachev. The signs held by the demonstrators made their feelings quite clear to anyone who cared to read them. Some of them were specifically addressed to the American guests: "Moscow has 15 colonies"; "The empire of evil is living"; "If being part of an empire is so great, why did America get out of one?"; "Columbus opened America, Bush opens Ukraine." George Bush responded emotionally to his reception. In his address to the Ukrainian parliament a few hours later, he told his audience, "Every American in that long motorcade—and believe me, it was long—was moved and touched by the warmth of the welcome of Ukraine. We'll never forget it." Whether the president and his entourage grasped that the city was welcoming them as allies against Moscow and Gorbachev, not as supporters of Gorbachev's reforms or his vision of a reformed union, is hard to tell.[15]

The people welcoming Bush were proponents of Ukrainian independence. They represented the sentiments of Kyiv residents and many millions of Ukrainians outside the city, and they had been organized by activists of a political organization called Rukh, the Ukrainian word for "movement." Rukh was born in the fall of 1989 as the People's Movement of Ukraine for Perestroika. It was modeled on the popular fronts created in the Baltic republics and originally enjoyed Gorbachev's strong support. In this organization, created on the initiative of former dissidents released from imprisonment on his orders and by leaders of the Ukrainian intelligentsia, Gorbachev saw a counterbalance to the conservative party leadership headed by Volodymyr Shcherbytsky. As Kravchuk later recalled, Shcherbytsky hated the word "perestroika." When, during one of his public meetings with Kyivans, Gorbachev told them that they should apply pressure on the apparatus from one side while he did so from the other, Shcherbytsky turned to his entourage, pointed his finger at his head, implying that all was not well with Gorbachev's mental health, and asked his advisers, "On whom, then, does he plan to rely for support?"[16]

Shcherbytsky was right. Rukh's support for Gorbachev did not last long. If originally the founders of Rukh professed loyalty to Gorbachev's program of reforms, in October 1990, at the second congress of the organization, they dropped the word "perestroika" from the organization's name and declared the achievement of Ukrainian independence as their primary goal. By that time Ukraine had already declared its sovereignty, allowing the Ukrainian parliament to override any all-Union law that conflicted with republican-level legislation. But the party apparatus, the security services, the military, and most of Ukraine's industry were still taking orders from Moscow. Rukh sought to do away with that subordination. Its leaders also protested against the prospect of Ukraine's participation in the reformed union advocated by Gorbachev. Bush's visit to Kyiv could either lend support to Rukh or bolster its opponents, depending on the position he took. The word that the Rukh leaders were getting on the subject was anything but positive. Rumor had it that Bush was coming to Kyiv to do Gorbachev's bidding.

On July 31, as Bush was negotiating with Gorbachev in Moscow, the Rukh leadership organized a press conference in Kyiv dedicated to the forthcoming visit. Those present included Ivan Drach, a talented poet and head of Rukh, and Viacheslav Chornovil, a dissident and longtime prisoner of the Gulag who now chaired the Lviv regional administration—the stronghold of the pro-independence movement in formerly Austrian and Polish western Ukraine. Next to them was the legendary former political prisoner Levko Lukianenko, a Moscow-trained lawyer who was first arrested in 1961 for using Marxist-Leninist arguments to advocate Ukrainian independence and spent more than a quarter century in Soviet labor camps. The former inmates of the Gulag had joined forces with representatives of the national intelligentsia to lead Ukraine first to Soviet-style sovereignty and then to full independence. They wanted Bush to back their effort.

The bald and bespectacled Drach, fifty-five years old, was the first to speak at the Rukh press conference. He praised Bush for the support he had offered the Soviet nationalities while serving in Ronald Regan's administration, but there the pleasantries ended. The rest of his statement was an attack on Bush's policy toward the Soviet republics in general and Ukraine in particular. "President Bush seems to have been hypnotized by Gorbachev," claimed Drach. "The Bush administration still talks of stability in a way that suggests our source of stability is Moscow. And we must remember that as president, Bush has consistently snubbed the democratic movements in the republics. . . . He has specifically refused meetings with Rukh leaders in Washington. He has specifically refused to meet with us here. I am afraid that Bush comes here as a messenger for the center."

The American president's refusal to hold a separate meeting with leaders of the opposition was the immediate reason for Rukh's dissatisfaction. When the Rukh leadership had approached the White House to request such a meeting, it received a rebuke: the leaders of Rukh would be invited to a luncheon for Bush hosted by Leonid Kravchuk and other communist leaders of Ukraine, but there would be no separate meeting. The leaders of Rukh were also annoyed by American statements that did not recognize the distinctive character of Ukraine and its culture. Reacting to a White House statement to the effect that Bush was traveling to Kyiv to find out more about Soviet life and culture, Drach declared that "President Bush has missed the point." He went on, "If he wants to see Soviet life and culture, he can see it in the Kremlin. In the Kremlin he can witness imperialistic culture and greed. This is Ukraine. We are not a sample of Soviet culture; we are examples of the legacy of Soviet greed, a nation raped by Gorbachev's center."[17]

Bush was under pressure from Gorbachev in Moscow and from the Rukh leaders in Kyiv. His assistants had removed the definite article before "Ukraine" in the speech he was about to deliver before the Ukrainian parliament, but the president was still worried about the reception of his address. On the way from the airport, he stunned Kravchuk by asking him to read his address and tell him whether anything had to be changed. The Ukrainian leader was more than impressed: he could not imagine any of the Soviet leaders from Moscow showing him such consideration. All of them, from Brezhnev to Gorbachev, came to tell Ukraine what to do, not to ask the people what they thought. Bush, the leader of the world's richest and most powerful country, was actually interested in Kravchuk's opinion. He also gave the former party apparatchik turned democrat a piece of advice that Kravchuk never forgot: look people right in the eye, and only then will you be able to tell whether they will vote for you or not. Kravchuk read the draft of Bush's speech in translation and suggested a couple of changes. The parts that would not sit well with his parliamentarians were too essential to the speech to be deleted. One had to wait and see how many deputies would be dissatisfied and how unhappy they might become.[18]

Kravchuk's short meeting with Bush before they headed for parliament reassured him that the guest from Washington was indeed treating Ukraine and its leadership with respect. Bush's talking points for the meeting with the Ukrainian leader included references to Ukraine's "economic might and size—roughly equivalent to France and Britain in population." The American president was supposed to tell his Ukrainian counterpart that "our sole diplomatic relations will continue to be with the center" and that he intended to maintain the closest possible relations with Gorbachev, for whom he had deep respect. That said, Bush was not going to influence the Ukrainian position on the union treaty one way or another. "I understand that you are delaying a final commitment to a Union treaty until you can finish writing your own constitution," Bush was supposed to tell his host. The reference was to the delaying tactics adopted by the

Ukrainian leadership with regard to the union treaty—the writing of a new constitution could take forever.[19]

Kravchuk and the Ukrainian leadership decided to use Bush's stopover in Kyiv to push for two things: the opening of a Ukrainian consulate in the United States (a US consulate had just opened in Kyiv) and economic investment of up to $5 billion. The latter goal was supposed to be promoted by an American grant of most-favored-nation trade status to Ukraine. Cooperation in dealing with the effects of the Chernobyl nuclear disaster was another issue. The Ukrainians had little to offer in return, apart from their country's cooperation in the United Nations—they were clearly ready to act as independent players in the international arena, which they were not. Unlike the opposition, the Ukrainian leaders were not asking for support for independence; nevertheless, they were moving essentially in the same direction.

Ukraine's leaders wanted the same things that Yeltsin wanted, perhaps even more ardently than he did, but they presented their wishes in a more tactful manner, and Bush, while taking the same line as in Moscow, was much more friendly in his remarks to the Ukrainian leaders. The welcoming Ukrainians on the streets of Kyiv and the Ukrainian voters back home clearly helped him find the right tone with his Ukrainian hosts. "As the Union treaty is worked out," said Bush to Kravchuk, "I understand it will allow more direct dealings with the republics. In the meantime, we can go forward with economic issues, with nuclear safety."[20]

It was close to four o'clock in the afternoon on August 1, following his meeting with the Ukrainian leadership and a luncheon attended by representatives of the opposition, when President Bush rose to address the Ukrainian lawmakers. The members of parliament, who interrupted their debate on the implementation of Ukrainian sovereignty to listen to Bush's speech, represented a population of 52 million, of whom more than 70 percent were ethnic Ukrainians and roughly 20 percent ethnic Russians. There were also close to half a million Jews living in Ukraine. Roughly half the population spoke Russian, while the other half spoke Ukrainian.

The western territories incorporated into the USSR after World War II—a good part of them had belonged during the interwar period to Poland and, before that, to Austria-Hungary—were a stronghold of Ukrainian nationalism. Their population voted in concord with that of the Baltic republics, which also had been annexed to the Soviet Union in the course of the war. The east voted not unlike the neighboring oblasts of the Russian Federation—it all depended on whether people lived in cities or villages. Big cities such as Kharkiv became strongholds of the democratic opposition, comparable in that regard to Moscow and Leningrad. The countryside was still under the spell of communist propaganda. In the Ukrainian parliament, the communists maintained a solid majority, 239 seats out of 450. The "national democrats," a category that included nationalists and liberals, elected by voters in the west and in the big cities of the east, including Kyiv, could count on 125 votes.[21]

The main theme of Bush's speech, which he delivered with a huge statue of Lenin behind his back, was the idea of freedom and the responsibility that comes with it. Bush introduced his theme with an observation on the etymology of the name "Ukraine." Carefully avoiding the use of the definite article, he said, "Centuries ago, your forebears named this country Ukraine, or 'frontier,' because your steppes link Europe and Asia. But Ukrainians have become frontiersmen of another sort. Today you explore the frontiers and contours of liberty." Contrary to the worst expectations of the Rukh leaders, Bush spoke of Ukraine—its people, history, and geography—as separate from Russia. It was a far cry from Nixon's speech in 1972, when at a dinner hosted for him by Ukrainian officials, Nixon had referred to "Soviet soil," called Kyiv the "mother of all Russian cities," and freely used the definite article before the country's name.[22]

What Bush said next was less to the liking of the Ukrainian opposition. The president's speech, while carefully crafted so as not to offend Ukrainian sensibilities, confirmed the worst predictions of Drach and his colleagues about the political import of Bush's visit to Kyiv. "Some people have urged the United States to choose between supporting President Gorbachev and supporting independence-minded leaders throughout the U.S.S.R.," stated the president. "I consider this a false choice. In fairness, President Gorbachev has achieved astonishing things, and his policies of glasnost, perestroika, and democratization point toward the goals of freedom, democracy, and economic liberty." The president then explained his understanding of "freedom," which was disheartening to Rukh:

"Freedom is not the same as independence. Americans will not support those who seek independence in order to replace a far-off tyranny with a local despotism. They will not aid those who promote a suicidal nationalism based upon ethnic hatred." There was no doubt remaining: the United States would not support Ukraine's drive for independence—its proponents were on their own.[23]

Bush's speech reflected current thinking in the White House. Nicholas Burns later recalled:

> I do not think anyone thought on the American side in summer 1991 of any realistic possibility that the Soviet Union would disintegrate. . . . There was relative trust between Gorbachev and Bush, we were working together on most issues fairly well, and we were very anxious to visit Kyiv to demonstrate our interest in the republics. . . . We wanted to a see a gradual weakening of the Soviet structure and gradual change and reform because we feared that if we put our direct support behind nationalist movements, it could turn to violence, which could compromise control over nuclear weapons in some republics, and we felt that stable decline was in our interest.[24]

The speech produced a mixed reaction in the Ukrainian parliament. The communist majority welcomed Bush's cautious approach; the prodemocratic opposition rejected it, as did their backers in the United States. Bush tried to placate Ukrainian Americans when he stated in his speech to the Ukrainian parliament, "If you saw me waving like mad from my limousine, it was in the thought that maybe some of those people along the line were people from Philadelphia or Pittsburgh or Detroit, where so many Ukrainian-Americans live, where so many Ukrainian-Americans are with me in the remarks I've made here today." He thought that the speech, which was about to be reprinted in Ukrainian newspapers in the United States, would make his voters happy. That was a miscalculation, to say the least.[25]

The Ukrainian American community had been mobilized by recent developments in Ukraine and did not support Gorbachev or the Ukrainian communist leadership. They supported Rukh, and if Rukh was unhappy, so were Ukrainian Americans. Few were aware of Gorbachev's attempts to stop Bush from visiting Kyiv and the efforts that Bush and his team had applied to make the visit possible.

On Sunday, August 4, three days after Bush's visit to Kyiv, a group of Ukrainian protesters marched to the White House with such slogans as "I am a Ukrainian American. I do not support George Bush" and "Mr. Bush: Ukrainian independence equals freedom for all minorities." Following an hour-long demonstration, the leaders submitted their grievances to the White House. Their letter ended with a direct threat to defeat Bush at the next election: "Mr. President, we have come to the sad conclusion that in this visit to Kiev, Ukraine, you have done Mr. Gorbachev's bidding well. However, Ukraine will become independent, in spite of the Gorbachev-Bush coalition, as sure as the sun rises. And we, your fellow Americans who you claimed were with you on your performance in Kiev, were not and are not with you. We will take the lesson we have learned to the election polls in 1992."[26]

Negative reaction to Bush's speech would not be limited to the Ukrainian American community. The most damaging criticism came in an article by William Safire, a *New York Times* columnist and former speechwriter for Richard Nixon, who called Bush's "dismaying 'Chicken Kiev' speech" one of the administration's greatest blunders. According to Safire, Bush had "lectured the Ukrainians against self-determination, foolishly placing Washington on the side of Moscow centralism and against the tide of history." Safire's derisory phrase, "'Chicken Kiev' speech," caught the imagination of the American public as a metaphor for indecisiveness in Bush's foreign policy. In a book of memoirs written jointly with President Bush, Scowcroft claimed that the president's reference to local despotism was directed not toward Ukraine but toward Moldova (Moldavia) and other Soviet republics. Jack Matlock, who had probably invested the greatest effort in the visit, discerned ill will on Safire's part, but also possible atonement. It was Safire, noted Matlock, who had drafted President Nixon's speech of 1972 that referred to Kyiv as the "mother of all Russian cities."[27]

ON AUGUST 1, 1991, there was virtually nothing, apart from the protests of former political prisoners and intellectuals hardly known outside Ukraine, to indicate trouble ahead for Bush and his advisers. After a round of applause from the communist majority in the Ukrainian parliament, the president and his entourage left the building in the company of Leonid Kravchuk and his aides. Their limousines proceeded to Babyn Yar (Russian: Babii Yar), a ravine near the

medieval Church of St. Cyril and the site of one of the most horren-
dous massacres of the Holocaust. "The long, slow, twenty-minute motorcade to Babi Yar was the best of the trip to Bush," read the media
pool report on the event. "Ukrainians lined the streets, five and six
deep. Unlike the Muscovites, they were SMILING. They waved at Bush
and everyone else in the motorcade."[28]

On the slopes of Babyn Yar on the outskirts of Kyiv, in late
September 1941, the Nazi Sonderkommando 4a gunned down close
to thirty-four thousand of Kyiv's Jews in the course of two days. The
executions were carried out in broad daylight. Gramophone music
played by the Nazis failed to drown out the cries of the victims, and the
experience brutalized the city's inhabitants. These were the first days
of the German occupation and the first victims of Babyn Yar. Before
the Red Army recaptured Kyiv in the fall of 1943, more than seventy
thousand new victims—Soviet prisoners of war, Ukrainian nationalists,
Roma, civilian hostages, and psychiatric patients—were executed on the
slopes of Babyn Yar. Before their departure the Nazis tried to conceal
their crimes, exhuming bodies, burning them, and then scattering the
ashes. They could not erase the memories of the survivors.

The Soviets investigated and documented the executions—at
the Nuremberg war crimes trials they reported some one hundred
thousand victims—but the original report was doctored to conceal the
fact that the first victims were Jews and that they were killed as part
of what would become known as the Holocaust. The Soviets treated
all victims as undifferentiated citizens of the USSR. A documentary
novel titled *Babii Yar*, by the talented Kyiv writer Anatolii Kuznetsov,
was published in 1966, with a quarter of its text deleted by the censors.
It was not published in full until 1970, after Kuznetsov emigrated to
the West. In 1976, a monument was finally erected at Babyn Yar to
commemorate the victims of the massacres. According to the official
version of events, it commemorated Soviet prisoners of war and
Soviet citizens in general.[29]

It was against the background of the Soviet-era memorial that
George Bush was preparing to deliver his speech honoring the dead.
"Look closely at the great bronze and granite monument that will
form a backdrop for Bush's speech," read the advance pool report
for the media. "At its top is the figure of a woman bending her head
to kiss her child. Only from the rear of the monument is the true

horror and tragedy of the scene revealed—the woman's hands are tied behind her."

In his speech at the memorial, Bush welcomed the new politics of memory in Ukraine that finally made it possible to recognize the victims of the Holocaust in their own right. "For many years, the tragedy of Babi Yar went unacknowledged, but no more," he said. "You soon will place a plaque on this site that acknowledges the genocide against Jews, the slaughter of gypsies, the wanton murder of Communists, Christians—of anyone who dared oppose the Nazi madman's fantasies." As he had done in his speech to parliament, Bush found a way to acknowledge the contribution made to the reevaluation of Soviet history by Mikhail Gorbachev and support his embattled partner in the Kremlin. He linked him to no less a figure in American history than Lincoln: "Abraham Lincoln once said: We cannot escape history. Mikhail Gorbachev has promoted truth in history."

"I was choked up when we went to the memorial at Babi Yar, where the Nazi occupiers had killed tens of thousands of Ukrainians, Jews and others," Bush later recalled. "Midway through my speech I faltered as I described the horrors of a day fifty years earlier." The president's speech was indeed full of heartbreaking details of the massacre, including the use of gramophones by the Nazi executioners. Barbara Bush listened to the speech seated next to simply dressed elderly women of peasant appearance, survivors of Babyn Yar, and those who had helped save their lives. Leonid Kravchuk was trying to calm his own emotions. As an eight-year-old boy in German-occupied Ukraine, he witnessed mass execution of Jews by Nazi machine gunners. A few months after Bush's visit, speaking at the ceremony marking the fiftieth anniversary of the Babyn Yar massacre, he would deliver part of his speech in Yiddish, and in a later interview he would state that not all his countrymen had behaved as they should have under the circumstances. The reference was to Ukrainian participation in the Holocaust.[30]

Bush's speech was very well received by those present at the ceremony. Ivan Drach and other Rukh leaders, who were among the first in Ukraine to recognize the significance of Babyn Yar in the Holocaust, welcomed the visit. The Ukrainian-Jewish alliance against the Soviet empire developed by political dissidents of both peoples in the Gulag was becoming a political reality thanks to Rukh, whose policies were heavily influenced by former dissidents. Rukh was in the forefront of those battling the still widespread anti-Semitism in Ukraine, and its political platform advocated Ukrainian-Jewish cooperation against the dictates of the center.[31]

The only people who seemed out of place at the ceremony were Gorbachev's representatives accompanying Bush on his trip to Kyiv—Vice President Gennadii Yanaev and the Soviet ambassador to Washington, Viktor Komplektov. Because all speeches in the course of the visit were delivered in either Ukrainian or English and all business was transacted in those languages, the Russian visitors were almost completely at a loss. Komplektov remarked during Bush's speech in parliament "that it was good that he understood English, otherwise he would have been unable to follow what was going on." According to his short biography in the president's briefing book, Yanaev spoke "some English." If that was indeed the case, it was not apparent in Kyiv. The Ukrainian officials spoke perfect Russian, but their switch to Ukrainian had symbolic meaning for the now officially sovereign republic.

The Americans went along and brought a Ukrainian interpreter. They also accommodated the Ukrainian request for a separate meeting between President Bush and Leonid Kravchuk that was not attended by Yanaev. According to Ed Hewett of the National Security Council, the Soviet vice president, who did not speak Ukrainian and probably did not understand most of what was said in English, was treated by the Ukrainian officials more like the "chairman of the All-Union Leprosy Association" than as a representative of the Union center. He was visibly bored and annoyed during the luncheon hosted by Kravchuk. But times had changed: it was now the center's turn to make itself useful to the republics, and Yanaev understood the new rules of the game.[32]

AT ABOUT 7:00 P.M. LOCAL TIME, Air Force One took off from Boryspil airport and headed for Washington. The visit was finally over. A major milestone had been reached on the long road to nuclear disarmament, a new policy formulated on the national self-determination of the Soviet republics, democracy supported, and help given to a friend in the Kremlin in order to maintain control over the crumbling former superpower. In Yanaev's Moscow-bound plane, Matlock and the Soviet vice president "toasted what had seemed to be a very successful visit by the American president." George Bush was looking forward to a well-deserved rest on his Maine estate in Kennebunkport. It had been a busy July. August promised to be slow and restful. That was the hope, never to be fulfilled.[33]

II.

THE TANKS OF AUGUST

4

THE PRISONER OF THE CRIMEA

"MIKHAIL, I HOPE YOU'RE WELL," were the first words of the virtual message that George Bush dictated into his small tape recorder. In his years as president, Bush kept an audio diary, with which he often shared thoughts and emotions that he did not wish to make public. On the evening of August 19, 1991, as he dictated another entry into his tape recorder, the president's mind was far from American shores: he was thinking of Mikhail Gorbachev. "I hope they've not mistreated you," continued the president. "You've led your country in a fantastically constructive way. You've been attacked from the right and from the left, but you deserve enormous credit. Now we don't know what the hell has happened to you, where you are, what condition you are in, but we were right to support you, I am proud we have supported you, and there will be a lot of talking heads on television telling us what's been wrong, but you have done what's right and strong and good for your country."[1]

The president was gathering his thoughts about a day that he called historic in his diary. In faraway Moscow, that day had seen the declaration of a state of emergency by Gorbachev's former allies, his ousting from power on grounds of alleged poor health, and the appearance of tanks in the streets. Bush had not expected any such turn of events after his return from Moscow a few weeks earlier. He had spent the previous night at his family estate, Walker's Point, in Kennebunkport, Maine, with only one major item on his agenda:

73

at 6:30 a.m., before Hurricane Bob hit the coast, he was planning to play eighteen holes of golf with Brent Scowcroft, who was staying at the Nonantum Hotel in Kennebunkport, and Roger Clemens, a celebrated pitcher for the Boston Red Sox. A few minutes after retiring, Bush was awakened by a telephone call from Scowcroft. The national security adviser was not calling about the golf game or the weather that threatened to derail it. As had been the case the previous summer, when Saddam Hussein invaded Kuwait, the news had to do with international politics and threatened to kill not just the game but the whole vacation: there had been a coup in Moscow.

Half an hour earlier Scowcroft had been lying peacefully in bed reading cables. The television set was tuned to the twenty-four-hour CNN news channel, and he heard the announcer say something about Gorbachev resigning for health reasons. It did not sound right: only a few weeks earlier Scowcroft had seen Gorbachev, apparently in excellent health, and he now began to listen more carefully. The next announcement from Moscow left no further doubt: the Soviet information agency, TASS, reported on Gorbachev's illness and the creation of a committee to deal with a state of emergency. Those in charge of the committee—a group of hard-liners led by Vice President Gennadii Yanaev—included the heads of the KGB and the military, Vladimir Kriuchkov and Marshal Dmitrii Yazov. All of them had been guests at Bush's reception in Moscow a few weeks earlier. Scowcroft called his deputy, Robert Gates, asking him to check the news with the CIA. He then summoned the deputy press secretary, Roman Popadiuk, who was staying in the same hotel, to draft a statement in case the report was not a hoax.

Scowcroft then called the president and told him what he knew. For the time being there was no independent confirmation from any government channel, including the CIA. "My God!" was Bush's first reaction. They discussed how to react: journalists were already knocking on the door of Popadiuk's hotel room. "The president's inclination was to condemn it outright, but if it turned out to be successful, we would be forced to live with the new leaders, however repulsive their behavior," wrote Scowcroft later. "We decided he should be condemnatory without irrevocably burning his bridges." Scowcroft was anything but optimistic: with so many powerful figures behind the reported coup, it would probably succeed. "Extra-constitutional" was the term Scowcroft suggested that the president use in any public reference to the coup. Before Bush made an attempt to go back to sleep, they agreed that Scowcroft would monitor the situation throughout the night and call him at 5:30 a.m. Popadiuk issued a brief statement to the press, admitting that the administration had no independent confirmation of what was going on in Moscow. He told Scowcroft that in the morning the president would have to speak to the press, and he could not comment on the coup from a golf course. "It might be raining in the morning anyway," responded Scowcroft. The game was definitely off.[2]

The morning brought little clarity, except that there was no doubt the coup had indeed taken place. What had happened to Gorbachev? What could now be expected? What was the plotters' agenda, and what did the coup mean for the future of Soviet-American relations and of the USSR itself? Everyone knew that the impact of such an event would be enormous, but no one could tell exactly what it would be.

As usual, the CIA covered all possible options. Its analysts suggested a 10 percent chance of a return to the pre-perestroika regime, a 45 percent chance of a stalemate between hard-liners and democrats, and a 45 percent chance that the coup would fail. The CIA was more skeptical than Scowcroft about the plotters' chances of success, partly because its people failed to detect any major preparations: the coup had been organized at the last moment and could not have been prepared very well. Still, it was anyone's guess how things would go. Bush spoke with Prime Minister John Major of Britain and President François Mitterrand of France. Like the American president, they had been taken completely by surprise. Bush told Mitterrand that Gorbachev too had been caught unawares. That was the line given him by Scowcroft earlier in the morning. "If they don't know, how the hell could we know?" dictated the president into his tape recorder that day. Still, it looked bad: not only had the CIA missed signs of the coming coup, but it had left the president and his national security adviser to learn the news from CNN. "The press is saying it was an intelligence failure," said Bush to Prime Minister Brian Mulroney of Canada later that morning.[3]

The State Department was unprepared as well. James Baker, on vacation in Wyoming, learned of the coup from the department's Operations Center one hour after Scowcroft heard of it on television.

As he received information from Washington and advice from his assistants, themselves on vacation and scattered all over the world, Baker made notes in his hunter's notebook. Its small pages were marked at the top with an observation appropriate for a vacation but hardly for international crisis management: "Hunter will do anything for a buck $." The first notes read, "No leverage. Certainly minimal"; "Will be hard to do business w/new guys for a while"; "Emphasize the lack of their political legitimacy." After that, there appeared to be some hope that the situation could be reversed. "Yeltsin is key guy," read one of the notes. "Should stay in touch with him. Portray us trying to get info. Touch base w/reformer."

The American embassy in Moscow was in the middle of a transition: Jack Matlock had already left, and his replacement, Robert S. Strauss, had not yet been sworn in. A Texan with close links to Bush and no knowledge of Russian or diplomatic experience of any kind, Strauss was supposed to act as the president's direct liaison with Gorbachev. Now it appeared that Gorbachev had been taken out of the picture before Strauss even entered the scene. Bush called the US chargé d'affaires, Jim Collins, who had already gone next door to the Russian parliament building, known in Moscow as the White House. He told the president that the building was open but there was no sign of Boris Yeltsin, who had opposed the coup. The Americans in Moscow were in no danger, reported the chargé d'affaires.

That was the only positive news Bush could give journalists crammed into a small room of the presidential compound, where they took shelter from the rain brought by Hurricane Bob. Bush expressed deep concern about the events in Moscow. He assured the reporters that the US government was carefully following the situation, but it was too early to say how things would develop. Answering a question, he noted that coups could fail: "They can take over at first, and then they run up against the will of the people." Following Scowcroft's advice, the president characterized the coup as "extra-constitutional" rather than unconstitutional. Bush's praise for Gorbachev and his accomplishments sounded like an elegy. He admitted that he had not tried to reach Gorbachev by phone. His main concern was whether the plotters would continue the withdrawal of Soviet troops from Eastern Europe begun by Gorbachev and honor START and other agreements on the control of nuclear arms. He said that US aid would be suspended as long as "extra-constitutional" rule continued, but there would be no further sanctions unless the new leaders departed from their commitments to other countries.

Still, Bush was reluctant to burn his bridges with the coup leaders. The president found some good words to say about Vice President Yanaev and declined to support Yeltsin's call for a general strike, despite a direct question from a journalist. Privately, Bush refused to believe that Yanaev was actually in charge of the coup. That was an impression he shared with Chancellor Helmut Kohl of Germany. Bush liked the Soviet vice president, whom he had met on his recent trip to Moscow and Kyiv. After coming back to Washington and learning that Yanaev was a fisherman, the president had sent him some fishing lures from his own supply. He did not know whether they had reached the purported leader of the plot. At the press conference, Bush shared his "gut feeling" that Yanaev was committed to reform but admitted that his actions pointed to the contrary. Bush noted, however—correctly, as it turned out—that it was not Yanaev but the KGB and army hard-liners who were calling the shots in the coup.[4]

The press conference was anything but a success, as Scowcroft immediately told the president. The reporters had been taken aback by the coolness of Bush's reaction and compared it to his response to the Tiananmen Square massacre by the communist government of China more than two years earlier. To control the damage, Bush decided, on Scowcroft's advice, to interrupt his vacation. He would leave Maine in front of television cameras and head for Washington to manifest his leadership and direct involvement in dealing with the international crisis. The image would change, but not the substance of the president's response. The most important thing on the minds of administration officials that day was to look tough in front of the television cameras without provoking the coup leaders into abandoning international agreements signed by Gorbachev. Helmut Kohl told Bush that he was worried about whether the withdrawal of Soviet troops from eastern Germany would continue. So did the East European leaders, who still had Soviet troops on their territories. The United States and its allies had managed to get much of what they wanted from Gorbachev, but would his successors continue to observe those arrangements?[5]

The American leaders had long been aware that the Soviet Union's policy of cooperation with the West might be short-lived, and Washington had planned accordingly. In January 1991, after hearing a CIA report on the latest developments in the Soviet Union, Secretary of State James Baker commented to his staff, "What you are telling us, fellas, is that the stock market is heading south. We need to sell." Baker meant locking in the gains of the unprecedented bull market in US-Soviet relations. In his memoirs he wrote, "'Selling' meant trying to get as much as we could out of the Soviets before there was an even greater turn to the right or shift into disintegration." This policy continued into the spring and summer of 1991. Robert Gates wrote in his memoirs that in the months leading up to the coup the administration was following the approach summarized by Brent Scowcroft at a national security briefing for the president on May 31, 1991: "Our goal is to keep Gorby in power for as long as possible, while doing what we can to help head him in the right direction—and doing what is best for us in foreign policy."

Now that Gorbachev was out of power, the task was not to forfeit what had been achieved during his tenure. The fall of the Berlin Wall in 1989 had led to the reunification of the two German states and symbolized the end of communism in Eastern Europe. Could the old walls dividing East and West be rebuilt by the new leaders in the Kremlin? No one knew. On August 19, 1991, the same day George Bush dictated his warm and compassionate virtual letter to Gorbachev, he also dictated the following into his tape recorder: "I think what we must do is see that the progress made under Gorbachev is not turned around. I'm talking about Eastern Europe, I'm talking about the reunification of Germany, I'm talking about getting the troops out of the pact countries, and the Warsaw Pact itself staying out of business. [[Soviet]] cooperation in the Middle East is vital of course, and we may not get it now, who knows?"[6]

Judging by his audio diary, Bush was struggling to reconcile the policies he felt he had to conduct in the interests of his country with the personal attachment he clearly felt for Gorbachev. In his thoughts, the president went back in time, trying to establish whether he or his administration could have done anything more to support Gorbachev and help him avoid the coup. Eventually he succeeded in convincing himself that nothing could have been done differently or better. In his diary that day, Bush was eager to answer critics who claimed that he had been too supportive of Gorbachev. He saw the coup as a vindication of his earlier policies vis-à-vis the Soviet center and the republics—represented by Gorbachev and Yeltsin. "If we had pulled the rug out from under Gorbachev and swung towards Yeltsin you'd have seen a military crackdown far in excess of the ugliness that's taking place now," wrote Bush in his diary.

A more difficult question to answer was whether the United States and its allies had done enough to support Gorbachev in London in July when he had asked for money. That question was raised by Prime Minister Brian Mulroney of Canada in a telephone conversation with Bush after the press conference. He reminded Bush of the question he had asked Helmut Kohl in London: "If a month from now, Gorbachev is overthrown and people are complaining that we haven't done enough, is what we're proposing the kind of thing we should do?" Kohl, who owed Gorbachev a debt for his role in the reunification of Germany and was the strongest advocate of granting the Soviet Union as many credits as possible, allegedly said, "Absolutely." Both Bush and Mulroney knew that Kohl's position at the G-7 meeting in London had been much more supportive of Gorbachev than their own, but afterward they took comfort in Kohl's change of heart as he indicated that Germany would go along with the United States and the rest of the G-7 in offering Gorbachev encouragement but little money. "Any doubt in your mind that he was overthrown because he was too close to us?" asked Mulroney. "I don't think there is any doubt," answered the president.[7]

GORBACHEV HAD PLANNED TO RETURN to Moscow from his summer vacation in the Crimea on August 19. He had flown there on August 4, about the same time that President Bush went to Walker's Point. Like Bush's estate, Gorbachev's vacation home was located by the sea, but whereas Bush went to Maine to avoid the heat of the American summer, Gorbachev went south to bask in the sun: like many Soviet citizens of his generation, he could not imagine a vacation without getting a suntan and swimming in the Black Sea. Unlike other Soviet citizens, however, he could afford to spend his vacation in what was considered utmost luxury by Soviet standards.

In 1988, a brand-new villa had been constructed for Gorbachev on the high bluffs of the Crimea near a settlement called Foros. Located in "greater Yalta," Foros was some forty kilometers from Livadia, where Franklin Roosevelt, Winston Churchill, and Joseph Stalin had conferred in 1945. The new mansion, known as State Resort No. 11 or the Sunrise Building, was constructed at a time when Gorbachev and his colleagues in the Politburo had launched a campaign against privileges for the party leadership and apparatus. When the Gorbachevs came to Foros in August 1991, Raisa ordered that crystal chandeliers be removed from beach houses near the sea. That did little to change the reality: it was a luxurious development indeed.

The Sunrise Building went up in record time on what previously had been bare rock. To make the environment more hospitable, thousands of tons of soil, along with bushes and trees, were brought there from afar. Every year, as winter rains and winds pushed soil down to the sea, new soil was brought in to replace what had been lost. The beach, created by removing rocks and adding hundreds of tons of sand, was connected with the main terrace by an escalator. To protect the mansion from the winds, which were especially strong there, part of the huge rock face was cut off to accommodate the building. The officers of the KGB bodyguard department, which oversaw construction and was charged with ensuring the security of the mansion, complained that it was difficult to protect from approaches by both land and sea, but the Gorbachevs loved it. As in previous years, in August 1991 they vacationed there together with their daughter's family—the thirty-four-year-old medical doctor Irina Vigranskaia, née Gorbacheva, together with her doctor husband, Anatolii, and their two young daughters.

August 18, the last day of Gorbachev's vacation, had begun for him like any other part of his Crimean holiday. He and Raisa woke up at about 8:00 a.m. and had breakfast, and at around 11:00 a.m. Mikhail and Raisa, whose movements were recorded by their KGB guards under the code names 110 and 111, went down to the sea. As always, Raisa went for a swim, but Mikhail remained on the beach: a few days earlier he had suffered an attack of lumbago and was now staying away from the water. As always, it was a working vacation for Gorbachev. After lunch he revised the speech he was going to deliver in Moscow on August 20 at the signing ceremony for the new union treaty, which was the result of many months of maneuvering and negotiation between the weakening center and the ever more assertive republics. At about 4:30 p.m. Gorbachev spoke by phone with one of his aides, Georgii Shakhnazarov, who was vacationing at a nearby resort and helping him draft the speech. It turned out to be the last phone conversation Gorbachev would have for the next several days.

A few minutes earlier, two KGB officers who had arrived in the Crimea together with the head of the bodyguard department of the KGB, General Yurii Plekhanov, ordered Tamara Vikulina, a telephone operator at the KGB-run government telephone center, to cut Gorbachev's lines. Vikulina asked them to allow her to place the last call—she had just told Gorbachev that she was connecting him with Shakhnazarov. The officers agreed. But once the call was over, all the lines linking Gorbachev's mansion with the outside world were cut, including the communications network that allowed the Soviet president to launch a nuclear attack. The president's nuclear briefcase would be sent to Moscow the next day, where it ended up in the hands of the plotters, who included the minister of defense, Marshal Yazov, and the chief of the General Staff, General Mikhail Moiseev, the bearers of two other nuclear briefcases. The Ministry of Defense became the sole master of the Soviet nuclear force.[8]

Gorbachev realized that something was wrong when Vladimir Medvedev, the chief of his personal security detail, came to his room around 4:45 p.m. and interrupted his afternoon newspaper reading with the announcement that there was a group of visitors from Moscow waiting to see him. Members of the group included his chief of staff, Valerii Boldin; two secretaries of the Central Committee of the Communist Party; and the commander of Soviet ground troops, General Valentin Varennikov. All except Varennikov were trusted aides long known to Gorbachev, but the Soviet president was clearly worried. He asked Medvedev how they had made their way to the heavily guarded compound. Medvedev replied that the group included General Plekhanov, the chief of all bodyguards, including Medvedev himself. What did they want? Medvedev could not answer that question. By then he already knew that a coup was under way. When Plekhanov had showed up in his office a few minutes earlier and asked that the delegation be taken to Gorbachev, Medvedev had first tried to reach the president by phone. The line was dead. "Now I understood," he later wrote, "this was the Khrushchev scenario. All communications had been cut."[9]

Gorbachev understood that it might be a coup after he told Medvedev to ask the guests to wait and then tried to call Moscow to find out what was going on. He wanted to reach the head of the KGB, his trusted ally Vladimir Kriuchkov. The telephone was dead. So was another, and another—all five, including the red telephone provided for Gorbachev as commander in chief of the Soviet armed forces. Now there could be no doubt: it was a coup, and not only had the visitors violated protocol by showing up without being summoned, they had also isolated the Soviet leader from potential allies outside. Gorbachev summoned Raisa and then his daughter and son-in-law to one of the bedrooms. After a short discussion, the entire family decided to stand by him, whatever decision he made. Gorbachev later wrote that he firmly resolved not to succumb to pressure and change his policies, no matter what the cost. It was a moment full of anxiety. "We all knew our history, its terrible pages," recalled Raisa Gorbacheva later.[10]

The last Soviet leader ousted by his aides had been Nikita Khrushchev, whose removal in 1964 was immediately recalled by Gorbachev's bodyguard. Khrushchev was lucky: his life was spared, and he was allowed to retire. All previous Soviet leaders, as well as Khrushchev's successor, Brezhnev, died in office—some under more than suspicious circumstances. There were persistent rumors that Stalin had been poisoned: he died at a time when he was preparing to strike out against his closest associates, including the head of the secret police, Lavrentii Beria. This alleged mastermind of Stalin's assassination was soon arrested by the military on Khrushchev's orders and shot after being accused of working for British intelligence. Leonid Brezhnev had died in 1982, when, according to some reports, he was preparing a transfer of power that would bypass the former head of the KGB, Yurii Andropov. According to Brezhnev's bodyguard, Vladimir Medvedev, for years Andropov (along with some other members of the Politburo) had been supplying Brezhnev with sleeping pills; Brezhnev died in his sleep. The Gorbachevs knew their history, or rather the Kremlin lore, very well.[11]

Given the political precedents, it was a good sign that the plotters had decided to talk before acting. After speaking to his family, Gorbachev went to see the uninvited guests. They were already in the building, some sitting on a couch, others wandering around the second-floor hall of the mansion, which they found spectacular. Then they saw Gorbachev. He was clearly suffering from lumbago and moving with difficulty. Gorbachev invited the visitors into his office and, turning to those with whom he felt most comfortable, asked in a low voice whether this was an arrest. They assured him that it was not. They told him that they had come to discuss the situation in the country. His demeanor changed. "Whom do you represent, and in whose name are you speaking?" asked Gorbachev once the plotters had crammed into his office, which had only two chairs for visitors. They were silent, not knowing what to say. He repeated the question. When they told him that they represented a committee including Kriuchkov, Yazov, and Yanaev, the president asked who had created the committee—the Supreme Soviet? They did not have an answer. Gorbachev had immediately identified the weakest spot in their position: the committee they represented was an "extra-constitutional" body at best.[12]

Valerii Boldin, the fifty-six-year-old chief of the presidential staff and the plotter who knew the president best, believed that Gorbachev felt somewhat relieved when he heard the names of the committee members. Gorbachev's main concern, argued Boldin in his memoirs, was that the visitors might represent not his indecisive aides but his impulsive archenemy, Boris Yeltsin. In the previous few days Gorbachev had often been on the phone with Kriuchkov, discussing the political situation in the country. Gorbachev was mainly worried that at the last moment Yeltsin would change his position and refuse to sign the union treaty. On August 14 he had had a long conversation with Yeltsin, trying to convince him not to succumb to the pressure of critics who were demanding a Russian referendum on the treaty. "On the whole we parted on good terms," wrote Gorbachev in his memoirs. "However, I could not get rid of the feeling that Yeltsin was holding something back."

When, a few days later, on August 16, Yeltsin went to Almaty to see the Kazakh leader Nursultan Nazarbayev, an ally of his, an alarmed Gorbachev called Valerii Boldin in Moscow to find out whether he knew anything about the visit. Gorbachev suspected a plot. "You understand what's going on. Independently, ignoring the opinion of the president of the USSR, local leaders are deciding matters of state. This is a conspiracy," he allegedly told his aide, who was already plotting with Kriuchkov and others to oust his boss. On August 18, the day the plotters showed up on the doorstep of Gorbachev's Foros villa, Yeltsin had issued a decree taking over any all-Union institutions responsible for supply chains on the territory of the Russian Federation. Gorbachev's principal concern at the time was how to deal with Yeltsin.[13]

Judging by Boldin's memoirs, in the last years of his rule Gorbachev put pressure on the KGB to wiretap Yeltsin's conversations, despite alleged protests by Kriuchkov, who reported that his people were refusing to do the job. Kriuchkov sent the transcripts to Boldin, who then arranged for their direct delivery to Gorbachev. The Soviet leader was worried about a possible alliance between his political opponents, among whom he listed not only Yeltsin but also his liberal adviser and the "grandfather of perestroika," Aleksandr Yakovlev, and the military. Gorbachev was especially disturbed by the violent end of Nicolae Ceaușescu's regime and the execution of the Romanian leader, along with his wife, by rebels in December 1989. There were discussions about establishing direct presidential control over the KGB directorate in charge of presidential bodyguards, but Gorbachev never acted on the idea. Instead, he dramatically increased the number of his bodyguards and their salaries. He also started to use an armored limousine more often. In August 1991 the bodyguards were still hired by and reported to Kriuchkov, not Gorbachev.

The Romanian events were very much on the minds not only of Gorbachev but also of his security chiefs, although they drew different conclusions from them. On August 18, 1991, surprised by the unexpected appearance of the plotters, Gorbachev's bodyguards had approached the arriving limousines armed with Kalashnikov automatic rifles. One of the bodyguards' commanders, General Viacheslav Generalov, had arrived with the plotters: he rushed toward them, telling them to put their rifles aside so as not to repeat the Romanian scenario, when Ceaușescu's guards provoked bloodshed that led to his execution. The guards obeyed Generalov's order and let the unannounced visitors pass their checkpoint. Gorbachev's main line of defense had failed. When he showed the plotters into his small office, he would not admit General Plekhanov, the chief of the KGB directorate. Gorbachev considered him a traitor who had tried to "save his own skin" by betraying the president.[14]

As Gorbachev sat in his study, facing the representatives of the plotters, it was not the loyalty of the guards but the treason of his most trusted associates that was his first concern. Against all odds, he was trying to win a political battle, not an armed confrontation that might well have ended tragically for him and his family. Once he learned that the plotters were not his political opponents but his heretofore sycophantic allies and aides, he not only felt psychological relief of sorts but also found himself in a position of strength. "I had promoted these people—and now they were betraying me!" wrote Gorbachev in his memoirs. He had managed to browbeat and keep these people under control before. Now he would not allow Plekhanov to enter his office. He told Boldin to shut up and called him a "prick" who had come to lecture him on the situation in the country.

The visitors were shocked by the forcefulness of Gorbachev's reaction to their proposals. They offered their boss a choice: either sign a decree declaring a state of emergency or transfer his powers temporarily to Gennadii Yanaev and stay in the Crimea for "health reasons," while they would do all the "dirty work" in Moscow. The plotters believed that Gorbachev, with whom many of them had discussed contingency plans for the implementation of a state of emergency in the past, would agree to one of these proposals. Gorbachev flatly refused to accept either of them. "If they were truly worried about the situation in the country, I told them," wrote Gorbachev in his memoirs, "we should convene the USSR Supreme Soviet and the Congress of People's Deputies. Let's discuss and decide. But let us act only within the framework of the Constitution and under the law. Anything else is unacceptable to me." Gorbachev was in his element—negotiating, maneuvering, trying to convince his opponents. He asked them to describe their plans and called their mission suicidal. "Think about it and pass it on to the comrades," he said to the visitors while shaking hands before their departure. To General Valentin Varennikov, the member of the delegation who was especially insistent on demanding the proclamation of a state of emergency, Gorbachev said, "Now, after such explanations, we obviously will not be working together."

After the delegation left, Gorbachev recounted the gist of the conversation to his family and his aide Anatolii Cherniaev, an old apparatchik with strong liberal convictions who was responsible for formulating many of Gorbachev's foreign policy initiatives. "He was calm, steady, and smiling," wrote Cherniaev in his diary a few days later. Still, Gorbachev could not get over the fact that his associates had betrayed him. He could not believe that Kriuchkov was among the plotters and was particularly shocked by the claim that they had been joined by Marshal Yazov. "But perhaps they wrote him in without asking him?" he wondered about his loyal minister of defense. Cherniaev was sympathetic but could not help mentioning that all the plotters were Gorbachev's people.[15]

THE VISITORS LEFT GORBACHEV'S Foros villa confused and depressed. The driver who took them to the mansion and then back to the airport later testified that on the way to Foros they were animated and talked about the weather. On the return trip they were angry and mostly silent. Boldin later regretted that there was no time left to swim in the sea, which was probably part of the original plan: a friendly talk with the president, who would sign one of the prepared documents, leaving enough time for a quick swim. Now they faced a different situation. On the flight back to Moscow, the Foros visitors had more than a couple of drinks to soothe their nerves. Before landing two and a half hours later, they had finished a big bottle of whiskey, which was served with pieces of lard, bread, and vegetables.

In Moscow they headed straight for the Kremlin. In the spacious office of Prime Minister Valentin Pavlov, once used by Joseph Stalin himself, they were welcomed by the leaders of the plot: KGB chief Kriuchkov, Prime Minister Pavlov, Interior Minister Boris Pugo, and Vice President Yanaev. Also present was Defense Minister Dmitrii Yazov, about whose loyalty Gorbachev had reassured President Bush a few weeks earlier. The news about Gorbachev's refusal to transfer his powers to Yanaev had already reached the plotters: the head of the KGB bodyguard department, General Plekhanov, had called Kriuchkov from the plane to let him know what had transpired in the Crimea. They were now waiting for the return of the delegation to hear a firsthand report and decide what to do next.[16]

Bespectacled, gray, and half bald, the sixty-seven-year-old Kriuchkov was an unlikely plotter. He was known for his outstanding work ethic, bureaucratic skills, and caution. An attorney who joined the Foreign Service in the early 1950s, he found a patron in Yurii Andropov after serving under his leadership at the Soviet embassy in Budapest during the 1956 Hungarian uprising. Kriuchkov followed his boss into the KGB in the 1960s, where he presided over the Soviet foreign spy agency for fourteen years, from 1974 to 1988. Gorbachev promoted Kriuchkov to head of the KGB in 1988. Kriuchkov had powerful supporters at the top, including Gorbachev's close ally Aleksandr Yakovlev. The reformers wanted to see the KGB headed not by an ideological watchdog, as in the past, but by someone with international experience who realized how far the Soviet regime had fallen behind the West and would therefore support reform.

Kriuchkov fit the bill, or so it seemed. Actually, his only service abroad had been his time in Budapest in the 1950s. The only Western spirit Kriuchkov truly appreciated was whiskey—a product to which ordinary Soviet citizens had no access. Robert Gates, then deputy director of the CIA, first discovered Kriuchkov's penchant for whiskey in December 1987, when he came to Washington to prepare Gorbachev's first visit to the United States. Gates, Colin Powell (then national security adviser to President Reagan), and Kriuchkov met for dinner in a Washington restaurant. When the time came to order drinks, Kriuchkov asked for a scotch. The interpreter, speaking English, asked for Johnny Walker Red, but Kriuchkov corrected him and said that he wanted Chivas Regal. "It was clear he was not a man of peasant tastes," Gates later recorded. To him, Kriuchkov looked more like a college professor than a chief of intelligence.[17]

There can be little doubt that Kriuchkov, like many of the other plotters, originally supported Gorbachev's perestroika, which they understood as a set of reforms intended to make the Soviet system more competitive without undermining its foundations. But once they realized that it threatened not only the party, to which the most pragmatic of them had no ideological attachment, but also the political structure of the state and their place in it, their attitude changed. Kriuchkov's change of outlook was noticed by Robert Gates, who met with him in Moscow in February 1990. After the meeting, Gates told James Baker, who was also in Moscow at the time, that Kriuchkov "was no longer a supporter of perestroika and Gorbachev had better watch out." The KGB head had told the visiting American official that "people were dizzy with change," perestroika had failed, the economy had deteriorated, and relations between national groups were going from bad to worse. "Kriuchkov seemed to have written off Gorbachev," remembered Gates later.[18]

What made Kriuchkov and the other plotters strike when they did was the threat to their own positions at the top of the power pyramid. Gorbachev later believed that the coup had been triggered by a wiretap of one of the most confidential discussions he ever had with Boris Yeltsin. That conversation took place in the late hours of July 29, 1991, one day before President Bush's visit to Moscow. The venue was the same villa in Novo-Ogarevo where Gorbachev and Bush would hold their talks two days later, and the conversation included one more republican boss, Nursultan Nazarbayev of Kazakhstan. They stayed in the building until midnight, discussing personnel changes that were supposed to follow the signing of the new union treaty on August 20. Nazarbayev would replace Prime Minister Valentin Pavlov in the new Union government. Yeltsin insisted on the removal of Kriuchkov and Yazov. Nazarbayev also wanted to get rid of Yanaev. Gorbachev felt uncomfortable discussing the fate of his aides but then gave his consent to the removal of Kriuchkov and interior minister Pugo, though not Yazov.[19]

The conversation had been taped on Kriuchkov's orders, and the head of the KGB now knew that his days in power were numbered unless he acted immediately. A coup could be organized only while the president was not in Moscow otherwise he would learn of the preparations. Back in 1964, Brezhnev and his associates had made a secret alliance against Khrushchev and planned their arrangements while he was on vacation. Two days after Gorbachev left for the Crimea, Kriuchkov summoned two of his officers and assigned them to prepare an assessment of likely public reaction to the introduction of a state of emergency. The results were not encouraging, as the KGB experts concluded that the response would be largely negative. The economic situation should be allowed to deteriorate further. But Kriuchkov knew that he had to act before Gorbachev returned to Moscow to sign the union treaty on August 20. There was of course some hope that the Gorbachev-Yeltsin alliance would fall apart before then. But once Gorbachev and Yeltsin confirmed their readiness to sign the treaty in a telephone conversation on August 14, Kriuchkov could not wait any longer.

That day he ordered his aides to prepare plans for introducing a state of emergency. On the following day he ordered wiretapping of the telephones of Yeltsin and other democratic leaders. On Friday, August 16, Kriuchkov discussed how to proceed in a series of meetings with his coconspirators held at KGB headquarters. On the August 17 the group, which included Kriuchkov and top party and government officials, met in a larger group at a KGB safe house known by the code name ABC. They began by asking Prime Minister Pavlov, who was not yet involved in the plot, whether he knew that he was to be removed from his position. Pavlov said that he was prepared to resign but nonetheless decided to join the plotters. Questioned after the coup, Pavlov and other participants in the meeting claimed that they did not discuss the ouster of the president—what they had in mind was simply going to the Crimea and convincing him to declare a state of emergency. On Sunday, August 18, they sent their delegation to Gorbachev. Before talking to him, they cut off his communications and arrested his bodyguards. Whether or not the enterprise was planned as a coup, it became one the moment they ordered his telephones disconnected.[20]

The delegation that had confronted Gorbachev at Foros arrived in the Kremlin soon after 10:00 p.m. on August 18. Marshal Yazov remembered a few days later that the report the plotters heard boiled down to the following: "He [[Gorbachev]] drove them out, refusing to sign any documents. Generally speaking, we have 'shown our hand,' so to speak. And if we are now dispersing empty-handed, then we are headed for the executioner's block, while you are free and clear." The reference was to those members of the conspiracy, including Yazov and Kriuchkov, who had stayed in Moscow, awaiting the results of the Crimean trip.

The plotters could reach no immediate agreement on a course of action. Gorbachev's refusal to let them do the "dirty work" for him had taken them by surprise. The Gorbachev they knew—a cunning politician, always maneuvering and shifting position depending on circumstances—was supposed to succumb under pressure. His demurral left the plotters in a precarious position. Going ahead with the implementation of the state of emergency meant breaking the law. Some in the room suggested that, given Gorbachev's refusal to support the coup, things should be left as they were. Boldin had his doubts. He told those gathered in the prime minister's office, "I know the president; he will never forgive such treatment." There was no way back, especially for those who had gone to the Crimea. The only hope was a transfer of presidential powers to Yanaev on health grounds.[21]

That had been plan B from the very beginning. Kriuchkov and the other plotters had no doubt that Yanaev would go along, but the vice president himself had known nothing about the plot until he entered the prime minister's office a few hours before the arrival of the delegation from the Crimea. Like the members of the delegation, Yanaev showed up at the meeting far from sober: known for his propensity to drink, he had been dragged away from a table at a resort near Moscow, where he had been visiting a friend. A few hours earlier, knowing nothing of the plot, Yanaev had told Gorbachev on the phone that he would meet him on his return to Moscow the next day. As the alcohol began to wear off, Yanaev felt anything but happy about being saddled with the whole "extra-constitutional" enterprise. Although he was empowered to take over from the president in case the latter was incapacitated, there was no proof that Gorbachev had any medical problem.

When a prepared copy of the one-sentence decree was produced by Kriuchkov, Yanaev balked: the president should come back and take care of business after recovering from his illness. Besides, he did not feel ready to take on the job. The plotters would not be put off. A takeover by the vice president was their only hope of legitimizing the coup, however thinly, and they pressed hard on Yanaev, citing the need to stabilize the situation and save the harvest. They would all pull together to get the job done: the only thing he had to do was sign the decree. When Kriuchkov, playing the good cop, told him softly, "Sign, Gennadii Ivanovich," he complied. The decree read, "In view of Mikhail Sergeevich Gorbachev's inability, for health reasons, to carry out the responsibilities of President of the USSR, and in accordance with Article 127 (7) of the USSR Constitution, the responsibilities of the President of the USSR have been transferred to the Vice President of the USSR, Gennadii Yanaev, beginning August 19, 1991." Then, as acting president, he signed a decree on the creation of the Committee for the State of Emergency, which included, apart from himself, Kriuchkov, Yazov, Pavlov, and other members of the conspiracy. The constitution was all but suspended: power in the country had been usurped by the committee.

The paperwork had been prepared ahead of time by Kriuchkov and his associates. For all their references to the constitution, none of the decrees were constitutional. Not only did Yanaev have no right to assume Gorbachev's powers—as the president was not incapacitated—but under the constitution even Gorbachev was not empowered to declare a state of emergency without the consent of the all-Union and republican parliaments. Besides, there was no reason to declare a state of emergency: no natural disasters, industrial catastrophes, or popular disturbances were recorded on August 18, 1991. The only emergency the drafters of the documents were able to come up with was the need to save the harvest, but even there, the situation was neither better nor worse than usual. But with the signing of the questionable papers by Yanaev and other members of the newly formed committee, the Rubicon had been crossed, and it was time to act. Yanaev and Prime Minister Pavlov, for their part, retired to Yanaev's office and drank until dawn. Others went to work establishing the state of emergency beyond the confines of Gorbachev's villa in Foros.

Vladimir Kriuchkov spent the rest of the night meeting with his deputies and commanders and organizing the implementation of the coup. It had been his idea to start with, and his people had been involved in drafting the relevant documents and making the first clandestine preparations. The time had come to involve the entire KGB apparatus. At 3:30 a.m. Kriuchkov called a general meeting of the KGB leadership to announce that perestroika was over. The democratic leadership had failed to keep the situation under control, he said, having in mind Gorbachev and his liberal advisers, and it was time to impose a state of emergency.[22]

THE FIRST NEWS ABOUT THE OUSTER of Gorbachev and the declaration of a state of emergency was broken by the Soviet media at 6:00 a.m. on August 19. Soviet radio and television made an announcement that shook the country: a state of emergency was being declared for a period of up to six months. There was no independent commentary and very little else in the way of news programming. Television and radio stations were ordered to work as they had done in days of mourning for deceased Soviet leaders. After the death of General Secretaries Brezhnev, Andropov, and Konstantin Chernenko between 1982 and 1985, the Soviet public was mainly fed broadcasts of classical music and ballet. Did the broadcast of *Swan Lake* on this occasion signify the death of yet another Soviet leader? No one could tell for certain. There was only the announcement of Gorbachev's ill health, unaccompanied by any medical report.[23]

Gorbachev, who had spent a sleepless night in Foros, learned of his ouster thanks to a small Sony radio that the plotters had failed to take away from him. "What a stroke of luck to have brought it along," wrote Raisa Gorbacheva in her Foros diary. "While shaving in the morning Mikhail Sergeevich uses it to listen to the 'Maiak' station. He brought it with him to the Crimea. The fixed receiver here in our residence is not working on any of the wavelengths. Only the tiny Sony is working." The whole Gorbachev family had spent a sleepless night. "Several large warships headed toward our bay," wrote Raisa. "The patrol ships came unusually close to the shore, stayed for about fifty minutes and subsequently left." She wondered what that might mean: "A threat? Isolation from the sea?" Neither she nor her husband knew the answer.[24]

The appearance of an unusual number of patrol ships near Gorbachev's mansion was one of the few facts that the CIA could provide to President Bush in addition to official Soviet reports about the ongoing coup. Another piece of information was that Gorbachev's plane had not left the Crimea. The Americans knew that Gorbachev was there, but no one could say what had happened to him. They could only hope for the best. But their optimism was limited, to say the least.

On the evening of August 19, President Bush dictated into his tape recorder his virtual letter to the distant Gorbachev: "As I sit here with all the best advice we can muster, I'm not sure that there's any chance that you, Mikhail, can come back. I hope that you never compromise yourself enough that if you come back you'll be under a cloud. I hope that Yeltsin, who's calling for your return, stays firm, that he's not removed by the power of this ugly right-wing coup." The words sounded like a prayer. It was anyone's guess whether it would be answered.[25]

5

THE RUSSIAN REBEL

BORIS YELTSIN WAS AWAKENED by his daughter Tatiana soon after 6:00 a.m. at his resort house in the government compound of Arkhangelskoe-2 near Moscow. He had slept barely five hours after returning from a visit with Nursultan Nazarbayev in Almaty. At first he could not understand what was going on, but when Tatiana told him about the coup, Yeltsin's first reaction was, "That's illegal." The news came as a complete shock. It was August 19, the first full day of the coup. The previous night his thoughts had been focused on the signing of the new union treaty. He was worried about what to expect from Mikhail Gorbachev once the treaty was signed: Would he try to set the Central Asian republics, which were loyal to him, against Russia? Now Yeltsin was facing an unprecedented situation. He sat glued to the television set, watching the announcers read the official statements of the Emergency Committee. It was clear that Gorbachev was not among the committee members. The treaty was off. What should he do now?

Yeltsin's wife, Naina, was the first to compose herself. "Boria," she said, addressing her husband by his nickname, "whom should we call?" Most of the Russian leaders were housed in the buildings nearby. Unlike Gorbachev's phones, Yeltsin's were still working, and he soon summoned his associates to his house. The visitors found Yeltsin deep in thought. Everyone agreed that it was a coup. Given the membership of the committee, the plotters had all the instruments of power in their hands. The Russian government, meanwhile, was a paper tiger. It had ministers and departments but no control over the army, the KGB, or the interior forces. The democratically elected mayors of Moscow and Leningrad (since September 1991 St. Petersburg) theoretically had the local police under their control, but nothing more. The first impulse was to enter into negotiations with the Emergency Committee, but that idea was soon rejected. The Russian leadership would instead appeal to the people.

Yeltsin and the members of his government began to draft the text of their appeal by calling a spade a spade: "On the night of August 18–19, 1991, the legally elected president of the country was removed from power." It declared the Emergency Committee unlawful and called on the "citizens of Russia to give a fitting rebuff to the putschists and demand a return to normal constitutional development." Yeltsin, Russian prime minister Ivan Silaev, and chairman of the parliament Ruslan Khasbulatov, the three Russian leaders who signed the appeal, called for a general strike until their demands were met: that Gorbachev be allowed to address the country and that the Soviet parliament be called into emergency session. The appeal was written by hand and then typed by Yeltsin's daughter Tatiana. It was now ready for distribution. Its main points were dictated over the phone to the Russian vice president, Aleksandr Rutskoi, who was then in Moscow. The deputy mayor of Moscow, Yurii Luzhkov, jumped into his car and sped off to the capital with a copy of the appeal. He had orders from Yeltsin to mobilize the citizens of Moscow against the coup.

It was now close to 9:00 a.m., and Yeltsin had to decide what to do next. Should he stay in Arkhangelskoe or go to Moscow? "We were afraid that we would be caught there," his prime minister, Silaev, later remembered, referring to Arkhangelskoe. That would have been easy to do in the remote compound, but there was the no less real danger that the Russian leaders would be arrested on their way to Moscow. Their bodyguards were reporting the appearance of KGB troops near the compound and the movement of tanks toward the capital and offered to smuggle Yeltsin out in a fisherman's boat on the Moskva River and then take him to Moscow by car. He refused. He would go openly in his presidential limousine to the White House, as Muscovites called the huge downtown building of the Russian parliament, from which he would lead the resistance. Yeltsin saw tears in his wife's eyes. As he put on a bulletproof vest and got ready to leave, she tried to stop him: "What are you protecting here with that bulletproof vest? Your head is still unprotected. And your head is the main thing." She added, "Listen: there are tanks out there. What's the point of your going? The tanks won't let you through."

Naina Yeltsina later recalled her husband's words: "No, they won't stop me." It was then that she became truly frightened. Yeltsin had a somewhat different recollection of his answer. "I had to say something," he wrote in his memoirs, "so I gave her my best shot: 'We have a little Russian flag on our car. They won't stop us when they see that.'" It is not clear from Yeltsin's memoir which Russian flag he had on his car—the official Soviet one, red with a narrow blue stripe, beneath which he had taken the presidential oath a few weeks earlier, or the old tsarist tricolor with white, blue, and red stripes, the official flag of the Russian Empire and later of the first democratic Russian revolution of February 1917, which toppled tsarism. Certainly it was the latter that became the symbol of Russian hope and identity in the days of the coup.

A few hours later, having made his way to the White House, Yeltsin climbed atop one of the tanks surrounding the parliament building to read his appeal to the people of Russia. Behind him, his aides unfurled a middle-sized Russian tricolor. "This improvised rally at the tank was not a propaganda gimmick," remembered Yeltsin later. "After coming out to the people, I felt a surge of energy and an enormous sense of relief inside." Yeltsin was now leading the opposition to a coup that allegedly wanted to save the Soviet Union. He was doing so in the name of Russia, under the traditional imperial colors—an unlikely leader of an even more unlikely revolt. Russia was rebelling against its own empire.[1]

FOR KGB HEAD VLADIMIR KRIUCHKOV, as for most of the plotters, the sleepless night of August 18 was followed by a day that was hectic but also full of excitement. Immediately after 5:00 a.m., he ordered the distribution of printed forms to military commanders for the detention of opposition leaders. Prime Minister Valentin Pavlov demanded the internment of a thousand activists, but Kriuchkov was not so relentless. There were about seventy individuals on his list, including Gorbachev's former liberal aides Eduard Shevardnadze and Aleksandr Yakovlev. There was also a short list of eighteen people, including the activists of Shield, an organization of former military officers whom the plotters considered most likely to organize mass protests. The "short list" did not include the name of Boris Yeltsin.

The Russian president was no friend of Gorbachev's, and the plotters hoped to win him over. Kriuchkov sent commandos from the KGB Alpha group to Yeltsin's cottage in Arkhangelskoe with the order to create conditions for Yeltsin's negotiations with the Soviet leadership. In plain language, that meant his arrest. But Kriuchkov soon changed his mind and called off the operation in Arkhangelskoe. Hopeful that the Soviet parliament would provide a veil of legitimacy for the coup, Kriuchkov was careful to avoid any rash action. The unprovoked arrest of such a high-profile figure as Yeltsin would doubtless raise questions in parliament. It was therefore decided to wait: if Yeltsin cooperated, he could be left free; if he did not, he could be arrested for violating the newly proclaimed laws once he made it fully apparent that he was opposed to the state of emergency and thus, it was hoped, had discredited himself in the eyes of the public. The plotters firmly believed that most people were tired of the anarchy of Gorbachev's rule and would side with them. Yeltsin was therefore allowed to proceed to Moscow on the morning of August 19: the Alpha operatives were under orders not to stop him.[2]

At 10:00 a.m., when the plotters gathered in Acting President Yanaev's office for the first regular meeting of the Emergency Committee, Kriuchkov told his colleagues that he had been in touch with the Russian president. The result was dismal: "Yeltsin refuses to cooperate. I spoke with him by telephone. I tried to make him see reason. It was useless." This was a clear setback but not a major reason for concern. The coup was proceeding as planned. By 6:00 a.m., tanks of the Taman division had surrounded the Ostankino television center and tower; an hour later the rest of the troops from the Taman and Kantemirovskaia divisions, familiar to Muscovites from their participation in the annual military parades on Red Square, began to move in. Altogether some 4,000 troops, more than 350 tanks, about 300 armored personnel carriers, and 420 trucks were rushed into the city. They converged on the capital just as Muscovites who had spent the weekend at their country houses were making their way back. The troops blocked major intersections and created havoc on the roads.

Yeltsin's limousine had managed to reach the center of town before army vehicles made the streets there almost impassable.

Muscovites cursed the traffic jams and the army but were generally friendly to individual soldiers. They talked with the young recruits, whose average age was nineteen. They also brought food and candy and bombarded the troops and officers with endless questions: Why did you come? Are you going to shoot? The soldiers did not know the answer to the first question but knew that they would not fire on civilians. As the plotters saw it, things were going their way. There were no demonstrations in Moscow, enterprises were working as usual, and Yeltsin's call for a general strike went unanswered. His speech from the top of a tank made an impressive picture, but there were relatively few people around the White House to listen to him. The situation outside Moscow seemed calm as well. Kriuchkov received regular reports from around the country. He later remembered, "It was calm everywhere. The first reaction aroused hope; there was even a kind of euphoria."[3]

With the troops safely in Moscow and the situation under control, the time had come to face the public and tell the Soviet people and the international community what the plotters wanted. Scores of foreign correspondents and a select group of Soviet reporters whose editors had the trust of the hard-liners were invited to a press conference at 6:00 p.m. in the press center of the Ministry of Foreign Affairs. There, a few weeks earlier, Bush and Gorbachev had held their press conference after the signing of the START treaty. Weary and under stress, Gennadii Yanaev, who had known nothing about the coup a day earlier and could hardly have imagined himself as its leader, was charged with selling it to the public. Kriuchkov, Yazov, and Prime Minister Pavlov refused to face the public—they would run the coup behind the scenes—but the rest of the plotters, including Interior Minister Boris Pugo, joined Yanaev behind a long table facing hundreds of foreign and domestic reporters.[4]

"Ladies and gentlemen, friends and comrades," said Yanaev as he opened the press conference, "as you already know from media reports, because Mikhail Sergeevich Gorbachev is unable, owing to the state of his health, to discharge the duties of President of the USSR, the USSR Vice President has temporarily taken over the performance of the duties of the President." He went on to stress the gravity of the political and economic situation in which the country found itself as a result of Gorbachev's reforms, and he promised to organize the broadest possible discussion of the new union treaty. After Yanaev was done, the floor was opened for questions, both to him and to other members of the committee. That afternoon the committee had ordered the closing of all liberal-leaning newspapers in Moscow. In the evening they would use their total control of state television to project the desired image of the coup and its objectives. The television cameras were in the hall. The plotters' calculation was simple: their own man would conduct the press conference, and even if foreigners asked uncomfortable questions, these would be offset by the "right" questions from loyal reporters.

The proceedings began well. The loyal correspondents asked questions designed to help Yanaev make his case in favor of extraordinary measures and against the actions undertaken by Boris Yeltsin. A *Pravda* correspondent said that Yeltsin's call for a general strike could "lead to the most tragic consequences." But the next question, which came from a foreign correspondent, opened a devastating salvo of inquiries. Ignoring the tone set by the Soviet reporters, their foreign counterparts bombarded Yanaev with questions about Gorbachev's health and pointed out the illegality of the coup. But the hardest blow on that score was delivered by a local journalist. Tatiana Malkina, a young reporter for *Nezavisimaia gazeta* (*Independent Newspaper*), one of the papers shut down by the plotters, had sneaked into the conference hall without an invitation. When the unsuspecting press secretary called on her, she shook the audience with the sheer audacity of her demeanor: "Could you please say whether or not you understand that last night you carried out a coup d'état? Which comparison seems more apt to you—the comparison with 1917 or with 1964?" The references were to the Bolshevik coup and the dismissal of Nikita Khrushchev.

Yanaev dodged the question, saying that neither precedent applied to this particular case. But the question that followed immediately from a foreign reporter was no less crushing: whether the plotters had consulted with the leader of the 1973 Chilean coup, General Pinochet. The audience burst into laughter and applause. The press secretary called for order. In answering further questions and countering accusations that the committee was acting unconstitutionally, Yanaev promised to have the Soviet parliament in session by August 26. He also went out of his way to assure the audience of his loyalty to his "friend, President Gorbachev," whose return after recovery he was eagerly awaiting. Before the conference Yanaev had received a message from Gorbachev, who demanded that his communications at Foros be restored and that a plane be made available to take him back to Moscow. The demand was rejected. Instead, the guards reconnected the television cable, making it possible for Gorbachev and his family to watch the press conference.[5]

The press conference was a failure for the plotters. Television cameras showed the whole country a tired apparatchik with a gray and less than healthy-looking face, an odd haircut designed to cover his baldness, a trembling voice, a runny nose, and restless hands that he did not know where to place. Yanaev, who was not well known in the country and was considered a nonentity by those who did know him, confirmed people's worst expectations. The press conference had shown people all over the country that the authorities could be not only argued with but even ridiculed. Later that evening it became apparent that the plotters did not have full control over Soviet television. The official news program *Vremia* (*Time*) included not only a reading of the Emergency Committee's statements and a report on the press conference but also a broadcast from the approaches to the White House, where Yeltsin's supporters were constructing barricades. Now everyone in Moscow knew that resistance was possible and where to go in order to join it.

The press conference highlighted a major problem facing the committee: it had no unquestioned leader. The mastermind of the coup was Kriuchkov, but formal authority belonged to Yanaev, who, as a seasoned apparatchik, was trying to save his place atop the Soviet pyramid in the only way he knew: by avoiding responsibility. Prime Minister Valentin Pavlov, having joined the committee and demanded harsh measures against his political opponents and strike participants, drank himself into an attack of hypertension and found safe haven in a hospital. Marshal Yazov and Interior Minister Pugo had been at each other's throats ever since their subordinates began to be deployed to crush pro-independence movements in the non-Russian republics, so neither of them was about to take responsibility for failures there. When Marshal Yazov's wife, Emma, came to see her husband at the

Ministry of Defense at the time of the press conference and begged him to quit the committee and call Gorbachev, he told her, "Emma, understand that I am alone." He shook his head in desperation as he watched the broadcast of the press conference. "Dima," said Emma, calling her husband by his nickname, "whom have you fallen in with? You always used to laugh at them!"[6]

As the plotters assembled in Yanaev's office after the press conference, the euphoria they had experienced a few hours earlier was gone. They now grasped that Yeltsin was a real danger to them and had to be dealt with. They decided to do something about that in the morning.

The morning of August 20 began for Yanaev and others with the reading of a fresh KGB memo on the errors they had made the previous day. The committee, wrote the KGB experts, had failed to enforce the state of emergency, locate and isolate opposition leaders, disrupt communications between opposition groups, and seize opposition media resources. And there was more bad news: chances were dwindling that the Soviet parliament would approve the committee's actions, as rumors were spreading among political insiders that Gorbachev was alive and well in his Crimean cage. That morning Kriuchkov, Yazov, and Interior Minister Pugo ordered their subordinates to prepare a plan for storming the White House.[7]

BORIS YELTSIN HAD SPENT all of August 19 in the White House. Naina Yeltsina, her younger daughter, Tatiana, and the rest of the family found safety in a small apartment on the outskirts of Moscow that belonged to Yeltsin's bodyguard.

They had left Arkhangelskoe in a hurry soon after Yeltsin's presidential limousine with the Russian flag on it sped off to Moscow. The family members got into a van brought by the guards. Boris and Maria, the young children of Yeltsin's elder daughter, Elena, were told that if the security personnel ordered them to lie on the floor of the van, they should do so without asking questions. "Mama, will they shoot us in the head?" asked the young boy. His question sickened the whole family. Although the van was inspected by KGB troops on leaving Arkhangelskoe, it was allowed to proceed to Moscow. When Tatiana called from a street telephone on the morning of August 20, she could not get through to her father. As she later recounted, she was told that "everything's normal. Papa has practically not slept at all, he is working constantly, and he is in a fighting mood."[8]

At the White House, Yeltsin was in his element. Projecting a sense of strength and a belief in ultimate victory, he provided the kind of leadership that the plotters could only dream of. A charismatic politician who could sense the mood of the masses, Yeltsin was willing to take risks that his competitors, including Mikhail Gorbachev, were not prepared to run. Like Abraham Lincoln and Winston Churchill, Yeltsin was at his best in times of crisis. Once the crisis passed, he often felt lost and depressed. That had been the case after his removal as Moscow party boss in the fall of 1987, when he tried to commit suicide by slashing his stomach with office scissors. He would treat his depressions with alcohol, surprising both supporters and opponents with erratic behavior. But Yeltsin was at his best in a crisis, and this time, too, he rose to the occasion.[9]

Apart from climbing on top of a tank, the Russian president had spent August 19 issuing decrees that declared the coup unconstitutional and established his authority over institutions and troops on the territory of the Russian Federation. The Soviet KGB, Interior Ministry troops, and the army were to follow the orders of the Russian president alone, declared the decrees and appeals. But privately he was preparing for the worst. The reports received that day by the members of the Emergency Committee did not lie: not only was there no general political strike, but no individual strikes were in evidence either. By the end of the day a few mines went on strike in the faraway Kemerovo region, but that did nothing to help the defenders of the White House.

Yeltsin's forty-four-year-old vice president, Aleksandr Rutskoi, was placed in charge of the White House defenses. Rutskoi was a former military pilot who had been shot down twice in Afghanistan. On one occasion he was captured by agents of Pakistani Inter-Services Intelligence and allegedly given an offer of immigration to Canada in return for cooperation with the CIA, but he remained loyal to his country. Rutskoi was released from captivity, awarded the star of Hero of the Soviet Union, and elected to the Russian parliament before being chosen by Yeltsin as his running mate in the presidential election of 1991. A maverick by nature and a trained military officer, Rutskoi was an ideal candidate to organize the White House defenses, which relied heavily on the expertise of former Afghan veterans. But neither Rutskoi's poorly armed men nor the makeshift barricades constructed by the Muscovites in imitation of the barricades built by Lithuanians around their parliament in January 1991 were capable of repelling an attack by Kriuchkov's commandos with the support of Yazov's tanks. Yeltsin, Rutskoi, and the rest of the Russian leadership were well aware of that. Their only hope was that the plotters would not dare to attack or, if they did, that the troops would not obey orders to shoot.[10]

Throughout the day, Yeltsin worked hard to win over the troops brought to Moscow by the plotters. The Russian president appealed to individual commanders, trying to bring them over to his side. One of his first calls from Arkhangelskoe had been to General Pavel Grachev, a forty-three-year-old Afghan veteran and commander in chief of Yazov's paratroop units. Yeltsin had met him during his presidential campaign a few months earlier. Back then, the young general had assured Yeltsin that he was prepared to defend the Russian government against any challenge to the constitution. Now the time had come to test the general's resolve to defend the constitution. Even if Grachev did not actually mean what he had said in the heat of the political campaign, Yeltsin had nothing to lose by trying. No coup was possible without the paratroopers, one of the few battle-ready units in the Soviet army, and at worst Yeltsin would learn what was going on among them. His contacts with real or potential adversaries went on throughout the coup.[11]

The main battle for the loyalty of the army was waged on the streets of Moscow. Muscovites, initially shocked by the appearance of tanks in their city, soon adopted a strategy that proved devastating for the coup: they simply charmed "the boys." Casual discussions with army veterans, pretty girls, and kindly grandmothers who shared whatever they had with the soldiers made them psychologically unfit for the task of crushing civilian unrest. The new class of Russian businessmen who supported Yeltsin and feared the loss of their enterprises at the hands of a new hard-line communist regime brought enough food and alcohol to the White House to keep up the spirits not only of its defenders but also of the troops stationed around Yeltsin's stronghold. Yazov was appalled. To eliminate the danger of fraternization, the army commanders began rotating their units around Moscow.

Nevertheless, Yeltsin made it as difficult as possible for Yazov and the people around him to command the loyalty of the troops. His first victory was achieved largely through the efforts of the Muscovites, whom Yeltsin was counting on to turn things around when he summoned them to a rally in front of the White House at midday on August 20.

Moscow Echo, an independent radio station whose journalists refused to be intimidated by the plotters, called incessantly on Muscovites to show up at the White House. The television reports of the previous evening had shown citizens where to gather. Still, it was a gamble. If people ignored the call for a meeting as they had ignored the call for a general strike, no barricade or reluctance on the part of the troops would save Yeltsin and the nascent Russian democracy from an imminent crackdown. As things turned out, people heard the call and showed up in staggering numbers. Yeltsin spoke from the balcony to close to one hundred thousand Muscovites who came to manifest their support for him and his struggle. They brought a huge Russian tricolor flag. Smaller flags decorated the balcony from which Yeltsin addressed the city and the nation. He spoke from behind the cover of bulletproof shields, and his aides soon whisked him inside, as they were afraid of possible snipers on the roofs of nearby buildings.

There was no shortage of speakers that day. For three hours one followed another, addressing the crowd that chanted, "Yeltsin, we support you," "Russia is alive!" and "Put the junta on trial!" The speakers included Gorbachev's former foreign minister, Eduard Shevardnadze, and Russia's best-known living poet, Yevgenii Yevtushenko, who read a poem featuring references to Pushkin and Tolstoy and describing the White House as "a wounded marble swan of freedom defended by the people" and swimming into immortality. Also in attendance was the world-renowned cellist Mstislav Rostropovich, who had heard the news of the coup in Paris and taken the first flight to Moscow. At the White House he first performed for its defenders and then grabbed a Kalashnikov assault rifle himself. Elena Bonner, the widow of Andrei Sakharov, father of the Soviet hydrogen bomb and longtime political dissident, made a splash with a personal anecdote from her life with Sakharov in exile. She had asked a KGB officer why the regime was writing lies about her husband. "It is written not for us but for the rabble," came the reply. "The junta is the same," argued Bonner.

"Everything they have said and written is for the 'rabble.' They think we are 'rabble.'" Bonner's listeners believed they were rabble no more. The organizers of the meeting appealed to its participants to stay and help defend the White House. Thousands responded to the call.[12]

AS THE RALLY AT THE WALLS of the Russian White House neared its end, Yeltsin suddenly got the boost he had been waiting for. On the city phone line, which had not been cut off by the KGB, he heard the voice of George H. W. Bush. It was a call that had been long in the making. On the afternoon of August 19, a few minutes before Bush made his first very cautious public assessment of the coup at his Kennebunkport compound, Andrei Kozyrev, Yeltsin's forty-year-old minister of foreign affairs, had summoned Jim Collins, the American chargé d'affaires in Moscow, to the Russian White House. He wanted to give Collins Yeltsin's letter to President Bush. "I appeal to you, Mr. President," wrote Yeltsin, "to call the attention of the entire world community, and primarily the United Nations, to the events which are occurring in the USSR and demand the restoration of the legally elected organs of power and the reaffirmation of the post of USSR President M. S. Gorbachev."[13]

By midmorning the text of Yeltsin's letter had already been received in Washington, and Deputy National Security Adviser Robert Gates dictated it over the phone to Brent Scowcroft, who was flying with the president from Maine to Washington. After a brief discussion, Bush and Scowcroft decided that the letter was sufficient reason to harden the administration's public stand on the coup. It fell to the ever cautious Scowcroft to provide this new emphasis. The general went to the back of the aircraft to talk to the press. In front of the cameras, he declared that all of the plotters were conservatives, the coup was intended to derail reforms, and the US administration had a negative attitude toward what he still called an "extra-constitutional" act. Although this fell short of Yeltsin's expectations, the administration was inching toward a tougher position on the coup and its perpetrators. Yeltsin's letter was the first official message to reach Washington from Moscow, but the Russian president was not the only Soviet leader knocking on Bush's door that morning.[14]

The Soviet ambassador, Viktor Komplektov, one of the few Soviet officials who had accompanied Bush on his visit to Kyiv a few weeks earlier, visited the State Department and then the White House to pass on letters from his new masters in the Kremlin. "I am sending this message to you at a point which is critical for the destiny of the Soviet Union and for the international situation in the whole world," began the letter to President Bush from Gennadii Yanaev. It expressed the plotters' resolve to carry out their anti-perestroika agenda, even as they promised to continue reform. At the very end of the text prepared by Kriuchkov's KGB experts, Yanaev added a short personal note that undermined the letter's assertions about Gorbachev's illness. "For your information," wrote Yanaev, "Mikhail Sergeevich [[Gorbachev]] is in complete safety, and nothing is threatening him." Komplektov handed Yanaev's letter to Gates, who happened to be the senior official on duty that morning in the White House. "I offered no pleasantries or polite conversation and tried to make the atmosphere as cold as possible," wrote Gates later, recalling his meeting with Komplektov.[15]

Gates was fresh from a conference of deputy heads of key government departments that he had convened in the White House Situation Room at 9:30 a.m. The participants in the meeting decided to change the tone of American pronouncements on the coup, moving toward condemnation of it. Their attitude was influenced by a report delivered by the deputy head of the CIA, Richard Kerr. The agency's analysts believed that they were dealing with an "incomplete" coup whose outcome was not yet clear. "As the morning progressed," Gates remembered later, "our sense in Washington was that something didn't smell right, something was amiss in Moscow. Why were all telephone and fax lines in and out of Moscow still working? Why was daily life so little disrupted? Why had the democratic 'opposition' around the country—and even in Moscow—not been arrested? How could the regime let the opposition barricade themselves in the Russian parliament building and then let people come and go? We began to think the coup leaders did not have their act together and that maybe, just maybe, this action could be reversed." They decided to strengthen the statement they had worked on by including the word "condemn." Gates checked with Scowcroft, who was still on his way to Washington, and added the all-important word to the text of the document. It made headlines in the evening news and saved the face of the administration, which had begun the day with declarations that smacked of appeasement.[16]

An even stronger statement condemning the coup was approved at a second Deputies Committee meeting convened by Gates in the Situation Room at 5:00 p.m. The meeting was attended by President Bush, National Security Adviser Scowcroft, and the chairman of the Joint Chiefs of Staff, General Colin Powell. By that time there was further evidence of the plotters' disorganization. The CIA's Richard Kerr summarized the agency's estimate as follows: "In short, Mr. President, this does not look like a traditional coup. It's not very professional. They're trying to take control of the major power centers one at a time, and you can't pull off a coup in phases." The new information indicated that the president could now go much further in condemning the coup. "We are deeply disturbed by the events of the last hours in the Soviet Union and condemn the unconstitutional resort to force," began the new document. It included a quotation from Yeltsin's letter to President Bush, demanding the "restoration of the legally elected organs of power and the reaffirmation of the post of USSR President M. S. Gorbachev."[17]

The quotation was a signal to Yeltsin that Bush had received his letter and was on his side, offering no support or recognition to the plotters. But the US president was still reluctant to call the Russian president. Given his unpleasant dealings with Yeltsin during his recent visit to Moscow, Bush did not hasten to contact him. He asked his aides to connect him with Gorbachev, but Gorbachev's telephone was silent. The US president had seen for himself how bitter the rivalry between Gorbachev and Yeltsin had become, and he did not want to do anything to provoke a new round of hostilities. Yet the progress of the coup left him little choice. On the evening of August 19, the presidential aides concluded that their boss would have to call Yeltsin.[18]

On the morning of August 20, with Gorbachev's telephones still silent, Brent Scowcroft drafted a memo providing a rationale for Bush's call to Yeltsin. The Americans had very little reliable information about the rapidly evolving situation in Moscow. Scowcroft told Bush that Yeltsin was "holed up in the RSFSR Building (his 'White House') with approximately 100 Russian deputies." There were also rumors that Yeltsin had already been arrested. Another rumor claimed that Gorbachev was in Moscow, wrote Scowcroft. American intelligence could not confirm any of those rumors, and the national security adviser wanted the president to get "first hand information on the current situation." There were also other reasons for the call. "Calling President Yeltsin this morning allows you to show support for him, and through him, for the constitutional process violated by the coup. The mere fact of your call will buoy him up," claimed Scowcroft. That was as far as the administration was prepared to go at the time in supporting Yeltsin's resistance to the coup. "It is important not even inadvertently to leave President Yeltsin with the impression that we can give more than general support," wrote Scowcroft. Yeltsin had to be reassured that the United States supported his call for the restoration of Gorbachev to power. The Americans would also try to communicate with the coup leaders to prevent the use of force.[19]

The call to Yeltsin miraculously went through soon after 8:00 a.m. Eastern Standard Time (EST) on August 20. "Just checking up to see how things are going from your end," began the president, apparently forgetting to greet his Russian interlocutor. "Good morning," responded Yeltsin, for whom it was late afternoon in Moscow. "Good morning," reiterated Bush, paying no attention to the time difference between Washington and Moscow, and then repeated his question: "I just wanted a first-hand report on the situation from your end." He stuck to his talking points, showing no excitement about managing to reach Yeltsin, who only a few minutes earlier had been presumed to be under arrest. Yeltsin did not mind. As Scowcroft had predicted, the call was a major boost to him. "The building of the Supreme Soviet and office of the President is surrounded," Yeltsin told Bush, "and I expect a storming of the building at any moment. We have been here 24 hours. We won't leave. I have appealed to 100,000 people standing outside to defend the legally elected government." The 100,000-person rally to which Yeltsin referred was drawing to a close at the walls of the Russian White House.

"You have our full support for the return of Gorbachev and the legitimate government," said Bush after Yeltsin's lengthy report on the coup and the opposition's demands. Urging Bush to rally world leaders in support of Russian democracy, Yeltsin also advised him against calling Yanaev, and the American president concurred. They agreed to get in touch the next day. Surprisingly, it was turning out to be an uplifting conversation not only for Yeltsin but also for Bush. "Good luck and congratulations on your courage and commitment.

We sympathize and pray with you. All the American people support you. What you're doing is absolutely right," said Bush in conclusion. The difference in tone from the cold initial exchange could not have been more striking.[20]

THE RESOLVE DEMONSTRATED by thousands of ordinary Muscovites gathered in front of the White House at the time of Bush's call gave Yeltsin grounds for cautious optimism. But there also were signs that the plotters were preparing an armed assault on the Russian parliament building. Before 2:00 p.m. Yeltsin had a visit from General Aleksandr Lebed, whose paratroopers were stationed around the White House, ostensibly to protect Yeltsin. Lebed had just received orders to withdraw, making the White House vulnerable to attack. He refused to follow Yeltsin's order to leave the battalion where it was. Lebed told the president about his military oath and explained that the only way to get around it was for Yeltsin to issue a decree appointing himself commander in chief. Yeltsin vacillated. Lebed also explained to the defenders of the White House the futility of their efforts. "All it would take would be the release of a few antitank guided missiles, and the plastic in the building would ignite," Yeltsin later remembered the general saying. "The fire would burn so fiercely that people would jump out of the windows."[21]

News that the assault was imminent began to reach the Russian White House in the late afternoon. A KGB man was brought to the defenders, claiming that his unit had received orders to attack the Russian parliament. This was confirmed by Yeltsin's aides, who were in touch with fellow Afghan veterans in the army and KGB. At 5:00 p.m. Vice President Rutskoi ordered that people gathered around the White House be organized into defense units. They declared the formation of the Russian (as distinct from Soviet) armed forces and called on young men to join them. Yeltsin finally decided to appoint himself commander in chief of the armed forces. Defectors were welcomed from units of the Soviet army, police, and KGB stationed in Moscow. The units were growing in number and strength. At 6:00 p.m. came the announcement that women were obliged to leave the White House. The radio station Moscow Echo was still on the air, calling on Muscovites to come to the parliament building and help save their democracy. People were responding.

As darkness fell on the city, there were some fifteen thousand people around the building. Among them was Theresa Sabonis-Chafee, a young graduate student from the Woodrow Wilson School of Public and International Affairs at Princeton University, who had arrived in Moscow in January 1991 and whose Russian was shaky at best. "I wandered among the crowds," she remembered later, "debating the merits of shouting, 'Comrades, I need an interpreter,' but decided I would rather be treated as a Russian among Russians." She was soon recruited into a unit guarding access to the White House. Expecting the army to use gas to disperse the crowd, the organizers started to hand out gas masks. "They created cordons of people with their arms linked," wrote Sabonis-Chafee later. "The first cordon was men only, until they realized that there were not enough large gas masks. Then women who could fit into the smallest-size gas masks also joined the first cordon. I ended up in the second cordon, controlling access to the drive-in entrance."

In the White House, the exhausted Yeltsin was ready to take a nap. Before he retired, his chief bodyguard, Aleksandr Korzhakov, presented him with a choice: if the expected attack came, either retreat to the basement or move to the nearby American embassy. In the basement, he told the president, "we will perish without outside assistance." In the embassy "we can take shelter for a long time and tell the whole world what is going on in Russia." Yeltsin said, "Fine." Korzhakov posted a guard with a rifle next to his office and sent the president to sleep in a doctor's office on the other side of the building. At the approaches to the White House, Theresa Sabonis-Chafee, having spent hours in the cordon checking other people's documents without ever showing her own American passport, fell asleep in a bus parked nearby.[22]

6

FREEDOM'S VICTORY

HE KNEW THAT HE WAS BEING FOLLOWED. On August 20, the second day of the coup, when Andrei Kozyrev, the foreign minister of the Russian Federation, headed for Sheremetevo International Airport on the outskirts of Moscow, his "escort" of undercover KGB officers accompanied him, as they had done the day before. Kozyrev was trying to catch a flight to Paris but did not have a ticket and was not sure whether he would be allowed to leave Moscow. He was on a special mission on behalf of the government that had barricaded itself in the Russian White House.

Boris Yeltsin had ordered his foreign minister to go abroad to rally support for the Russian opposition among Western leaders and the public. His ultimate destination was the United States—more precisely, the New York headquarters of the United Nations. If it came to the worst and Yeltsin himself was killed or arrested, Kozyrev was to set up a Russian government-in-exile. Yeltsin also sent a group of his loyal lieutenants to Sverdlovsk in the Urals, his home city and power base—the "geographic center of Russia," as he later described it to George Bush—to set up an alternative government center in one of the area's Cold War–era Soviet bunkers. In Moscow Kozyrev was leaving behind his wife and a young daughter from his first marriage. His chances of seeing them again anytime soon were nil. The KGB officers following Kozyrev did not attempt to prevent him from buying a ticket and leaving the country. They had no orders to that effect. Kriuchkov had nothing against the leaders of the opposition, including Yeltsin himself, leaving the country. Kozyrev got the impression that the KGB men were telling themselves, "We'll let him go." So he went.

The three-hour flight to Paris gave Kozyrev an opportunity to collect his thoughts. A career diplomat who had been admitted to the prestigious Moscow Institute of International Relations (with the help of the KGB, as he later acknowledged), Kozyrev, like his boss, Boris Yeltsin, began to question Soviet ideology and practice when he found himself in an American supermarket during his first trip abroad. It was not the mere abundance of food that struck the young Soviet diplomat but the fact that the customers were ordinary people, many of them black or Latino. It was one thing for a loyal Soviet subject to admit that the West could provide a wealth of products to the capitalist elite but quite another to realize that blue-collar workers and minorities, allegedly exploited by those elites, had access to goods that Soviet apparatchiks could only dream about.

Then he got a copy of Boris Pasternak's *Doctor Zhivago*, a novel prohibited from distribution in its author's homeland, and read it in a single day, sitting on a bench in New York's Central Park. One of the many ironies was that he read the Russian novel in English. He left it on the bench, afraid to take it to the Soviet diplomatic compound where he was staying. To his surprise, Kozyrev found nothing anti-Soviet in the book. Why, then, was it banned? Eventually he concluded that the regime of which he was a product, and which he was serving with distinction, did not allow its subjects the right of opposition or even autonomy. Pasternak was not anti-Soviet; he simply had not toed the party line. Along with *Doctor Zhivago*, Kozyrev left on the Central Park bench his belief in the system to which he officially continued to belong. Privately, as he himself expressed it, he eventually became an *antisovetchik*, the term the KGB used to describe dissidents.

In the Foreign Ministry, Kozyrev was one of the young diplomats who slowly but surely pushed their bosses, Eduard Shevardnadze and Mikhail Gorbachev included, to go on from a broadly defined policy of glasnost to a public embrace of freedom of speech and human rights as internationally recognized. Kozyrev never trusted Gorbachev, who remained for him a dedicated communist and party apparatchik. Yeltsin, who had openly rebelled against the party, was different. In the summer of 1990 Kozyrev made his choice. He left a coveted position as head of a directorate in the Soviet Foreign Ministry under Shevardnadze to take up the post (then largely ceremonial) of foreign minister of the Russian Soviet Federative Socialist Republic. The ministry had absolutely no representation abroad and, unlike the parallel structures in Ukraine and Belarus, was not even involved in the activities of the United Nations: Ukraine and Belarus, along with the Soviet Union, were UN members, while Russia was not. Kozyrev knew that by joining Yeltsin and his team he was going into opposition, but he had a vision of a new, democratic Russia and was prepared to take the risk.

At his confirmation hearings in the Russian parliament, the then thirty-nine-year-old foreign-minister-to-be formulated his vision as follows: "Democratic Russia should and will be just as natural an ally of the democratic nations of the West as the totalitarian Soviet Union was a natural opponent of the West." Then came the coup. Kozyrev's men, whom he took with him to the Russian Foreign Ministry from the Soviet one, stood behind Yeltsin. They strongly believed in the vision of a democratic Russia allied with the West. The real question now was whether the West saw it the same way. Did Western leaders even realize that the real struggle was no longer between Gorbachev and the party hard-liners but between democratic Russia and the military junta that threatened freedom all over the world?[1]

Kozyrev had his task cut out for him. Western leaders, while disturbed by the news from Moscow, were initially reluctant to condemn the coup or raise their voices in support of the imprisoned Gorbachev, to say nothing of supporting Yeltsin's appeal for an all-Russian political strike. In Paris, Kozyrev's current destination, President François Mitterand made a statement on the morning of August 19 that all but recognized the coup as a fait accompli. The same sentiment was shared by the Canadian minister of foreign affairs, Barbara McDougall. President Bush's first statement on the morning of August 19 was also short of a condemnation of the coup. On the evening of that day, Vice President Gennadii Yanaev even praised Bush's nonconfrontational approach at the press conference for foreign correspondents broadcast throughout the Soviet Union. It was a major disappointment for Kozyrev and Yeltsin's entourage. And all this in spite of Kozyrev's frantic efforts on the first day of the coup to rally Western support for Yeltsin and his demand to put down the anticonstitutional coup and restore Gorbachev to power.

Upon his arrival in Paris, Kozyrev called Allen Weinstein, the director of the Washington-based Center for Democracy and the future archivist of the United States, to dictate a statement of his own. Weinstein was not a member of the Bush administration, but Kozyrev apparently knew no one in the White House or in the State Department to whom he could turn at that crucial moment. Weinstein proved an excellent choice. A native of the Bronx and the son of Jewish immigrants from the Russian Empire, he cared deeply about developments in the Soviet Union and had good connections in the media. On the following day Kozyrev's statement, perhaps edited by Weinstein, appeared in the *Washington Post*.

In his statement, the Russian foreign minister claimed that the original lukewarm reaction to the coup by leaders of the democratic world had made the plotters believe that they had succeeded in deceiving the West. "More recent statements from President Bush, Prime Minister John Major and other Western leaders," continued Kozyrev, "have corrected that misconception. It is crucial that the West continue to condemn the coup attempt and not recognize—or promise eventual recognition to—the plotters." He went on: "President Gorbachev must be restored immediately as the President of the Soviet Union, and the West should demand immediate and direct contact with him as well as international medical experts to assure his health."[2]

Neither Yeltsin nor Kozyrev fully trusted Gorbachev, whom many in Moscow suspected of playing a double game—using his former aides to do the dirty work of crushing the democratic opposition and then returning to Moscow as the savior of the nation. But calling for Gorbachev's return meant exposing the plotters' greatest weakness— the lack of constitutional and legal justification for their arbitrary ouster of a legitimate head of state. The "bring back Gorbachev" strategy provided Yeltsin with the kind of legitimacy his earlier actions had lacked in the eyes of the West. It also appealed to the hearts and minds of the Western public, still dizzy with the Gorbymania of the late 1980s. When Bush finally called Yeltsin on the second day of the coup, he told the besieged Russian president that he supported his call for Gorbachev's return. Bush and Yeltsin now had a joint agenda that went beyond the long-term strategy of building democracy. Its two main objectives were to stop the coup and save Gorbachev.

The "recent statement" by President Bush that, according to Kozyrev, "corrected the misconception" about the West's complacency with regard to the coup was made at a Rose Garden press conference opened by Bush on August 20 at 10:35 a.m. EST, two hours after his telephone conversation with Yeltsin. "The unconstitutional seizure of power is an affront to the goals and aspirations that the Soviet peoples have been nurturing over the past years," he declared. There followed a piece of news that electrified the audience: "I have this morning spoken with Boris Yeltsin, the freely elected leader of the Russian Republic, and I assured Mr. Yeltsin of continued U.S. support for his goal of the restoration of Mr. Gorbachev as the constitutionally chosen leader. Mr. Yeltsin is encouraged by the support of the Soviet people and their determination in the face of these trying circumstances. He expressed his gratitude for our support of him and President Gorbachev." The White House correspondents wanted details, but there was little the president could add. One of the questions went to the core of the dilemma facing the administration: "Mr. President, what kind of support, though, are you going to give Yeltsin, or are you—just have to stay on the sidelines and offer verbal encouragement?" Bush stuck to the line already announced: support would be limited to encouragement of the opposition and pressure on the plotters, who would have a hard time surviving without Western economic assistance. But privately, Bush was already prepared to go further.[3]

After the press conference, Bush went to the Oval Office, where he was joined by his advisers to discuss what more could be done to support Yeltsin. Every hour brought additional news about challenges to the coup. There were unconfirmed reports to the effect that the coup leaders were facing their first defections: Prime Minister Valentin Pavlov had reported himself ill, and Marshal Dmitrii Yazov had allegedly resigned from the Emergency Committee. There were also divisions among the military commanders and leaders of major republics, including such heavyweights as Nursultan Nazarbayev of Kazakhstan and Leonid Kravchuk of Ukraine, who declared themselves against the coup. Considering these developments, Bush and his advisers agreed to increase pressure on the regime. The general statement on denying legitimacy to the coup plotters took on specific features. The new American ambassador to the USSR, Bob Strauss, who had just been sworn in and was about to go to Moscow, was instructed not to present his credentials to the new leaders. The broadcasters at the Voice of America (VOA) were asked to help Yeltsin spread his message across the Soviet Union. They obliged.[4]

The Voice of America had three correspondents in the Soviet Union—two in Moscow and one in Vilnius. The station was on the air fourteen hours a day, broadcasting to all parts of the Soviet Union, from the Baltics in the west to the Kamchatka Peninsula in the Far East. It began covering the coup twenty minutes after the takeover was announced on Soviet radio and television. VOA listeners in the Soviet Union were able to hear Yeltsin's statement condemning the coup on the morning of August 19. What could be done to increase the impact of VOA broadcasts on the situation? Soon after 5:00 p.m. on August 20, the US Information Agency, responsible for VOA broadcasting, faxed a report to the White House on changes made in the broadcast schedule in the course of the second day of the coup. "Fifteen new transmitter hours were added today to increase frequencies and beef up VOA's Russian signal—hours per day are unchanged at 14, but the signal is now louder and easier to catch." The VOA switched to all-news coverage, with almost hourly live reports from its Moscow correspondents.

On the following day, VOA reports from the streets of Moscow were relayed through a Finnish cell phone network recently installed in the Soviet capital. "The unusual routing of his [[a correspondent's]] voice reports by phone," stated another report to the White House, "was Moscow street—VOA office—London—Washington—Greenville transmitters—U.K. relay—Soviet listener, all in milliseconds." Broadcasts of the Voice of America and other Western media, including the BBC, became a principal source of information for Soviet citizens on the actions of Boris Yeltsin and the opposition forces. In the capital they supplemented information provided by the radio station Moscow Echo, and in the provinces they were the only source of news about resistance to the coup. According to a US Information Agency report sent to the White House during the coup, "With only nine newspapers now reportedly publishing in the USSR, and republic and other independent radio and TV stations virtually pre-empted by official Soviet transmissions, American and other Western media will be playing an increasingly important role in informing Soviet audiences." When Dan Rather of CBS News asked one of his guests, a specialist in Soviet politics, "How would news of Yeltsin's call for a general strike get to audiences in the USSR?" the answer he got was, "The Voice of America will do the job." Indeed it did.[5]

IT WAS AT 5:35 P.M. ON AUGUST 20 that news of automatic gun-fire around the Russian White House and in close proximity to the American embassy reached James Baker in the State Department. There was little that the secretary of state could do about the rapidly unfolding events in Moscow. "I've seldom felt so powerless in my life," remembered Baker later. As he flew across the Atlantic that night to attend a NATO meeting in Brussels next morning, he "kept waiting for the other shoe to drop, for the Ops Center or Sit[[uation]] Room to call with news that KGB and Interior Ministry troops had attacked and overrun the barricades, killing Yeltsin in the process."[6]

Around the same time as news of the shooting in Moscow reached Baker, Marshal Dmitrii Yazov returned to his office at the Ministry of Defense from a late-night meeting of the Emergency Committee in the Kremlin in the worst possible mood. In Moscow it was the early morning of August 21. The meeting, which had begun at 8:00 p.m. the previous day, had revealed deep divisions within the committee. It began with a stunning proposal from Gennadii Yanaev, who read the text of a statement denying rumors of a planned attack on the White House. He wanted it broadcast on radio and television. Those present, who included quite a few government officials and politicians sympathetic to the coup, could not help noting that the statement came as a complete surprise to Yazov, Kriuchkov, and other members of the committee.

The plan to attack the White House had been commissioned by Yazov and Kriuchkov on the morning of August 20. By midday they had a detailed plan. Paratroopers and units of riot police would surround the White House at night and disperse the crowd, making way for commandos of the KGB Alpha unit and army unit B. The commandos would storm the White House, blasting their way through with grenade launchers, clear the premises, and arrest Yeltsin. The operation, code-named Thunder, would take place at 3:00 a.m. on August 21. The army units taking part would begin to converge on the White House at midnight. Yazov promised reinforcements. The plotters now had only to wait for darkness. This was to be Yeltsin's last night of freedom. Upon being arrested, he would be taken to the state hunting grounds in Zavidovo, where Leonid Brezhnev had once hunted wild boars with foreign dignitaries, including Henry Kissinger, Richard Nixon's national security adviser and, later, secretary of state. To the commandos, some of whom had stormed the presidential palace in Kabul in December 1979, the whole operation looked like a piece of cake.[7]

But now there appeared to be dissension at the very top of the plotters' pyramid. Yanaev, the acting Soviet president and formal leader of the plot, was hedging his bets so as to avoid responsibility for the coming assault. If anything went wrong—and many things could go wrong—he would be safe from reproach, a responsible leader who refused to condone violence against his own people. Once the second-tier officials invited to the Emergency Committee meeting were released and the plotters were left alone in the room, Yanaev's demeanor suddenly changed. He no longer tried to play the liberal. Like everyone else, he voted for Yeltsin's arrest. The assault on the White House would go forward as planned, but the conduct of the meeting left serious doubts in Yazov's mind. Were the others trying to use the army to do their dirty work, which would make him a scapegoat? If so, it would not be the first time that the army had been used and then blamed for decisions made by politicians.[8]

The military thought that had been the case in Vilnius in January 1991. Troops were sent in against protesters and then blamed for the violence once millions of Soviet citizens saw the television footage and Gorbachev ordered a stop to the operation. Gorbachev had then told his aides that Kriuchkov and Yazov were good for nothing. The military brass was enraged. Liberals such as Yazov's deputy minister and Air Marshal Yevgenii Shaposhnikov were appalled by the very idea of using the army against the civil population. "After Vilnius, after the images seen on television of one of our soldiers beating a civilian with the butt of a machine gun, I understood that a decisive and final end had to be put to that," he wrote a few years later. Officers never suspected of liberal sympathies, such as the paratroop commander General Pavel Grachev, were appalled by the duplicity of the political leadership. On the evening of August 20, Grachev told Shaposhnikov with regard to the planned attack on the White House, "Let them just hint that I be the one to give the order, and I'll send them packing."[9]

The thinking of the military commanders was very much informed by their earlier experiences of being used against civilians. In Tbilisi in April 1989 and in Vilnius in January 1991, the government had ordered them to crush pro-independence demonstrations but refused to take any responsibility when things went wrong and people were injured or even killed. In both cases, the government had blamed the military. Now the same could happen in Moscow. Besides, the situation in Moscow presented the generals with a new challenge. In the Baltics and the Caucasus, largely Russian and Slavic elite units had been unleashed against non-Russian protesters. In Moscow, they would have to be used against Russians. Under such circumstances, would the troops follow orders? Yeltsin's supporters not only plied the troops with attention but also overwhelmed them with lectures on the nature of democracy and patriotism. They told the young boys not to shoot at their compatriots.

The issue of Soviet versus Russian identity now came to the fore. When paratroopers commanded by General Aleksandr Lebed, who were the first to arrive at the White House on August 19, declared themselves Soviets, one of the defenders responded, "What the hell is Soviet?" Iain Elliott, a reporter for the US-funded Radio Liberty, later described a scene that he witnessed on the streets of Moscow. A drunken man, "ripping open his shirt and thrusting his naked chest against the muzzle of a Kalashnikov in the hands of a nervous teenager . . . shouted: 'You won't shoot us, will you? After all, we're Russian and you're Russian.'" Theresa Sabonis-Chafee, who stayed in the cordon around the White House on the night of August 20, later remembered that those who declared themselves "for Russia" were considered "ours" and allowed to pass. On the same evening, General Grachev, who was still vacillating between the two sides, had told Yeltsin's messenger to convey to the president of Russia that "he was a Russian and would never allow the army to spill the blood of its own people."[10]

Yet blood would indeed soon be spilled. The first shots were fired at midnight. On the square in front of the White House, Michael Hetzer, the editor of the *Guardian,* a Moscow weekly produced for the benefit of the foreign community and expatriates, noted the time: it was 12:00 a.m. on August 21. News spread immediately among the White House defenders that tanks were circling to attack the parliament from the embankment of the Moskva River. "At 12:10 a.m. more shots could be heard over the hill on the Ring Road," wrote Hetzer a few days later in his newspaper. "This time the sound, fast and regular, was unmistakably automatic gunfire. 'They're coming!' one woman cried. 'The bastards are coming.' Later there was another burst of gunfire and then several terrific explosions."[11]

General Valentin Varennikov, who had confronted Gorbachev in Foros on the evening of August 18, was now back in Moscow after a short stopover in Ukraine and was prepared to confront Yeltsin. He dispatched troop carriers toward the White House and was busily arranging the landing of commandos on the roof of the Russian parliament building. The first shots were fired by soldiers of the Taman division, who were passing the White House on Varennikov's orders to take up positions near the Soviet Foreign Ministry in preparation for the assault. As the armored troop carriers entered the underpass beneath Kalinin Avenue, they were suddenly ambushed by defenders of the White House, who thought that the assault had already begun. The exit from the underpass was blocked by trolley buses. Although the lead carrier made it through the barricade, the others were trapped in the narrow tunnel.

The defenders of the White House, some of them veterans of Afghanistan, knew what had to be done to incapacitate the armored vehicles. They threw pieces of fabric onto the narrow observation openings, blocking the drivers' view. The young and inexperienced soldiers, feeling trapped, began to rotate their gun turrets in an effort to dislodge the attackers. The soldiers were soon assaulted with Molotov cocktails that set the vehicles ablaze. Soldiers from the burning troop carriers jumped out, shooting into the air. Their bullets hit armor plate and the walls of the underpass, ricocheting into the crowd. One soldier burned his hands as he tried to put out the flames on his uniform, but the others escaped unharmed. They left three lifeless bodies on the pavement: an Afghan veteran, his skull crushed by a troop carrier, and two more defenders killed by bullets. Many others were wounded.[12]

Marshal Yazov learned of the first casualties after his return from the meeting of the Emergency Committee, where he suspected that Gennadii Yanaev and others were hedging their bets. Now it seemed that everyone was free and clear but Yazov. It was his people, the military, not KGB or police units, who had opened fire on ordinary Russian citizens. After grimly listening to the report on developments at the White House, Yazov ordered his deputy, "Give the command to stop!" The news that the army would take no part in the planned assault on the White House was met with disbelief by Kriuchkov. Those gathered in his office in the early hours of the morning of August 21 accused the military of cowardice. But some were actually relieved: these included senior officers charged with carrying out the attack, who might have ended up bearing personal responsibility for casualties. The commander of the Interior Ministry forces declared that if the army was not participating, neither would his troops.[13]

The KGB commandos were also refusing to storm the White House. The all-powerful espionage organization was crumbling under Kriuchkov's feet. If one trusts claims made later by Vladimir Putin, the future president of Russia, that day the KGB chief received an unexpected call from St. Petersburg. Mayor Anatolii Sobchak, who supported Yeltsin, asked what had happened to the letter of resignation submitted a year earlier by his deputy, the thirty-eight-year-old KGB lieutenant colonel Vladimir Putin. That day Putin allegedly submitted his second letter of resignation. His allegiance was to Sobchak, not to the coup leaders. As Putin recalled later, he respected Kriuchkov, but "when I saw the criminals on the screen, I understood immediately that it was all over: they were done for."

Some of Putin's biographers question his claim to have submitted the letter during the coup, suggesting that he did so later, once the coup had collapsed. During the decisive days of August, his critics say, Putin was playing a wait-and-see game, trying to figure out which way the pendulum would swing. Even if Putin's critics are right, his behavior during the coup was not exactly what Kriuchkov expected of his subordinates. Too many KGB officers were sitting on the proverbial fence, waiting to see whether the coup would succeed. Putin shared the plotters' goal of saving the country but not their outdated methods. "In the days of the putsch all the ideals and goals that I had on going to work in the KGB collapsed," confided the future president of Russia in an interview that he gave eight years later.[14]

Faced with defections on all fronts, Kriuchkov had no choice but to call off the assault. "Well, the operation has to be canceled," he told his subordinates. By that time a heavy rain prevented a helicopter landing on the roof of the White House, and the last-ditch attempt to send commandos in plainclothes to the White House had been foiled by the vigilance of the defenders of the Russian parliament. Kriuchkov finally ordered that telephone lines to the building be cut: a prolonged siege of the White House was now on the agenda.

But around 8:00 a.m., Yazov called his commanders and ordered a complete withdrawal of troops from Moscow. This came as a major surprise to Kriuchkov and the other members of the Emergency Committee. The plotters descended on the Ministry of Defense, trying to convince Yazov to change his order. He was accused of cowardice and treason, but his answer remained the same: shooting people was no solution. If the army stayed in Moscow, said Yazov, there would be new clashes, and if even one tank was set on fire, with forty shells inside it, there would be a major disaster. Yazov told his co-conspirators that he was not about to become another Pinochet—the Chilean dictator known in the Soviet Union as a symbol of martial law and tyranny.[15]

NEWS OF THE WITHDRAWAL OF TROOPS from Moscow soon reached the exhausted defenders of the White House, causing jubilation in their ranks. Earlier that night, on hearing the first shots, Yeltsin's chief bodyguard, Aleksandr Korzhakov, had rushed to the doctor's office to awaken the Russian president, who was asleep in his clothes. It did not take him long to get up and follow Korzhakov into an elevator and then into the garage. Yeltsin's first thought was, "That's it. The storming had begun." The aides put a bulletproof vest on him and seated him in the back of the presidential limousine.

Korzhakov ordered that the gate be opened. They were going to the American embassy across the square. By that time the Americans had been warned and were keeping their embassy gates open. Korzhakov's people made a gap in the barricades to let the limousine through. A few short minutes, and Yeltsin would be in the safety of the American embassy. But before the car could start, the president came fully awake. "Where are we heading?" he asked his bodyguard.

"What do you mean, where?" answered the surprised Korzhakov. "To the American embassy. Two hundred meters, and we're there."

"What embassy?" responded the no less surprised Yeltsin. "No, we don't need any embassy; let's turn back."

Korzhakov ordered the driver to wait. Yeltsin's "fine," which he had given Korzhakov a few hours earlier, was now reversed—and, as was often the case with Yeltsin, reversed in the most dramatic way and at the last possible moment.

Yeltsin's political instinct took primacy over the instinct for survival. Whatever the risk of arrest or death during the assault on the White House, he wanted to survive politically. That could not be achieved by hiding in the American embassy. "It would mean I had gotten myself to a safe place but had left them under the gun," remembered Yeltsin later. He was also sensitive to Russian national pride, which he had mobilized so skillfully in the months leading up to the coup. "Despite our respect for the Americans, people in our country don't like it when foreigners take too active a hand in our affairs," wrote Yeltsin in his memoirs. That was certainly an understatement. Many of his voters still thought in Cold War terms, seeing the United States as their country's main adversary. The years of Gorbachev's perestroika had done relatively little to dispel such sentiments, while the Soviet retreat from Eastern Europe and economic troubles at home only added to resentment of the rich West in general and the United States in particular.

Yeltsin would spend the night in the basement of the White House, listening to occasional automatic gunfire outside and waiting for the assault to begin. He was joined in the White House basement by the democratic leaders of Moscow. There was the mayor, Gavriil Popov, and his deputy, Yurii Luzhkov. The deputy mayor came along with his pregnant young wife, who brought home-cooked food and a sense of calm that was in short supply in the besieged building.[16]

At 5:00 a.m., when the curfew was lifted by the military authorities in Moscow, the American chargé d'affaires, Jim Collins, got a chance to survey the previous night's battlefield. "The half-dozen BMP's which had become trapped in the Kalinin [[Avenue]] underpass after midnight had surrendered to the RSFSR forces," wrote the diplomat to Washington. An unidentified source inside Yeltsin's White House (the name is blacked out in the text of the embassy report released by the US archives) called the embassy after 6:00 a.m. to report that paratroopers heading for the White House had stopped after Russian officials approached their commander.

News of the army's retreat was confirmed around 8:00 a.m. by a fax forwarded to the embassy by the Russian information service. According to the fax, the military authorities in Moscow had ordered the withdrawal of troops at "full speed." One of the senior commanders stated that the military would not attempt to seize the White House "tomorrow or the day after tomorrow." The coup seemed to be fizzling. The crowd that Collins had seen near Yeltsin's White House around 5:00 a.m. was shrinking as many of the defenders left for home. Collins told the American personnel who had spent the tumultuous night in the embassy's office building that it was safe to go back to their living quarters.[17]

While news of the troop withdrawal came as a complete surprise to most of the White House defenders, there are indications that Yeltsin and people around him learned of it earlier. It is known that at some point Kriuchkov, the KGB chief, personally called Yeltsin to inform him that the assault had been called off. Besides, Yeltsin apparently knew more about the plotters and their plans than they supposed. A few years after the events at the Russian White House, an American official told the Pulitzer Prize–winning investigative journalist Seymour M. Hersh that President Bush had ordered American intercepts of telephone communications between the plot leaders and Soviet military commanders to be shared with Yeltsin.

"The Minister of Defense and the KGB chief were using the most secure lines to reach the military commanders," wrote Hersh, quoting his source. "We told Yeltsin in real time what the communications were. The bulk of the theater commanders weren't taking the calls." According to Hersh, a communications specialist was sent from the American embassy to Yeltsin's White House to set up secure communications with the Soviet military commanders. "Yeltsin was able to warn them to steer clear," said Hersh's unnamed source.[18]

Neither Bush nor members of his administration mentioned the transfer of intelligence to Yeltsin in their memoirs. If it actually happened, then it contravened a law signed by the president four days before the coup that made it illegal to authorize covert operations in foreign countries without informing the Senate. With most intelligence-related materials of the Bush administration still classified and unavailable for research, one can only speculate whether such sensitive information, revealing American capacity to eavesdrop on the most secret communications of the Russian military brass, was indeed transferred to Yeltsin and, if so, whether it influenced his behavior and the outcome of the coup. There is no hint of secret deals in the transcripts of Bush's telephone conversations with Yeltsin.

On August 21, Bush reached Yeltsin by phone from his compound in Kennebunkport, to which he had returned after his short visit to Washington. It was 8:30 a.m. in Maine and 3:30 p.m. in Moscow. As Bush later recalled, Yeltsin sounded more confident than he had the previous day. He had survived the night and, in the words of Robert Gates, had turned into "a key figure as never before." Bush asked the Russian president whether he could do anything at that point to assist him: "We are anxious to do anything helpful, not counterproductive. Do you have any suggestions?" Yeltsin had no additional requests: "Unfortunately, other than propagandizing our plight and moral support and statements I can't see anything for you, technical or any other way, to help us at this point." Referring to his plans to arrest the plotters, Yeltsin said, "I can't give you the details about it over this phone." Bush replied, "I understand."[19]

The Russian president's main worry now was not a possible assault on the White House but the political maneuvering of his opponents. He told Bush that a Russian delegation had been sent to the Crimea along with two of Gorbachev's loyal aides to meet with the imprisoned president. "Unfortunately," continued Yeltsin, "forty minutes before our group departed, 5 of the junta including Yazov flew out before us. What they want to do is intercept Gorbachev and either force him to sign a paper or take him to points unknown. What I'm trying to do is work with Kravchuk [[head of Ukraine]] to intercept them and have them land in Simferopol in the Crimea and not let them get to him [[Gorbachev]] first." Yeltsin also reported that his opponents were lobbying members of the USSR Supreme Soviet, which would go into session on August 26, to provide legal foundations for the actions of the Emergency Committee. The coup, it appeared from Yeltsin's analysis, might fail militarily but succeed politically. The key figure deciding the fate of the coup might again be Mikhail Gorbachev.

In the previous few days, Yeltsin had managed to expose the illegality of the coup and establish his own legitimacy by demanding Gorbachev's release. As far as he and those around him were concerned, it was a gamble. Many in Yeltsin's entourage still believed that Gorbachev was not a victim of the plotters but the instigator and puppet master of the coup. What would happen if the plotters got to Gorbachev first and convinced him to join them? The Russian delegation had to head them off. Yeltsin sent his vice president, General Aleksandr Rutskoi, with a group of officers armed with Kalashnikov assault rifles to the Crimea. He also wanted the commander of the Soviet air force, Air Marshal Shaposhnikov, who had supported him throughout the coup, to divert the plotters' airplane from its route or force it to land and allow the Russian plane to arrive first. But Shaposhnikov was powerless, as no one but the head of the General Staff could order the presidential plane to land.

For the plotters and their opponents alike, the position that Gorbachev would take under the new circumstances was of paramount importance. Those who managed to "save" Gorbachev first would determine the success or failure of the coup and the political—perhaps even physical—survival of the main players on the Soviet political stage. "Now there are three aircraft flying in that direction, trying to get there first," said Yeltsin to President Bush about the planes racing to the Crimea. The third plane belonged to the Speaker of the Soviet parliament, Anatolii Lukianov, who had backed the coup but was now eager to show his independence from the plotters. In Washington, James Baker received a report that James Collins of the US embassy in Moscow had tried to fly to the Crimea with Rutskoi but was late for the departure.[20]

MEANWHILE, SHORTLY AFTER 1:00 p.m. Moscow time, Marshal Yazov hugged his wife, Emma, and headed for the airport. He was finally ready to follow the advice she had given on the first day of the coup: to abandon the plotters and go talk to Gorbachev. When Yazov told members of the Emergency Committee that he was not only ordering the troops out of Moscow but also going to the Crimea to see Gorbachev, Kriuchkov tried to stop him. This attempt failed, and the KGB chief changed his mind and said that he would go along. Kriuchkov wanted to be the first to talk to the president they had betrayed and make an alliance with him against their now even more powerful and threatening rival, the president of Russia. During the flight they learned that Yeltsin had ordered their arrest. Gorbachev was now their only hope. Kriuchkov told his colleagues, "Gorbachev can't be so stupid as not to understand that without us he is nothing."[21]

Late in the afternoon, a procession of limousines carrying Kriuchkov, Yazov, and a number of Gorbachev's former aides approached the Soviet president's compound in Foros. Like the delegation that had come three days earlier, this one was accompanied by the head of the KGB bodyguard department, General Yurii Plekhanov. At about 5:00 p.m. the gates of the heavily guarded compound opened to admit the visitors from Moscow. But then something unexpected happened. Two of Gorbachev's bodyguards, armed with Kalashnikov assault rifles, suddenly emerged from nearby bushes and ordered the cars to stop. General Plekhanov jumped out of his car and ordered them to let the vehicles pass: "What, aren't you letting the head of security through?" But the guards did not react. They would follow only Mikhail Gorbachev's orders. Raisa Gorbacheva, disturbed by the noise from the driveway, came out of her bedroom. The entrance to Gorbachev's office was blocked by one of his guards. "Will you allow no one to pass here?" she asked in an exhausted tone. "No one else will come through here," came the answer.

Raisa Gorbacheva was visibly shaken by the experience of the previous days. Exhausted by sleepless nights, she had suffered a stroke and lost partial control of one of her arms. Although the family appeared calm after the messengers from Moscow left the villa on August 18, pressure had begun to mount the next morning once the plotters announced that Gorbachev was ill. It became almost unbearable after the Gorbachevs watched the Emergency Committee's press conference on the evening of August 19. If others had reacted with guarded optimism, thinking that such people were incapable of holding power for very long, the Gorbachev family had become even more anxious. The reporters' persistent questions about Gorbachev's health and Yanaev's repeated assurances that what he most wanted was to have his boss return to Moscow triggered suspicions that the plotters would try to change the reality to match their statements—in other words, to make Gorbachev sick. That night Gorbachev taped an address to the country, condemning the coup and exposing the plotters' lies about his health. The four small tape cassettes had to be smuggled out of the heavily guarded compound—not an easy task by any measure. And now, after three days full of concern and anxiety, came the news that a delegation was arriving to see for itself what had happened to Gorbachev.

This time Gorbachev learned of his former aides' imminent visit before they entered the premises. Raisa noted in her diary that her daughter and son-in-law had heard a BBC broadcast claiming that Kriuchkov had agreed to let a delegation fly to the Crimea to check on Gorbachev's health. This was worrisome news. "We consider this a sign that the worst is to come," wrote Raisa in her diary. "Within the next few hours actions may be carried out to translate the infamous lie into reality. Mikhail Sergeevich had ordered the guards to block the drives leading up to the house as well as its entrance and not let anyone in without his permission; to be ready for action and to use force if necessary." All hope now rested in the remaining members of the security detail. The day after the plotters had paid their unexpected visit to Gorbachev, the guards had promised to stand by their commander in chief to the end. They were now intent on showing how serious they were about defending the president whom they had failed to protect when he was first threatened.

The guards' decisive actions had the desired effect on the visitors: Plekhanov held back his men, telling them that the guards were indeed prepared to shoot. The plotters then told the guards that they wanted to see the president and peacefully retired to the guesthouse, waiting for a summons from him. Gorbachev's loyal aide Anatolii Cherniaev, informed about the plotters' arrival by his secretaries, rushed to tell Gorbachev not to receive the visitors. Gorbachev assured him he would not: "I . . . gave them an ultimatum: if they do not turn on the communications, I will not talk to them. And now I will not do so anyway." When the plotters restored the communications system, Kriuchkov was first on the line. Gorbachev refused to talk to his former aide. He got in touch with the chief of the General Staff, General Mikahil Moiseev, and ordered him to ensure that the plane carrying the Russian Federation's delegation landed safely in the Crimea—the plotters were making preparations to ambush it on landing. The commander of the Kremlin garrison was informed that he could take orders from no one but Gorbachev. The minister of communications was ordered to cut the plotters' lines. The president was again in charge.

After the plotters gave in to Gorbachev's demand and restored his communications, his main goal, apart from regaining control over the military and security forces, was to assess the new political situation and decide on a further course of action. Gorbachev's aide Vadim Medvedev, who reached him by phone from Moscow late in the afternoon of that day, later remembered, "The president said that he had already made a number of calls to Moscow and to several republics and that he would now be speaking to Yeltsin." By the afternoon of August 21, Gorbachev had fully reemerged as a powerful force in Soviet politics. Not only the plotters but also the Yeltsin democrats felt that they needed him and his political clout. Gorbachev was now prepared to pick winners and losers. Theoretically, he could try to make a deal with the plotters, as they hoped he would do. Instead, Gorbachev threw his weight behind Yeltsin.[22]

Then, most unexpectedly, came a call from Washington. On Brent Scowcroft's orders, the US military had tried over and over to reach Gorbachev, and finally they succeeded. Once Gorbachev was on the line, they rushed to find George Bush. "There is a God!" said the chief communist of the Soviet Union to the American interpreter Peter Afanasenko. "I have been here four days in a fortress."

Bush also referred to the Almighty when he heard Gorbachev's voice: "Oh my God, that's wonderful, Mikhail."

"I have to congratulate you and the position you took from the first minute. You have been stalwart," Gorbachev told Bush generously (or, rather, on the basis of insufficient evidence, given Bush's statements immediately after hearing of the coup). "Thanks for taking [[time]] off from your vacation. You affected everyone with your strong statements, except Gaddafi"—the eccentric Libyan dictator had not been reticent about expressing his support for the coup.

Barbara Bush soon joined her husband. "Barbara is here and sends her love to Raisa," announced Bush.

Gorbachev was moved: "George, thank you and Barb both for your position of principle, but also for your humanity and friendship." Cherniaev, who was present during the Bush-Gorbachev conversation, later remembered that "it was a joyful exchange."

Gorbachev told Bush, "We want to keep going ahead with you. We will not falter because of what has happened. One thing is that this was prevented by democracy. This is a guarantee for us."

Bush was pleased. "I'll get that message out to the whole world now," declared the jubilant American president.

Less than an hour after Gorbachev got off the phone, George Bush was already talking to the press. He told the correspondents crammed into a small room of his house at Kennebunkport that he had spoken with the Soviet president, who was in good physical condition, was back in charge, and had "stated his sincere appreciation to the people of the United States and others around the world for their support for democracy and reform." In closing, he said, "All in all, it's a very, very positive development." The president had much to celebrate: his carefully calculated strategy of supporting the nascent Russian democracy without immediately burning his bridges with the plotters had worked exceptionally well.[23]

The Russian delegation, led by Vice President Rutskoi, arrived at Foros after 8:00 p.m. Raisa Gorbacheva, who saw people with assault rifles accompanying Rutskoi, asked whether they had come to arrest the Gorbachevs. No, Rutskoi assured her, they had come as liberators. Unlike the plotters, whom Gorbachev had left waiting for hours, Rutskoi was received right away. Gorbachev's aide Anatolii Cherniaev noted in his diary that the meeting between Gorbachev and the "Russians" would be engraved in his memory for the rest of his life: "I look at them. Among them are those who repeatedly swore at M.S., argued with him, got angry, and protested in parliament and in the press. But now misfortune has suddenly brought it about that they are at one, and vital to the country in just that way. I even said aloud, observing that general celebration and embracing: 'The union of the Center and Russia has taken place without any union treaty.'" The warm reception dispelled any doubts the Russians may have had about Gorbachev's attitude. Until the very end, Yeltsin and those around him did not know for sure whether Gorbachev was behind the plotters or not. People on the streets of Moscow were surprised when Gorbachev's translator, Pavel Palazhchenko, told them that the president had indeed been isolated by the plotters. But one look at the devastated Raisa Gorbacheva sufficed for Rutskoi to conclude that this was no political game: the isolation had been real.[24]

Gorbachev left for Moscow with Rutskoi and his delegation on the Russian plane. Rutskoi had convinced him that it was much safer than the Soviet presidential plane, which the plotters might try to shoot down. The latter plane was the one on which most of the plotters flew back to Moscow. Yazov cursed the moment he had agreed to join the committee and called himself an old fool. He was resigned to his fate and received the news of his arrest with calm and dignity. Kriuchkov's hopes initially rose when he was asked to fly on the same plane as Gorbachev and the "Russians." But he was searched before boarding, and no one but the guard would speak to him during the flight—he was used as a human shield to prevent an attack on the plane that many believed he might have arranged ahead of time. On landing, Kriuchkov was surprised to be arrested by Russian and not all-Union authorities. Upon arrival in his temporary prison, a guarded building in one of the resort compounds near Moscow, Kriuchkov asked for whiskey but received none. Times were changing.[25]

III.

A COUNTERCOUP

7

THE RESURGENCE OF RUSSIA

THE REPORTERS AND OFFICIALS WHO GATHERED at Vnukovo airport near Moscow in the early hours of August 22 to welcome the president on his return from Crimean detention saw a tired but upbeat Gorbachev descend the steps of the plane. The guards kept their Kalashnikov machine guns at the ready—a reminder of the severity of the ordeal that the president and his family had just endured and a sign that the danger might not yet be over.

Gorbachev was followed by Raisa and other family members, including their granddaughters Kseniia and Anastasiia. Raisa looked shaken and depressed. She still lacked the full use of one hand and would be hospitalized two days later. Gorbachev's thirty-four-year-old daughter Irina, a medical doctor by training, who had been calm and composed throughout the ordeal, burst into tears on finding herself in the safety of the presidential limousine. Only the two granddaughters seemed oblivious to what was going on around them. Gorbachev later remembered that the younger one, Anastasiia, had been least affected during the first days of the coup: "She understood nothing, ran around, and demanded to be taken to the beach." On the flight back to Moscow, the girls slept peacefully on the cabin floor.[1]

While Gorbachev's family sat waiting in the presidential limousine, the president addressed the media. He spoke mostly about the Crimean captivity and promised to say more about it in the days to come. But he also gave an assessment of the new political situation and the tasks awaiting him. "The main thing," said Gorbachev before the television cameras, "is that all we have done since 1985 has already produced real results. Our society and people have become different, and that was the main obstacle in the way of the escapade undertaken by a group of individuals. . . . And this is the greatest victory of perestroika." He thanked Boris Yeltsin personally for his stand during the coup and expressed special appreciation to the *Rossiiane*—the citizens of the Russian Federation—for their attitude. Looking to the future, Gorbachev stressed the need for continuing cooperation between the center and the republics in order to overcome the current political and economic crisis. He did not call for the immediate signing of the union treaty, which had triggered the coup and been derailed by it. He spoke instead about the need for "understanding."[2]

"We are flying to a new country," Gorbachev had said to his aides on board the Russian plane taking him to Moscow. He probably did not realize how right he was. Thousands of Muscovites who awaited Gorbachev near the Russian White House for a good part of the night of August 22 did not get to see him. Either he was not informed about their presence or he was too exhausted to address them after his seventy-two-hour ordeal. At about 4:00 a.m. the Russian vice president, Aleksandr Rutskoi, told the jubilant crowd that Gorbachev was free and that the arrests of the plotters had begun. For one reason or another, on that night Gorbachev, who by refusing to back the plotters had provided justification for those resisting the coup, failed to address the people who had made his return possible.[3]

There were many things in the postcoup situation that Gorbachev apparently failed to grasp or fully appreciate. One of them was the dramatically increased power of the street in Soviet politics. The masses that had occupied the streets and squares of Moscow during and immediately after the failed coup had become a force in their own right. They were also a potent weapon in the hands of Boris Yeltsin and his allies, who could speak to the masses, direct their actions, and make use of their support in political battles at the top. Gorbachev could not. The activism of the masses was indeed a product of his policies of perestroika and glasnost, but it was not his ideals that Muscovites had defended at the approaches to the Russian parliament during the days and nights of the coup. People did not want to "restructure" an old way of life; they wanted to build a new one.

In the next few days Gorbachev would miss his chance to become a new kind of politician and would lose the all-important first round in his contest with Boris Yeltsin, the ever more powerful new master of Russia. This loss would have a profound impact on the future of the Soviet Union.

IN HIS MEMOIRS, Gorbachev skips August 22, which one of his key advisers at the time, Vadim Medvedev, later considered a day of lost opportunities. On the first morning after his return from Crimean captivity, Gorbachev took some badly needed rest. At noon he drove to the Kremlin, where he summoned his closest advisers. The main question on the agenda was that of cadres. The president got busy removing plotters and their supporters from governmental posts and replacing them with people whom he believed he could trust. The appropriate presidential decrees were drafted by aides in Gorbachev's presence, typed up, and immediately signed by him. The first priority was replacement of the head of the KGB and the ministers of interior and defense—there Gorbachev could not procrastinate. These were the pillars of presidential power at a time of crisis, and in the aftermath of the coup, Gorbachev needed those pillars more than ever.[4]

Eager to fill vacant cabinet posts as soon as possible, Gorbachev promoted deputies of former ministers who he believed were not implicated in the coup. As acting minister of defense he appointed General Mikhail Moiseev, who had made a strong impression on President Bush and his advisers during his visit to Washington in the spring of 1991. Bush twice asked Yeltsin during their telephone conversations at the time of the coup whether Moiseev had "behaved" or not. Yeltsin said that he had not; Gorbachev thought otherwise. The position at the helm of the KGB was entrusted to Leonid Shebarshin, the head of Soviet foreign intelligence and a specialist on the Middle East, who had spent the first day of the coup playing tennis, thereby sending a signal that his office had nothing to do with the plot masterminded and administered by his colleagues. The minister of the interior, Boris Pugo, who had committed suicide earlier that day, was replaced by his deputy. What now seemed paramount was not the closeness of Gorbachev's new appointees to the coup leaders, who were no longer a threat, but their distance from Yeltsin, who was reemerging as Gorbachev's main rival for power.[5]

The new ministerial appointments produced the first major crisis in Gorbachev and Yeltsin's postcoup relations. While Gorbachev was drafting and signing new decrees, Yeltsin was rallying the masses. At noon he addressed a crowd of thousands of "victors" in Moscow, declaring the red, blue, and white Russian imperial tricolor the official flag of the Russian Federation. Yeltsin's chief bodyguard, Aleksandr Korzhakov, later recalled the reaction of his boss once he learned about Gorbachev's prompt appointment of new ministers: "Naturally, such audacious independence exasperated Yeltsin. He decided to redo everything in his own way." The Russian president now considered himself, not Gorbachev, the master of the situation.

The ministers responsible for the military, police, and secret services could decide the political future not only of the country but also of Yeltsin himself. For these positions the Russian president wanted people who were either loyal to him or at least not fully dependent on and indebted to Gorbachev. Yeltsin's main weapon in his counteroffensive against the weakened Gorbachev was information on the behavior of senior government officials during the coup that Gorbachev lacked. When the Russian president learned from television reports about the appointment of new chiefs of the security agencies, he immediately called Gorbachev: "Mikhail Sergeevich, what are you doing? Moiseev was one of the organizers of the coup, and Shebarshin is a man close to Kriuchkov, the chief coordinator of the coup." Gorbachev tried to maneuver his way out of the difficult situation. "Yes, it's possible I've gone off track, but now it's too late. All the newspapers have published the decree; it's been read over television." Yeltsin was not prepared to back down. He told Gorbachev that he would come to see him in his office the next day.[6]

Canceling Gorbachev's decree was part of Yeltsin's game plan. Getting the Soviet president's approval of his own decree enhancing the economic autonomy, if not outright independence, of the Russian Federation in the Union was the other part. Gorbachev annulled the plotters' decrees but recognized the validity of Yeltsin's decrees signed under the extraordinary conditions of the coup. Now Yeltsin claimed that on August 20 he had signed a decree on Russia's economic sovereignty. According to that decree, as of January 1, 1992, all enterprises on Russian territory would be transferred to the jurisdiction and operational control of the Russian Federation. The Russian president also decreed measures to create a Russian customs service, form Russian gold reserves, and subject the exploitation of natural resources to licensing and taxation by Russian authorities. It was a ploy designed to make Gorbachev approve a decree that he would not otherwise have countenanced, as it undermined the economic foundations of the Union. The decree could not have been and was not signed on August 20. It bore no sign of having been drafted while the president awaited the storming of his premises.

That was not all. A separate decree signed by Yeltsin on August 22, the day on which Gorbachev resumed his functions as president of the USSR, banned the publication of *Pravda* and other newspapers that had supported the coup. Yeltsin clearly overstepped his jurisdiction by firing the general director of the all-Union information agency TASS and establishing Russian government control over Communist Party media outlets on Russian territory. These measures went far beyond the rights ascribed to the Russian Federation by the draft union treaty that had been derailed by the coup. They left no doubt that as far as Russia was concerned, the treaty was dead. But Yeltsin was not content with taking more sovereign rights for Russia. Having saved Gorbachev from the plotters, he was subjecting the Soviet president to a new captivity. Gorbachev's aide Vadim Medvedev referred to Yeltsin's actions in the first days after the coup as a countercoup.[7]

When Yeltsin raised the question of ministerial appointments with Gorbachev during their tête-à-tête on August 23, the Soviet president tried to play for time. Responding to Yeltsin's demand for Moiseev's dismissal, he said, "I'll think of how I can correct it."

Yeltsin refused to leave his office: "No, I won't leave until you do it in my presence. Have Moiseev come here right away and send him into retirement." Yeltsin's hand was strengthened when he received a note through his bodyguards that Moiseev had ordered the destruction of documents pertaining to the Defense Ministry's involvement in the coup. The note bore the name and telephone number of the officer in charge of shredding the papers. Yeltsin ordered that the number be called and then handed the telephone receiver to Gorbachev: "Order the senior lieutenant to stop destroying documents. Let him put everything under guard." Gorbachev followed what amounted to an order. He did likewise when Yeltsin insisted on calling in Moiseev.

"Explain to him that he is no longer a minister," he told the Soviet president. The humiliated Gorbachev followed Yeltsin's order.[8]

The new minister of defense, appointed on Yeltsin's recommendation, was Air Marshal Yevgenii Shaposhnikov, who had opposed the coup and made his position known to Yeltsin and his entourage. Yeltsin now had his man in charge of the Soviet military. He also negotiated the appointment of Vadim Bakatin, a Gorbachev ally who had supported Yeltsin during the coup, as the new KGB chief. Furthermore, Yeltsin insisted on the removal of Aleksandr Bessmertnykh, the Soviet foreign minister, who had reported himself ill while the coup was in progress. Also dismissed was the acting minister of internal affairs whom Gorbachev had appointed the previous day. "I had told him that the coup had taught us a bitter lesson and therefore I had to insist that he not make any personnel decisions without first obtaining my consent," recalled Yeltsin, describing his conversation with Gorbachev about ministerial appointments. "He looked at me intently, with the expression of a person backed into a corner." It was a countercoup indeed. Yeltsin was forcing Gorbachev to appoint either his own people or those he considered well disposed to him personally. The appointments of Shaposhnikov and Bakatin would turn out to be crucial in the months leading up to the disintegration of the USSR.[9]

Gorbachev was clearly in retreat. He was confused, and his position was undermined by accusations that he himself had been behind the coup. On August 22, when correspondents of the Moscow daily *Argumenty i fakty* (*Arguments and Facts*) hit the streets of the capital to ask passersby what they thought of the president of the USSR, the subtext of the question was perfectly obvious: Did people believe that Gorbachev was behind the coup? One of the four people interviewed that day did not trust Gorbachev, another trusted him, and the other two gave him the benefit of the doubt but did not trust him completely—after all, those leading the coup had been his own protégés. What Yeltsin was saying about his new ministerial appointees or senior officials in the Central Committee might well be true: having spent the three critical days of the coup in isolation, Gorbachev was now in no position to check facts or disprove allegations. Recalling his first ministerial appointments, Gorbachev wrote in his memoirs, "Such errors were due to the lack of information. Much would be disclosed only months later and certain issues have not been fully clarified to this day."[10]

MIKHAIL GORBACHEV returned to Moscow determined to regain his position not only as president but also as head of the party. At the televised press conference on the evening of his return, he declared himself an adherent of the socialist idea; castigated his close aide and an intellectual father of perestroika, Aleksandr Yakovlev, for abandoning the party; and proclaimed his determination to continue the renewal of the party on a democratic basis. In July he had forced a new party program on the Central Committee that would reform the Communist Party along European social democratic lines. Now, with the hard-liners on the run after the defeat of the coup, he believed that the reform could be carried out successfully.

In his memoirs, Gorbachev explained his logic at the time as follows: "The break-up of the party was inevitable at a certain stage, because of the different ideological and political tension in its membership. I advocated proceeding by democratic means: convening a congress in November and making an amicable divide. According to some opinion polls, the version of the program adopted by me and my followers was favored by nearly a third of the party members." The party Gorbachev envisioned could have up to 5 million members. But he soon found himself with no party at all. His opponents used their power over the street to shut down the activities of the Central Committee of the Communist Party.[11]

Major popular demonstrations began in Moscow on the day of Gorbachev's return, August 22. In the course of that day, the crowds swelled with liberal supporters of the democratic revolution, most of whom had not dared to show up during the acute stage of the conflict, as well as with city youth in search of adventure and excitement. Liquor was freely available, making the crowds more unruly. Those managing the crowds came from the Moscow city administration—all ardent supporters of Yeltsin during the coup. They succeeded in preventing the increasingly aggressive throng from storming the KGB buildings, which were protected by sharpshooters, by offering an alternative: the removal of the monument to "Iron Felix"—the founder of the Soviet secret police, Felix Dzerzhinsky—that dominated Lubianka Square in front of KGB headquarters. The ploy worked.[12]

American embassy staffers who reached the KGB building late in the afternoon got the best view of the scene. When one of them told the demonstrators that he was an American, he was thrust through the crowd toward the center of the square so that he could see the whole event from the first row. At first the demonstrators wanted to pull the statue down with a truck. But then the Moscow authorities asked the crowd to wait for cranes to arrive, explaining that the statue was too heavy. If it toppled, it could crash through the ground into the Moscow subway system. The warning worked, and the statue was removed a few hours later with Krupp cranes.

"Finally," reported the American diplomats to Washington, "just before midnight, the final bolts were cut, and the cranes were moved into position to lift the statue from its base. When the statue was lifted from the pedestal the crowd broke into cheers and began chanting 'Down with the KGB,' 'Russia,' and 'Executioner.' All three KGB buildings were dark throughout the event. Whenever an office light was turned on the crowd began pointing and shouting until it went out. People in the crowd remarked, 'They are afraid of us.'" The night came to an end without riots or major incidents.[13]

Then came the morning of August 23. Yeltsin's lieutenants seemed to be in control of the crowds and were in no hurry to send the demonstrators home, realizing their political importance for the moment. They warned the crowds that the hard-liners were preparing a new attack on the White House. Marshal Shaposhnikov, who would be appointed minister of defense in a few hours, reacted to the rumor by placing the air force on high alert. Meanwhile, a crowd gathered around a police station on Petrovka Square, and the boldest began to climb the iron fence around the building. A riot was in the making, with a possible seizure of weapons. Moreover, there was no supreme authority in charge of the police: the minister of the interior, Boris Pugo, had committed suicide; his replacement, appointed by Gorbachev, had been rejected by Yeltsin; and Yeltsin's appointee had not yet been approved by Gorbachev and the republican leaders. The situation might well have gotten out of hand.[14]

The Moscow city authorities, who had opposed the coup and enjoyed great trust among Muscovites, took charge of the situation, as they had done the previous night. Their solution was to divert the masses toward the Communist Party headquarters, located a few kilometers away from the Petrovka police station. "The mayor needs your help. Everyone to the Central Committee," said one of the city officials to the crowd. Many were unhappy to be thwarted when they had almost gotten their hands on the policemen and their weapons, but a good part of the crowd of Muscovites, used to seeing the party as the source and main symbol of power, obeyed the official's call.

While the earlier targets of the crowd's rage—the KGB and the police—had been directly and visibly implicated in the coup, the party, whose leadership had never publicly declared its attitude, was a still larger prize. The protesters were rebelling not just against the coup authorities but against the party-run state itself. Antiparty slogans had mobilized Muscovites to take part in meetings and demonstrations over the previous few years, and now they worked just as the city authorities hoped they would. The crowds moved in the direction of the Old Square—the complex of buildings belonging to the Central Committee of the Communist Party of the Soviet Union.

That day, while Gorbachev and Yeltsin bargained for ministerial positions at the Kremlin, real power in the country and the capital rested with Gennadii Burbulis, a forty-six-year-old grandson of Latvian immigrants who had grown up in Yeltsin's native Sverdlovsk. A former university professor of Marxist political economy and, since the beginning of perestroika, a democratic organizer and an anticommunist to boot, Burbulis had recently been appointed by Yeltsin to the post of secretary of state, the second-highest office in the Russian hierarchy. This gave him control over the presidential administration and a good part of the government. On August 23, Burbulis was running Russian affairs from an office in the White House. He communicated with Yeltsin, then in session with Gorbachev and republican leaders at the Kremlin, through notes passed to the Russian president by his bodyguards. It was he who told Yeltsin about the shredding of documents at the Defense Ministry, giving him grounds to demand the dismissal of Gorbachev's appointee to the ministry.

Now Burbulis applied the same tactic—accusations of shredding documents and covering up participation in the coup—to undercut Gorbachev in his own sphere and shut down the operations of the Communist Party, where neither Yeltsin, who had left the party several years before, nor the republican leaders had any real influence. Burbulis sent Gorbachev (then in session with Yeltsin) a note claiming that party officials were shredding documents implicating them in the coup and demanded permission for a temporary shutdown of the Central Committee premises. Shredding was indeed going on, although the machines broke down when party apparatchiks, eager to destroy all traces of their participation in the coup, failed to remove paper clips. Apparently in an attempt to appease Yeltsin, Gorbachev signed the memo, thereby authorizing the closure of the Central Committee buildings. His fate as head of the party was now sealed, and his position as president was weaker than ever before.

Moscow city officials rushed to the party headquarters with the paper signed by Gorbachev, demanding that the confused and frightened party apparatchiks close their offices and go home. The crowds besieging the building echoed that demand. When Nikolai Kruchina, the head of the Central Committee staff, told the Moscow officials that he could not just shut down the operations of the entire Central Committee, they pointed to the window and the crowds outside: "They will tear everyone inside here to pieces, unless you go quietly," barked one of the officials at Kruchina. "Stop playing the fool. Do as you're told!" The senior party official, visibly shaken, turned red. There were not enough KGB guards to put up effective resistance. So Kruchina gave up and ordered his deputy to lead the Moscow city representatives to the civil defense announcement system in the building. "By agreement with the president, in view of recent events, a decision has been made to seal the building. You have one hour in which to leave. You may take your personal belongings with you, but everything else is to be left behind," went the announcement.

The crowds were jubilant. As the party apparatchiks started to leave the building, the city officials appealed to the demonstrators not to "give any pretext to those who would like to sow any disorder here." "Shame! Shame!" chanted the Muscovites as thousands of party employees left the building in utmost humiliation. The Moscow city party secretary, Yurii Prokofiev, who on the last day of the coup had demanded that the plotters give him a pistol so that he could shoot himself, was verbally abused and even kicked but was then taken under police protection and driven away in a taxi. The demonstrators, who searched officials as they left the building, showed off their loot—smoked fish and sausages that some party officials had tried to smuggle out, these being delicacies hard to come by at the time.[15]

THE SHUTDOWN OF PARTY headquarters in downtown Moscow coincided with Gorbachev's greatest public disaster of his long political career. In the afternoon, he met with a group of deputies to the Russian parliament in what was supposed to be an informal setting. In fact, it was broadcast on television. He began by thanking the Russian parliament and Yeltsin personally for standing up to the coup. He revealed that he had signed a decree promoting Aleksandr Rutskoi, a colonel at the time of the coup, to the rank of general. To appease Yeltsin, Gorbachev read aloud an excerpt from the minutes of a cabinet meeting of August 19, at which all but two of his ministers had supported the coup.

But the Soviet president was also eager to save what remained of his power. He called on the Russian deputies to help him salvage the Union: "Today, after emerging from this crisis, the Russians must act together with all the other supreme soviets of the other republics and the peoples of the other republics. Otherwise they would not be Russians." The allusion was to the traditional imperial role of the Russians in the Russian Empire and the Soviet Union. None of this sat well with the deputies, who took Gorbachev's appeal to act in conjunction with other republics as an attempt to check Russia's drive toward democracy and market reform by harnessing it to the Union bandwagon. The deputies bombarded Gorbachev with questions about his own complicity in the coup and demanded that the Communist Party, his real power base, be declared a criminal organization. Gorbachev went on the defensive. "This is just another way of carrying on a crusade or religious war at the present time," he told the deputies. "Socialism, as I understand it, is a type of conviction which people have and we are not the only ones who have it but it exists in other countries, not only today but at other times."

Then came a question about the ownership of all-Union property on the territory of the Russian Federation and the decree on Russia's economic sovereignty signed by Yeltsin. "You today said that you would sign a decree confirming all my decrees signed during that period," said Yeltsin, referring to the measures he had signed during the coup.

Gorbachev knew he was in trouble. "I do not think you have tried to put me in a trap by bringing me here," he responded. Gorbachev went on to say that he would sign a decree confirming all Yeltsin's decrees of the coup period except the one dealing with all-Union property. "I will issue such a decree after signing the [[union]] treaty," he said to Yeltsin. This was not merely a delaying tactic. Gorbachev was trying to keep Yeltsin on the hook: signature on the union treaty first, property second.

The Russian president did not like what he heard. His ruse of backdating the decree had failed, but he had a trump card in hand and knew how to use it against Gorbachev. "And now, on a lighter note," declared Yeltsin in front of the cameras, "shall we now sign a decree suspending the activities of the Russian Communist Party?" Yeltsin used the pronoun "we" to refer to himself. Gorbachev was stunned. All party organizations in Russia were suddenly on the chopping block. Without them, his already dwindling powers would be reduced to almost nothing. After realizing what was going on, he asked his "ally," "What are you doing? . . . I . . . haven't we . . . I haven't read this."[16]

The Russian president took his time signing the decree temporarily banning Communist Party activity on Russian territory. When Gorbachev told him that he could not ban the party, Yeltsin responded that he was only suspending its activities. Welcoming the decree with applause and chants of approval, the Russian deputies went on with their interrogation of the trapped Soviet president. Gorbachev found it hard to recover from Yeltsin's blow. "At that encounter," he remembered later, "Yeltsin was gloating with sadistic pleasure." This was a side of Yeltsin's personality that the public had not previously seen—not the popular leader who picked up on the mood of the masses, nor the calculating politician who valued personal loyalty, nor yet the sensitive man who cared about those around him, but Yeltsin the predator. One of Yeltsin's principal advisers later recalled his impression of his boss's sudden attack on the Soviet president: "a cruel, malicious, wicked scene."[17]

Yeltsin had scored another major victory in his contest with Gorbachev to control the levers of power. With the reversal of the appointments of security ministers and suspension of the activities of the Communist Party, Gorbachev all but lost his influence in the country and his power base.

Once the decree was signed, Yeltsin tried to charm his victim. At the end of the meeting the victorious Yeltsin publicly took Gorbachev under his protection, assuring the deputies that the Soviet president was committed to the prosecution of those complicit in the coup. Once the meeting was over, Yeltsin told Gorbachev, "Mikhail Sergeevich! We have been through so much—such events, such turmoil! You had a hard time of it in Foros, and we didn't know how that putsch of the Extraordinary Committee would turn out, and our family members, and Raisa Maksimovna . . . Let's have a family get-together. Naina Iosifovna, Raisa Maksimovna . . . "

Gorbachev looked at Yeltsin in bewilderment, probably not knowing whether to take him seriously. "No, not now," he told Yeltsin. "We shouldn't do that."[18]

ON THE EVENING OF THE SAME DAY, August 23, George Bush and Brent Scowcroft were watching a televised relay of Gorbachev's meeting with the Russian deputies and Yeltsin's humiliation of his rival. "It's all over," was Scowcroft's comment. Gorbachev, he told the president, was "not an independent actor anymore. Yeltsin is telling him what to do. I do not think Gorbachev understands what's happened." George Bush agreed: "I am afraid he may have had it." The banning of the Communist Party was an important milestone in the ideological competition between the United States and the Soviet Union, and seasoned cold warriors such as Bush and Scowcroft had every reason to celebrate. But more important for the moment was its significance for Gorbachev's political survival.[19]

Bush had seen it coming. The first signs of the new political situation in Moscow had become apparent on August 21, with the jubilant Yeltsin calling from the Russian White House for the first time since the coup. He sounded like a man completely in charge, as in fact he was. "As we agreed, I'm reporting on the latest events," began Yeltsin after a brief greeting.

"Please do," responded Bush.

"Russian Prime Minister Silaev and Vice President Rutskoi," began Yeltsin, "have brought President Gorbachev back to Moscow unharmed and in good health. I am also reporting to you that Defense Minister Yazov, Prime Minister Pavlov, and KGB Chairman Kriuchkov have been taken into custody." Silaev, who had spent the decisive night of the

White House siege at home, returned to his president the next day and was now back at the center of the action. Bush encouraged Yeltsin with occasional remarks indicating his interest. Yeltsin went on: "And, upon my order, with sanction, the prosecuting Attorney General of the Soviet Union has begun a case against all conspirators."

A country in which the all-Union attorney general was acting on the orders of the president of Russia was obviously not the old Soviet Union. But for now it was all about celebrating the defeat of the coup. "My friend, your stock is sky-high over here," said Bush to Yeltsin. "You displayed respect for law and stood for democratic principles. Congratulations. You were the ones on the front line, who stood on the barricades—all we did was support you. You brought Gorbachev back intact. You restored him to power. You have won a lot of friends around the world. We support and congratulate you on your courage and what you've done. If you will now accept some advice from a friend—get some rest, get some sleep."[20]

Sleep was the last thing on Yeltsin's mind. It was 9:20 p.m. EST on August 21 in Kennebunkport and early in the morning of August 22 in Moscow. Yeltsin had just declared the coup defeated and thanked the defenders of the Russian White House. He had a brand-new day ahead of him, one he was eager to use to consolidate his power, no longer in confrontation with the coup leaders but in competition with Gorbachev. The battlefield was not limited to Moscow, Russia, or the Soviet Union. It also included the Western capitals and platforms provided by international organizations. Yeltsin supporters there presented a striking dilemma not only to the Russian and Soviet public but also to Western leaders: either support Yeltsin as a democratically elected politician devoted to radical reform or remain loyal to Gorbachev and bid farewell not only to democracy but also to reform.

On that day Yeltsin's young foreign minister, Andrei Kozyrev, arrived in Strasbourg at the invitation of the Council of Europe. His main message to the European leaders was, "The time has come to separate the sheep from the goats in Soviet politics." This was a major change from a few days earlier. To begin with, the new message included no gesture to Gorbachev. On the contrary, according to an American diplomatic report, Kozyrev "repeatedly criticized 'some people' in positions of authority who are not committed to democratic ideals and lack legitimacy because they have never been elected." The reference was clearly to Gorbachev, who had been elected president of the USSR by parliament, not by popular vote, as was the case with Yeltsin. Kozyrev was also skeptical that Gorbachev had "the psychological resources to initiate truly radical reforms." Kozyrev, went the report, "commented that Gorbachev was in the grip of a 'syndrome of fear.'" Gorbachev would do anything for reform, said Kozyrev, but only within the system. "He is afraid that he and his family would become nobodies—cease to exist—if the system that now supports them collapses."[21]

THE SOVIET PRESIDENT'S DOWNFALL became complete on Saturday, August 24. On the morning of that day, he and Yeltsin attended the funeral of three young men who had died defending the White House on the night of August 20. Gorbachev tried to use the occasion—his first appearance before Muscovites since his return from the Crimea—to express his gratitude to those who had defended democracy. He was also eager to show the all-Union flag, awarding the title of Hero of the Soviet Union posthumously to the three men. The crowd was moved, but Yeltsin, the real hero of resistance to the coup, managed to steal Gorbachev's thunder. The Russian Federation had no awards of its own, and he had no authority to grant them. Yeltsin simply asked the mothers of the three young men to forgive him for not being able to save their sons. Once again, he won the day.[22]

After the funeral, Gorbachev went to the Kremlin to sign a number of decrees. With one of them he dissolved the cabinet and replaced it with a committee chaired by Yeltsin's prime minister, Ivan Silaev. With another decree, Gorbachev resigned as general secretary of the party, citing the attitude of its leadership during the coup. He also advised his former party colleagues to dissolve the Central Committee and asked local party organizations to decide their own fate. As president of the USSR, Gorbachev signed a decree placing Communist Party property under the control and protection of local soviets. Gorbachev was no longer prepared to lead a banned party that constituted no threat to him, as he believed it had earlier, and which represented no asset in the political struggle he had begun to wage immediately after the coup. He would devote pages of his memoirs to an attempt to prove that it was the party apparatus that had betrayed him in August 1991, not the other way around.[23]

The party apparatchiks were foot soldiers but hardly the driving force behind the coup—by the summer of 1991 they were too demoralized and disorganized to become its true leaders—and the Emergency Committee's appeal to the people made no mention whatever of the party or its policies and ideals. It was the KGB and military officers who had led the coup. As a group, however, the apparatchiks had stood to benefit most from a successful coup, which was supposed to reverse Yeltsin's decree banning party cells at state enterprises. At a meeting of the Central Committee secretariat on August 13, 1991, five days before the coup, the party bosses had discussed ways to deal with the decree.

The coup had seemed the only way to restore the party's monopoly of political power. But with the coup a failure and Gorbachev resigning from the highest party post, the political force that had ruled the country with an iron fist, and often with a blood-smeared club in its hands, was going down to defeat without bloodshed. Some blood was spilled, to be sure, but it was that of party establishment figures who decided to end their lives rather than stand trial.[24]

The first to depart was Boris Pugo, the minister of the interior, whose police formations and troops had been directly involved in the coup. On the morning of August 22, Russian officials reached him on the phone at home and asked for a meeting. When a four-man group including Gorbachev's economic adviser Grigorii Yavlinsky showed up at Pugo's home, an old man with obvious signs of dementia opened the door and let them in. It was Pugo's father-in-law. One of the visitors saw a pool of blood on the floor. They then entered the bedroom, where the fifty-four-year-old Boris Pugo lay on the bed, killed by a gunshot. Instead of waiting to be arrested, he had committed suicide. Next to him, near the bed, sat his mortally wounded wife. She reacted to questions but could not say anything. Valentina Pugo would die soon in a Moscow hospital. In a suicide note written earlier that morning, Boris Pugo asked forgiveness of the members of his family: "This is all a mistake. I lived honestly all my life."

Another supporter of the coup, Marshal Sergei Akhromeev, committed suicide in his Kremlin office a few days later. He had been one of the Soviet negotiators of arms reduction treaties with the United States. On August 19, the first day of the coup, the sixty-eight-year-old

Akhromeev, then Gorbachev's adviser on military affairs, interrupted his summer vacation in Sochi to return to Moscow and report to his new boss, the acting president of the USSR, Gennadii Yanaev. He told Yanaev that he shared the Emergency Committee's agenda and was prepared to help in its realization. Akhromeev was entrusted with the task of collecting and analyzing information on the situation in the regions. Yanaev also asked him to prepare a draft of his address to the Soviet parliament. Akhromeev worked on both tasks with enthusiasm.

In a letter he wrote to Mikhail Gorbachev before committing suicide, the marshal explained his reasons for supporting the coup: "Beginning in 1990 I was convinced, as I am convinced today, that our country is headed for perdition. Soon it will be dismembered. I looked for a way to say that aloud. . . . I understand that as a marshal of the Soviet Union I have violated my military oath and committed a military crime. . . . Nothing remains for me but to take responsibility for what I have done." To his suicide note Akhromeev attached a fifty-ruble banknote—money he owed the Kremlin cafeteria for lunches there.[25]

Vadim Medvedev, a Gorbachev aide who had known both Pugo and Akhromeev well, later commented on their suicides: "I understand their tragedy: I knew Boris Karlovich [[Pugo]] well as a man of integrity in his own way, devoted to a particular idea, foreign to political intrigue or careerism. Nor do I have any doubt about the honesty of Sergei Fedorovich." Both Pugo and Akhromeev believed in communist ideals and the indivisibility of the Soviet state. Akhromeev had fought for it in the Second World War. Pugo, the son of a "Latvian sharpshooter"—one of Lenin's crack troops fanatically devoted to the revolution—had spent a good part of his life at the helm of the Latvian KGB and then of its Communist Party, stamping out nationalist dissent. The coup had given them hope of saving the world that had brought them up and given them career opportunities, high positions, and, last but not least, identity. For people such as Pugo and Akhromeev, its failure meant both personal fiasco and the collapse of their universe. Suicide released them from a world that regarded them not as heroes and saviors but as criminals who had acted against their own people and betrayed their president.[26]

On the evening of Sunday, August 25, one day after Gorbachev stepped down as general secretary of the Soviet Communist Party and signed a decree on the transfer of party property, and the day on which Yeltsin signed his own decree seizing that property, Nikolai Kruchina, the sixty-three-year-old chief of staff of the Central Committee, went to his old office to discuss the property transfer with representatives of the Moscow government. The meeting, which ended soon after 9:00 p.m., did not go well for Kruchina. Normally a friendly individual, he surprised his KGB guard when, on his return from the Central Committee, he did not greet him as usual. Looking depressed and withdrawn, Kruchina went to his fifth-floor apartment in an exclusive building in downtown Moscow. He bade his wife goodnight and told her that he still needed to do some work. Soon after 5:00 a.m. on August 26, Kruchina stepped onto his balcony and jumped to his death.

Kruchina committed suicide not because he was disillusioned with the ideals of the Communist Party or the actions of its leaders and members but because he felt that he had broken his oath of loyalty to his boss and, judging by what we know today, was afraid of an investigation into the party's finances. The meeting that put Kruchina into a mood of depression on the evening of August 25 ended on a very worrisome note for him: as the man responsible for party finances, he had signed almost every major document authorizing secret transfers of party funds to business ventures both at home and abroad. When Vasilii Shakhnovsky, the Moscow city official who met with Kruchina that evening, told him, "We'll need to have a special discussion about party finances," the party's chief of staff went pale. He abruptly ended the conversation, promising to return to the subject the next day. For him, that day never came.

Party finances were the one thing that the chief of the party staff was not prepared to discuss with Russian officials. As later investigations showed, some of the party money had been transferred abroad, according to memos signed by Kruchina, for "good" communist causes, including clandestine support for communist parties and movements all over the world, from the United States to Afghanistan. But most of the transfers went to the new commercial banks and shady enterprises created by party apparatchiks and their business cronies during the last two years of Gorbachev's rule. Having been maneuvered out of office, the party officials were seeking to convert their political power into financial resources. This strategy offered them a comfortable life outside the party apparatus and saved the country from a prolonged and potentially bloody struggle with the numerous and well-entrenched ruling class, which otherwise would have had everything to lose and nothing to gain from the transition. Still, the process was not bloodless. Kruchina became one of its first victims.[27]

8

INDEPENDENT UKRAINE

NO ONE COULD TELL HOW MANY PEOPLE there were: thousands, tens of thousands, perhaps as many as a hundred thousand. The Ukrainian parliamentary deputies making their way through the crowds to the parliament building were in no position to count. It was the sunny Saturday morning of August 24, the day on which Yeltsin upstaged Gorbachev at the funeral for the defenders of the White House and on which the Soviet leader stepped down as head of the Communist Party. What would happen in Kyiv that day would send a shock wave around the Soviet Union considerably greater than the one set off by that day's events in Moscow. The second Soviet republic would declare its complete independence from the Union.

The Kyivan crowds had not gathered in the city's downtown on August 24 to defend parliament, as had been the case in Moscow a few days earlier, but to condemn the communist parliamentary majority for its covert support of the coup. The previous day Yeltsin had signed a decree banning the Communist Party of Russia in full view not only of the confused Gorbachev but also of millions of excited television viewers all over the Soviet Union. Many of those gathered in Kyiv believed that the same should be done in Ukraine. The leaflets that summoned them called the Communist Party a "criminal and anticonstitutional organization whose activities must be brought to an end." The people responded. Many brought along blue-and-yellow national flags and placards calling for a Nuremberg-style trial for the Communist Party.[1]

The fate of the party was not their only concern; otherwise people would have gathered at the building of the Ukrainian party's Central Committee, only a few blocks from parliament. They did not do so because it was no longer in the party's power to grant or revoke what they wanted. Carrying placards that read "Ukraine is leaving the USSR," they demanded independence for their country. Only parliament could deliver that. The crowds, consisting largely of supporters of Ukrainian opposition parties, were in a resolute mood. Only a few weeks earlier, many of those on parliament square had lined the streets of Kyiv to welcome President George Bush to the Ukrainian capital. At that time they had carried placards with the same demand: now, however, they were directed not toward an American visitor whom they implicitly trusted but toward their own domestic nemesis—the communist apparatchiks, whom they did not trust at all.

John Stepanchuk, the acting consul general of the United States in Kyiv, who had been directly involved in preparations for Bush's visit and was now in charge of the consulate there, had difficulty making his way through the crowds at the parliament building that morning. "There were thousands of people surrounding it, angry people," he remembered later. "Angry at the Communists, angry at everything. They were just gathered there. They thought I was a Communist because I was dressed in a suit. So one woman started pulling my jacket calling 'hanba,' 'shame.' They thought I was one of the guilty." The communist majority inside the parliament building suddenly found itself a besieged minority. Stepanchuk, seated in a diplomatic booth, "could see that the Communists were all glued to the window watching these crowds come closer and closer, wondering if they would ever leave the building alive." The communist members of parliament "were all nervous, and smoking, walking around. This was the atmosphere of tension. It was known, of course, that Kravchuk would make a speech, but no one knew how far he would go."

Leonid Kravchuk, the silver-haired Speaker of the Ukrainian parliament, who had made a positive impression on President Bush a few weeks earlier and then seemed to be in full control of the institution, was now clearly on the defensive. Not only the Communist Party but also his own behavior during the coup was now being questioned and put on trial. His own fate—the outcome of that day in parliament, outside its walls, and all over the country—would depend on the attitude Kravchuk adopted. With the crowds outside parliament chanting, "Shame on Kravchuk," the Speaker was fighting for his political life.[2]

WHAT HAPPENED IN MOSCOW on August 18, 1991, caught Leonid Kravchuk by surprise. It presented a major challenge to his grip on power in Ukraine and to the movement for Ukrainian sovereignty with which he had closely associated his name and his political fortunes. On the morning of August 19, he learned about the overthrow of Gorbachev from his main political rival, the first secretary of the Communist Party of Ukraine, Stanislav Hurenko, who called Kravchuk at his suburban residence to summon him to Central Committee headquarters. There was to be a meeting with the Emergency Committee's strongman, the tough-talking General Valentin Varennikov, who had arrived in Kyiv after his encounter with Gorbachev in the Crimea.

Kravchuk refused. "I immediately grasped where power was now moving," he remembered later. "I said: 'Stanislav Ivanovych, the point is that the state is embodied in the Supreme Soviet, and I am the head of the Supreme Soviet. If Varennikov wants to meet, then we shall meet in my office at the Supreme Soviet.'" Hurenko had to agree. This represented Kravchuk's first, modest victory over his rival. Just one year earlier, the fifty-five-year-old Hurenko, as first secretary of the Central Committee, had been considered a step above Kravchuk in the republican hierarchy. But with Ukraine declaring sovereignty in the summer of 1990, the role of parliament and its Speaker, traditionally known as the head of the presidium of the Supreme Soviet, had grown enormously, making Kravchuk the republic's principal figure. This was now the trend in all the Union republics, although it was not so pronounced in Central Asia, where local heads of party Central Committees also became Speakers of parliament.

Kravchuk later remembered that while waiting for Hurenko and Varennikov to arrive, he felt defenseless: no military or police units reported to the head of parliament, and the only force he had at his disposal consisted of three guards with handguns. Varennikov's sudden arrival in Kyiv showed how ephemeral was the power of the head of a republic that had declared its sovereignty and set its own laws above those of the Union. Kravchuk had no doubt that he was being faced with a coup. Gorbachev's alleged illness was a sham: Kravchuk had seen him in the Crimea a few weeks earlier. On the evening he visited Gorbachev in Foros, they had polished off a 0.75-liter bottle of lemon vodka with the help of Gorbachev's son-in-law. Kravchuk did not conceal his skepticism about the Emergency Committee's claim with regard to Gorbachev's poor health from anyone with whom he chanced to speak, and later that day he mentioned the bottle of vodka at a meeting with World War II veterans. Finally the guests arrived, with Hurenko preceding Varennikov and his entourage.[3]

The host and his guests sat around the long table—military on one side, civilians on the other, Varennikov directly across from Kravchuk. Varennikov was the first to speak. "Gorbachev is ill; power in the country has gone over to a newly created agency, the Emergency Committee on the Extraordinary Situation," he said, according to a participant in the meeting. "From 4:00 a.m. on August 19, in the interests of public safety, a state of emergency has been declared in Moscow in connection with the deterioration of the situation in the capital and the danger of disturbances. I have come to Kyiv in order to sort out the situation directly and, if necessary, to recommend the declaration of a state of emergency in at least a number of regions of Ukraine." Varennikov specified Kyiv, Lviv, Odesa, and one of the cities in the western region of Volhynia.

The civilians on the other side of the table reacted as if shell-shocked. There was complete silence for at least a minute. Hurenko showed no emotion. The silence was finally broken by Kravchuk, who seemed poised and confident without being aggressive. "We know you, Valentin Ivanovich, as the USSR deputy minister of defense, a respected individual, but you have shown us no credentials," said Kravchuk in response. "Besides, we have not yet received any instructions from Moscow. And, finally, the most important point: the declaration of a state of emergency throughout Ukraine or in a particular region is a matter for the Supreme Soviet—that is what the law requires. We are informed that the situation both in Kyiv and in the regions is fairly calm, requiring no extraordinary measures."[4]

Varennikov had come to Ukraine because the plotters in Moscow were apprehensive about Rukh—the pro-independence alliance of Ukraine's opposition parties—and its possible actions against the coup in Kyiv and western Ukraine. "There is no Soviet power in western Ukraine; it's all Rukh," declared Varennikov. "It is imperative to declare a state of emergency in the western oblasts. Strikes are to be stopped. All parties except the CPSU are to be shut down, along with their papers; meetings are to be stopped and dispersed. You are to take extraordinary measures so that people do not think you are following the previous course. . . . The army is in full battle readiness, and we will take every measure, including bloodshed." Kravchuk insisted that there was no need for a state of emergency. If the general thought there was, he could go to western Ukraine and see for himself that calm prevailed there.[5]

Varennikov changed his line. "You are a man of authority; a great deal depends on you, and I am asking you personally," he said to Kravchuk, "that you, first of all, make an appearance on television, then on radio, and appeal to the people to remain calm, taking account of what has already been proclaimed." After Hurenko and the others left Kravchuk's office, leaving him one-on-one with the general, Kravchuk asked him as an old acquaintance (they had attended the same meetings of the Central Committee in Kyiv when Varennikov served in Ukraine), "Valentin Ivanovich, once you succeed, are you going to bring back the old system?" He had in mind the pre-perestroika political order and relations between the center and the republics. The general responded in the affirmative: "We have no other choice." This answer spoke volumes to Kravchuk. As he remembered later, he realized at that moment that a victory for the Emergency Committee would not mean keeping things as they were but would actually lead to turning back the clock, perhaps all the way back to the times of mass persecution.

The putschists would have nothing to lose, and their victory would mean not only the end of Kravchuk's political career but also his possible imprisonment. Unlike Hurenko, Kravchuk was in no position to gain anything politically by siding with the coup, but neither was he prepared to rebel like Boris Yeltsin in Moscow. His strategy was different: to do everything in his power to avoid giving the military a pretext to introduce a state of emergency in Ukraine.

"Presentiment suggested to me," remembered Kravchuk later, "that it was necessary to gain time, to avoid any unnecessary moves, and all would be well." It was a wait-and-see attitude for which he would later be severely and justly criticized.[6]

Kravchuk's stand was largely shared by the Ukrainian government. None of its members genuinely supported the coup, recalled the liberal-minded deputy prime minister, Serhii Komisarenko. At a meeting of the government presidium called that day, Komisarenko himself described the actions of the Emergency Committee as "openly anticonstitutional." However, if there was lack of support for the committee's actions, there was no lack of fear. The government soon created a special commission along the lines proposed by Varennikov, although its purpose was somewhat different from the one that he suggested. The title of the government decree establishing the commission indicated the main concern of its creators: "On the Establishment of a Temporary Commission to Prevent Extraordinary Situations." If a state of emergency was declared in Ukraine, then real power would be taken away from the parliament and government, where it had rested until then. Once lost, it would never be regained. The commission's main task was to keep the opposition quiet and shut out the Emergency Committee and the military.[7]

The only man at the top of the Ukrainian power pyramid who had much to gain from the coup, the first secretary of the Central Committee, Stanislav Hurenko, returned to party headquarters after meeting with Kravchuk and Varennikov to find a telegram from Moscow urging party committees to support the coup. He called in the leading party officials for a meeting and informed them of the state of affairs and the plan of action: a special memo should be prepared on the basis of the telegram received from Moscow and sent to the local party committees, instructing them to offer all possible support to the coup. The memo prepared at Hurenko's bidding was many times longer than the telegram from Moscow, indicating the agitation of the Ukrainian party apparatus. The Ukrainian Central Committee instructed party cadres on the ground that support of the Emergency Committee was their most important task, ordered them to prohibit any meetings or demonstrations, and stressed that preservation of the Soviet Union was among the main tasks of the party. The actions of the Emergency Committee, wrote the leaders of the Communist

Party of Ukraine, "correspond to the attitudes of the overwhelming majority of toilers and are consonant with the principled position of the Communist Party of Ukraine."[8]

Meanwhile, Kravchuk began his all but impossible balancing act, trying to please everyone while retaining the power he already had. He addressed the country on Ukrainian radio and television late in the afternoon of August 19. The idea of an address had been suggested by Varennikov, but the Ukrainian leader had his own agenda. Kravchuk refused either to support or to condemn the coup. He appealed for calm and pleaded for time, which was allegedly needed to assess the situation. "That is to be done by a collective agency elected by the people," he told the audience. "But there is no question that in a state founded on law everything, including the declaration of a state of emergency, is to be done on the basis of the law." He declared that a state of emergency would not be introduced in Ukraine. "Kravchuk urged Ukrainians," reads an American diplomatic dispatch from Kyiv, "to demonstrate wisdom, restraint and courage, and above all not to antagonize Moscow, which could make the situation worse."[9]

Kravchuk tried, less successfully, to take the same line in a brief interview with the all-Union television news program *Vremia*. There he shocked the Soviet audience by saying that "what happened had to happen, perhaps not in such a form." He argued that a situation in which neither the center nor the republics had enough power to deal with urgent economic and social issues could not last forever. Kravchuk also characterized the coup as a lamentable development that, given the tragic history of Ukraine, raised people's concern about the possibility of a return to the totalitarian past. Despite these caveats, the general impression created by Kravchuk's interview, which ended with a statement on the need to maintain the working rhythm of the economy, was that at best he was trying to take both sides of the issue and at worst he was supporting the coup. Contrasted with reports on the same program about Yeltsin's open resistance and the declaration by President Mircea Snegur of Moldova that his republic would continue to press for independence, Kravchuk's maneuvering looked like indirect support for the coup.[10]

THE COUP CAME AS A COMPLETE surprise not only to Ukrainian government officials but also to the leaders of the Ukrainian "national democrats," the members of the liberal opposition who had welcomed President Bush to Kyiv a few weeks earlier with the slogan of Ukrainian independence. The session of parliament that Bush had addressed on August 1 was long over, and the deputies had dispersed all over Ukraine, working in their constituencies or taking well-deserved vacations. Viacheslav Chornovil, a longtime prisoner of the Gulag and now head of the Lviv regional administration in western Ukraine, spent the days leading up to the coup in Zaporizhia, an industrial city of nine hundred thousand in the southern part of the country.

Chornovil was the leading democratic candidate in the presidential elections announced by parliament a month earlier, and Zaporizhia seemed the perfect place to launch his campaign. In the summer of 1991 Zaporizhia was chosen as the site of the second all-Ukrainian Chervona Ruta (Red Rue) song festival, which combined traditional folk music with a rock and underground music culture that was breaking free of Soviet restraints. The finale of the music festival took place at the local soccer stadium on the evening of August 18, the same evening on which the plotters paid a surprise visit to Gorbachev in the neighboring Crimea. It turned into a major celebration of Ukrainian culture and emerging, previously suppressed trends in music but was completely ignored by the local communist administration. The next morning participants and guests, including Chornovil and quite a few nationaldemocratic leaders, were supposed to leave the city. For many of them the departure became an ordeal as thousands of guests, alarmed by news of the coup, stormed the airport and the railway and bus terminals in an effort to get to Kyiv as soon as possible.[11]

On the morning of August 19, the first day of the coup, Chornovil was awakened when a journalist staying in the same hotel knocked on his door to tell him that there had been a coup in Moscow. To Chornovil, who had spent more than fifteen years in Soviet prisons and internal exile, the fact that he was learning of the coup from a journalist and not a KGB officer was already good news. "The putsch must not be serious if I'm still sleeping here, still dreaming some dream, and not in a prison cell," said Chornovil to his awakener.

John Stepanchuk, the acting American consul in Kyiv, who had also attended the Red Rue festival and was staying in the same hotel as Chornovil, soon came to his room. He witnessed Chornovil making phone calls to KGB and military headquarters in the city of Lviv, where he had been elected head of the local administration, to find out what was happening. The commander of the Carpathian military district told Chornovil that his forces were essentially opposed to the coup and that he would not interfere with the workings of democratic governments in the western Ukrainian oblasts as long as they refrained from declaring a general strike. Chornovil assured the commander that he would do his best to maintain peace in western Ukraine.[12]

Chornovil's first reaction to the coup was basically the same as Kravchuk's: both were eager to make a deal with the military, exchanging peace on the streets for its noninterference in government affairs. That was the strategy also adopted by Yeltsin's close ally Anatolii Sobchak, the democratically elected mayor of Leningrad. With the help of his deputy, Vladimir Putin, Sobchak made a deal with the military and the KGB, exchanging relative peace on the streets for neutrality of the security forces that reported to Kriuchkov and Yazov. This was a strategy meant to preserve the political gains of perestroika. But Chornovil's reaction, dictated largely by his role as head of the regional administration in the largest center of western Ukraine, was not shared by many opposition leaders in Kyiv, some of whom called for active resistance.[13]

The highest-placed reformist leader in the Ukrainian parliament, Deputy Speaker Volodymyr Hryniov, went on radio that morning to condemn the coup in the strongest possible terms. He later remembered his attitude at the time: "I understood perfectly that if the *nomenklatura* officials came to an understanding with one another, there would be no one to come to an understanding with me about anything." An ethnic Russian elected from the city of Kharkiv in eastern Ukraine, Hryniov represented an all-Union trend in the Ukrainian opposition. He and his supporters closely associated themselves with Boris Yeltsin and the Russian liberal democrats without sharing their Russia-first attitude. Hryniov and the constituency he represented—the urban intelligentsia of Ukraine's Russified east and south—stood for a democratic Ukraine in a Russia-led confederation. Hryniov's allies were among the first to raise the flag of resistance to the coup in such cities as Zaporizhia.[14]

Chornovil and other national democrats were caught between Kravchuk's vacillations and the radical position taken by Hryniov and Yeltsin's other allies in Ukraine. It took a while for Rukh, the nationaldemocratic umbrella organization consisting of a number of democratic parties and associations, to come up with a statement. It appeared only on the second day of the coup, but it was strong and unequivocal in its condemnation and called on the citizens of Ukraine to prepare for a labor strike that would paralyze the country's economy. For the Ukrainian national democrats, the moment of indecision had passed. That day the Lviv regional council declared the coup unconstitutional. So did the Kharkiv city council in eastern Ukraine, and the miners of the Donets Basin were getting ready for a strike. Rukh announced a general political strike to begin at noon on August 21. In cities all over Ukraine, democratic activists distributed Yeltsin's appeal for resistance. People were glued to their radios, listening to the Voice of America, BBC, and other Western stations. The news coming from the Moscow White House was more and more worrisome. No one knew whether Russian democracy would survive the night.[15]

ON AUGUST 21, THE THIRD and decisive day of the coup, Leonid Kravchuk was awakened before 4:00 a.m. by a call from one of the opposition deputies demanding an emergency meeting of the presidium, the ruling body of parliament. News had reached him that army units had begun an attack on the Russian White House. Kravchuk was noncommittal, as always: there was nothing they could do about the situation in Moscow in the middle of the night, so the meeting would have to wait until the start of the working day. By the time Kravchuk reached his office that morning, the situation had changed dramatically. The news from Moscow left little doubt that the coup was unraveling and that Yeltsin, hitherto a virtual prisoner in the White House, was emerging victorious.

Kravchuk immediately did what the opposition deputies had been demanding for days: he jumped on Yeltsin's bandwagon. He later claimed that he had kept in touch with the besieged Russian leader and his entourage throughout the coup. The Ukrainian Speaker was the first republican leader whom Yeltsin had called on the morning of August 19. Although he failed to convince Kravchuk to join forces in resisting the coup, he received assurances that Kravchuk would not recognize the Emergency Committee. Kravchuk never formally violated his promise to the Russian leader. On the last day of the coup, Yeltsin told George Bush that he believed he could trust Kravchuk.

It seemed that Kravchuk was again on the right side of history. But that was not the impression shared by the leaders of Ukrainian opposition forces. The people pouring into the main square of Kyiv at the news of the defeat of the coup were chanting, "Yeltsin, Yeltsin! Down with Kravchuk!" The day that began for the Ukrainian Speaker with worries about a possible crackdown by the putschists ended with worries about his political future in an environment fully dominated by the national democrats.[16]

On August 22, the day of Gorbachev's return to Moscow, Kravchuk finally agreed to summon parliament to an emergency session. He presented his agenda for the session at the press conference he called that day to explain his vacillation during the coup. Kravchuk wanted parliament to condemn the coup, establish parliamentary control over the military, KGB, and police on Ukrainian territory, create a national guard, and withdraw from negotiations on a new union treaty. "It isn't necessary for us to rush into signing the union treaty," said Kravchuk to the press. "I believe that at this moment the Soviet Union needs to form a government for this transitional period, maybe a committee or council, perhaps with nine people or so, which could protect the actions of democratic institutions. All political forms must be re-evaluated. However, I do believe that we should urgently sign an economic agreement." Kravchuk was not speaking of independence. His agenda was the complete destruction of the Union center as it had existed before the coup and its replacement by a committee of republican leaders. It was a program of confederation.[17]

The next day Kravchuk left for Moscow to meet Gorbachev, Yeltsin, and the other republican leaders. The visit followed the scenario he had described to the press on the previous day. In Gorbachev's presence, the committee of republican leaders agreed on the appointment of new ministers of defense and interior, as well as the head of the KGB. They also discussed the composition of the new executive committee that was to replace the old Soviet government. There was one catch: all the new appointments were made by the Russian president. Yeltsin had not blocked Gorbachev's appointments of national security ministers in order to allow anyone else to reap the fruits of his victory.

The first impression was that the republican leaders did not mind Yeltsin's rapid accession to virtually dictatorial powers in the Union to which they all still belonged. Experienced politicians raised in a tradition of party subordination and Byzantine intrigue, they voiced no disagreement with the now dominant Russian president, who was their traditional ally against the weakening center. They were also unanimous in condemning the coup that many of them had supported only a few days earlier. Nor did they voice any objection to Yeltsin's assault on the party to which they belonged. That day the leaders of Kazakhstan, Nursultan Nazarbayev, and Tajikistan, Kakhahr Makhamov, resigned from the Politburo and the Central Committee of the party.[18]

But the republican leaders were not entirely on Yeltsin's side. While they were forced to surrender to Yeltsin on every issue and every government appointment he made, they also promised Gorbachev that they would cooperate in progressing toward a new union treaty. The official communiqué, published the next day in the central press, placed special emphasis on their interest in signing such a treaty. That day Gorbachev told the American ambassador, Bob Strauss, "As far as our federation is concerned, we have confirmed that we will proceed toward a Union treaty. Moreover, we have decided this time that we shall sign it together, all the republics, and not one by one." Signing the new union treaty as a group, continued Gorbachev, meant that "some will have to wait a bit as compared with previously established deadlines. But Ukraine, for example, will have to make haste with its decision."[19]

In fact, Leonid Kravchuk was not prepared to make haste. When Gorbachev, referring to George Bush's "Chicken Kiev" speech, told the Ukrainian leader that even the American president could see that Ukraine's drive for independence had no "historical prospects," Kravchuk seemed noncommittal. He also refused to take the bait when Gorbachev tried to flatter Ukraine with the new prominence of its leaders in Union structures and play them against Yeltsin. When Gorbachev asked Kravchuk whether the Ukrainian prime minister, Vitold Fokin, would make a good head of the interim Union government—the position that Yeltsin wanted for Russia's prime minister, Ivan Silaev—Kravchuk responded evasively: Fokin was an excellent choice but probably would not want to leave Ukraine. Indeed, Fokin had said no to Gorbachev.[20]

What Kravchuk witnessed that day in Moscow must have made him more sympathetic to the idea of Ukrainian independence

than ever before. He went to Moscow determined to replace the
all-Union government with a republic-dominated committee, but
Yeltsin's success in removing Gorbachev's nominees from the new
government and his sudden decision to suspend the activities of the
Russian Communist Party changed the political landscape in Moscow
no less than did his victory over the coup leaders two days earlier.
Instead of Gorbachev's weak Union center, a strong center controlled
by Yeltsin was emerging. Neither Kravchuk nor his colleagues in the
Ukrainian government and party wanted any part of a Yeltsin-run
Union. They did not think that a power-sharing agreement like that of
Nikita Khrushchev's and Leonid Brezhnev's times could be restored;
besides, during the last years of Gorbachev's rule they had become
accustomed to a degree of freedom previously undreamed of. As they
saw it, the center was bringing them nothing but uncertainty and
trouble, now more than ever before. Kravchuk was now faced with an
unexpected challenge that once again put his survival skills to the test.

During the coup the Ukrainian Speaker had first gained the
reputation of a man who needed no umbrella: he could make his
way between raindrops without ever getting wet. Twenty years
later, asked about the validity of the joke, Kravchuk responded with
uncharacteristic candor: "In principle, that's quite right: I am flexible
and diplomatic; I rarely tell people the truth to their face; I very rarely
open up. Experience teaches that there are situations in politics in
which any frankness or openness can be used against you." In this
response he was more candid than one can expect of most politicians.
On August 23, 1991, Leonid Kravchuk, the man who had walked
between raindrops, was coming home from Moscow to face a flood.
This time he might need not an umbrella but a life vest. It was anyone's
guess whether he would find one.[21]

AS THOSE GATHERED AROUND THE Ukrainian parliament on
the morning of August 24 chanted, "Shame on Kravchuk!" the visibly shaken Speaker of parliament told the deputies—his words were
transmitted live to those at the walls of parliament—that he had never
recognized the legitimacy of the coup. He went on to propose a number of laws intended to strengthen Ukrainian sovereignty and advocated by the opposition. "It is imperative to adopt laws on the status
of the armed forces now deployed on the territory of the republic,"

he told the deputies. "The interior forces, the Committee for State Security [[KGB]], and the Ministry of Internal Affairs must be subordinate to the head of the Ukrainian state. Moreover, they must not be involved in any all-Union structures. There can only be a question of coordinating activity. Appropriate laws on these matters must be adopted. The question of separating the party from the law-enforcement agencies of the republic must also be resolved."[22]

The national democrats wanted more. Their parliamentary leader, the academician Ihor Yukhnovsky, demanded independence. Then the writer Volodymyr Yavorivsky read a brief text titled "Act of Declaration of Independence" and asked that it be put to a vote. Parliament was thrown into confusion. The chief communist of Ukraine, Stanislav Hurenko, asked for a break. Kravchuk went along, declaring a recess so that parliamentary factions could formulate their positions on the issue. Those most in difficulty were the communists.[23]

The principal author of the draft declaration of independence was Levko Lukianenko, the head of the Ukrainian Republican Party, by far the best-organized political force of the period. Lukianenko had spent more than a quarter century in the Gulag for his dedication to Ukrainian independence. He was an embodiment of Ukraine's sacrifice in the struggle for freedom, and the democratic deputies wanted him to be the first to read the declaration. It was only because of the commotion in the democratic ranks that the honor fell to Yavorivsky. A few weeks before the coup, during President Bush's luncheon with Ukrainian political leaders, Lukianenko had approached him and given him a note with three questions. Two of them dealt with the Ukrainian opposition, and the third, concerning Ukrainian independence, read (in shaky English) as follows: "Now that inevitable disintegration of the Russian empire is a fact, whether the government of the USA the most powerful state in the world can help Ukraine to become a full-right subject of international relations?"

On the flight back to the United States, Bush had dictated a memo to his Soviet expert, Ed Hewett, concerning Lukianenko's questions. "At the lunch in Kiev today," read the memo, "Levko Grigorovich Lukyanenko very politely addressed first me, and then Chairman Kravchuk. He is a deputy in the Ukrainian Supreme Soviet. He spent twenty years in jail as a dissident, and now he represents the independence movement, Narodna Rada [[People's Council]]." Bush asked Hewett to prepare a response. On the question of international recognition of Ukraine, Hewett's draft of August 5 gave the standard American position on the issue: a change in the structure of the USSR could "occur only through peaceful and good faith dialogue between the republics and all-union leaders."[24]

Lukianenko no longer believed in dialogue. He did believe, however, that the defeat of the coup presented a huge opportunity to make a breakthrough to his goal. At a general meeting of democratic deputies on the morning of August 23, Lukianenko surprised his colleagues by proposing that the question of Ukrainian independence be placed on the agenda of the emergency session of parliament. "The moment is so unique that we should solve the fundamental problem and proclaim Ukraine an independent state," he later recalled saying in his appeal to the deputies. "If we do not do this now, we may never do it. For this period in which the communists are at a loss is a brief period: they will soon get back on their feet, and they have a majority."

Knowing how ephemeral their real power was, the democratic deputies accepted Lukianenko's argument and entrusted him with the task of drafting the declaration. "There are two approaches to the document that we can write," said Lukianenko to a fellow deputy whom he had handpicked as a coauthor. "We can write it either as a long or a short document. If we write it as a long document, then it will inevitably prompt discussion; if we write a short one, then it has a chance of prompting less discussion. Let's write the shortest possible document so that we give them as little as possible to discuss about where to put a comma or what has to be changed." And they did just that. It was not "quite the 4th of July," joked the acting US consul in Kyiv, John Stepanchuk, later about the brevity of the declaration of Ukrainian independence. Nevertheless, when Lukianenko presented the freshly drafted text to his colleagues in the democratic caucus, they agreed with his reasoning. With few editorial changes, the text was approved for distribution among the deputies at the opening of the emergency session.[25]

While supporting Lukianenko's initiative to put the question of independence to a parliamentary vote, the democratic caucus was split concerning its proper place on the agenda. Some deputies, including the highest-ranking democrat in parliament, Deputy Speaker Volodymyr Hryniov, wanted voting for independence to take place only after a vote on suspension of the activities of the Communist Party. Hryniov was concerned that unless the ban was approved first, Ukrainian independence would result in the creation of a communist-dominated state. His view was shared by some democratic deputies from Kyiv. But what were the chances of a communist-dominated parliament banning the party and then voting for independence? None, thought Lukianenko and others who supported him. They stood for independence first and decommunization second, even if it would take a while to bring about the latter. One deputy even said that he was prepared to spend ten years in prison as long as it was a Ukrainian prison. Not many of his colleagues had such resolve, but those who shared Lukianenko's opinion gained the upper hand in the caucus.[26]

Whereas the democrats came to the parliamentary session with a more or less consolidated position on independence, the communists were taken by surprise. The break in the session that Hurenko requested and Kravchuk granted allowed them to discuss the issue for the first time as a group. Traditionally staunch opponents of independence, they now found themselves in difficulty. Long gone were the times when the communist majority in parliament constituted a unified force. Kravchuk and the communist faction that supported him had long been pushing for sovereignty and were now prepared to embrace complete independence. As the nervous and disoriented communist deputies met in the cinema hall of the parliament building, their leader, Stanislav Hurenko, called on them to support independence or find themselves and the party in trouble.

The conservative members of the communist caucus knew that they had been all but abandoned by their leadership in Moscow, with Gorbachev resigning as general secretary earlier that day and the party leadership at a loss. As far as they were concerned, Yeltsin had declared open season on communists, and it was only a matter of time before the "witch hunt," as Gorbachev called it, reached Ukraine. In fact, it was already there—the crowd of a hundred thousand around the parliament building was demanding independence and was ready to put them on trial. Would it be satisfied with independence alone? Many hoped that conceding independence might shield them from the anticommunist tsunami rolling in from Russia and leave them in charge of Ukraine.

Those still wavering abandoned their doubts when representatives of the opposition showed up at their meeting and suggested a compromise: the vote on independence would be confirmed by a popular referendum to be conducted on December 1, simultaneously with the presidential elections. That sounded to many like an ideal solution: a vote in favor of independence would give them immediate protection, while a referendum lay in the future and might not actually take place. The communists would therefore support Lukianenko's declaration.[27]

During the break Kravchuk called Moscow, seemingly following the long tradition of Ukrainian communist leaders seeking the elder brother's approval for even minor decisions. This time, however, the shoe was on the other foot. Kravchuk informed both Yeltsin and Gorbachev about the developments in the Ukrainian parliament and told them that the vote in favor of independence was inevitable. Yeltsin accepted the news calmly, but Gorbachev was clearly upset. He eventually told Kravchuk that it did not much matter what the Ukrainian parliament voted for, as the March 1991 referendum in Ukraine had shown overwhelming support for the Union. Parliament could not overrule the referendum results. Kravchuk agreed. After the phone call, he threw his weight behind the idea of ratifying a parliamentary vote on independence by a referendum. One referendum would thus be annulled by another. It seemed that the canny Kravchuk might again manage to satisfy all parties involved.[28]

With the one-hour break concluded, Kravchuk was prepared to put the declaration of Ukrainian independence to a vote. That day he became a strong promoter of the act, seeing in it a way out of the current political crisis. His patriotic inclinations should also be taken into account. "What did I feel as we worked on that historic document?" Kravchuk recalled later. "I simply felt happy." He worked hard to convince those reluctant to vote yes. Knowing that the two main caucuses were split on the issue, he met with representatives of regional groups; as he later remembered, he told those from the west not to be disoriented by demands to disband the party first and vote for independence second. No one knows what he was telling the communists, but his message was clear: he wanted them to vote for independence.

There was only one obstacle left on the road to Lukianenko's long-dreamed-of Ukrainian independence—the lack of a quorum in the parliamentary chamber. Kravchuk waited for the deputies to return, which proved to be a slow process. For proponents of independence, every minute seemed like a week. Rumor had it that Kravchuk had ordered the closing of the secret tunnel that linked the parliament to the nearby building of the Ukrainian Central Committee, thereby making it impossible for communist deputies to leave parliament without facing angry crowds. Finally, the number of registered deputies exceeded three hundred. Who would read the text of the declaration? Kravchuk suggested Lukianenko, but his liaison with the People's Council, the poet Dmytro Pavlychko, all but ordered Kravchuk to read the text. Pavlychko wanted the resolution to be proposed by the Speaker himself; otherwise the communists might change their mind. Kravchuk, under attack for having vacillated during the coup, was now on the spot and had to agree.[29]

He read out the text: "In view of the mortal danger hanging over Ukraine in connection with the coup d'état of 19 August 1991 in the USSR, and continuing the thousand-year tradition of state-building in Ukraine, . . . the Supreme Soviet of the Ukrainian Soviet Socialist Republic solemnly declares the independence of Ukraine and the creation of an independent Ukrainian state—Ukraine. . . . This act takes effect from the moment of its approval."[30]

Kravchuk asked the deputies to vote. A moment later, the numbers of those who had voted for and against the declaration appeared on the huge screen behind him. The chamber suddenly exploded with chants. As the deputies rose and began hugging one another, it became hard to tell democrats and communists apart. A state of elation engulfed the chamber. The Ukrainian parliament had voted for independence, with 346 deputies in favor, 2 opposed, and 5 abstaining. It was five minutes before 6:00 p.m. The crowd outside roared its approval. Foreign diplomats rushed to their consulates to file reports. "The Fat Lady Has Sung," read the title of the report on Ukrainian independence by the Canadian consul, Nestor Gayowsky.[31]

At 9:00 p.m. the democrats' symbol of victory, the blue-and-yellow Ukrainian national flag, was carried into the chamber—this after crowds had chanted for hours, "Put the banner on the parliament building!" Petro Stepkin, the conductor of a Cossack choir from

Zaporizhia, where the song festival had been held a few days earlier, had lost his voice from incessant chanting outside the building. Although he and other proponents did not manage to raise the blue-and-yellow flag to the summit, they got it into the chamber. It was a compromise typical of Kravchuk. Against the wishes of communist deputies who still considered the flag an emblem of nationalism, not patriotism, Kravchuk allowed the banner to be brought in, allegedly in recognition of the democratic victory in Moscow: Viacheslav Chornovil claimed that that particular banner had been atop one of the tanks defending the Russian parliament. The communists could not say no to a victory flag from Moscow, even after Moscow had abandoned them.[32]

9

SAVING THE EMPIRE

O N THE AFTERNOON OF AUGUST 28, one week after Russian vice president Aleksandr Rutskoi flew to the Crimea to save the president of the Soviet Union, he headed south yet again, this time to save the Soviet Union itself. Promoted by Gorbachev from colonel to major general after the success of his first mission, Rutskoi was on his way to Kyiv to deal with a crisis that had erupted in Russo-Ukrainian relations after Ukraine's declaration of independence. The plan was to keep Ukraine within the Union by raising the prospect of partitioning its territory if Ukraine insisted on independence.

Reporting on this new mission of Rutskoi and his colleagues, a correspondent for the pro-Yeltsin *Nezavisimaia gazeta* wrote, "Today they have the opportunity to inform the Ukrainian leadership of Yeltsin's position that, given Ukraine's exit from membership in 'a certain USSR,' the article of the bilateral agreement on borders becomes invalid." Translated into plain language, this meant that Russia was denouncing its existing treaty with Ukraine, its neighbor, and threatening Ukraine with partition of its territory. "It is expected," continued the newspaper account, "that independence will be declared today at a session of the Supreme Soviet of the Crimea." The independence of the Crimea, an autonomous republic within Ukraine, could set off a process of partition that might lead to a violent confrontation between the two largest Soviet republics.[1]

The plane carrying Rutskoi to Kyiv took off from Vnukovo airport, on the outskirts of Moscow. The vice president was accompanied by Yeltsin's close adviser Sergei Stankevich, who had helped remove the Felix Dzerzhinsky monument from downtown Moscow a few days earlier. But the "Russians" were not the only members of the delegation sent from Moscow to reason with the rebellious Ukrainian deputies. They were joined by "Soviets"—members of the USSR Supreme Soviet or parliament, which had begun its deliberations in Moscow a few days earlier. A few hours before the plane carrying Rutskoi and Stankevich took off, a session of the Supreme Soviet devoted to an investigation of the plotters' activities had been abruptly called upon to deal with an emergency. The deputies temporarily put aside their differences to select representatives for the Russo-Ukrainian negotiations and send them to Kyiv. "This was something of a sign of trouble, one of the last warnings to the Union parliament, which was, objectively speaking, one of the few remaining pillars of the disintegrating Union," wrote *Izvestiia* the next day.

The Soviet parliamentary delegation included Yeltsin's close ally Anatolii Sobchak, the mayor of Leningrad and a strong believer in the Union. According to the same *Izvestiia* article, that day Sobchak had called on the deputies "to concentrate on the main thing: not to allow the spontaneous disintegration of structures of Soviet power and to put an end to unproductive discussions of questions not pertaining to the danger of the country's collapse." Sobchak was accompanied by a member of the Soviet parliament representing Russia and two elected from Ukraine. They rushed from the Kremlin to the airport, hoping to catch the departing plane of the Russian vice president. No one could have imagined such a situation only a few days earlier. Russia and Ukraine, whose leaders had forged a strong alliance before the coup and managed to preserve it during the darkest days of August, were now quarreling over their borders. And conversely, Russian and all-Union politicians previously divided by seemingly unbridgeable differences were now working together to save the Union. Moreover, the leading role in that attempt belonged to Yeltsin, not to Gorbachev. In fact, Gorbachev was not in the picture at all.[2]

THE SHIFT IN YELTSIN'S POSITION from undermining Gorbachev and the Union center to collaborating with the former and supporting the latter was a direct outcome of his victory in the campaign he had waged against Gorbachev ever since the Soviet president's return from the Crimea. On August 22, when Gorbachev tried to tell the Russian deputies that Russia would not be Russia if it did not try to hold the republics together, he was booed and verbally insulted. By August 28, when the joint Russian-Soviet delegation departed for Kyiv, Yeltsin's victory seemed all but complete: he had replaced Gorbachev as the most powerful figure not only in Russia but also in the Union itself. Keeping it together suddenly became one of his main concerns. Trying to get more concessions from the center while Gorbachev was calling the shots in the Kremlin was one thing; conceding the independence of Union republics in the wake of the implosion of the center was quite another. Neither Yeltsin nor his advisers were ready for that, either psychologically or politically. They were prepared to let the Baltics go and hoped that the Central Asian republics would stop demanding subsidies from the center, but no one in Yeltsin's entourage had ever imagined releasing Slavic Ukraine—a nightmare scenario.[3]

The declaration of Ukrainian independence produced a shock wave throughout the Soviet Union, dramatically altering the political landscape. Ukraine, which had declared its sovereignty in the summer of 1990 only in the wake of Yeltsin's Russia, now took the lead in the drive for independence among those republics whose leaders still remained loyal to the Union. The Baltic republics, Armenia, and Georgia, which declared independence before Ukraine, were all controlled by forces opposed to the old communist regime. Kravchuk's Ukraine became the first country with a communist-dominated legislature to make such a declaration, clearing the way for other republics run by the communist or former communist *nomenklatura*. On August 25, the day after Ukraine's parliament voted for independence, a similar declaration was made by Belarus; on August 26 came one by Ukraine's other neighbor, Moldova. Faraway Azerbaijan would proclaim its independence on August 30. It would be followed the next day by Kyrgyzstan and a day later by Uzbekistan. Not only Gorbachev but also Yeltsin looked on in horror and astonishment as one republic after another declared its independence.[4]

None of the republics that declared independence after August 24 adopted a Ukrainian-style provision for a referendum to ratify the declaration, but then, none of them had any immediate intention of leaving the Union. What, then, were the practical consequences of the declarations? For the time being, the major difference between sovereignty and independence was that if sovereignty gave republican laws priority over all-Union ones, independence made it possible to disregard all-Union laws entirely. Only republican laws were now valid. The formal independence of the republics also meant the emergence of more powerful republican leaders.[5]

August 24 marked a turning point, not only because of the declaration of Ukrainian independence but also because, on the same day, the three Baltic republics, Estonia, Latvia, and Lithuania, received recognition of their independence from Yeltsin himself. The Russian president signed three letters that same day recognizing the independence of Russia's western neighbors without attaching any conditions or questioning the newly independent states' Soviet-era borders. His action left hundreds of thousands of ethnic Russians, most of whom had moved to the region after World War II, beyond the borders of Russia and the Union. Their concerns did not seem to be those of Yeltsin's government.

The new, democratic Russia refused to use force, economic pressure, or legal and diplomatic tricks to keep the Baltic republics in the Soviet Union. Territorial issues and minority rights did not seem to be significant issues at the time. In previous years, many members of Russian communities had opposed independence for the republics they called home. They joined the Moscow-sponsored and communist-run Interfronts, which welcomed Moscow's crackdown on Baltic independence in early 1991. Their leaders, who had openly supported the coup in Moscow, now feared revenge on the part of local majorities. Yeltsin's Russian government largely ignored their worries. Its allies were national democrats in Tallinn, Riga, and Vilnius, not Russian minorities who had sided with the Kremlin conservatives.[6]

Many in the non-Russian republics of the Union wondered whether the Baltic example set a precedent for Russia's dealings with other republics. It soon became apparent that it did not. The Baltics held a special place in the hearts and minds of Yeltsin's democrats, and Russian diplomatic recognition did not extend to all the Soviet republics that had declared their independence before or during the coup. Georgia, which had declared independence on April 9, 1991, much earlier than Estonia or Latvia, was not granted recognition. It was not clear whether Ukraine's declaration of independence would place it in the same camp as the Baltics or Georgia. Given that Yeltsin's reaction to Kravchuk's phone call on the eve of the independence vote in parliament was much calmer than Gorbachev's, there was some hope that Ukraine's position would be treated with respect and understanding in Russia. As it turned out, there was only a weekend pause. Kravchuk called Yeltsin with the news on Saturday, which meant that Russian reaction would not come until Monday, August 26, when the session of the Soviet parliament promised by the plotters on the first day of the coup finally convened in Moscow.

At the opening session a deputy from Ukraine, Yurii Shcherbak, read a Russian translation of the declaration of Ukrainian independence. Later he considered that moment the greatest in his life, but at the time he was almost frightened of his own words. Absolute silence suddenly fell on the normally busy chamber. It seemed to him that people's faces went pale. Gorbachev, red faced, rose and left the hall. Gorbachev's loyal adviser Vadim Medvedev recorded in his diary that on that day representatives from the republics spoke "with one voice of independence, the needlessness of the center, and the liquidation of Union structures."

Proponents of the Union sounded the alarm. A neighbor of Shcherbak's in the chamber, Anatolii Sobchak, went to the podium to state that "under the cover of this talk about national independence they are trying to retain these communist structures, but with a new face." He declared that what he was witnessing was insane, as the USSR was a nuclear power and its partition might lead to nuclear anarchy. Sergei Stankevich, another member of the delegation and deputy mayor of Moscow, expressed the hope that his Ukrainian friends would not do damage, presumably to the cause of democracy. A Russian moral authority, academician Dmitrii Likhachev, declared that the uncontrolled collapse of the Union could lead to border wars.[7]

Many in Yeltsin's camp treated Ukrainian independence not as an act aimed at the weakened center but as a stab in the back of democratic Russia, which had emerged victorious in the battle with the communist Goliath. Besides, the sudden shift of political power in Moscow created a situation unimaginable only a few days earlier. So far the Russian Federation had been in the forefront of rebellion against the center, working hand in hand with the Baltics and adopting laws on its sovereignty ahead of Ukraine, Belarus, and most other Soviet republics. Russia had now all but taken over the center and was faced with the unexpected task of what to do with the Union.

As Sobchak, Stankevich, and Likhachev joined forces in an attempt to save the Union in the Soviet parliament, Boris Yeltsin ordered his press secretary, the forty-two-year-old economist-turned-journalist Pavel Voshchanov, to prepare a statement to the effect that "if any republic breaks off Union relations with Russia, then Russia has the right to raise the question of territorial claims." This was a complete reversal of the policy adopted only two days earlier vis-à-vis Baltic independence. Voshchanov remembered later that when it came to relations with the non-Russian republics, Yeltsin was eager "to put Gorbachev to shame," as the latter had failed to keep those republics in line. To his chagrin, the Russian president soon found himself in the same situation as Gorbachev. "The Russian president was wounded," remembered Voshchanov. "And at that point the idea was born to give the negotiating partners a 'hint' that 'Yeltsin, as you will see, is no Gorbachev.'" The declaration of Ukrainian independence and the process that it unleashed made the task especially urgent.[8]

Pavel Voshchanov did as he was told. After the draft of the presidential statement was ready, he read it to Yeltsin over the phone. The statement released to the press read as follows: "The Russian Federation casts no doubt on the constitutional right of every state and people to self-determination. There exists, however, the problem of borders, the nonsettlement of which is possible and admissible only on condition of allied relations secured by an appropriate treaty. In the event of their termination, the RSFSR reserves the right to raise the question of the revision of boundaries." The statement did not name the republics with which Russia might have territorial disputes, but when Voshchanov was asked during the press conference which countries Yeltsin had in mind, he responded by naming Ukraine and Kazakhstan. He recalled later that the contested areas included territories that had earlier belonged to Russia: the Crimea and the Donetsk region of Ukraine, Abkhazia in Georgia, and northern territories of Kazakhstan.[9]

In fact, the Crimea was the only region transferred from Russia in the 1950s. The transfer took place in 1954, when, in commemoration of the tercentenary of the extension of Moscow's protectorate over Cossack Ukraine, the Crimea was reassigned by Moscow to Ukraine. By that time two hundred thousand of the peninsula's indigenous Crimean Tatars had been exiled to Central Asia. Most of the remaining inhabitants were ethnic Russians, but the peninsula was geographically and economically tied to Ukraine. The transfer made sense from the viewpoint of the central planners in Moscow, and the authorities in Russia and Ukraine went along. The Crimea was, however, the exception on Voshchanov's list of contested territories: the others had never belonged to the Russian Federation. That applied to the Donets Basin (Donbas) of eastern Ukraine, which had been part of the independent from Russia Ukrainian state and then of the Union republic, and to Abkhazia, which in Soviet times had been either formally independent or an autonomous part of Georgia. No territory was formally transferred from the Russian Federation to Kazakhstan, which became an autonomous republic in the 1920s and, in the next decade, a Union republic of the USSR.[10]

The crisis in Russo-Ukrainian relations produced an opening for the embattled Gorbachev. Speaking at a session of the Soviet parliament that day, he told the deputies that he would do everything in his power to keep the Union together. "There can be no territorial problems within the Union," declared Gorbachev. "But their emergence cannot be ruled out when republics leave the Union." Voshchanov's statement was welcomed also by leaders of the Russian democratic camp. Many believed that Ukrainian and Belarusian independence amounted to little more than an effort by local party elites to cling to power, and in the struggle against those elites, democracy had to show its teeth. Gavriil Popov, the democratic mayor of Moscow and Yeltsin's close ally, appeared on central television to claim that he supported Yeltsin's position on secessionist republics and that border questions would have to be decided by referendum in the border regions. He referred specifically to the Crimea, Odesa, and Moldovan Transnistria. The irony of the situation was that the elites in the regions mentioned by Popov had welcomed the coup, and most of their inhabitants showed no sympathy for the democratic Russian leaders in Moscow.[11]

But not everyone in Moscow applauded Yeltsin and Voshchanov. On the day after the publication of Voshchanov's statement, seven prominent democratic figures led by Yurii Afanasiev and Elena Bonner, whose anticoup credentials were beyond reproach, signed an appeal titled "We Welcome the Fall of the Empire." They acknowledged that the leadership of some republics leaving the Union was dominated by communists who had supported the coup and were prone to oppress their own people, but this was to be resisted by coordinated action with other democratic powers, not by restoring the empire. "Most dangerous of all," wrote Afanasiev, Bonner, and their colleagues, "are statements about possible territorial or property claims by Russia on neighboring republics in the event of the dissolution of the USSR." The authors of the appeal stated that the way toward the creation of a new community of democratic republics on the ruins of the former empire was through peaceful dissolution of the USSR. The appeal presented a clear challenge to the position taken by the Russian leadership. It also offered a bold vision that would be crucial to Russia's search for a new policy toward the Union center and the former Union republics in the months to come. Few appreciated its importance at the time.[12]

The new line of the Russian government, expressed in the Voshchanov statement, was met with deep concern also by the leaders and legislators of Ukraine, Moldova, and Kazakhstan. Ukraine was most threatened and therefore made its position known more quickly than any other republic directly or potentially affected by the new Russian attitude. On August 27, the day on which the Voshchanov statement was issued, the Rukh association of Ukrainian democratic parties fired off a statement of its own. It accused the "newly democratized leaders of Russia" of "imperial aspirations" akin to those manifested by the Bolsheviks in 1917. At that time, under the banner of proletarian revolution, the Bolsheviks had crushed the young Ukrainian independence movement and destroyed its democratic institutions. This historical parallel was echoed by a document issued the same day by the presidium of the Ukrainian parliament. It declared that Ukraine had no territorial claims on Russia but was prepared to discuss possible Russian claims on the basis of the Russo-Ukrainian treaty signed by Yeltsin in November 1990. That treaty guaranteed the existing border between Russia and Ukraine. Leonid Kravchuk called a press conference to release the presidium's statement, informing journalists that he had called Yeltsin to discuss the Voshchanov statement. The next day, the Russian president ordered Rutskoi and Stankevich to go to Kyiv to deal with the situation.[13]

THE MEMBERS OF THE JOINT Russian/all-Union delegation that flew to Kyiv on the afternoon of August 28 to explain the position of the Russian president and his democratic supporters to the leadership of the newly independent country had their task cut out for them. Their main goal was to derail or postpone Ukrainian independence, not to claim contested territories. "Do you think we need those territories?" a member of Yeltsin's inner circle had asked a surprised Voshchanov. "We need Nazarbayev and Kravchuk to know their place!" Their proper place was, of course, in the Union, together with Russia and under its control.

A member of the Soviet parliament, Yurii Shcherbak, who flew to Kyiv together with Rutskoi and his colleagues as one of the delegates representing the Union bodies, later remembered something that Anatolii Sobchak had said to him: "Don't you Ukrainians think of separating from Russia: we are one, after all." According to Shcherbak, not only Sobchak but also Stankevich regarded the proclamation of Ukrainian independence with utmost suspicion. Rutskoi, who spoke good Ukrainian, was especially condescending. "So, you topknots [[*khokhly*]], you've decided to separate, have you?" he asked the representatives of Ukraine, using a derogatory term for the Ukrainian nationality.[14]

Before boarding the plane, Shcherbak called Kyiv to warn his colleagues there about the arrival of the Moscow delegation. Immediately, Ukrainian radio broadcast two appeals from the Ukrainian parliament. The first called on all political forces in Ukraine to unite in defense of independence. The second appeal assured the sizable national minorities that Ukrainian independence was no threat to their rights. That day the presidium also issued a decree placing military recruitment centers all over Ukraine under the republic's jurisdiction. The Ukrainian leadership was consolidating its political position and preparing citizens for an impending diplomatic confrontation with Russia.

As the Russian plane made its way to Kyiv, Ukrainian radio broadcast a third appeal. A Rukh leader went on the air to summon Kyivans to the parliament building in order to defend Ukrainian independence. More people responded to the call than had come to the Ukrainian parliament during its vote for independence, and soon the building was surrounded by Kyivans eager to defend what still remained a dream. Shcherbak was himself shocked to see how many people showed up, resolved to defend their newly declared independence.[15]

It is not clear what kind of reception Aleksandr Rutskoi and his colleagues expected in Kyiv, but it was not the one they received. A member of the delegation, Sergei Stankevich, later remembered, "In Kyiv they did not let us out of the plane for half the day, interrogating us about the purpose for which we had come to the independent state." Rutskoi appealed to Slavic solidarity and declared that the purpose of the visit was to work out a program for the development of Russo-Ukrainian relations in light of the declaration of Ukrainian independence.

Only after these assurances had been given was the delegation taken to parliament. Instead of being met by members of the presidium, dominated by former communists, the delegates were welcomed by the leaders of the democratic bloc. Sobchak and Stankevich found themselves across the table from their old friends and allies in the Ukrainian democratic camp. The latter sought to convince their Russian counterparts that an independent Ukraine was anything but a safe haven for the Communist Party. Stankevich assured the members of the "reception committee" that the Moscow delegation was not going to raise territorial questions, and it did not question Ukraine's right to independence. That reassurance broke the ice.[16]

After the meeting with the democratic deputies, the Russian representatives and Soviet parliamentarians sat down with the official Ukrainian delegation, led by Leonid Kravchuk. Their meeting would last long into the night. From time to time the participants would come out to tell the crowd of people around the parliament building how the negotiations were going and try to calm them down. Sobchak's attempts to appeal to the people over the heads of their unyielding leaders produced disastrous results. When he told the crowds, "It is important for us to be together," they responded by chanting, "No!" "Shame!" "Ukraine without Moscow!"

After midnight, when Kravchuk and Rutskoi finally called a press conference to report on their deliberations, the results favored the Ukrainian leadership. The two countries agreed to create joint structures to manage the transition and work on economic agreements. The Ukrainians were happy with the outcome; the Russians were not.

"The talks were difficult," recalled Stankevich. "We did not come up with a formula of association," meaning that they had found no common ground for continuing existence in the same state. That was bad news indeed for the future of the Union. Its two largest members could not agree on a formula for coexistence that would satisfy both parties. Time would show that even Ukrainian accession to the agreement was provisional—the Kyiv politicians were already seeking a formula for what later became known as a "civilized divorce."[17]

The outcome of the late-night deliberations in Kyiv that disappointed Stankevich encouraged Nursultan Nazarbayev, who was upset about the Russian takeover of the Union government and wanted to take control of Soviet armed forces in his republic. That day the Kazakh leader fired off a telegram to Yeltsin requesting that Rutskoi's delegation visit Kazakhstan. It read, "Given that so far the press has carried no clearly expressed renunciation on Russia's part of territorial claims on contiguous republics, social protest is growing in Kazakhstan, with unforeseeable consequences. This may force the republic to adopt measures analogous to those of Ukraine." The threat to follow the Ukrainian example and declare outright independence, voiced by the leader of another nuclear republic, worked. Rutskoi, Stankevich, and Sobchak had their plane refueled and flew east instead of returning to Moscow. In Almaty, the capital of Kazakhstan, they signed a declaration analogous to the one negotiated in Kyiv. At his press conference with Nazarbayev, Rutskoi assured journalists that there were no territorial problems between Russia and Kazakhstan.[18]

In Kyiv and Almaty alike, the Russian officials did their best to dissociate themselves from Voshchanov's statement, treating it as the act of a rogue official. This turn of events came as a complete surprise to the politically inexperienced press secretary, who later wrote,

I shall never forget the strange feeling: I turn on the television set and hear Rutskoi and Stankevich speaking to the assembled Kyivans, calling down curses of every description on the "uppity press secretary who will get what's coming to him, you may be sure of that." I waited anxiously until Rutskoi got back to Moscow. I go to his office: "Sasha, why are you making a scapegoat out of me?" The vice president puts a bottle on the table. "Ah, Pavel, son, what can I do? That's the dirty work you and I have to do!"

But it was not only Rutskoi and Stankevich but also Yeltsin himself, after having approved the statement, who tried to disown the failed political initiative. "I got a call from none other than Boris Nikolaevich [[Yeltsin]]," remembered Voshchanov later. "He had never spoken to me so severely in all the years of our acquaintance and cooperation. 'You made an extremely serious error!' . . . Then it turned out that, having made the statement, I should have clammed up, as if I had lost my tongue, and not named the disputed territories under any circumstances." Voshchanov was left to pay the price.[19]

By August 28, a mere two days after Yeltsin and the new Russian deputies had reduced Gorbachev to submission and all but taken over the Union center, the victors found themselves in great difficulty. Kravchuk and Nazarbayev, who were supposed to have been reminded of their place in the Union hierarchy, were evidently refusing to fall into line. It was becoming clear that the non-Russian republics were not just pawns in a chess game between the Russian president and his Soviet counterpart. They had agendas of their own, and their combined forces were too strong to be kept in check by two main players at odds with each other. The formerly united Russian forces were now in disarray. Some of Yeltsin's advisers wanted to take the place of the Union center in negotiations with the republics; others suggested strengthening the unequal Yeltsin-Gorbachev alliance. There were also those who saw no sense in fighting for a Union that would leave out Ukraine and Belarus but include the "undemocratic" Central Asian republics. And, finally, there were those outside Yeltsin's immediate circle who welcomed the fall of the empire and called for the dissolution of the USSR, no matter what the consequences.[20]

The setback in the Russian offensive against the increasingly obstinate republican leaders and the confusion in Yeltsin's ranks came at a time when Yeltsin himself felt completely exhausted, as was often the case after periods of extreme stress and feverish activity. Even before the crisis over the recognition of Soviet-era borders between republics, he announced to his aides that he was leaving Moscow for a two-week vacation. "After the putsch and the personnel changes," recalled Yeltsin's chief bodyguard, Aleksandr Korzhakov, "Boris Nikolaevich wanted a rest." On August 29 he was spotted in the Latvian capital, Riga, at the opening of the Russian embassy there. Journalists wondered what had brought him to Latvia in the midst of an ongoing crisis in Moscow. It turned out that the exhausted Yeltsin had decided to take his vacation at a Baltic seaside resort near Jurmala, now beyond the borders of Russia and the Union alike. It was the last time that a Moscow leader would vacation in the Baltics.

"Boris Nikolaevich and I walked the beach and delighted in the sea air," remembered Korzhakov. "Seagulls cried, children dug out pieces of amber on the shore, and it seemed that the sleepless nights at the White House and the grueling battle with political opponents had all taken place long ago, in another time dimension." Over the next few days, Yeltsin would call his associates, sign papers, and occasionally come to Moscow to take part in the Congress of People's Deputies, the Union superparliament, which was called into session on September 2, 1991. But his absence from Moscow created an opening for rivals to regain some lost ground.[21]

THE GROWING CRISIS in relations between the Russian leadership and the republics allowed Gorbachev and his advisers, who seemed to have been swept from the scene only a few days earlier, to attempt a political comeback. Gorbachev's return to center stage in Soviet politics began at a session of the Soviet parliament on August 28, the day Yeltsin left for Latvia and the Rutskoi delegation flew to Kyiv. That day, for the first time since the coup, he found himself under attack for being subservient to Yeltsin and the Russian leadership because he supported the appointment of Yeltsin's prime minister, Ivan Silaev, as head of the all-Union government. Gorbachev's economic adviser Vadim Medvedev noted in his diary entry for the Autust 28, "The greatest passions are swirling around the creation of Silaev's committee. People are saying that because of that committee, Union agencies are being supplanted by Russian ones. The president is being accused of acting at the dictate of the Russians."

Ivan Silaev came to Gorbachev's rescue, explaining that the republics would be invited to join his committee. That explanation did not sit well with many deputies, whom Gorbachev was now asking to rubber-stamp the liquidation of the cabinet, a body they had created less than a year earlier by amending the existing constitution. Gorbachev maneuvered this way and that but eventually allowed himself his first critical remarks about the Russian president and his actions since the coup. He said that once the coup was over, neither the Russian president nor the Russian parliament or government had the right to violate the constitution by claiming the prerogatives of the central government. Specifically at issue was the Russian attempt to take over the Soviet central bank in the chaos that followed the defeat of the coup. Gorbachev's advisers protested. Later that day, Yeltsin signed a decree suspending the takeover. Gorbachev and his circle were glad to claim their first victory over their Russian nemesis.[22]

The next major victory for Gorbachev came on September 2, the opening day of the Congress of People's Deputies of the USSR, the Soviet superparliament that had the authority to change the constitution. The meeting began with Nursultan Nazarbayev reading a "Statement of the President of the USSR and the Supreme Leaders of the Republics." It became known as 10 + 1, with 10 standing for the number of republics that subscribed to the statement and 1 for the center, represented by Gorbachev. A few days earlier Moscow newspapers had been full of articles claiming that Russia, and not the Union center, should be the 1 in the formula 9 + 1 or 10 + 1, but few Congress deputies were open to that idea. Nazarbayev's statement brought the center back into the equation and put Gorbachev back in the game. That was the Soviet president's main achievement.

The statement itself was the product of a compromise that reduced the actual importance of the center in all-Union affairs to a degree unimaginable before the coup. Produced at a meeting between Gorbachev and the leaders of the republics the previous evening, it reflected the new political reality—the growing power of Yeltsin in Moscow and of the republican leaders in all-Union affairs. Leonid Kravchuk came to Moscow to say that Ukraine was implementing its declaration of independence, but before it was confirmed by referendum, he was prepared to take part in negotiations on the union treaty—just in case the declaration was not approved. Earlier he had informed the Russian president, who was insisting on a federal structure for the Union, that the only structure acceptable to Ukraine was confederal. Nazarbayev, asserting that Ukraine's declaration of independence had rendered the old federal Union obsolete, also threw his support behind the idea of confederation. It envisioned the Soviet Union not as a state in its own right but as a coalition of states that would create joint bodies for the conduct of foreign and military policy.

With the leaders of the two largest non-Russian republics presenting a united front, Gorbachev and Yeltsin had little choice but to give in to their demand. The Nazarbayev statement, prepared and signed by Gorbachev, Yeltsin, and other leaders of the Soviet republics, called for a new union constitution and proposed a set of measures for the so-called transitional period. They included the replacement of the Supreme Soviet and the Congress of People's Deputies with a Constitutional Assembly composed of representatives of the republican parliaments; the creation of a State Council, the new executive body, consisting of the Union president and the leaders of the republics; and the formation of an Economic Committee made up of representatives of the republics, to replace not only the now defunct cabinet but also the controversial Silaev committee.

In addition, Nazarbayev proposed that a new union treaty be signed and comprehensive economic and security agreements be concluded among the republics to guarantee the rights and freedoms of their citizens. The republics declared their intention to join the United Nations. Appearances to the contrary, Nazarbayev's statement turned out to be a blueprint for the takeover of the center not by one republic, as Yeltsin had attempted, but by all of them. Like Yeltsin's takeover bid, it was directed against the existing constitution, which was declared irrelevant. To the surprise of the delegates, the declaration demanded that the Congress of People's Deputies endorse this assault on the constitution and then dissolve itself. In their memoirs, both Gorbachev and Yeltsin refer very favorably to the Nazarbayev statement and defend its constitutionality. At the time, they also did their best to have the Congress of People's Deputies approve the document and dissolve itself.[23]

After Nazarbayev read the text of the statement, a recess was abruptly announced, without giving the deputies an opportunity to ask questions or express their opinions. Shock prevailed in the chamber, but the break gave some deputies time to cool off and prevented an explosive reaction. Gorbachev's close ally Vadim Medvedev, who took part in the session, wrote in his memoirs, "In essence, such decisions are inevitable as a last chance to save the country. On the outside, of course, they do not look very democratic, but then, that is the nature of the situation." This was a breathtaking understatement, and many in the Soviet superparliament had no intention of yielding. The debate would last four days.[24]

"The president of Kazakhstan, Comrade Nazarbayev, whom I respect, is being offered the role of the legendary sailor Zhelezniak," declared Deputy A. M. Obolensky from the podium of the congress. He was referring to the forcible dissolution of the Russian Constitutional Assembly in early 1918 by a Bolshevik military unit headed by a sailor of the Baltic Fleet, Anatolii Zhelezniakov. "The leadership of the republics," continued Obolensky, "has made its destructive contribution to the final dismantling of Soviet power. Perhaps it is time we stopped treating the Constitution like a common strumpet, accommodating it to the pleasure of the new courtier!" Whether Obolensky had Yeltsin or Gorbachev in mind, he ended with a demand for the latter's resignation. Yeltsin, who was back from the Baltics and chairing that particular session, later recalled that "words like *treachery, conspiracy, plundering of the country*, and so on were hurled from the speaker's platform."

But after days of debate, Gorbachev and the leaders of the republics finally bullied the Congress of People's Deputies into submission. According to Yeltsin, "Gorbachev always had trouble restraining himself when people said such nasty things around him, and when they finally drove him to the wall, he went to the podium and threatened that if the Congress didn't dissolve itself, it would be disbanded. That cooled the ire of some of the speakers, and the proposal for the council of heads of states went through without a hitch." The Congress thus approved the Nazarbayev memorandum and dissolved itself, but not before getting a concession of sorts: while the superparliament would be gone, the Supreme Soviet, or regular USSR parliament, which had no right to amend the constitution, would stay in place. Gorbachev later expressed satisfaction with that decision. After all, it left him with one more Union institution to rely on in his battles with the republican leaders.[25]

The Congress completed its work on September 5. The next day Gorbachev convened the first meeting of the State Council, consisting of him and the republican leaders. "In the new reality," remembered Yeltsin, "Gorbachev was left with only one role: the unifier of the republics that were scattering." One way or another, Gorbachev was back, performing a clearly diminished but still significant role that satisfied both Yeltsin and the leaders of the non-Russian republics for the time being. In late August one of those leaders, the Speaker of the Armenian parliament, Levon Ter-Petrosian, had explained the nature of the new arrangement in an interview with the Moscow weekly *Argumenty i fakty*: "If Yeltsin allows the reanimation of the center, then Gorbachev has a chance to stay. But for now Gorbachev is necessary as a stabilizing factor."[26]

The active phase of the struggle between the Union center and the republics was over. Those republics that were not yet ready to leave the Union gained time to make their final decision. The Russian president's recognition of Baltic independence had closed one chapter by encouraging the sovereignty of the republics and their rebellion against the center. The declaration of Ukrainian independence opened a new chapter in which Russia began to feel responsible for the fate of the center and the republics alike. Soon after the Soviet superparliament adopted the Nazarbayev statement, Yeltsin signed a decree canceling passages of his earlier decrees that had infringed on Union rights. Gorbachev and Yeltsin had reached an interim agreement: they now shared responsibility for maintaining the empire.

Boris Yeltsin and his administration soon moved into one of the Kremlin buildings. He demanded and received the same type of VIP armored limousine that Gorbachev used. "Both presidents cooperated, striving for compromise," recalled Yeltsin's bodyguard Aleksandr Korzhakov. "Mikhail Sergeevich had the advantage over Boris Nikolaevich not in the Kremlin but at his suburban residence in Ogarevo. The heads of the other Union republics would gather there. Gorbachev drank his favorite Armenian Jubilee cognac and behaved like a tsar at table. Yeltsin was angry with him and made sharp remarks, but Boris Nikolaevich's colleagues did not support him." Dual power, not seen in Russia since the Revolution of 1917, had reemerged in Moscow. No one could tell how long the power sharing in the Kremlin would last or what would happen if one party decided to break the deal that was keeping the shaky Union together.[27]

The two Kremlin presidents were brought and kept together by two factors now beyond their control: the leaders of the non-Russian republics, who did not want either of them to become more powerful than the other, and the president of the United States, who remained loyal to Gorbachev and looked to the Gorbachev-Yeltsin alliance for hope that a weakened but still stable Soviet Union would continue to exist. For Yeltsin, as had been the case during the coup, the only way to build up his relations with Bush and thus with the West in general was to show willingness to cooperate with Gorbachev. "For the time being, for now, Gorbachev and I are close," said Yeltsin to the visiting American ambassador, Bob Strauss, on August 24. Yeltsin asked Strauss to convey to the American president that he and Gorbachev were working together. Strauss summarized his impressions from the visit as follows: "This is a man who is conscious of his authority and new stature, but also someone who wants to convey the message that he is working with Gorbachev—from a position of strength."[28]

IV.

SOVIET DISUNION

10

WASHINGTON'S DILEMMA

GEORGE H. W. BUSH WAS SITTING on the sea terrace of his Kennebunkport home, enjoying the warm weather and watching seagulls on the rocks from which he often fished. It was early afternoon on September 2, 1991, the day the Congress of People's Deputies began its deliberations in Moscow. A few hours earlier, Bush had announced to the world that the United States was resuming its diplomatic relations with the Baltics—the former Soviet republics of Estonia, Latvia, and Lithuania—which had now regained their independence of the interwar period. The Baltics played an important role in American thinking about the fate of the Soviet Union. For months the White House had pushed for official Soviet recognition of the independence of Lithuania. Now, with diplomatic relations restored, the question was, what next? Should Washington support the drive of the other republics for independence, or should it try to save whatever was left of the Soviet Union? This would become the main question on the administration's agenda in the weeks and months to come.[1]

September 2, 1991, was the last day of the president's vacation, and he had just finished his lunch with a glass of sherry. Bush was in a reflective mood. "Forty-seven years ago this very day I was shot down over the Bonin Islands," he dictated into his tape recorder. "So much has happened, so very much—in my life and in the world." On September 2, 1944, an Avenger aircraft piloted by the twenty-year-old Lieutenant (j.g.) George H. W. Bush took off from the USS *San Jacinto* as one of four torpedo bombers attacking Japanese installations on the island of Chi Chi Jima. Bush's plane was hit by Japanese antiaircraft fire before reaching its target, but the young lieutenant made it to the island, dropped his bombs, and headed back to the aircraft carrier. With fire engulfing the plane, Bush and his two crewmen bailed out in the middle of the ocean. Only two of their parachutes opened, and Bush turned out to be the only survivor: he was picked up by an American submarine after floating for four hours in an inflated raft. Lieutenant Bush was awarded a Distinguished Flying Cross and went on to a career with enough momentous events to fill three, if not more, lives—his own and those of the two comrades he lost in battle.[2]

The world had indeed changed a great deal in almost half a century. In September 1944, America's mighty ally, Joseph Stalin, completed his takeover of Romania and Bulgaria, and Stalin's commanders launched major offensives to recapture Tallinn and Riga, the capitals of Estonia and Latvia, which had been annexed by the Soviet Union in the summer of 1940 but occupied by the Nazis after Hitler's invasion of the USSR. The Franklin D. Roosevelt administration had refused to recognize the Soviet annexations, but in December 1943 Roosevelt told Stalin that he would not start a war with him over the issue. This statement amounted to de facto recognition of the Soviet takeover, later tacitly confirmed at the Yalta Conference in early 1945. The United States walked a fine line throughout the Cold War, accepting de facto Soviet control of the Baltics but refusing to recognize the USSR's sovereignty over the region. The Estonian, Latvian, and Lithuanian diplomatic missions in the United States were closed, but the American government recognized the sovereign authority of the three Baltic legations and worked with them during the Cold War.[3]

Nicholas Burns, a thirty-five-year-old staffer at the National Security Council (NSC) and White House liaison to the American Baltic communities, remembered later,

> We were very focused on the Baltic states from the beginning. We never accepted their forcible incorporation into the Soviet Union. We accepted Soviet sovereignty in Armenia, Turkmenistan, in Ukraine, but we never accepted it in the Baltic states. We kept Baltic legations open; we protected the Baltic gold given to us in 1940.

There was very strong sentiment in the US Congress that the Baltic states should be free, and there was a very strong and active Baltic community called the Joint Baltic American National Committee, and I met with them very frequently as a White House staffer. Our administration very much wanted to support Baltic rights.[4]

Long-standing, if not always active, American support for Baltic independence was part and parcel of US foreign policy thinking during the Cold War era. According to that view, the independent Baltic states of the interwar period belonged to the ranks of nations unlawfully taken captive by the Soviet Union. Similar treatment was not extended to Moldova, western Ukraine, and western Belarus, which had been incorporated into interwar Romania and Poland, but they were also annexed by the USSR at the same time as the Baltic states after the Molotov-Ribbentrop Pact of 1939. There was a peculiar logic in that distinction: unlike the Baltic states, none of the latter territories were independent during the interwar period or recognized as such in international law. Thus, in the minds of US foreign policy experts, the Baltic states received special treatment that put them in the same category as Poland, Hungary, and Czechoslovakia. By that logic, Soviet withdrawal from Eastern Europe would not be complete until the Baltic states had regained their independence.[5]

This was hardly a view shared or even fully understood in Moscow. For the Soviets, the Baltics were not part of Eastern Europe but former possessions of the Russian Empire lost during the Revolution of 1917 because of imperialist intervention. They had recovered them as a result of the Molotov-Ribbentrop Pact, lost them again in 1941, and reconquered them in the bloody war with Hitler. In Moscow's view, the Western Allies had accepted this new geopolitical reality at the Teheran and Yalta conferences. Letting the Baltics go was unimaginable to those Soviet leaders who were locked into the Cold War mind-set and believed that by taking over the region they had redressed the injustice done by the West to Russia in the aftermath of the revolution. A more immediate reason to keep the Baltic republics was that allowing their secession would create a precedent for other Soviet republics and spell the end of the USSR. As Soviet foreign minister Eduard Shevardnadze once told Jack Matlock, the Balts were not the only ones who had been taken and kept by force.[6]

Using force once again was an option that Gorbachev and his hard-line advisers had tried but did not fully manage to implement. The main foreign policy obstacle before them had been the position of the United States and other Western states. The cost of the use of force in the Baltics was explained to Gorbachev in the plainest possible language by George Bush in the aftermath of the Soviet military crackdown there in early 1991. In a letter delivered by Ambassador Matlock to Gorbachev on January 24, Bush made continuing American economic cooperation and assistance to the crumbling Soviet economy dependent on Soviet behavior in the Baltics.

"I had hoped to see positive steps toward the peaceful resolution of this conflict with the elected leaders of the Baltic states," wrote the US president.

> But in the absence of that and in the absence of a positive change in the situation, I would have no choice but to respond. Thus, unless you can take these positive steps very soon, I will freeze many elements of our economic relationship including Export-Import credit guarantees; Commodity Credit Corporation credit guarantees; support for "Special Associate Status" for the Soviet Union in the International Monetary Fund and World Bank; and most of our technical assistance programs. Further, I would not submit the Bilateral Investment Treaty or Tax Treaty to the United States Senate for consent to ratification when and if they are completed.

One paragraph of the letter presented the history of US economic assistance to the Soviet Union through the prism of Soviet treatment of the Baltics. "I honored your personal request and signed the Trade Agreement in spite of the economic blockade that the Soviet Union had imposed on Lithuania," wrote Bush. "You gave me assurances that you would take steps to settle peacefully all differences with the Baltic leaders. Several weeks later, you lifted that blockade and began a dialogue with Lithuanian and other Baltic leaders. From that time on, our cooperation in the economic sphere had expanded, culminating in the steps that I took on December 12 in response to the difficult circumstances that your country faced as winter approached." But the Soviet military crackdown in the Baltics, argued Bush, made continuing economic assistance impossible. "Unfortunately," read the letter, "in view of the events of the last two weeks—resulting in the death of at least twenty people in the Baltic states—I cannot, in good conscience, and indeed, will not continue along this path."[7]

"No one wishes to see the disintegration of the Soviet Union," wrote George Bush to Gorbachev in the same letter. He was not trying to mislead the Soviet president. Bush and his administration indeed did not intend to kill the Soviet Union by pushing for Baltic independence. In 1988, when Soviet deputy foreign minister Anatolii Adamishin asked US Deputy Assistant Secretary of State Thomas Simons, "Please, please, please don't open a second front in the Baltics," he was told that the United States had no intention of doing so, as it was not US policy to encourage the breakup of the Soviet Union. That remained true in 1989, 1990, and even 1991. But whatever Bush thought about his and his administration's actions, pushing for Baltic independence actually amounted to encouraging the breakup of the Union.

Gorbachev's reliance on Western economic assistance in the last two years of his rule was among the factors that obliged him to deal with the Baltic crisis by granting the rebellious republics ever greater autonomy. That was a slippery slope. According to the Soviet constitution, which, with the start of perestroika, had ceased to be a dead letter in the Soviet political process, the Baltic republics had the same rights as all other Union republics, including the three largest of them—Russia, Ukraine, and Kazakhstan. When Gorbachev and his advisers proposed legislation granting the Baltics special rights, the leaders of other republics felt discriminated against and demanded equality. When Gorbachev and the central government resisted such demands, the republics began to take them on their own. This was the logic behind the successive declarations of republican sovereignty that began with Estonia in the fall of 1988 and engulfed the Soviet Union as a whole by the summer of 1990. The postcoup declarations of independence also followed the Baltic example.[8]

As the White House understood quite well, encouraging Baltic independence also meant undermining Gorbachev and thus US interests in other parts of the world. Baltic demands for independence ran counter to the US global agenda. "We've got so much at stake that it affects the others in the world, and it affects us," wrote Bush to Gorbachev on January 23, 1991, with regard to the Baltic issue. "Arms control comes to mind, but so [[do]] Afghanistan, Cuba, Angola, and many other regional questions. Then you have the natural wariness of the Germans and the Poles, all of whom don't want to see a reversal of any kind with the Soviet Union." In short, as noted by Robert Gates, then a deputy national security adviser, the Bush administration had bigger fish to fry: the drive for Baltic independence could jeopardize the American-Soviet dialogue.[9]

But there was also an issue of domestic American politics. Bush, who was never fully trusted by the Republican Right, had to pay close attention to the aspirations of the American Balts. "I took a great deal of flack in the press, from leaders in the US Baltic communities, and from 'experts' that I was too accommodating, accepting Gorbachev's 'new thinking' and reforms at face value," he recalled years later. On the eve of Bush's trip to Moscow and Kyiv in July he received a letter, signed by forty-five members of Congress, urging him to use the summit to "effectively press the Soviets for direct and substantive talks with the leaders of the Baltic states."

Questions about Baltic independence had been introduced in Bush's talking points not only with Gorbachev but also with Boris Yeltsin and Leonid Kravchuk, two other Soviet leaders he expected to meet during the trip. But Gorbachev cited Soviet law, which, as Bush knew, made secession almost impossible. The US president found himself between two fires—on one hand Gorbachev, maneuvering but unyielding on the issue of Baltic independence; on the other, ever more persistent critics at home. Given the pressure from Baltic émigré organizations in the United States and their supporters in the Republican Party, it is easy to imagine that President Bush and his advisers were simply doing what domestic US politics was forcing them to do, hoping that the pieces of the foreign policy puzzle would somehow ultimately fall into place.[10]

In a manner of speaking, they did. The collapse of the coup revived Bush's hopes that Gorbachev could actually set the Baltic republics free. "A cautious Gorbachev," he said, dictating his diary entry for August 21, "has to worry less about the problem of his political right—military, KGB, etc. And maybe we can get a breakthrough on Cuba, Afghanistan, Baltics, etc." The Baltic states, all of which had declared their independence before or during the coup, needed a decision of the Union parliament to make independence fully legitimate, and the

Baltic leaders once again turned for help to the American president. "Should you, Mr. President, advise M. Gorbachev to support such a resolution," read a letter sent to Washington soon after collapse of the coup by the leader of the Lithuanian parliament, Vytautas Landsbergis, "perhaps this question would be solved quickly and positively." Landsbergis believed that this was Gorbachev's last chance to prove his democratic credentials. "We do not know whether M. Gorbachev will stay in his position for any length of time, although he may still manage to participate in the question of Baltic independence and save political face to some extent," argued Landsbergis. He asked Bush for immediate "renewal of recognition for Lithuania."[11]

The pressure on Bush to grant US recognition to the Baltic states had been mounting ever since the collapse of the coup. On August 23, Republican senator Slade Gorton of Washington wrote to Bush, demanding recognition and claiming that "any possible tie—any bond between those nations and the Soviet Union—was certainly destroyed by the military action taken against them." The senator had in mind the introduction of the state of emergency in the Baltic republics during the coup. The United States was indeed lagging behind in recognition of the independence of the Baltic states. Smaller countries, led by Iceland, began granting recognition almost immediately after Estonia and Latvia made their declarations on August 20 and 21, respectively. Yeltsin had Russia follow suit on August 24. Bush then cabled Gorbachev to tell him that the United States could not wait and would recognize Baltic independence on August 30. Gorbachev asked him to hold off until September 2, hoping that his State Council would recognize the Baltics on that day. It turned out, however, that the new council would not meet until September 6.[12]

Bush could not wait any longer. He made his announcement on the date Gorbachev had originally requested, September 2, the last day of his Kennebunkport vacation. After lunch, enjoying the sea view from his terrace, Bush dictated into his tape recorder, "Today I had a press conference. I recognized the Baltics. I called the presidents of Estonia and Latvia, having talked to Landsbergis of Lithuania a couple of days ago. I told them what we were going to do. I told them why we have waited a few days more. What I tried to do was use the power and prestige of the United States, not to posture, not to be the first on board, but to encourage Gorbachev to move faster on freeing the Baltics." In a letter sent to Landsbergis a few days earlier, he wrote, "We never recognized the forcible incorporation of Lithuania into the Soviet Union, and we are proud that we stood with the Lithuanian people during the many difficult times of the last fifty-one years."[13]

WHAT TO DO WITH the Soviet Union was the question at the top of President Bush's agenda when he returned from vacation in early September. The problem was that neither Bush nor his advisers had a clear vision of what they should do next: the White House was as reactive as ever in its treatment of the rapidly developing situation. There was a belief that this was the only reasonable position under the circumstances. Perhaps it was. The president, by his own admission, "did not consider it at all useful for the United States to pretend we could play a major role in determining the outcome of what was transpiring in the Soviet Union." Bush and his national security adviser, Brent Scowcroft, were concerned that too much activity on the part of the United States could result in another coup. "Demands or statements by the United States could be counterproductive and galvanize opposition to the changes among the Soviet hard-liners," wrote Bush and Scowcroft later.[14]

On September 5, the day the Congress in Moscow decided to ditch the Soviet constitution and dissolve itself, Bush convened the National Security Council. Security issues—cuts to nuclear arsenals and security of the Soviet stockpiles—dominated the agenda, but a good part of the meeting was devoted to discussing the broader Soviet strategy that the White House so far lacked. The president opened the meeting by stating that "with the Baltics free at last, and the rush of other independence declarations, it was a complex situation." Indeed it was. The administration made a clear distinction between its policy toward the Baltic republics and that toward the rest of the Soviet Union. What was good for the Baltics was considered bad for Ukraine. But even if one opted to side with the center against the republics, where was that center to be found—with Yeltsin and his young revolutionaries or with Gorbachev and his seasoned liberal reformers? The press had long been criticizing Bush for backing Gorbachev and neglecting Yeltsin. Should he fully engage with Yeltsin now? "Although Yeltsin was a hero, a genuine hero, how would he look a month from now?" wrote the president and his national security adviser years later, recalling the dilemma.[15]

That day Bush asked his aides for advice but also let them know that he preferred caution. "We should not act just for the sake of appearing busy," he told the gathering. The only person in the room who seemed to be out of sympathy with Bush's cautious approach was the fifty-year-old secretary of defense, Richard Cheney, who took part in the National Security Council meeting. Unlike Scowcroft and the president, Cheney believed that the United States could and should influence the situation in the Soviet Union. "I assume these developments are far from over," he told the gathering. "We could get an authoritarian regime still. I am concerned that a year or so from now, if it all goes sour, how we can answer why we didn't do more." He favored a proactive strategy: "We ought to lead and shape the events."[16]

Cheney pushed for strengthening the administration's ties with the Soviet republics, which would in fact encourage the dissolution of the USSR, which in turn would diminish the Soviet threat and, in time, the Pentagon's budget. The secretary of defense did not make a distinction between the independence of the Baltic states and that of Ukraine. He believed that the United States should support the new nations if they wanted to be independent. For the time being, he suggested opening American consulates in all the Soviet republics. For him, the fact that American and G-7 humanitarian aid was channeled through the center—a point raised by Scowcroft—was "an example of old thinking." In their memoirs, Bush and Scowcroft characterized Cheney's proposal as nothing but "a thinly disguised effort to encourage the breakup of the USSR."

It fell eventually to James Baker, who was a personal friend of Bush's and, as everyone in the White House knew, exercised significant influence on his thinking, to respond to Cheney's challenge. Like Cheney, Baker believed that the American position could influence developments in the Soviet Union. "While events will be determined on the ground, our *words* will—as they clearly did during the coup— have a great impact on how leaders act," read a memo prepared for Baker by his staffers. Before the meeting of the National Security Council, Baker had released to the press five principles on which US policy in the region was to be based. It was a message to the leaders of the former Soviet republics about American expectations of them.

These included the peaceful character of national self-determination; inviolability of existing borders; respect for democracy and the rule of law; respect for human rights, especially those of ethnic minorities; and, last but not least, respect for the international obligations of the USSR—the State Department was decidedly opposed to scrapping the START agreement that had just been negotiated with Gorbachev.

Baker and his State Department advisers did not want to let Gorbachev down after what he had done to improve Soviet-American relations. To them, Gorbachev and the people around him were known, likable, and predictable. No one in the State Department was well acquainted with Boris Yeltsin or his minister of foreign affairs, Andrei Kozyrev, not to mention the leaders of the other republics. People close to Eduard Shevardnadze had warned the US secretary of state that the center was collapsing and nationalism was on the rise. A State Department memo prepared for Baker after the coup pointed to "the real possibility that these current declarations of independence will now lead to territorial, economic and military disputes between republics." "We ought to wait on the consulates [[for the republics]] and do what we can to strengthen the center," said Baker at the NSC meeting. He was also eager to point out the potential problems that the disintegration of the Soviet Union might entail, especially the prospect of violence and bloodshed, as well as the possibility of nuclear proliferation.[17]

Cheney was not convinced by what he heard. He felt that the administration was missing emerging opportunities. "What should we be doing now to engage Ukraine?" he asked, raising the major problem presented by the declaration of independence on the part of the Soviet Union's second-largest republic. "We are reacting."

President Bush asked whether Ukraine would join the Union. "Out," answered Cheney. "The voluntary breakup of the Soviet Union is in our interest. If it's a voluntary association, it will happen. If democracy fails, we're better off if they're small," he argued.

Baker responded, "The peaceful breakup of the Soviet Union is in our interest. We do not want another Yugoslavia."

Scowcroft, siding with Baker, asked the secretary of state whether he would support the Union if the alternative was bloodshed. "Peaceful change of borders is what we're interested in, along the lines of [[the]] Helsinki [[Accords]]," came the predictable answer.

Scowcroft followed up, "But if there's bloodshed associated with the breakup, then should we oppose the breakup?" Baker advocated a continuation of existing policy, working with republican leaders without encouraging a breakup. Cheney disagreed: in his view, more could be achieved by intensifying contacts with the republics.

The only agenda item on which President Bush suggested action that day—an extremely important item—was nuclear disarmament. The chairman of the Joint Chiefs of Staff, General Colin Powell, who took part in the meeting, believed that as long as nuclear arms were in the hands of the Soviet military and not the politicians, they were safe. Powell's years of involvement in nuclear diplomacy had introduced him to many top Soviet commanders, whom he now tended to trust. He distrusted the new wave of political leaders and did not favor the transfer of nuclear weapons from other republics to Russia. With the center still in place and the army still in control, the United States had one—perhaps final—opportunity to achieve something in nuclear diplomacy with the USSR. Bush asked Cheney to prepare a proposal for the reduction of nuclear arsenals. This would help save money and show that the Bush administration was not merely reacting to developments in the Soviet Union. Bush decided to push as hard as possible in an already familiar direction—that of nuclear disarmament. That was what the American people wanted, and Gorbachev was still in a position to deliver. They would try to keep the Soviet Union going as long as possible.[18]

JAMES BAKER CAME TO appreciate the scope of the changes in the Soviet Union since the collapse of the coup when he flew to Moscow for the September 10 opening of a human rights conference under the auspices of the Council for Security and Cooperation in Europe (CSCE). He found the experience "surreal." Next to the Russian White House, he saw barricades and flowers placed in memory of the three young men who had died less than three weeks earlier. At the conference, he listened to a speech by the foreign minister of Lithuania. "If two months ago," he wrote to George Bush, "someone had told us an independent Lithuanian Foreign Minister would be making a very positive speech to a CSCE meeting in Moscow in September, we would have asked what he was smoking."

Human rights had been a thorn in the side of the Soviet foreign policy establishment ever since the Helsinki Accords of 1975, when the Soviet Union accepted the obligation to respect human rights on its territory. Ignoring those obligations, the Soviet authorities had jailed political dissidents who tried to monitor human rights in the USSR. This turned the issue into a tool of Western propaganda against the USSR and a dirty word in the Soviet political lexicon. It was only under Gorbachev that Soviet officials began to warm up to the idea of respect for human rights. With dissidents released from prison, running popular fronts, and even taking power in the Baltics and other Soviet republics, the human rights conference in Moscow underscored the enormousness of the change taking place in the Soviet Union.[19]

There was much to please and amaze American and other Western visitors to Moscow in September 1991. Human rights were just one example; openness to Westerners was another. James Baker would meet with Ivan Silaev, Yeltsin's prime minister and de facto head of the new Union government, in the same office (previously occupied by Stalin) where the now imprisoned prime minister Valentin Pavlov and the hard-liners had plotted their move against Gorbachev on the night of August 18. Baker also visited the old office of the former head of the KGB, Vladimir Kriuchkov. The new man in charge of the building, Gorbachev, and Yeltsin's liberal appointee Vadim Bakatin, awaited the American secretary of state at the curb and welcomed him inside after admitting to the press that he was "a little nervous."

Gorbachev and Yeltsin were as friendly to the American visitor as their subordinates and the leaders of the republics were. Baker was eager to return to the American precoup agenda and push for things that President Bush had not managed to obtain from Gorbachev at the Moscow summit. With the Baltics finally free, these included canceling Soviet aid to the Moscow-backed regimes in Afghanistan and Cuba. "Given the highly uncertain Soviet future," recalled Baker, "we were in even more of a hurry to 'lock in' gains then and there." He made it apparent to Gorbachev and Yeltsin that American economic aid depended on the withdrawal of Soviet support for Cuba and Afghanistan. "They jumped at my offer, and indeed were almost competitive in trying to be cooperative," wrote Baker in his memoirs. Gorbachev, who no longer represented the Communist Party, told the

American secretary of state, "Yes, we spent eighty-two billion dollars on ideology."

Baker was amazed when Gorbachev agreed not only to terminate Soviet aid to Cuba but also to announce his decision at the joint press conference they were about to hold in the Kremlin. This was done without consulting Fidel Castro. It was a major coup for American foreign policy: all Soviet army servicemen were to be withdrawn from Cuba, and aid would be cut off as of January 1, 1992. The same deadline was set for the ending of Soviet aid to Afghanistan. Upon hearing Baker's request, Yeltsin responded, "I will tell Gorbachev to do it." He then called the Soviet president and assured Baker that the deadline would be accepted. The agreement, in which both the Soviet Union and the United States committed themselves to ending assistance to their respective clients in Afghanistan, was announced in Moscow the next day.

The pro-Soviet Afghan leader Mohammad Najibullah was informed of the withdrawal of the annual Soviet aid package six hours before the Moscow announcement, and he presented a brave face. Najibullah would be out of power in a few months and hanged by the Taliban in September 1996. Pictures of his corpse in the world media were a sign of trouble to come, but in September 1991 no one predicted the subsequent tragic turn of events in Afghanistan. Baker could take satisfaction in a major victory. When the US ambassador, Bob Strauss, passed him a piece of paper with a note reading, "These 2 meetings today are really pretty historic!" Baker returned it with his own comment: "That's the understatement of the day!"[20]

Why were the Soviets so accommodating? The new Soviet foreign minister, Boris Pankin, the only Soviet ambassador to publicly condemn the coup before it was over, who was then rewarded with the top diplomatic job, explained the concessions to the United States as follows:

We looked to the US for economic assistance and were prepared to make many concessions to achieve it—hence our compliance with independence for the Baltic states. Our retreat from the Third World and downgrading of our relations with Cuba fit the same pattern. On the one hand we could no longer afford to maintain these kinds of relationship; on the other we strove to present their

abandonment as badges of good intent. Both the Americans and
we dressed up our statements in terms of détente, but for our part
it was economic imperatives that drove us, as the Americans perfectly well understood.

Pankin had good reasons to emphasize the economic factor when
he sat down a few years later to write his memoirs and tried to recall,
analyze, and justify his foreign policy. Even so, the same memoirs
indicate that there was something more than pure realpolitik driving
Soviet behavior in the international arena in the fateful autumn of
1991. The other important factor was an ideological revolution that led
to the rejection of anything related to the former communist vision
of the world and the international role of the USSR. This revolution,
which had been brewing for years among liberally inclined officials in
the offices of the International Department of the Central Committee
and the corridors of the Foreign Ministry, was unleashed by the
failure of the coup.

Not only Yeltsin but also Gorbachev was in full agreement with
the new trend. At his first meeting with Pankin, Gorbachev said, "We
must change priorities, get rid of prejudices. Yasser Arafat, Gaddafi—
they call themselves our friends, but only because they dream of
us returning to the past. Enough double standards." Communist
ideology was thus all but expunged from Soviet foreign policy. The
liberal thinking closely associated with newfound Soviet admiration
for the economic and cultural achievements of the United States
became central to the Soviet foreign policy process.[21]

"We longed to be accepted," wrote Pankin. "In those days the
common obsession that gripped our entire leadership was with the
idea of becoming a 'civilized state.'" The desire for acceptance informed
Pankin's behavior during his first meeting with Baker. He began by
handing Baker a copy of an internal memo that he had prepared for
Gorbachev, spelling out Soviet readiness to reverse every position taken
on issues ranging from Afghanistan to Eastern Europe, Israel, and Cuba.
Pankin probably wanted to indicate that henceforth Soviet diplomacy
would have no secrets from the "civilized world." As the surprised
Baker examined the memo, Pankin told him, "I hope we can come to
a common understanding on many of these issues. But I want to make
one request: even if the agreement we reach is closer to your original

position than to ours, please avoid the temptation to tell the press that these are concessions extracted by you. All this stems from the ideas and positions of the people who are running our foreign policy today."[22]

This sounded like an aspiration to be more Catholic than the pope. Baker was probably in no position to appreciate the full scope of ideological reasons for this fire sale of Soviet foreign policy assets, but the economic ones were quite apparent. Ivan Silaev, who headed the Economic Committee now functioning as the interim Union government, told Baker that the economic situation was "grave." His main task was not to improve it—that was beyond the government's capacity—but to prevent it from growing worse. Gavriil Popov, the democratic mayor of Moscow and a staunch supporter of Yeltsin during the coup, told Baker that in reality there was no central government. The republics and large municipalities such as Moscow were on their own. "Moscow cannot support itself through the winter," he admitted, and then asked for help, mentioning in particular eggs, powdered milk, and mashed-potato mix. "Some of this material is stored by your army, which throws it out after three years. But a three-year shelf life is all right for us." Baker was stunned. "It was a sobering admission of the problems faced by the country whose leader once talked about 'burying' the West," he wrote in his memoirs. The mayor of St. Petersburg, Anatolii Sobchak, and his aide Vladimir Putin, whom Baker visited on his brief stop in the former imperial capital, were equally concerned about the coming winter.

After meeting with the new democratic leaders, who wanted change but were clearly unprepared to govern the country, Baker wrote to Bush suggesting a Marshall Plan for the Soviet Union in all but name. "The simple fact is we have a tremendous stake in the success of the democrats here. Their success will change the world in a way that reflects both our values and our hopes. . . . The democrats' failure would produce a world that is far more threatening and dangerous, and I have little doubt that if they are unable to begin to deliver the goods, they will be supplanted by an authoritarian leader of the xenophobic right wing."[23]

THE BIG ISSUE that came up in almost all Baker's discussions in Moscow was that of relations between the center and the republics. The new minister of defense, Yevgenii Shaposhnikov, asked Baker,

"Please do not be in a hurry to recognize all these new republics." Baker was not. With no clear strategy enunciated by the Bush White House, he was free to conduct his own policy. Baker's talks in Moscow and St. Petersburg seemed to confirm his earlier assumption that the democrats were concentrated in the center; helping the center therefore meant helping democracy. Baker told everyone in the Soviet Union who would listen that some arrangement had to be made between the center and the republics so that the West would know with whom to deal on economic reform and humanitarian aid.

Baker managed to host a dinner for the prime ministers of the republics. It was a striking difference from March 1991, when the initiative of the US ambassador, Jack Matlock, to gather the leaders of the republics for a meeting at his embassy had been torpedoed by Gorbachev and his people. Now Baker was the only political leader trusted by the heads of the republics to be an honest broker. He used the occasion to smooth over contradictions and alleviate tension and distrust between the new cohorts of Soviet leaders. He acted as a go-between for the center and the republican leaders. By assuring Prime Minister Vitold Fokin of Ukraine that humanitarian aid would be distributed to all the republics, Baker obtained his commitment that Ukraine would sign the economic treaty with Russia and the other post-Soviet republics.[24]

What Baker did in Moscow vis-à-vis the republics had the full support of the president. George Bush did almost everything diplomatically possible to keep the Soviet Union alive. It was no easy task. He got an opportunity to assess the dimensions of the problem on September 25, when he welcomed his former Kyiv host, Leonid Kravchuk, the head of the Ukrainian parliament, to the White House. Three days earlier, five thousand demonstrators representing local Ukrainian American organizations had gathered in Lafayette Park, across from the White House, to manifest their support for Ukrainian independence and urge Bush, then still under attack for his "Chicken Kiev" speech, to change his attitude toward independence for the Soviet republics. "You were last with the Baltics. Be first with Ukraine," read one of the demonstrators' signs.

Bush found Kravchuk more self-confident and much less agreeable than he had been in Kyiv less than two months earlier. During Bush's visit, Kravchuk had agreed with him on the need to resist what the

American president called "suicidal nationalism." Bush was still in the same frame of mind, opposing independence for every Soviet republic except the Baltics, but Kravchuk had clearly shifted position. His support for Ukrainian independence had become something more than a tactical move by a party apparatchik threatened by the democratic victory in Moscow. "Independence is forged by the people. And on December 1 [[the date of the impending referendum]] the people will confirm our independence and we will begin building a new nation—Ukraine," he told the North American media.[25]

Having embarked on selling the idea of Ukrainian independence to the world, Kravchuk used his invitation to the White House as an opportunity to make his case to the world's most powerful political leader. His verdict on the Soviet Union was not the one that Bush and his advisers wanted to hear: "The Soviet Union is virtually disintegrating. There is no national government. There is no Supreme Soviet of the Soviet Union." Kravchuk concluded his presentation by stating, "The Union cannot exist in any serious form. There is a struggle for power there, and we cannot be part of a union in which there are some members more powerful than others." His reference was clearly to the Gorbachev-Yeltsin alliance and the role that Russia aspired to play in the new Union. Kravchuk requested support for Ukrainian democracy, which he understood as the drive for national independence. He also wanted direct diplomatic ties, the opening of a Ukrainian trade mission in the United States, and eventually the recognition of Ukrainian independence. Kravchuk did not come only to ask for favors. He had also something to offer: Ukraine, he said, aspired to be a nuclear-free country.

Bush was not impressed. In his memoirs he wrote that Kravchuk "did not seem to grasp the implications and complexities of what he was proposing." On the previous day Bush had met with the Soviet foreign minister, Boris Pankin, who assured him that while the immediate postcoup period had seen a rush for independence by the republics, in the last few weeks republican leaders had realized that they had to work together. That was not the impression one would get from talking to Kravchuk. According to Bush's memoirs, the Ukrainian leader gave him "a taste of the dissatisfaction the republics felt for the Union." Bush promised Kravchuk support for democracy and economic reform, as well as food and humanitarian assistance.

He also gave him what was by now the standard American line on center-republic relations: the United States did not presume to shape the changes taking place in the Soviet Union but wanted political clarity there. It also wanted a viable economic plan. Recognition of Ukraine, unlike that of the Baltic states, would have to await the results of the referendum.

The conversation, scheduled for forty-five minutes, had now lasted an hour and a half, and Bush signaled that time was running out. Kravchuk rushed to make his final plea—one that took Bush by surprise. Thanking him for the offer of food and humanitarian aid, Kravchuk said that Ukraine needed investment and technology instead. This was very different from what Bush and Baker heard from the representatives of the Soviet center, who were begging for food supplies. "We have a difficult situation," said Kravchuk. "The Soviet Union has received food assistance, but Ukraine has not. Now we must pay these [[all-Union]] debts. While the Soviet Union was getting assistance, we were sending 60,000 tons of meat and milk to the Soviet Union [[at nominal prices]]. . . . Our request is that you give us credits. We'll buy technology. We'll invite businessmen to invest in Ukraine. We'll work." Kravchuk's statement reflected the simple fact that Ukraine was a food-producing republic, not a food-importing one, and its interests differed from those of other republics. Commerce and investment, not food aid, was Ukraine's highest priority.

Drawing aside the veil of American impartiality with regard to relations between the center and the republics, Bush asked Kravchuk a direct question that revealed the underlying premise of American policy at the time: "Do you see that there must be an economic union with the center or not? We think that is a necessary step to encourage investment." "I would be glad to have that if the center could do something," responded Kravchuk. "But the center is incapable of doing anything. We're losing time. The Soviet Union is a huge country. It is impossible to pursue economic reform at a rapid pace in the entire country."

The two leaders parted ways without reaching an understanding. The Ukrainian visitor sought to be as gracious as possible in his subsequent comments to the press, which accused Bush of being completely in Gorbachev's corner. "I am convinced that President George Bush is beginning to change his way of thinking," he told the press. Later, Kravchuk summed up Bush's position as follows: he wanted the Soviet Union to go on. The security of the nuclear arsenals was always at the top of his agenda. Kravchuk respected that position, as he believed that it corresponded to the interests of those who had elected Bush to govern their country.[26]

GEORGE H. W. BUSH indeed wanted the Soviet Union to survive. It was essential to his security agenda, which remained focused on Soviet nuclear weapons, just as it had been at the height of the Cold War. By the time the president met with the increasingly difficult Kravchuk, Dick Cheney and his experts at the Department of Defense had prepared the proposal for nuclear disarmament that Bush had requested at the NSC meeting three weeks earlier. It was immediately sent to American allies in Western Europe and to Gorbachev in Moscow. On September 27, Bush called Prime Minister John Major of Britain, President François Mitterrand of France, and Chancellor Helmut Kohl of Germany to explain his initiative and ask for support. He also called Gorbachev. At first glance, the proposal constituted a unilateral offer by the United States to reduce its nuclear arsenal by removing tactical nuclear weapons and getting rid of multiple independently targeted reentry vehicles (MIRVs) on intercontinental ballistic missiles (ICBMs). In reality, the proposal was designed as an invitation to the USSR to do the same. As Scowcroft told the secretary-general of NATO, Manfred Woerner, "We are not planning negotiations. This is a unilateral move. Of course, if the Soviets reject our proposals, we may have to reconsider."[27]

Ultimately, the success of the proposal depended on the Soviet response. In his telephone conversation with Gorbachev on September 27, Bush told the Soviet leader, "We'll spell out what we do. In some categories, we'll spell out how the Soviet Union could take similar steps. For example, we cancel ICBMs except for single warheads, and would like to say that the Soviet Union is doing the same thing."

Gorbachev seemed interested but avoided any specific commitment. "George, thank you for those clarifications," he told the US president. "Since you're urging that we take steps, I can only give an answer in principle—since there is much that must be clarified—and that answer is a positive one." Bush said that he understood and asked whether he could announce that Gorbachev's initial reaction was positive. Gorbachev gave his consent.[28]

Gorbachev spoke to Bush in the presence of top Soviet military officers with whom he had just finished studying the text of the American proposal. General Vladimir Lobov, the new chief of the Soviet army General Staff, was more than skeptical. According to Scowcroft, the proposal to remove tactical nuclear weapons served immediate American interests in more than one way. In Germany, American weapons of that class had been rendered obsolete by German unification: if fired, they would now hit the eastern territories taken over by Bonn. In South Korea, the Seoul government wanted such weapons out in order to engage North Korea on the diplomatic level. Elsewhere in the Pacific, the governments of Japan and New Zealand objected to nuclear-armed American ships in their ports. Given the American offer to remove tactical nuclear weapons unilaterally, problems associated with long negotiations and subsequent verification were eliminated.

According to Gorbachev's foreign policy adviser, Anatolii Cherniaev, who was present during the telephone call, "[[General]] Lobov tried to 'exert pressure': it was supposedly disadvantageous to us; they will deceive us; I see no reciprocity, and so on—even though Mikhail Sergeevich pointed a finger at Bush's text, arguing the opposite." After his conversation with Bush, Gorbachev entertained the generals by sharing his impressions of a play that he and his wife had seen a few days earlier. It was based on Thornton Wilder's 1948 novel *The Ides of March*. Gorbachev told the surprised generals that he saw analogies between the last days of the Roman Republic and the times they were living in. "There is in him a mixture of artlessness and a clever pretense of credulity with the new generals," noted Cherniaev in his diary. One way or another, Gorbachev eventually convinced his new military chiefs to go along. They turned out to be much more agreeable than their predecessors.

Boris Pankin wrote in his memoirs that "after the putsch of August 1991, many of the military were embarrassed by their own tacit sympathy for its aims, if not active support. So the quiescence of the Soviet military made it easier for us to be imaginative." In that vein, Cherniaev credited Bush's proposal to the international influence of Gorbachev's "new thinking," which he himself had helped shape. "Do you not see in this any emergence of a new US policy, new relations with us, results of new thinking?" he asked the ever suspicious generals after the Bush-Gorbachev teleconference. Apparently they did not. Cherniaev's statement would come as a surprise to the Americans as well, but not to Gorbachev. He kept believing in his transformative influence on the very nature of international politics.

Eight days later, on October 5, Gorbachev called Bush not only to accept the challenge but also to invite him to go further down the road to nuclear disarmament. He proposed a one-year ban on nuclear testing and an invitation to other nuclear powers to join the United States and the Soviet Union in reducing their nuclear arsenals. The Soviets would get rid of their tactical nuclear weapons, negotiate on the MIRVs, and unilaterally cut their ground forces by seven hundred thousand. It was now the Americans' turn to be surprised and check the new proposals with their generals. "There were some differences in our positions," recalled Bush, "but on balance it was very positive and forthcoming." Bush's gamble had worked. While the Soviets, like the Americans, were of course trying to make a virtue of necessity in cutting their military budgets, there is no question that both countries benefited, as did the world at large. Their agreement in the fall of 1991 created a basis for the START II treaty, which Bush and Yeltsin would sign in January 1993.[29]

A few days later, when Bush again called the National Security Council into session, there was good news to share. The plan to reduce nuclear arsenals that they had discussed at the previous meeting was now working. Nevertheless, the course of developments in the Soviet Union was as murky as ever, and the dilemma of whom to support, the center or the republics, was no closer to a solution. As discussion of these problems resumed, Dick Cheney again sought to change the existing strategy of supporting the center. "It was still Cheney against the field," remembered Robert Gates, who took part in the meeting. Despite general agreement on the need to support democracy and economic reform, there was no consensus on how best to do so. "Support for the center puts us on the wrong side of reform," argued Cheney. James Baker disagreed: "The guys in the center *are* reformers." Baker summed up his argument by stating, "We should not establish the policy of supporting the breakup of the Soviet Union into twelve republics. We should support what *they* want, subject to *our* principles." The meeting ended with no clear decision, which meant a continuation of the balancing act between the center and the republics, Gorbachev and Yeltsin.[30]

11

THE RUSSIAN ARK

"THANK YOU FROM THE BOTTOM OF MY HEART," said Boris Yeltsin to George Bush before putting down the receiver. The American president had called to ask about his health and offer medical assistance. It was September 25, early afternoon in Russia. A few days earlier, Yeltsin, still exhausted after his August brush with destiny, had felt chest pains. The brief vacation he had taken a few weeks earlier did not alleviate his condition. He needed more rest. "I have been reading in the papers that you may require some medical attention," said Bush when he heard Yeltsin's voice on the other end of the line. "I would like to offer you the best hospital facilities in Washington, D.C. if that would have any appeal to you."

After the collapse of the August coup, George Bush had adopted a practice of calling both Kremlin presidents, Gorbachev and Yeltsin. "We knew that Gorbachev was weakening, we knew that Yeltsin was strengthening, and President Bush began to juggle our relations with Gorbachev and Yeltsin," recalled Nick Burns, the NSC staffer who was often a note taker on Bush's calls to Moscow. "We made a very concerted effort to work together with Gorbachev and Yeltsin. So every time that President Bush talked to Gorbachev he would usually follow up with a call to Yeltsin." Yeltsin was clearly moved by these signs of attention. "Mr. President, thank you," he said to Bush at the end of their telephone conversation on September 25. "I am very grateful. Thank you for your personal attention to me. I don't know how to find the words to thank you." The two presidents agreed not to reveal the substance of their conversation to the press, in order, as Yeltsin said, "not to worry people too much."[1]

That day people in Russia read media reports not about Yeltsin's health but about his diplomatic achievements in the North Caucasus, where he and Nursultan Nazarbayev of Kazakhstan had negotiated a cease-fire between Azerbaijan and Armenia in Nagornyi Karabakh— the site of the first ethnic conflict to erupt in the USSR during the perestroika era. "We had a tough mission to Nagornyo-Karabakh, but we brought the two sides to the table and signed a protocol," Yeltsin told Bush on the phone. He also let him know that he was taking another short vacation. That day the presidential spokesman, Pavel Voshchanov, declared that Yeltsin would go on vacation "not for relaxation but so that he can work on his further plans and on a new book in calm surroundings."

Relaxation and the need for medical treatment were in fact the main reasons for his absence from the capital for the second time in less than a month. Yeltsin vacationed at a government mansion, Bocharov Ruchei, near Sochi on the Black Sea. He made no substantive progress on his new book of memoirs, but he had plenty of time to consider his "further plans" and discuss them with his numerous visitors. His chief bodyguard, Aleksandr Korzhakov, arranged tennis matches and Russian saunas for the president, but rumors reached Moscow that he was drinking heavily. "They say he would get blind drunk," noted Gorbachev adviser Anatolii Cherniaev in his diary. "And the only ambulance in town stood ready near the dacha."[2]

Whether the rumors were true or not (one could hardly expect Gorbachev's aides to be too kind to Yeltsin), the Russian president's disappearance from Moscow came at a most unfortunate time for the new Russian government. "It was as if Napoleon had repaired to the Riviera to compose poetry after routing the Austrian and Russian armies at Austerlitz," commented one of the president's supporters in the Russian parliament. "The country was heading for collapse," recalled Yeltsin's principal adviser at the time, Gennadii Burbulis. With the Union government in shambles and the Russian government not yet in control, no one was in charge. "And that situation of power without power, of responsibility without resources could not continue indefinitely," argued Burbulis many years later. "One way or another, an effective government had to be established quickly. But Yeltsin took off for Sochi."[3]

He left behind three competing centers of power, one around Mikhail Gorbachev and two others within his own government. With Yeltsin out of town, they found themselves at one another's throats. One part of Yeltsin's government wanted to embark on a radical course of political and economic reform, which would mean severing economic ties with the other republics. Another wanted to move ahead slowly, coordinating Russia's efforts with the rest of the former Union. Gorbachev, for his part, wanted to restore the old Union under a new name, with as strong a center as possible. While the central authorities were in disarray, the Union republics stopped transferring taxes to Moscow, using their newly acquired right to issue currency in order to buy industrial products in Russia. Food was becoming more and more an issue in Russia's industrial centers. October 1991 would become the crucial month in deciding the country's future course and the prospects of the Soviet Union. Yeltsin had to make a choice. He took his time.[4]

THE SPLIT WITHIN THE RUSSIAN government became public with the resignation on September 27 of Ivan Silaev, the Russian premier, who had doubled since late August as head of the interim Soviet government. He had found himself in an impossible situation, simultaneously representing the center and the Union's largest republic. The leaders of the other republics accused him of favoring Russia, while members of the Russian government claimed that he was advancing the interests of the center. Attacks on Silaev from within his own government intensified after he issued a letter recommending the suspension of a number of Yeltsin's decrees concerning the takeover of all-Union property and the introduction of Russian customs duties. Silaev wanted the decrees, many of them issued immediately after the August coup, suspended until consultations could be held with the other republics. His opponents saw his letter as an attempt to restore the old center.[5]

Faced with a choice between Russia and the Union, Silaev eventually chose the latter. He was helped in that decision by Yeltsin himself, who called him in mid-September and suggested that he remain in charge of the all-Union economic administration. At the top of the Russian power pyramid, Silaev lost a bureaucratic battle to Yeltsin's immediate entourage—people whom the Russian president had brought to Moscow from his native city, Sverdlovsk. In private conversation with James Baker, Nursultan Nazarbayev referred to them as the "Sverdlovsk mafia." They included the second most influential person in Russia after Yeltsin himself, State Secretary Gennadii Burbulis, as well as the head of the presidential administration and the first deputy head of government. While Silaev advocated a cautious approach to reform and its coordination with the other republics, Burbulis argued for what became known as "shock therapy," an aggressive reform effort associated with rapid liberalization of prices and an initial sharp decline in living standards, which had been tried successfully in Poland.[6]

Burbulis and his supporters—who included the Russian foreign minister, Andrei Kozyrev, and the information minister, Mikhail Poltoranin—put Russia's interests first, seeking to grab as much power as possible from the center and to do so as quickly as they could. They were not willing to hold up Russian reform so as to accommodate republics that rejected their strategy or were as yet unprepared to join Russia on the road to rapid economic and social transformation. Burbulis placed his hopes for reform in the group of young economists who had been working since late August on an assessment of the economic situation.[7]

The economists were based in a government resort in the village of Arkhangelskoe, where Yeltsin and his entourage had awoken on August 19 to news of the coup in Moscow. The group was led by Yegor Gaidar, a rising thirty-five-year-old scholar who had served during the perestroika years as economic editor of the Communist Party's two main publications, the journal *Kommunist* and the newspaper *Pravda*. The boyish, moon-faced Gaidar was born into the world of Soviet privilege. Both of his grandfathers were famous authors. One of them, Arkadii Gaidar, was by far the most popular Soviet writer of children's literature; every Soviet teenager read his best-selling 1940 novel *Timur and His Team*, describing the battles of the book's main character, Timur, with hooligans in a dacha settlement near Moscow. Timur was in fact the name of Arkadii Gaidar's son and Yegor Gaidar's father, who grew up to become a high-ranking Soviet naval officer and a military correspondent for *Pravda*. Yegor spent a good part of his childhood and youth abroad, first in Yugoslavia and then in Cuba, where his father was stationed as a reporter.

In 1980 Yegor Gaidar graduated from the prestigious Moscow University with a postgraduate degree in economics, joined the Communist Party, and went to work in economic institutes and think tanks in Moscow. His main obsession became Soviet economic reform, which he modeled on the market transformations then taking place in Yugoslavia and Hungary. Perestroika allowed Gaidar to popularize his reformist views in the party's main publications. He also established his own research institute and emerged as the leader of a small group of young economists developing a reform program for the all-Union government. According to Gorbachev's economic adviser Vadim Medvedev, Gaidar "took part in many situation analyses and brainstorming sessions in the presidential apparatus." For months, Gorbachev had been playing with the idea of radical economic reform, and he had even thrown his support behind a 500 Days Program for the transition to the market proposed in August 1990 by a team of economists led by Stanislav Shatalin. Eventually, however, he settled for a watered-down version with no mechanism or timetable for implementation.[8]

After the failed August 1991 coup, the Russian presidential administration became Gaidar's main client. His principal contact and promoter there was Gennadii Burbulis, whom Gaidar met for the first time in the besieged White House when he came to defend the nascent Russian democracy. In late August Gaidar was among the early supporters of the takeover of all-Union institutions by the Russian government, which he saw as the only hope for the continuation of the Union. "Gorbachev immediately gives up his post and passes it on to Yeltsin as president of the largest republic of the Union," Gaidar later said, describing his scenario for saving the empire. "Yeltsin legitimately subordinates Union structures to himself and, wielding his then absolute authority as leader of the whole Russian people, ensures the merger of the two centers of power."

Gaidar's vision was not realized at the time, for which he blamed the indecisiveness and passivity of the Russian government. A few weeks later, that very same government was giving Gaidar and his team an undreamed-of opportunity to test their economic models and finally move from words to actions in the sphere of market reform. They had been pushing for such an opportunity for months, but the Gorbachev government had dragged its feet. Now the situation was so bad that the Russian government had to act. Gaidar and his group went to work. They believed that if something was not done immediately to stabilize the situation, the collapse of the economy would become not only inevitable but irreversible in a month or two.[9]

As Gaidar later wrote, it became clear to him and his circle early on that "there can be no effective economic union without a political one. And there was obviously no chance of restoring one quickly." They therefore concluded that Russia would have to go it alone. Their first priority was to liberalize prices in order to revive collapsing markets and create incentives for state and collective enterprises to start trading again. But liberalization would inevitably lead to a collapse of the financial system unless the government drastically cut its own expenditures, including subsidies for food products. That could produce a social explosion, but the young economists believed that neither they nor the politicians had any other viable alternative— they had to take the risk. They hoped that their shock therapy would jump-start the dying economy, opening the way for privatization of state property and a full transition to a market economy.[10]

Along with other members of the Russian government, Burbulis visited Gaidar and his team at their Arkhangelskoe resort and concluded that there was no alternative to their shock therapy. If Yeltsin did not try to implement it, despite the obvious risks, his popularity would soon evaporate like Gorbachev's, and a popular revolution would drive him and his entourage out of office. Burbulis asked for specifics: Gaidar and the young economists came up with their estimates and proposals. After discussing them at the Russian State Council, Burbulis flew to Sochi to sell the plan for saving the Russian economy and Yeltsin's presidency to the president himself. The memo he brought to Yeltsin was titled "Russia's Strategy for the Transition Period," but it became better known as the "Burbulis Memorandum." No one could tell how Yeltsin would react to the plan. "Everyone waited, as they say, not by the day but by the hour to see what would happen there," recalled Burbulis later.[11]

Burbulis and Yeltsin spent long hours on the shore of the Black Sea discussing the plan. Aleksandr Korzhakov supplied them with food. "The situation was actually extreme in the sense that the legacy we inherited was monstrous," remembered Burbulis. "And Boris

Nikolaevich understood that very well." Sitting on a deck chair, Burbulis argued that Gaidar's economic plan was their only hope.

Yeltsin's first reaction was a blunt refusal: "I can't do it. What do you mean?"

But Burbulis insisted. As he later summarized his response, "What was good was that in Gaidar's papers the idea was immediately accompanied by steps and an instrument. A law, then a decree; a decree, then a law, a resolution. And it was clear what was being proposed and how to do it."

One of Gaidar's basic premises was that Russia could not afford to subsidize the other republics: Russian resources were needed to overcome the current crisis and make a giant leap into the market economy without causing social upheaval. This in turn raised questions about the need for a Union center, not only in political terms but also in economic ones. "Objectively, Russia does not need an economic center standing over it and busying itself with the redistribution of its resources," read the memo. "But many other republics are interested in such a center. Having gained control of property on their own territory, they are trying to use all-Union agencies to redistribute Russia's property and resources in their own interests. Given that such a center can exist only with the support of the republics, it will objectively carry out a policy, regardless of the composition of its cadres, that runs counter to Russia's interests."

At some point Burbulis asked Yeltsin, "What are we to do with the republics?" and then gave his own answer: "We will cooperate mildly with them, but we have no food or drink to offer."

Yeltsin eventually began to incline toward Burbulis's proposal. "What, only that way and no other?" he asked.

Burbulis insisted, "No other way."

Yeltsin asked again, "Is there another possibility?" Burbulis said no. The president finally gave in: "If there is nothing else, then that is how we will proceed."

In Sochi Burbulis met members of the competing group within the Russian government, made up of Silaev's allies, who were trying to convince Yeltsin to follow a more cautious strategy, but he flew back to Moscow with new hope for the future. If Yeltsin put Burbulis's memo into effect, then Russia would embark on something unprecedented in its history: instead of putting the empire first, it would start building its own ark to survive the coming flood.[12]

AS HAD HAPPENED in August 1991, Yeltsin's unexpected departure from the capital created a political opportunity for Gorbachev. He wanted to return to center stage in Soviet politics, and his main instrument for doing so was the idea of a new union treaty, which he wanted the leaders of the republics to sign as soon as possible.

Gorbachev's first postcoup meeting with Yeltsin and the leaders of the other republics, which took place on August 23, had left no doubt that not only the old Union but also the old union treaty that triggered the coup were now dead. In the days following the meeting, Gorbachev called one of his top advisers, Georgii Shakhnazarov, and asked whether he was working on a new union treaty. The question took Shakhnazarov by surprise: "It never entered my head to do so." He doubted whether negotiations could be resumed.

Gorbachev insisted, "If we sit with our hands folded, we will lose everything. They will tear the country to hell." Shakhnazarov pointed out that the republics would now want more from the center. "Definitely," Gorbachev told Shakhnazarov, "but for our part, we should explain to them that without the Union not one of them will survive. Not even Russia. It will be bad for everyone."[13]

On September 10, with James Baker in Moscow, Gorbachev convinced Yeltsin to rejoin the negotiating process. Yeltsin agreed on condition that the new union treaty create a confederation—a decentralized entity in which the center would deal largely with issues of defense and foreign relations. That was also the position taken earlier by Kravchuk of Ukraine and, after the collapse of the coup, by Nazarbayev of Kazakhstan. Although Gorbachev wanted a new union, not a confederation, he had no choice but to take Yeltsin's offer. In late September, with Yeltsin out of Moscow, Shakhnazarov met with Burbulis and Yeltsin's legal adviser, Sergei Shakhrai, to discuss the parameters of the new treaty. Burbulis gave Gorbachev's adviser an introduction to the new order of precedence: the days when "Russia, as a 'donor,' the savior of the Union, would lie down on the embrasure to cover any breach in it" were over. Russia needed time "to look after itself and gather strength."

Burbulis and those around him did not believe that Gorbachev's attempts to revive the all-Union market offered a solution to the Union's economic problems or served Russian interests. The republics were flooding Russian banks with ever more worthless money in order to drain Russia of its natural resources. "That is why we must save Russia and strengthen its independence, separating ourselves from the rest," argued Burbulis and Shakhrai. "After that, when it is back on its feet, everyone will rally to it, and the question [[of the Union]] can be resolved again," they assured the representative of the Union center. For now the Russians wanted a confederation, not an entangling union. They also wanted Russia to become the legal successor to the USSR, which would give it primacy in the confederation. They were prepared to work toward that goal with the center, which they considered an intermediary with the republics. This arrangement would allow Gorbachev to remain in politics, if not in power. "We understand," said Burbulis, "that Gorbachev is an outstanding reformer, and that he is playing a major role on the world stage, as before. And if a negotiating process is announced according to the Russian scenario, then coordinating structures will be required in order to produce a defense strategy and develop diplomatic agencies. No one can carry out that function better than Gorbachev."[14]

Translated into plain language, Burbulis's proposal meant the following. The revolutionary takeover of the center by Russian institutions immediately after the coup had failed. Because of the position taken by the leaders of the Union republics and George Bush, Yeltsin was obliged to work with the center. His advisers were prepared to turn the center into an ally. If Gorbachev cooperated, he could provide a screen for Russian hegemony in the Union and help maintain it. The Russian proposal was formally based on confederal principles, corresponding in that sense to the informal Yeltsin-Gorbachev agreement reached a few weeks earlier. But that was not what Gorbachev wanted from the impending negotiations. His ultimate goal was a union state with a strong center, and he was prepared to bend every effort to get it.

While Yeltsin vacationed in Sochi, the struggling Soviet president gained unexpected support from two of his staunchest allies: the mayors of Moscow, Gavriil Popov, and of St. Petersburg, Anatolii Sobchak. Their millions of citizens depended on food supplies from the Union republics to survive the winter, which required the prompt restoration of all-Union ties. Gorbachev was their only hope to achieve that. "Leningrad has been taken off the Union and republican supply network; we have ceased to receive provisions from Ukraine and Kazakhstan," reported Sobchak at a meeting of Gorbachev's political council on October 2. "In return for what we supply, I could feed ten Leningrads. If this does not change, I will forbid the shipping of tractors to Ukraine and cut off supplies to the republics that do not carry out their obligations." Vladimir Putin, then Sobchak's aide in charge of foreign relations, later recalled Sobchak's anger at what was going on in Moscow. "What are they doing? Why are they destroying the country?" he said to Putin.[15]

Although the republican leaders in Russia, Ukraine, and Kazakhstan had serious reservations about plans to create a new union, most of them agreed on the need for an economic agreement to reestablish a common market. Gorbachev originally declared that the economic treaty would be signed before the political one. But with only a few days left before a meeting of republican prime ministers scheduled for October 1 to discuss the economic treaty, he abruptly changed course and began to insist that the political treaty be signed before the economic one. His hope was that economic necessity would force the republican leaders to endorse his draft union treaty.

This sudden shift of position created consternation not only among the republican leaders but also in Gorbachev's own camp. Grigorii Yavlinsky, the chief architect of the economic agreement, was prepared to resign. When he told Anatolii Cherniaev what was going on, Gorbachev's loyal aide exploded. "What has he done? Has he gone off his rocker?" wrote Cherniaev in his diary. "There will be no union treaty! What is wrong with him: does he not see that Russia is provoking this so that [[the other republics will]] go off in all directions, and then Russia, 'in splendid isolation,' will proceed to dictate its conditions to them, to 'save' them by getting around Gorbachev, who will be completely unnecessary!!!"[16]

Gorbachev apparently believed that he could get away with sudden shifts like the one described by Cherniaev because both the Russian president and the republican leaders needed him. The republics were uneasy about Yeltsin's hegemonic behavior and wanted the center to restrain Russia's growing ambitions. Yeltsin, on the other hand, needed the center as an instrument through which he could influence the behavior of the republics. Feeling the shift in the political situation, Gorbachev again began to use the tactic that had worked so well with the party apparatchiks—threatening resignation. "I will not take part in a funeral for the Union," he told Yeltsin a few days before the Russian president's departure for Sochi. The tactic did not work. It actually backfired. Nazarbayev, the host of the economic forum, which took place on October 1, 1991, rejected Gorbachev's proposal to link an economic agreement with a political one, maintaining that the economic agreement should be primarily among the republics. Gorbachev was effectively shut out of the meeting, which turned out to be a success: the prime ministers of eight Soviet republics, including Russia and Kazakhstan, initialed a treaty intended to restore commercial and economic ties between the republics.[17]

AS HE HAD OFTEN DONE in the past, Gorbachev refused to give up. He insisted on adding a political treaty to the agenda of a State Council meeting scheduled for October 11 that involved the heads of the republics and was to discuss economic cooperation. He also asked his advisers to send the new draft union treaty to the republics. Prepared by Shakhnazarov and Sergei Shakhrai, who represented Yeltsin, the draft reflected a confederal vision. But before it went to the republics, Gorbachev insisted on further changes. He wanted to replace references to a "union of states" with "union state," add provisions for a union constitution, and arrange for the election of the union president by popular vote, not by the parliamentary assembly. Shakhnazarov was opposed to making any changes, reminding Gorbachev that he had already agreed to a confederation, which meant a "union of states," not a "union state." Gorbachev was not pleased, retorting, "You are going to lecture me? I don't need you to tell me that: I studied it in university. . . . The point now is not the wording but the essence of the matter. Be so good as to write 'union state.' I do not want to hear any objections." The draft with Gorbachev's changes was sent to the republics.[18]

To Gorbachev's great disappointment, the political treaty was removed from the agenda of the State Council meeting of October 11. Leonid Kravchuk of Ukraine told Gorbachev that the Ukrainian parliament had voted to suspend its participation in negotiations on the new union treaty until the referendum of December 1, when

Ukrainians would vote on their independence. Gorbachev was visibly upset by this major change in Ukraine's position. Kravchuk had previously taken part in the discussions on the premise that if the referendum did not confirm parliament's vote for independence, Ukraine would join the Union, which Kravchuk envisioned as a confederation. Now Ukraine was withdrawing from negotiations altogether. Gorbachev proposed that the State Council issue an appeal to the Ukrainian parliament, asking it to suspend its decision not to participate in the preparation of the treaty.

"The Ukrainian parliament will confirm its decision," responded Kravchuk.

"God be with you, and we will cleanse our soul!" was Gorbachev's reply.[19]

With political union off the table, the economic agreement took center stage at the State Council deliberations on October 11. The presentation on the agreement was made by Grigorii Yavlinsky, Gorbachev's main economic adviser. This was Yavlinsky's third attempt to convince those in power to accept his vision of economic transformation. The first one was undertaken in 1990 with the development of the 500 Days Program for the market transformation of the Soviet economy. After initially embracing the program, Gorbachev had abandoned it in the fall of that year. In July 1991, working with Jeffrey Sachs of Harvard University, Yavlinsky had prepared another plan for economic reform to be presented at the G-7 summit in London. It was dismissed by first world leaders as insufficient. Now Yavlinsky presented a revised program, adjusted to the new circumstances of a crumbling Union.

Anatolii Cherniaev, who attended the meeting, thought Yavlinsky did an excellent job of presenting the draft treaty to the council. He termed Yavlinsky's performance "literacy instruction and cultural enlightenment for the illiterate republican presidents." Cherniaev was appalled by what he regarded as the inability of the republican leaders to grasp the basic principles of a market economy. "The primitivism is striking," recorded Gorbachev's aide in his diary. Cherniaev was perfectly right to note that few of the republican leaders, who had risen through party ranks under the Soviet command economy, had a good knowledge of the principles of a market economy. But they clearly understood the interests of their republics and their own interests as leaders when they insisted on joint republican control over the central bank, despite Yavlinsky's best efforts to persuade them otherwise.[20]

The position taken by the leaders of the republics boded nothing good for the common financial space, and it did not sit well with Cherniaev or with Boris Pankin, the Soviet foreign minister (and also a product of the Moscow liberal establishment), both of whom attended the meeting. Pankin later expressed in his memoirs the shock he felt on witnessing the debates at the State Council: the formerly all-powerful center "was now squeezed into a single room, and a good half of it was represented by the leaders of independent republics." Pankin looked with horror upon the new leaders defining the fate of whatever was left of his country. "Who were these unfamiliar new men on the State Council? Who were these new khans from the outer regions of the Soviet Union?" he wrote in retrospect.

Pankin characterized Kravchuk, who reminded him of one of Gogol's characters, as a "plumpish" man with a "strong sense of self-satisfaction and self-importance." Ayaz Mutalibov, the leader of Azerbaijan, struck Pankin as "a teenage street thug who had grown up and lost touch with his bad companions but never quite shed his old habits." Saparmurat Niyazov of Turkmenistan reminded him of "a chairman of a first-class collective farm," and Askar Akaev of Kyrgyzstan, of "a local educator from the 1920s." The forty-six-year-old Akaev was in fact one of the leading Soviet specialists in optics and a former head of the Kyrgyz Academy of Sciences. He was also the only Central Asian president who opposed the coup. To Pankin, all the republican presidents shared one key trait—they were provincials who had no idea how to run a great country.[21]

Both Pankin and Cherniaev felt desperate. For decades they and their cohort of educated and liberal-minded apparatchiks had had to serve party bosses sent to Moscow by the provincial party elite. In Gorbachev, they had finally found a provincial with an amazing aptitude for learning and changing both himself and the country according to their standards. But Gorbachev was now sinking fast, along with the country they loved. Before their very eyes, power was devolving to a pack of colonial administrators whom they found even less enlightened than the old elite, which had acquired some elements of imperial sophistication after spending years in Moscow. The barbarians were taking over Rome.

Yeltsin, who had just returned to Moscow from his Sochi vacation, sat silent for most of the State Council meeting. "Throughout the six hours of the State Council, Yeltsin, as sullen as he was wont to be at the Politburo, did not open his mouth," noted Cherniaev in his diary. The Russian president had good reason for his attitude. Although he had privately endorsed the Burbulis Memorandum, which set Russia on the path of economic reform irrespective of the wishes and economic needs of other republics, he was politically in no position to come out against the agreement, which allowed the republics to issue currency on their own terms and, as Burbulis believed, flood Russia with worthless rubles and deplete it of its resources. One reason for Yeltsin's silence was that his government was still divided on the issue of economic reform. Another was the promise he had given Gorbachev to support the economic agreement. And then there was a promise he gave to President Bush.

George Bush had unexpectedly called Yeltsin in Sochi late in the evening of October 8, two days before Yeltsin's return to Moscow. He repeated his previous offer to Yeltsin: the Russian leader could come to the United States for medical treatment if necessary. But that was not the main reason for his call. The White House was alarmed by news from the US embassy in Moscow indicating that the Russian government was withdrawing its support for the economic treaty. "Clearly this is an internal matter, not really any of my business," said Bush. "But I just wanted to share one thought with you. Some voluntary economic union could be an important step for clarifying who owns what, and who's in charge, thus facilitating humanitarian assistance, and any economic investment which might be forthcoming." Bush was trying to cajole the Russian president into the economic union with a promise of humanitarian help.

Yeltsin admitted to Bush that his government was split on the issue but promised that he would do his best to sign the economic treaty. Knowing Bush's attachment to Gorbachev, or perhaps even suspecting that Bush might be acting on behalf of the Soviet president, Yeltsin stressed that he was working together with Gorbachev. "I called President Gorbachev," Yeltsin told Bush, "and we agreed that on October 11 we will get together in Moscow, hear reports, and then Russia will sign the treaty." Yeltsin presented this as an actual sacrifice of Russia's interests. "We understand we have the least to gain; as a matter of fact we might even lose something," he told Bush. "But we'll sign because of the bigger political goal—to save the Union. As President I do have that right, even though it may be tough to get through the Supreme Soviet for approval."[22]

On the face of it, Yeltsin kept his promise to Bush. On the evening of October 18 the Russian president went to the Kremlin along with the leaders of the other republics to sign the treaty declaring the creation of an economic community of "independent states." An uneasy compromise was reached on control of the central bank and coinage of currency: the all-Union bank was to be administered by a commission of representatives of the central and republican banks, but the latter had to accept limits on the amount of currency they could issue. There was no indication, however, that Yeltsin intended to honor the treaty: he said right away that Russia would not ratify the treaty unless thirty additional agreements on specific issues important to Russia were signed as well.[23]

Earlier that day the Russian president had given a speech that threw a wrench into the restoration of the former Union. He announced that Russia was cutting off funds to most all-Union ministries, noting that "the task is to do away with the remains of the unitary imperial structures as quickly as possible and create inexpensive interrepublican ones." In September, Russia had nationalized oil and gas enterprises on its territory and taken over the revenue they had previously contributed to all-Union coffers. By enriching Russia and bankrupting the Union, the Russian leaders gained a potent new weapon to use against the center. In mid-October, the Russian parliament voted to declare the decisions of all-Union bodies, including Gorbachev's State Council, nonbinding on the Russian Federation. Yeltsin issued a similar decree with regard to Gosplan, the all-Union economic planning body. Bush's call made Yeltsin sign the economic agreement, but there was little that the American president could do to ensure that Yeltsin would actually honor it or that his actions would not lead to the further weakening of the Union.[24]

YEGOR GAIDAR WAS in Rotterdam at the invitation of Erasmus University when he received an urgent call to come back home: Yeltsin wanted to see him. Gaidar knew what the call might mean— the end of his comfortable life as an academic adviser and the beginning of perhaps the most unpopular and painful reform in Russian history. Although Gaidar did not look forward to overseeing it, he was not prepared to reject the prospect. When he told his father what might await him, the old man, who had served as a Soviet military correspondent in Cuba and Afghanistan, could not conceal his horror. Schooled in the Stalinist dogma that freedom meant the recognition of necessity, the elder Gaidar gave his blessing: "If you are certain that there is no other way, then do as you think best."[25]

Gaidar believed, as did Burbulis and his entourage, that the plan they proposed was the only way to prevent economic collapse. He also believed that Yeltsin was the only politician prepared to take a risk and implement his reforms. "For a politician, Yeltsin has a decent understanding of economics and is generally aware of what is going on in the country," wrote Gaidar, recording his first reactions to the meeting he had with the Russian president after returning from Amsterdam. "He understands the tremendous risk associated with the initiation of reforms, and he understands how suicidal it is to remain passive and await developments." Gaidar's friends believed that he had fallen under the spell of Yeltsin's personality and would remain charmed for years.[26]

Yeltsin was no less impressed by his young guest. He saw him as a representative of the Russian intelligentsia who, "unlike the dull bureaucrats in the government administration, would not hide his opinions" but defend them no matter what. Another quality of Gaidar's that Yeltsin found attractive was his ability to explain complex economic issues in simple terms. "Listening to him," wrote Yeltsin, "you would start to see the route we had to take." He also had a program that no one else was proposing and a group of people ready to implement his plan—a quick, decisive reform that would produce results within a year. Furthermore, Gaidar made Yeltsin believe that if he did not do something drastic about the economy, he would share the fate of Gorbachev, who kept promising reform but never delivered it and was now on his way out.[27]

Burbulis, who had brought Gaidar and Yeltsin together, believed that they had immediately forged a cultural bond. Like most Soviets of his generation, Yeltsin knew and admired the writings of Gaidar's paternal grandfather, Arkadii Gaidar; like the natives of the Ural region, he had the highest regard for the writings of Gaidar's maternal grandfather, Pavel Bazhov, the author of a collection of tales based on Ural folklore and titled *The Malachite Casket*. "It was a bonding of the rarest sort," said Burbulis, recalling the first meeting between Yeltsin and Gaidar. "There was a sudden realization: we are from the same lands, the same volcanic origins, the same root." The growing Sverdlovsk mafia in the Kremlin was finding recruits in the most unexpected places.

The common roots that Burbulis mentioned were not only geographic but also ideological. Both of Gaidar's grandfathers were devoted Bolsheviks who had fought in the Revolution of 1917. Burbulis believed that Gaidar and Yeltsin shared the particular historical and cultural matrix of early Bolshevism. "There was the utopianism, the mythology of Bolshevik daring, and service to an idea—this is also present in that fellow," remarked Burbulis about Gaidar. "And that historico-cultural and socio-romantic code—it was all there in compressed form." Both of Gaidar's grandfathers had helped suppress peasant uprisings against communist rule. Now their grandson had chosen to lead the country back to a world in which the private property defended by the rebellious peasants would rule supreme. In both cases, the process was extremely painful. The Bolshevik wholesale assault on capitalism was now to be followed by a similar assault on the communist economic system. Yegor Gaidar would take no prisoners.[28]

ALTHOUGH YELTSIN had given his assent to the Burbulis Memorandum on the Sochi beach, he did not publicize it and probably did not make a final decision on it until his meeting with Gaidar. But once he made up his mind, developments proceeded with breathtaking speed. Yeltsin prepared to present his reform plan and request special powers for its implementation at a session of the Russian Congress of Deputies—the Russian superparliament—scheduled for October 28. A few days before the session, news of the content of the reform and of Yeltsin's speech reached the Gorbachev circle. On October 22, Gorbachev's aide Vadim Medvedev noted in his diary, "It seems that a general liberalization of prices will be announced, and that without any connection to tougher banking regulations on currency circulation or limitations on budgetary deficits. . . . The next few days will show where things are heading, but the Russian leadership is obviously inclined toward the extreme choice—full independence for the republic."[29]

While Gorbachev was left in the dark about what to expect from Yeltsin's impending speech, Yeltsin called Bush on October 25 to inform him about the coming major turn in Russian policy, "following the tradition between us in talking about very important matters." He said, "I will announce substantial economic plans and programs and say that we are ready to go quickly to free up prices, all at the same time, privatization, financial and land reform. All this will be done during the next four to five months, maybe six months. It will be a one-time effort. It will increase inflation and lower living standards. But I have a popular mandate and am ready to do this. We'll have results by next year." Yeltsin offered to send his foreign minister, Andrei Kozyrev, to Washington to explain the Russian reform plan, and Bush expressed interest in meeting him. "It sounds like an ambitious program. I congratulate you on a tough decision," he said. They ended the conversation as old friends, with Yeltsin informing Bush that he had benefited from his two-week vacation. "I am full of energy, playing tennis, and my heart is good," he assured Bush. "I am fine."[30]

Bush spoke with Yeltsin on October 25, 1991. Three days later, on October 28, the Russian president addressed his parliament with probably the most fateful speech in its short history. "I turn to you at one of the most critical moments in Russian history," said Yeltsin at the beginning of his address, which lasted close to an hour and was titled "An Appeal to the Peoples of Russia and to the Congress of People's Deputies of the Russian Federation." "It is being decided at this very time what Russia and the country as a whole will be like in the years and decades to follow; how present and future generations of Russians will live. I resolutely call on you to embark unconditionally on the path of deep reforms and for support from all strata of the population for that resolution." Yeltsin declared that the government was planning to free prices and cut spending, including food subsidies.

The first stage will be the hardest. There will be some reduction in the standard of living, but uncertainty will finally disappear, and a clear prospect will emerge. The main thing is that in deeds, not words, we will finally begin to emerge from the quicksand that is pulling us in ever deeper. If we embark on this path today, we will already have results by autumn. If we do not take advantage of this real chance to reverse the unfavorable course of events, we will doom ourselves to poverty and a state with a centuries-old history to destruction.

"Reforms in Russia are the path to democracy, not to empire," continued Yeltsin, taking up the subject of relations between the Union center and the republics. He announced that Russia would cease to finance most Union ministries by November 1, a mere three days after his speech. Interrepublican institutions would be limited to coordinating relations among the republics, and Russia would not allow the restoration of the old all-powerful center. But Yeltsin was not giving up on the Union entirely. He encouraged Ukraine, whose leadership refused to sign the economic treaty, to join the economic union and threatened that any republics conducting a policy of "artificial" separation from Russia would be charged world prices for Russian resources. He hoped that the former Soviet republics would also sign a political agreement. In the absence of such an agreement, said Yeltsin, Russia would declare itself the legal successor of the USSR and take over all-Union institutions and property—a move opposed by the leaders of Ukraine and Kazakhstan, among others.[31]

On the following day, Yeltsin asked the Russian parliament to grant him special powers for a year. There would be no elections in 1992, no matter what the results of the transformation. He would personally lead the government and bear full responsibility for the success of the reform. All his requests were granted. "The most popular president is finally prepared for the most unpopular measures. The kamikaze group will be led by Yeltsin," ran the lead article in *Nezavisimaia gazeta*.

The reaction in the non-Russian republics was cautious at best. "Uzbekistan receives some 60 percent of its goods from beyond its borders; a great deal comes from Russia," said Islam Karimov of Uzbekistan. "Hence the liberalization of prices in the RSFSR will affect Uzbekistan, and we will be obliged to take defensive measures." That sounded like an end not only to the old Soviet Union but also to the economic agreement that was supposed to keep the common market in existence.[32]

The Russian ark was leaving the Soviet dock.

12

THE SURVIVOR

IN LATE OCTOBER THE CUSTODIANS OF the Palacio Real de Madrid, the official residence of the king of Spain, received a request from the state administration to remove one of its most magnificent paintings from its walls. The canvas, which featured Charles V, the early-sixteenth-century Holy Roman emperor and king of Spain, was not going for restoration. It was to be stored in a warehouse. The palace was being readied for the opening of an international summit on the Middle East scheduled for October 29, and the depiction of a Christian ruler massacring Muslims was clearly inappropriate for the occasion. Madrid had been chosen over Washington, Cairo, Geneva, and The Hague as the most appropriate venue for the first high-level meeting between Israeli and Palestinian leaders in more than forty years. They agreed to meet with the leaders of Egypt, Syria, and other countries of the region to discuss peace—the beginning of a process that would ultimately lead to the Oslo Accords in 1993 and the longest peace in recent Israeli history.[1]

There would have been no Madrid conference without the new spirit of cooperation between the United States and the Soviet Union, the two Cold War superpowers that had competed in the Middle East for decades, funding and arming opposing sides in the Arab-Israeli conflict. George Bush and Mikhail Gorbachev served as official cosponsors of the conference. "President Bush and President Gorbachev request your acceptance of this invitation," read the letter addressed to potential participants, including the heads of European and Middle Eastern states and the leadership of the Palestine Liberation Organization. They all agreed to come or send high-level delegations.

The agreement to call a conference was reached during George H. W. Bush's visit to Moscow in July. Paving the road to Madrid had begun eight months earlier in Paris. European heads of state met there in November 1990 with the leaders of the United States and Canada for what was dubbed the peace conference of the Cold War. They took advantage of recent developments in Eastern Europe, the fall of the Berlin Wall, and the disappearance of the Iron Curtain to approve the Charter of Paris for a New Europe—a document that bridged the East-West divide in institutional and ideological terms, laying solid foundations for the establishment of the Organization for Security and Cooperation in Europe.[2]

James Baker believed that it was there and then that the Cold War had indeed come to an end. His belief was based not so much on the signed Charter of Paris as on the actions of the Soviet Union, whose leaders had agreed for the first time since the Yalta Conference of 1945 to work together with the United States in solving a major international crisis—the invasion of Kuwait by Saddam Hussein's Iraq a few months earlier. In Paris, responding to a direct request from President Bush, Mikhail Gorbachev agreed to cosponsor a resolution of the United Nations Security Council authorizing the use of force against Saddam Hussein. Gorbachev overruled his hard-line advisers and kept his word, giving Bush and an international coalition of states the opportunity to attack Saddam, drive him out of Kuwait, and place Iraq under siege.[3]

After the United States' victory in the Gulf War, the American stake in the region grew tremendously, creating an opportunity for Washington to push for a peace conference between Israel and its Arab neighbors. The Soviet Union supported the initiative, which took on new momentum after the failure of the Moscow coup and the appointment of Boris Pankin as Soviet foreign minister. The Soviets, who had abrogated diplomatic relations with Israel after the Six-Day War of 1967, restored them in October 1991. To Washington's surprise, they did so without consulting Syria, their main ally in the region. Events in the Middle East were going America's way. That month, President Bush commented on the new Soviet policy to a visiting Middle Eastern dignitary, the emir of Bahrain: "We don't see them coming back to threaten our interest in the Middle East." James Baker would begin his numerous meetings with Middle Eastern leaders, from Prime Minister Yitzhak Shamir of Israel to President Hafez al-Assad of Syria, with the same confident phrase: "The Soviets remain fully on board."[4]

Mikhail Gorbachev was definitely on board with America's plans for the future of the Middle East, but developments in the USSR were putting into question the commitments he was about to make in the international arena. This precarious situation echoed another recent dramatic development in international politics. The Paris summit of November 1990, which opened the road to the Madrid peace conference, turned out to be the last international conference attended by Prime Minister Margaret Thatcher of Britain. While she attended the negotiations in the French capital, a vote took place in her own party caucus in the British parliament that forced her to resign. For the British, this was a reprise of the Potsdam Conference at the end of the Second World War, when Winston Churchill was abruptly removed from office by British voters. Now there were well-grounded fears that Madrid could become the last international conference of another heavyweight in international politics—Mikhail Gorbachev.

"Reports [[arrived]] recently that he might not be around long," recorded Bush in his diary on the eve of his departure for Madrid. "The briefing book indicates this might be my last meeting with him of this nature. Time marches on." A few minutes earlier, Bush had dictated into his tape recorder,

> It is clear to me that things are an awful lot different regarding Gorbachev and the Center than they were. He's growing weaker all the time. I am anxious to see what his mood is. He is still import-ant in nuclear matters, but all the economic stuff—it looks to me like the republics have been more and more asserting themselves. It will be interesting to figure out his mood. I remember not so long ago how he couldn't stand Yeltsin. How he up at Camp David [[in June 1990]] made clear he didn't think Yeltsin was going anywhere. But now all that has changed.[5]

Gorbachev was not in good humor as he left Moscow for Madrid on the afternoon of October 28. Yeltsin was now at the center of attention in the Soviet capital. The forthcoming US-Soviet summit and the international peace conference that would normally have dominated the news were now secondary issues. And whatever coverage made it into the media was often unfavorable to Gorbachev. "'Emissary of non-existent state' was typical of the headlines in the Moscow press," recalled Soviet foreign minister Boris Pankin. Gorbachev was acutely sensitive to such slights. In Madrid a reporter asked him an innocent question: "Since your departure from Moscow, who is taking your place in Moscow?" The Soviet president took offense. "I'm still the president," he responded. "Nobody is taking my place. Everybody else is doing what they're supposed to be doing and carrying out their functions. . . . Nobody is going to take me out of the action."[6]

Raisa Gorbacheva agreed to accompany her husband on his trip to Madrid. She had partially recovered from her August stroke, but her eyesight had deteriorated. The Crimean experience would haunt her for the rest of her life. With Yeltsin now in the Kremlin, she ceased to go there. As Gorbachev's power visibly waned, she found the people around him less accommodating than before. She had a clash with Gorbachev's loyal assistant Anatolii Cherniaev, who was now avoiding his boss's wife. Initially he refused to go to Madrid for that reason, but Gorbachev made him come. On the flight to Madrid, as Cherniaev and other presidential aides discussed the summit, Raisa sat reading on a couch at the other end of the cabin.

Her own book, *I Hope,* which appeared in the United States in September, made it onto the *New York Times* best-seller list, but there were few people present with whom to share the excitement. Barbara Bush, who had inspired her to write the book by bringing her to the Wellesley College commencement in June 1990, was not coming to Madrid. This in itself reduced the significance of the coming US-Soviet encounter, lowering its status from that of an official visit to a working visit. Until the very end, the Soviet side did not know who would be waiting for the Gorbachevs when they landed in Madrid. Then news reached the presidential plane that Prime Minister Felipe González of Spain and his wife, Carmen Romero, had come to the airport. "I sensed that this news cheered up the president a little," remembered Boris Pankin.[7]

González showed genuine respect for the Soviet president. It was a meeting of two allies and confidants, if not friends. Gorbachev had a natural affinity for González, the son of a farmer who had become general secretary of the Spanish Workers' Party and eventually prime minister. González, for his part, had genuine respect for Gorbachev. On hearing of the August coup, he took the most principled stand of any Western leader. While François Mitterrand of France came near to accepting it as a fait accompli and Bush was indecisive at first, González immediately released a communiqué, which he drafted himself, denouncing the event as a coup d'état. Now he told Gorbachev, "Mikhail, during those days I had the impression that the West had accepted what had happened as a fait accompli and was ready to resign itself to it."

González believed that having once shown readiness to write Gorbachev off, the Western leaders might well do so again. "I conclude that today Western political leaders are in doubt about the ability of the Soviet Union to preserve itself and, therefore, proceed from the possible scenarios, including the disintegration of the USSR," González told Gorbachev. "It's quite depressing." González's words impressed Gorbachev strongly enough for him to reproduce them a few years later in his memoirs. During his last years in office, as things deteriorated at home, Gorbachev would take comfort in visits abroad and exchanges with his Western friends. Those times were coming to an end. Even in the West, he was no longer exactly on home turf. He was cutting a diminished and increasingly pathetic figure.[8]

Alexander M. Haig, the former secretary of state in the Reagan administration, went on record with a political obituary for Gorbachev: "Mr. Gorbachev is yesterday's leader, to whom we owe a great debt because he didn't resort to force to prevent the breakup of the empire, but as far as the future is concerned, is history." Journalists on both the American and Soviet sides knew who was really running the show in Madrid. *Pravda* reported on a briefing in which the head of protocol of the Spanish Foreign Ministry told reporters, "The music is requested by the Americans, the ballet ensemble consists of the conference participants, and we make the stage available to them." The same sentiment was expressed in a *New York Times* article that discussed, among other things, the white tent installed at the entrance to the Soviet embassy, where Bush and Gorbachev met before the conference. "The tent tactic said something about the diminution of Soviet power," wrote Alan Cowell. "Americans proposed it, Spaniards stitched it and Soviets agreed to it."[9]

GORBACHEV MET WITH BUSH for a working lunch in the new building of the Soviet embassy on October 29, the day after his arrival in Madrid. The meeting "was warm, even cordial, especially while the cameras were rolling," remembered Gorbachev's foreign minister, Boris Pankin. The encounter began with the two men catching up on developments since their last meeting in July. Discussion naturally turned to the coup, raising the insecurities Gorbachev had felt at the time.

"It was stupid to try to overthrow you," said Bush to Gorbachev.

"This is what generals do sometimes," responded Gorbachev, pointing jokingly at General Scowcroft.

"If Brent Scowcroft wants my job, or Baker for that matter, they can have it," offered Bush.

But the joke wore thin for Gorbachev. "I don't want to abandon my job," he said to Bush.

The statement prompted Bush to raise an eventuality that could not be ignored: "This may be an improper question, but do you have a concern about a second attempted takeover?" Gorbachev answered that he believed the odds were on his side. He pinned his hopes on the signing of a new union treaty.

While Gorbachev did his best to communicate his cautious optimism about the Soviet future to the American president, Bush showed greater interest in nuclear security than in anything else. He wanted to reduce the Soviet nuclear arsenals as much as possible while Gorbachev was still in a position to do so. "I'd like to hear your view," said Bush. "This is a situation where the center has a role, and you have a stake."

Gorbachev assured Bush that there was nothing to fear. "George," he said, "a lot of what you hear in the press is not reliable. The press may have a duty to say such things." He went on to say that despite inflated political rhetoric, Leonid Kravchuk had committed Ukraine to seek nonnuclear status. So had Nursultan Nazarbayev of Kazakhstan, and Yeltsin had just recently avowed that he was in favor of central control over the military.[10]

But whereas nuclear weapons were at the top of the American agenda, money headed the Soviet one. Gorbachev wanted massive US assistance. "We all understand what is at stake," he said. "What happens with the Union will have consequences for the whole world." Gorbachev spoke explicitly: "Let me be very frank. $10–$15 billion is not much for us, and repayment is not a serious problem." This was not an amount that the Americans were prepared to consider. "I can tell you what I can do now," answered Bush, "$1.5 billion for the winter while you sort out the union-republic situation. If that is insulting to you, I will go back and consult and see what might be done." Gorbachev responded that he needed $3.5 billion to deal with the food crisis before the new harvest. James Baker joined the conversation and signaled that the United States could offer no more than Bush had just done. Allegedly, he told Gorbachev's interpreter, Pavel Palazhchenko, in private, "Take a billion and a half in ready cash; take it before we reconsider. Too little? We can't give any more."

That was the end of the aid package negotiations. The position of the republics with regard to the Soviet debt, which they had not taken on and were not eager to pay, concerned Bush and his advisers, who were under growing pressure to do something, if not to save Gorbachev then to protect the population of his country from possible hunger. The Bush administration was prepared to open its purse more widely than anyone could have suggested a few months earlier, but only to feed the hungry and help avert a social explosion that could bring the hard-liners back and put nuclear weapons in the wrong hands. For Gorbachev, who had tried and failed to persuade Bush to come up with major financial assistance at the July G-7 summit in London, the American proposal probably did not come as a surprise. He would later even express some satisfaction with Bush's offer.

Even though Bush and Gorbachev were agreed that the main task of the Madrid peace conference was to provide an opportunity for the two sides in the Middle East conflict to meet and begin discussions, the conference itself got surprisingly little attention at their preliminary meeting. Bush wanted the Soviets to keep encouraging the Syrian and Palestinian leaders to take part in the peace process. Gorbachev promised his assistance while making his own requests. The Soviet global agenda was now dwindling to the Slavic and Orthodox world, the traditional arena of the tsars and the focus of Russian foreign policy in decades to come. Gorbachev wanted the United States to persuade its Turkish allies to be more accommodating in dealing with the Greek Cypriots and to get the United Nations more involved in resolving the Yugoslav crisis, which had already claimed its first victims. He made little headway: Bush promised no support with regard to Cyprus and was skeptical about Yugoslavia.[11]

Not surprisingly, most of the questions at the press conference that Bush and Gorbachev held after their meeting dealt with the situation in the Soviet Union, not the Middle East peace process. Cherniaev recorded in his diary, "Bush tried to avoid making a show of the difference in weight categories, and Mikhail Sergeevich was not one who would have allowed it. . . . He acted as if nothing was amiss." But according to Pavel Palazhchenko, that made little impression on the audience. "As they watched Gorbachev," he wrote later about the reaction of the American delegation, "their expressions were skeptical, cold and indifferent. . . . To them he [[was]] already a goner." That day Palazhchenko had a feeling that "an era was definitely coming to a close." Boris Pankin blamed Bush for showing little support for his counterpart. He felt that despite appearances, something important was missing. "It gradually dawned on me what was wrong," Pankin recalled. "Gorbachev was irritated and concerned by media speculation about the disintegration of the Soviet Union and his own precarious position. He knew that President Bush was receiving much the same information that he was, and he expected Bush to give some indication of support, to send some signal. But Bush sent no signal."[12]

If Bush did send a signal, Pankin was in no position to hear it. He was in a sour mood in Madrid. He was about to become a minister without a ministry. News had reached him in the Spanish capital that in his speech on economic reform, Yeltsin had put Pankin's ministry on the chopping block, demanding that it be reduced to a tenth of its size and even threatening to cut off funding altogether.

On the eve of the Madrid conference, the announcement of planned cuts made by the Russian foreign minister, Andrei Kozyrev, caused an uproar in Washington. Bush and James Baker instructed the US ambassador in Moscow, Bob Strauss, to meet as soon as possible with Kozyrev to discuss the unexpected cuts to Pankin's ministry. With the Madrid conference about to start in a few days, Yeltsin's apparent drastic reduction of the all-Union center, including its international arm, presented a major threat to American plans for a peace settlement between Israel and the Palestinians. Kozyrev assured Strauss that what he had said was merely an expression of his frustration with the ministry's policy of ignoring Russia. The problem seemed to have been resolved. But now, in Madrid, Pankin learned that despite Kozyrev's assurances to the contrary, Yeltsin had gone ahead and announced the cuts.[13]

Pankin tried to maintain a brave face, telling the international press that "Boris Nikolaevich must have been speaking figuratively," but the situation was spinning out of control. His subordinates in the Soviet Ministry of Foreign Affairs began a mutiny. A petition demanding Pankin's return to Moscow was signed by some of the ministry's most prominent employees and reached the minister in Madrid. The petition "had the nerve to say that rather than establishing peace in the Middle East I should hurry back home and set about saving the Foreign Ministry," recalled Pankin. He refused to do so. He would return only when he believed that his world mission was fully accomplished.[14]

The Foreign Ministry petition highlighted the gap between the grand façade of Soviet diplomacy and the misery of the Union government's everyday existence. The collapse of Union institutions, which was gathering speed in Moscow, seemed a nightmare that many in Madrid—not only members of the Soviet delegation—simply wanted to forget. After all, it was interfering with the realization of a dream that Western leaders had cherished for generations, that of establishing lasting peace in the Middle East. Now, when that dream seemed within reach, the partner they were counting on to make the process work was about to disappear.

The Americans worked hard to keep the dream alive by helping the Soviet center send representatives abroad and play its role in the grand Middle Eastern gala. The Soviets rose to the occasion. Like old aristocrats who had lost all their possessions to nouveaux riches but would not give up their extravagant lifestyle, the Soviet leaders came to Madrid for their last ball. Everyone appreciated their presence, but the conference itself was considered an exclusively American success. In the dozens of congratulatory letters received afterward by its main organizer and promoter, James Baker, there was no mention whatever of the Soviet Union.[15]

THE TRUE HIGHLIGHT of Gorbachev's visit to Madrid was the dinner he attended with Bush and Felipe González at the invitation of the Spanish king, Juan Carlos. There the Soviet leader got all the emotional support he was longing for. In his memoirs, Gorbachev called the dinner and the four-hour conversation "truly unique" and "amazingly candid." He and Raisa, who later departed with the queen, leaving the four men alone, recalled their ordeal in the Crimea. Juan Carlos, himself a survivor of a military coup and head of a country with its own nationality problems, represented most vividly by Basque separatism, could not have been more supportive. So was Felipe González. The dinner hosted by the Spanish king made the whole trip worthwhile for Gorbachev. Despite all the problems and humiliations, the Madrid conference ultimately accomplished what all his previous foreign visits had done for him: it boosted his morale and helped recharge his batteries for the continuing fight back home.[16]

Another psychological boost came from a most unexpected quarter: President François Mitterrand, who invited the Gorbachevs to visit him at his modest estate in southern France on their way back to Moscow. They accepted. Unlike González, who had stood by Gorbachev during the first and most difficult hours of the coup, Mitterrand had made an initial statement that many interpreted as de facto recognition. He had corrected his position by the end of the day, and the people around Gorbachev blamed the faux pas on the Soviet ambassador in Paris. Now Mitterrand insisted on seeing Gorbachev. He wanted to support his struggle to preserve the Union and did so more than once during the Soviet leader's impromptu visit to his estate.

"History teaches us through the centuries," he told Gorbachev, according to Cherniaev's diary, "that France needs an ally to maintain the European balance. . . . We are great friends of today's Germans. But it would be very dangerous if there were a soft underbelly north or east of Germany. Because the Germans will always be tempted to penetrate in those directions." Gorbachev could not have agreed more. Indeed, the two leaders agreed on almost everything, including the threat of German economic expansion, the unduly cozy relations between the United States and Israel, and the need to preserve Yugoslavia. They discussed the new architecture of Europe, almost always seeing eye to eye.[17]

Gorbachev was obviously in his element. As the two presidents were joined by their wives and assistants, he kept talking over cognac and coffee served after dinner. "Mitterrand," remembered Cherniaev, "sitting in a large chair, infrequently 'stopped' the meandering conversation with significant observations . . . with a benevolently condescending smile on his weary face." Cherniaev, one of the architects of Gorbachev's concept of a "common European home" and the European destiny of the Soviet Union, wrote in his diary about the meeting of "two great Europeans at the end of a terrible century, so different and so understandable to each other." But even he could not avoid noting the difference between Mitterrand's private and public behavior. At the press conference that followed their informal talks, Mitterand, like Bush before him, offered very little support for Gorbachev. Such, at least, was the impression of Gorbachev's assistants. "His friends are writing him off," said Palazhchenko to Cherniaev.

On the flight home, Gorbachev gathered a small group of advisers over lunch to share his thoughts on the visit and chart a course for the future. He was pleased and inspired by what he saw as the Western leaders' concern about the future of the USSR. His best strategy, argued Gorbachev, would be to support Yeltsin in his economic reform efforts while pushing ahead with the new union treaty. Everyone agreed. "One person on the plane who seemed pessimistic about the chances of success was Raisa Gorbacheva," wrote Palazhchenko later. "She was not saying much, but it was clear she had grave concerns on her mind."[18]

LIKE GORBACHEV'S RETURN to Moscow after his ordeal in the Crimea, his return from Madrid was to some degree a landing in a different country. Once again, the country was being transformed by Boris Yeltsin. His decision to initiate radical economic reform, which Gorbachev had never had the stomach for and now had no time to implement, made a strong impression on everyone, including Gorbachev's own advisers. "These days are probably decisive after all," noted Anatolii Cherniaev in his diary after his return from Madrid. "Yeltsin's report at the RSFSR congress is certainly a breakthrough to a new country, to a different society."

Yeltsin was eager to show that he meant what he had said in his speech to the Russian parliament. Russia cut funding to the majority of Union ministries. University professors went without paychecks and students without scholarships. Cherniaev expected that by mid-November there would be fifty thousand unemployed ministry officials in Moscow alone. It was the first time that he and his staff in the presidential administration had not received their paychecks:

with Russia withdrawing its funding, there was no money left in the Union coffers. Food shortages became a daily reality. Reinvigorated after his return from Madrid, Gorbachev sensed an opportunity to regain some of his lost political ground. On November 4, at the State Council meeting attended by the leaders of the Union republics, he attacked Yeltsin for his ill-conceived plan for implementing reform.[19]

"Look at what has happened already," said Gorbachev, referring to the consumer panic created by Yeltsin's price liberalization. "Generally, 1,800 [[metric]] tonnes of bread per day are sold in Moscow. But yesterday, it was already 2,800 tonnes! Goods are being snapped up at a furious rate. Stores have started to hold back goods. The markets are deserted: sellers are waiting for prices to rise." Gorbachev launched his attack before Yeltsin entered the room—he was running late—but continued after Yeltsin eventually arrived for the meeting. "That's what always happens when you lag behind events," declared Gorbachev in Yeltsin's presence. "Those around the table looked at each other in amusement," recalled Boris Pankin. "The roles had switched, and now it was Gorbachev reproaching Yeltsin for wasting time."[20]

Gorbachev used the aura of world leader that he had partially recovered in Madrid to advance his main cause—the preservation of the Union. "The West fears the breakup of the Soviet Union," he told the republican leaders. "I assure you that this was the main subject of all my talks in Madrid. They can't understand what's happening here. Just when we are finally on the road to democracy and clearing the debris of totalitarianism. . . . They say the Soviet Union has to be preserved as one of the pillars of the international system." Yeltsin was not impressed. He derailed Gorbachev's attempt to renew discussion of the union treaty by demanding that participants stick to the agenda, which did not include an item on the treaty. But the Russian president showed no hostility toward the idea of union in general. He even voiced support for the continuing existence of joint armed forces. Gorbachev's spokesman, Andrei Grachev, came to the conclusion that Yeltsin had no immediate plans to destroy the Soviet Union.[21]

In the following days Gorbachev extended his offensive against the Russian president by assuming his traditional role of protector of the autonomous republics within the Russian Federation against the "tyranny" of the Russian government. The case in question was Yeltsin's treatment of Chechnia. On Saturday, November 9, in the middle of a four-day holiday break to mark the anniversary of the 1917 Bolshevik Revolution, Anatolii Cherniaev found his boss in his office working the telephones. "What is he doing, what is he doing?" said Gorbachev to Cherniaev, referring to Yeltsin. "There would be hundreds of people killed if it were to start."

The previous evening, central television had announced the Russian president's signing of a decree introducing a state of emergency in Chechnia, a former autonomous republic within the Russian Federation that had recently declared independence. Now Gorbachev was consulting with his security ministers, trying to prevent bloodshed. "I am told that the governor whom he [[Yeltsin]] appointed there has refused to carry out his role," continued Gorbachev to Cherniaev. "Parliament as well. All the factions and groupings that were holding discussions and bickering among themselves have [[now]] united against the 'Russians.' The fighters are already assembling women and children to go in front of them when the troops approach. Idiots!" The last word was meant for Yeltsin and his team.[22]

The roots of the Russo-Chechen conflict that flared up in November 1991 and subsequently engulfed the entire North Caucasus went back to the Russian conquest of the region in the nineteenth century. During World War II, Joseph Stalin ordered all Chechens resettled to Kazakhstan as punishment for their alleged disloyalty. Nikita Khrushchev allowed the Chechens and the Ingush, another North Caucasian people with whom the Chechens shared an autonomous republic and experience of exile, to return to the North Caucasus in the late 1950s. Three decades later, the implementation of perestroika and glasnost allowed the Chechens to assert their identity and make claims for sovereignty and independence. In that regard, they were not very different from other Soviet nationalities.[23]

In June 1991, after Yeltsin's victory in the Russian presidential elections, the Chechen National Congress, a pro-independence organization established in the fall of the previous year, proclaimed a Chechen national republic separate from Ingushetia. A forty-seven-year-old major general named Dzhokhar Dudaev emerged as its leader. A month earlier he had resigned as commander of the Soviet strategic bomber division based in Estonia, where he witnessed the movement of that Baltic republic toward sovereignty and independence. Dudaev wanted the same for his homeland. His people were only slightly less numerous than the Estonians: according to the Soviet census, there were close to 1 million ethnic Estonians and approximately 750,000 ethnic Chechens in their respective homelands. Russians and other Slavs constituted between a quarter and one third of the population in each republic. But there were also significant differences between Estonia and Chechnia. The former had the status of a Union republic, and its right to independence was recognized and promoted by Bush and Yeltsin alike. Chechnia, on the other hand, was a self-proclaimed republic whose right to existence, let alone independence, was recognized by no one.[24]

During the August coup, Dudaev supported the Russian president. "We took control of the situation, organized armed units, localized the MVD [[Ministry of Internal Affairs]] and the KGB, and took over the troops, communications, and railway junctions," recalled Dudaev, summarizing the report he had sent to Yeltsin at the time. The failure of the coup in Moscow strengthened Dudaev's hand in Chechnia but did not make him its leader: officially, power remained in the hands of the established politicians who had supported the plotters. On September 6 Dudaev staged a coup in Groznyi, the capital of the republic. His supporters stormed and took over government buildings. The head of the republican parliament was forced to resign, and the mayor of Groznyi jumped to his death from his office window when the rebels took it over. He became the first high-profile victim of a conflict that would eventually claim hundreds of thousands of lives.[25]

Yeltsin and his advisers, who included Ruslan Khasbulatov, an ethnic Chechen and acting Speaker of the Russian parliament, found themselves in a difficult situation. Their opponents in Chechnia, the old Communist Party cadres, were opposed to Chechen independence, while their supporters, led by Dudaev, were for it. In September and early October Groznyi was visited by scores of Yeltsin's advisers, including Ruslan Khasbulatov and Vice President Aleksandr Rutskoi. The compromise they helped negotiate led to the dissolution of the old republican parliament. Elections were soon organized, but to the disappointment of the Russian authorities, these were not elections to the new republican parliament.[26]

On October 27, in elections boycotted by ethnic Russians and justly criticized for numerous violations of electoral law, General

Dudaev was elected president of Chechnia. His first decree declared the political sovereignty of Chechnia. It looked like the beginning of the disintegration not just of the Soviet Union but also of the Russian Federation. On November 7, Yeltsin countered with a decree proclaiming a state of emergency in Chechnia. On the following day, interior troops were dispatched to Khankala airport, near Groznyi. Fifteen hundred soldiers in police uniforms were supposed to enter Groznyi, depose the new government, and arrest Dudaev and his entourage. On November 8 the entire country learned of Yeltsin's decree on the evening news. It was out in the open.[27]

The Chechens refused to be intimidated and pushed for complete independence from Russia. On the following day, General Dudaev was officially inaugurated as the first president of Chechnia. One day later he issued a decree annulling Yeltsin's proclamation of a state of emergency. The local police began to go over to the rebels, who took over police and KGB installations and began arming the militia— one of Dudaev's earlier decrees had ordered the mobilization of all men age fifteen to fifty-five. Soviet military units in Chechnia were surrounded in their barracks, and Russia's railway connections with the Transcaucasian republics of Armenia, Azerbaijan, and Georgia were blocked.

On November 10, to attract international attention to the Russian actions in Chechnia, three armed Chechens hijacked a Soviet plane with 171 passengers on board and rerouted it to Turkey. Leaving the frightened hostages at the Ankara airport, the hijackers flew on to Groznyi, where they were welcomed as national heroes. It was the first act of terrorism perpetrated in the name of Chechen independence by the twenty-six-year-old Shamil Basaev, who had been among the defenders of the Russian White House a few months earlier. Several years later, he would lead the takeover of the Budennovsk hospital in Gorbachev's native Stavropol region of Russia, holding all its patients hostage.[28]

Vice President Aleksandr Rutskoi, who was charged by Yeltsin with overseeing the entire military operation in Chechnia, found himself in difficulty. Dudaev's successful mobilization of pro-independence forces was only one of the problems facing Rutskoi and his men. No less serious was the sabotage of their orders by Soviet authorities. The Soviet interior minister, Viktor Barannikov, who had previously been the interior minister of Russia, voiced his opposition to the use of his forces in Chechnia. This was a major blow to Rutskoi's plans. The police and interior forces were the only asset available to the Russian leadership to enforce the state of emergency in Chechnia. The army was under Union jurisdiction, and the Russian officials decided early on not to use it in Groznyi. The KGB also was under Union jurisdiction. Without the cooperation and support of the all-Union ministries, Rutskoi had no chance of implementing Yeltsin's decree.

That realization came rather late. When Rutskoi and the Speaker of parliament, Ruslan Khasbulatov, began calling the Union security ministers for help, they all refused, citing Gorbachev. On November 7, Yeltsin had signed a letter to Gorbachev merely informing the Soviet president of his decision to use force in Chechnia, with no request for advice or assistance. The letter also stated that Yeltsin would be informing the secretary-general of the United Nations of his decision. Yeltsin and those around him had clearly misjudged the degree of Russia's independence from the Union. They could cut their financing of Gorbachev's office and all-Union ministries, humiliate and ridicule him in the media, and make the Soviet presidency irrelevant in economic and social affairs, but Gorbachev still held a monopoly on the representation of Moscow's international interests and controlled the Soviet armed forces, secret services, and, as it turned out, interior troops. With the security ministers unwilling to commit their troops to Yeltsin's operation, Gorbachev afforded them a perfect cover to ignore Rutskoi's commands.[29]

With the Chechnia operation in jeopardy, the presidium of the Russian parliament went into session to discuss the situation. On November 9 it issued two decrees. One instructed the Russian president to take full control of interior troops on the territory of the Russian Federation; the other blamed problems associated with the implementation of Yeltsin's decree on the Union ministers. "To propose that the president of the RSFSR assess the actions of the heads of the executive agencies," read the decree. In plain language, that meant firing the Union ministers. The problem was that Yeltsin had no authority over them. After demanding in vain that the presidium of the Russian parliament court-martial Viktor Barannikov, the Union interior minister, Rutskoi finally decided to call Gorbachev.

Anatolii Cherniaev, who was in Gorbachev's office at the time, recorded in his diary that Gorbachev first listened to Rutskoi's outburst but then laid the receiver aside for ten minutes and read the papers on his desk, allowing Rutskoi to vent his frustration. Then, according to Cherniaev, he told the Russian vice president, "Aleksandr, calm down, you are not at the front. To carry out a blockade starting from the mountains, surround and block them so that not one Chechen gets through, arrest Dudaev and isolate the others—what's wrong with you? Don't you see what will come of this? . . . I have information here that no one in Chechnia is supporting Yeltsin's decree. They have all united against you. Don't go off your rocker." Gorbachev was back in the game and once more in his element.[30]

With no support from the center, the Russian authorities gave the order on November 10 for the withdrawal of interior troops already in Groznyi. The Russian parliament voted to annul Yeltsin's decree proclaiming a state of emergency. Aleksandr Rutskoi, who had allegedly prepared the decree and was charged with its implementation, bore the blame for the debacle. Yeltsin ordered his press secretary, Pavel Voshchanov, to prepare a press release stating that the president had always supported a political solution to the Chechen problem. "You know, there are those among us who will crush Chechnia with tanks as easily as they bombed villages in Afghanistan!" the president told his press secretary. The reference was to Rutskoi, who, like his main adversary, General Dudaev, was an Afghanistan war veteran.[31]

Boris Yeltsin had spent the decisive days of the Chechnia crisis at Zavidovo, a hunting resort near Moscow. November 7 was October Revolution Day, lavishly celebrated by the Soviet elite. Yeltsin had been part and parcel of that elite too long not to develop a special regard for the holiday, which was still on the Soviet and Russian official calendars. His celebration of the event apparently lasted more than one day. On November 9, when Gorbachev wanted to convene a meeting with Yeltsin to discuss the Chechen crisis, he had to abandon the idea after reaching Yeltsin by telephone in Zavidovo: the Russian president was drunk. "As soon as I started talking to Boris Nikolaevich," said Gorbachev to Cherniaev, "I grasped after a few seconds that talking was pointless: he was incoherent." Gorbachev later told Khasbulatov, who had called to demand the restoration of order in Chechnia, that the meeting had to be postponed because Yeltsin was "not himself."[32]

Yeltsin's decision, whether conscious or unconscious, to isolate himself at the most crucial moment in the first Chechen crisis and leave the implementation of his decree to his assistants clearly had a major impact on its outcome. The man who had mobilized his forces to resist the proclamation of a state of emergency a few months earlier was nowhere to be found when it came time to carry out the same thing in one of the Russian territories. Only he could wrest the armed forces away from Gorbachev, but he refused or was incapable, for the moment, of doing so. Like Gorbachev in the Baltics earlier that year, Yeltsin in Chechnia was not willing to give full support to his hardliners. In both cases, external factors played a role: Bush had stayed Gorbachev's hand, and now Gorbachev had stayed Yeltsin's.

The new Russia's first show of force had ended in an embarrassing public display of the limits of Yeltsin's power. Gorbachev, on the other hand, could relish his victory. According to Cherniaev, "Yeltsin's fumble with the state of emergency for Chechnia 'inspired' him." But Gorbachev was not prepared to exploit his opponent's faux pas to the full. He told his advisers, "I will save him; that affair cannot be allowed to impair his authority." Yeltsin's cooperation was crucial to Gorbachev's struggle for survival—his own and that of the Soviet Union. Without Yeltsin's support, there would be no Union. In his memoirs, Gorbachev recalled what he told Yeltsin with regard to the events in Chechnia: "Remember, our state is held together by two rings. One is the USSR, the other is the Russian Federation. If the first is broken, problems for the other will follow."[33]

THE NEW UNION TREATY was finally placed on the agenda of the State Council, which was scheduled to meet on November 14, a few days after the Chechnia debacle. On the eve of the meeting Gorbachev allowed his chief negotiator on the treaty, Georgii Shakhnazarov, to go to London to participate in a dialogue with former US secretary of state Henry Kissinger organized by the Japanese newspaper *Yomiuri Shimbun*. It was a notable change of heart for Gorbachev, who only a few weeks earlier had refused Shakhnazarov's request to visit the United States, claiming, "What's wrong with you? What do you mean, the USA? We'll sign the Union treaty, and you can go the day after that."

Shakhnazarov had protested that the treaty would not be signed before December. Gorbachev disagreed. But now he let his assistant go.[34]

In late October, on the day after Yeltsin's economic reform speech in parliament, Shakhnazarov had given Gorbachev a memo that directly challenged the latter's vision of the new Union as a single state with a strong center and a constitution binding on all. "At this moment it is practically impossible to revive the Union state," wrote Shakhnazarov.

> Except for Nazarbayev [[Kazakhstan]] and Niyazov [[Turkmen-istan]], practically all the republics have irrevocably decided to prove to themselves and the whole world that they are independent. With his last statement Yeltsin, too, has crossed the Rubicon. And he is right, of course: Russia has no other way out. It should not grab its fleeing partners by the coattails, not plead with them or compel them but look after itself. Once Russia revives, they will come back, and if not all of them do, then let them go with God. It will suffice to hold on to the states contiguous with Russia in the zone of its political and economic influence."

This was the program presented to Shakhnazarov by Gennadii Burbulis, Sergei Shakhrai, and the other Russian negotiators. It would eventually become the basis for Russian policy vis-à-vis the former Soviet republics.

Shakhnazarov also argued that it was futile to insist on the revival of a strong Union center and that Gorbachev would be better off focusing on the role allocated to him by Yeltsin and other republican leaders— that of commander in chief of the armed forces, chief negotiator on nuclear issues, coordinator of the republics' international policy, and intermediary in disputes between the members of the new union. "Mikhail Sergeevich," wrote Shakhnazarov, "this is one of those fateful moments that may resound very heavily for the country and for you as the individual who brought about a historic change of course. Not to recognize the need at least temporarily to renounce excessive demands concerning the Union state would mean committing a tragic error."[35]

Shakhnazarov not only set forth his disagreements with Gorbachev and proposed his solutions but also submitted his de facto resignation. "Conscience does not allow me to continue a line that I consider mistaken and fruitless," he wrote in the memo. Gorbachev did not accept the resignation: instead, he let Shakhnazarov go debate with Kissinger. If an aide could not be counted on for complete support when the treaty came up for a crucial discussion at the State Council, then it was safer to send him off to London. The problem was that Shakhnazarov was not the only aide who had lost faith in Gorbachev's strategy. On November 13, one day before the fateful council meeting at Gorbachev's retreat at Novo-Ogarevo, Anatolii Cherniaev noted in his diary, "The union treaty that will be on the agenda in Novo-Ogarevo will not pass. I have read the new version! But Kravchuk will not come at all . . . And no one will come from Ukraine. Revenko [[Gorbachev's chief of staff]] made long entreaties to all the presidents to show up. . . . And by evening it was still not clear whether they would do so. All this looks like a rearguard action on Gorbachev's part." Despite the open and secret defections of his most trusted aides, Gorbachev remained undeterred. He would fight to the end to have the State Council pass his version of the union treaty, which provided for a strong Union center.[36]

The discussion of the treaty by the State Council on November 14 initially confirmed Shakhnazarov's worst fears. With the support of other republican leaders, Yeltsin protested against the creation of a union state with its own constitution. Even though Kravchuk had stopped attending State Council meetings back in October, Yeltsin had no problem in gaining the support of most leaders of the republics (they included Nursultan Nazarbayev of Kazakhstan), who kept coming to Moscow. Gorbachev, who had officially agreed to conduct negotiations on the basis of the confederative idea, openly moved away from the federation/confederation dichotomy. "A union state," he told the gathering. "I insist categorically. If we do not create a union state, my prognosis is trouble for you."

Yeltsin would not yield: "We will create a union of states."

Gorbachev went all out, threatening to leave the meeting. "If there is no state, then I will take no part in this process," he told the gathering. "I can abandon it right now. This is my principled position. If there is not going to be a state, I consider my mission concluded. I cannot support something amorphous."

Yeltsin and other members of the council tried to convince Gorbachev of the advantages of a confederative version of the treaty. In a confederation, they argued, the armed forces, transportation system, ecological and space programs would be controlled from the center. Gorbachev would not listen. He stood up and began collecting his papers as an indication that he was about to leave. The republican leaders panicked and called for a break. Yeltsin met privately with Gorbachev, and they reached a compromise: the Union of Sovereign States, as the new structure was to be called, would constitute a "democratic confederative state." It would not have a constitution, but its president would be elected by the people of the entire union.

Despite all the shortcomings of the new draft, Gorbachev was extremely satisfied: he had not managed to obtain a constitution, but he had secured a provision on the election of the president. The republican leaders agreed to initial the new union treaty at the next meeting of the State Council. Boris Pankin, who was present at Novo-Ogarevo, noted a "restless but happy look on Gorbachev's face." As the members of the State Council headed for the exits, no one could say whether they would speak to the press or not, but Gorbachev's press secretary arranged the reporters in such a way as to block the exits. The Soviet president brought the republican leaders to the microphone one by one to make statements in support of the union state. "We have agreed that there will be a Union—a democratic confederative state," declared Yeltsin.[37]

Gorbachev could feel triumphant. He seemed to have achieved something that no one, including his closest advisers, had thought possible. His interpreter, Pavel Palazhchenko, watched the press conference on television. In his memoirs, he wrote, "To almost everyone's surprise, Gorbachev did look like a winner in the late evening of November 14, as Yeltsin and others spoke into the microphones on live television, repeating the phrase, 'The Union will exist. There will be a Union.' Watching the live broadcast with my colleagues, I felt that they, like me, were surprised Gorbachev had pulled it off."[38]

V.
VOX POPULI

13

ANTICIPATION

MIKHAIL GORBACHEV WAS SITTING in his office at the government resort of Novo-Ogarevo. It was the afternoon of November 25, eleven days after the previous meeting of the State Council and the day of its next meeting. This time he had done it—he had not just threatened to walk out on a meeting but had actually done so. Now he was anxious to learn what the next minutes would bring. Much had changed in and around Moscow since November 14, when he put Yeltsin and other leaders of the republics in front of television cameras and had them say that there would be some form of union in the future.

The main change was in the mood of the policy makers. Everyone was awaiting the Ukrainian referendum, scheduled for December 1, and everyone except Gorbachev was predicting a landslide in favor of independence. That was the opinion of the Ukrainian leaders, Boris Yeltsin and his fellow leaders of the republics, and George Bush and his advisers in Washington. Within the next few days, the Ukrainian factor would dramatically change the balance of forces between the republics, their relations with Gorbachev, and Bush's relations with the Soviet leader. The first sign of the coming change was the behavior of the presidents of the republics who gathered in Novo-Ogarevo on November 25 to discuss the new union treaty proposed by Gorbachev.

On that day, they were supposed to endorse the text of the union treaty that they had debated and agreed upon at the previous meeting of the State Council. Problems began, as always, with Yeltsin, who again raised the question of the nature of the future union. He claimed that the term agreed on last time, "confederative state," was meaningless. The treaty should stipulate instead the creation of a union or confederation of sovereign states: otherwise the Russian parliament would not ratify it.

The leaders of Belarus, Uzbekistan, and Turkmenistan supported Yeltsin. They refused to endorse the treaty and offered instead to submit it to their parliaments without their signatures, effectively dissociating themselves from the text. Gorbachev was furious, accusing Yeltsin of going back on his word given at the previous meeting. "So what?" responded Yeltsin, who told the media the day after the November 14 meeting that he had compromised too much. "Time is passing. In groups and committees of the [[Russian]] Supreme Soviet . . . [[the text]] was discussed, and they say that such a draft will not make it through." As if that were not enough, Yeltsin pointed to the elephant in the room—the absence of representatives from Ukraine. He doubted that Ukraine would agree to join a "confederative state." "There will be no union without Ukraine," declared Yeltsin.

The Speaker of the Belarusian parliament, the fifty-six-year-old Stanisłaŭ Shushkevich, a member of the Belarusian democratic opposition and an opponent of the August coup, argued that the republican leaders needed ten more days to study the treaty because of its importance. The postponement would also make it possible for Ukraine to join. "Let's wait until December 1," suggested Yeltsin. Gorbachev tried to turn the Ukrainian factor around. "If we decline," he said, referring to the endorsement of the union treaty, "it will be a gift to the separatists." His argument fell on deaf ears. Gorbachev finally lost his nerve and decided to resort to his tried-and-true maneuver of threatening to leave. "If you consider the agreement unnecessary, say so clearly," he told the republican presidents. "Perhaps you should meet separately and decide. Or stay here, and we shall leave you. . . . Get a feeling for what is more important to you— the people or the separatists." With a few more parting words, he left the room, accompanied by his assistants.

Gorbachev spent close to an hour in his office. Would the rebel republican leaders come to their senses and call him back? In April, he had walked out of a meeting of the Central Committee of the

Communist Party after a motion was made to vote on his ouster as general secretary. The committee backed down, annulling the vote, and Gorbachev regained control of the party. But the situation now was more complex. No one was trying to unseat him either as leader of a long-gone party or as head of a state in shambles. They were simply refusing to rebuild the state, and without it he had no role to play and no country to rule. They were also reluctant to come to his office and invite him back. Clearly, the republican leaders had decided to take their time and not rush after him.

After discussing the situation, they sent their representatives to Gorbachev—Yeltsin, whom Gorbachev considered, not without reason, the main culprit of the revolt, and the more agreeable Shushkevich. Yeltsin was not happy to go, but Shushkevich had a hidden agenda. As they made their way to Gorbachev's office through the glassed-in corridor of the building, enjoying the golden forest panorama, Shushkevich reminded Yeltsin about his earlier invitation to visit Belarus to discuss economic relations between the two republics. He offered to host the Russian president at a government hunting resort called Belavezha (White Tower), near Brest. Yeltsin agreed.

"So we've come to the khan of the Union—take us under your high hand," said Yeltsin to Gorbachev on entering his office. Gorbachev, apparently feeling relieved and vindicated, responded in the same vein: "You see, Tsar Boris, everything can be settled by honest cooperation." They were alluding to late-medieval Russian history, when the country's rulers recognized the suzerainty of the khans of the Golden Horde. The parallel was inaccurate, to be sure: the Russian princes began to call themselves tsars only after throwing off the overlordship of the khans. The tsars recognized no authority above their own, and "Tsar Boris" was not about to deviate from that tradition. As Gorbachev later told his advisers, Yeltsin spoke to him "turning up his nose, almost spitting." What Yeltsin and Shushkevich brought Gorbachev was at best a face-saving proposal: the republican leaders would leave the reference to a "confederative" state in the text of the union treaty, but it would go to the republican parliaments for discussion without their signatures. This was not the kind of compromise for which Gorbachev had been hoping.

Gorbachev returned to the conference room to continue the meeting. After it was over, he went in front of the television cameras to present the State Council's decision to send the treaty to the parliaments for discussion as an endorsement of the document. Few were taken in by the move and the play on words. As Gorbachev later recalled, journalists asked, "Who was responsible, who disrupted the endorsement." He was silent. Privately he was sure that Yeltsin had not acted alone. According to Anatolii Cherniaev, the Soviet president had long suspected a "conspiracy between Yeltsin and Kravchuk to bring down the Union from both sides."[1]

GORBACHEV HAD ALREADY FOUND the Ukrainian leadership obstinate earlier. After the coup, as the Ukrainian elite closed ranks around Kravchuk and polls showed growing public support for independence, Kravchuk grew bolder. His visit to Canada and the United States in September left no doubt of his commitment to independence. The last meeting of the State Council that he attended, in October, dealt with economic issues, not the union treaty. At that meeting, he told the council that the Ukrainian parliament had passed a resolution suspending the republic's participation in negotiations on the new union treaty until after the referendum. The Ukrainian deputies had indeed voted to boycott all Union institutions, opting for direct ties with individual republics. As far as they were concerned, the Union was effectively dead.[2]

But Gorbachev thought otherwise. He never gave up on the rebellious republic. The son of a Russian father and a Ukrainian mother, he regarded the prospect of a Russo-Ukrainian breakup as a personal tragedy. Although Gorbachev considered himself a Russian, he knew and loved to sing Ukrainian folk songs. He also believed that he understood the mood of Ukrainian society better than anyone else. "Don't be silly, Leonid Makarovych!" he would tell Kravchuk over the phone. "Your referendum will certainly fail: in March, 70 percent voted for the Union." Gorbachev was referring to the Ukrainian vote in support of renewed union during the all-Union referendum of March 1991. There were some sinister notes in Gorbachev's appeals for Russo-Ukrainian unity. Again and again in his private conversations with aides and foreign leaders, as well as in his public appeals, he threatened Ukrainians with the possibility of ethnic conflict, de facto raising tensions, if not inciting actual conflict, among Ukraine's minorities.[3]

Using the ethnic card to derail the referendum was an idea proposed to Gorbachev by his adviser Georgii Shakhnazarov in a memo of October 10, 1991. Shakhnazarov was disappointed that after the disintegration of the Communist Party there was no political force in Ukraine prepared to stop what he called the "Galician nationalists." He was also unhappy that the Russian leadership decided not to press territorial claims against Ukraine. Shakhnazarov proposed that Gorbachev "not only publicly repeat but also lend an official tone to Russia's position with regard to the Crimea, the Donbas, and southern Ukraine." He wrote, "It should be stated plainly and clearly, without constraint, that those regions are historical parts of Russia, and it does not intend to renounce them if Ukraine should wish to cease being part of the Union."

Among Shakhnazarov's other suggestions was the launching of an anti-independence campaign in the Crimea and southern and eastern Ukraine. "In agreement with Comrade [[Nikolai]] Bagrov," wrote Shakhnazarov with reference to the head of the Crimean parliament, "to activize work in the Crimea. The whole population of the republic should know that if Ukraine announces its exit from the Union, the Crimea will cease to be part of Ukraine the very next day and will be annexed to Russia." Shakhnazarov suggested the creation of a special group in the presidential administration headed by the well-known Ukrainian poet Borys Oliinyk and sending scores of Russian celebrities on anti-independence tours in Ukraine. Gorbachev, who in previous years had used state funds to set up and support bogus political parties advancing his own political agenda, now had no resources to implement even half of Shakhnazarov's proposals; by October, speeches and interviews were all that were left to him. In his discussions with George Bush in Madrid in late October, Gorbachev referred to Ukraine's Russian problem, suggesting it as one of the reasons Ukraine would not leave the Union.[4]

BY THE TIME OF THE MADRID CONFERENCE in late October and early November, Ukrainians featured ever more prominently not only on Gorbachev's agenda but also on Bush's domestic radar. Gorbachev's interpreter, Pavel Palazhchenko, later remembered that during the dinner hosted by King Juan Carlos of Spain, who made such a favorable impression on Gorbachev, Bush peppered the Soviet president with questions about Ukraine. "Do you think Kravchuk will win the elections?" he asked Gorbachev, who assured Bush that Kravchuk would indeed win. "And do you think after that he will join you in some kind of Union or association?" came the next question. Gorbachev responded that he was not sure about Kravchuk, but he knew that Ukraine and Russia would stay together: "These two nations are branches of the same tree. No one will be able to tear them apart." Bush changed the subject to the coming presidential elections in the United States. Palazhchenko, who noted Bush's visible concern about their outcome, saw no connection between these subjects of dinner conversation—the Ukrainian and American presidential elections. In fact, there was one.[5]

The president's relations with the Ukrainian community in the United States had never recovered from his "Chicken Kiev" blunder in August. On November 5, Ukrainian attacks on the president, earlier regarded as little more than a political nuisance, grew into a major political problem. On that day, in a special election to the US Senate, Pennsylvania voters defeated Dick Thornburgh, the former US attorney general and Bush's handpicked candidate to replace Senator John Heinz, who had died in a plane crash earlier that year. The Democratic candidate, Harris Wofford, whose campaign was run by Bill Clinton's future electoral gurus Paul Begala and James Carville, came from behind to score a decisive victory over the Republican favorite. The loss was a major embarrassment for President Bush: Thornburgh had resigned as attorney general, convinced that he would win the seat.

Since Thornburgh was considered to be the president's man, Democratic strategists had done their best to link him to Bush, whose popularity was slumping in the polls after having reached an all-time high immediately after the Gulf War. The economy, which had begun a slide into recession, was the main culprit, but political issues were also involved. The polls showed that voters of East European descent, who had supported the Republican Party during the Cold War, were now switching sides in response to what they regarded as the administration's indecisiveness, first on the issue of Baltic independence and now on that of Ukraine, Armenia, and other Soviet republics. Democratic hopefuls for the presidency were jumping on the ethnic bandwagon. Governor Bill Clinton of Arkansas criticized the administration for not supporting the republics' drive for independence. Something had to be done immediately to stop the defection of East European voters from the Republican camp.[6]

Having supported the Republican Party in the Cold War, Ukrainian Americans now believed that the party was betraying them. After Bush's "Chicken Kiev" speech, they had promised retaliation at the voting booths, declaring strong opposition to the administration in their newspapers and at their meeting halls. Their traditional Republican allies were unable to get the attention of the White House. A letter of September 16 to President Bush from Senator Hank Brown (R-Colo.), urging the White House to recognize Ukrainian independence on the basis of the parliamentary declaration, went unanswered.

Ukrainian community leaders mobilized their followers to lobby not only Republican but also Democratic representatives. Their lobbying efforts on the Hill finally came to fruition on November 21, when the US Senate passed a resolution sponsored by Senator Dennis DeConcini (D-Ariz.) urging the administration to recognize Ukraine following the December 1 referendum. DeConcini was not shy about attacking his Republican opponents in the administration. "After supporting Baltic independence for 50 years, to our country's shame, the U.S. government was only the 37th to finally recognize those brave nations," declared DeConcini. "This pattern of hypocrisy must not be repeated with respect to Ukraine."[7]

The *Ukrainian Weekly,* the leading Ukrainian American newspaper, which was usually well disposed toward the administration, was now full of articles and letters attacking Bush for not helping Ukraine and, indeed, hindering its drive toward independence. "It Would Be Prudent, George," read the headline of the newspaper's editorial on November 24, demanding speedy American recognition of Ukrainian independence. Writing in the same issue, Myron B. Kuropas, the newspaper's columnist and former special assistant to President Gerald R. Ford, took aim at Bush's national security adviser, General Brent Scowcroft.

"It was he who, because of personal slight, underestimated Boris Yeltsin's popular appeal in Russia. It is he who helped write President Bush's remarks in Kiev. It is he who out of admiration for Mikhail Gorbachev is fighting to preserve the Soviet Union," wrote Kuropas.

He was wrong about Scowcroft's admiration for Gorbachev as the main source of his thinking about the fate of the Soviet Union. But Scowcroft indeed despised Yeltsin, had coauthored Bush's "Chicken Kiev" speech, and upon his return from Madrid had declared to his aides that although Gorbachev was now a mere ghost of the former center, US policy had to be conducted in such a way as not to do him any harm.[8]

That was about to change. Throughout the last two weeks of November, the US national security policy team held numerous meetings to discuss the situation. There was agreement on one point: everyone expected an overwhelming vote for independence in Ukraine and knew that it would mark a watershed in US policy toward the Soviet Union. But there was little else on which Bush's foreign policy advisers could agree. The lines drawn between the Department of Defense and the State Department in September remained almost intact. Dick Cheney, pushing as always for closer ties with the republics, was now urging the speedy recognition of Ukraine. Stephen Hadley, then an assistant to Paul Wolfowitz in the Defense Department, said later, "We had a view that without Ukraine a retrograde Russia would never reconstitute the Soviet Union. It would never become the threat posed by the Soviet Union because of the enormous resources and population and geography of Ukraine. So that would become an important element of U.S. policy—putting aside all the principles that were all-important—from the strategic standpoint an independent Ukraine became an insurance policy."[9]

James Baker advocated a more cautious approach that would benefit the Soviet center and Gorbachev. Baker's main authority on the issue was still Eduard Shevardnadze, whom Gorbachev had called back to government in mid-November to replace Boris Pankin. Shevardnadze, who had much more weight in both internal Soviet and international politics than his predecessor, was concerned about a possible Russo-Ukrainian conflict over the Crimea and eastern Ukraine—the potential problem to which Gorbachev had alerted Bush in Madrid. Baker wanted to postpone recognition of Ukraine, even if its people voted for independence, and to use such recognition as a carrot with which the United States could influence the policies of Ukrainian leaders on such sensitive issues as nuclear arms.

Then there was the position of General Scowcroft. "An overall caution marked Scowcroft," wrote the White House deputy press secretary, Roman Popadiuk. "Although sympathetic, he was reluctant to push the national cause of the individual Soviet republics too much to the front." Popadiuk, who would become the first American ambassador to independent Ukraine, was somewhat critical of Scowcroft's overcautious approach but also recognized the reasons behind it. "For one superpower to support the dismantlement of another could only create a backlash and lead to direct political conflict," he wrote later.[10]

On November 25, the day on which Yeltsin and the leaders of the Soviet republics refused to initial Gorbachev's new union treaty, the *Washington Post* ran an article titled "U.S. Officials Split over Response to an Independent Ukraine." It brought the divisions in the administration into the open, characterizing Baker as opposed to the recognition of the soon-to-be independent country. Baker was furious, suspecting Cheney staffers of leaking information to the press. Although the article quoted both State Department and Department of Defense officials, the leak came from the Defense side. Speaking on condition of anonymity, a Pentagon insider told reporters that the time had come for the United States to "get on the ground floor" with nations that had already decided to recognize Ukraine. The decision had to be made ahead of the NATO Council meeting scheduled for the end of the week.[11]

The next day, proponents of early recognition of Ukrainian independence mobilized their supporters in Congress. A large group of congressmen from both sides of the aisle threw their weight behind Cheney. Their letter to President Bush, among whose signatories were such up-and-coming stars of American politics as Newt Gingrich, Nancy Pelosi, Leon Panetta, and Rick Santorum, read, "We know that you are now considering the advice of several members of your administration, including Defense Secretary Dick Cheney, that the US be among the first to recognize Ukrainian independence. Mr. President, this is wise counsel. It is vitally important that America side with the people of Ukraine, in favor of freedom and democracy, instead of helping to prop up a Kremlin still being run by barely reconstructed Communists." The latter reference was to Gorbachev and his circle. "Those who argue that continued Kremlin control over military, economic and social policies in Ukraine somehow benefits the United States are wrong. America now has the opportunity to move quickly toward negotiations with an independent Russia and an independent Ukraine for wholesale destruction of nuclear weapons, as well as implementation of sweeping free-market reforms. Let us be in the vanguard of this movement, rather than clumsily trundling behind." The congressmen urged Bush to show the resolve he had demonstrated in the Gulf War.[12]

For the proponents of Ukrainian independence in the administration and elsewhere, the timing of the letter was perfect. On November 26, when it was dispatched, the president conducted a decisive meeting with his foreign policy advisers. With a meeting of the North Atlantic Council to discuss the Ukrainian situation scheduled for the next day and political pressure for the recognition of Ukrainian independence growing at home, Bush and his advisers finally agreed on their strategy. They would recognize Ukraine, although the recognition would be not immediate but delayed a few weeks. The president would send a special emissary to Kyiv immediately after the referendum to assure the Ukrainian leadership of American support for their newfound freedom.

In his memoirs, Baker put the best possible spin on the compromise reached at the meeting, writing that those taking part had accepted the State Department proposal for "delayed recognition." In his handwritten notes on the back of the photocopy of the *Washington Post* article about the split in the administration, Baker wrote, "Kozyrev says *moderates* in Russia support our approach—mistake to say 'no' or *quickly* 'yes'—same for moderates in Ukraine." He marked the following sentence with multiple asterisks: "Run a risk by rushing to recog[[nition]]—chaos + civil war—whereas wait for couple of weeks *is no risk*."[13]

That day a cable with talking points for the North Atlantic Council meeting was sent to the American ambassador at NATO headquarters in Brussels. The authors of the cable predicted a solid pro-independence vote in the forthcoming Ukrainian referendum and expected the Ukrainian government to assert its independence immediately afterward. According to the cable, "The question for us is not whether to recognize Ukraine, but how and when." Its authors argued against setting preliminary Western conditions for recognition. "We do not favor imposing conditions on Ukraine that it must meet before we are willing to grant recognition and diplomatic relations," read the cable. "Instead, we believe NATO collectively and each of us individually should communicate certain factors to Ukraine which we will take into consideration making our individual decisions."

The requirements put forward in the cable included maintaining the existing central command over nuclear forces located in Ukraine, the commitment of the country's leadership to its proclaimed goal of becoming a nuclear-free state, and adherence to the international treaties signed by the USSR on arms control, as well as to the Helsinki Accords, with their provisions for the recognition of post–World War II borders and pledges to uphold and protect human rights. The drafters of the cable were well aware that the decision on Ukrainian independence would set a precedent for American and NATO policy toward other Soviet republics, including Georgia and Armenia.[14]

After the fateful November 26 meeting in the White House, George Bush could finally begin restoring ties with the Ukrainian community and, by extension, with other voters of East European background. The first step in that direction had been made a few days earlier by the newly appointed head of the CIA, Robert Gates. On November 17, a few weeks after taking office, Gates delivered the keynote address at a Ukrainian American community dinner at the New York Plaza Hotel. The occasion was the honoring of the highest-ranking Ukrainian American in the Bush administration, White House deputy spokesman Roman Popadiuk, with the "Ukrainian of the Year" award, bestowed on him by the New York–based Ukrainian Institute of America.

Judging by the public reaction, Gates's speech was a success. Ralph Gordon Hoxie, a prominent New York educator and head of the Center for the Study of the Presidency, who attended the event, later congratulated Gates on an "outstanding" address that captivated him with its Jeffersonian contrast between democracies and tyrannies. Gates used the opportunity to bridge the gap between the administration and the Ukrainian American community. He also had a chat with Hennadii Udovenko, the head of the Ukrainian mission at the United Nations. Later *US News & World Report* attributed the Bush administration's decision to recognize the results of the Ukrainian referendum to the position taken in internal debates by the new head of the CIA.[15]

The leaders of the Ukrainian American community were invited to the White House on the morning of November 27, the day after the administration decided to recognize Ukrainian independence. The group of fifteen met for half an hour with Bush, Scowcroft, Ed Hewett of the National Security Council, and other foreign policy advisers in the Roosevelt Room. It was led by Taras Szmagala, a Cleveland native, longtime Republican supporter who headed the Ukrainian National Association, and publisher of the *Ukrainian Weekly*, which had recently been so unfriendly to Bush. In 1988 Szmagala had chaired the American Ukrainians for Bush committee. In September 1991 he had been among the members of the US delegation led by Bush's brother Jonathan to mark the fiftieth anniversary of the Babyn Yar massacre.

Now Szmagala told the president that Ukrainian independence was inevitable and that US recognition of it was the Ukrainian American community's "gut issue." Bush was reminded of his support for Ukrainian national self-determination back in the 1970s and early 1980s, but, according to the *Ukrainian Weekly* report on the meeting, no mention was made of his "Chicken Kiev" gaffe. The Ukrainian American community leaders presented Bush with an appeal from the Rukh leadership in Ukraine to support their country's drive toward independence and stop giving financial assistance to Gorbachev, who was waging a media war against their cause—a war that, in the opinion of the Rukh leadership, could turn into open aggression. "Who will assume responsibility for possible aggression of Gorbachev against Ukraine?" asked the Rukh leaders.[16]

George Bush was happy to tell his long-suffering Ukrainian American supporters that his administration had decided to recognize Ukraine. His caveats that it would not be done immediately were lost on his audience, which heard what it most wanted to hear—there would be recognition after all. Finally, those in attendance had something definite to tell their friends in Ukraine and fellow community members who had been criticizing them for staunchly supporting the Republicans even as the Republican president purportedly built up Gorbachev and sold Ukraine down the river. Once they left the White House, the community leaders rushed to tell reporters of Bush's pledge that the United States would "salute Ukrainian independence" and "move forward" with its recognition. "No timetable was mentioned," reported the *Washington Post*.[17]

The news of Bush's readiness to grant Ukraine recognition was soon confirmed by a White House official who mentioned, speaking off the record, that the decision had been made at a White House meeting the previous day. He presented the decision as a compromise between the positions advocated earlier by Cheney and Baker. James Baker, once again outmaneuvered on the issue of Ukrainian independence, blamed the leaders of the Ukrainian community and the press for ignoring "the nuances of our position." In his memoirs, George Bush wrote with regret about the news being "leaked" to the press, but Robert Gates, who had earlier shared Baker's cautious stand on the issue, simply recorded in his memoirs that "events and expediency overtook a principled approach." He refused to blame the Ukrainian American community leaders for the leak.

Indeed, it could not have come as a surprise to Bush and his advisers that the leaders of the Ukrainian American community talked to the press after the meeting, and the media could hardly have been expected to engage in hairsplitting on the nuances of the administration's position in light of the major change in the administration's policy. With the Republicans losing a safe seat in Pennsylvania, Bush's own popularity sliding in the polls, and voters of East European descent loudly voicing their discontent, the White House could ill afford to maintain its previous support for Gorbachev, now described by Scowcroft as little more than a "ghost of the center." The change in course, personally unpleasant to George Bush but politically necessary, had to be made sooner or later. Gorbachev was going down, and the danger was that he might drag the American president into a political abyss along with him.

The "leak," which the White House not only immediately confirmed but also elaborated on by providing additional details about the decision-making process, was a convenient way to tell the country and the world about a major shift in US foreign policy—the abandonment of Gorbachev and his Union project. In a breach of long-established tradition, Gorbachev was not consulted or warned of the announcement. Formally speaking, there was no announcement at all.[18]

ON NOVEMBER 30, three days after the White House leak and
the day before the Ukrainian referendum, President Bush called
Mikhail Gorbachev to explain the turn in American policy, of which
Gorbachev was already aware. It was a conversation neither leader was
looking forward to. When Gorbachev's aide Anatolii Cherniaev told
him that Bush had requested a telephone conversation, Gorbachev
was not pleased. "What for?" he asked Cherniaev. "I won't be here."
Only after some hesitation did he agree to take the call: "Let them put
it through wherever I happen to be." Gorbachev felt betrayed by his
American counterpart. The leak from the White House undermined
his ongoing campaign against Ukrainian independence, in which he
had claimed the full support of George Bush and other Western leaders. Now the mirage of Western backing suddenly disappeared, exposed as a bluff and giving Ukrainians one more incentive to vote and
then push for independence.[19]

Gorbachev's interpreter, Pavel Palazhchenko, had first heard the
news on CNN. "Whatever the details of the decision made by Bush," he
told Cherniaev, "this announcement is a real blow." Cherniaev agreed.
He drafted a public response on Gorbachev's behalf, claiming that the
news from Washington "arouses bewilderment." The statement failed
to achieve its goal even in Moscow, to say nothing of Washington.
It was criticized on the front page of *Izvestiia*, which was normally
loyal to Gorbachev. The author of the article maintained that while
the Washington leak could indeed be treated as meddling in Soviet
affairs on the eve of the referendum, Gorbachev's public repudiation
of the White House made little sense when the polls showed that more
than 80 percent of Ukrainians supported independence. The *Izvestiia*
article appeared next to a piece titled "Ukraine: One Day Before
Freedom Achieved Through Suffering." If anyone was out of step with
reality, it was Gorbachev, not Bush. But Cherniaev was proud of his
work, suspecting that Gorbachev's statement had played its role in
prompting Bush to call his abandoned ally on November 30.[20]

When the call finally went through, Bush told Gorbachev right
away that he was calling on the issue of Ukraine and was concerned
by statements coming recently from the Soviet side—a clear reference
to Cherniaev's declaration. "You know our tradition as a democratic
nation. We must support the Ukrainian people," said Bush. He tried
to sweeten the pill: "It would seem to us that recognizing Ukrainian

independence could well bring them back into the union treaty process." After listening to Bush, Gorbachev went over to the attack. "I won't hide that the leak from the White House saying that serious consideration was being given to recognizing the independence of the Ukraine by the U.S.—especially because that leak came on the eve of the referendum—that this was taken negatively," he said to Bush. "It appears that the U.S. is not only trying to influence events but to interfere."

Gorbachev continued by declaring that the Ukrainian vote for independence should not be treated as a vote for secession. He brought up events in Yugoslavia. "If someone in Ukraine says that they are seceding from the Union, and someone says they are supporting them," said Gorbachev, alluding to Bush's readiness to recognize Ukraine, "then it would mean that 12 million Russians and members of other peoples become citizens of a foreign country." He indicated that Yeltsin's claims to Ukrainian regions bordering on Russia and the situation of Russian minorities in the Crimea and the Donbas coal region of eastern Ukraine were potentially explosive issues. Gorbachev was following the recommendations given him on Ukrainian minorities by Georgii Shakhnazarov the previous month.

Anatolii Cherniaev, who was present during the conversation, summarized Gorbachev's argument as follows: "Independence is not secession, and secession is Yugoslavia squared and raised to the tenth power!" Gorbachev asked Bush to take care not to embolden the separatists. "Every state of the U.S. is sovereign, but we deal with the United States as a strong state," he said to Bush.

"Very true," responded the American president, but he was not prepared to yield an inch. "The recognition of the aspirations of Ukrainians to be independent will pave the way to resolve these thorny issues standing in the way of political and economic reforms," he said. Bush assured Gorbachev that he was not out to make things more complicated for him. "I'm under a little pressure at home," said Bush, referring to his domestic Ukrainian problem. "I can't understand what you have been through, but people are piling on me, so I can understand a little of what you're experiencing."

There was no dialogue: the conversation consisted of two monologues. Although the interlocutors avoided an open conflict, both knew that their positions were incompatible. The telephone call could do little to draw them closer. The political alliance between Bush and Gorbachev was now a thing of the past. Cherniaev regarded James Baker, who participated in the conversation on the American side, as more sympathetic than Bush to Gorbachev's plight and the future of the Union. "Baker is freer in his judgments and less subject to pressure from all kinds of lobbyists, more frank!" wrote Cherniaev in his diary later that day. After the conversation he sat down to draft a press release about it. Gorbachev was eager to use the fact of the call itself, if not its content, to his political advantage on the eve of the Ukrainian referendum. He tried to offset Bush's indirect leak to the press a few days earlier with his own leak. The goal of the statement, according to Cherniaev's diary, was "to put the squeeze on Kravchuk and Co."[21]

FOR GORBACHEV, THE DIFFICULT conversation with Bush followed on the heels of a no less difficult meeting with Boris Yeltsin, whom he considered the source of most of his recent troubles. That morning Gorbachev had begged Yeltsin to save the Union from looming default: the Russians, who were now in control of oil and gas revenues, had stopped financing Union structures. The world's second superpower was broke. Gorbachev still commanded the military and the diplomatic corps but had no money to pay either or even to cover the salaries of his own staff.

The Union coffers were empty. On the previous day, at a session of the Union parliament, Gorbachev had asked the deputies to approve his June decree ordering the Central Bank to issue 68 billion rubles in credits to state institutions and enterprises. He had also asked for approval of new credits in the amount of 90 billion rubles. This was, in effect, a request to print more money, and it did not sit well with many of the deputies. While one chamber of the Union parliament passed a resolution to issue the credits, parliament as a whole, under the influence of the Russian deputies, would not approve it. The Russian government, ready to launch a radical economic reform, wanted to avoid another round of inflation at all costs. The Gorbachev administration was bereft of funds. "Russia, in effect, blocked the acceptance of an extraordinary Union budget at the end of the year," wrote Gorbachev's economic adviser Vadim Medvedev in his diary. "This led to a mass nonpayment of salaries to institutions on the [[Union]] budget."[22]

On that same day the State Bank ceased all payments to Union institutions, including the army and the presidential administration. The sole exception was the Ministry of International Relations, now headed again by Eduard Shevardnadze. Yeltsin, mindful of the negative reaction of Western leaders to his earlier plans to cut the ministry's funding, continued to bankroll it from Russian coffers. Ministry officials sounded the alarm, expecting a takeover by Russia, but Gorbachev was powerless. "What could we do?" wrote Cherniaev in his diary. "Russia still has the wherewithal to pay, but M[[ikhail]] S[[ergeevich]] has nothing!"

At his meeting with Yeltsin and his advisers on November 30, Gorbachev had no cards to play. His only hope was to shame his opponents into giving him the money. "The case was presented as follows;" wrote Cherniaev in his diary, "the 'center' cannot be left with no means of support." At the end of the four-hour session Yeltsin agreed to release some funds. His economic advisers were to figure out exactly how that would be done. While Gorbachev spoke with Bush on the phone in his office, the experts met in the adjacent Walnut Room, so called because of its paneling, previously used for meetings of the Politburo. The problem they were trying to solve could scarcely have been imagined, except perhaps as a nightmare, by the Soviet leaders meeting in that room in the heyday of their Cold War rivalry with the United States.[23]

The Union was on its deathbed. It was no longer even bleeding: when it came to finances, all the blood was long gone. The solution negotiated by Gorbachev was at best a whiff of oxygen. But despite all the disappointments of the previous few days, he was not giving up. In his conversation with Bush, Gorbachev was eager to report one of his rare political successes—on the previous day his efforts to save the Union had gained the full support of his political consultative council, which included the mayor of St. Petersburg (formerly Leningrad), Anatolii Sobchak, and the "grandfather of perestroika," Aleksandr Yakovlev. The council members, many of them founders of the Interregional Group, the first democratic bloc in the all-Union parliament, would now back Gorbachev's efforts to save the Union. Some of them spoke about creating a formal opposition to what was regarded as Yeltsin's intention to destroy the USSR.

Yeltsin's longtime ally, Sobchak, went on television that evening with a strong statement in support of the Union. But the council members were hardly an influential voice in the new Russia. They never formed the opposition bloc that they discussed with Gorbachev, and their ability to influence public opinion was limited at best. Yegor Yakovlev, a council member who had been appointed head of the Soviet Television and Radio Administration after the coup, was losing control of his own staff. "Yegor Yakovlev complained that television is being 'taken away' from him," noted Cherniaev in his diary. "He is no longer master there. And the 'Russians' are now in charge." Cherniaev then added, with regard to the television news program aired on November 29, "There were comments blatantly offensive to M[[ikhail]] S[[ergeevich]] concerning his 'Ukrainian policy.'"[24]

A few days earlier, Cherniaev and Aleksandr Yakovlev, two liberal party apparatchiks, had concluded that, as Cherniaev noted in his diary, "whether we like it or not, there is no alternative to Russia's breakthrough to independence. Gorbachev's efforts to save the Union are hopeless spasms." On November 29, the day on which Gorbachev received support from Sobchak and other leaders of perestroika, Cherniaev sent his boss a draft address to the Union parliamentarians with an appeal to vote for the new union treaty. Privately, he noted, "I don't believe in it myself. . . . Yet I came up with the words!" The same day, he forwarded a memo to Gorbachev in which he did believe, advising him to "redirect his role toward international affairs and the defense of culture . . . to represent his world prestige at home and draw support from it, not relying either on the Union treaty or on the decisions of congresses that elected him and confirmed the election after the putsch, nor on the Constitution of the USSR!" This was not a plan to save the Union but an attempt to salvage Gorbachev himself as a historical figure, if not a political one.[25]

Gorbachev, for his part, was reaching out to anyone who would listen, predicting that the dissolution of the Union would mean a human disaster of epic proportions. In an interview with the Belarusian *People's Newspaper*, Gorbachev made one of his habitual references to Yugoslavia, where the conflict between Serbs and Croats had forced hundreds of thousands of men, women, and children to abandon their ancestral homes and flee the conflict area. He thought that the Yugoslav tragedy would pale in comparison to what could happen in the Soviet Union if new national boundaries were to create a host of ethnic minorities. His argument focused on the Russians—the former masters of the empire—and the discrimination they could face in newly independent states.

"Seventy-five million people live outside the bounds of their 'small fatherlands,'" asserted Gorbachev, referring to the ethnic homelands of Soviet nationalities and the intermingled population of the Union. "What, then, are they all second-class citizens? And let them not lull us with assurances that everything will be guaranteed in bilateral agreements signed by the republics. I do not believe that they will solve the problem. We must preserve a state that will provide a legal defense for every individual." Gorbachev then referred to the Russian-speaking inhabitants of the region, who could not fully participate in the political process without knowledge of the local languages. "Willy-nilly, it's turning out that certain citizens living in the Baltic republics are being reduced to something in the nature of a second class," he told the journalist.

Even though the Belarusian reporter asked questions openly critical of Yeltsin, inviting Gorbachev to lash out against his main political opponent, the Soviet president did not rise to the bait. Whatever he thought of Yeltsin, in public he made an effort not to attack him. Gorbachev was much less restrained when it came to Leonid Kravchuk. Referring to Kravchuk's bid for Ukraine's presidency, he told the reporter, "Generally speaking, a wonderful republic . . . But look at how they are exploiting the idea of independence: in my judgment, by no means only for the purpose of an election campaign." Then Gorbachev played his minorities card, claiming that he wanted to see Ukraine united, while drawing attention to Ukraine's large Russian minority. "And if they intend to separate Ukraine from the Union," argued Gorbachev, "what are the twelve to fifteen million Russians living there supposed to do, and who needs it, anyway? I am for self-determination without the destruction of the Union."[26]

Kravchuk and his supporters in Ukraine believed that by constantly expressing concern about the fate of the eastern regions of Ukraine, Gorbachev was in fact trying to stir up interethnic conflict in the republic and exploit it to save the Union. But the question of what would happen to the Russian minority in Ukraine was more than a propaganda ploy on Gorbachev's part. Even those in his entourage who had already given up on the Union were concerned about the prospect of partitioning what was regarded as Russia's historical territory. "In general there would be nothing amiss if it were not for Ukraine and for the Crimea, which cannot be given up," noted Cherniaev in his diary.[27]

The answer to Gorbachev's and Cherniaev's concerns would be given by the forthcoming Ukrainian referendum. Those around Gorbachev did not believe that the Crimea and other regions of Ukraine with a sizable Russian population would vote for independence. It was a paradoxical situation. The future of the Russia-dominated Union depended on the Ukrainian vote, which in turn depended on the ethnic Russian vote in eastern and southern Ukraine.

George Bush and Mikhail Gorbachev at a press conference after signing the START1 agreement on the reduction of nuclear arsenals. Gorbachev managed to persuade his military to agree to unprecedented cuts in the Soviet nuclear arsenal despite the lack of funds from the West. Kremlin, Moscow, July 31, 1991. (Corbis)

Barbara Bush and Raisa Gorbacheva had an agenda of their own in Moscow. The two first ladies got along exceptionally well. They are shown here in June 1990 at Wellesley College (Wellesley, Massachusetts), where they took part in a commencement ceremony in the course of the Gorbachevs' visit to the United States. (Corbis)

The party crasher. Boris Yeltsin tried to play host at a Kremlin reception in honor of George and Barbara Bush officially hosted by the Gorbachevs. Kremlin, Moscow, July 30, 1991. (ITAR-TASS Photo Agency)

President Bush greeting Chairman Kravchuk. "Look people in the eye and you can figure out right away whether they will vote for you," Bush told the future president of Ukraine, Leonid Kravchuk. Kravchuk took that advice to heart, winning the Ukrainian presidency and independence for his country in December 1991. Boryspil airport near Kyiv, August 1, 1991. (Corbis)

The rebel. Boris Yeltsin mounts a tank and declares the putsch unconstitutional. Bush was originally reluctant to support Yeltsin but, with Gorbachev detained by the plotters, had no choice but to throw his support behind the Russian president. Yeltsin's chief bodyguard, Aleksandr Korzhakov, is to his left. Moscow, August 19, 1991. (Corbis)

The army refuses to shoot at fellow citizens. General Aleksandr Lebed speaks to defenders of the Russian White House, Yeltsin's headquarters in downtown Moscow, on August 20, 1991. Privately he told Yeltsin that if he wanted the army on his side, he would have to declare himself commander in chief of the Russian armed forces. Yeltsin followed the general's advice and won. (Corbis)

"Dear Mikhail," wrote Bush on this photograph. "Here we are in Maine thinking about you in the Crimea. Thank God you and Raisa were safe and sound. Sincerely, George." Bush is shown speaking with Gorbachev by telephone after his communication lines were restored on the afternoon of August 21, 1991. Walker's Point, Kennebunkport, Maine, August 21, 1991. (Corbis)

"We are returning to a different country," said Gorbachev on the flight to Moscow after his imprisonment in the Crimea. He did not know how right he was. In the next few days Boris Yeltsin would strip him of most of his powers. Gorbachev is shown returning to Moscow on the night of August 22, 1991. Behind him are Raisa, who suffered a stroke during the imprisonment, and one of Gorbachev's granddaughters. (Corbis)

President Bush meeting with (right to left) Secretary of Defense Dick Cheney, Secretary of State James Baker, White House Chief of Staff John H. Sununu, and National Security Adviser General Brent Scowcroft during the First Gulf War in early 1991. A few months later, Cheney clashed with the rest of the Bush team over American policy toward the crumbling Soviet Union. He wanted the USSR gone as soon as possible. (George Bush Presidential Library and Museum)

Time is up. Russian prime minister Ivan Silaev and future Ukrainian president Leonid Kravchuk check their watches as a worried Mikhail Gorbachev looks on. In the fall of 1991 Gorbachev found it increasingly difficult to deal with the two largest Soviet republics. Kremlin, Moscow, 1991. (ITAR-TASS Photo Agency)

With Russia and Ukraine against him, Gorbachev courts the Kazakh leader, Nursultan Nazarbayev. Both men wanted to preserve the Soviet Union. Here a worried Yeltsin looks on as Gorbachev talks with Nazarbayev during the signing of the economic agreement in Moscow, October 18, 1991. (Corbis)

The Russian ark. Boris Yeltsin shakes hands with his economic guru, Yegor Gaidar. Russia will go its own way, at least when it comes to economic policy. The rest of the republics can follow or get out of the way. Russia would get them back once it saved itself, argued Yeltsin's advisers. Moscow, 1991. (ITAR-TASS Photo Agency)

The survivor. Gorbachev's last appearance on the international scene. Participants in the Middle East Peace Conference descend the stairs of the Royal Palace, Madrid, Spain, October 30, 1991. Behind Gorbachev is his short-lived foreign minister, Boris Pankin; behind Bush is the main architect of the conference, James Baker. In the center is Prime Minister Felipe González of Spain. He told Gorbachev that Bush and other Western leaders had written him off during the coup. (George Bush Presidential Library and Museum)

The Slavic trinity. The leaders of the three Slavic republics decide to dissolve the USSR, Belavezha Hunting Lodge, December 8, 1991. Left to right: the contented Leonid Kravchuk of Ukraine, the confused Stanislaŭ Shushkevich of Belarus, and the always decisive Boris Yeltsin of Russia. He is bracing himself for a stormy meeting with Gorbachev the next morning in Moscow. (ITAR-TASS Photo Agency)

Bush and Baker, friends and confidants, shown here in November 1990. In the fall of 1991 they decided to back Gorbachev no matter what. In December 1991 Baker traveled to Moscow, Kyiv, Minsk, Almaty, and Bishkek to find out what was actually going on in the Soviet Union. He reported back to Bush, recommending that he endorse the creation of the Commonwealth of Independent States. (George Bush Presidential Library and Museum)

Christmas in Moscow. Gorbachev reads his resignation speech. Now it is official: the last empire has disappeared from the political map of the world. Kremlin, Moscow, December 25, 1991. (ITAR-TASS Photo Agency)

The storyteller. President Bush reads Christmas stories to his grandchildren on December 24, 1991. Next day he would fly to Washington to address the nation on the occasion of Gorbachev's resignation and declare American victory in the Cold War. (George Bush Presidential Library and Museum)

14

THE UKRAINIAN REFERENDUM

Leonid Kravchuk spent the last days of November campaigning. The referendum scheduled for December 1 was to be
held concurrently with Ukraine's presidential election, and Kravchuk,
who wanted to become president of independent Ukraine, had to win
both races.

An experienced party apparatchik but a novice public politician,
Kravchuk remembered the advice given to him by George Bush
during his July visit to Kyiv: look people in the eye, and you can figure
out right away whether they will vote for you. Kravchuk did not go
knocking on doors like a Western politician, but neither did he avoid
contact with all sorts of people. At one point it almost cost him his
life. As he visited a local department store in the central Ukrainian
city of Vinnytsia, the head of his security detail told him that
thousands of people had gathered on the square in front of the store
to see him. Neither his own security detail nor the local police had
enough personnel on hand to control the crowd, which was estimated
at twenty thousand. Kravchuk refused to leave through the back
door. "To flee like a thief from people, many of whom would soon be
voting for me?" he wrote in his memoirs. "That would be nonsense!"
A rookie campaigner, he overruled his guards and went to talk to the
people on the square.

His political instincts were immediately rewarded with cries of
"Hurrah for Kravchuk!" But the huge crowd, with people at the back

pushing those in front to get a glimpse of the man at the center, was becoming ever more restless. The Ukrainian Speaker suddenly felt excruciating pain and heard a crack—it was his finger. Someone in the crowd had grabbed Kravchuk's hand in an unsuccessful attempt to shake it and broke his finger. "As I looked around, things began to look somewhat frightening," Kravchuk wrote. "It seemed that if the rather uncertain militia cordon did not hold, we would simply be crushed." Kravchuk made his way out of the square as the locals continued to chant "hurrah"—a sign of approval of him personally and of the policies he advocated. He got out of Vinnytsia with new confidence in his victory, but his finger was broken, and his shoes were ruined: as his bodyguards dragged him through the crowd, he had dug in his heels so as not to lose balance. This was an aspect of democratic campaigning on which Bush could not have offered advice; who would have thought that the former Soviet officials did not know how to control a crowd?[1]

In early November, one month before the elections, Kravchuk was leading in the polls with more than 30 percent of the popular vote. His closest rival, a former political prisoner and now head of the Lviv regional administration, Viacheslav Chornovil, was trailing him with slightly more than 12 percent of the projected vote. Kravchuk's competitors believed that the deck was stacked against them, as their opponent had the full support of the state apparatus in the center and regions alike. Indeed, he was not only part and parcel of the establishment but also, under the circumstances, its favorite son and last hope. The former communist elite, initially either hostile to independence or wary of it, now fully embraced it. In August, the communist majority in the Ukrainian parliament had voted for independence on condition that the decision be ratified three months later by a referendum. This gave them an opportunity to change their minds if necessary, but there were no developments after August 24 that required a change of course.[2]

To be sure, the vote for independence did not save the party, which had been not just suspended but completely outlawed in Ukraine in late August 1991, months before it was fully banned in Russia. The process, however, was quite different. There was no public humiliation of party officials; nor were they deprived of former party property. Instead, one group of party officials calmly transferred party property to another group: it came under the jurisdiction of the local soviets, regional and city councils controlled more often than not by former communist officials. For most of the former communist elite, independence became a new religion and Kravchuk its prophet, who would save them from the rage of Yeltsin, as well as from that of the democrats and nationalists in their own backyard. These two elements—Kravchuk and independence—were complementary parts of the ticket that would allow them to stay in power. They would do anything to support independence if Kravchuk became president and anything to undermine it if he lost to his rivals either from the pro-Yeltsin democratic camp or from the nationaldemocratic camp.[3]

KRAVCHUK HAD HIS TASK cut out for him. Soon after the declaration of Ukrainian independence in August, it became clear that he had to find a way to convince the voters that despite his communist past he was the best candidate to lead them and the country into sovereignty. He also had to convince them to vote for independence. To achieve that goal, he had to appease the regional elites and dissuade them from playing the separatist card; to calm the sizable national and religious minorities, who might be afraid to remain in a Ukrainian-dominated country without the intermediacy and protection of the Union center; and to win over the commanders of Soviet military units, whom the Union or Russian leadership could use as a Trojan horse against Ukrainian independence.

The task of convincing the voters that he was the best candidate for the presidency of Ukraine seemed the easiest one. Since there were five presidential candidates competing with Kravchuk, the democratic vote in Ukraine was split several ways. The urban intelligentsia from the Russified east, which had voted for democrats of Yeltsin's stripe during the perestroika years, found a spokesman in the second deputy Speaker of parliament, Volodymyr Hryniov. An ethnic Russian and a product of the democratic awakening in the city of Kharkiv on the border with Russia, Hryniov was an early and resolute opponent of the coup. He was also one of few deputies who voted against independence on August 24, not because he opposed independence per se but because he did not want the country to be ruled by communists. However, with the Communist Party officially outlawed, Hryniov embraced the idea of an independent Ukraine, believing that this was what most people wanted at the time. As he subsequently recalled, "It was quite clearly apparent in the course of the election campaign that the mood of the people was oriented on the independence of Ukraine. When you meet the masses, you cannot disguise the mood."[4]

The main candidate from the nationaldemocratic bloc, Viacheslav Chornovil, contrasted himself with Kravchuk by telling his life story, claiming that he had always been anticommunist and had not trimmed his views to fit circumstances. A longtime political dissident, first arrested in 1967, Chornovil had had more than enough time in prison camps to think about what kind of Ukraine he wanted and would be able to build. He believed that an independent Ukraine would have to become a federal state. When Chornovil became head of the Lviv regional administration after the first democratic elections in the spring of 1990, he promoted the idea of a Ukrainian federation in which Galicia, a historical region composed of three oblasts with its administrative center in Lviv, would have autonomy. But on the presidential trail he downplayed federalism, claiming that at the moment it undermined the goal of independence.[5]

For some of Chornovil's rivals in the nationaldemocratic camp, this was too little, too late. Levko Lukianenko, the principal author of the Ukrainian declaration of independence, continued to argue that Chornovil was a federalist and that federalism was harmful to Ukraine, as it would encourage Russian imperial ambitions and provide a legal foundation for separatism. Chornovil, the official candidate of Rukh, and Lukianenko, the head of Rukh's strongest and best-organized political force, the Ukrainian Republican Party, went their separate ways, creating a wedge in nationaldemocratic ranks that benefited Kravchuk. The Ukrainian nationaldemocratic vote was split even further when some members of that camp came out in support of Kravchuk. Many early proponents of Ukrainian independence from the ranks of the intelligentsia believed that his election was the only chance for Ukraine to emerge united and independent.[6]

For many in the Ukrainian intelligentsia, Kravchuk represented the lesser evil. Those from the national camp suspected that if not closely watched, he might cave in to pressure from Moscow. Pro-Yeltsin democrats from the Hryniov camp considered him too cozy with the nationalists. Neither group could forget his recent communist past.

Even so, those who did not believe that Chornovil or Hryniov could win were prepared to hold their noses and vote strategically for Kravchuk. As Larysa Skoryk, a nationaldemocratic member of parliament, explained to a Canadian correspondent of the *Ukrainian Weekly*, Kravchuk was the man of the hour and right for the job. He was the only pro-independence candidate capable of talking to the communist elite, as he had fully demonstrated during the vote for independence on August 24. According to Skoryk, Kravchuk knew that there was no way back. "He is an extremely clever person," she told the reporter. "To say that this is a man with high moral values, I cannot. . . . But, on the other hand, is the given moment really one which demands heroics, or is it a moment where super diplomacy is needed?"[7]

AS KRAVCHUK WROTE in his memoirs, winning the presidency would be meaningless unless Ukraine voted for independence. One thing he did not want was to become governor-general of a province ruled from Moscow. Very early in the campaign, with his position as front-runner consolidated and secure, Kravchuk decided that his best strategy was to campaign not for himself but for Ukrainian independence. This worked well with voters. There was a steady growth in the number of those who favored independence: 65 percent in late September; close to 70 percent of those polled and more than 80 percent of those intending to vote in the election by early November. It was most important that the number exceed the threshold of 70 percent—the level of support among Ukrainian voters for a renewed union registered in the March 1991 referendum initiated by Gorbachev. That result was Gorbachev's main weapon in his struggle to keep the Soviet Union alive.

Kravchuk faced a formidable challenge. Not only did he have to beat the results of the March referendum, he also needed to obtain a yes vote of at least 50 percent in every region of Ukraine. Otherwise, the legitimacy of Ukrainian independence would be challenged both at home and in Moscow, to say nothing of the West. Nothing could be left to chance. Kravchuk and his supporters deliberated for some time on the wording of the question that they would ask on December 1. Pollsters told them that if people were asked not only whether they supported independence but also whether they approved the August declaration of independence adopted by the Ukrainian parliament, the results were usually better. The word "independence" had been discredited by decades of Soviet propaganda in eastern Ukraine. But parliament's sanction was giving the word and concept a new legitimacy that appealed to conservative voters. On the eve of the referendum, the presidium of parliament issued an appeal to the population of Ukraine, making one last point in the debate. It said that not supporting independence meant supporting dependence. Few people wanted their republic to remain dependent on Moscow.

One of the main problems faced by proponents of Ukrainian independence—from Kravchuk and Hryniov to Chornovil and Lukianenko—in their respective campaigns was the country's regional and cultural diversity. This was the card that Georgii Shakhnazarov proposed Gorbachev play to stem the growing pro-independence tide in Ukraine and the problem that Gorbachev never tired of mentioning to anyone who would listen. While pollsters predicted a strong vote for independence in Ukraine as a whole, the degree of support varied from region to region. Support was strongest in Galicia, which had formerly been ruled by Austria and Poland. In Ternopil oblast in Galicia, more than 92 percent of those polled favored independence. Kravchuk's native Volhynia, which had been part of Poland during the interwar period but never part of Austria-Hungary, was not far behind, with close to 88 percent of the projected vote favoring independence. Kyiv and central Ukraine had jumped on the independence bandwagon as well, but support for independence in some of Ukraine's eastern and southern provinces was barely above 50 percent. Those were the regions that had been fully colonized only in the nineteenth century under the rule of the Russian Empire and had experienced a major influx of ethnic Russians in the Soviet period. There, Kravchuk was significantly ahead of his main rival, Viacheslav Chornovil. His election was an assurance for many that if independence actually came, it would not take the form of radical nationalism.[8]

On October 23 Kravchuk flew to Ukraine's most independent-minded region, the autonomous republic of the Crimea, to convince the local parliament to support Ukrainian independence. The Crimea, a peninsula connected to Ukraine's mainland by a strip of land seven kilometers wide and divided from Russia by the four and a half kilometers of the Kerch Strait, had belonged to the Russian Federation before 1954. It was transferred to Ukraine during the rule of Nikita Khrushchev for economic reasons and was one of twenty-five Ukrainian oblasts until February 1991. That changed after the Crimean referendum of January 1991, which endorsed not only autonomy for the Crimea but also its right to be a signatory to the new union treaty. In early 1991 Gorbachev and the center were busy building up the status of the autonomies in order to counterpose them to sovereignty-minded leaders of the Union republics. The tactic worked only to a degree. When in August 1991 Gorbachev invited Nikolai Bagrov, the Speaker of the Crimean parliament, to come to Moscow for the signing of the union treaty, Bagrov politely declined the invitation. It was already clear to everyone that Ukraine would not participate in the agreement.

But the Ukrainian leaders' problems with the Crimea in the fall of 1991 were not all of Gorbachev's making. In February 1991, the Kyiv authorities agreed to grant the Crimea autonomous status partly because it was the only region of the country where ethnic Ukrainians were a minority (a quarter of the population). More than 67 percent of the population consisted of ethnic Russians, who dominated Crimean politics and culture. There were no Ukrainian-language schools in the Crimea, few ethnic Ukrainians used the Ukrainian language in everyday life, and only half claimed Ukrainian as their native tongue—an indication that their Ukrainian identity was anything but strong. An additional concern for the Kyiv authorities was the presence in the Crimea of officers and sailors of the Soviet Black Sea Fleet and military retirees opposed to Ukrainian independence. The Crimean Tatars, who had been deported from the peninsula by Stalin in 1944 on charges of collaboration with the Nazis during the German occupation, were beginning to return to their ancestral homeland, adding new complexity to the ethnic balance.[9]

Kravchuk came to the Crimea on the day when its parliament was scheduled to vote on the law regulating the local referendum that was to put the question of the Crimea's secession from Ukraine to a popular vote. He managed to convince the Crimean parliament to postpone the adoption of the law and cancel the referendum. His argument was simple: if the Crimea was an autonomous part of Ukraine, its parliament would have enough power to solve the region's problems without interference from Kyiv. The former communist elite, who had worked with Kyiv since 1954, agreed to postpone the vote on the law. Their opponents in parliament, represented by the Republican Movement of the Crimea, which favored the referendum, were outvoted.

The Republican Movement's leader, Yuri Meshkov, one of the few Crimean deputies who had opposed the August coup, declared a hunger strike in protest. He defined the conflict in parliament as a struggle of democracy against communism. But not everything was clear-cut in Crimean politics. Soon four women journalists—one Ukrainian, one Tatar, and two Russians—began their own hunger strike to protest the escalation of ethnic hatred in the Crimea by Meshkov's supporters. Kravchuk's line eventually prevailed: there would be no separate referendum on Crimean independence. Crimean voters would go to the polling stations to answer just one referendum question: whether they supported Ukrainian independence. Unlike Yeltsin in the case of Chechnia, Kravchuk managed to keep the autonomous Crimea within his republic by political means.[10]

The Crimea, which had gained autonomy in early 1991 and was now given special consideration by Kyiv, was envied by local elites in the Transcarpathian oblast of Ukraine, which had belonged to Czechoslovakia before the war. They, too, wanted autonomy. Odesa in the south and the Donbas coal region in the east were prime candidates for similar status. With federalism becoming a dirty word in the Ukrainian presidential election, Viacheslav Chornovil promised the Odesa elites a free economic zone. Kravchuk toured the country with a different message, offering broad economic autonomy for Ukrainian historical regions, of which he counted twelve. The local elites had to settle for what he was offering, as most of them were not about to vote for Chornovil. Rumor had it that if Kravchuk lost, the regional elites in the east and south would declare themselves independent of Kyiv.

Centrifugal tendencies in the regions were one of the challenges facing Kyiv in the run-up to the December referendum. The impact that those tendencies would have on Ukraine's relations with its neighbors, Soviet and non-Soviet, was another. After the statement made in late August by Yeltsin's spokesman, Pavel Voshchanov, it had become clear that, depending on the results of the referendum, Russia was prepared to make claims on the Crimea and possibly on eastern regions of the country. Hungarians in Transcarpathia looked to their ethnic brethren across the border, and a Romanian movement was gaining strength in northern Bukovyna, a largely Ukrainian-populated region that had belonged to Romania during the interwar period. And if the Czechoslovak and Hungarian elites were not making any claims on current Ukrainian territories, the Romanian parliament was much less accommodating.

On the eve of the Ukrainian referendum, Romania's parliament adopted a resolution calling for nonrecognition of the results in northern Bukovyna, which it called an "ancient Romanian land." The Ukrainian foreign minister, Anatolii Zlenko, learned of the Romanian resolution as he was on his way to Bucharest for his first official visit there. He decided not to proceed and left the train in the middle of the night, before it crossed the border. The next morning the foreign minister of Romania, who was not informed of his Ukrainian guest's sudden change of plans, waited for him in vain at the Bucharest train station. The Ukrainians treated the question of their territorial integrity very seriously. In fact, they had no other choice: postwar Ukraine included territories that had belonged to Poland, Czechoslovakia, Romania, and Russia before 1939.[11]

Foreign claims on Ukrainian territory, like those of Russia and Romania, and centrifugal tendencies among Ukraine's diverse regions were closely linked to the question of Ukraine's ethnic minorities. The Russians were the largest group, accounting for 11 million people, settled largely in urbanized eastern and southern Ukraine. Their concerns were on the minds of Kravchuk and the other presidential candidates whenever they campaigned in the Crimea or southeastern Ukraine. The message they all delivered was roughly the same: they wanted Russians in Ukraine to feel even more comfortable than they would in Russia. Many did. The closeness of the two East Slavic languages, Russian and Ukrainian, and the fact that most ethnic Ukrainians in eastern urban centers switched to Russian in their daily lives made the Russo-Ukrainian divide all but invisible and gave the Russians confidence about their future in an independent Ukraine. Many of them had lived in Ukraine for generations and had intermarried with Ukrainians. As a group, they were not hostile to the idea of Ukrainian independence and were prepared to be persuaded of its advantages.

Ukraine's Russian population could see that the Soviet Union was not working; the economy was in free fall. Everyone in Ukraine, including the Russians, was ready to try something else. Marta Dyczok, a graduate student from Oxford University who was freelancing for the *Guardian* while doing her archival research in Ukraine, traveled the country on assignment for the newspaper in an effort to grasp the mood of the people. Later she summarized what she learned as follows: "Listening to people before and after the coup, it was that desire for change that was really, really strong. That was the bottom emotion that we heard everywhere. Enough of this confusion, enough of this corruption, enough of this. We want something else. The thing that was being offered as a change was Ukraine becoming independent."[12]

In his appeal to voters, Kravchuk put the main emphasis not on ethnocultural nationalism but on economic independence, drawing on the myth, ingrained in the minds of the country's inhabitants, of Ukraine as an economic superpower and breadbasket of Europe that was now feeding Russia and the rest of the Soviet republics. Ukrainian newspapers featured a story—which turned out to be completely false—that experts at the Deutsche Bank considered Ukraine the Soviet republic with the greatest economic potential. With living standards in Ukraine higher than those in the Russian provinces for most of the Soviet period and the Ukrainian consumer market for agricultural goods doing much better than the Russian market in the fall of 1991, it did not take much to persuade Ukrainian citizens of all nationalities to choose independence and thus economic prosperity.

The need for political and economic independence became self-evident when in November the Soviet central bank cut payments to Ukraine, making it difficult for many Ukrainian institutions and enterprises to pay wages and salaries. Yeltsin's speech on economic reform destabilized the consumer market in Russia, causing prices to rise and goods to disappear from stores in the Soviet capital. Muscovites, whose salaries were paid by the Russian government, headed south by train to buy agricultural products in Ukraine. In response, cash-strapped Ukrainians and Russians in the traditionally Russia-friendly east of the country physically protected their markets and low prices on agricultural goods by not allowing travelers from the north to leave train stations on their arrival. Clashes between the two groups became an everyday occurrence in Ukrainian industrial centers such as Dnipropetrovsk. Independence seemed the only way out of the conundrum, whatever one's ethnic origin.[13]

Jews were Ukraine's second-largest minority, accounting for half a million Ukrainian citizens. They were among those most discriminated against during the last decades of Soviet rule, and it was with regard to them that the Ukrainian authorities sought to demonstrate their newfound tolerance. In October 1991, with national democrats on the offensive and former communists on the run, the Ukrainian authorities sponsored the first public commemoration of the massacre of the Jews of Kyiv in the Babyn Yar ravine in the fall of 1941. For tens of thousands of Jews who attended the ceremony, it was the first time in their lives that they could publicly manifest their Jewish identity. For tens of thousands of non-Jews, it was the first time that they publicly recognized and embraced the suppressed identity of their neighbors.

Gorbachev sent a personal representative to the event at Babyn Yar—the "grandfather of perestroika," Aleksandr Yakovlev. Bush sent a delegation of prominent Americans, headed by his brother Jonathan. Kravchuk met with the delegation and spoke at the event, preaching tolerance and respect for human rights and human life. "Dear friends!" said Kravchuk to the multiethnic and multireligious audience. "The history of relations between the Ukrainian and Jewish peoples is complex and dramatic. It has had its bright and dark pages. Not one of us has the right to forget anything. But we should remember not in order to reopen old wounds but so that we never let them happen again. May our memories include more often that which unites us and not the differences between our peoples." Kravchuk, who had witnessed a massacre of Jews in Volhynia and knew about the participation in the Holocaust of Ukrainian policemen recruited by the Nazis, finished his speech in Yiddish after offering his apologies to the Jewish people on behalf of the Ukrainian nation.[14]

On November 1, the Ukrainian parliament adopted a Declaration on the Rights of Nationalities of Ukraine that guaranteed equality to citizens of all origins. On November 16, a thousand delegates gathered in Odesa to take part in the All-Ukrainian Inter-ethnic Congress, jointly organized by Rukh and the Ukrainian parliament. The delegates overwhelmingly adopted a resolution supporting Ukrainian independence—only three votes were cast against it. A *Los Angeles Times* reporter was amazed to see a Hassidic Jew and a Ukrainian dressed in Cossack style, with a saber at his side, attending the same congress and peacefully promoting their respective causes in front of the Odesa opera house. It was a marked difference from Ukraine's previous attempt to gain independence. In January 1918, Jewish delegates to the Ukrainian parliament, who had earlier supported autonomy, voted against independence. What followed was a split in the pro-democratic alliance, years of civil war, and numerous pogroms and massacres that left deep scars in Jewish memory. Now both nationalities saw a common solution to their respective problems. In November 1991, Jewish support for independence registered at 60 percent, slightly above the Russian figure of 58.9 percent.[15]

On November 20, Kravchuk addressed the first all-Ukrainian religious forum. The former self-described chief atheist of Ukraine (under his supervision, the ideology department of the Central Committee of the Communist Party of Ukraine oversaw the country's religious organizations) asked forgiveness of religious leaders, not on behalf of the defunct party but on that of the state he now represented. As communism and atheism lost their ideological appeal and religion returned to the public sphere, religious denominations began to play an ever more important role in society. Ukraine, which accounted for two-thirds of all Orthodox Christian parishes in the USSR and was home to most Soviet Protestants, was considered the Bible Belt of the Soviet Union. It had become a religious battleground with the arrival of perestroika and glasnost. Kravchuk called for interreligious toleration and support for independence. He wanted religious leaders to work toward the independence of their religious institutions but to avoid strife in doing so. On November 20, leaders of sixteen religious organizations in Ukraine pledged their support for government policy on religion. It was, in effect, a gesture of support for independence.[16]

THE FATE OF THE SOVIET ARMY on the territory of Ukraine was another of Kravchuk's major concerns. Kravchuk had realized how defenseless the Ukrainian authorities were against the Soviet military when General Valentin Varennikov visited him in his parliamentary office on the first day of the coup. After the coup collapsed, the Ukrainian authorities immediately set about forming a national guard by taking over Interior Ministry troops on their territory. But that was hardly enough to deter Soviet army formations stationed in Ukraine and commanded from Moscow. Ukraine, considered the second echelon of Soviet defense structures in case of global war (the first was Soviet-controlled Eastern Europe), was home to Soviet army units totaling seven hundred thousand men.

On August 27, three days after the declaration of Ukrainian independence, Kravchuk called a meeting of senior Soviet military commanders posted in Ukraine. He wanted them to accommodate the new political reality of Ukrainian independence and begin the formation of independent Ukrainian armed forces. The military brass did not believe that the decision of the Ukrainian parliament affected them. With support from Moscow, they argued that the Soviet army should remain united under a single command. Kravchuk's call for military reform gained a positive response from only one senior officer who attended the meeting. He was Major General Kostiantyn Morozov, the forty-seven-year-old commander of an Air Force army stationed in Ukraine. An open-minded officer sympathetic to the movement for democracy in Ukraine, Morozov was the only officer in the room who had boycotted the directives of the coup leaders to put their troops on the alert. Now he became the only officer at the meeting to suggest that an independent Ukraine should establish its own armed forces. That made him a marked man with no prospect of advancement or even of remaining at his current post.

Like his former subordinate General Dzhokhar Dudaev, who left the Soviet military in the spring of 1991 to lead the Chechen republic toward independence, Morozov was now solidly in the anti-Moscow camp. He had reached a point of no return, and his life and career would henceforth be associated with the idea of Ukrainian independence. A week after the August 27 meeting, the Ukrainian parliament voted overwhelmingly to appoint Morozov as Ukraine's first minister of defense. Morozov shared the vision of Ukraine as a nuclear-free state and was ready to give up the world's third-largest nuclear arsenal. He was opposed, however, to transferring nuclear weapons to Russia and wanted them dismantled in Ukraine. Morozov's confirmation by parliament became a certainty when he answered a question from Dmytro Pavlychko, who, apart from chairing the foreign relations committee, headed the Society for the Promotion of the Ukrainian

Language. Asked whether he would master Ukrainian, Morozov, who spoke to parliament in Russian, answered in the affirmative. He told Pavlychko that he would be happy to do so with the help of the society. The answer charmed the national democrats, who were uncertain whether they could entrust the defense of their not yet fully born country to a general with a typically Russian surname.

Morozov was in fact a native of Ukraine and half Ukrainian by birth. Born and educated in the Russified eastern part of the country, where most of the population spoke Russian or a mixture of Russian and Ukrainian, he had studied standard Ukrainian in school but had not used it in more than thirty years of military service. His appointment to Kyiv to command air force district was a major error on the part of the General Staff in Moscow. According to an unwritten law of the Soviet military, under no circumstances could ethnic Ukrainian officers be allowed to serve in positions of high authority in Ukraine. The same rule applied to other ethnic groups in their native republics. General Dzhokhar Dudaev, the future leader of independent Chechnia, served under Morozov's command in Ukraine but was not allowed to hold command positions in his native land. Even in Ukraine, his promotion to the rank of general was not free of problems. He was accused of nationalism for dancing the *lezginka,* a national dance of many ethnic groups in the Caucasus, upon learning of the promotion.

Morozov got around the restrictions on Soviet ethnic minorities because, according to his documents, he was Russian, not Ukrainian. When he declared his support for Ukrainian independence in the autumn of 1991, his commanders in Moscow, including his former patron, Marshal Yevgenii Shaposhnikov, now the Soviet minister of defense, could not believe their ears. Shaposhnikov twice asked Morozov whether he was indeed Ukrainian. Morozov responded half jokingly that an error had apparently made its way into his personal file. For his commanders, as Morozov recalled later, half Russian meant Russian. His case underlined the complexity of Russo-Ukrainian relations and the blurring of the two cultures and identities as Russification of ethnic Ukrainians gathered speed in the course of the twentieth century. In the Soviet Union, people of mixed ethnic parentage, including Morozov, could choose their nationality at will. Many chose Russian as their passport nationality but, having been born and raised in Ukraine, considered the latter their true homeland. Morozov was one of them.[17]

Language, identity, and loyalty were three major issues that Morozov had to tackle in his capacity as chief architect of the Ukrainian armed forces. The importance of language came to the fore in October 1991 when he met a visiting American academic, Zbigniew Brzezinski. The former national security adviser to President Jimmy Carter came to Kyiv on the eve of the Ukrainian parliament's adoption of a resolution on the country's nonnuclear status. After his official conversation with the newly appointed minister of defense, Brzezinski asked Morozov whether they could speak privately. As Morozov remembered later, he agreed but was somewhat puzzled—he did not speak English, and Brzezinski was not prepared to switch to Russian. Eventually they found a way to communicate: Brzezinski, being of Polish origin, spoke Polish, while Morozov spoke Ukrainian. They understood each other perfectly well. One of the questions Brzezinski asked privately dealt with the language of Ukraine's armed forces: should it be Ukrainian or Russian? Morozov replied that it would be difficult to switch, but he felt that the language should be Ukrainian. Brzezinski liked what he heard and said something to Morozov that would be carved in the latter's memory forever: "The order to defend the nation should be given in the national language."[18]

For the time being, however, language would have to wait, not only because the minister of defense himself was still taking private Ukrainian lessons but also because the model of recruitment that Morozov and Kravchuk had chosen to implement did not include or even allow for the prompt introduction of a new language regime. It would have been possible only if Ukraine had followed the Baltic example, where the governments of the newly independent states demanded the withdrawal of Soviet troops from their territory and recruited their armed forces from scratch. Kravchuk and Morozov considered that infeasible in Ukraine. The Soviet army of seven hundred thousand had nowhere to go. Russia was still struggling and would struggle for years with the task of repatriating and resettling troops withdrawn from Eastern Europe. Kyiv had no choice but to take command of Soviet troops and Ukrainize them in the process.

This was relatively easy when it came to draftees: soldiers recruited in Ukraine would replace those from other republics. Nor was there a problem with noncommissioned officers, who were all local. But the officer corps had been recruited from all over the Soviet Union. Morozov and his people did not intend to follow the nationality policy of the old Soviet army. Passport nationality would be only one of the criteria for deciding the fate of a given officer. He would not necessarily stay in Ukraine if he was a passport Ukrainian and/or be sent away if he was a passport Russian or Armenian. What mattered no less was the officer's place of birth and family ties, as well as other links to Ukraine. Last but not least, the officer would have to manifest a desire to serve Ukraine. If those criteria were met, he would be welcome: language acquisition could wait. Kravchuk was trying to build a political nation out of Ukraine's multiethnic population, and Morozov was recruiting the Ukrainian officer corps on the same principle.

Nuclear arms presented another challenge to the idea of Ukrainian independence. Morozov wanted an independent Ukrainian army, but initially neither he nor his political masters challenged the principle that nuclear forces on Ukrainian territory should be commanded from Moscow. That view was shaken by a conversation with another of Morozov's new American acquaintances, the national security adviser and secretary of state in Richard Nixon's administration, Henry Kissinger. At their first meeting, Kissinger seemed half asleep, but the questions he asked the minister showed a mind working in unexpected ways. When Kissinger inquired what Morozov and the Ukrainian leaders were going to do with the nuclear arms and strategic armed forces on their territory, Morozov answered as he had always done: strategic arms would be under the central control of Moscow. The apparently sleepy Kissinger asked a blunt follow-up question: "And what, then, is independence?" The question overturned all of Morozov's previous thinking on the issue. Ukraine could not take over strategic nuclear forces on its territory without becoming an international pariah, but if its leaders were serious about independence, they could not allow major military formations in their country to report to Moscow rather than to Kyiv. This was the origin of Morozov's conclusion that the strategic forces should be transferred to Russia: better to lose them than to keep a Trojan horse inside the country.

For most of the autumn of 1991, Morozov's plans for the Ukrainian armed forces remained little more than a vision. The Moscow authorities rejected the idea of Kyiv's takeover of military formations based in Ukraine, proposing that Morozov remain the commander of Soviet airborne troops there (and continue to take orders from the General Staff) while moonlighting as an official of the Ukrainian government. As Morozov recalled, they could not bring themselves to pronounce the title "minister of defense." He requested the transfer from Moscow of a number of General Staff officers who were natives of Ukraine and had volunteered to help build its army. They were sent to Kyiv but distrusted thereafter by their former colleagues.

Morozov established his headquarters in the offices of a former party building in downtown Kyiv. The office was severely understaffed and underfunded. Morozov communicated with his people on the ground mainly by telephone, and the Ukrainian diaspora in North America donated a couple of fax machines. At first he drove the car that he had used as commander of airborne troops. Morozov's small staff relied on volunteers in individual military units stationed in Ukraine to collect information about what was going on there. In some units, his officers worked virtually under cover. Morozov himself was barely tolerated by the commanders of Ukrainian military districts, all of whom held military rank higher than his.

In November, a rumor began to make the rounds that General Viktor Chechevatov, the commander of the Kyiv military district and one of the officers who had visited Kravchuk during the coup as part of General Varennikov's entourage, had issued an order to arrest Morozov. There were also reports that Gorbachev had approved military maneuvers to be held in Ukraine by units stationed there on November 28, two days before the referendum. Although Morozov condemned those plans, he had little control over what the military would do on the territory of the state that he now served as minister of defense.[19]

ON THE MORNING of Sunday, December 1, Kravchuk dropped his ballot into a box at a polling station in central Kyiv to the flashes of dozens of cameras belonging to Ukrainian and foreign correspondents catching the historic moment. Like many of his compatriots, Kravchuk voted in the morning. Early reports from polling stations indicated that the turnout was good.

The countryside, where most people were early risers, led the way. In the village of Khotiv, south of Kyiv, between 70 and 80 percent of registered voters had cast their ballots by 10:00 a.m. A local woman who informed Western correspondents of this fact burst into tears. She was proud of her fellow villagers, and there was no doubt in her mind that they had voted for independence. In Kyiv, as in the villages, many went to vote with members of their families, taking children along. Some were reluctant to go home after voting and stayed near the polling stations, discussing the possible outcome of the referendum and its significance. Ukrainian Americans and Canadians who had come to their ancestral homeland to help with the historic vote were moved by the experience. Chrystyna Lapychak of the *Ukrainian Weekly* expressed the feelings of many of her fellow Ukrainian Americans when she told an Associated Press correspondent, "I felt that ghosts were present that day in all of those places—ghosts of people who were not fortunate enough to have lived to vote. All of our ancestors were there, everyone who had ever suffered, who had ever dreamed that their grandchildren would see freedom. We are those grandchildren."[20]

Yurii Shcherbak, a minister in the Ukrainian government, had read the declaration of Ukrainian independence from the podium of the all-Union parliament in Moscow in late August. He remembered later that different political forces and social groups came together to vote for independence. Each had its own hopes and expectations: the national democrats were intent on independence and rapid cultural Ukrainization; the former communist leaders wanted a safe haven for themselves and their families, free from Moscow's control; and most of the population, convinced that Ukraine was the richest republic of the Union, wanted to separate from poor and unpredictable Russia, with its political and military conflicts. The success of the Ukrainian Americans, who had managed to commit President Bush to the recognition of Ukrainian independence even before the vote took place, gave confidence to the Ukrainian elites that independence could be not only proclaimed but also achieved.[21]

The results of the referendum exceeded the expectations of the most optimistic supporters of Ukrainian independence. The turnout on December 1 was 84 percent, and more than 90 percent of voters supported independence. Gorbachev had called Kravchuk a dreamer when he predicted that no less than 80 percent of voters would back independence, but even Kravchuk did not expect what actually happened. A week before the referendum, when Stepan Khmara, a deputy of the parliament and a former prisoner of the Gulag, told him that support would exceed 90 percent, Kravchuk replied that he was crazy. Khmara turned out to be right: the final result was 90.32 percent in favor of independence.

As predicted by the pollsters, a virtually unanimous vote for independence was recorded in Ternopil oblast in Galicia, where the turnout exceeded 97 percent, and close to 99 percent of voters supported independence. In Vinnytsia, the city in central Ukraine where Kravchuk had almost been stampeded by his admirers a few weeks earlier, the vote for independence exceeded 95 percent. Support was less impressive but still very strong in the east and south. In Odesa oblast, more than 85 percent voted for independence. In Luhansk oblast, which was part of the Donbas region and the easternmost oblast in Ukraine, the vote for independence exceeded 83 percent. In neighboring Donetsk oblast, it reached almost 77 percent. Even in the Crimea, so troublesome to the Ukrainian authorities, more than 54 percent voted in favor. In Sevastopol, the base of the Soviet Black Sea Fleet, the figure was 57 percent.

Kravchuk learned the first results of the referendum at about 2:00 a.m. on December 2. There was now no doubt that the pro-independence campaign conducted by Kravchuk and his rivals would produce an independent state for one of them to lead. As expected, Kravchuk was in the lead in all Ukrainian oblasts except Galicia, where the winner was Viacheslav Chornovil. Nationwide, Kravchuk received 61 percent of the vote over Chornovil's 23 percent. Kravchuk's strongest showing was in Luhansk oblast, where he gained more than 76 percent of the vote. In the Crimea, he won with 56 percent against Chornovil's 8 percent. Despite Gorbachev's grim predictions, Ukraine was not divided by ethnic strife or local separatism. Later that morning, when Kravchuk called Gorbachev to report on the results of the referendum and the presidential election, Gorbachev could not believe what he was hearing. He congratulated the Ukrainian leader on his victory in the presidential race but did not mention the referendum.[22]

On the following day, Gorbachev tore up a draft appeal to the citizens of Ukraine prepared by his adviser Georgii Shakhnazarov. By now, Shakhnazarov had stopped making suggestions on how to use the ethnic card to undermine the drive for Ukrainian independence and had fully embraced the Russian position on the Ukrainian referendum. Those around Yeltsin had bowed to the inevitable and were prepared to endorse the results. Shakhnazarov's draft had included congratulations to the Ukrainians on their "historic choice." Gorbachev ordered his other aide, Anatolii Cherniaev, to prepare a new draft, including such statements as "All are independent, but not all turn independence into a weapon against the Union. . . . Misfortune awaits the Ukrainians—both those who live there and those scattered around the country. . . . That goes even more for Russians." Cherniaev obliged. The next day Gorbachev published an appeal to parliamentarians throughout the Soviet Union. "Every one of you has the right to reject the Union," read the appeal. "But it requires that those chosen by the people consider all the consequences." He warned the deputies against interethnic conflict.

Cherniaev was in Gorbachev's office on the evening of December 2, when the Soviet president placed a call to Yeltsin. In response to Gorbachev's offer to meet and discuss the new situation, perhaps with Kravchuk and the leader of Kazakhstan, Nursultan Nazarbayev, the Russian president said, "Nothing will come of it anyway. Ukraine is independent." He suggested a four-member union consisting of Russia, Ukraine, Belarus, and Kazakhstan. Gorbachev flatly refused: "And what would be my place in it? If that's the deal, then I'm leaving. I'm not going to bobble like a piece of shit in an ice hole." Gorbachev would not countenance a union that left him dependent on Yeltsin and reduced him to playing a supporting role to his nemesis. Yeltsin would not tolerate a union in which Gorbachev could tell him what to do.[23]

On December 3, 1991, George Bush asked his assistants to connect him with Leonid Kravchuk. He wanted to congratulate the newly elected president of a newly independent country on his personal victory and the overwhelming vote in favor of independence. Bush told Kravchuk that Americans welcomed the emergence of a new democratic nation and would send an envoy to discuss nuclear disarmament, border issues, human rights, and the rights of minorities. Kravchuk had good news for Bush: Yeltsin had already been in touch with him, and Russia had recognized Ukrainian independence. He would meet with Yeltsin on the following Saturday to discuss the new situation and coordinate policy.[24]

15

THE SLAVIC TRINITY

GEORGE BUSH FIRST LEARNED ABOUT the planned meeting of Russian and Ukrainian leaders from Boris Yeltsin, with whom he spoke on the eve of the Ukrainian referendum. The Russian president took Bush by surprise when he said that in order to preserve good relations with Ukraine, Russia should recognize its independence right away if the vote in favor exceeded 70 percent.

"Right away?" asked Bush.

"Yes, we need to do it immediately," responded Yeltsin. "Otherwise our position is unnecessarily unclear, especially since we are approaching the new year and a new reform. Gorbachev does not know about this. He still thinks Ukraine will sign."

Yeltsin thought otherwise. "Right now the draft union treaty has only seven states ready to sign up—five Islamic and two Slavic (Byelorussia and Russia)," he told Bush. He explained that if Ukraine did not join the Union, Russia would be in trouble: "We can't have a situation where Russia and Byelorussia have two votes as Slavic states against five for the Islamic nations." A few minutes later he added, "I am now thinking very hard with a very narrow circle of key advisers on how to preserve the Union, but also how not to lose relations with Ukraine. Our relations with Ukraine are more significant than those with the Central Asian republics, which we feed all the time. On the other hand, we can't forget the Islamic fundamentalist factor."

While skeptical about the prospects of the union treaty promoted by Gorbachev, Yeltsin was optimistic about the future of Russo-Ukrainian relations and a possible new union that would include the two countries. "I think the new Ukrainian president will not begin negotiations with Gorbachev but will begin talks with Russia," he told Bush. Yeltsin in fact spelled out to Bush his position on the forthcoming meeting with Leonid Kravchuk. He did not want to join the new union without Ukraine but could not imagine Russia without some form of union relationship with that republic. Thus he would start negotiations with Ukraine outside the framework of the new union treaty endorsed by Gorbachev. As for the Central Asian republics, he wanted to reduce subsidies to them but maintain a presence there in one form or another. For now, the Russian president's main concern was secrecy. Yeltsin asked Bush not to reveal the content of their conversation to anyone, meaning Gorbachev. Bush agreed.[1]

What Yeltsin presented to Bush was nothing if not a bold new policy: Russia was no longer threatening Ukraine with dismemberment, as it had in late August. On the contrary, it was embracing Ukrainian independence and would negotiate a union deal with a sovereign Ukraine behind Gorbachev's back. It was clear that this would trash Gorbachev's hopes for a reformed Soviet Union, but it was not at all clear what the new union between Russia and Ukraine would mean in practice. What would be its conditions, and would Russia be able to offer the Ukrainian elites something they could not get from Gorbachev and had failed to attain under de facto independence? And if the two leaders found a compromise, would it satisfy the Muslim republics? No one, including Yeltsin, seemed to know the answers to those questions. The hope was that they would be provided during the forthcoming meeting between the Russian and Ukrainian presidents.

Yeltsin issued a statement recognizing Ukrainian independence on December 2, when the initial results of the referendum were made public. Russia became the third country to do so, after Poland and Canada. Yeltsin wanted Kravchuk to negotiate with him, not with Gorbachev, and he needed clarity vis-à-vis Ukraine before embarking on radical reform in Russia. The Russian president wanted to meet with his Ukrainian counterpart outside Moscow and out of Gorbachev's sight, and an opportunity conveniently presented itself soon after the Ukrainian referendum. It came in the form of Yeltsin's official visit to Belarus, which Yeltsin and the Speaker of the Belarusian parliament, Stanislaŭ Shushkevich, had discussed between sessions of one of the meetings of the State Council chaired by Gorbachev at Novo-Ogarevo. The visit was originally planned for November 29 but then postponed with an eye to the Ukrainian referendum. It would now take place on December 7 and would become the single most important event, after the Ukrainian referendum, to decide the fate of the Soviet Union.[2]

ON THE MORNING of Saturday, December 7, Yeltsin arrived in Minsk, the capital of Belarus, at the head of the Russian delegation, which included the second most powerful Russian government official, State Secretary Gennadii Burbulis; Deputy Prime Minister Yegor Gaidar, in charge of economic reform; Minister of Foreign Affairs Andrei Kozyrev; and Yeltsin's legal adviser, Sergei Shakhrai. At forty-six, Burbulis was the oldest in the group of advisers. The two youngest, Gaidar and Shakhrai, had turned thirty-five. The official goal of the visit was to sign agreements between Russia and Belarus, with the supply of Russian oil and gas heading the agenda. But in his speech to the Belarusian parliament, Yeltsin let the deputies know that his visit to Minsk was only the first leg of the trip and that fostering Russo-Belarusian cooperation was only one of its aims. "The leaders of the Slavic republics will consider four or five variants of the Union treaty," said Yeltsin to the Belarusian parliamentarians. "Perhaps the meeting of the three heads of state will be historic."[3]

What variants did Yeltsin have in mind? One of them came from his foreign minister, Andrei Kozyrev, who drafted a four-page memo for his boss on the possible structure of a reformed union. It was, however, put together in haste and was anything but a blueprint for future policy. On the night before he left for Minsk, Kozyrev had met at the Savoy Hotel in Moscow with his primary contact in the West during the August coup, Allen Weinstein, a former history professor at Boston University and the director of the Washington-based Center for Democracy. The Russian foreign minister quizzed his American friend on the differences between federation, association, and commonwealth. On the same day, while taking part in a meeting with the visiting Hungarian prime minister, József Antall, Gennadii

Burbulis drew up schemes for the future organization of the post-Soviet space. One scheme suggested a loose confederation of all the former Soviet republics except the Baltics; another, a union of Russia, Ukraine, Belarus, and possibly Kazakhstan.[4]

The idea of a Slavic union had first been proposed by one of Russia's best-known authors of the Soviet era, Aleksandr Solzhenitsyn. A former prisoner of Stalin's forced-labor camps, author of *The Gulag Archipelago*, which was widely acclaimed in the West and prohibited in the Soviet Union, and a winner of the Nobel Prize in literature, Solzhenitsyn had been expelled by the Soviet authorities in 1974. Living in exile in Vermont, in 1990 he wrote a treatise titled "Rebuilding Russia." It began with the following statement: "The clock of communism has stopped striking. But its concrete building has not yet come crashing down. For that reason, instead of freeing ourselves, we must try to save ourselves from being crushed by its rubble." Solzhenitsyn was an old-style Russian nationalist who still thought of Russians, Ukrainians, and Belarusians in prerevolutionary terms, as part of one Russian nation. He suggested that the Russians, as he broadly defined them, should slough off the burden of empire and create a state of their own, including Russia, Ukraine, Belarus, and the northern portions of Kazakhstan colonized by Slavs, which Solzhenitsyn called "Southern Siberia."[5]

"Rebuilding Russia" was published in September 1990 in the largest-circulation Soviet newspaper, *Komsomol'skaia pravda* (*Komsomol Truth*), and was widely discussed in the USSR. A few months later, the idea took on very practical significance when the leaders of the three Slavic republics and Kazakhstan sent Gorbachev a memorandum proposing the creation of a union of sovereign states that other Soviet republics could join. Gorbachev killed the idea, executed his political turn to the right, and, after the use of military force in the Baltics, became a virtual hostage of the hard-liners in the old Soviet leadership. In March 1991 Boris Yeltsin, Leonid Kravchuk, and the Belarusian leaders began negotiations on the creation of a Slavic union. These came to a halt after Gorbachev's defection from the hard-liners' camp and his sudden overture to the republican leaders, which included endorsement of a new union treaty.

Yeltsin suggested the idea of a Slavic union to Gorbachev immediately after the Ukrainian referendum, but the Soviet leader would not listen. He needed the Central Asian republics to save his own union project and maintain his hold on power. In Yeltsin's camp, meanwhile, no one knew what to expect from Kyiv. Burbulis later remembered that after the referendum, when he and others in the Russian government began "to write and call all those Ukrainian freemen, we soon got the feeling that we had to get organized, as the key question was, above all, how to deal with Ukraine in its euphoria."[6]

KRAVCHUK FLEW TO MINSK with a small number of advisers for a rendezvous with the Russian president on the afternoon of December 7, the same day Yeltsin arrived in Belarus. On the morning of that day Kravchuk met with a special representative of President Bush, Assistant Secretary of State Thomas Niles. He told the American visitor that he was taking with him to Minsk a package of proposals that could lead to the signing of bilateral agreements with Russia and Belarus and potentially to the creation of a community of states akin to the European Union. Judging by Kravchuk's memoirs, the Ukrainian leadership wanted only one thing at that point: to make its independence a political reality. But to achieve that, the Ukrainians needed Russian cooperation. The referendum results were Kravchuk's main trump card in the fast-approaching political contest with Yeltsin. "At this meeting," remembered Kravchuk later, "the difference in principle consisted in the fact that I arrived armed with the results of the expression of all-Ukrainian will. Moreover, I already possessed the status of president."[7]

Among those accompanying the freshly minted Ukrainian president on his trip to Minsk was Prime Minister Vitold Fokin, a fifty-nine-year-old mining engineer from eastern Ukraine. Like Yeltsin's former prime minister, Ivan Silaev, Fokin was a product of the Soviet planned-economy apparatus, and although he supported the idea of Ukraine's economic autonomy and even independence, he was concerned about the consequences of the disintegration of a single economic space encompassing the former Soviet republics. The Ukrainian nationaldemocratic forces were represented by two members of the oppositional bloc in the Ukrainian parliament. They came from the republic's intellectual establishment. Academician Mykhailo Holubets, who specialized in forestry and ecology, and Volodymyr Kryzhanivsky, a construction designer, had entered politics during the first free elections in the spring of 1990. In parliament they joined the nationaldemocratic People's Council and were in opposition to Kravchuk and his communist base before the August coup.

In Minsk the Ukrainian delegation was welcomed by the Speaker of the Belarusian parliament, Stanislaŭ Shushkevich. "We were given a very warm welcome at the airport," recalled Mykhailo Holubets. "The head of the Supreme Council of Belarus, Stanislaŭ Shushkevich, a professor of physics, is an extraordinarily pleasant man, a marvelous diplomat, and a wise head of state." Holubets clearly recognized a kindred spirit. Shushkevich's rise to the highest post in the republic was the result of perestroika and, ultimately, of the failure of the coup. Born in Minsk in 1934, Shushkevich had dedicated most of his life to research and teaching, gaining a second doctorate in radioelectronics at the age of thirty-six—a major accomplishment by the standards of the time. In 1986 he became vice president of his alma mater, Belarusian State University.

Perestroika gave a tremendous boost to Shushkevich's career. In 1989 he was elected to the all-Union parliament, where he joined the democratic Interregional Group, led by one of the most prominent Soviet dissidents and the father of the Soviet hydrogen bomb, Andrei Sakharov; a historian and communist apparatchik turned radical critic of the communist regime, Yurii Afanasiev; and the future democratically elected mayors of Moscow and Leningrad (St. Petersburg), Gavriil Popov and Anatolii Sobchak. In the following year he was also elected to the Belarusian parliament, where he became first deputy Speaker. In August 1991 Shushkevich resisted the coup and signed an appeal against the plotters. In September, as the hard-liners lost control of parliament in the aftermath of the coup, Shushkevich was elected Speaker of parliament and de facto head of the Belarusian state.[8]

Belarus was known in the USSR as a major producer of electronics for the Soviet military-industrial complex. It was considered a well-to-do republic, partly because of the achievements of its dairy farming, which supplied the local population with milk, butter, and cheese at a time when those products were in short supply in other parts of the Soviet Union. The Belarusian agricultural idyll came to an abrupt and tragic end on April 26, 1986, with the explosion of a reactor at the Chernobyl nuclear power station, just south of the Belarusian border in neighboring Ukraine. In the first days after the disaster, prevailing winds brought close to 70 percent of the station's radioactive material to Belarus, poisoning one-fifth of its arable land. Still self-sufficient in agricultural production, Belarus was heavily dependent on Russia and other republics when it came to energy. Ensuring supplies of Russian oil and gas was therefore the main concern of the Belarusian leaders during Yeltsin's visit to Minsk in December 1991.[9]

When the Ukrainian plane landed in Minsk on the afternoon of December 7, Shushkevich suggested to Kravchuk the Belarusian agenda for the political component of the forthcoming meeting: issuing a declaration stating that Gorbachev had lost the capacity to rule, that negotiations on the new union treaty had reached an impasse, and that the economic and political situation was becoming ever more grim. Shushkevich had discussed this idea with Yeltsin earlier in the day, when the Russian president arrived in Minsk. But Kravchuk seemed unimpressed and told Shushkevich that there was no need for him to come to Belarus for such a statement. Shushkevich did not know what to say. He had nothing else on his agenda. He told Kravchuk that Yeltsin would join them later in the day at the Viskuli hunting lodge in western Belarus.[10]

"Why Viskuli?" asked the surprised Kravchuk. Shushkevich responded that it would be pleasant to escape the pressure of everyday government business and the attention of journalists. Viskuli was one of the state-run hunting lodges built for the top Soviet leadership during the Khrushchev era. It is only eight kilometers from the Polish border, in the Belarusian part of the Belavezha Forest. Before World War I the region was part of the Russian Empire, and during the interwar period it belonged to Poland. It went to the USSR on the basis of the Molotov-Ribbentrop Pact of 1939. During World War II, the Belavezha Forest was a theater of partisan warfare and served as a refuge for local Jews fleeing the Holocaust.[11]

In 1957, during Nikita Khrushchev's rule, the Belavezha Forest was declared a state reserve. That year Khrushchev first went there for his hunting vacation. The locals later remembered Khrushchev as a good marksman, second only to his Hungarian counterpart Janos Kádar. Another politician who loved coming to Viskuli was Khrushchev's successor, Leonid Brezhnev. The game most prized by Belavezha hunters was a rare breed of European bison known in Polish and

Belarusian as the *zubr* (wisent). Few hunters managed to kill a *zubr*, most being satisfied with wild hogs, but all of them tried a variety of buffalo-grass vodka called Zubrovka. In June 1991, Belavezha was suggested to Gorbachev as a venue for his meeting with German chancellor Helmut Kohl, but they met in Kyiv instead. In December, the Belarusian hosts prepared unlimited supplies of Zubrovka for the forthcoming Slavic summit in Viskuli.[12]

On arrival in Viskuli, the Ukrainian delegation went hunting without waiting for Yeltsin to arrive—a show of "insubordination" that was duly noted by Yeltsin's chief bodyguard, Aleksandr Korzhakov. He wrote later about the Ukrainian president, "He always sought to make a show of 'independent' behavior; to emphasize his own independence. By contrast, Stanislaŭ Shushkevich, as host, received his guests with demonstrative friendliness." Shushkevich did his best to smooth over the jarring effect of Yeltsin's "goodwill gift" presented to the Belarusian parliament earlier in the day. It was a seventeenth-century tsarist charter to the Belarusian city of Orsha, taking it under Russian protection. What Yeltsin and his advisers regarded as an instance of Russo-Belarusian friendship to be emulated in the future was perceived by the democratic opposition in the Belarusian parliament as a symbol of Russian imperialism. Yeltsin's gift was met with shouts of "Shame!" The Russian president was at a loss and later blamed advisers for the incident.[13]

Yeltsin came to Viskuli in the company of the Belarusian prime minister, Viacheslaŭ Kebich. In the Belarusian power tandem, consisting of the Speaker of parliament and the prime minister, the latter was the more powerful figure. Like Kravchuk, the fifty-five-year-old Kebich had been born in what was then interwar Poland, but his career, linked with industry rather than ideology, resembled that of Yeltsin more than that of Kravchuk. Kebich rose through the ranks of Soviet industrial management to become the first director of a Minsk high-tech enterprise and then secretary of the Minsk city committee of the Communist Party. At the beginning of Gorbachev's perestroika, he became deputy head of the Belarusian government, and in 1990 he was appointed prime minister. Kebich was the establishment candidate for Speaker of the Belarusian parliament in September 1991, but in the postcoup atmosphere he failed to gain the support of the suddenly radicalized deputies and accepted Shushkevich's election as a temporary compromise. With Shushkevich formally at the top, Kebich maintained control over the Belarusian government, composed of former managers of industrial enterprises and party apparatchiks. He hoped to become president of Belarus once such a post was established, as it had been in Russia and now in Ukraine.[14]

THE TRIPARTITE SLAVIC SUMMIT began on the evening of December 7, 1991, with dinner for the three delegations. Yeltsin was late for dinner, making the others wait for him. Once he joined the group, the Russian president found himself sitting directly across from Kravchuk, and the two immediately formed a nexus, reducing the other participants, including the leaders of Belarus, to the role of witnesses to the negotiation process. Their conversation lasted more than an hour. Others participated only with occasional remarks or attempts to influence the tone of the conversation by delivering toasts hailing the friendship of the three East Slavic nations.

Yeltsin began by honoring the promise he had given Gorbachev a few days earlier, when he informed the Soviet president about his forthcoming meeting with the Ukrainian and Belarusian leaders. He placed on the table the text of the union treaty negotiated by Gorbachev and republican leaders in Novo-Ogarevo a few weeks earlier and on behalf of the Soviet president invited Kravchuk to sign it. Yeltsin added that he would sign immediately after Kravchuk. "I recall that Kravchuk smiled wryly after hearing out that preamble," wrote the Belarusian foreign minister, Petr Kravchenka, subsequently recording his observations. The deal offered by Gorbachev and brought to Viskuli by Yeltsin offered Ukraine the right to modify the text of the agreement, but only after signing it. It was a trap, even if Kravchuk had been prepared to join the Union on his particular conditions. But he was not. Gorbachev offered nothing new, and Yeltsin brought nothing to Belavezha but Gorbachev's agreement. Kravchuk said no.[15]

Kravchuk then reached for his main negotiating weapon. To recapture the initiative, he presented Yeltsin and Shushkevich with the results of the Ukrainian referendum. "I did not even expect," he recalled later, "that the Russians and Belarusians would be so impressed by the results of the vote, especially in the traditionally

Russian-speaking regions—the Crimea and southern and eastern Ukraine. The fact that most non-Ukrainians (and there were fourteen million of them in the republic) gave such active support to political sovereignty turned out to be a true discovery for them."

According to Kravchuk, Yeltsin was particularly impressed. "What, did the Donbas also vote for it?" he asked.

"Yes," responded Kravchuk, "there is no region in which the votes were fewer than half. As you see, the situation has changed substantially. We have to look for another solution."

Yeltsin then took a different tack, referring to the common history, traditions of friendship, and economic ties linking Russia and Ukraine. Petr Kravchenka was under the impression that the Russian president was sincere in his attempt to save whatever was left of the Union. "But Kravchuk was unyielding," recalled Kravchenka. "Smiling and calm, he parried Yeltsin's arguments and proposals. Kravchuk did not want to sign anything! His argumentation was as simple as could be. He said that Ukraine had already determined its path in the referendum, and that path was independence. The Soviet Union no longer existed, and parliament would not allow him to create new unions of any kind. And Ukraine needed no such unions: the Ukrainians did not want to exchange one yoke for another."[16]

Gennadii Burbulis, Yeltsin's right-hand man, also credited Kravchuk with burying the idea of a new union. "Here, indeed, Kravchuk was the most insistent and the most stubborn of all in rejecting the Union," he remembered later. "It was very hard to convince him of the need for even minimal integration. Although he is a reasonable man, he felt bound by the referendum results. And Kravchuk explained to us a hundred times that for Ukraine there was no problem of a union treaty—it simply did not exist, and no integration was possible. It was out of the question: any union, even a reformed one, with or without a center." The discussion had reached an impasse. Yeltsin's legal adviser, Sergei Shakhrai, later remembered that the representatives of Rukh in the Ukrainian delegation grumbled, "There's nothing at all for us to do here! Let's go back to Kyiv." According to a different account, Kravchuk allegedly said to Yeltsin, "And who will you be when you return to Russia? I'll return to Ukraine as the president elected by the people, and what will your role be—that of Gorbachev's subordinate, as before?"[17]

Kravchuk believed that the turning point was reached when, in response to his refusal to sign the union treaty, Yeltsin declared that without Ukraine he would not sign it either. It was then that they began looking for a new structure to take the place of the Soviet Union. Petr Kravchenka credited the Ukrainian prime minister, Vitold Fokin, with changing the course of the discussion. Fokin could not directly contradict Kravchuk but found another way to express his opinion. As Kravchenka recalled, "Fokin, constantly citing [[Rudyard]] Kipling, began to speak of the call of blood, the unity of fraternal peoples, and of the fact that we had the same roots. He did so very correctly, in the form of gentle remarks and toasts. And when Kravchuk started up and began to dispute, Fokin cited economic arguments." Only then did Kravchuk allegedly say, "Well, given that the majority is for an agreement . . . let's think what this new structure should be like. Perhaps, indeed, we shouldn't disperse."[18]

The conversation around the table moved into a more constructive phase. Yeltsin insisted that the meeting should produce something more than talk. The Russian president suggested that the experts work out a draft agreement of a treaty between the three Slavic republics, to be signed by the leaders the next day. Everyone agreed. Viacheslaŭ Kebich later remembered that Yeltsin asked Sergei Shakhrai and Andrei Kozyrev whether they had anything prepared. They responded that they had nothing but very preliminary drafts. He ordered the Young Turks to get together with the Belarusians and Ukrainians and draft a new agreement. When the experts left, Yeltsin vented his hatred of Gorbachev, who, according to the Russian president, had lost credibility both at home and abroad, making Western leaders worry about the uncontrolled disintegration of the Soviet Union and nuclear arms on the loose. According to Kebich, Yeltsin told the gathering, "Gorbachev has to be removed. Enough! . . . No more playing the tsar!"

For the Belarusians, the outcome of the meeting was a complete shock. They were preparing a statement intended to warn Gorbachev that if he did not accommodate the republics, the country would fall apart. At most they were contemplating the possibility of forming a looser union . . . but no union at all? No one in the Belarusian leadership had expected such a turn of events. "After dinner almost the whole Belarusian delegation gathered in Kebich's little house; only Shushkevich was missing," recalled one of Kebich's bodyguards,

Mikhail Babich. "They began to say that Ukraine did not want to remain in the USSR, and so we had to think of what to do now; how to draw closer to Russia." It would appear that the strategic decision was made on the spot: Belarus would follow Russia into a new union or out of the existing one. After dinner, the Belarusians invited members of both delegations to relax in a steam bath. The Ukrainians declined, but most of the Russian delegation, including Gaidar, Kozyrev, and Shakhrai, accepted.[19]

The Russo-Belarusian bond grew even stronger as the Young Turks, accompanied by Petr Kravchenka and other Belarusian experts, gathered in Gaidar's cottage after the sauna to work on the text of the agreement. The Ukrainians did not come, but their position was the elephant in the room that no one could ignore. It was taken into account even in the proposed title: "Agreement on the Creation of a Commonwealth of Democratic States." "Union" was out; "commonwealth" was in. At dinner that evening, the Ukrainians had been particularly insistent on outlawing the word "union." "Kravchuk even asked that the word be prohibited," recalled Gennadii Burbulis. "That is, it should be stricken from the lexicon, from consciousness, from experience. Given that there was no union, there was no union treaty either." The word "commonwealth," on the other hand, did not have negative connotations; in fact, it had positive ones. Petr Kravchenka wrote later that at their drafting session he and his colleagues "thought of the British Commonwealth of Nations, which seemed just about the ideal example of postimperial integration."

After agreeing on the title of the document, the experts did not know where to start. Gaidar saved the situation by producing the draft of a Russo-Belarusian treaty: the Russian delegation had taken it along for bilateral negotiations with the Belarusians in Minsk. "Gaidar took his text," recalled Kravchenka, "and, with our help, began to rework it from a bilateral to a multilateral one. That work took a good deal of time and continued until about five in the morning." Gaidar wrote out the whole text by hand: there were no typewriters or typists in the residence. At 5:00 a.m. the security people left the premises in search of both. They would not come back for hours. By the time the draft was ready and the participants in the night session could finally go to bed, it was 6:00 a.m. Moscow time, and they heard Radio Moscow beginning its daily broadcast with the Soviet anthem. As the choir sang the familiar words, "Great Rus' has forever bound together the indissoluble union of free republics," the representatives of Great and White Russia collapsed onto their beds, completely exhausted by the efforts they had made to turn the "eternal" union into a timebound one. It was the beginning of the last day of the existence of the USSR.[20]

The new round of negotiations began on the morning of December 8, after breakfast, which witnessed a curious show of Russo-Belarusian friendship. Yeltsin presented Shushkevich with a watch in gratitude for what he called "support of the Russian president." The previous evening, Yeltsin had almost fallen down the stairs after dinner but was supported at the last moment by Shushkevich. Before breakfast, the Russian and Belarusian experts showed the draft agreement on which they had worked all night to their well-rested Ukrainian counterparts. The latter approved the draft with one caveat—the commonwealth was to be one of "independent" rather than "democratic" states. Everyone agreed: full democracy was still a dream for most of the Soviet republics.[21]

After breakfast, which included "Soviet"-brand champagne, the three Slavic leaders gathered in the billiard room, which had been turned into a conference hall. The format chosen for the negotiations, with Yeltsin and Burbulis speaking for Russia, Shushkevich and Kebich for Belarus, and Kravchuk and Fokin for Ukraine, was advantageous to the Ukrainian president. Yeltsin's influential aides, including Gaidar, Kozyrev, and Shakhrai, would be in the adjacent room along with their less prepared Ukrainian and Belarusian counterparts. Kravchuk immediately took control of the whole negotiating process, volunteering to draft the new agreement and all but ignoring the draft prepared by the Russo-Belarusian team of experts the previous night. "I took a blank sheet of paper, a pen, and said that I would write," remembered Kravchuk later. "That was how we began. We wrote and edited ourselves, without assistants. According to the old protocol, there had never been anything like it—heads of state writing government documents themselves."[22]

The previous night, Kravchuk had refused to let his people join the Russo-Belarusian expert working group. In fact, he believed that he had no one to dispatch, recalling later, "I had no experts." If his prime minister, Vitold Fokin, was loath to bury the Soviet Union, his Rukh advisers were more than eager to do so but lacked political experience and legal expertise. Kravchuk could rely on his negotiating skills and the results of the Ukrainian referendum, Yeltsin's hatred of Gorbachev, and the desire of the Young Turks to move ahead with Russian economic reform as soon as possible. During the working dinner of the previous night he had played his cards well, single-handedly winning the first round of negotiations with his flat refusal to sign Gorbachev's treaty or join any kind of reformed union. That forced Yeltsin to switch gears and start thinking about a different kind of agreement. Kravchuk now managed to present the very idea of an agreement as a concession on his part. Letting his people join the Russians and Belarusians in drafting the agreement would have meant committing himself to a particular draft, becoming part of the process; Kravchuk wanted to remain the arbitrator of its results.[23]

Kravchuk had with him brief handwritten notes. These were the old drafts of the Slavic union treaty prepared on his and Yeltsin's initiative in early 1991 but rejected by Gorbachev. They had been revised in the fall of 1991 by Kravchuk's experts in the Ukrainian parliament, and he had studied them the previous night: he did not go to bed until three o'clock in the morning. His main counterpart on the Russian side turned out to be Burbulis, who had notes of his own hidden in one of his pockets. The principals, with the document prepared during the night session by the Russian and Belarusian experts in front of them and handwritten notes besides, began to discuss its text article by article. The Ukrainian delegate Mykhailo Holubets, who spent the morning of December 8 in the advisers' room, remembered later that for the first thirty or forty minutes there was no sound from the billiard room. Then, clearly concerned by something, Burbulis and Fokin came out for brief consultations with the experts. Another fifteen minutes passed, and finally the experts heard a "hurrah"— the principals had agreed on the first article of the treaty. At Yeltsin's initiative they raised glasses of champagne in triumph. The process went smoothly after that.[24]

The Agreement on the Establishment of a Commonwealth of Independent States consisted of fourteen articles. The three leaders agreed to create the Commonwealth and recognize the territorial integrity and existing borders of each now independent republic. They declared their desire to establish joint control over their nuclear arsenals. They also declared their willingness to reduce their armed forces and strive for complete nuclear disarmament. The prospective members of the Commonwealth were given the right to declare neutrality and nuclear-free status. Membership in the Commonwealth was open to all Soviet republics and other countries that shared the goals and principles declared in the agreement. The coordinating bodies of the Commonwealth were to be located not in Moscow—the capital of Russia, the old tsarist empire, and the vanishing USSR—but in Minsk, the capital of Belarus.

The three leaders guaranteed the fulfillment of the international agreements and obligations of the Soviet Union, while declaring Soviet laws null and void on the territory of their states from the moment the agreement was signed. "The operation of agencies of the former USSR on the territory of member states of the Commonwealth is terminated," read the final paragraph of the agreement. It was a natural concluding statement for a document that began with the following declaration: "We, the Republic of Belarus, the Russian Federation (RSFSR), and Ukraine, as founding states of the USSR that signed the union treaty of 1922 . . . hereby establish that the USSR as a subject of international law and a geopolitical reality ceases its existence."[25]

The idea that the three founding republics of the Union could not just leave it but had to dissolve it altogether belonged to Yeltsin's legal adviser Sergei Shakhrai. The Soviet constitution guaranteed the right of republics to leave the Union—a right realized in September 1991, after long struggle, by the three Baltic republics. But Shakhrai's argument went further: Russia, Ukraine, and Belarus were not only leaving the Union but dissolving it. The Soviet Union had been formed in December 1922 by four Soviet socialist republics: Russia, Ukraine, Belarus, and the Transcaucasian Federation, which included the future republics of Georgia, Armenia, and Azerbaijan. When the Transcaucasian Federation was abolished in 1936, it was up to the three remaining founding members of the Union to decide the question of its future existence—so went Shakhrai's argument.[26]

According to Kebich, the statement on the dissolution of the Soviet Union was added to the document at the initiative of Burbulis after the whole text had already been approved by the principals. Burbulis allegedly told a surprised Yeltsin that the document lacked an article. "We should begin by denouncing the union treaty of 1922," argued Burbulis. "Only then will our accords be absolutely correct from the legal viewpoint." The principals agreed. If leaving the Union along with Russia and Belarus was good enough for Kravchuk, that solution did not satisfy Yeltsin, as it not only divorced Russia from a good part of its former empire without giving it any legal means of maintaining influence there but also left Gorbachev in charge of the rump Union. If Russia left the USSR but the Union was not dissolved, then Gorbachev could stay in Moscow, the seat of the Union and the capital of a Russia no longer in the Union. The struggle between him and the Russian president would continue, becoming uglier than ever. Dissolving the Union completely was the only solution that satisfied Yeltsin and his team.[27]

THE SIGNING CEREMONY in Viskuli took place at 2:00 p.m. in the lobby of the hunting lodge. Tables were brought from other rooms and chairs from the living quarters. Kebich was assigned to find a tablecloth, which was eventually located in the dining hall. His next task was to prepare the journalists for what was promised to be a very short ceremony. Yakov Alekseichik, one of the few media representatives in attendance, noticed that Yeltsin was "not quite in good form." The "Soviet"-brand champagne with which Yeltsin had celebrated every article in the agreement was clearly affecting something more than the process of dissolving the Soviet Union. The newspaper reporters were advised not to ask Yeltsin any questions. But once the ceremony was over, Yeltsin, who was in a good mood, decided to say a few words to the journalists. At that moment, the spokesman for the Belarusian prime minister, following his superior's earlier instructions, suddenly interrupted Yeltsin: "Boris Nikolaevich, there is no need to say anything: everything is clear!" Yeltsin was taken aback. "Well, if it's all clear to you . . . ," he said to the journalists, and abruptly left the room. The press conference was over.[28]

Kravchuk remembered Yeltsin being under a lot of stress that day. He was thinking ahead and counting his allies and enemies in the now inevitable clash with Gorbachev. "Boris Nikolaevich was visibly nervous," wrote Kravchuk in his memoirs. "He was afraid that Gorbachev might win Nazarbayev over to his side." Nursultan Nazarbayev of Kazakhstan was the most influential Central Asian leader, and Gorbachev had previously countered initiatives from the Slavic leaders by drawing support from the Central Asian republics.

Moreover, Kazakhstan was the only other republic (apart from Russia, Ukraine, and Belarus) with nuclear arms on its territory. It also had a large Slavic population and had been regarded in the past as a possible member of a Slav-dominated union. Yeltsin ordered his people to call Almaty, then the capital of Kazakhstan, but they were informed that Nazarbayev was in the air, on his way to Moscow. "I urged Boris Nikolaevich not to worry, sensing that this process could no longer be reversed," remembered Kravchuk later. His assurances did not have the desired effect.[29]

Yeltsin was adamant: he insisted on speaking with Nazarbayev before the Kazakh leader met Gorbachev in Moscow. He placed his chief bodyguard, Aleksandr Korzhakov, in charge of making the arrangements, but there was little Korzhakov could do before Nazarbayev landed in Moscow. His attempt to convince the head of air traffic control at Vnukovo airport in Moscow to call Nazarbayev's airplane failed, as the general bluntly replied that he had a different boss and would not accept orders from the head of Yeltsin's security detail. In his memoirs, Korzhakov wrote, "Dual power is fraught with danger because people do not recognize a single authority in that period. Gorbachev was no longer taken seriously; people mocked him. But Yeltsin did not have access to the levers of power." Later it became known that on Gorbachev's orders air traffic controllers had been prohibited from connecting anyone with the president of Kazakhstan while he was en route.[30]

Yeltsin finally reached Nazarbayev by phone after the Kazakh leader landed in Moscow. He did his best to persuade him that the Commonwealth was in fact a realization of his idea of 1990 about forming a quadripartite union. Nazarbayev promised to come to Viskuli. Kebich even sent a car to the airport to meet his old friend, but there was no sign of Nazarbayev. First came the news that he had to refuel his plane, then that he would go not to Viskuli but to Minsk, and not immediately but on the following day. Rumor had it that Gorbachev had convinced him to stay in Moscow by offering him the post of prime minister of the crumbling USSR. "The news that Nazarbayev would not come depressed everyone," recalled Petr Kravchenka, the Belarusian foreign minister. "At that point we could only start guessing what arguments Gorbachev had found to make Nazarbayev change his plans. Was Gorbachev getting ready to resort to outright force? And here the head of Belarusian KGB, Eduard Shirkovsky, made an ominous comment: 'After all, it would take just one battalion to nail all of us here.'"[31]

Shirkovsky was not joking. Earlier that day he had approached Prime Minister Viacheslaŭ Kebich: "Viacheslav Frantsevich, this is a coup d'état pure and simple! I have reported everything to Moscow, to the Committee [[for State Security]] . . . I am awaiting Gorbachev's command."

Kebich was petrified when he heard this. "I would not call myself one of the timid sort," he remembered later. "But that report gave me the creeps, and my hands went cold." Kebich asked the secret police chief, "Do you think the command will come?"

The KGB man had no doubt: "Of course! We're faced with high treason, betrayal, if we are to call things by their right names. Don't misunderstand me: I could not help reacting. I swore an oath."

That was not what Kebich wanted to hear. "You might at least have warned me!" he said.

Shirkovsky replied, "I was afraid that you wouldn't agree. And I didn't want to involve you anyway. If anything happens, I'll take full responsibility." Clearly, he was doing his best to serve two masters.[32]

Kebich never told Shushkevich about his exchange with Shirkovsky. It is not out of the question, however, that he said something to Yeltsin or Kravchuk. Yeltsin and the others decided that it was time to leave Belavezha. With Nazarbayev remaining in Moscow, there was no doubt that Gorbachev knew about the outcome of the Viskuli negotiations. Communications between Viskuli and the rest of the world were now restored: the journalists had been given an opportunity to send their reports to their press agencies and newspapers. Publicity was the best means of preventing a possible assault. While the delegates gathered in the lobby of the hunting lodge waiting for departure to the airport, the leaders of the now independent states met in Yeltsin's quarters. The first call they made was to the man who had real power to arrest them, the Soviet minister of defense, Yevgenii Shaposhnikov. In the aftermath of the August coup, it was Yeltsin who had insisted on Shaposhnikov's appointment to that post, and in the months leading up to the Viskuli meeting, the minister had demonstrated his loyalty to the Russian president.

Yeltsin reached Shaposhnikov by phone sometime before 10:00 p.m. Moscow time. He informed the Union minister that the three Slavic countries were forming a new entity—the Commonwealth of Independent States. Over the phone, he quoted parts of the agreement dealing with the military. Shaposhnikov was pleased with the section on strategic forces, which were to remain united under a single command. Yeltsin had one more argument in his arsenal to cement Shaposhnikov's loyalty to him and steer him away from Gorbachev. Among the documents that the three Slavic presidents signed that day was a decree on the formation of the Commonwealth Defense Council. The council's own first decree appointed Shaposhnikov commander in chief of the Commonwealth's strategic forces. He accepted the nomination. He believed that "the initiative of the leaders of the three republics has evidently made things more definite and helped society make its way out of the dead end in which it found itself."[33]

Immediately after his conversation with Yeltsin, Shaposhnikov was reached by the surprisingly well-informed Gorbachev. "Well, what's new?" he asked. "After all, you've just spoken with Yeltsin. What's going on in Belarus?" Shaposhnikov did not know what to say. "He wriggled and squirmed like a grass snake on a frying pan," remembered Gorbachev later, "and finally said that they had telephoned him to ask how he envisaged the joint armed forces in a future state structure. It was of course a lie." According to Shaposhnikov, Gorbachev told him, "I warn you, don't butt into what doesn't concern you!" He then hung up the receiver. Sergei Shakhrai later claimed that Gorbachev tried to reach the commanders of the military districts that evening. With the de facto defection of the minister of defense, he was apparently trying to rally support from Shaposhnikov's subordinates. He failed. Gaidar later commented that Gorbachev could not find one regiment loyal to him. Yeltsin and his people were also talking to military commanders on the ground. One such call from Viskuli was mistakenly directed to Gorbachev's press secretary, Andrei Grachev—Yeltsin's aides were trying to get in touch with Pavel Grachev, Shaposhnikov's first deputy and Yeltsin's savior during the August coup.[34]

In Viskuli, with Shaposhnikov on their side, the three leaders considered calling Gorbachev. Yeltsin refused to do so, and the task was given to Shushkevich, as host of the meeting. But before Shushkevich was able to reach Gorbachev, Yeltsin placed a call to none other than President George Bush. According to Kebich, Yeltsin deliberately called Bush before anyone could speak to Gorbachev, He allegedly told those who suggested talking to Gorbachev first, "By no means! First of all, the USSR no longer exists, Gorbachev is not the president and cannot tell us what to do. And second, to avoid any surprises, it's best that he find out about it as a fait accompli that can no longer be reversed." Shushkevich supported the idea. According to Kebich, he saw the call to Washington as a guarantee against possible retaliation from Moscow. Kravchuk later explained the call in the same terms. "It was done so that the world would know where we were and what documents we were approving," he remembered later. "For any eventuality, as they say."[35]

It was soon after 10:00 p.m. Moscow time that Yeltsin reached Bush in Washington. The Russian foreign minister, Andrei Kozyrev, who placed the call, first had to explain who he was and why he was calling—he was still a little-known figure in Washington. According to the American memorandum of the conversation, the call lasted for almost half an hour, from 1:08 to 1:36 p.m. Washington time. Yeltsin informed Bush about the decision reached in Belarus. He put special emphasis on the desire of the Slavic leaders to maintain joint control over nuclear arms and their acceptance of the international obligations of the Soviet Union. Yeltsin told Bush that he had just spoken with Shaposhnikov and obtained the approval of Nazarbayev, who was supposed to fly to Minsk to sign the agreements. Whether Yeltsin was still under the impression that Nazarbayev would attend or was simply spinning the situation in the way that worked best for him, he spoke to Bush on behalf of four Soviet republics, not three. "This is very serious," said Yeltsin. "These four states form 90 percent of the national product of the Soviet Union." Yeltsin admitted that Gorbachev had not yet been informed of their decisions. As always, Bush was very cautious. He let Yeltsin do the talking, responding to his monologue with an occasional "I see." He promised to study the text of the agreement and then give his reaction to it. Yeltsin's main goal was accomplished: Bush had received the message and had not rejected the initiative out of hand.[36]

Shushkevich had the most thankless task imaginable: telling Gorbachev that the country over which he thought he presided had ceased to exist. He later remembered,

I informed him in a few words: "We've signed such and such a declaration, and its contents come down to the following . . . We hope for a constructive continuation of this approach and see no other." Gorbachev: "Do you realize what you've done?! Do you understand that the world community will condemn you? Angrily!" I could already hear Yeltsin talking to Bush, "Greetings, George!' and Kozyrev interpreting. Gorbachev continued: 'Once Bush finds out about this, what then?" And I said, "Boris Nikolaevich has already told him; he reacted normally . . . " And then, at the other end of the line, Gorbachev silently made a scene. . . . And we said goodbye.

Gorbachev was furious and demanded to talk to Yeltsin. "What you have done behind my back with the consent of the US President is a crying shame, a disgrace!" said Gorbachev to Yeltsin, according to his memoirs.[37]

Gorbachev wanted to see all three Slavic leaders in Moscow the next day. Neither Kravchuk nor Shushkevich was eager to go to Moscow. Yeltsin, for his part, had no choice. It was agreed that he would speak to Gorbachev on their behalf. "I can't stand to go back," said Yeltsin to Kravchuk before leaving Viskuli. Someone pointed out to him and Kravchuk that their planes could be shot down on Gorbachev's orders once they left the Viskuli-area air base. According to rumors that reached American diplomats, Yeltsin arrived in Moscow early in the morning of December 9 completely drunk and had to be carried off the plane.

In the Soviet (now Russian) capital, Gorbachev's loyal aide Anatolii Cherniaev listened to the midnight news. "Midnight," he recorded in his diary. "The radio has just reported that Yeltsin, Kravchuk, and Shushkevich have declared the end of the existence of the Soviet Union as an object of international law."[38]

The Ukrainian president's plane was registered as flying to Moscow, while in fact it set off for Kyiv. While in Viskuli, as a precaution, Kravchuk had placed no calls and did not tell his family about his travel plans. When he finally reached his residence outside Kyiv, he saw armed men on the premises. He did not know what to expect and was prepared for the worst. It turned out that the men had been sent to protect him. Once safely home, he told his wife what had happened in Viskuli. "So we're no longer in the Union?" asked Antonina Kravchuk. "What, is it all over?" He answered, "So it would seem." Kravchuk did not return a call from Gorbachev that night. He no longer felt that the Soviet president was his boss.[39]

The Belarusian leaders decided to stay in Viskuli rather than fly to Minsk, the capital of Belarus, which the three Slavic leaders had designated as the capital of the Commonwealth as well. They went to bed immediately after returning to the hunting lodge. In the nearby village of Kameniuki, on the edge of the Belavezha Forest, the head of the game reserve, Sergei Baliuk, came home late at night and awakened his wife with the shocking news: "The Soviet Union has fallen apart!" For a while his wife could not comprehend the news. "Half awake, I could make no sense of what had happened or what to do," recalled Nadezhda Baliuk. "But he was so agitated and nervous, constantly repeating, 'There is no more Soviet Union, no more.'"[40]

VI.

FAREWELL TO THE EMPIRE

16

OUT OF THE WOODS

SHORTLY BEFORE NOON ON MONDAY, DECEMBER 9, 1991, the day after the signing of the Belavezha Agreement, Boris Yeltsin arrived at the Kremlin in a heavily guarded procession of automobiles. He was coming to see Mikhail Gorbachev, the president of the now allegedly defunct Soviet Union. Yeltsin's bodyguards were prepared for the worst. Their chief, Colonel Aleksandr Korzhakov, had a gun in the front seat of his Niva sport utility vehicle, the Soviet equivalent of a Jeep. Korzhakov and a subordinate accompanied Yeltsin to Gorbachev's office and remained in the reception room face-to-face with Gorbachev's own bodyguards throughout the meeting, which lasted almost two hours. The concern was that what Gorbachev had refused or been unable to do in Belavezha—arrest the instigators of the dissolution of the USSR—he would start now, in the Kremlin. Before the meeting, Yeltsin had called the Soviet leader and asked for a guarantee of safe conduct. "What, have you gone crazy?" exclaimed Gorbachev. "Not I, perhaps, but someone else," responded Yeltsin.[1]

When Gorbachev's aide Vadim Medvedev had reached his boss by mobile phone on his way to the Kremlin earlier that day, the Soviet president showed his bellicose attitude. As Medvedev reported about a paper that he had prepared at Gorbachev's request on economic reasons for maintaining the Union, Gorbachev responded, "What's needed now are not arguments but something else." Gorbachev had begun the day by meeting with his legal experts. "Mikhail Sergeevich is in a rage, saying that he will resign; that he will tell them all where to go, and so on . . . that he will 'show them,'" Anatolii Cherniaev learned from one of the Kremlin staffers who attended the meeting. But when the Russian vice president, Aleksandr Rutskoi, taken aback by the Belavezha decisions, rushed to Gorbachev's office and demanded the arrest of the "drunken threesome" on charges of treason, Gorbachev refused. He instead asked Georgii Shakhnazarov to draft an address to the nation "dotting all the *I*'s and speaking plainly about the role of Kravchuk and the other participants in the Minsk agreements."[2]

Gorbachev had expected Kravchuk, along with Yeltsin and Shushkevich, to come to his office. "Let them explain it to the whole country, to the world, and to me," said Gorbachev to his press secretary, Andrei Grachev. "I have already spoken with Nazarbayev— he is outraged and also waiting for an explanation from Yeltsin." Nazarbayev and Yeltsin were supposed to see Gorbachev at noon, but neither Shushkevich nor Kravchuk showed any inclination to do likewise. The Belarusian Speaker called Gorbachev's chief of staff, Heorhii Revenko, to let him know that he was not coming. According to Revenko, Shushkevich told him, "almost sobbing," that he had to catch up on sleep and think things through—everything had gone so quickly in Belavezha. He would come, however, if Gorbachev and Yeltsin decided that they needed him. A few minutes later, Gorbachev would cite that vague promise to tell Kravchuk that Shushkevich was coming to Moscow.

Kravchuk had never returned Gorbachev's midnight call, so the Soviet leader decided to call him again. "So, are you coming to Moscow?" was Gorbachev's first question. When Kravchuk gave a polite but negative answer, Gorbachev used every argument he could think of to change his mind. "What is this?" Kravchuk later remembered Gorbachev saying. "You are a member of the [[State]] Council [[of the USSR]]. How can you? . . . The Union still exists." Kravchuk responded that the Union was no more. "Does that mean you're not coming?" asked Gorbachev, rather shocked. The usually polite and evasive Kravchuk was direct this time and said no. To himself, he thought, "Enough traveling for me and the others." The conversation was over. "Well, all right," said Gorbachev with a sigh of disappointment, and he hung up the receiver. Kravchuk later remembered that one reason not to travel to Moscow was his suspicion that a trap was being set. "I felt," he wrote in his memoirs, "that they would not let us go; that they would keep us there until we renounced the agreement signed at the Belavezha reserve." The possibility of arrest had also been on Yeltsin's mind ever since he departed Viskuli.[3]

When Yeltsin left his guards in the reception area and entered Gorbachev's office, the Soviet president was already waiting for him in the company of Nazarbayev, who despite his earlier promises had never gone to Viskuli or even to Minsk and was now, to all appearances, in Gorbachev's camp. Yeltsin began by telling Gorbachev that he had tried to sell Kravchuk on any conceivable union treaty, starting with a four- or five-year agreement and ending with Ukraine's associate membership in a Slavic union. Since Kravchuk had remained obdurate, the Commonwealth of Independent States was the only possible solution under the circumstances, argued Yeltsin. The main issue on Gorbachev's mind, however, was not the creation of the Commonwealth but the dissolution of the Soviet Union. "The three of you got together, but who gave you any such authorization?" said Gorbachev, according to the account that he gave a group of advisers later that day. "The State Council gave no instructions; the Supreme Soviet gave no instructions."

Yeltsin protested and threatened to leave. Gorbachev stopped him, but the tone of the discussion did not change much. To Gorbachev's question, "Tell me what I am to say to people tomorrow," Yeltsin responded, "I will say that I am taking your place." He accused Gorbachev of conspiring with Vice President Aleksandr Rutskoi of Russia behind his back. "You conspired with Bush," shot back Gorbachev. "And so it went—forty minutes of squabbling; I even felt ashamed to be present there," recalled Nazarbayev later. The Soviet president demanded that a referendum be held on the future of the Union, but the stormy meeting ended with a compromise solution: the text of the Belavezha Agreement was to be sent to the republican parliaments for study and evaluation. Yeltsin told Kravchuk afterward, "I would never again want to have such a conversation with anyone else."[4]

Gorbachev did not attempt to arrest Yeltsin, but neither was he giving up. He believed that the newly created Commonwealth was illegitimate and would not last, while the Union could and should be saved. The next two weeks in Moscow would witness the highest human and political drama since the failure of the August coup, with Gorbachev and Yeltsin contending for the support of the republican leaders, their parliaments, top military commanders, and the international community in a struggle whose stakes were the future of the Soviet Union and the world political order. There was only one person in Moscow to whom the worrying leaders were prepared to listen: the visiting US secretary of state, James Baker. The problem was that for some time neither Baker nor his boss in the White House, George Bush, knew what to make of the new situation and whether to endorse or torpedo the newly created Commonwealth.

MIKHAIL GORBACHEV STILL believed that it was in his power to save the crumbling Soviet Union. He started by restoring relations with the minister of defense, Marshal Yevgenii Shaposhnikov, whom he had warned the previous evening not to get involved in politics. Now he changed his tune. "Perhaps," he said to the marshal after meeting with Yeltsin and Nazarbayev, "we shall have one more meeting at Novo-Ogarevo and propose that the union treaty be signed by those wishing to do so." That day Gorbachev also met with the leaders of Turkmenistan and Tajikistan. But the leaders of Uzbekistan and Kyrgyzstan ignored Gorbachev's summons to come to Moscow and asked Nazarbayev to return to Almaty. Rumors were spreading there about the possibility of establishing a Muslim or Central Asian confederation to counter the Commonwealth founded at Belavezha.[5]

That evening, television announcers read Gorbachev's statement on the Belavezha Agreement. It was a product of his uneasy discussion with advisers after the meeting with Yeltsin and Nazarbayev. Everyone agreed that Gorbachev could not remain silent and had to make his position known to the public. But what should he say? Gorbachev's aides, who attended a reception that evening at Spaso House, the residence of the US ambassador, denounced the agreement as a second coup, but the statement eventually signed by Gorbachev and read on television was pointedly nonconfrontational. Gorbachev welcomed the return of the Ukrainian leadership to the negotiating table and praised articles of the agreement that ensured the continuing existence of a common economic, security, and cultural space. He stressed, however, that while every republic had the right to leave the Soviet Union, three republican leaders could not decide the fate of the entire USSR on their own. Gorbachev wanted the Belavezha Agreement to be discussed in the Union and republican parliaments and suggested that a new referendum be held on keeping the USSR in existence.[6]

Anatolii Cherniaev, who had not been summoned for consultations, heard the statement on television. He was more than skeptical that anything would come of Gorbachev's proposals. In his diary, he recorded, "Even if the people's deputies collect half the signatures [[required to authorize a referendum]], that will be of no avail. Nicholas II was man enough to renounce the throne. Three hundred years of dynastic rule. M[[ikhail]] S[[ergeevich]] cannot understand that his day is done. He should have left the scene long ago . . . to maintain his dignity and respect for what he has accomplished in history."[7]

On the other side of the globe, in Washington, George Bush and members of his staff were following the drama unfolding in Moscow with concern. "We were somewhat surprised by December 8, by the meeting of Yeltsin, Kravchuk and Shushkevich," recalled National Security Council staffer Nicholas Burns. "We did not expect a definitive statement that they would secede from the Soviet Union. . . . We were surprised, but we knew that this was probably going to be the end, that if these three republics were determined to leave there was very little way that the Soviet Union would hold together. I think it was the first time it became very, very clear that the Soviet Union was going to be disintegrating rather shortly." What worried the American president most was the possible involvement of the military in a clash between Gorbachev, on one hand, and Yeltsin and his allies in the republics, on the other.

On the evening of December 9, Bush dictated into his tape recorder, "Now we hear from Gorbachev, saying that the whole deal by Yeltsin is illegal. 'We need a referendum, we need the people to speak.' And, I find myself on this Monday night, worrying about military action. Where was the Army—they've been silent. What will happen? Can this get out of hand? Will Gorbachev resign? Will he try to fight back? Will Yeltsin have thought this out properly? It's tough—a very tough situation." The last time Bush had had such worries was during the August coup. Back then he could not reach Gorbachev and believed for some time that Yeltsin was out of reach as well. He could now call both of them, but what good would that do under the circumstances?[8]

Bush's concern about the possible involvement of the military was anything but a figment of his imagination. One thing that Gorbachev still had going for him was his formal title of commander in chief of Soviet military forces, and he was not above using that trump card in his confrontation with Yeltsin. On the morning of December 9, he had called Marshal Shaposhnikov in an effort to rebuild relations, which had been damaged during their telephone confrontation the previous night over the news from Viskuli. On Tuesday, December 10, Gorbachev summoned district military commanders to the Ministry of Defense. Speaking in Shaposhnikov's presence but over his head, Gorbachev called on the military brass to support him as commander in chief in preserving the Soviet Union. He could not help but lecture them on the importance of Soviet patriotism. It did not work. Shaposhnikov and his supporters were clearly consolidating their position in the ministry. On that day, Shaposhnikov removed two deputy ministers of defense from their posts. Gorbachev returned from the meeting with little hope that the army would support him. His aides later admitted that the generals' attitude had been hostile.[9]

According to a Russian proverb, "Bad news does not travel alone." That same day, December 10, Gorbachev learned that the parliaments of not only rebellious Ukraine but also the much more cautious Belarus had ratified the Belavezha Accords. In Ukraine the ratification came with a number of amendments—twelve altogether—that put in question even the few "integrationist" articles smuggled into the agreements by Yeltsin's Young Turks at Viskuli. Kravchuk managed to sell the agreement to parliament but faced strong opposition to any proposal that would put Ukraine back into Russia's orbit. Even some members of his cabinet, including Defense Minister Kostiantyn Morozov, opposed the agreement.[10] In Belarus, the agreement was met with mild criticism from both pro-Union and pro-independence politicians. But most deputies supported the agreement. This was true even of Aliaksandr Lukashenka, the future president of Belarus, who would later denounce the Belavezha Accords. "He congratulated me and shook my hand with the words 'Way to go, guys! You've done really well,'" recalled the Belarusian foreign minister, Petr Kravchenka, writing about his exchange with Lukashenka on the day of the ratification.[11]

After returning from the Ministry of Defense, where he was rebuffed by the generals, Gorbachev gathered his advisers from the Political Consultative Committee—a body he had created in the fall to improve his political standing—for a discussion of the rapidly deteriorating situation. With the military option off the table and the republics beginning to ratify the Belavezha Accords, Gorbachev's hopes of saving the Union and staying in power were dwindling with unprecedented speed. He opened the meeting with another piece of depressing news: without so much as consulting him, Yeltsin had subordinated the service responsible for government communications to himself. "They took over, and that's all there is to it," Gorbachev told his allies.

The main question on the agenda was what to do next. Yevgenii Primakov, the new head of the Soviet foreign intelligence service, now separated from the KGB, summarized the situation: "We have no means of settling this by force. We can't rely on the army. International powers will cooperate with the republics."

But Foreign Minister Eduard Shevardnadze told Gorbachev what he wanted to hear: "Resignation will be interpreted as an abdication of responsibility."

Gorbachev was prompt to agree: "They would say that I ran away." The Soviet president decided to stay and fight, against all odds.[12]

The next day, December 11, witnessed a further weakening of Gorbachev's position. Alarmed by his rival's meeting with the commanders, Yeltsin arranged his own meeting with the military brass. It went exceptionally well for the Russian president. "At first we did not know how we would react," recalled one of the participants in both meetings, "but Mr. Yeltsin knew what to say—after all, he has fought an election, and Mr. Gorbachev hasn't." Yeltsin also could promise the military what Gorbachev could not—a significant raise in officers' salaries, which had been reduced to virtually nothing by the high inflation of the previous months. Furthermore, he vowed to lead society out of the political and economic chaos prevailing under Gorbachev. That same day, Yeltsin delivered another blow to Gorbachev's plans. The Russian parliament adopted a resolution recalling their deputies from the Union parliament, forestalling Gorbachev's use of it as an instrument against the Belavezha Accords. Gorbachev protested, but to no avail.[13]

On the next day, December 12, following the example of their Ukrainian and Belarusian colleagues, the Russian deputies voted to denounce the union treaty of 1922 and ratify the Agreement on the Establishment of a Commonwealth of Independent States. Yeltsin called on the deputies to support both proposals. He presented the Belavezha Agreement not as an empire killer but as an empire savior. "In today's conditions," he said, "only a Commonwealth of Independent States can ensure the preservation of the political, legal, and economic space built up over the centuries but now almost lost." Yeltsin also assured the deputies that the Commonwealth was open for other Soviet republics to join: "We have sought to take account of the interests not only of the three republics but of all possible future members of the Commonwealth. I cannot agree that it is based on any ethnic principle. We treat peoples of various nationalities with equal respect." The Russian deputies supported Yeltsin: 188 voted in favor, 7 abstained, and only 6 voted against, including the head of the now banned Russian Communist Party, S. A. Polozkov.[14]

As Yeltsin was addressing the Russian parliament, Gorbachev met with journalists to deny rumors of his imminent resignation. "What right do we have to slice up the Fatherland like a pie?" he said to them. "We come into this world for sixty or seventy years, but our state was built over ten centuries; generations will live after us, yet we have begun slicing up the Fatherland like a pie. So what: will we slice the pie, drink, and have a snack? No, do not expect that of me." His last hope was the session of the Union parliament scheduled to meet later that day. It was a faint hope. Gorbachev was unable to address the session for lack of a quorum. "In the afternoon," wrote Gorbachev's aide Vadim Medvedev in his diary, "an attempt was made to convene a session of the Supreme Soviet. But it no longer has legal status, as a number of republics have recalled their deputies." Then came the results of the vote in the Russian parliament—a devastating blow. "I believe it was after the Russian parliament's decision to approve the Minsk agreement that Gorbachev decided not to resist the process that had taken on its own momentum," wrote Gorbachev's interpreter, Pavel Palazhchenko, in his memoirs.[15]

Even before the Belavezha meeting, one of Gorbachev's advisers, Nikolai Portugalov, had prepared a memo arguing in favor of Gorbachev's resignation in anticipation of the collapse of the Union structures. "The name and authority of the President of the USSR, a great Russian reformer, should in no case be associated, either now or in history, with the catastrophe that is about to befall our Fatherland," wrote Portugalov. He called on Gorbachev to follow in the footsteps of French president Charles de Gaulle and step down after explaining to the Soviet public his disagreement with the new leaders of the republics. "That way out is not only the most dignified but also the most rational, the most politically appropriate, for it alone preserves the real possibility of a return to power at the call of the Fatherland and its peoples." How could that come about? Portugalov explained, "Yeltsin's popularity continues to fall; Gorbachev's popularity will rise as his prophecy [[of economic and political collapse]] begins to come true. The West will give him material assistance."[16]

It is not clear whether Gorbachev actually read this memo. But on the evening of December 12, the day the Russian parliament voted to approve the Belavezha Agreement and dissolve the Union, Gorbachev called in Anatolii Cherniaev, whom he knew to be in favor of his resignation. "He was sorrowful," wrote Cherniaev in his diary that day. "He asked about my impressions of the Russian parliament, which had ratified the Belavezha Agreement. . . . He was taken aback by the insults of the cosmonaut Sevastianov, who had declared from the rostrum of parliament that the document was weak, but it was a good thing that the 'Gorbachev era' was over. . . . He asked for a 'handwritten' draft of a farewell speech to the people." Rumors of Gorbachev's impending resignation had flooded Moscow since the day of the Belavezha Accords, but this was the first sign that Gorbachev was preparing for such an eventuality.[17]

ON DECEMBER 12, the day Gorbachev asked Cherniaev to prepare his resignation speech, James Baker woke up at 4:30 a.m., concerned about a line in a speech that he was to deliver later that day. It was 2:30 p.m. in Moscow; the Russian parliament was voting to ratify the creation of the Commonwealth of Independent States, and it was that new and unknown entity that would not let Baker rest. He suddenly realized that the draft of his speech announcing a major shift in American foreign policy made no mention whatever of the Commonwealth. The text referred to the emerging post-Soviet space as "Russia, Ukraine and the other republics." Should he include the Commonwealth as well? Was it a viable institution? How long would it last, or would it be replaced by something else? No one knew. Baker called his aide Margaret Tutwiler, awakening her at that early hour and asking whether the text of the speech had been released to the press. It had not, allowing Baker to make a last-minute change. He came up with what he later called a "painful phrase": "Russia, Ukraine, the other republics and any common entities."[18]

The venue selected for the speech was meant to underscore its message of a significant change in policy. Princeton, New Jersey, was not only the home of Princeton University, from which Baker had earned his undergraduate degree in 1952, but also the base of operations for the Cold War's most famous thinker on international relations, George F. Kennan. The eighty-seven-year-old dean of international relations and intellectual father of "containment," which had defined US policy toward the USSR for a good part of the Cold War, was sitting in the front row, waiting to hear Baker's speech. The secretary of state began by praising Kennan for designing a policy that had borne fruit—containment, he argued, had worked. The Soviet Union was no more. "The state that Lenin founded and Stalin built held within itself the seeds of its demise," declared Baker.

The Soviet collapse, he went on, had brought a new world into existence, and the United States had to take advantage of the "new Russian Revolution" to build long-term relations with its former adversary.

If during the Cold War we faced each other as two scorpions in a bottle, now the Western nations and the former Soviet republics stand as awkward climbers on a steep mountain. Held together by a common rope, a fall toward fascism or total chaos in the former Soviet Union will pull the West down too. Yet equally important, a strong and steady pull by us now can help the Russians, Ukrainians and their neighbors to gain their footing, so that they, too, can climb above to enduring democracy and freedom. Surely we must strengthen the rope, not sever it.

Baker later wrote that he wanted to achieve two major goals in Princeton: to signal a departure from Cold War policies and to declare a shift in US relations with the Soviet Union, from the center and Gorbachev to the republics. Baker declared that the United States was prepared to deal only with those leaders who abided by a set of principles including the establishment of centralized control over the Soviet nuclear arsenals, nuclear disarmament on the part of all republics except Russia, and commitment to democracy and a market economy. Accordingly, Western and particularly American aid to the republics would depend on their leaders abiding by those principles. The secretary of state spent most of his time explaining the need for American assistance and describing its nature and extent. He paid special attention to humanitarian aid, claiming that the winter of 1991–1992 could become as crucial to the course of world history as the Russian winters of 1812, 1917, and 1941. The first helped defeat Napoleon, the second brought the Bolsheviks to power, and the third contributed to the defeat of Nazism. If the winter of 1991 turned out to be cold and hungry, it might well nullify the accomplishments of what Baker called a "new Russian Revolution."[19]

The university setting of Baker's speech, along with a good part of its content—humanitarian aid and economic assistance to a European enemy turned ally—and, finally, its rhetoric of support for freedom and democracy could not but remind one of a speech delivered forty-four years earlier by another secretary of state, George Marshall. In 1947, Marshall went to a commencement ceremony at Harvard University to announce a massive aid package intended to rebuild a Europe devastated by World War II, while securing its democratic future and alliance with the United States. That historical parallel was not lost on James Baker. He had begun to advocate a major economic aid package for the nascent democratic republics in September 1991, after visiting Moscow, St. Petersburg, and Almaty in the aftermath of the August coup. At that time, he wrote to President Bush about the need for strong support of democratic leaders and their policies in the crumbling USSR. "What may be at stake is the equivalent of the postwar recovery of Germany and Japan as democratic allies, only this time after a long Cold War rather than a short, hot one," he wrote from Moscow, drawing a parallel between the aftermaths of two wars and implicitly advocating a similar American response.[20]

Baker's aides in the State Department had increased their efforts to push through a major economic assistance package after the Ukrainian referendum. The notes prepared for Baker prior to his meeting with Bush on December 4 read as follows: "A pivotal point. We have to help the democrats—succeed. Next few months may determine their fate. We can't look like we did nothing to help them. Can't be unilateral effort. Need to catalyze and mobilize others." Baker added the word "republics" where his assistants referred to the "democrats." He also made a marginal comment on the reference to the $400 million to be spent on dismantling the Soviet nuclear arsenals: "We spent trillions over 40 years. This is a small investment in *our security.*"

It is not clear how much success Baker had with the president on December 4, but the notes prepared for his planned meeting with Bush on December 11 included an impatient appeal to the latter to throw his support behind a major economic assistance package that would create "pockets of success" in places where democratic reformers were active, such as St. Petersburg, ruled by Anatolii Sobchak. The appeal, drafted by one of Baker's aides, used the parallel of the American victories in World War II and the Cold War to drive its point home. Oddly enough, the point was attributed to Gorbachev's economic adviser, Grigorii Yavlinsky:

> I watched your Pearl Harbor speech, and one line struck me very hard. You said, "we crushed totalitarianism, and when that was done, we helped our enemies give birth to democracies. We reached out, both in Europe and in Asia. We made our enemies our friends, and we healed their wounds, and in the process, we lifted ourselves up." I was struck because I think we face the same situation today. We've won the Cold War peacefully. Now, we have to decide, as Yavlinsky says, what to do with the people we've defeated. . . . We face a great opportunity and equally great danger.

The author of the notes tried to convince Bush to do what Harry Truman had done—to go to the American people and sell a major new plan of economic assistance abroad. "You have passed the first two tests—liberating Eastern Europe and liberating Kuwait—but now historians will view those as footnotes to your reaction to present crisis," went the notes, appealing to Bush's sense of history. "You need to make the case to the American people about why internationalism, not isolationism, is the road to peace and prosperity. . . . [[T]]hey need to know that as Commander-in-Chief you are doing everything you can to make sure those nuclear weapons do not get loose. Nukes scare people. They trust you do something about it."[21]

Baker's appeal, if it was ever presented to Bush in the form suggested by the notes, had limited success. In 1991, Bush's administration allocated close to $4 billion in credit export guarantees for food supplies and agricultural products to be shipped to the Soviet Union. Still, the United States lagged behind the European Union, especially when it came to direct grants. Seventy percent of all aid to the Soviet Union was coming from Western Europe. By early 1992, Germany alone had allocated close to $45 billion for economic assistance to the USSR, a good part of it to help the Soviet army leave German soil. The equivalent of a Marshall Plan, for which Baker had advocated and Russian reformers had hoped, did not materialize. There were a number of reasons the Bush administration did not follow in the footsteps of Harry Truman and his advisers. The most immediate one was economic and financial hardship at home. In 1947, the US economy was riding the wave of the post–World War II boom, with the United States accounting for 35 percent of world GDP. By 1991, that share had been reduced to 20 percent, and the US economy had hit the bottom of an economic recession.[22]

The Bush administration did not have the kind of bipartisan congressional support for major spending that Truman and Marshall had built up in the mid-1940s. Neither American politicians nor the general public considered the Soviet collapse an existential threat to the United States, as the rise of Soviet power had been regarded after World War II. In the fall of 1991 the United States was deep in the recession and thus in no position to spend freely. Many Americans expected the end of the Cold War to produce a financial "peace dividend," not another drain on the economy. Even the strongest promoters of increased aid to the former Soviet Union were more than cautious about offering anything beyond humanitarian assistance. Thus, Baker urged a common effort of all Western countries to assist the former Soviet republics. "Baker Presents Steps to Aid Transition by Soviets," ran the headline of the *New York Times* report by Thomas Friedman published on November 13. "But He Doesn't Mention Any Large Increase in U.S. Funding," specified the subtitle, cooling readers' expectations.[23]

The notes prepared for Baker on December 13 for his next meeting with the president were less than enthusiastic. Whoever wrote them had obviously run out of steam, if not hope. "You may wish to discuss your upcoming trip, especially preparing the way for humanitarian support we'll need in the future. This could include military logistics and supplies," read the notes. Baker's aides were clearly unhappy with the White House's treatment of their proposals. Dennis Ross, the director of the State Department's Policy Planning Staff and a drafter of Baker's Princeton speech, had sent the secretary of state the text of the speech on December 6 with what Baker considered an "unusual blunt note." The note not only advocated a shift away from the policy of containment and from Gorbachev as a relevant figure in Soviet politics but also vented frustration with other branches of the administration. "Few have understood the stake," wrote Ross, according to a crossed-out passage in an early version of Baker's memoirs, "and they have killed almost every good idea we've had in the last three months."[24]

Baker's Princeton speech was timed to inaugurate his tour of the crumbling Soviet Union, which would include stopovers in Moscow as well as the capitals of Kyrgyzstan, Kazakhstan, Belarus, and Ukraine. It was designed to articulate American policy in the wake of the Ukrainian referendum, but events on the ground had developed so quickly that last-minute revisions were needed. As the State Department finally prepared to shift away from the center toward the republics, news of the creation of the Commonwealth added one more layer of complexity. Figuring out what exactly the Commonwealth would mean for the future of the Soviet Union, the independence of the individual republics, and the fate of the Soviet nuclear arsenals became one of the main tasks of the impending trip. "I wondered," wrote Baker, recalling his thoughts on the eve of his departure for Moscow on December 14, "whether it would be possible to find any solid footing in a country dissolving into chaos."[25]

It was chaos indeed. Baker remembered later that the US embassy in Moscow was struggling to find gas to fuel its cars. Sheremetevo International Airport on the outskirts of Moscow, where the secretary of state landed, was one of the few Soviet airports still operating: many were closed for lack of fuel, and most flights were canceled at the others. On December 13, the issue of the *New York Times* that published extensive excerpts from Baker's Princeton speech on page A24 featured an article titled "Moscow Misery" on page 1. An event recounted in the article had taken place in Yeltsin's home city, Sverdlovsk, now renamed Yekaterinburg—the name it had before the Russian Revolution. "This week in Yekaterinburg in the Urals," read the article, "'people exhausted by more than 24 hours of waiting, unable to sit, get anything to eat, or obtain information in the terminal' took charge of a plane that had been delayed for hours and ordered its crew to fly to the Crimea." Chaos prevailed in the vast country, poor in the requisites of daily living but with no shortage of nuclear arms and a history replete with violence and disorder.[26]

SOON AFTER NEWS of the Belavezha Accords shook the Kremlin and reverberated throughout the world, Michael R. Beschloss and Strobe Talbott, two distinguished American foreign policy pundits, boarded a plane for Moscow to interview Mikhail Gorbachev. The invitation had come from people in Gorbachev's immediate circle. Beschloss, the author of several books on the American presidency, and Talbott, a foreign affairs columnist for *Time* magazine who had translated Nikita Khrushchev's memoirs in his student years and was an expert on Russia and Eastern Europe—the area he would cover as special coordinator and then deputy secretary of state in the cabinet of President Bill Clinton, a friend from student days—accepted eagerly. The two were working on a book about the end of the Cold War, but the Soviet president wanted to give an interview to *Time* magazine. They could accommodate him on that. "Gorbachev tried one last time to mobilize his sole remaining constituency—his Western audience," wrote Beschloss and Talbott later.[27]

On the afternoon of December 13, when Pavel Palazhchenko brought Beschloss and Talbott, along with *Time* magazine Moscow bureau chief John Kohan, to Gorbachev's office, they expected to witness (as they later wrote) Gorbachev's swan song. They were surprised to see instead a man who was anything but defeated. Depressed the previous evening by the news of the Russian parliament's ratification of the Belavezha Agreement, Gorbachev was back on his feet by morning. To their only half-joking question of whether he would still be in power on Monday, when *Time* magazine was to run part of the interview, Gorbachev responded with laughter: "On Monday? I am sure I will!"

Gorbachev was still clearly hurt by Yeltsin's decision to call George Bush from Belavezha before calling him. "There was no need to draw Bush into this," he said to Beschloss and Talbott. "It's a question of Yeltsin's moral standards. I cannot approve or justify this kind of behavior." More directly, Gorbachev criticized the American administration's readiness to bypass him and establish relations with the republican leaders. He credited himself with having launched the international careers of some of those leaders. "Well, if Gorbachev is sending these people over here, that must mean that Gorbachev is finished, and we should side with the new leaders," said the Soviet president, summarizing his understanding of Western attitudes. "Things are in flux here," he continued, clearly offended. "While *we're* still trying to figure things out, the United States seems to know everything already! I don't think that's loyalty—particularly toward those of us who have favored partnership and full-fledged cooperation."[28]

While Gorbachev had all but given up on his American friends, his aides still believed that they were his best bet for staying in power. On December 15, two days after the interview, Beschloss and Talbott accepted an invitation from Gorbachev's interpreter, Pavel Palazhchenko, to an informal lunch in his apartment on the outskirts of Moscow. After lunch, Palazhchenko asked his wife to leave the room and then told the surprised Beschloss and Talbott that he wanted them to write down a confidential message for the American leadership. As dictated by Palazhchenko, it read,

The president [[Gorbachev]] is keeping all of his options open. It is possible that he might accept some role in the Commonwealth. But he will not accept it if it is done in a humiliating way. The leaders of the United States and the West should find a way to impress on Yeltsin and the others the benefits of keeping the president involved and the importance of doing so in a way that is not offensive to his dignity. At the same time, it is quite possible that he will be a private figure within a few weeks. Some people

are fabricating a [[criminal]] case against him. It is important that
Yeltsin not have anything to do with that and that he not permit
anything to happen that would harm the president. Once again,
the leaders of the United States should impress that point on him.
The above is a personal view, never discussed with the president.

Palazhchenko assured Beschloss and Talbott that he was not
speaking on behalf of Gorbachev. He would not divulge the source of
the message but was very precise about the addressees. The note was
to be delivered to either George Bush, James Baker, or Baker's close
associate in the State Department, the director of policy planning,
Dennis Ross. Palazhchenko later recalled that he had decided to send
a message to the American leadership on the advice of a colleague
who had extensive connections among the Soviet elite and later
worked for Yeltsin. The colleague told Palazhchenko that there was "a
team searching frantically for 'compromising material,' and the coup
plotters will quite likely change their stories to help frame him." "Him"
meant Gorbachev. The instigators of the August coup did indeed
claim that they had declared a state of emergency with Gorbachev's
tacit approval.[29]

Palazhchenko's initiative was the desperate act of a loyal servant
trying to rescue his boss and save his own job in the process. But
despite the sheer drama of his choice, he was knocking on an already
open door. Two days earlier, on December 13, George Bush had
conveyed to Yeltsin the American concern for Gorbachev's future.
When Yeltsin called Bush to report on the ratification of the Belavezha
Agreement by the Russian, Ukrainian, and Belarusian parliaments,
the US president asked his Russian counterpart, "Boris, what do you
think Gorbachev will do?"

Yeltsin made it clear that he would not offer Gorbachev any job
in the Commonwealth. "We will not have the position of President of
the Commonwealth," he told Bush. "We will all be equals."

Bush returned to the Gorbachev question at the very end of the
conversation. "As this evolution takes place, I hope it will be in a
friendly manner," he told the Russian president.

Yeltsin assured Bush that Gorbachev would be treated with
respect. "I do guarantee, I promise you personally, Mr. President,"
declared Yeltsin, "that everything will happen in a good and decent

way. We will treat Gorbachev and Shevardnadze with great respect. Everything will be calm and gradual with no radical measures."

Bush was satisfied with the response. "Wonderful," he said. "I am glad to hear that."[30]

Soon after that conversation, Bush made a courtesy call to Gorbachev. Gorbachev lashed out against Yeltsin and republican leaders for rejecting him by forming the Commonwealth, which he called the work of amateurs. "Gorbachev's fury was obvious," recalled Bush. "He spoke rapidly, recounting the events since November 25."

For all his outrage over what he considered a betrayal on Yeltsin's part, Gorbachev did not preclude cooperation with the new body. "How do I see my role in the future?" he asked himself in the phone conversation with Bush. "If the Commonwealth is an amorphous organization with no mechanism for foreign policy and defense and economic interaction, then I do not see any role for myself." The message was clear: he was ready to help, but the Commonwealth would need to have interstate bodies to coordinate its activities and thus a place for him as one of its leaders.[31]

After the conversation, Bush turned to Brent Scowcroft and asked his national security adviser, "This really is the end, isn't it?" Scowcroft agreed, "Yeah, Gorbachev is kind of a pathetic figure at this point." In the telephone log, the transcript of the president's teleconference with Gorbachev was marked for the first time as a conversation not with the president of the USSR but with the president of the former Soviet Union.[32]

ON THE AFTERNOON of December 15, soon after Palazhchenko dictated his message to the surprised Beschloss and Talbott, the US airplane carrying James Baker and Dennis Ross—two of the possible addressees of the top-secret note—landed at Sheremetevo International Airport. Talbott, with Palazhchenko's note in hand, rushed to the Penta Hotel in downtown Moscow to see Ross and deliver the message. He told Ross that it came from a person in Gorbachev's entourage but did not give the name. Ross rightly assumed that the message came from Palazhchenko. His second guess was Aleksandr Yakovlev. When Ross brought Talbott's note to Baker, who was staying in the same hotel (built for the 1980 Olympics, which had been boycotted by the United States), the secretary of state remarked to his adviser, "Well, we've got to follow up on this. . . . We've got to raise it with both Yeltsin and Gorbachev. Still, we can't get in the middle of it."[33]

Three months had passed since Baker's last visit to Moscow in early September. At that time he had enjoyed the warm weather and been uplifted by the general euphoria following the collapse of the August coup. The weather this time was cold and gloomy, like the political atmosphere, at least when it came to his friends in Gorbachev's entourage. Baker's meeting schedule reflected the new realities in and around the Kremlin. His first visit would be not with the Soviet foreign minister, his old friend Eduard Shevardnadze, but with Shevardnadze's Russian counterpart, Andrei Kozyrev. They had first met in Brussels immediately after the coup, when Kozyrev fled Moscow to rally international support for Yeltsin's cause. Since then his influence had grown dramatically, and by November 1991 he had eclipsed the Soviet foreign minister at that time, Boris Pankin. Shevardnadze's return to head the Soviet Foreign Ministry on Smolensk Square in downtown Moscow did nothing to change that trend.

Kozyrev was not looking forward to Baker's visit. He had more than enough on his plate and did not see how the US secretary of state could help the Russian government sort out relations with its post-Soviet neighbors. "December was a terrible month, given the amount of work with the former republics," recalled Kozyrev. "And on top of that, Baker barged in. At that point he was entirely out of place, as we were trying to take care of our own business." Baker descended on Kozyrev's office in the former building of the Communist Party's Central Committee with a score of his State Department advisers. He peppered Kozyrev with questions on how the Commonwealth was supposed to work, starting with control over nuclear weapons and armed forces and ending with the formulation of a joint foreign policy and the desirability of having the Commonwealth recognized as an international entity. Kozyrev gave Baker the by now standard line that establishing the Commonwealth was a way of stopping the uncontrolled disintegration of the Soviet Union, but he offered nothing more specific.

Kozyrev wanted diplomatic recognition by the United States of the members of the Commonwealth. Baker was in no hurry to promise recognition, which he considered the main carrot that the United States could offer Russia and other republics in exchange for satisfying US requirements on security, democracy, and market reform. He noted that Kozyrev kept referring to the USSR as a former state and was not pleased with this treatment of what he considered an existing entity. The US foreign policy team was not yet emotionally prepared to let the USSR go. Members of Baker's staff soon began asking questions of their own, to which Kozyrev had no satisfactory answers. He later acknowledged that confusion ruled the day in the Russian leadership of the time: "Of course, we had no order at all. Everything was done on the fly. No normal government, nothing."[34]

Later that evening, Baker shared his frustration about Kozyrev and the Commonwealth with Shevardnadze. They met for a private dinner in the apartment of a Georgian friend of Shevardnadze's, the sculptor Zurab Tsereteli. "In a room walled by boldly colored abstract paintings, we met around a white plastic table with multicolored patio furniture," recalled Baker. In years to come, Tsereteli would become one of the most popular but also most hated sculptors in Russia—his monuments to Russian leaders would be erected in downtown Moscow, St. Petersburg, and other Russian cities, their monstrosity denounced by some as a blight on the existing architectural ensemble. The characters he depicted in bronze ranged from tsars—Peter I and Nicholas II—to Joseph Stalin and Vladimir Putin. Sitting in Tsereteli's bizarrely decorated and furnished apartment, Baker finally found a sympathetic ear in Shevardnadze, who shared his opinion of the Commonwealth: while it seemed the only way out of the existing impasse, nevertheless, as Baker put it, "the parties to this new Commonwealth don't know exactly where they are going." He was also pleased to have his old friend endorse his position that American recognition of Commonwealth member states should be contingent on their handling of military issues.[35]

The next day, Baker took his questions about the Commonwealth, its future, and control over nuclear weapons to the only man in Moscow who was in a position to answer them, Boris Yeltsin, whose performance made a strong and positive impression on the American guest. Yeltsin insisted that their meeting take place in St. Catherine's Hall in the Kremlin, where Gorbachev had received distinguished foreign officials. He brought with him not only members of his government, including the Young Turks Yegor Gaidar and Andrei

Kozyrev, but also two top ministers of Gorbachev's crumbling cabinet: the minister of defense, Marshal Yevgenii Shaposhnikov, and the minister of the interior, General Viktor Barannikov. Yeltsin's people had intrigued journalists on the eve of the meeting by suggesting that they watch who would accompany Yeltsin. The reference was to the two Union ministers, whose appearance in Yeltsin's entourage was designed to send a clear signal both to Baker and to the domestic audience about who was now really in charge at the Kremlin.

Yeltsin began the meeting by welcoming Baker to "a Russian building on Russian soil." He then brought a level of clarity to the issues of the Commonwealth, nuclear control, and humanitarian aid that Kozyrev had failed to offer the previous day. First of all, he announced that on December 21 the Commonwealth would be joined by the Central Asian republics. He told Baker that Russia would take over key Union ministries, replace the Soviet Union on the United Nations Security Council, and exercise sole control over nuclear arms throughout the Commonwealth. In the presence of Shaposhnikov, Yeltsin declared his desire to someday merge the Commonwealth's armed forces with those of NATO. Like Kozyrev before him, Yeltsin wanted the United States to recognize Russia, Ukraine, and Belarus as independent states and acknowledge Russia as the successor to the Soviet Union in the international arena.

Baker was pleased to hear direct answers to the questions he had asked Kozyrev the previous day—the foreign minister had probably briefed Yeltsin ahead of time on the questions that interested Baker. Alerted by Palazhchenko's message of the day before, Baker was anxious to raise the "Gorbachev issue" with Yeltsin. The Russian president told his guest that media speculation about Gorbachev possibly becoming commander in chief of the Commonwealth was groundless. Yeltsin was much more responsive to the notion that Gorbachev should be treated with respect. When Baker said that rumors had reached him about possible criminal prosecution of Gorbachev and that such a turn of events would not be understood or welcomed by the United States, Yeltsin was quick to show goodwill to his vanquished rival. "Gorbachev has done a lot for this country," he told Baker. "He needs to be treated with respect and deserves to be treated with respect. It's about time to become a country where leaders can be retired with honor!"

The sensitive issue of centralized control over nuclear arms was discussed by Baker and Yeltsin in a confidential part of the meeting without their advisers. Yeltsin told Baker that currently there were three nuclear briefcases with launch codes: one with Gorbachev, another with Shaposhnikov, and the third with Yeltsin himself. For a nuclear launch to take place, all three would have to authorize it. Yeltsin's presentation implied that Gorbachev no longer had sole power to decide such issues: Yeltsin was already involved, and it was hard to imagine him agreeing with Gorbachev about anything, let alone a nuclear launch. What Yeltsin foresaw, with the USSR gone and the Commonwealth taking its place, was a reduction in the number of nuclear briefcases, not an increase. "Will remove telephone and briefcase from Gorby before end of December," noted Baker on his Soviet-made notepad, which had the word "Moskva" at the top. Yeltsin explained that Gorbachev's case would be taken away from him, but the leaders of the nuclear republics—Ukraine, Kazakhstan, and Belarus—would be not given their own briefcases. "The leaders of Ukraine, Kazakhstan and Byelorussia do not understand how these things work, that's why I'm telling only you," said Yeltsin. "They'll be satisfied with having the telephones." Baker found that explanation satisfactory.

At the end of the conversation, Yeltsin promised to provide Baker with a list of officials with whom the United States could deal in delivering humanitarian aid. Baker decided not to ask questions that would embarrass the Russian president, and so he crossed out the following paragraph of his negotiations checklist: "Right now we can't even ship food under CCC [[Commodity Credit Corporation agreement]] because your side is unable to pay the freight cost it agreed to cover. And you need to figure out how you are going to pay for the CCC credits that come due in January. If you default, we're legally required cut you off. That would be disastrous."

Overall, Baker was satisfied with the results of the meeting. Yeltsin's confidence, the clarity of his presentation, and his direct responses to questions that Kozyrev had had trouble answering the previous day made a strong impression on Baker. It was then, listening to the Russian president, that he apparently crossed the line between his political and emotional attachment to the USSR and acceptance of the Russian-led Commonwealth as its substitute. Comparing his meeting with Yeltsin to the meeting he had later in the day with Gorbachev,

Baker wrote in his memoirs that on that day he "saw firsthand the Soviet Union's past and Russia's future."[36]

Kozyrev, by contrast, was highly dissatisfied with the meeting, not out of jealousy toward his boss but because he thought that Yeltsin had missed a unique opportunity to negotiate large-scale economic assistance from the United States, settling instead for humanitarian aid. Before the meeting, Kozyrev had discussed economic assistance with Yeltsin's economic guru, Yegor Gaidar, and they agreed that Kozyrev would ask Yeltsin to give Gaidar a chance to present Russian desiderata to Baker. It never happened. According to Kozyrev, when Baker asked whether Yeltsin wanted humanitarian aid to be given only to Russia, Yeltsin responded, "Why, no. Ukraine and all the republics should receive humanitarian assistance." This came as a shock to the Young Turks. "Yegor and I almost jumped out of our skin during that discussion," recalled Kozyrev. "I asked him, 'Yegor, was that what you wanted?' He said: 'No, that's not it.' I said: 'Let Yegor speak.'" Yeltsin refused to give his economic guru an opportunity to present his case. "No one could speak when he was speaking," remarked Kozyrev about Yeltsin.

Kozyrev had clearly misread the signals given by the American secretary of state on the previous day. There was no Marshall Plan in the works. Humanitarian aid and technical assistance were the extent of the help that the United States was able and willing to offer Russia and the other republics at the time. When Kozyrev saw Baker off at the Moscow airport on December 17—and, given the exceptionally cold weather, handed the American his fur hat—he was disappointed that Baker was leaving with a mere request for humanitarian aid and not one for a substantial economic assistance package. "And so he took off wearing my hat, clutching humanitarian assistance between his teeth, and worked on that," recalled Kozyrev years later with obvious regret. It was a good deal, exchanging a hundred-dollar Soviet hat for hundreds of millions in American humanitarian assistance, but it was not the deal that Kozyrev had been dreaming of.[37]

BEFORE DEPARTING MOSCOW, Baker had returned to the Kremlin for a meeting with the man who had changed his country and the world so dramatically that neither had a place for him any longer. There was a sensitive issue that Baker had to keep in mind while meeting with Gorbachev in his office on the third floor of the Senate Building. Three days earlier, on December 13, when Bush had placed a courtesy call to Gorbachev, the Soviet leader told his American counterpart, "George, I think Jim Baker's Princeton speech should not have been made, especially the point that the USSR had ceased to exist. We must all be more careful during these times." Gorbachev had confused Baker's Princeton speech with his earlier television remarks, in which the secretary of state said, "The Soviet Union as we have known it no longer exists." Baker had made those remarks after the Belavezha summit of the three Slavic leaders and tried to be as careful as possible under the circumstances, but Bush decided to appease Gorbachev nevertheless. "I accept your criticism," he told the Soviet president. After the conversation, Gorbachev called Anatolii Cherniaev and told him that he had given Bush "a thrashing for his conduct."[38]

Baker now had to deal with the offended Gorbachev. But the meeting went unexpectedly well for him. Gorbachev did not show that his feelings were hurt and only once allowed himself to refer to American missteps, in very general fashion. "Maybe there have been some mistakes, some grave blunders on my part and some on yours," he told Baker, who interpreted the observation as a possible reference either to the White House leak on the recognition of Ukrainian independence or to his own remarks on television. If Gorbachev showed any indignation, it was with regard to Yeltsin and the creators of the Commonwealth, whom he accused of staging a coup. Gorbachev fully understood his own precarious situation, and the difference between his demeanor and Yeltsin's could not have been more striking. "Where Yeltsin had swaggered," recalled Baker, "Gorbachev was subdued." Baker assured Gorbachev of American support for him. "Whatever happens, you are our friends," he told Gorbachev and his advisers. "And it makes us very sad when we see, as we do on this visit, that you are being treated with disrespect. I'll tell you frankly: we are against it." He did not mention Yeltsin's assurances that Gorbachev would be allowed to retire "with honor."[39]

While obviously bitter about his treatment by Yeltsin, Gorbachev showed readiness to work with the republican leaders. A note prepared by Anatolii Cherniaev for his meeting with Baker said that the creation of the Commonwealth had produced a new situation. "I want myself and my longtime colleagues," said Gorbachev, referring to Aleksandr Yakovlev and Eduard Shevardnadze, who were present at the meeting, "to help establish the future of the Commonwealth and continuity of succession." He also told Baker that he had agreed with Yeltsin on a time frame for handing over power. For all their reservations about the Belavezha Accords, both Gorbachev and Baker recognized that the Commonwealth was a reality, and both attempted to board its bandwagon. But whereas Baker was a welcome guest and an important partner, Gorbachev was seen as an impostor and a party crasher from whom everyone wanted to distance himself.[40]

17

THE BIRTH OF EURASIA

O N DECEMBER 17, THE DAY JAMES BAKER left Moscow, Mikhail Gorbachev and Boris Yeltsin met to discuss the transition of power from Union to Commonwealth authorities. "The presidents agreed that the process of managing the transition of Union structures to their new capacity should be completed by the end of this year," read an article in the next day's issue of the pro-Yeltsin *Rossiiskaia gazeta* (*Russian Newspaper*). "By that time, the activity of all Union structures is to be terminated: some of them are to go over to the jurisdiction of Russia, and the rest are to be liquidated." By mid-December it had become obvious to all the political actors that there would be no new union. Even Gorbachev realized that the project was dead. Its place would be taken by the Commonwealth. According to the pollsters, its creation was supported by 68 percent of the citizens of the Russian Federation. The question that still remained unanswered was, What kind of Commonwealth?[1]

The answer would come from the leaders of the Slavic and Central Asian republics, who were gathering in Almaty, the capital of Kazakhstan, on December 21 to discuss the new political reality created by the Belavezha Agreement. Yeltsin had already told Bush that the Central Asian leaders would join the Commonwealth, but it was not clear in what capacity and on what conditions. Gorbachev pinned all his hopes of staying in power on the Almaty meeting. He wanted the Central Asian presidents to turn the Commonwealth into a much more centralized polity than the one envisioned by Yeltsin, Kravchuk, and Shushkevich in Viskuli. As had often been the case since 1989, he expected that the "radicalism" of Russian politicians would meet its match in the conservatism of representatives of the Central Asian republics.

Gorbachev miscalculated. While most of the Central Asian presidents, including the leaders of the two largest republics, Nursultan Nazarbayev of Kazakhstan and Islam Karimov of Uzbekistan, did not welcome the creation of the Slavic Commonwealth, they saw no benefit in antagonizing Russia. They bore enough grudges against the former Union and had enough ambition to become independent rulers to throw their full support behind the idea of a Commonwealth that included their republics.

WHILE GORBACHEV AND YELTSIN had opposite expectations for the Almaty summit, it fell to James Baker to be the first outsider to test attitudes toward the Commonwealth on the part of the Central Asian leaders. On the morning of December 17, he embarked on a complicated journey that would take him from Moscow to Brussels through Central Asia, Belarus, and Ukraine. It was a punishing schedule. He would leave Moscow at 9:00 a.m. on December 17, arrive in Bishkek, the capital of Kyrgyzstan, at 3:30 p.m., leave it at 7:55 p.m., and arrive in Almaty, the capital of Kazakhstan, forty minutes later. His last appearance before the press was scheduled for 11:38 p.m. that same day. The next morning he was to fly to Minsk, the capital of Belarus, arriving there at 1:00 p.m. and going on to Kyiv, with his arrival scheduled for 5:55 p.m. He was to leave Kyiv on the morning of December 19 at 6:45 a.m. in order to make a 9:00 a.m. meeting in Brussels.[2]

The visit to Kyrgyzstan was first on Baker's itinerary. "In a region more prone to warlords than Jeffersonian democrats, the president of Kyrgyzstan, Askar Akaev, was an anomaly who genuinely believed in democracy and free markets," wrote Baker in his memoirs, explaining the rationale behind his stopover in Bishkek. "I felt my visit there would be an important symbol for Akaev and the Muslims in this region that the United States was ready to support their reforms." A former president of the Kyrgyz Academy of Sciences, Akaev indeed stood out among the new generation of republican leaders, all of whom, with the notable exception of his fellow scientist Stanislaŭ Shushkevich of Belarus, were former Communist Party bosses. And the US secretary of state's visit was indeed a big boost for him and his country, which was about to be born. As Baker later remembered, when the president of Kyrgyzstan saw him descending from his plane at the Bishkek airport, he "had his hands clasped in fists above his head as though he had just won the welterweight boxing title."

What Akaev told Baker was exactly what he wanted to hear from a Central Asian republican leader: Akaev was all for the Commonwealth, as he considered Russian help essential in dealing with the threat posed by radical Islam and the growing influence of neighboring China. He did not plan to acquire nuclear arms and did not think that his country needed a military force of more than a thousand troops. Kyrgyzstan would be armed instead with the five principles that Baker had proclaimed in the wake of the August coup as guidelines for the post-Soviet governments. In short, Kyrgyzstan would become a willing and enthusiastic participant in the new world order envisioned by the US secretary of state. Baker left Bishkek for Almaty thinking that "with our enormous moral authority with many of these republics and their leaders, the United States had a unique responsibility to support reform efforts."[3]

Less than hour later, Baker landed in Almaty. This was his second visit to Kazakhstan in little more than three months—he had last been there in mid-September, during his postcoup fact-finding mission to the USSR. His return underscored the importance of the republic and the political acumen of its leader. The president of Kazakhstan, fifty-year-old Nursultan Nazarbayev, was running the only non-Slavic republic with nuclear arms on its territory, had considerable influence in Soviet politics, and was eager to establish direct political and economic relations with the West. The future of the Soviet Union and the Commonwealth, as well as control of nuclear arms, which was paramount for the American leadership, all depended in large degree on the attitude of the Kazakh president.

Lagging behind many of his fellow republican leaders in declaring his country's independence, Nazarbayev had caught up with them after the Belavezha summit. After attending a stormy meeting between Gorbachev and Yeltsin on December 9, Nazarbayev decided to shift his support from Gorbachev to Yeltsin and his political weight from the all but defunct Soviet Union to the increasingly viable Commonwealth. *Rossiiskaia gazeta* described Nazarbayev's new position as follows: "He advised against speculating on the subject of opposition between Slavic and Asian republics. First, because it is dangerous; second, because he himself is acutely opposed to agreements based on the national, ethnic principle and considers them a throwback to the Middle Ages. Third, because he sees no anti-Kazakh or similar motives in the desire of three Slavic states to find optimal forms of cooperation."

After leaving the Kremlin, Nazarbayev rushed home to speed up the process of making Kazakhstan an independent state. The Union was living out its last days, and if Kazakhstan wanted to play any role in the Commonwealth or any other regional organization, it had to have all the formal attributes of national independence. On December 10, the Kazakh parliament renamed the Kazakh Soviet Socialist Republic the Republic of Kazakhstan. Later that day, Nazarbayev swore an oath of allegiance as the first elected president of the republic—the elections had taken place on December 1, the same day that Ukrainians voted for independence and elected Leonid Kravchuk as their president. On December 16, the Kazakh parliament proclaimed independence without submitting the matter to a referendum. As some newspapers suggested, in effect the Ukrainians had voted on December 1 not only for their own independence but also for that of Kazakhstan.[4]

James Baker wanted to see Nazarbayev in order to discuss nuclear arms and the future of the Commonwealth. He was prepared to offer the same carrots that the US administration was ready to give the other leaders of the Soviet republics: humanitarian aid and technical assistance. He conducted his negotiations with Nazarbayev on the basis of standard points prepared by his staff for meetings with all post-Soviet presidents. They included a list of American expectations concerning nuclear arms and conventional forces, resolution of border disputes, and economic cooperation. They also listed the amount of American aid for the Soviet Union: pledges of humanitarian assistance of up to $3.5 billion since December 1990. In December 1991 the crumbling Soviet state was supposed to receive supplies valued at $600 million as part of the pledged amount. Nazarbayev apparently showed little interest in the aid package. He wanted recognition of his country's independence and foreign investments. "Send me advisers and investors, not money," he told Baker.[5]

Nazarbayev was also forthright in showing his displeasure with what he interpreted as American support for the dissolution of the USSR. "Yeltsin told the whole world that he had called President Bush and that President Bush had immediately supported what he had done," confided Nazarbayev to Baker. "If it's true, I would say only that since President Bush is respected by the whole world, one has to consider the weight of his words very carefully. What did the president think of the legality of that move by them? What did he think of the constitutionality of this? In August, the reaction of the United States was very clear. And the US view is important to everybody. Now what we have is Yeltsin trying to legitimize his actions by getting President Bush to do so for him."[6]

Baker assured Nazarbayev that Bush had remained neutral, giving no support to Yeltsin and his counterparts. The secretary of state recalled later that while Nazarbayev was clearly hurt by his initial exclusion from the Belavezha summit, he was prepared to make his peace with that. "They have all apologized, and it's over," he told his American visitor, referring to Yeltsin, Kravchuk, and Shushkevich. He was now all for the Commonwealth and was working hard to convince his fellow Central Asian presidents to join it. "Once again, I am going to have to get into being a firefighter," he told Baker, referring to the political storm touched off by the Belavezha Agreement. "I am going to have to get them all together."

There was one major condition on which the Central Asian leaders were ready to join the Commonwealth: they were to be treated as its founding members, and the whole treaty was to be signed anew with their participation. Nazarbayev also wanted a separate treaty between the four nuclear republics on the control of nuclear arms. Those words must have been music to Baker's ears. "When I got to my room that night at 3:00 a.m., I felt that my three hours with Nazarbayev were among the best I had had thus far," he recalled. Baker wanted Nazarbayev to succeed. As he explained the next day to Stanislaŭ Shushkevich in Minsk, "By an association of the Central Asian republics with the Slavic republics, the Central Asians could serve as a bridge between West and East and a secure buffer against the spread of radical Islamic fundamentalism."[7]

WHILE THE AMERICANS were interested in extending the Slavic Commonwealth into Central Asia for reasons related to nuclear arms and militant Islam, the motivations of the Central Asian leaders for joining the Belavezha Agreement were much more diverse and complex. Nuclear arms were an issue only for Nazarbayev, and radical Islam was only one of the factors that influenced the Central Asian leaders, most of whom were former party bosses. At the center of their thinking was Russia. Traditionally, their relations with Moscow were ones of subordination and dependence, and while they were eager to end the former, they were not in a position to terminate the latter entirely.

On December 17, the day Baker arrived in Almaty, Nazarbayev presided over a mass downtown rally to mark two occasions: the declaration of the country's independence by the republican parliament one day earlier and the fifth anniversary of the anti-government protests in Almaty on December 16 and 17, 1986. The protests had involved Kazakh youth and proceeded under national slogans—the very first indication of rising ethnic tensions in the Soviet Union. The young people, largely students of Almaty institutions of higher learning, went into the streets to protest Moscow's appointment of an ethnic Russian as leader of the republic's party and state apparatus, a post earlier occupied by a Kazakh. The appointment of Gennadii Kolbin was part of Gorbachev's plan to remove from power party cadres closely associated with Leonid Brezhnev and his corrupt rule.

To establish his control over the republics and regional elites, Gorbachev relied on party cadres from Russia. A year earlier, Boris Yeltsin had been transferred from Sverdlovsk to Moscow to take over the capital from the Brezhnev loyalist Viktor Grishin. Now Kolbin, who had been Yeltsin's rival in Sverdlovsk in the 1970s, was moved from the post of first party secretary in the city of Ulianovsk on the Volga to Kazakhstan. With Gorbachev's blessing and assistance, the "Sverdlovsk mafia" was taking over with the goal of rooting out corruption and increasing the power of the new general secretary over a country badly in need of political and economic reform.[8]

But whereas Yeltsin's appointment to the helm of the Moscow city administration was welcomed by the Moscow public, Kolbin's "election" as first secretary of the Communist Party of Kazakhstan at Moscow's insistence met with hostility on the part of the Kazakh populace and elite alike. The main reason was quite simple: in trying to clamp down on old party cadres and corruption, Gorbachev had violated the unwritten contract between the center and the republics that had existed since Stalin's death—the leader of any republic was to be drawn from its titular nationality. Gorbachev was changing gears and proposing to run the Soviet Union directly from the Kremlin, bypassing local elites. But Almaty was not Moscow. Republics had more rights than cities, and republican party and cultural elites were not about to yield their hard-won local prerogatives to a starry-eyed upstart in the Kremlin.[9]

There were rumors that senior officials in the republican party apparatus and government, who had much to lose with the arrival of a Moscow appointee in their capital, encouraged ethnic Kazakh students to rebel. Nazarbayev, an ethnic Kazakh, was then head of the republic's government and one of the obvious candidates for the post of first secretary of the Kazakh Communist Party. Some have argued that he was behind the student protests. If so, he managed to remain unnoticed in Moscow. At the height of the protests he spoke to the students, asking them to disperse. When diplomacy failed, he backed those who argued for harsh measures. The protest, which took place a few months before the start of Gorbachev's glasnost, was crushed. There were casualties, and thousands of students were arrested, interrogated, and expelled from the universities.

Nazarbayev, a former metallurgical engineer who had begun his education in Leonid Brezhnev's hometown, Dniprodzerzhynsk, in Ukraine—a fact that he mentioned with pride to underscore his internationalist bona fides—managed to maintain his position in the republican leadership. His time to claim the highest office would come in the summer of 1989, when he was elected first secretary of the Kazakh party with Gorbachev's blessing. The contract between the center and the republican elite in Kazakhstan, violated by Gorbachev a few years earlier, was now restored. This occurred at a time when the republican elite was preparing not only to regain the status it had held under Brezhnev but also to claim new ground in competition with Gorbachev, now weakened by his own political reforms. In the spring of 1990, less than a year after becoming first secretary, Nazarbayev took over as president of Kazakhstan, receiving his mandate, like Gorbachev, not from the masses but from parliament.

President Nazarbayev had to be very careful in deciding how much sovereignty and independence to take under the circumstances. When it came to the political and ethnic balance in Kazakhstan, he was in a much harder spot than any of his republican counterparts. The republic, whose titular nationality and leaders were Kazakh, was largely non-Kazakh in ethnic composition. Of Kazakhstan's 16.5 million inhabitants, Kazakhs constituted only 6.5 million. Russians were the next-largest ethnic group, with more than 6 million; Ukrainians, linguistically and ethnically close to them and often culturally Russified, constituted the third-largest ethnic group, numbering slightly less than 1 million. In the 1980s the Kazakhs were the fastest-growing ethnic group in the republic, but the Slavs remained a majority. The Slavs were generally better educated, formed a majority in urban centers, and flaunted their superiority as masters of the republic. "If you traveled around my country," confided Nazarbayev to Baker during his visit to Almaty in September 1991, "you would see Russian kids beating up Kazakh kids. That's how it was for me. It's not easy to live with them."[10]

The precarious ethnic composition of Kazakhstan was the result of Soviet ethnic engineering and economic policies. In the early 1930s, the ethnic composition of the republic was affected by Soviet agricultural policies and, in particular, by a brutal campaign of forced collectivization. More than 1 million Kazakhs, or a quarter of their entire population, perished in the famine of 1930–1933. The 1950s brought an influx of hundreds of thousands of Slavs, who arrived as part of another agricultural campaign—the colonization of the "Virgin Lands" launched by Nikita Khrushchev and implemented with the help of a then rising star in Soviet politics, Leonid Brezhnev. They wanted to make the steppes of northern Kazakhstan arable in order to solve the problem of chronic food shortages in the USSR. While the food problem remained unsolved, the ethnic composition of Kazakhstan was further changed in favor of the Slavs.[11]

Upon assuming presidential office in 1990, Nazarbayev was caught between a rock and a hard place: on one hand, rising Kazakh self-awareness and nationalism; on the other, growing separatist tendencies among the Slavs, who were settled largely in northern Kazakhstan. While pushing for his republic's legislative sovereignty and economic autonomy, he lent no open support to either Kazakh or Slavic nationalism. Balancing between the two groups, he managed to consolidate power in Almaty and become an influential power broker in Moscow. Nazarbayev gained the respect of Yeltsin and Gorbachev, Kravchuk, and Shushkevich, and his word counted for a good deal among the leaders of the Central Asian republics. The collapse of negotiations on the new union treaty and the formation of the Commonwealth of Independent States tested Nazarbayev's ability to maneuver without appearing to waver.

Nazarbayev could not unilaterally declare the independence of Kazakhstan against the wishes of its Slavic majority, but neither could he embrace the Commonwealth as constituted in Belavezha: that would mean 6.5 million Kazakhs sharing the new political entity with more than 200 million Slavs. One could easily predict the consequences of that arrangement for the Kazakh elite's influence in the Commonwealth, to say nothing of the Kazakh national and cultural identity. Even less attractive was the vision of Kazakhstan's future offered by Aleksandr Solzhenitsyn, the spiritual father of the Slavic Union, which many believed to have come into existence in Belavezha. Solzhenitsyn was a proponent of the "reunification" of northern Kazakhstan with Russia. As Nazarbayev affirmed later, even if he had come to Belavezha on December 8, he would not have signed the agreement in its existing form.[12]

Nazarbayev was not prepared to sign the Commonwealth treaty with the Slavic presidents alone, but he was happy to do so if joined by other Central Asian leaders. On December 12, he flew to Ashgabat, the capital of the neighboring Muslim republic of Turkmenistan, to take part in a meeting of the five presidents of the Central Asian republics. On the agenda of the meeting, hosted by President Saparmurat Niyazov of Turkmenistan, was the question of the Central Asian response to the creation of the Slavic Commonwealth. Niyazov proposed the formation of a Central Asian confederation as a counterbalance to the Slavic Union created in Belavezha. Nazarbayev was among those who argued against it. He wanted the Central Asian republics to join the Commonwealth created by the three Slavic leaders.

"We gathered at Niyazov's quarters in Ashgabat," recalled Nazarbayev, "and discussed the situation until 3:00 a.m.: whether we should refuse to accept the dissolution of the Union and recognize Gorbachev as president—but what kind of Union could there be without Russia? Or should we create a Central Asian confederation—that was what Niyazov proposed, but then, we have one economy, one army, one and the same ruble [[with Russia]], 1,150 nuclear warheads in Kazakhstan. . . . How could we engage in a confrontation with Russia?" The idea of a Central Asian confederation probably would have been advantageous to Niyazov's own republic, which was rich in natural gas and had a population of only 3.5 million, the absolute majority of whom were Turkmen. But the prospect of complete separation from Russia and other Slavic republics could deepen the emerging division between Slavs and Kazakhs in Kazakhstan and might very well mean the end of Kazakhstan in its current borders, with the subsequent realization of some form of Solzhenitsyn's scenario.[13]

Crucial to the outcome of the late-night debate in Ashgabat was the position taken by the fifty-three-year-old leader of Uzbekistan, Islam Karimov. Uzbekistan was Central Asia's most populous republic. With close to 20 million inhabitants, it was third in the Soviet Union, after Russia and Ukraine. The Uzbeks, numbering more than 14 million, had a comfortable majority over non-Uzbeks: their largest ethnic minority, the Russians, came a distant second, with somewhat more than 1.6 million. While not threatened by Russians or Slavs at home, the Uzbek elite had had difficult relations with Moscow in the last years of Soviet rule. Moscow had never tried to send an ethnic Russian to rule non-Slavic Uzbekistan, as was attempted in Kazakhstan, but it did much to alienate the Uzbek elite with its relentless drive against corruption—a drive that, for a number of reasons, focused on Uzbekistan.[14]

The investigation of the "Cotton Case," which soon became known as the "Uzbek Case," began under Yurii Andropov and resumed with new vigor under Gorbachev. The facts uncovered by the Moscow investigators in Uzbekistan were staggering. The first secretary of the Uzbekistan Communist Party was accused of taking bribes from fourteen individuals in the total amount of 1.2 million rubles. Some of the bribes, claimed the prosecutors, had been handed over in St. George's Hall of the Kremlin Grand Palace during sessions of the USSR

Supreme Soviet. The system that generated millions of dollars in bribes in Uzbekistan was created by Shoraf Rashidov, the first secretary of the republic's Central Committee and a nonvoting member of the Moscow Politburo, who ran the republic from 1961 to 1983.

In the mid-1970s, responding to increasing demands from Moscow for production quotas of cotton—Uzbekistan's main export product—and encouraged by that year's bumper crop, Rashidov made a public pledge to his patron, Leonid Brezhnev, that from then on his republic would produce 6 million tons of cotton per annum. At best, it could in fact produce only two-thirds of that amount, and in a bad year, no more than 3 million tons. Rashidov's future and the careers of those around him were under threat. Rashidov ordered every available plot of land to be used for growing cotton and forced the entire population of the republic, including children and teenagers, to work in the fields, irrespective of their main occupation. The results were disappointing at best—the harvest never reached 6 million tons.[15]

Like European imperial powers in their overseas colonies, the Soviets in Uzbekistan wanted "white gold," as cotton was then known in Soviet parlance. While cotton was grown and produced in Uzbekistan, the main textile facilities were in Russia. Thus Uzbekistan exported cotton and imported textiles, at a great loss to its economy. The leaders of Uzbekistan then found a colonial solution to the imperial problem. It was called bribery. If the missing 2 or 3 million tons per annum could not be produced in the republic, decided Uzbek officials, they could be "added" to the official reports.

The scheme involved tens of thousands of individuals at all levels, from collective farms to high offices in the government and the Central Committee. Money received from the center for allegedly produced cotton was redistributed in Uzbekistan in the form of bribes. Millions of rubles also went to directors of textile factories and state and party officials in Russia, who confirmed the receipt of cotton never produced or pretended not to know what was going on. Uzbekistan became the homeland of the first hundred Soviet-era millionaires and a breeding ground of organized crime. Andropov and then Gorbachev gave their consent to the arrests of those involved in the scheme. With thousands of people under investigation, many began to regard the criminal prosecution as an assault on the entire republic, whose leaders were considered by their defenders to be guilty of nothing more than trying to fulfill the wishes of their colonial masters.

Islam Karimov, who became the leader of Uzbekistan in 1990, shared the feelings of his countrymen. Like many in Uzbekistan, he regarded the "Cotton Case" as a form of political persecution. In September 1991, he convened a congress of the Communist Party of Uzbekistan, now renamed the Popular Democratic Party, which adopted a resolution exonerating the communist leaders of Uzbekistan of any wrongdoing. "They have labored honestly and with a clear conscience for the good of the Motherland and can look their people in the eye directly and openly," read the resolution. In late December 1991, a few days before being elected to the newly created presidency of his country, Karimov pardoned every individual prosecuted as a result of the investigation. By that time it had become known as the "Uzbek Case" and served as a symbol of Uzbek suffering under the communist regime.[16]

Karimov showed much more independence than Nazarbayev during the Gorbachev-initiated talks on the new union treaty. He often sided with Yeltsin and Kravchuk in derailing Gorbachev's efforts (generally supported by Nazarbayev) to tie the republics more closely to the center. After the August coup he moved swiftly to remove the veneer of communist ideology from Uzbek society, demolishing monuments to communist leaders and rechristening squares and streets originally named after them. He declared, however, that Uzbekistan was not ready for democracy, crushed nascent opposition, and proclaimed that his inspiration was the political and economic model of neighboring China. Despite this move away from Moscow, Karimov was unhappy with what had happened at Belavezha. He later would express his displeasure directly to Yeltsin concerning the separate agreement between the Slavic presidents. But during the lengthy discussion in Ashgabat on the night of December 12–13, 1991, Karimov supported Nazarbayev and others who were arguing against the creation of what Moscow journalists were already calling the "Muslim Charter."

Karimov's motives for joining the Commonwealth were different from Nazarbayev's. Like the president of Kyrgyzstan, Askar Akaev, Karimov needed Russia and the Commonwealth as allies against Islamic fundamentalism and rising China. But even more, he needed

Russian textile factories to process Uzbek cotton. Without them, the Uzbek economy would collapse in a matter of weeks. Talking to reporters after the end of the Ashgabat meeting, Karimov rejected suggestions of a second-class citizenship status awaiting the Muslim republics in the Slavic Commonwealth. He told reporters that "the only way to escape a secondary role [[for those republics]] is to turn Central Asia into a highly developed region with its own processing industry."[17]

Even though they were unhappy about the exclusively Slavic character of the Belavezha meeting, Nazarbayev, Karimov, and their colleagues saw no alternative but to support—in each case for a different combination of political, economic, social, ethnic, and security reasons—the course adopted at Belavezha by Russia and its Slavic neighbors. At Ashgabat, the Central Asian leaders not only agreed to join the Commonwealth but also came up with a face-saving way to do so. "Having discussed the matter, we adopted a declaration of the leaders of the five republics," Nazarbayev told journalists after the end of the meeting, "which states the following: 'We treat with understanding the effort of the leaders of the republics of Belarus, Russia, and Ukraine to establish a Commonwealth of Independent States in place of the previously disenfranchised republics. Our main condition is the entry of all republics of the CIS as founders, that is, on the basis of absolutely equal rights.'"[18]

THE ALMATY SUMMIT, which, as many expected, would decide the fate of both the crumbling Union and the not yet fully established Commonwealth, was scheduled for Saturday, December 21. It was to be held at the Palace of Friendship in Kazakhstan's capital, where in early November the leaders of twelve Soviet republics had met for their first summit without Gorbachev to sign an economic agreement. This new meeting would also take place without Gorbachev. But how many leaders would come to Almaty was not clear until the very end, and the journalists who descended on the capital of Kazakhstan—almost five hundred in all—to cover the last Soviet and first post-Soviet summit of the republican presidents were kept guessing. "The talk now is that not just eight but nine or ten states will take part," wrote a reporter for the Moscow newspaper *Izvestiia*. "It is expected that the Minsk 'trio' and the Ashgabat 'quintet' will be joined by Armenia and perhaps Moldova." On the eve of the meeting, news reached Almaty that Ayaz Mutalibov of Azerbaijan, a country locked in bloody battle with Armenia over Nagornyo-Karabakh, was also on his way.[19]

What the presidents of republics with different interests—sometimes even at war with one another, such as Armenia and Azerbaijan—were bringing to the table and what to expect from the meeting were anyone's guesses. The only political leader to go public with his agenda for the Almaty summit was the one who was not invited to attend—Mikhail Gorbachev. He was left with no vehicle but that of a public statement to present his views and concerns and try to influence the outcome. After the ratification of the Belavezha Agreement by the Russian parliament and the Ashgabat declaration of the leaders of the Central Asian republics, Gorbachev had no choice but to reconcile himself to the idea of the Commonwealth. On December 17, the day on which Baker left Moscow and Gorbachev held his all-important meeting with Yeltsin about the transfer of power, the Soviet president declared to the media that his position coincided 80 percent with that of Yeltsin.

The content of the remaining 20 percent was revealed on the following day, when Gorbachev published an open letter to the participants in the Almaty summit. Gorbachev wanted the Commonwealth to become a subject of international law, take part in international relations, and have a common citizenship. He also argued for the creation of a unified military command and a common foreign policy agency that would take care of Soviet legal obligations abroad and USSR representation in the United Nations Security Council. He proposed the creation of Commonwealth institutions to coordinate economic and financial policy, as well as academic and cultural activities. Finally, he suggested dropping the reference to independent states from the title of the new organization and calling it the "Commonwealth of European and Asian States."[20]

The letter left little doubt that while Gorbachev accepted the word "commonwealth," he actually wanted to re-create a looser version of the polity envisioned in his now defunct union treaty. At best, he was finally prepared to agree to the principles of confederation advocated by Yeltsin and Nazarbayev and briefly accepted by Kravchuk after the failure of the August coup. But it was too late: the train of confederation had long since left the station. The text of the open letter was drafted by Anatolii Cherniaev, whose version Gorbachev preferred to the one prepared by his other aide, Georgii Shakhnazarov. According to Cherniaev, Shakhnazarov's draft was "composed in thoroughly 'constructive' tones—benevolent, conciliatory, offering wishes of success." Was Gorbachev concerned with making a statement of principle, regardless of the political consequences? Or was he still hoping to be offered a major role in the Commonwealth, which would keep him afloat politically? In his memoirs, Gorbachev does not comment on his intentions, stating only—and not without bitterness—that his letter "had no effect whatsoever."[21]

One day after Gorbachev issued his letter, Russian newspapers published a translation of Yeltsin's interview with the Italian newspaper *La Repubblica,* which left Gorbachev little hope of a political future. To the question "Will Gorbachev play any role in the Commonwealth?" the Russian president gave an unequivocal answer: "No. We shall treat him with the dignity and respect that he deserves, but because we have decided to complete the transition phase in our country by the end of December, he should also make his decision by that deadline."[22]

Yeltsin's vision for the Commonwealth institutions was much more modest than Gorbachev's. "Perhaps a Council of Heads of State, a Council of Heads of Government, and a Defense Council will be established, comprising the heads of the independent states," wrote Yeltsin's chief aide, Gennadii Burbulis, outlining Russian desiderata for the Almaty meeting after the Russian cabinet discussed the matter on December 18. On the same day, the government reviewed alternative designs for the new Russian coat of arms. It was decided to go back to the symbol of imperial Russia, the double-headed eagle. Burbulis told the press that of the two designs discussed at the meeting, the ministers decided to choose the eagle that looked less threatening. The last thing Russia wanted at that point was to frighten away its potential partners in the Commonwealth.[23]

The character of the new Commonwealth institutions and the scope of their authority were of great concern to Leonid Kravchuk of Ukraine. For some time it was not clear whether he would attend the meeting at all. At Belavezha, Kravchuk had insisted that Ukraine would not accept any Commonwealth institutions that limited its independence. He had won the day. Now that arrangement suddenly appeared to have been called into question: judging by the statements of Yeltsin's aides, Russia was eager to "deepen" the deal and strengthen the integrationist aspect of the Commonwealth. Kravchuk was not pleased. He faced strong opposition in his government, parliament, and society at large to what many considered a sellout of Ukrainian national interests, perpetrated almost immediately after the country had won its long-sought independence. Many questioned the intentions of the former communist apparatchik who had led his nation to independence and then, without so much as consulting the cabinet or parliament, signed an agreement to establish what looked to many like a reincarnation of the Soviet Union.

A poll conducted in Moscow, Kyiv, and Minsk after the signing of the Belavezha Agreement indicated that only 50 percent of respondents in Kyiv supported it, as compared to 84 percent in Moscow and 74 percent in Minsk. Kyivans who favored the creation of the Commonwealth did so largely for economic reasons, not because they were inspired by the notion of political unity of the three Slavic nations. Of those polled in Kyiv, 54 percent linked their hopes for a better economic future with the Commonwealth, as compared to 44 percent in Minsk and 38 percent in Moscow.[24]

After the Central Asian presidents proposed to cancel the old treaty and sign a new one, Kravchuk indicated that he was in no hurry to go to Almaty. As always, he played his weak hand exceptionally well. By showing no interest in renegotiating accords, Kravchuk put everyone on edge. If the Central Asian republics did not want to lose Russia, Russia did not want to lose Ukraine. Yeltsin had been opposed to signing Gorbachev's union treaty without Ukraine because it would have left Russia almost one-on-one with the Central Asian Muslim republics. The Commonwealth without Ukraine, as he saw it, was quite a similar proposition. Baker visited Kravchuk in Kyiv on December 18, and their conversation began with Kravchuk's plea for American support of Ukrainian independence. When Kravchuk told Baker that he would go to Almaty, the US secretary of state was greatly relieved.[25]

Unlike Kravchuk, the Belarusian leader, Stanislaŭ Shushkevich, was eager to take part in the Almaty meeting. Soon after signing the Belavezha Agreement, he issued a statement to the effect that the Commonwealth was not meant to be an exclusive Slavic club and was open for other republics, including the Central Asian ones, to join. But the Belarusians did not want to extend the Commonwealth at any price. They came up with the idea that only republics not involved in violent conflicts on their territory could be invited to join the Commonwealth. That approach would automatically exclude Moldova, which was trying to rein in its predominantly Slavic region of Transnistria; Azerbaijan, which was striving to retain its predominantly Armenian-settled region of Nagornyo-Karabakh; Armenia, which was involved in the Karabakh conflict; and probably Georgia, where the opposition was engaged in street fights with government forces, and such regions as Abkhazia and North Ossetia, predominantly non-Georgian in ethnic composition, were demanding the right to self-determination. In theory, even Russia, with its deepening crisis in Chechnia, could be barred from Commonwealth membership if the Belarusian proposal was adopted at the Almaty summit.[26]

Quite apart from the Belarusian proposal, the Almaty meeting had to take a stand on the breakaway regions. As the date of the Almaty meeting drew closer, two breakaway regions, Transnistria in Moldova and Nagornyo-Karabakh in Azerbaijan, applied for membership in the Commonwealth before their "home" republics did so. Meanwhile, Russia recognized the independence of Moldova and Armenia in their Soviet-era borders. This did little to defuse tensions in the breakaway regions. The revolt of autonomies against their "parent" republics, so greatly encouraged by Gorbachev's center in 1990–1991, was in full swing now that the Soviet Union was nearing its final hour.

As one would expect, given the Union republics' earlier troubles with autonomist movements, at the Belavezha meeting the presidents of Russia, Ukraine, and Belarus had declared their support for "legitimate" authorities in the republics. On Russia's initiative, they had issued a statement supporting the Moldovan leadership in its effort to crush Slavic separatism in Transnistria. The Slavic presidents were insisting on the inviolability of existing borders and placing legal principle above ethnic solidarity with fellow Slavs. Their unanimity on those points would help prevent a "Yugoslavia with nukes," as the Soviet Union was being described in Gorbachev's doomsday scenarios.[27]

While the Slavic republics were at peace with one another, the others were not. Ethnic warfare in the non-Slavic regions of the once united country was becoming more intense and dragging units of the Soviet army into the conflict. On December 9, the day after the signing of the Belavezha Agreement, Moldovan forces clashed with the Transnistrian militia in the border city of Bender. The Transnistrian forces enjoyed the support of the Soviet Fourteenth Army, formally still under Gorbachev's authority. In the next few days, clashes took place in the Transnistrian town of Dubasari. In Azerbaijan, on December 18, President Ayaz Mutalibov took command of all military formations on the territory of his republic. He wanted Soviet army units to either acknowledge his authority or leave Azerbaijan. On the following day, the Armenians of Nagornyo-Karabakh formed their own self-defense committee, which took charge of local militias cooperating with Soviet troops under Gorbachev's tutelage. President Levon Ter-Petrosian of Armenia issued his own decree strengthening ties between local Armenian authorities and Soviet army units on the territory of the republic. Whereas Azeris saw the Soviet army as a potential enemy, Armenians considered it an ally.[28]

The civil war against which Gorbachev had warned Ukrainians on the eve of their referendum was breaking out in other republics. For the time being, it was limited to the Caucasus and the Slavic-Roman frontier in Moldova. In the following year, it would spread into Tajikistan.

THE ALMATY SUMMIT began as planned at 11:30 a.m. on December 21 at the Palace of Friendship in the capital of Kazakhstan. The participants were supposed to give new meaning to the old Soviet cliché of the friendship of peoples. They managed to do so. They faced enormous problems at home and abroad, but there was also hope that their meeting—the largest such gathering since the failed coup—would show the former Soviet republics a way out of the impasse of the previous several months.

The Commonwealth meeting offered the republican leaders a sorely needed negotiating platform that Gorbachev and his meetings on a new union treaty had failed to provide. Marshal Yevgenii Shaposhnikov was the first to admit this. "It was the first meeting in many months of all heads of Union republics in such a complement," he wrote in his memoirs. "The very fact that everyone came, with the exception of the leaders of the Baltic republics and Georgia, which sent an observer, spoke volumes. I compared this meeting with many others—meetings of the State Council of the USSR and consultations at Novo-Ogarevo, at which some leaders failed to show up for a variety of reasons."[29]

Formally a minister in Gorbachev's government, Shaposhnikov held the only official Commonwealth post so far established—commander in chief of its military forces. Having accepted the office from Yeltsin immediately after the signing of the Belavezha Agreement, Shaposhnikov was now presiding over a quickly disintegrating army. His problems in that regard were not limited to the attempts of the presidents of the North Caucasus republics of Azerbaijan, Armenia, and Georgia to establish some form of control over Soviet troops on their territory or the efforts of leaders of the breakaway regions of Transnistria and Nagornyo-Karabakh to do the same in their jurisdictions.

No less dangerous to the unity of the armed forces was the decision of the president of the so far peaceful republic of Ukraine to declare himself commander in chief of Soviet troops on Ukrainian soil. On December 6, Shaposhnikov's former protégé Kostiantyn Morozov, who was Kravchuk's minister of defense, had sworn an oath of allegiance to Ukraine. In response to Shaposhnikov's subsequent attempt to order Soviet troops to swear allegiance to Russia, Kravchuk had pushed ahead with plans to administer the oath of allegiance to Ukraine to troops stationed on Ukrainian territory. Those plans had been suspended for the moment, but Shaposhnikov expected that the Ukrainians would raise the question in Almaty. Miraculously, they did not.[30]

The participants in the Almaty summit focused on two big subjects: the dissolution of the USSR and the creation of a new Commonwealth that would now include not three but eleven republics. It took the heads of the post-Soviet states only three and a half hours to agree on the principles of the new international structure, which would include most of what remained of the Soviet Union after the departure of the Balts. By 3:00 p.m. the final drafts of the agreements had been sent to the typists, and two hours later they were signed at an official ceremony. At the insistence of the Central Asian republics, the leaders of the post-Soviet states, including Russia,

Ukraine, and Belarus, signed the declaration on the formation of the Commonwealth anew. Now all present in Almaty were founding members of the Commonwealth.

Most of the decisions were adopted on the initiative of the Russian delegation. First, the presidents agreed to form two coordinating institutions: the Council of Presidents and the Council of Prime Ministers. They also agreed to abolish all remaining Soviet ministries and institutions—an issue of paramount importance to Yeltsin in his ongoing struggle with Gorbachev. Russia also received the participants' approval to declare itself the successor to the USSR, which meant, among other things, permanent membership in the Security Council of the United Nations. The agreement on joint control of nuclear arsenals was in full accord with the scheme that Yeltsin had described to Baker a few days earlier in Moscow: only the president of Russia could authorize a launch of nuclear weapons, while the other presidents with a nuclear arsenal would be consulted but would have no technical ability to order a launch. By July 1992, tactical nuclear arms would be moved from Ukraine, Belarus, and Kazakhstan to Russia for disassembly. The leaders of all four nuclear republics, including Kravchuk, Nazarbayev, and Shushkevich, endorsed that solution.[31]

The meeting proved so successful because its agenda was limited to issues on which all could agree. The others were postponed until the next summit, scheduled for December 30 in Minsk, the capital of Belarus and still the capital of the Commonwealth. Kravchuk, the most skeptical and reserved of all the participants, went along. He agreed to leave Shaposhnikov in charge of all strategic and tactical nuclear arms until the next summit, not insisting on the creation of an independent Ukrainian army. Nor did he object to the resolution making Russia the legal international successor to the Soviet Union, which meant that Ukraine would forfeit its share of Soviet property abroad.

The Almaty agreement offered Ukraine compensation in the form of the almost immediate liquidation of the USSR as a subject of international law, which cleared the way for recognition of Ukrainian independence by the United States and other Western countries that were still sitting on the fence. The most important point for the Ukrainian delegation was that, despite Gorbachev's insistence, the

Almaty meeting did not create any superstate structures or infringe on Ukrainian sovereignty by establishing joint Commonwealth citizenship. Moreover, the Commonwealth Defense Council, created ad hoc in Belavezha for the sole purpose of appointing Shaposhnikov commander in chief and luring him away from Gorbachev, was now tacitly dropped from the books. Leonid Kravchuk later recalled with satisfaction that at the press conference following the summit, its host, Nursultan Nazarbayev, "rose and, with no emotional ado, announced in businesslike fashion that we had all reached a decision: the Union no longer existed, the CIS was a fact, and we should now proceed to build new relations."[32]

HIGH ABOVE THE ATLANTIC, on a US aircraft heading for Washington, James Baker took a call from distant Almaty. Nursultan Nazarbayev was calling the secretary of state to report on the results of the summit. "The Alma-Ata meeting is over," he told Baker. "Eleven republics participated in the meeting." He added that the Central Asian republics had joined the Commonwealth, while Russia, Ukraine, Belarus, and Kazakhstan had agreed to maintain unified control over their nuclear arsenals. Tactical nuclear weapons would soon be transferred to Russia, and the rest of the nuclear republics would become nuclear-free by the end of the decade.

Baker was more than pleased. "Let me tell you how grateful I am for your call and your very full report," he told the Kazakh president. "It is consistent with everything that you and I discussed with the Republic leaders." Nazarbayev thanked Baker but said that his achievement had not come easily. "You have done remarkably well," responded Baker. He promised the former communist boss speedy recognition of his republic's independence.[33]

"Time will determine the true meaning of the agreements signed in Alma-Ata," declared the Moscow newspaper *Izvestiia*. If the long-term significance of the meeting was still unclear to participants and observers, its importance was grasped instantaneously by someone whose immediate future depended directly on its outcome. On the following day, Gorbachev's aide Anatolii Cherniaev noted in his diary, "Yesterday was the day of the Alma-Ata slaughter. A turning point, evidently, comparable to October 25, 1917, and with equally undetermined consequences." Cherniaev was referring to the Bolshevik takeover in St. Petersburg seventy-four years earlier—an event that had changed the fate of his country and the history of the world. He and his boss, Mikhail Gorbachev, were about to enter the final, and probably the most dramatic, if not tragic, stage of their political careers.[34]

18

CHRISTMAS IN MOSCOW

O N THE MORNING OF MONDAY, DECEMBER 23, the first work-day since his return to Moscow from Almaty, Boris Yeltsin went to see Mikhail Gorbachev to complete the unfinished business of the transfer of power. Yeltsin no longer feared for his safety, as he had after Belavezha. Armed with the Almaty decision on the liquidation of all institutions of the former USSR and the agreement of all the republican leaders to hand over to Russia Soviet assets and legal rights abroad, Yeltsin was eager to clear the decks and remove Gorbachev from the scene as soon as possible. Their original agreement, reached only a few days earlier, stipulated that the transfer of power would take place before mid-January. In Almaty the republican presidents had agreed that proposals on the liquidation of Soviet institutions be submitted for their next meeting in Minsk on December 30. But Yeltsin did not want to wait even for that date. He was apparently eager to come to Minsk as the sole leader of Russia, as Kravchuk was of Ukraine or as Islam Karimov, whose presidential elections were scheduled for December 29, would be of Uzbekistan.

Yeltsin had discussed Gorbachev's future with the republican presidents in Almaty. All had agreed that he should be treated with respect and allowed to step down with a retirement package appropriate to his presidential status. Yeltsin had asked the presidents to share the expense of supporting Gorbachev in retirement. But

Yeltsin's chief bodyguard, Aleksandr Korzhakov, later recalled that even though Gorbachev was president of the USSR as a whole, "they all delicately avoided the problem, hinting that Russia was a rich country and could feed Gorbachev and all his retinue." At the press conference in Almaty, Yeltsin declared that the presidents had decided not to treat Gorbachev as his Soviet predecessors had been treated, that is, as an enemy of the people, only to be rehabilitated afterward, but rather to deal with him in a civilized manner. "Civilized manner" was a general term, and, given that Gorbachev was "assigned" to Yeltsin at Almaty, it was up to the Russian president to define exactly what it meant.[1]

When Yeltsin arrived at the Kremlin on December 23, Soviet and American television producers who happened to be on the scene asked the two presidents for permission to film their greetings: Gorbachev agreed, but Yeltsin refused. There would be no handshake before the television cameras. Yeltsin showed who was boss by appearing at Gorbachev's quarters on short notice and making his former patron postpone all his plans for the day. By that time, Gorbachev was all but resigned to his fate. He had earlier told Chancellor Helmut Kohl of Germany that if the Commonwealth was approved in its current form at the Almaty summit, he would resign. His open letter to the summit participants had been his last attempt to influence politics in the crumbling Soviet Union and perhaps prolong his own political life. It achieved neither.

After the letter was published in the media, Gorbachev had focused on his plan B, which was resignation. As the republican presidents were gathering in the Almaty Palace of Friendship to begin their summit, Gorbachev summoned to his office his two remaining political allies, Aleksandr Yakovlev and Eduard Shevardnadze, along with his aide and speechwriter Anatolii Cherniaev. He asked them to help him edit his resignation speech, and they spent two hours working on the text. It would be their last speechwriting assignment for Gorbachev. "We became engrossed in the editing," noted Cherniaev in his diary, "as if . . . we were composing another speech for the Supreme Soviet, or something of the sort. Arguing over words, we seemed to forget that we were preparing a death notice."[2]

WHEN YELTSIN SHOWED UP unexpectedly on the morning of December 23, Gorbachev was getting ready to tape his final address to the citizens of an already nonexistent Soviet Union. The taping had to be canceled. The meeting began in the former Politburo Walnut Room with only Gorbachev and Yeltsin present, but after some time the heads of the two presidential administrations were called in to take account of the agreements made by the two presidents. The negotiations were anything but pleasant or easy. According to various reports, they lasted from six to eight hours. Yeltsin and Gorbachev eventually agreed on the timetable for the transition of power. Gorbachev would deliver his resignation speech in two days, on the evening of December 25. After that, he would sign decrees relinquishing his posts as president of the USSR and commander in chief of the Soviet armed forces. Yeltsin and Shaposhnikov would visit him afterward to take possession of his nuclear briefcase. Gorbachev's aides were then supposed to vacate their offices in four days, by December 29. The red Soviet flag would be lowered on the Kremlin tower for the last time on December 31. The Kremlin would begin the new year with a new flag and a new master.

As the meeting proceeded, Gorbachev called in Aleksandr Yakovlev to facilitate the negotiations. One of the intellectual fathers of perestroika, he had been abandoned by Gorbachev in the summer of 1990 to appease the hard-liners in the Soviet leadership. He was subsequently expelled from the Politburo and then from the party. Yakovlev returned to Gorbachev after the failed August coup, in which he gave vocal support to Yeltsin. Both Gorbachev and Yeltsin trusted Yakovlev, which made him an ideal intermediary in one of the most sensitive discussions ever to take place between the two rivals. Yakovlev later remembered that both men behaved with dignity and that the tone of the meeting was "businesslike, with mutual respect." He also added a qualifier: "They argued at times, but without irritation."

With Yakovlev's help, the two presidents agreed on a political cease-fire. Gorbachev would not criticize Yeltsin during the most difficult months of the coming economic reform. Yeltsin would allow Gorbachev to create and run his own foundation, which was supposed to support research on social, political, and economic matters but stay out of politics per se. For days before the meeting, Gorbachev had fantasized about a "RAND Corporation" of his own, funded by Western foundations, which would cooperate with think tanks in the West. He invited Cherniaev and his other aides and allies, including Yakovlev, to work for the new foundation. They had their doubts, but Yakovlev helped Gorbachev negotiate a deal with Yeltsin according to which the latter turned over to the future foundation a complex of buildings administered before the coup by the Central Committee of the Communist Party and used as training grounds for foreign communist cadres. It included classrooms, cafeterias, gyms, and a hotel. "At that point, Yeltsin obviously had no idea of the actual dimensions of the complex," recalled his bodyguard and confidant Aleksandr Korzhakov.[3]

The meeting also involved the transfer of the presidential archive. In Yakovlev's presence, Gorbachev turned over to the new master of the Kremlin the contents of one of his safes—secret documents that had been passed on from one head of party and state to another since Joseph Stalin. They included the map that accompanied the secret protocols of the Molotov-Ribbentrop Pact of 1939 and the materials of the internal investigation of the Katyn Forest massacre of tens of thousands of Polish prisoners of war by NKVD troops in the spring of 1940. Gorbachev had publicly claimed that there were no documents in the Soviet archives on the fate of the Polish officers, but the materials had been in his safe all along. There were other, no less sensitive documents, including KGB reports on Lee Harvey Oswald and the assassination of President John F. Kennedy, which showed that the KGB had nothing to do with the plot.

Yeltsin later claimed that he refused to take the documents and thereby continue the conspiracy to keep the party's dirty laundry secret. "Those were foreign-policy matters, one more sordid than the other," confided Yeltsin later to the former Soviet foreign minister Boris Pankin. "I said: 'Stop. Please! Just hand these papers to the Archives, and they'll make you sign for them. I do not intend to be held responsible for them. Why should I take charge of all these matters? You are no longer the general secretary, while I have not been one, and will not be.'" It was an attempt to make a clean break with the past. Yeltsin's aides, who collected the files once the meeting was over, would indeed turn them over to the archives. At least, most of them. Aleksandr Korzhakov later wrote that Yeltsin kept some of the documents in his personal safe. The break with the past was not as clean as it seemed at first glance.[4]

Then there was the issue of Gorbachev's retirement. The negotiators agreed that he would retire with his current salary, which, although extremely high by Soviet standards four thousand rubles—amounted to a mere $40 at the black-market exchange rate at the time. He was also assigned a country house located on a sixteen-hectare wooded lot outside Moscow, an apartment somewhat smaller than the one he occupied at the time, two cars, and a staff of twenty, including cooks, waiters, custodians, and bodyguards. Yeltsin also allowed some members of Gorbachev's circle, including the former Russian prime minister, Ivan Silaev, to privatize their state dachas at a significant discount. One thing Yeltsin did not promise Gorbachev was immunity from prosecution. Two days later, he told the media that if Gorbachev felt he was guilty of something, the time to confess was immediately.

At the end of the meeting, the clearly exhausted Gorbachev retired to a private room behind his office. "God grant that no one find himself in his position," Yakovlev said to Yeltsin. The two stayed for another hour. As Yakovlev later recalled, they "drank and talked heart to heart." When Yakovlev went to check on Gorbachev in the private room, he found his boss in distress. "He was lying on the couch, with tears in his eyes," recalled Yakovlev. "You see, Sash, this is how it is," said Gorbachev, calling Yakovlev by his nickname. "I consoled him as best I could," wrote Yakovlev later. "But I, too, felt a tightness in my throat. I was overcome with tears of pity for him. I was choked by the feeling that something unjust had happened. A man who just yesterday had been the tsar of cardinal changes in the world and in his own country, who had decided the fates of billions of people on earth, was now the helpless victim of history's latest caprice." Gorbachev asked for water. He wanted to be alone. Yakovlev left the room.[5]

Yeltsin left Gorbachev's quarters more confident than ever. Yakovlev watched as Yeltsin "firmly paced the parquet floor, as if on a parade square." He wrote in his memoirs, "It was a conqueror's march." Upon returning to his office with the secret documents from Gorbachev's archive brought along by his aides, Yeltsin placed a call to George Bush. He wanted to report on the results of the Almaty summit and the transition of power he had just accomplished.

"Hello, Boris, Merry Christmas," Yeltsin heard at the other end of the line. He wished Bush a merry Christmas in return. He then turned to business. The news on the unified nuclear command and the pledges of Ukraine, Belarus, and Kazakhstan to become nonnuclear states were the centerpieces of his presentation on the Almaty summit. He also told Bush about Gorbachev's retirement package. "Gorbachev is satisfied," Yeltsin reported to Bush. "As we agreed with you, we are thus trying to show respect for him. I repeat that he is satisfied, and I have already signed the decree on all these matters."

Yeltsin next addressed the question of control over the nuclear button. "After President Gorbachev announces his resignation on December 25, nuclear control will be passed to the President of Russia in the presence of Shaposhnikov. There will be no single second break in control of the button." Bush expressed his appreciation.

After delivering the kind of news he knew Bush wanted to hear, Yeltsin used the opportunity to lobby the American president for speedy recognition of his new country and transfer of the Soviet seat in the United Nations Security Council to Russia. He also wanted to speed up the delivery of American humanitarian aid. Bush promised to work on all three issues. He also agreed in principle to Yeltsin's proposal for a bilateral summit. Yeltsin had completed his coup. In all but name, he was now the sole master of the Kremlin.[6]

ON CHRISTMAS DAY 1991, officially his last day in office, Gorbachev intended to follow the scenario agreed upon with Yeltsin two days earlier. At 7:00 p.m. he would give his farewell speech, then sign the resignation decrees and, finally, transfer the nuclear codes.

The choice of Christmas Day for Gorbachev's farewell address was somewhat accidental. When Yeltsin's unexpected visit to Gorbachev on December 23 derailed the planned taping of the resignation speech, the Soviet president had suggested to the head of the USSR Television and Radio Administration, Yegor Yakovlev, that he do a live broadcast in the next day or two. He wanted to get it over with as soon as possible and suggested December 24. But Yakovlev advised his boss to wait one more day. He told him that Christmas Eve was the most important part of the holiday, and he wanted television viewers to celebrate that day in peace.

The viewers Yegor Yakovlev had in mind were all abroad. Orthodox Christmas, to be celebrated thirteen days later according to the Julian calendar, would not come until January 7. Yakovlev had good reason to worry about Western viewers and forget his own domestic audience. Despite his title, he was no longer in control of the Soviet television industry—his realm was now ruled by Yeltsin's people. The only crews he could provide for taping in the last days of Gorbachev's rule were American ones. "If, in those final days, Yegor Yakovlev had not brought in ABC, which was literally spending its days in the hallways, filming anything that turned up . . . then M[[ikhail]] S[[ergeevich]] would have remained in an information blockade until his very last in the Kremlin," noted Anatolii Cherniaev in his diary. The ABC team he had in mind was led by a legend of American broadcasting, Ted Koppel. Apart from Koppel and his ABC team, there was CNN, which had obtained exclusive rights to broadcast Gorbachev's resignation speech outside the USSR. The CNN team was led by its then president, Tom Johnson.[7]

Working with the American producers and cameramen was no easy task for Gorbachev's officials, since it involved both linguistic and cultural barriers. Gorbachev and the people around him believed that Christmas Eve, not Christmas Day, was the more important holiday in the West. That belief came from their own Eastern Christian tradition: in Russia, Ukraine, Belarus, and other historically Orthodox countries of the region, the main celebration of the holiday takes place at Christmas Eve dinner. And there turned out to be another complication—to the staffers' surprise, not everyone in the West celebrated Christmas.

On the morning of December 25, when a friendly Kremlin official approached Koppel and his ABC producer, Rick Kaplan, offering Christmas greetings, Kaplan, who was Jewish, responded, "To me you have to say 'Happy Hanukkah.'" The official was confused, never having heard the word. "Why would I have to say Happy Honecker?" he asked Kaplan, having in mind the ousted East German communist leader Erich Honecker, whose name was all over the Soviet press as he sought to avoid extradition from the crumbling USSR to a now united Germany. The Americans laughed. No, Kaplan was not talking about Honecker: he was referring to a Jewish holiday all but unknown in Russia.[8]

Gorbachev's aides realized that they had chosen the wrong date for the resignation speech when they tried to place Gorbachev's final call in his capacity as president of the USSR to George Bush at Camp David. The US embassy in Moscow was closed for the holiday, and the Soviet Ministry of Foreign Affairs was already in Yeltsin's hands. Gorbachev's interpreter, Pavel Palazhchenko, managed to reach the State Department's operations desk by using a regular Moscow telephone line. He scheduled the call for 10:00 a.m. EST, which was 5:00 p.m. in Moscow—two hours before Gorbachev's resignation speech. The call came through soon after George and Barbara Bush, together with their children and grandchildren, had finished opening their Christmas presents.

"Merry Christmas to you, Barbara and your family," began Gorbachev. "I had been thinking about when to make my statement, Tuesday or today. I finally decided to do it today, at the end of the day." Anatolii Cherniaev, who was present during the conversation and pleased that Bush had agreed to take a call on Christmas Day, was also happy with the tone of the conversation. He recorded his impressions in his diary: "M[[ikhail]] S[[ergeevich]] conversed in an almost familiar manner . . . 'Russian style' . . . 'as friends.' . . . But Bush also 'departed' from his reserve for the first time, offering many words of praise." According to the American transcript of the conversation, Bush recalled one of Gorbachev's visits to Camp David. "The horseshoe pit where you threw that ringer is still in good shape," he said. "Our friendship is as strong as ever and will continue to be as events unfold. There is no question about that," he told the Soviet president.⁹

There was also the business component of the call: Gorbachev and Bush discussed the transfer of control over Soviet nuclear forces from Gorbachev to Yeltsin. Bush would later be surprised to learn that Gorbachev had allowed Ted Koppel and the ABC crew to film the whole conversation from the Moscow side. The presence of television crews in Gorbachev's office seemed bizarre not only to Bush but also to Gorbachev's own aide, Pavel Palazhchenko, who later wrote in his memoirs, "It felt a little unreal—while the president was putting the final touches on the text of his address and the decree passing to Yeltsin control of the Soviet Union's nuclear weapons, American television technicians were coming and going busily, checking their wires and microphones. Who could have thought that this—all of this—were possible just a year ago?"¹⁰

There was a certain symbolism in the fact that Americans were now at both ends of the line. With his telephone call to Bush,

Gorbachev was effectively acknowledging the United States as the sole remaining superpower on the face of the earth. Ironically, it was also the Americans who provided Gorbachev with a pen to sign his resignation decrees. As he prepared to sign, Gorbachev discovered that his pen was not working properly. Tom Johnson, the president of CNN, who had led his crew into the Kremlin, offered his own Mont Blanc ballpoint—a twenty-fifth wedding anniversary present from his wife. Gorbachev hesitated. "Is it American?" he asked Johnson. "No, sir, it is either French or German," came the answer. Gorbachev signed the decrees with a pen produced by a German company founded in Hamburg before World War I. As if to underline the new power of the United States, it was given to a Soviet politician by an American businessman.[11]

Gorbachev's resignation address, which started as planned at 7:00 p.m. Moscow time, was the first of his speeches to be broadcast live not only to a Soviet audience but also to the world at large. The first task was performed by Soviet state television, which had finally shown some interest in Gorbachev; the second, by CNN. Gorbachev's press secretary, Andrei Grachev, later remembered that Gorbachev's voice was on the verge of trembling when he began his address, but he soon regained self-control. Cherniaev was happy with his boss's performance. "He was calm," noted Cherniaev in his diary. "He did not hesitate to consult the text, and everything turned out right from the start."

Cherniaev had special reasons to be happy with Gorbachev's performance. The text that Gorbachev did not hesitate to consult was largely written by Cherniaev himself. Another version, written by Aleksandr Yakovlev, which Cherniaev regarded as full of bitterness and self-pity, had been rejected. It included the following sentences: "And let it remain on the conscience of those who are now casting stones at me and allowing themselves to engage in vulgarity and insults. Decent people will remind them, I hope, where they would have been if everything had remained the same." Gorbachev also turned down a version written by his press secretary, Andrei Grachev. It criticized the presidents of the rebellious republics and claimed that without a center, cooperation between the non-Russian republics and Russia would be all but impossible: "An equal political union, for instance, between tiny Moldova and gigantic Russia is impossible in principle. Russia's obvious economic advantage is a basis for looming Russian imperialism." Grachev proposed that Gorbachev use the address to go over the heads of the presidents of the newly independent republics and appeal for popular support in reforming the federal state.

Gorbachev clearly tried to avoid a direct confrontation with Yeltsin. Cherniaev, however, was proud that in the final version of the speech, he had managed to restore some of the boldest parts of it. They included the statement that the USSR should not be dissolved without a referendum, a line that everyone knew would anger Yeltsin and that Gorbachev had initially crossed out during the editing process. What Cherniaev heard later from his own circle convinced him that he had done the right thing. Those close to Cherniaev were telling him that the speech was the very soul of "dignity and nobility." Aleksandr Yakovlev, whose version of the speech was rejected by Gorbachev, was of a different opinion. "This is the typical delusion of someone devoid of self-analysis," he commented later. "He did not come out of that psychological cul-de-sac where he put himself, having taking offense with the whole world."

"Dear Compatriots and Fellow Citizens!" Gorbachev began his address. "Given the situation that has come about with the formation of the Commonwealth of Independent States, I am ceasing my activity in the office of president of the USSR. I am making this decision for reasons of principle." It was anyone's guess how resignation because of the liquidation of the Union and the office of its president was to be reconciled with resignation for reasons of principle. No less confusing were the sentences immediately following: "I came out firmly for independence, the freedom of peoples, and the sovereignty of the republics. But at the same time for maintaining the Union state and the integrity of the country." How one could simultaneously support freedom, sovereignty, and even independence for the republics and unity for the state that tried to prevent them from acquiring sovereignty and independence was probably also beyond the intellectual grasp of the television audience. Along with Cherniaev, Gorbachev was caught up in the political rhetoric of the last years of the Soviet Union, when "sovereignty" was understood as something other than "independence" and neither term meant among the Soviet political class what it did to the rest of the world.

Gorbachev spoke much more coherently about the accomplishments of his rule: the end of the Cold War, the dismantling of the totalitarian system, the democratization of Soviet politics, and the opening of the country to the world. But few Soviet citizens were prepared to give him credit. Many could no longer endure even the sound of Gorbachev's voice, as his endless talking throughout his years in power had accompanied a steady decline in their standard of living. Some felt sorry for him, but almost no one wanted him to stay. For Cherniaev, Gorbachev cut a tragic figure. Indeed he was. A visionary and a man of great accomplishment, he changed the world and his country for the better by his actions but failed to change himself. A democrat at heart, he never faced a popular election and outstayed his welcome at the head of the country that was crumbling under his feet.[12]

All that remained for Gorbachev to do once his speech was over was to transfer his nuclear briefcase to Yeltsin. The Russian president was supposed to come to Gorbachev's office in the company of Marshal Shaposhnikov and the officers in charge of the briefcase to complete the transfer. When, after a brief interview with CNN, Gorbachev returned to his office, Shaposhnikov was waiting for him in the anteroom, but there was no sign of Yeltsin. The reason was that Yeltsin had called Shaposhnikov as the latter watched Gorbachev's resignation speech on television and told him that he would not go to Gorbachev's office. Yeltsin wanted Shaposhnikov to handle the entire transfer on his own.

It turned out that Yeltsin was outraged by the content of Gorbachev's speech, which made no reference to the transfer of power to him and assigned all credit for the Soviet Union's democratic development to Gorbachev alone. After watching the speech for a while, the enraged Yeltsin turned off the television set. As far as he was concerned, the truce concluded two days earlier had expired. Yeltsin saw no reason to do something he did not want to do in the first place—to pay Gorbachev a visit as president of the Soviet Union. After the negotiations of December 23, he had told his aides that he would never go back to see Gorbachev in his office. Now Gorbachev seemed to have given Yeltsin an excuse to avoid a final show of deference.

Yeltsin passed on his new offer to Gorbachev: he would meet him, but only on "neutral territory," in St. Catherine's Hall. It was all about who would have to come to whom. Gorbachev, whom his aides found redfaced and agitated after his conversation with Shaposhnikov, refused to go to the hall, which was used for the reception of foreign delegations. He would not defer to Yeltsin, and besides, in his mind, the USSR and Russia were not foreign states. Shaposhnikov eventually made arrangements for Gorbachev and Yeltsin to transfer the nuclear codes without seeing each other. The actual ceremony took place in a Kremlin corridor, with one set of officers surrendering the codes and the other set accepting the nuclear briefcase. They saluted one another in the presence of a CNN crew whose cameras were already packed.

Now that one agreement with Gorbachev had been broken, Yeltsin decided to break another. He ordered the lowering of the red Soviet flag flying over the cupola of the Senate Building in the Kremlin, originally scheduled for December 31, to take place immediately. Gorbachev finished his speech at 7:12 p.m. Less than half an hour later, the flag was taken down. Gorbachev was appalled. "Even in the first minutes after stepping down I was faced with impudence and a lack of courtesy," he wrote in his memoirs. Gorbachev wanted to keep the Soviet banner taken down from the Senate Building flagpole as a memento, but he was unable to do so. It was taken away by Kremlin custodians who no longer obeyed his orders. After seventy-four years of Soviet rule, the red banner was replaced by the red, white, and blue flag of Russia. The Commonwealth had no flag of its own: if one was going to be adopted, it would have to be raised in Minsk, not Moscow.[13]

After the official business of the transfer of nuclear codes was over, Gorbachev and his closest advisers, including Cherniaev, Aleksandr Yakovlev, and Yegor Yakovlev, marked the occasion with a glass of cognac. Then they moved what was developing into an ad hoc party from Gorbachev's office to the Walnut Room, where they were joined by Gorbachev's press secretary, Andrei Grachev. As Grachev would recall later, the ex-president "had his last farewell supper in the Walnut Room in the company of a mere five members of his 'inner circle,' having received not one telephone call with an expression, if not of thanks, then at least of support or sympathy from those politicians of the new Russia or the henceforth independent states of the CIS who owed him everything." The only leaders who had called Gorbachev in the previous few days to convey their good wishes for a life away from presidential office were Westerners: Chancellor Helmut Kohl of a now united Germany, Prime Minister John Major of Britain, and, half an hour before his resignation speech, Hans-Dietrich Genscher, the German foreign minister.

In his own memoirs, Mikhail Gorbachev would put a more positive spin on his last supper at the Kremlin: "Together with me were the closest friends and colleagues who shared with me all the great pressures and drama of the last months of the presidency." What definitely united those drinking cognac and eating cold cuts in the former Politburo meeting room on the last day of Gorbachev's presidency was their belief in perestroika—the revolutionary changes in society that they all had helped Gorbachev bring about. Andrei Grachev later recalled the mood around the Politburo table as both solemn and sad: "There was something of a feeling of a big thing accomplished. There was a kind of feeling of everyone sharing." They left the Kremlin after midnight, looking to the future with some hope but mainly with concern. Gorbachev asked Cherniaev to tell his contact in the German publishing industry not to transfer to Moscow Gorbachev's honorarium for the German translation of his book on the August coup. No one knew what the next day would bring.[14]

WHEN GORBACHEV AND HIS AIDES left the Kremlin in the early hours of December 26, it was still Christmas Day in Washington. George Bush, who had taken a telephone call from Gorbachev in the morning at his Camp David retreat, flew to Washington later that day to address the nation from the Oval Office. His live address was scheduled for 9:00 p.m. EST, which was the early morning of December 26 in Moscow. The major television networks hastily canceled or rescheduled some of their programs to accommodate what many expected would be a historic announcement.[15]

While everyone had been anticipating Gorbachev's eventual resignation, which seemed inevitable after the Almaty summit, no one had known exactly when it would come. On December 23, when Yeltsin paid his surprise visit to Gorbachev to arrange the transfer of power, Ed Hewett, the Soviet expert at the National Security Council, and his assistant Nick Burns were putting the finishing touches on a draft of a statement that President Bush was to make in response to Gorbachev's forthcoming resignation. Hewett, Burns, and others in the administration had wanted Bush to give a speech explaining to the nation the significance of the Soviet collapse, but Bush was reluctant. Burns believed the president did not want to make things even more difficult for Gorbachev than they already were. Then came word from General Brent Scowcroft that indeed there would be no speech, and Hewett and Burns got busy working on a statement intended to pay tribute to Gorbachev's contribution to history and his role in the peaceful ending of the Cold War.

The statement praised the Soviet president for "the revolutionary transformation of a totalitarian dictatorship and the liberation of his people from its smothering embrace." It also paid tribute to Gorbachev's role in international affairs. He had "acted boldly and decisively to end the bitter divisions of the cold war and contributed to the remaking of a Europe whole and free." As examples of US-Soviet cooperation on world issues, the statement singled out the Gulf War, the peace settlements in Nicaragua and Namibia, and progress on the Israeli-Palestinian talks. "As he leaves office," read the text prepared for Bush, "I would like to express publicly and on behalf of the American people my gratitude to him for years of sustained commitment to world peace, and my personal respect for his intellect, vision, and courage."[16]

Burns forwarded the text to Dennis Ross and Tom Niles in the State Department, asking for their comments by 2:00 p.m. that day. "The president would like to issue a statement on the day Gorbachev resigns," read the cover note. The draft aroused no questions or objections from the State Department or anyone else. Ed Hewett and Nick Burns could look forward to a restful Christmas Eve and Christmas Day. But their holiday plans were overturned on Christmas Eve when George Bush, already at Camp David, arranged a teleconference with his advisers, including James Baker, Brent Scowcroft, White House spokesman Marlin Fitzwater, and pollster Robert Teeter—a sign of the impending presidential campaign— to discuss the administration's response to Gorbachev's expected resignation. They approved the statement prepared by Hewett and Burns, but Scowcroft felt that Gorbachev's resignation, which the latest news from Moscow suggested would happen on Christmas Day, was "too important to kiss off with a statement from Marlin's office." He believed that the president should make a televised address to the nation. Bush finally agreed.

Then came the question of the text of the presidential address. Teeter, who was considering the impact of such an address on public opinion and liked the draft prepared by Hewett and Burns, came up with a solution: "Get those two guys who wrote the statement to turn it into a speech." Scowcroft and Fitzwater reached Hewett and Burns at home and told them, "Merry Christmas! We need a speech by nine o'clock tomorrow morning." Burns had one thing to do before writing the speech. He and his family—his wife, Elizabeth, and their three young daughters, Sarah, age eight, Elizabeth, five, and Caroline, a year and a half—were ready to celebrate Christmas Eve. They had a tradition of putting milk and cookies out for Santa Claus. Once they had done so, Burns left home and headed for the White House to work on the speech that he wanted the president to deliver and the nation to hear.

Hewett and Burns worked on the draft speech until 3:00 a.m. on Christmas Day. "I am afraid that the final death throes of communism forced me to work not only on Christmas Eve but also on Christmas Day on the president's speech that evening," wrote Burns a few days later to one of his acquaintances. "That was not a popular event with Libby and the girls, but I'll try to make it up to them!" The telephone began ringing at Burns's home soon after 8:00 a.m. on December 25. These were calls from Bush's staff at Camp David. There were revisions to the speech, and revisions to the revisions. He ended up fitting them together and editing the final text, working on it through the rest of the day. He was also a note taker on the telephone call that Gorbachev made to Bush that day. It was hard for anyone in the US government whose Christmas Day was ruined by Gorbachev's sudden resignation to credit the notion that he had actually chosen that date because he wanted Americans to spend Christmas Eve in peace.[17]

At 9:01 p.m. on Christmas Day, George Bush delivered his address to the nation. It lasted seven minutes. "Good evening, and Merry Christmas to all Americans across our great country," began Bush.

"During these last few months, you and I have witnessed one of the greatest dramas of the 20th century, the historic and revolutionary transformation of a totalitarian dictatorship, the Soviet Union, and the liberation of its peoples," continued the president. "For over 40 years, the United States led the West in the struggle against communism and the threat it posed to our most precious values. This struggle shaped the lives of all Americans. It forced all nations to live under the specter of nuclear destruction. That confrontation is now over. The nuclear threat, while far from gone, is receding. Eastern Europe is free. The Soviet Union itself is no more. This is a victory for democracy and freedom. It's a victory for the moral force of our values."[18]

While a good part of Bush's statement on Gorbachev's resignation, released on the same day, was incorporated into the television address, its interpretation of the meaning of that event was quite different. The change of interpretation, in fact, could hardly have been more profound. In the first statement, the ending of the Cold War was presented as a joint effort, achieved with Gorbachev's active participation. In the television address, it was his resignation that heralded the end of the Cold War, which had come about through the victory of the United States. An ally in bringing the Cold War to a conclusion was turned into a defeated enemy. Until the last weeks of the existence of the USSR, Bush had resisted its disintegration and tried to keep Gorbachev in power at all costs. But now that Gorbachev had resigned, Bush and his team were ready to take the credit for something they had worked hard to avoid—the loss of a reliable junior partner in the shaping of the post–Cold War world. One of the reasons for this reversal was Bush's flagging presidential campaign. Another was a sense of jubilation among his aides.

Nicholas Burns later remembered that he and Ed Hewett received only general guidelines regarding the content of the speech. The rest was very much a representation of what they knew to be the feelings of the American leadership as the Soviet Union disintegrated and their own feelings about the Soviet collapse. "We felt exhilarated," remembered Burns,

we felt positive, we were relieved, very, very happy, for two things: we had avoided the Third World War, a catastrophe, and our democratic values had triumphed in Europe, and America's commitment to Europe had triumphed. There was no love lost for the

Soviet Union. Despite good personal relations with Gorbachev and Shevardnadze, many of us viewed it as an evil empire, as in Reagan's words. And that is why the speech that Ed and I drafted that evening was meant to convey the triumph of democracy, triumph for the United States and the European peoples against communism.[19]

The president used the occasion of his Christmas speech to declare recognition of the newly independent states that had come into existence on the ruins of the Soviet Union. "The United States recognizes and welcomes the emergence of a free, independent, and democratic Russia, led by its courageous president, Boris Yeltsin," announced Bush. Not only did Russia receive recognition and a promise of immediate establishment of diplomatic relations, with the ambassador to the USSR becoming the ambassador to Russia, but it also got US support in obtaining the USSR's seat in the United Nations Security Council. A group of post-Soviet countries, including Ukraine, Belarus, Kazakhstan, and Kyrgyzstan—the four non-Russian states visited by Baker a few days earlier—as well as the much-lobbied-for Armenia, were granted recognition and a promise of speedy establishment of diplomatic relations. The rest of the former Soviet republics—Moldova, Turkmenistan, Azerbaijan, Tajikistan, Georgia, and Uzbekistan—were promised establishment of diplomatic relations once they assured the United States of their compliance with Baker's principles, as the other post-Soviet republics had done.[20]

On the afternoon of December 26, when George Bush met with the press in the Briefing Room of the White House, there was no question dealing specifically with Gorbachev. The president himself mentioned Gorbachev only once, when discussing the control of nuclear arsenals. Nuclear security and delivering humanitarian aid to Russia and other post-Soviet states were not just at the top of the media's agenda but accounted for all the questions concerning the former Soviet Union. Whereas Gorbachev was mentioned once, Yeltsin was referred to six times. The Soviet Union was rapidly being consigned to the past, as far as the American media and, by extension, the American public were concerned.[21]

A few days later, James Baker took time to draft a personal letter to Mikhail Gorbachev, paying tribute to his accomplishments. In it he all but recognized Gorbachev's leadership in ending the Cold War. "You saw the folly in superpower competition and in the isolation of your country from the rest of the world," wrote Baker in his "Dear Mikhail" letter.

> Your speech to the United Nations in 1988 ushered in a new era in world politics. With every step you took, you asked the United States to join you to build a new world. We were ready to do so and to build a new partnership between our nations as well. And we did that in a remarkable way—in Afghanistan, Central America, Cambodia, Namibia, the Persian Gulf and the Middle East. In addition, we cooperated not just to control arms, but to eliminate them. And to bring the risk of nuclear war to its lowest point since such arms were invented. Most importantly, together we saw the map of Europe transformed—peacefully and democratically. We saw Germany united and the people of Central and Eastern Europe set free to determine their own future. And as I said on many occasions, none of this would have happened without your leadership. Your place in history will forever be secure.[22]

EARLY IN THE MORNING on Friday, December 27, Kremlin custodians came to Gorbachev's office on the third floor of the Senate Building to change the sign on the door from "President of the Soviet Union, Gorbachev Mikhail Sergeevich" to "President of the Russian Federation, Yeltsin Boris Nikolaevich." Soon after 8:00 a.m. Yeltsin himself showed up at the threshold of the coveted office in the company of his chief adviser, Gennadii Burbulis; the head of the Russian parliament, Ruslan Khasbulatov; and his propaganda and information chief, Mikhail Poltoranin. What happened then we know of from the largely secondhand accounts of Gorbachev's supporters.

Yeltsin entered Gorbachev's office in a manner that left no doubt who was in charge. "Well, show it to me," he told the secretary on duty. His glance then fell on the desk, where he believed something was missing. "There used to be a marble desk set here," he said to the secretary. "Where is it?" The terrified public servant explained in a trembling voice that Gorbachev had never used ink pens and preferred felt ones, so there had never been an ink set on his desk. "Well, all right," said Yeltsin, dropping the matter, "and what's over there?" He walked into the inner sanctum that former general secretaries and the Soviet president had used for relaxation. Once there, Yeltsin began to pull drawers out of a desk. One of them happened to be locked. He demanded the keys. It took a while before the right custodian was located. Finally, extra keys were found and the drawer unlocked. It was empty. "Well, all right," said the disappointed Yeltsin. He then returned to the office, where he and his entourage sat around a conference table and opened a bottle of whiskey to celebrate the takeover of the last remaining fortress on their enemy's territory. It was 8:30 a.m. in the morning. Several minutes later the victors left the conquered and now appropriately marked territory in a good mood, laughing. The departing Yeltsin told the still shocked secretary, "Look at me! I'll come back later today!" Indeed he did, returning to sign a number of decrees in the presence of the media.[23]

"This was the triumph of plunderers—I can find no other word for it," wrote the appalled Gorbachev in his memoirs. He learned of the invasion from a secretary who called to tell him what was going on in the Kremlin. According to his earlier agreement with Yeltsin, the president of the USSR could use his office until Sunday evening. But as far as Yeltsin was concerned, the deal was off. The Russian president simply could not wait to move into the office historically associated with supreme power in the country. On Monday, December 30, he had to be in Minsk at the first working summit of the leaders of the Commonwealth of Independent States. He wanted Gorbachev out before then. "Long farewells make for too many tears," he wrote later.[24]

By the time Gorbachev entered the Senate Building that day, the whiskey party was over. He was mortified. He had scheduled an interview with Japanese journalists for that morning, and now he had to look for a different office. His old one still featured a red flag in the corner, but it was no longer his. The humiliated ex-president gave the interview in the office of his former chief of staff. Anatolii Cherniaev, who described in his diary the takeover of Gorbachev's last refuge, was appalled by Yeltsin's behavior, but he was also less than kind to Gorbachev. "Why humiliate oneself that way; why does he 'go' to the Kremlin? . . . The flag has already been changed above the cupola of the Sverdlovsk Hall [[the Catherine Hall in the Senate Building]], and he is no longer president! A nightmare! And that one [[Yeltsin]] is more and more of a boor. He tramples ever more rudely."[25]

Yeltsin indeed seemed unable to control his desire for revenge—this despite his solemn promises to Bush and Baker that he would treat his rival with dignity. He began his attack even before Gorbachev completed his resignation speech. In the afternoon of December 25, as Gorbachev was putting the finishing touches to the text of his address, he received a disturbing call from home. The panic-stricken Raisa Gorbacheva was calling her husband to inform him that Kremlin officials had shown up at their Moscow apartment, demanding that it be vacated in two hours. This was a breach of every agreement Gorbachev had made with Yeltsin a few days earlier. Gorbachev had agreed to move to a smaller apartment, but not before he formally left office. The transition period they had come to terms on was to last into the New Year, and a bit of civility, not to say leniency, could well be expected even after that. But now his family was being evicted even before he signed his resignation papers! Gorbachev was furious. According to Anatolii Cherniaev, who was present when Raisa Gorbacheva called her husband, the president "flew into a rage; his face went red; he made one phone call, then another, and let loose a stream of curses." Yeltsin's officials backed down, and the move was postponed until the following day. Gorbachev was free to speak with Bush and then deliver his address.[26]

The next morning Gorbachev, who had returned home late after the ad hoc farewell party with his aides, had to deal with the reality of the unexpected move. He later described the scene at home: "Heaps of clothes, books, dishes, folders, newspapers, letters, and God knows what lying strewn on the floor." When Gorbachev came to work at the Kremlin that day, he looked depressed. It took a while before his security detail managed to get a limousine to bring him to the Kremlin—the car that Yeltsin had allowed him to keep as part of the deal made the previous Monday. It was also next to impossible to get a truck to move their belongings from the apartment. Gorbachev's daughter, Irina, recalled that he wanted to call Yeltsin and protest the actions of his underlings. "After all, we agreed with him on everything like decent people!" he told his family. But Raisa Gorbacheva was against it. "There is no need to phone anyone or ask anyone for anything. Better to die with Irina, but we will pack up and move. People will help us."[27]

Raisa and Irina Gorbachev packed the family belongings with the assistance of the bodyguards who had protected them at Foros. After their Crimean imprisonment, they were prepared for the worst: Raisa had burned her personal correspondence with Mikhail, and Irina, her diaries. "After all, we had been living the whole most recent period as if in someone else's house," recalled Irina, thinking of the months leading up to Gorbachev's resignation. "Everything hung by a slender thread. We did not know which of the powers that be—the KGB or the democrats—would break into it." Raisa now took special care in packing the books she had kept on the shelves in alphabetical order by author. Among them were gift books from Margaret Thatcher and a volume of the Ukrainian poet Taras Shevchenko, adored by her father. In her book *I Hope,* released in the United States only a few months earlier, Raisa quoted lines from Shevchenko that now seemed particularly appropriate to the occasion and were cited in that context by Conor O'Clery in his book about the last day of Gorbachev's presidency: "My thoughts, my thoughts, what pain you bring! Why do you rise at me in such gloomy rows?"[28]

Gorbachev had every reason to be appalled by the harassment to which he and his family were subjected by Yeltsin's subordinates. But this was not so different from the treatment that the old regime had reserved for its former officials. Those who vacated positions at the top of the Soviet power pyramid never did so of their own volition— they either died in office or were removed in disgrace. That tradition continued into the Gorbachev period. Aleksandr Yakovlev recalled in amazement the breathtaking speed with which his privileges as a member of the Politburo were taken away once he was removed from office with Gorbachev's approval: "As soon as I was elected to the Politburo, I was driven home in another car with my bodyguards, but no sooner had Gorbachev accepted my resignation than the car was taken away, and I was told to leave the dacha by 11:00 the next morning."[29]

The brutal haste with which Yeltsin took over Gorbachev's office and had his family evicted from their living quarters became known in Moscow, casting Yeltsin and his team in a negative light. In his memoirs, Yeltsin took issue with "rumors circulated by the press that we literally threw the former general secretary's possessions out of his Kremlin office." He claimed that the Gorbachevs were given sufficient time to move to their new quarters and blamed possible excesses on friction between clerks, "inevitable" under the circumstances. One of those "clerks," Yeltsin's chief bodyguard, Aleksandr Korzhakov, recalled telling Gorbachev's bodyguards on an almost daily basis to remind their boss of the need to vacate his country house. The reason, according to Korzhakov, was quite simple. Barvikha-4, as Gorbachev's country dwelling was known to security personnel, was the only government residence outside Moscow that had all the communications equipment required to house the leader of the country and the commander in chief of its armed forces. "There were no [[other]] buildings of that kind near Moscow," recalled Korzhakov.[30]

Sooner or later the president of the USSR indeed had to be "evacuated" from the government facilities he occupied, but Yeltsin went out of his way to make the process as painful as possible for Gorbachev and his family. Did he want the Gorbachevs to experience at least part of the pain that he and his wife, Naina, had felt when they were harassed by Gorbachev and his men? In November 1987, when Yeltsin was recovering in a Moscow clinic after his defeat at a Politburo meeting and a botched suicide attempt, Gorbachev sent KGB bodyguards to drag him out of his hospital bed to a meeting of the Moscow city party committee, which would remove him from his post as first committee secretary. Yeltsin told Gorbachev that he could not walk without assistance, but the general secretary dismissed his protests, as he did those of his minister of health, who pointed out the seriousness of Yeltsin's condition. When guards came to the hospital to escort Yeltsin, who had just been injected with powerful analgesic and antispasmodic medicine, the desperate Naina Yeltsina told them that they were behaving like Nazis. She wanted them to tell Gorbachev that he was a criminal.[31]

The drama of Mikhail Gorbachev's last days in office exposed with brutal clarity the depth of distrust and sheer hatred that had existed between him and his nemesis, Boris Yeltsin. But the significance of their personal conflict should be kept in proper perspective. In the end, it was not up to Gorbachev and Yeltsin alone to decide whether the Soviet Union would live or die. The real conflict was between the emerging institutions of independent Russia and the other Soviet republics. With Ukraine leaving the Union no matter what, Yeltsin and his aides faced the choice of either continuing to carry the imperial burden on their own or quitting the empire. They decided to do the latter. The personal rivalry between Gorbachev and Yeltsin sped up the process.

EPILOGUE

"MR. SPEAKER! THE PRESIDENT of the United States!" announced the House sergeant at arms at the top of his voice, and the chamber of the House of Representatives exploded in applause. A slim six-foot-two man in a gray suit, sporting a blue-gray striped tie, somewhat narrow by today's standards, appeared in the doorway. Escorted by select members of the House and Senate, he began to make his way to the House clerk's desk. Smiling, he shook hands, exchanged greetings, and from time to time pointed his finger at congressmen, senators, and members of government who were eager to catch a glimpse of him and speak a word or two. They applauded him long after he reached the clerk's desk. The man at the center of attention was clearly pleased. He had promised his audience that this day he would speak about "big things," "big changes," and "big problems." He kept his promise.

It was a few minutes past 9:00 p.m. on Tuesday, January 28, 1992. President George H. W. Bush was about to deliver his third and, as anticipated by the press, most important State of the Union address, with millions of Americans in the television audience. He was expected not only to reflect on one of the most extraordinary years in his presidency and the whole post–World War II history of his country but also to sketch out policies for the future of that country and the world. When the applause finally subsided, Bush told the audience, "You know, with the big buildup this address has had,

I wanted to make sure it would be a big hit, but I couldn't convince Barbara to deliver it for me." The chamber again exploded in applause, with members of the joint session of Congress rising to their feet.

The normally dry and reserved Bush had clearly hit a home run with this self-deprecating joke. Barbara, with her silver-gray hair and broad, grandmotherly face, was seated in the first row of the balcony next to the nation's most celebrated evangelist, Billy Graham. It was true that she possessed an appeal her husband lacked. But this time he rose to the occasion—his address, prepared with the help of media consultants, some of whom had coached him during the previous presidential campaign, included powerful lines that would bring members of his audience to their feet again and again.[1]

A part of the address that made both Republicans and Democrats eager to show their solidarity with the president was his report on American foreign policy and the positive transformation of world politics that had come about since his previous State of the Union address in January 1991. Bush's successes in the international arena were recognized by friend and foe alike. "We gather tonight at a dramatic and deeply promising time in our history, and in the history of man on earth," declared Bush. "For in the past 12 months, the world has known changes of almost biblical proportions."

He referred to the dramatic events of 1991—a year that began with the Americans and their allies launching Operation Desert Storm against Saddam Hussein's Iraq and ended with the collapse of the Soviet Union. "Communism died this year," Bush told the jubilant gathering. He then continued, "But the biggest thing that has happened in the world in my life, in our lives, is this: By the grace of God, America won the Cold War." These words were greeted with cheers and a standing ovation. The president capitalized on the point a few moments later, when he declared that "the Cold War didn't 'end'—it was won."

George Bush went on to pay tribute to the sacrifices made by American soldiers and taxpayers to achieve the victory. He concluded with an emotional reference to a future generation of Americans: "And so, now, for the first time in 35 years, our strategic bombers stand down. No longer are they on round-the-clock alert. Tomorrow our children will go to school and study history and how plants grow. And they won't have, as my children did, air-raid drills in which they crawl under their desks and cover their heads in case of nuclear war. My grandchildren don't have to do that, and won't have the bad dreams children once had in decades past. There are still threats. But the long drawn-out dread is over." The chamber again rocked with applause.

Bush did not stop with a declaration of victory in the long struggle of the Cold War. He also presented his vision of the new role that the United States was destined to play in the new era. "A world once divided into two armed camps now recognizes one sole and preeminent power, the United States of America," declared the triumphant Bush. He also outlined the ways in which he was going to use this newly acquired power. "As long as I am President, I will continue to lead in support of freedom everywhere, not out of arrogance, not out of altruism, but for the safety and security of our children. This is a fact: Strength in the pursuit of peace is no vice; isolationism in the pursuit of security is no virtue." The chamber once again welcomed his words with applause. The message was loud and clear: the United States had vanquished the Soviet Union, emerged victorious in the Cold War, and was now destined to rule the world.[2]

This rhetoric was quite different from the carefully calibrated and much more humble statements issued by Bush and his advisers before Gorbachev's resignation on December 25, 1991. The new tone was a direct outcome of the presidential election campaign that was heating up in the United States. Linking the very recent fall of the USSR, America's former enemy, with the end of the Cold War, which by the administration's own account had occurred at least a year or two earlier, became a new electoral strategy. Trying not to make things more difficult for Gorbachev at home, in 1990 President Bush had refrained from what some of his advisers called a "dance on the [[Berlin]] Wall" after the reunification of Germany. At that time there was still the possibility of resistance by hard-liners in the USSR, where the Baltic republics were struggling for their sovereignty, and in Eastern Europe, which was still de facto occupied by the Soviet army. But now those constraints were gone, and the sense of victory was greater than ever. The joint Bush-Gorbachev declarations made in December 1989 on Malta about the end of the Cold War, as well as White House statements to the effect that the July 1991 meeting of the two presidents in Moscow was the first post–Cold War summit, were forgotten. The loud protests of Gorbachev, who felt robbed of his role in bringing the conflict to an end, were ignored, at least in public. Allegedly, Bush told Gorbachev in private "not to pay any attention to what he would say during the presidential campaign." In October 1992 Gorbachev told the *New Yorker*, "I suppose these are necessary things in a campaign, but if this idea is serious, then it is a very big delusion."[3]

The "victory in the Cold War" electoral strategy did not work very well. The country was stuck in economic recession, and polls indicated that the president, who had been enormously popular less than a year earlier—immediately after the end of the Gulf War, he enjoyed the support of 89 percent of the public—was rapidly losing support as the presidential election of 1992 drew closer: according to a *Washington Post* article commenting on Bush's State of the Union address, more than half of those polled disapproved of his performance. Like another wartime leader, Winston Churchill, Bush failed to capitalize on his foreign-policy success. In both cases, the voters wanted change at home.

Like Churchill before him, Bush tried to shape public memory of the war he had helped to end. The memoir that he wrote was coauthored with his national security adviser, Brent Scowcroft. Doubtless they tried to be as objective, as possible about the subject. But the chronological frame of their narrative, defined by the dates of Bush's presidential term, dictated its own logic. Within that frame, it made perfect sense to conclude their story of the end of the Cold War not with the demolition of the Berlin Wall in 1989 but with the collapse of the Soviet Union in late 1991. It was at that point, with Gorbachev's final phone call to the president on Christmas Day 1991, that they concluded their book of memoirs, *A World Transformed*.[4]

By publishing memoirs and giving interviews throughout the 1990s, members of the Bush administration helped create a narrative of the end of the Cold War that was directly linked to the collapse of the Soviet Union, conflating the two events without taking explicit credit for the latter (given the role that the White House played in the attempts to save the Soviet Union). Some members of the administration felt that they had been all but robbed of a well-deserved sense of victory. "George Bush," wrote Robert Gates in his memoirs, which also happened to end with the events of late 1991, "who refused 'to dance on the Wall,' was not about to declare victory in the Cold War. There was no national celebration such as would follow the Persian Gulf War. . . . We had won the Cold War, but there would be no parade." According to Gates, one of the reasons for the lack of an all-out victory celebration was the simple fact that "in December 1991 there was no agreement in Washington that the United States had, in fact, helped the USSR into an early grave."[5]

Ambassador Jack F. Matlock, who represented the Bush administration in Moscow between 1987 and 1991 and left Moscow on the eve of the August coup, has argued repeatedly that the end of the Cold War, the collapse of communism, and the fall of the Soviet Union were related but different things. "The U.S. attitude differed greatly in regard to those three events, and our contribution to them differed greatly," remarked Matlock on one occasion. According to the former ambassador, the United States wrote the score for the end of the Cold War and helped to bring down communism by promoting human rights, but the end of the conflict was also in the interest of the Soviets, and the downfall of communism was largely their achievement, not the Americans'. When it came to the fall of the Soviet Union, the US administration supported independence for the Baltic republics but wanted the rest of the Soviet Union to go on existing indefinitely. "The point is that we did not bring down the Soviet Union," argued Matlock, "though some people would like to take credit for it now, and some of the chauvinists in Russia would like to accuse us of it. It just isn't true."[6]

IF THE FALL OF THE SOVIET UNION was not—or not primarily—the work of the American administration and was not synonymous either with the end of Soviet communism or with American victory in the Cold War, then what led to the sudden collapse of one of the most powerful countries the world had ever seen? "Reviewing the history of international relations in the modern era, which might be considered to extend from the middle of the seventeenth century to the present," wrote one of the most astute practitioners and scholars of the Cold War, George F. Kennan, in 1995, "I find it hard to think of any event more strange and startling, and at first glance more inexplicable, than the sudden and total disintegration and disappearance from the international scene, primarily in the years 1987 through 1991, of the great power known successively as the Russian Empire and the Soviet Union."[7]

What seemed inexplicable to Kennan at the time was hardly a puzzle to some of Gorbachev's former advisers. "What actually happened in the USSR that year was what happened in 'their day' to other empires when history exhausted their potential," wrote Anatolii Cherniaev in retrospect, summing up the outcome of 1991. By that reasoning, the Soviet collapse simply concluded a process that had begun in earnest at the dawn of the century and was accelerated by the two world wars: the disintegration of world empires and their disappearance from the political map. The heirs of the tsars were the last to lose their imperial possessions, following the former masters of the Habsburg, Ottoman, British, French, Portuguese, and a few minor land-based and maritime empires. What seems so special about the Soviet Union is that very few people considered it an empire during its lifetime or were prepared to treat it as anything but a nation-state. Even Cherniaev's comments came after the Soviet collapse.[8]

Whether the Soviet Union was an empire or not—the debate on this still continues—it died the death of an empire, splitting along lines roughly defined by ethnic and linguistic boundaries. While there are important differences in the ways other world empires disintegrated, there are also striking similarities, especially when it comes to the Soviet and British experiences. In 1945 Stalin demanded and received two additional seats in the United Nations General Assembly for Ukraine and Belarus, republics that were treated by participants in the Yalta Conference on a par with the British dominions. They did not compare with British dominions such as Canada and Australia with regard to autonomy and self-rule, and their ethnic composition, distinct from that of Russia, also differentiated them from typical American states (at Yalta, President Franklin Roosevelt tried to negotiate the accession of two American states to the United Nations—an idea rejected by the American public).

Like the British dominions, the Soviet republics left their metropolis in 1991 under the leadership of their own "native" leaders and institutions. As was true of other twentieth-century dominions and colonial possessions, some of the Soviet republics left the Union core not against the wishes of the dominant nation but in accordance with them: the leaders of the Russian Federation wanted the Central Asians to go once Ukraine left the Union. Also, as in the case of other European empires, it was the question of extending citizenship rights, particularly voting rights, to residents of the Soviet republics that made the continuation of the empire in its existing form all but impossible.[9]

Despite Gorbachev's best efforts to prove otherwise, electoral democracy turned out to be incompatible with the continuing existence of the Soviet state. It is often overlooked that the dissolution of the Soviet Union was an outcome of electoral politics. The Soviet colossus fell less than three years after the introduction of semi-free elections in the former realm of the Romanovs for the first time since 1917, the year of the Bolshevik coup in St. Petersburg. The fall of the Soviet Union took place as a direct outcome of the Ukrainian referendum of December 1, 1991, in which more than 90 percent of those taking part voted for independence. That vote overruled the results of the previous referendum, held in March 1991, in which more than 70 percent voted for continuing participation in the Union on condition of far-reaching reform. The Union lived or died depending on the vote of its citizens. Even the secret decision of the three Slavic presidents in December 1991 to dissolve the Soviet Union was approved by large majorities in the democratically elected parliaments of Russia, Ukraine, and Belarus. By contrast, the attempt to save the Soviet Union in its old form was made not through democratic channels but in the form of a coup that failed on the steps of the Russian parliament building three days after its launch.

The arrival of electoral democracy dramatically changed the Soviet political landscape and influenced the decisions of the leaders, who now depended on popular support and elite consensus to stay in power. While limiting the choices available to the new leaders, democracy also empowered those of them who had the support of their electorates. Although it was the people who voted, it was their political leaders, both in the center and in the Soviet republics, who formulated questions for the referenda and interpreted their results. As Gorbachev argued more than once, the dissolution of the USSR was never put to a referendum vote. Did the vote for Ukrainian independence mean the dissolution of the Soviet Union? That was a question for the leaders to decide. Democracy shunted aside leaders who failed to obtain a mandate to rule though the electoral process. The outcome of the competition between the popularly elected president of Russia, Boris Yeltsin, and the president of the USSR, Mikhail Gorbachev, appointed to his position by parliament—a struggle that reached its crescendo in the last months of 1991—shows the decisive power of electoral politics over the main actors of the drama reconstructed in this book.

Mikhail Gorbachev unleashed a reform that showed the predilection of modern revolutions for eating their own children. If the French Revolution was an inspiration to the Bolsheviks, Western liberalism supplied the ideas and language for Gorbachev's perestroika. Like many before him in Russia, Gorbachev looked to the West for solutions to his country's problems, which manifested themselves in an inability to compete with the West in economic, social, and, eventually, military terms. Ever since the rule of Peter the Great in the early eighteenth century, Russian elites had sought to adopt Western models in order to catch up with the West. Again and again these models would come into conflict with Russia's society and non-Westernized populace. Some segments of the Russian elite tried repeatedly to change both through military coups, such as the one staged by guards officers in December 1825; liberal reforms, such as those introduced by Tsar Alexander II in the second half of the nineteenth century; or bloody revolutions, such as the one launched by Vladimir Lenin in 1917. Gorbachev's reforms were the latest attempt to catch up with the West by emulating it.

Like his immediate predecessors, Gorbachev did not think that he lived in or ruled over an empire. But his attempts to centralize his rule, eliminate widespread corruption in the Central Asian republics, and bring in a new breed of Russian managers including Boris Yeltsin and his onetime rival, Gennadii Kolbin, only alienated republican elites, setting off the first anti-Moscow riots in decades. Gorbachev pushed the republican bosses and their retinues even further away by unleashing glasnost, opening the party to media criticism, and forcing the communist elites to earn their right to stay in power by facing elections. As the elites in the Russian regions and the non-Russian republics found themselves dealing with nationalist revolts and democratic challenges to their power, they came to depend more on the ballot box than on the supreme boss in the Kremlin. It was only a matter of time before they challenged Moscow's rule, demanding autonomy and then independence. With the elites turning their backs on him and nationalists and liberal intellectuals demanding more freedoms, Gorbachev soon had no one to rely on but the army. In the last years of the USSR it would be employed more than once, allegedly without the knowledge of the commander in chief, in one Union republic after another. In March 1991 it would be brought onto the streets of Moscow to intimidate Boris Yeltsin and his supporters.

The fact that until the August coup Gorbachev was not only president of the USSR but also general secretary of the Communist Party made it difficult to distinguish the collapse of communism from the fall of the USSR. It has been argued that after the banning of the party, which allegedly served as a glue binding the republics, there was nothing else to hold the Union together. In fact, by the time of the August coup the party was no longer holding anything together, as its leaders in the republics turned into leaders of republican parliaments and, in many cases, presidents not beholden to Moscow. Party bosses who had already become presidents or would soon do so, such as Islam Karimov of Uzbekistan, were now pushing if not for the independence of their republics then for a confederative restructuring of the Union.

Yeltsin's ban on the Communist Party did not cut the ties linking Moscow to the republics, which barely mattered any more outside the Soviet army and the KGB, but provoked a revolt of former party elites against what they regarded as a new coup in Moscow aimed at them. Consultations between Gorbachev and Yeltsin, on one hand, and republican leaders, on the other, continued after the ban on the party, following an established trajectory that no longer had anything to do with the party or the decisions of its governing bodies. Gorbachev managed to maneuver the party out of supreme power long before it was banned in Russia—it was an easy target and scapegoat for the coup, which was led largely by the KGB and the army brass.

In his public pronouncements and, later, in his memoirs, Gorbachev all but monopolized the role of defender of the Soviet Union. He claimed that signing his union treaty was the only way to save the Union, while his opponents were out not only to get him but also to destroy the Union. That was true in many cases but not all. The real struggle in Moscow was being waged not between proponents and opponents of the existing Union but between two visions of a future union. After the coup, Gorbachev rejected the idea advanced by Boris Yeltsin's advisers to turn the Union into a confederation. Formally he was obliged to accept the confederation principle put forward by Yeltsin as a basis for any future negotiations on the fate of the Union, but in practice he resisted it until after the Belavezha Agreement, when it was too late even for a confederation.

The dividing line between proponents of the two visions of the Union passed not only between Gorbachev and Yeltsin but also through Gorbachev's own camp. Gorbachev's aides Georgii Shakhnazarov and Anatolii Cherniaev were skeptical about their boss's efforts to make the republican leaders sign the new union treaty. The Soviet Union's last minister of defense, Marshal Yevgenii Shaposhnikov, considered it a major error on Gorbachev's part that he did not take the idea of confederation seriously. "If Gorbachev had gone halfway to meet the tendencies that comprised the idea of confederation, with common consent that the center should have a monopoly on communications, transport, defense, a joint foreign policy, and other components of social life and activity common to all the republics, who knows in what state structure we would be living now," wrote Shaposhnikov later in the decade. Like the other top military commanders, he refused to back Gorbachev when the latter asked for the military's help to save his model of the Union before and then after the Belavezha Agreement.[10]

BORIS YELTSIN EMERGES from our reconstruction of the last months of the history of the Soviet Union as a much more complex figure than might be suggested by the popular image of him as the grave digger of communism, killer of the Union, and founder of modern Russia. Yeltsin and his advisers felt much more affinity with the Union than is usually allowed for in commentary about them. Not even the most radical of Yeltsin's advisers had the dissolution of the USSR on their original agenda. "Initially, the task was not to destroy the Soviet Union," recalled the most influential of them, Gennadii Burbulis. "The task was to seek out the capabilities and resources to govern the Russian Federation according to all the rules of an effective administration." Back in the spring of 1990, according to Burbulis, it was the impossibility of bringing about change by means of the conservative Union parliament that had forced the leaders of the democratic opposition to concentrate on Russian politics. Yeltsin's election as Speaker of the Russian parliament turned that institution into a vehicle for realizing the political goals of the democratic deputies.

Until the coup, Yeltsin's goal was to wrest as many powers and resources from the center as possible, including legal ownership of the Russian Federation's vast natural resources. Yeltsin achieved that goal in late July 1991. The coup threatened his newly acquired powers and control over the resources of Russia, of which he was now the president. But the defeat of the coup gave Yeltsin and his advisers a chance to return victorious to the all-Union political space that they had earlier abandoned and to implement their reforms throughout the Union. Yeltsin, who had prevented the coup plotters from saving the USSR, now adopted that mission himself. With the central bureaucracy defeated and its leader, Gorbachev, weakened, the Yeltsin supporters launched a hostile takeover of Union structures. The ones they could not or did not want to take over, such as the Communist Party, were destroyed. This hostile takeover of the center by a leader much more powerful and dynamic than Gorbachev caused the other republics to rebel, declaring their independence. Yeltsin had to back down. The attempt to take over the Union gave way to negotiations on a confederative structure that would give Russia enough power to implement economic and social reform on its own, free of any restraints on the part of the conservative elites of the non-Russian republics.

Yeltsin's advisers and supporters envisioned Russia as an ark for the salvation of the nascent Soviet democracy and its program of economic reform. In that sense they resembled the Bolsheviks of the Lenin era, who saw Russia as an ark for the salvation of the world proletarian revolution and its program of universal social and economic transformation. One of the many differences between those two visions was that in 1917 Lenin argued that, in the interest of the world revolution, the Marxists of the multiethnic Russian Empire should stick together, while now the Russian democrats believed that they had better prospects of succeeding on their own. This made a good deal of sense from the economic viewpoint. If during the Russian Revolution Lenin claimed that the revolution would not survive without Ukrainian coal, in 1991 the Union's greatest riches, especially its vast mineral resources, were on the territory of the Russian Federation, not in the republics. The death of the Soviet Union differed from that of other empires in that the resource-rich metropolis cut off its former colonial possessions from easy access to those resources. Russia stood to benefit from the loss of its imperial possessions more than any other empire of the past. Yeltsin and his people not only knew that but counted on it.[11]

It would be hard to exaggerate the importance of the personal rivalry between Gorbachev and Yeltsin for the fall of the USSR. The two were never shy about voicing their mutual grievances at the time or afterward. In his memoirs, the Russian president discussed the psychological reasons for his unwillingness to step into Gorbachev's political shoes and take over his position at the helm of the Soviet Union. Gorbachev, in his memoirs, accused Yeltsin of dissolving the Union for the sole purpose of getting rid of him as president of the USSR. The prospect of being a figurehead in a confederative Union dominated by Russia and Yeltsin was clearly unacceptable to him. Some authors in contemporary Russia tend to see the Gorbachev-Yeltsin rivalry as the main reason for the collapse of the Soviet Union. Others, like the former strongman of the August coup, General Valentin Varennikov, believed that not only Yeltsin but the republican leaders in general simply could not abide Gorbachev, who had fooled them time after time. There is no doubt that Yeltsin's sense of being wronged by the Communist Party leadership, and by Gorbachev in particular, played an important role in his embrace of the Russian democratic agenda. But overall it was that agenda, defined in political, economic, and social terms, that drove his policies and defined his political choices.[12]

For all his dislike of Gorbachev, Yeltsin consulted with him before his trip to Belavezha and began negotiations with Leonid Kravchuk of Ukraine by offering him the Gorbachev-approved plan for a reformed Soviet Union. It was the position of the Ukrainian leader backed by the December 1 referendum on the independence of Ukraine that turned out to be crucial in deciding the fate of the Soviet Union. Neither Gorbachev nor Yeltsin imagined a viable Union without Ukraine. It was the second Soviet republic after Russia in population and economic contribution to the Union coffers. The Russian leadership, which was already skeptical about bearing the costs of empire, could be persuaded to do so only together with Ukraine. Besides, as Yeltsin told George Bush on more than one occasion, without the Slavic Ukraine, Russia would be outnumbered and outvoted by the Central Asian republics, most of which, with the notable exception of Kazakhstan, relied on massive subsidies from the Union center.

WHEN IT COMES TO ASSIGNING either blame or credit for the disintegration of the USSR, fingers are usually pointed at Russia and its revolt against the center. While this factor is clearly important, it turns our attention almost exclusively to the Gorbachev-Yeltsin confrontation, which diminished in significance as a factor in deciding the fate of the USSR as the events of the August coup receded into the past. By December 1991, Russia had effectively taken over the Union institutions or made them impossible to operate without Russian consent and support. The outcome of the battle between Russia and the Union center was decided before the Ukrainian referendum of December 1, 1991, and the Belavezha Agreement of December 8 of that year. It was Russia's relations with Ukraine, the second-largest Soviet republic, and not those with the anemic Union center, that would prove crucial to the future of the Soviet empire in the last weeks of its existence.

Leonid Kravchuk, born in interwar Poland, presided over the drive for independence by a republic whose nationalist mobilization was quite similar to that of the Baltic republics. In western Ukraine, which, like the Baltics, had spent the interwar years outside the USSR, the democratic elections of 1990 led to the complete expulsion of the old local elites from the business of government. Western Ukraine, annexed by the Soviet Union after the Molotov-Ribbentrop Pact of 1939, was never fully digested by the mighty Soviet Union. It is easy to imagine that the USSR might still exist in one form or another even today if Joseph Stalin had not concluded the "nonaggression pact" with Hitler in August 1939 and then claimed half of Eastern Europe. It would probably still be around, though without its Baltic provinces, if at Yalta Stalin had accommodated Franklin Roosevelt's desire to leave the city of Lwów (Lviv) in Poland. Stalin insisted on transferring it to Ukraine. In the late 1980s, Lviv became the center of nationalist mobilization for Ukrainian independence. It was as difficult to imagine Ukrainian independence without Lviv as to imagine the Soviet Union without Ukraine in the fall and winter of 1991.

If in western Ukraine the situation reminded one of the Baltics, in the east it was akin to what was happening in Moscow, Leningrad (St. Petersburg), and the mining regions of Russia. In the central and eastern parts of Ukraine, which constituted part of the Soviet Union from its inception, the old communist elites struggled to survive against a rising tide of unrest led by striking miners of the Donbas and the liberal intelligentsia, which took over the city councils in the big industrial centers. Thus, in both east and west, the old Ukrainian elite felt abandoned by the Union center and had to make deals with opposition forces to stay in power.

Back in 1922 the USSR was created with an eye to accommodating Ukraine. The Union emerged as a state with a powerful center whose goal in the first decade of its history was to keep the Ukrainians in and the Russians, the formerly dominant ethnic group, down. Decimated in the wake of the Great Ukrainian Famine of 1932–1933, the Ukrainian communist elites bounced back after World War II, becoming Russia's de facto (but not de jure) junior partner in running the Soviet empire. Influential if not dominant in Moscow during the rule of Nikita Khrushchev and Leonid Brezhnev, Ukrainian elites were removed from the center of power under Gorbachev.

Despite their grudges against the new leader and his policies, the Ukrainian party apparatchiks remained loyal to the idea of the Union until the August coup, and some of them did so even afterward. Yeltsin's attempt to take over the center in the wake of the failed putsch threatened the Ukrainian elites with a situation in which the imploded center would leave them one-on-one with a powerful Russia no longer subject to any restraint. While Gorbachev was still trying to co-opt Ukrainians into all-Union structures, offering the second position in the party to a Ukrainian apparatchik before the coup and the office of prime minister in the future Union to a Ukrainian government official afterward, Yeltsin had no plans of that nature. And the Ukrainians were no longer interested in them anyway. It was the Ukrainian elites' insistence on the independence of their country and the unwillingness and inability of the Russian elites to offer the Ukrainian leadership an attractive integrationist alternative short of a Russia-dominated confederation that led to the fall of the Soviet Union.

There was little hope for Russo-Ukrainian accommodation after the coup. The Aleksandr Rutskoi mission sent to Kyiv by Yeltsin in late August 1991 failed to achieve its objectives and stop Ukraine's drive toward independence. By October, Kravchuk stopped coming to Moscow, and his fateful meeting with Yeltsin in Belavezha in December had to be organized by Belarusian intermediaries.

The Soviet Union never turned into an analogue of the Austro-Hungarian Empire, which extended its life in the nineteenth century by obliging the Austro-German elites to share the spoils and responsibilities of running the empire with their Hungarian counterparts. Aleksandr Solzhenitsyn's vision of a Slavic Union that some believed could materialize after Belavezha was in fact a blueprint for the creation of a greater Russia, not a recognition of the differences between Russia and Ukraine or a proposal of partnership. As the Ukrainian population voted for independence with astounding unanimity, Kravchuk presented not only Gorbachev but also Yeltsin with a fait accompli—Ukraine was leaving the Soviet Union. At Belavezha the Russian and Ukrainian presidents negotiated the exit conditions and a new modus vivendi.

Gorbachev's inability to regain power after the coup, Yeltsin's clumsiness in his original attempt to take over the Union center, his subsequent decision to go ahead with Russian economic reform without the other republics, and, finally, Kravchuk's dogged insistence on independence left most of the republics that had not yet declared their desire to leave the Union in a difficult position. The Belarusian leaders hosting the Belavezha summit told Yeltsin and Kravchuk that they would support whatever decision the two reached. Privately they knew that under any circumstances they would have to stick with Russia, if only because of their republic's dependence on Russian energy supplies. Nursultan Nazarbayev, the president of Kazakhstan and host of the Almaty meeting on December 21, shared that position. It was not Russian resources that were on his mind but the Russian and Slavic population of his republic, which outnumbered its titular nationality, the Kazakhs. The leaders of the other Central Asian republics also could not imagine the Union proposed by Gorbachev if it did not include Russia. There was a chain reaction: Ukraine did not want to be in the Union, Russia could not imagine the Union without Ukraine, and the rest of the republics that still wanted to be in the Union could not imagine it without Russia. The Central Asian leaders were all but expelled from the empire by their imperial masters and now had no choice but to join the Commonwealth.

Unlike the Soviet Union, the Commonwealth structure allowed much more flexibility in defining the level of political, economic, and social integration between the republics. It was varied levels of integration of the non-Russian territories into the imperial center that distinguished the former Romanov empire from the Soviet Union. Whereas in the Russian Empire Finland or the Kingdom of Poland could have special rights and privileges not accorded to the Russian or Ukrainian provinces, in the Soviet Union all republics, from tiny Estonia to huge Russia, were equal in constitutional terms. Giving certain rights to Estonia was impossible without giving the same rights to Russia. It was this characteristic of Soviet federalism that made the disintegration of the Soviet Union all but inevitable once the movement for independence gathered speed in the Baltics, western Ukraine, Caucasus, and Moldova.

THE INABILITY of the Soviet leaders to discriminate between the Union republics in constitutional terms was one of the realities of Soviet political life that George H. W. Bush and his advisers in Washington never fully grasped. They kept pushing for the independence of the Baltic republics, convinced that the Soviet Union could not only survive but do very well without them. Their argument was about fairness and legality: the United States had never recognized the annexation of the Baltic states after 1939, and they should now be set free. The rest of the republics should stay as they were. That was a difficult proposition to sell to other republics. George Bush tried in vain to do so in his "Chicken Kiev" speech in the Ukrainian parliament, whereas he succeeded in making it difficult, if not impossible, for Gorbachev to employ the coercive power of the state still at his disposal to establish martial law in the Baltics for a lengthy period. And surgical applications of force were no longer effective. With the price for prolonged use of force made prohibitive by Western pressure, Gorbachev had no choice but to play according to the constitutional rules.

In the final analysis, George Bush's policies contributed to the fall of the Soviet Union, but they often did so irrespective of the desires of his administration, or even contrary to them. The push for Baltic independence is only one example of the unforeseen consequences of American actions. There is little doubt that by helping to save Gorbachev after the coup and pushing Yeltsin to cooperate with him, the United States prevented Yeltsin from either completely taking over the Union center or forcing Gorbachev to negotiate a confederation agreement in September or October 1991, when Kravchuk and the Ukrainian leaders were still attending gatherings of republican leaders convened by Gorbachev. In November, a few weeks before the Ukrainian referendum, the Bush administration continued to apply pressure on Yeltsin, trying to keep him from doing away with the Union government, especially its foreign policy branch, the Ministry of Foreign Affairs. It was only in late November that the Bush administration allowed the leak of news about the coming recognition of Ukrainian independence, pushing the dying Soviet Union over the brink. This time the administration knew the consequences of its action.

Why did George H. W. Bush and his advisers do as they did? Bush's personal attachment to Gorbachev, whom he respected as a man and a politician, is of course part of the explanation, but much more important was the administration's desire to keep Gorbachev and the Soviet Union afloat as long as possible. The immediate goal, as formulated by James Baker in early 1991, was to extract maximum concessions from the dying Soviet behemoth in the realm of arms control and international relations. The strategy worked exceptionally well. The withdrawal of Soviet assistance from Moscow-backed governments in Cuba and Afghanistan, Moscow's agreement to make deep cuts in its nuclear arsenals, and Gorbachev's support for the US-proposed peace settlement of the Arab-Israeli conflict were among the accomplishments of Bush's Soviet policy in the fall of 1991.

But the most important American concern was the safety of the Soviet nuclear arsenals, which, it was believed in Washington, were much safer under the central control of the Soviet military, with whom the chairman of the Joint Chiefs of Staff, Colin Powell, and other American commanders had worked in the years of Gorbachev's rule. Here the administration's policies also met with success. One of the first points made by Yeltsin when he called Bush from Belavezha in December 1991 was to inform him of the agreement of the Slavic presidents on joint but centralized control over Soviet nuclear arms. Last but not least, there was a related concern about the peaceful dissolution of the USSR, especially when it came to the nuclear-armed republics of Russia, Ukraine, Kazakhstan, and Belarus. Despite Gorbachev's concerns and grim predictions, the Soviet Union never turned into Yugoslavia with nukes. Russia never became Serbia, and Yeltsin, unlike Slobodan Milošević, never tried to gather what many in Russia considered historical Russian lands, now in the possession of other republics, by force.

The main credit for the peaceful dissolution of the Union should go to the policies of Boris Yeltsin and the cautious stand on Russian minorities taken by Leonid Kravchuk and Nursultan Nazarbayev. But the American contribution to that process was by no means insignificant. By coordinating his position with the leaders of Western Europe, Bush managed to avoid a situation akin to the one that occurred in Yugoslavia, when Germany encouraged the drive for independence by Slovenia and Croatia, while the rest of the Western powers remained undecided on the issue. In the case of the Soviet Union, Bush was able to get all the Western leaders on board and served as spokesman for their common position. To be accepted in the West, the leaders of the republics had to do what Bush wanted them to do with regard to nuclear arms, borders, and minorities. American expectations were spelled out in the early fall of 1991 by James Baker and followed in spirit, if not to the letter, by the leaders of the Soviet republics.

While losing the battle to save the Soviet Union as a junior partner in the international arena, the Bush administration helped orchestrate its peaceful dissolution. This was no small accomplishment, especially if one thinks of the bloody ends of other empires. On a certain level, history had indeed come to an end—not in the sense of a final victory of liberalism, as declared by the leading American political scientist Francis Fukuyama in his best-selling book *The End of History and the Last Man* (1990), but in the disappearance of the old European empires. The United States, born of rebellion against an empire and an archenemy of colonialism throughout the world, unexpectedly found itself presiding over the dissolution of a country often labeled the last world empire. The Americans thus accomplished their anti-imperial purpose without really wishing to do so.[13]

THERE IS EVERY REASON to see 1991 as a major turning point in world history, and nowhere does this seem more obvious than in the former post-Soviet space, where many present-day trends in international relations, domestic politics, and economic relations continue to develop in the shadow of the year that some call an *annus mirabilis*, while others, including President Vladimir Putin of Russia, associate it with the "greatest geopolitical catastrophe of the century."[14]

It was in 1991 that the Russian leadership set a policy on the use of military force by which it abided until the Russo-Georgian war of 2008. While the Union republics were allowed to go without a fight, autonomous republics such as Chechnia were not. The Russian leaders learned a lesson from the Soviet collapse and established a new federal system in which some members of the Russian Federation, such as Chechnia or Tatarstan, could have more rights than others. That helped preserve a semblance of unity in the Russian state during the first difficult post-Soviet decade. Coercion and flexibility, the latter having been in short supply in the Soviet Union, became the hallmarks of the new Russian policy of dealing with rebellious autonomies. While crushing the drives of their own autonomies for independence, the Russian leaders took a page from Gorbachev's book of 1990 and 1991 when he played the leaders of the Russian autonomies against Boris Yeltsin and tried to support rebellious autonomies in other post-Soviet states, including Abkhazia and South Ossetia in Georgia and Transnistria in Moldova.

What is now considered Vladimir Putin's invention—an aggressive policy of integrating former Soviet republics into common institutions and opposing Ukraine's and Georgia's membership in NATO and structures affiliated with the European Union—also harks back to the events of 1991. Many of Yeltsin's advisers regarded the Commonwealth not as an instrument of divorce but rather as a means of Russian control over the post-Soviet space. They believed that Russia needed to free itself from the burden of supporting a traditional empire, but in twenty years, once it recovered from its economic and political problems, the republics would come back to Russia of their own free will. Some republics, such as Belarus, did come back and joined Russian-led political, economic, and military organizations. But others did not, and a semblance of a new Cold War between Russia and the West all but materialized in the wake of the 2003 Rose Revolution in Georgia, which resulted in the coming to power of the Western-educated president Mikheil Saakashvili, and the 2004 Orange Revolution in Ukraine, which saw the election of the pro-Western president Viktor Yushchenko over his Russian-backed and -funded competitor. Today, as in 1991, the former republics most politically distant from Russia are the Baltic states, while the country on which prospects for the reintegration of post-Soviet space under Moscow's auspices most depend is Ukraine.[15]

The origins of American policies that shaped international relations during the first decade of the twenty-first century also go back to 1991, when James Baker persuaded Gorbachev and Yeltsin to withdraw support from the Afghan government of Najibullah. Afghanistan soon became a no-man's-land, a country of warlords, saved from chaos and daily violence by the Taliban. The peace at home, enforced by religious zealots, brought destruction abroad, as Osama bin Laden turned the former graveyard of the Soviet army into his backyard. The response by the administration of the forty-third president of the United States, George W. Bush, to the challenge of 9/11 was also greatly informed by the experiences and lessons that the members of his administration drew from the events of 1991.

In the last months of 1991, as the fall of the USSR unfolded before CNN television cameras, the Bush administration's experts began making preparations for a new world in which the Soviet Union would be a much smaller factor in world politics or might even disappear altogether. The planning was entrusted to Secretary of Defense Dick Cheney and placed under the direct supervision of Undersecretary of Defense Paul Wolfowitz. The new doctrine produced by the Pentagon experts reflected the view presented in George H. W. Bush's State of the Union address of 1992: the Cold War did not just end but was won. The United States now had a special mission in the world defined by its new status as the sole global superpower. The geographical and political limits imposed on that vision by its former Cold War adversary no longer applied.

A few weeks after Bush's address of January 1992, when elements of the Wolfowitz Doctrine were leaked to the press, it turned out that the special mission was not only to support freedom throughout the world, as the president had claimed, but also to prevent the emergence of any potential rival on the world scene, if necessary by means of preventive war. This was the template for the foreign policy adopted by George W. Bush. In March 2003 he ordered American troops into Iraq to forestall a threat that never existed—alleged weapons of mass destruction that were never found. The invasion removed Saddam Hussein from power, but at the ultimate price of killing more than 190,000 people and destabilizing the country and the region. It cost the United States the lives of close to forty-five hundred military personnel and at least thirty four hundred civilian contractors.[16]

George W. Bush believed that America had won the Cold War, and he praised the "moral clarity" that had made the victory possible. In November 2003, after the initial success of the Iraq invasion, Bush gave a speech marking the twentieth anniversary of the National Endowment for Democracy. In it he credited American resolve for the fact that the "global nuclear standoff with the Soviet Union ended peacefully—as did the Soviet Union." In this triumphalist narrative he found inspiration for his plan of bringing democracy to the Middle East and transforming the Muslim world. "And now we must apply that lesson in our own time," the president argued in the same speech. "We've reached another great turning point—and the resolve we show will shape the next stage of the world democratic movement."[17]

The next stage never came. It was displaced by the nightmare of the long and bloody occupation of Iraq. In many ways, the road to the Iraq War had begun in 1991. It was not only the desire to finish the Gulf War of 1990–1991 by toppling Saddam Hussein's regime but also a deep-seated belief in the power of the United States as the country that won the Cold War by wiping its main adversary off the world map that informed the decisions of those who ordered American forces into Iraq in March 2003.

Acknowledgments

Like one of the characters in this book, the Russian foreign minister Andrei Kozyrev, I left Moscow on the second day of the coup, August 20, 1991. He was on a flight to Paris, while I took the Aeroflot flight to Montreal. Until we landed, no one knew whether the plotters in Moscow (or, rather, the Aeroflot authorities) would allow the plane to go all the way to Canada or reroute it to Havana. They never did what many on my flight were afraid of—they let us fly all the way to our destination. More important, they lost control not only over our plane but also of the situation on the ground in Moscow.

By the next day, there was no longer a coup to worry about. My colleagues at the University of Alberta in Canada, where I was scheduled to teach as a visiting professor, were excited about the events in the Soviet Union and wanted me to teach a course on the USSR in crisis, focusing on the fate of Russian and Soviet democracy and its final victory over totalitarianism. Coming from Ukraine and being aware of the importance of national mobilization in that Soviet republic, I offered instead to teach a course on the nationality question in the USSR. My hosts were skeptical. The nationality question appeared to be marginal, with no clear relation to what was going on in Moscow, or at least that was how the events were viewed by many in North American academia. I insisted, and they dropped their objections.

By the time my course ended in December 1991, there was no Soviet Union anymore. Instead of exemplifying the triumph of democracy, it disintegrated into fifteen republics. Unlike many of my North American colleagues, I realized the importance of the "national question" in the USSR and closely followed the drive of the Soviet republics toward independence. Like them, however, I was taken aback by the speed of developments and had little understanding of the peaceful but revolutionary process that took place between the defeat of the coup and the triumph of democracy on the streets of Moscow in August and the dissolution of the Soviet Union in December.

The existing literature on the collapse of the Soviet Union, written by journalists, political scientists, and, in the past decade, by historians, offers little help in explaining what exactly happened in the Soviet Union during my Canadian sabbatical. It turned out that I had little choice but to write this book in order to understand what actually took place in the Soviet Union and in the world during the last months of 1991 and why it happened. To answer these and many other related questions, I relied on the help and assistance of many people.

I would like to begin here with participants in the events who agreed to be interviewed for this book. They include President Leonid Kravchuk of Ukraine; the Speaker of the Belarusian parliament, Stanislaŭ Shushkevich; the minister of defense of Ukraine, General Kostiantyn Morozov; the deputy of the Soviet parliament, Ukrainian writer, and later diplomat Yurii Shcherbak; the American ambassador to Poland and, later, to Pakistan, Thomas Simons; and National Security Council staffer, and later ambassador to Greece and undersecretary of state, Nicholas Burns. I am also grateful to those who helped me arrange the interviews: Marshall Goldman, Marta Dyczok, Lubomyr Hajda, and Leonid Poliakov.

Secretary of State James Baker gave permission to use his papers in the Mudd Manuscript Library at Princeton University. Ambassador Burns read the entire manuscript and provided exceptionally useful comments and corrections. Deputy Foreign Minister Anatoly Adamishin of the Russian Federation read the book and did not raise major objections. I am also grateful to my Harvard colleagues Mark Kramer and Mary Sarotte and to my graduate student Elizabeth Kerley for their comments on various drafts of the manuscript.

Terry Martin, Charlie Maier, and Erez Manela commented on my papers and presentations based on research for this book, as did Blair Ruble of the Woodrow Wilson International Center for Scholars in

Washington, Vlad Zubok of the London School of Economics, and Olga Pavlenko of the Russian University for the Humanities. Their advice helped me greatly in crystallizing my argument, cutting less important parts of the manuscript, and avoiding mistakes. As always, my friend and longtime editor Myroslav Yurkevich did a wonderful job of "Englishing" my prose.

I am grateful to the Department of History for granting me a sabbatical in the fall of 2011 to work on the book and to the Ukrainian Research Institute and the Davis Center for Russian and Eurasian Studies for providing financial support. Special thanks go to my colleague Tim Colton, with whom I co-taught the seminar "Imperial Legacies and International Politics" in the 2012–2013 academic year, and to the Davis Center fellows and graduate students who took that course. I learned a lot from Tim and from the seminar participants about Soviet and post-Soviet politics and the ways in which they have been interpreted in the last few decades.

Princeton University archivist Daniel J. Linke helped me to secure permission to use Secretary Baker's papers at the Mudd Manuscript Library. Alexei Litvin was very helpful with getting access to the archive of the Gorbachev Foundation. Mikhail Prezumenshchikov, Peter Ruggenthaler, Yurii Shapoval, and Volodymyr Viatrovych advised me on the former Soviet, Russian, and Ukrainian archives. I am grateful to Evgenia Panova at the International Department of the ITAR-TASS Photo Agency and to Oscar Espaillat at Corbis Images for help in selecting the illustrations for this book.

My literary agent, Jill Kneerim, not only helped me find an excellent publisher for the manuscript but also helped make my argument as clear as possible not only to specialists in the field but also to a broader readership. One could not wish for a more supportive and enthusiastic publisher and editor than Lara Heimert, who took an immediate interest in the manuscript and, together with her highly motivated, friendly, and energetic team, turned it into a book. At Basic Books I am especially grateful to Roger Labrie, whose editing made my prose more lucid, and to Katy O'Donnell, who helped guide the book through the editorial process. Like all my previous books, this one could not have been written without the interest, support, and advice of my wife, Olena.

Notes

INTRODUCTION

1. George H. W. Bush, "Address to the Nation on the Commonwealth of Independent States," December 25, 1991, George Bush Presidential Library and Museum, Archives (hereafter Bush Presidential Library), Public Papers, http://bushlibrary.tamu.edu/research/public_papers.php ?id=3791&year=1991&month=12; George H. W. Bush, "State of the Union Address," January 28, 1992. C-SPAN http://www.c-spanvideo.org/program /23999-1

2. "Statement on the Resignation of Mikhail Gorbachev as President of the Soviet Union," December 25, 1991, Bush Presidential Library, Public Papers, http://bushlibrary.tamu.edu/research/public_papers.php?id=3790 &year=1991&month=12.

3. Apart from Bush's own pronouncements, see Brent Scowcroft's comments in George Bush and Brent Scowcroft, *A World Transformed* (New York, 1998), 563–564, and Robert M. Gates in his *From the Shadows: The Ultimate Insider's Story of Five Presidents and How They Won the Cold War* (New York, 1996), 552–575.

4. Ellen Schrecker, "Cold War Triumphalism and the Real Cold War," in Ellen Schrecker, ed., *Cold War Triumphalism: The Misuse of History After the Fall of Communism* (New York, 2006), 1–26; Bruce Cumings, "Time of Illusion: Post–Cold War Visions of the World," in Ellen Schrecker, ed., *Cold War Triumphalism*, 71–102; "Tainy mira s Annoi Chapman, no. 79. Gibel' imperii," YouTube video posted by ChannelProXima, February 13, 2013, www.youtube .com/watch?v=T1zr8Fr1Nbs; "Sekretnyi stsenarii razvala SSSR i Rossii v planakh TsRU," YouTube video posted by AndreyFLKZ, January 31, 2013, www.youtube.com/watch?v=PfeiGv6IkQc.

5. On the Soviet Union as a multinational state, see Richard Pipes, *The Formation of the Soviet Union: Communism and Nationalism, 1917–23* (Cambridge, MA, 1997); Terry Martin, *The Affirmative Action Empire: Nations and Nationalism in the Soviet Union, 1923–1939* (Ithaca, NY, 2001); Francine

Hirsch, *Empire of Nations: Ethnographic Knowledge and the Making of the Soviet Union* (Ithaca, NY, 2005).

6. For the interpretation of the Soviet collapse as the fall of an empire and the role of political nationalism in that process, see Roman Szporluk, *Russia, Ukraine, and the Breakup of the Soviet Union* (Stanford, CA, 2000); Dominic Lieven, *Empire: The Russian Empire and Its Rivals* (New Haven, CT, 2002), ch. 9; Mark R. Beissinger, *Nationalist Mobilization and the Collapse of the Soviet State* (Cambridge, 2002), 4; Jane Burbank and Frederick Cooper, *Empires in World History: Power and Politics of Difference* (Princeton, NJ, 2010), ch. 13.

7. David Remnick, the author of the Pulitzer Prize–winning *Lenin's Tomb: The Last Days of the Soviet Empire* (New York, 1994), devotes only two and a half pages to that important concluding chapter of Cold War history; Michael Dobbs, the author of the widely acclaimed *Down with Big Brother: The Fall of the Soviet Empire* (New York, 1997), six pages; Stephen Kotkin in his thought-provoking *Armageddon Averted: The Soviet Collapse, 1970–2000* (Oxford, 2001), five pages.

8. Kotkin, *Armageddon Averted*, introduction and ch. 4; Stephen Kotkin, *Uncivil Society: 1989 and the Implosion of the Communist Establishment* (New York, 2009), preface; David A. Lake, "The Rise, Fall, and Future of the Russian Empire: A Theoretical Interpretation," in Karen Dawisha and Bruce Parrott, eds., *The End of Empire? The Transformation of the USSR in Comparative Perspective* (Armonk, NY, 1997), 30–62; Timothy J. Colton, *Yeltsin: A Life* (New York, 2008), chs. 8 and 9.

CHAPTER 1

1. David Reynolds, *Summits: Six Meetings That Shaped the Twentieth Century* (New York, 2007), 1–102.

2. "U.S.-Soviet Relations and the Moscow Summit," July 26, 1991, C-SPAN, www.c-spanvideo.org/program/19799-1; Treaty Between the United States of America and the Union of Soviet Socialist Republics on the Reduction and Limitation of Strategic Offensive Arms, July 31, 1991. US Department of State, http://www.state.gov/www/global/arms/starthtm/start/start1.html.

3. John Lewis Gaddis, *The Cold War: A New History* (New York, 2006); Henry Kissinger, *Diplomacy* (New York, 1996), 423–732; Vladislav M. Zubok, *A Failed Empire: The Soviet Union in the Cold War from Stalin to Gorbachev* (Chapel Hill, NC, 2007), 1–226.

4. Scott Shane, "Cold War's Riskiest Moment," *Baltimore Sun*, August 31, 2003.

5. "Atomic War Film Spurs Nationwide Discussion," *New York Times*, November 22, 1983; Ronald Reagan, *An American Life* (New York, 1990), 585–586; Beth A. Fisher, *The Reagan Reversal: Foreign Policy and the End of the Cold War* (Columbia, MO, 2000); Ronald Reagan, "Address to the Nation and

Other Countries on United States–Soviet Relations, January 16, 1984," http://www.reagan.utexas.edu/archives/speeches/1984/11684a.html.

6. Barbara Bush, *A Memoir* (New York, 1994); George Bush, *All the Best, George Bush: My Life in Letters and Other Writings* (New York, 2000); Webster Griffin Tarpley and Anton Chaitkin, *George Bush: An Unauthorized Biography* (Joshua Tree, CA, 2004).

7. "Remarks at the Arrival Ceremony in Moscow, July 30, 1991" and "Remarks by President Gorbachev and President Bush at the Signing Ceremony for the Strategic Arms Reduction Talks Treaty in Moscow, July 31, 1991," Bush Presidential Library, Public Papers, http://bushlibrary.tamu.edu/research/public_papers.php?id=3256&year=1991&month=7.

8. Michael R. Beschloss and Strobe Talbott, *At the Highest Levels: The Inside Story of the End of the Cold War* (Boston, 1993), 411; George Bush and Brent Scowcroft, *A World Transformed* (New York, 1998), 510–511.

9. "Mikhail Sergeevich Gorbachev," Trip of President Bush to Moscow and Kiev, July 30–August 1, 1991, Bush Presidential Library, Presidential Records, Office of the First Lady, Scheduling, Ann Brock Series: Moscow Summit, Monday 7/29/91 to Thursday 8/1/91—Moscow and Kiev, no. 4.

10. Archie Brown, *The Gorbachev Factor* (Oxford, 1997); Andrei Grachev, *Gorbachev's Gamble: Soviet Foreign Policy and the End of the Cold War* (Cambridge, 2008); Raymond L. Garthoff, *The Great Transition: American-Soviet Relations and the End of the Cold War* (Washington, D.C., 1994); Don Oberdorfer, *From the End of the Cold War to a New Era: The United States and the Soviet Union, 1983–1991* (Baltimore, 1998).

11. Walter Goodman, "Summit Image: Hardly a Mikhail and George Show," *New York Times*, August 1, 1991; Gene Gibbons, "Pre Advance Pool Report, Moscow Summit, July 29–August 1, 1991, July 25, 1991," Bush Presidential Library, Presidential Records, White House Office of Media Affairs, Media Guide to the President's Trip to the USSR—Summer 1991.

12. Goodman, "Summit Image"; Bush and Scowcroft, *A World Transformed*, 511; Beschloss and Talbott, *At the Highest Levels*, 415.

13. Beschloss and Talbott, *At the Highest Levels*, 411–412; "Memorandum of Conversation. Extended Bilateral Meeting with Mikhail Gorbachev of the USSR, July 30, 1991," Bush Presidential Library, Memcons and Telcons, http://bushlibrary.tamu.edu/research/pdfs/memcons_telcons/1991-07-30 —Gorbachev%20[1].pdf.

14. Strobe Talbott, "Mikhail Gorbachev and George Bush: The Summit Goodfellas," *Time*, August 5, 1991.

15. Beschloss and Talbott, *At the Highest Levels*, 405–406.

16. *Jane's Strategic Weapons Systems*, issue 50, ed. Duncan Lennox (Surrey, 2009), 161–163; "Study Details Catastrophic Impact of Nuclear Attack on US Cities," *Space War*, March 23, 2007, www.spacewar.com/reports/Study

_Details_Catastrophic_Impact_Of_Nuclear_Attack_On_US_Cities_999
.html.

17. Pavel Palazhchenko, *My Years with Gorbachev and Shevardnadze: The Memoir of a Soviet Interpreter* (University Park, PA, 1997), 292–293; Bush and Scowcroft, *A World Transformed*, 508–509; "Beseda Gorbacheva s Dzh. Bushem v Londone, 17 iiulia 1991 goda," in *V Politbiuro TsK KPSS po zapisiam Anatoliia Cherniaeva, Vadima Medvedeva, Georgiia Shakhnazarova (1985–1991)* (Moscow, 2000), 695–696.

18. "Memorandum of Conversation. Extended Bilateral Meeting with Mikhail Gorbachev of the USSR, July 30, 1991," Bush Presidential Library, Memcons and Telcons, http://bushlibrary.tamu.edu/research/pdfs/memcons _telcons/1991-07-30—Gorbachev%20[1].pdf

19. Bush and Scowcroft, *A World Transformed*, 511–512; David Remnick, "All Substance, No Style Makes a Dull Summit: Businesslike Bush Forsakes the Flourishes," *Washington Post*, July 31, 1991.

20. Goodman, "Summit Image," *New York Times*, August 1, 1991.

21. Remnick, "All Substance, No Style"; Ann Devroy, "First Lady: Bush Must Run Again: 'For Country's Sake,' She Tells Interviewers," *Washington Post*, August 1, 1991; White House, Office of the Press Secretary, Interview of Ms. Bush by Steve Fox, ABC, July 31, 1991, Bush Presidential Library, Presidential Records, National Security Council, Nicholas R. Burns and Ed A. Hewett Files: POTUS Meetings March 1991–July 1991: Moscow Summit, July 1991, no. 1.

22. "Raisa Maksimovna Gorbachev," Trip of President Bush to Moscow and Kiev, July 30–August 1, 1991; Raisa Gorbacheva, *Ia nadeius'* (Moscow, 1991); Anatolii Cherniaev and Vitalii Gusenkov, Memo for Mikhail Gorbachev on the Program of His Visit to the United States from May 29 to June 4, 1990, Gorbachev Foundation Archive, fond 2, no. 8288.1; Anatolii Cherniaev, *Sovmestnyi iskhod. Dnevnik dvukh ėpokh, 1972–1991 gody* (Moscow, 2008), 939; "Raisa Gorbachev to Join Barbara Bush at Wellesley," *Harvard Crimson*, May 18, 1990; "Wellesley Students Hail Raisa Gorbachev," *New York Times*, May 20, 1990.

23. Barbara Bush, Address to Soviet Children, July 1991, Trip of President Bush to Moscow and Kiev, July 30–August 1, 1991; Francis X. Clines, "Red Square Is Beautiful. That's Agreed," *New York Times*, July 31, 1991; J. Y. Smith, "Raisa Gorbachev, Activist First Lady Dies," *Washington Post*, September 20, 1999; Barbara Bush, "Eulogy: Raisa Gorbachev," *Time*, October 4, 1999.

24. Beschloss and Talbott, *At the Highest Levels*, 415; Galina Markova, *Bol'shoi kremlevskii dvorets* (Moscow, 1981).

25. Bush and Scowcroft, *A World Transformed*, 514; "Remarks by President Gorbachev and President Bush at the Signing Ceremony for the Strategic Arms Reduction Talks Treaty in Moscow, 31 July 1991," Bush Presidential

Library, Public Papers, http://bushlibrary.tamu.edu/research/public_papers. php?id=3256&year=1991&month=7.

26. Bush and Scowcroft, *A World Transformed*, 514; R. W. Apple Jr., "Summit in Moscow: Bush and Gorbachev Sign Pact to Curtail Nuclear Arsenals, Join in Call for Mid-East Talks," *New York Times*, August 1, 1991.

27. Mikhail Gorbachev, *Memoirs* (New York, 1995), 624.

28. Gorbachev, *Memoirs*, 624; Cherniaev, *Sovmestnyi iskhod*, 968–969.

29. Internal Points for Bessmertnykh Meeting, July 28, 1991, James A. Baker Papers, box 110, folder 5; Bush and Scowcroft, *A World Transformed*, 514–515.

30. Esther B. Fein, "Summit in Moscow: The God (of Technology) That Failed," *New York Times*, August 1, 1991.

CHAPTER 2

1. Strobe Talbott, "Mikhail Gorbachev and George Bush: The Summit Goodfellas," *Time*, August 5, 1991; "At Big Moment, Little Earpiece Fails," *New York Times*, August 1, 1991.

2. George Bush and Brent Scowcroft, *A World Transformed* (New York, 1998), 514–515; "Toasts at a Dinner Hosted by President Bush in Moscow, 31 July 1991," Bush Presidential Library, Public Papers, http://bushlibrary.tamu .edu/research/public_papers.php?id=3256&year=1991&month=7.

3. Bush and Scowcroft, *A World Transformed*, 510–514; Pavel Palazhchenko, *My Years with Gorbachev and Shevardnadze: The Memoir of a Soviet Interpreter* (University Park, PA, 1997), 305–306; "Dmitriy Timofeyevich Yazov," The Trip of President Bush to Moscow and Kiev, July 30–August 1, 1991, Bush Presidential Library.

4. Mikhail Gorbachev, *Memoirs* (New York, 1995), 624–625; Palazhchenko, *My Years*, 300–301; Michael R. Beschloss and Strobe Talbott, *At the Highest Levels: The Inside Story of the End of the Cold War* (Boston, 1993), 413; Bush and Scowcroft, *A World Transformed*, 512; Jack Matlock, *Autopsy on an Empire: The American Ambassador's Account of the Collapse of the Soviet Union* (New York, 1994), 564.

5. Gorbachev, *Memoirs*, 624–625; Palazhchenko, *My Years*, 300–301; Beschloss and Talbott, *At the Highest Levels*, 413; Bush and Scowcroft, *A World Transformed*, 512; Jerry Seib, "Pool Report no. 11. Bush, Gorbachev—and Yeltsin—Go to Dinner. Moscow, USSR, Tuesday, July 30, 1991," Bush Presidential Library, Presidential Records, National Security Council, Nicholas R. Burns Files, Subject Files: Moscow Summit—Press Releases, Fact Sheets, Remarks, no. 2; Matlock, *Autopsy on an Empire*, 564.

6. For biographies of Yeltsin, see Timothy J. Colton, *Yeltsin: A Life* (New York, 2008), and Leon Aron, *Yeltsin: A Revolutionary Life* (New York, 2000).

Cf. Boris Yeltsin, *The Struggle for Russia,* trans. Catherine A. Fitzpatrick (New York, 1994).

7. "Boris Nikolaevitch Yeltsin," The Trip of President Bush to Moscow and Kiev, July 30–August 1, 1991, Bush Presidential Library.

8. Colton, *Yeltsin,* 183–184; Petr Aven and Al'fred Kokh, "El'tsin sluzhil nam!," interview with Gennadii Burbulis, *Forbes* (Russian edition), July 22, 2010, www.forbes.ru/node/53407/print.

9. Anatolii Cherniaev, *Sovmestnyi iskhod. Dnevnik dvukh épokh, 1972–1991 gody* (Moscow, 2008), 862–863, 968; Gorbachev, *Memoirs,* 601–602.

10. Oleg Shenin, "Ot partii zhdut énergichnykh deistvii," draft of a speech delivered at a meeting of secretaries of republican, regional, and oblast committees, January 24, 1991, Rossiiskii gosudarstvennyi arkhiv noveishei istorii (Russian State Archives of Recent History, hereafter RGANI), fond 89, op. 23, no. 2, 25–26.

11. "TsK KPSS. Ob obstanovke v partiinoi organizatsii sovetskikh uchrezhdenii v g. Zheneva (Shveitsariia)," RGANI, fond 89, op. 20, no. 23, 1–6; *Economic Survey of Europe,* no. 3 (2003): 125.

12. Mark R. Beissinger, *Nationalist Mobilization and the Collapse of the Soviet State* (Cambridge, 2002), 147–199.

13. Quoted in Edward W. Walker, *Dissolution: Sovereignty and the Breakup of the Soviet Union* (Lanham, MD, 2003), 88.

14. *Soiuz mozhno bylo sokhranit'. Belaia kniga. Dokumenty i fakty o politike M. S. Gorbacheva po reformirovaniiu i sokhraneniiu mnogonatsional'nogo gosudarsta,* 2nd ed. (Moscow, 2007), 150–155; Yegor Likhachev, *Inside Gorbachev's Kremlin* (New York, 1996); Archie Brown, *The Gorbachev Factor* (Oxford, 1996); Archie Brown, *Seven Years That Changed the World: Perestroika in Perspective* (Oxford, 2007).

15. *V Politbiuro TsK KPSS po zapisiam Anatoliia Cherniaeva, Vadima Medvedeva, Georgiia Shakhnazarova (1985–1991)* (Moscow, 2000), 499, 529; Beissinger, *Nationalist Mobilization,* 405.

16. Roman Szporluk, "Dilemmas of Russian Nationalism," in *Russia, Ukraine and the Breakup of the Soviet Union* (Stanford, 2000), 183–228; Beissinger, *Nationalist Mobilization,* 390–396, 401–416; Walker, *Dissolution,* 78–81.

17. Eduard Shevardnadze to James Baker, Moscow, January 20, 1991, James A. Baker Papers, box 102, folder 35.

18. Cherniaev, *Sovmestnyi iskhod,* 862–863.

19. Gorbachev, *Memoirs,* 326–347, 569–607; Walker, *Dissolution,* 55–136.

20. Szporluk, "Dilemmas of Russian Nationalism," 188–198; Cherniaev, *Sovmestnyi iskhod,* 947, 961; Valerii Boldin, *Krushenie p'edestala. Shtrikhi k portretu M. S. Gorbacheva* (Moscow, 1995).

21. *Soiuz mozhno bylo sokhranit',* 268–283.

22. "President. USSR. Designated Gifts," Bush Presidential Library, Presidential Records, Office of the First Lady, Scheduling, Ann Brock Series: Moscow Summit, Monday 7/29/91 to Thursday 8/1/91—Moscow and Kiev, USSR [[3]].

23. Colton, *Yeltsin*, 171–173; Boris Yeltsin, "Quotation of the Day," *New York Times*, September 11, 1989.

24. Robert M. Gates, *From the Shadows: The Ultimate Insider's Story of Five Presidents and How They Won the Cold War* (New York, 1996), 478–479; Bush and Scowcroft, *A World Transformed*, 141–143; Beschloss and Talbott, *At the Highest Levels*, 103–104.

25. Gates, *From the Shadows*, 503; Bush and Scowcroft, *A World Transformed*, 142–143; Colton, *Yeltsin*, 172.

26. "Luncheon with President Mikhail Gorbachev of the USSR," July 30, 1991, Bush Presidential Library, Memcons and Telcons, http://bushlibrary .tamu.edu/research/pdfs/memcons_telcons/1991-07-30—Gorbachev%20[2] .pdf.

27. "Memorandum of Conversation. Meeting with Boris Yeltsin, President of the Republic of Russia," July 30, 1991, Bush Presidential Library, Memcons and Telcons, http://bushlibrary.tamu.edu/research/pdfs/memcons_telcons/1991-07-30--Yeltsin.pdf; "The White House Office of the Press Secretary. Remarks of President Bush and President Yeltsin in Press Availability," July 30, 1991, Bush Presidential Library, Presidential Records, National Security Council, Nicholas R. Burns and Ed A. Hewett Series: POTUS Meetings, March 1991–July 1991: Moscow Summit, July 1991, no. 1.

28. Beschloss and Talbott, *At the Highest Levels*, 412–413; "Points to Be Made for Meeting with President Yeltsin," Bush Presidential Library, Presidential Records, National Security Council, Nicholas R. Burns Series, Subject Files: POTUS Trip to Moscow and Kiev, July 27–August 1, 1991, no. 1; G. Alimov, "Ukaz o departizatsii nachnet deistvovat' s 4 avgusta. Bush-Yeltsin-Gorbachev," *Argumenty i fakty*, no. 30 (August 30, 1991): 7; Jessica Lee, "Pool Report no. 10. President Bush Visits Boris Yeltsin and Stops at Tsereteli Studio," Moscow, USSR, Tuesday, July 30, 1991, Bush Presidential Library, Presidential Records, National Security Council, Nicholas R. Burns Series, Subject Files: Moscow Summit—Press Releases, Fact Sheets, Remarks, no. 2.

29. Bush and Scowcroft, *A World Transformed*, 509; Alimov, "Ukaz o departizatsii," 7.

CHAPTER 3

1. "Nuclear Weapon Effects from Hiroshima to Nagasaki to the Present and Beyond: A Broad-Gauged Analysis with New Information Regarding

Simultaneous Detonations and Firestorms," Nukefix, www.nukefix.org /weapon.html.

2. Jack Matlock, *Autopsy on an Empire: The American Ambassador's Account of the Collapse of the Soviet Union* (New York, 1994), 464–465; Michael R. Beschloss and Strobe Talbott, *At the Highest Levels: The Inside Story of the End of the Cold War* (Boston, 1993), 408–410.

3. Sergei Solodkin, "Glavredu udalos' razdobyt' v Londone sensatsionnye zapisi besed Mikhaila Sergeevicha s inostrannymi politikami," *Glavred*, October 5, 2009, http://www.glavred.info/archive/2009/10/05/163604-3.html.

4. "Russians Divided over Baltics' Independence," April 12, 1991, USIA Research Memorandum, National Archives and Records Administration, RG 306, box 49, M 52–91.

5. George Bush and Brent Scowcroft, *A World Transformed* (New York, 1998), 512; "Implications of Alternative Soviet Futures," National Intelligence Estimate, NIE 11-18-91 (June 1991), http://www.foia.cia.gov/docs/ DOC_0000265647/DOC_0000265647.pdf; Matlock, *Autopsy on an Empire*, 565–566.

6. Author's interview with Nicholas Burns, Harvard University, June 15, 2012; Beschloss and Talbott, *At the Highest Levels*, 414–415; Handwritten Notes on the Killing of Lithuanian Border Guards Passed by Brent Scowcroft to James Baker on July 31, 1991, James A. Baker Papers, box 110, folder 5; Bush and Scowcroft, *A World Transformed*, 513–514; Mikhail Gorbachev, *Memoirs* (New York, 1995), 623.

7. "Richard Nixon/Frank Gannon Interviews," May 13, 1983, Day 5, Tape 1, 00:01:59, www.libs.uga.edu/media/collections/nixon/nixonday5.html; Conrad Black, *Richard M. Nixon: A Life in Full* (New York, 2008), 814.

8. Von Hardesty and Bob Schieffer, *Air Force One: The Aircraft That Shaped the Modern Presidency* (New York, 2005), 127–154; Bush and Scowcroft, *A World Transformed*, 515; Beschloss and Talbott, *At the Highest Levels*, 415–416.

9. Matlock, *Autopsy on an Empire*, 567; Beschloss and Talbott, *At the Highest Levels*, 416; "Remarks to the Supreme Soviet of the Republic of the Ukraine in Kiev, Soviet Union," August 1, 1991, http://bushlibrary.tamu.edu/research /public_papers.php?id=3267&year=1991&month=8.

10. Gibbons, "Pre Advance Pool Report, Moscow Summit, July 29–August 1, 1991, July 25, 1991"; Susan Page, "Pool Report, Pool H," Bush Presidential Library, Presidential Records, National Security Council, Nicholas R. Burns Series, Subject Files: Moscow Summit—Press Releases, Fact Sheets, Remarks, no. 1; Matlock, *Autopsy on an Empire*, 567.

11. Volodymyr Lytvyn, *Politychna arena Ukraïny: diiovi osoby ta vykonavtsi* (Kyiv, 1994); *Ukraïna: politychna istoriia XX–pochatok XXI stolittia*, ed. Volodymyr Lytvyn et al. (Kyiv, 2007), 875–947; Lina Kushnir, "Valentyna Shevchenko: Provesty demonstratsiiu 1 travnia 1986-ho nakazaly

z Moskvy," *Ukraïns'ka pravda*, April 25, 2011, http://www.istpravda.com.ua
/articles/4db5d3966b581/view_comments/.

12. Page, "Pool Report, Pool H."

13. "Leonid Makarovich Kravchuk," The Trip of President Bush to Moscow
and Kiev, July 30–August 1, 1991; author's interview with Leonid Kravchuk, Kyiv,
September 1, 2011, http://www.istpravda.com.ua/articles/2011/09/10/53558/view
_print; Vahtang Kipiani and Volodymyr Fedoryn, "Kravchuk: 'Shcherbyts'kyi
skazav: Kakoi durak pridumal slovo perestroika?'" *Ukraïns'ka pravda*,
September 13, 2011; Valentyn Chemerys, *Prezydent. Roman-ese* (Kyiv, 1994);
David Remnick, "Ukraine Split on Independence as Republic Awaits Bush
Visit," *Washington Post*, August 1, 1991.

14. "Remarks at the Arrival Ceremony in Kiev, Soviet Union," August 1,
1991, http://bushlibrary.tamu.edu/research/public_papers.php?id=3265&
year=1991&month=8; Matlock, *Autopsy on an Empire*, 568.

15. Bush and Scowcroft, *A World Transformed*, 510–511; Matlock, *Autopsy
on an Empire*, 569; Anatolii Cherniaev, *Sovmestnyi iskhod. Dnevnik dvukh
ėpokh, 1972–1991 gody* (Moscow, 2008), 957–958; Chrystyna N. Lapychak,
"Bush Notes Importance of Republics in Historic Trip to Ukrainian Capital,"
Ukrainian Weekly, August 4, 1991, 1; Page, "Pool Report, Pool H"; George H.
W. Bush, "Remarks to the Supreme Soviet of the Republic of the Ukraine in
Kiev, Soviet Union," August 1, 1991, Bush Presidential Library, Public Papers;
Beschloss and Talbott, *At the Highest Levels*, 417.

16. Author's interview with Leonid Kravchuk, Kyiv, September 1, 2011;
Kipiani and Fedoryn, "Kravchuk: 'Shcherbyts'kyi skazav.'"

17. Ivan Drach, "My vitaiemo Dzhordzha Busha—iak prezydenta SShA
i ne pryimaiemo ioho iak moskovs'koho ahitatora," in *Polityka: statti, dopovidi,
vystupy, interv'iu* (Kyiv, 1997), 324–327. Cf. "Rukh Chairman Ivan Drach's
Remarks to President Bush," *Ukrainian Weekly*, August 11, 1991, 3.

18. Author's interview with Leonid Kravchuk, Kyiv, September 1, 2011.

19. "Points to Be Made for Meeting with the Ukrainian Chairman Leonid
Kravchuk," Bush Presidential Library, Presidential Records, National Security
Council, Nicholas R. Burns Files, Subject Files: POTUS Trip to Moscow and
Kiev, July 27–August 1, 1991, no. 3.

20. "Memorandum of Conversation. Meeting with Ukrainian Supreme
Soviet Chairman Leonid Kravchuk," August 1, 1991, Bush Presidential
Library, Memcons and Telcons, http://bushlibrary.tamu.edu/research/pdfs
/memcons_telcons/1991-08-01--Kravchuk.pdf; "Proposals of the Ukrainian
SSR for Possible Directions of Trade-and-Economic Cooperation Between
the Ukrainian SSR and USA," Bush Presidential Library, Presidential
Records, National Security Council, Nicholas R. Burns and Ed Hewett
Files: POTUS Meetings, March 1991–July 1991: Moscow Summit, July 1991,
no. 1.

21. For a survey of Ukrainian history, see Paul Robert Magocsi, *A History of Ukraine*, 2nd ed. (Toronto, 2010). On Ukraine's road to independence, see Bohdan Nahaylo and Victor Swoboda, *Soviet Disunion: A History of the Nationalities Problem in the USSR* (New York, 1990); Bohdan Nahaylo, *The Ukrainian Resurgence* (Toronto, 1999).

22. George H. W. Bush, "Remarks to the Supreme Soviet of the Republic of the Ukraine in Kiev, Soviet Union," August 1, 1991, Bush Presidential Library, Public Papers. Cf. Richard Nixon, "Toast at a Dinner in Kiev," May 29, 1972, The American Presidency Project, www.presidency.ucsb.edu/ws/index .php?pid=3440#axzz1QonAP09C; author's interview with Nicholas Burns, Harvard University, June 15, 2012.

23. Bush, "Remarks to the Supreme Soviet of the Republic of the Ukraine in Kiev, Soviet Union," August 1, 1991.

24. Author's interview with Nicholas Burns, Harvard University, June 15, 2012.

25. George H. W. Bush, "Remarks to the Supreme Soviet of the Republic of the Ukraine in Kiev, Soviet Union," August 1, 1991, http://bushlibrary.tamu. edu/research/public_papers.php?id=3267&year=1991&month=8.

26. *Ukrainian Weekly*, August 11, 1991.

27. "The Moscow Coup," *Washington Post*, August 20, 1991; William Safire, "After the Fall," *New York Times*, August 29, 1991; William Safire, "Bush at the UN," *New York Times*, September 16, 1991; William Safire, "Putin's 'Chicken Kiev,'" *New York Times*, December 6, 2004; "Bush Sr. Clarifies 'Chicken Kiev' Speech," *Washington Times*, May 23, 2004; Bush and Scowcroft, *A World Transformed*, 15–16; Matlock, *Autopsy on an Empire*, 570–571, 798.

28. Ann McFeatters, "Pool Report No. 21. Pool from the Supreme Soviet Session to St. Sophia to Babii Yar. Kiev, USSR, August 1, 1991," Bush Presidential Library, Presidential Records, National Security Council, Nicholas R. Burns Series, Subject Files: Moscow Summit—Press Releases, Fact Sheets, Remarks, no. 1.

29. Anatolii Kuznetsov, *Babii Iar: A Document in the Form of a Novel*, trans. David Floyd (London, 1970); Victoria Khiterer, "Babi Yar: The Tragedy of Kiev's Jews," *Brandeis Graduate Journal* 2 (2004): 1–16.

30. Gibbons, "Pre Advance Pool Report, Moscow Summit, July 25, 1991"; Bush and Scowcroft, *A World Transformed*, 516–517; George Bush, "Remarks at the Babi Yar Memorial in Kiev, Soviet Union," August 1, 1991, Bush Presidential Library, Public Papers, http://bushlibrary.tamu.edu/research/public_papers .php?id=3268&year=1991&month=8; interview with Leonid Kravchuk in *Rozpad Radians'koho Soiuzu. Usna istoriia nezalezhnoï Ukraïny 1988–91*, tape 9.

31. Oleksandr Burakovs'kyi, *Rada natsionalnostei Narodnoho rukhu Ukraïny (1989–1993)* (Edmonton, 1995); Oleksandr Burakovs'kyi, "Rukh,

ievreï, Ukraïna. Rozdumy inorodtsia," *Kyïv*, nos. 1–2 (1997): 93–125; interview with Yaakov Bleich in *Rozpad Radians'koho Soiuzu. Usna istoriia nezalezhnoï Ukraïny 1988–91,* tape 2 , http://oralhistory.org.ua/interview-ua/470/.

32. Beschloss and Talbott, *At the Highest Levels,* 417; "Gennadiy Ivanovich Yanayev," The Trip of President Bush to Moscow and Kiev, July 30–August 1, 1991.

33. Matlock, *Autopsy on an Empire,* 571; Bush and Scowcroft, *A World Transformed,* 517.

CHAPTER 4

1. George Bush and Brent Scowcroft, *A World Transformed* (New York, 1998), 526.

2. Ibid., 520; Michael R. Beschloss and Strobe Talbott, *At the Highest Levels: The Inside Story of the End of the Cold War* (Boston, 1993), 422–423; "Statement by Deputy Press Secretary Popadiuk on the Attempted Coup in the Soviet Union," Bush Presidential Library, Public Papers, http://bushlibrary.tamu.edu/research/public_papers.php?id=3313&year=1991&month=8.

3. "Telephone Conversation with Prime Minister Brian Mulroney of Canada, August 19, 1991," Bush Presidential Library, Memcons and Telcons, http://bushlibrary.tamu.edu/research/pdfs/memcons_telcons/1991-08-19 —Mulroney.pdf.

4. "First Statement on Soviet Coup," August 19, 1991, www.c-spanvideo.org /program/20705-1; Beschloss and Talbott, *At the Highest Levels,* 429–430; James A. Baker with Thomas M. DeFrank, *The Politics of Diplomacy: Revolution, War and Peace, 1989–1992* (New York, 1995), 514–518; "Assorted JAB Notes from Events Related to Attempted Coup in USSR, 8/12–8/22," James A. Baker Papers, box 110, folder 6; Bush and Scowcroft, *A World Transformed,* 504–505, 515.

5. Bush and Scowcroft, *A World Transformed,* 521–522; "Telcon with Jozsef Antall, Prime Minister of Hungary, August 19, 1991," Bush Presidential Library, Memcons and Telcons, http://bushlibrary.tamu.edu/research/pdfs/memcons _telcons/1991-08-19--Antall.pdf.

6. Baker, *The Politics of Diplomacy,* 475; Robert M. Gates, *From the Shadows: The Ultimate Insider's Story of Five Presidents and How They Won the Cold War* (New York, 1996), 502; Bush and Scowcroft, *A World Transformed,* 521–522.

7. Bush and Scowcroft, *A World Transformed,* 521–522; "Telephone Conversation with Prime Minister Brian Mulroney of Canada, August 19, 1991," Bush Presidential Library, Memcons and Telcons.

8. Vladimir Medvedev, *Chelovek za spinoi* (Moscow, 1994), 253–260, 269–273; "Gorbachevskaia dacha 'Zaria' v Forose", http://www.foros-yalta .com/?id=288; Valentin Stepankov and Evgenii Lisov, *Kremlevskii zagovor. Versiia sledstviia* (Moscow, 1992), 17, 56, 135–143.

9. Medvedev, *Chelovek za spinoi*, 278.

10. Michael Dobbs, *Down with Big Brother: The Fall of the Soviet Empire* (New York, 1997), 377–379.

11. Jonathan Brent and Vladimir Naumov, *Stalin's Last Crime: The Plot Against the Jewish Doctors, 1948–1953* (New York, 2004), 313–325; Medvedev, *Chelovek za spinoi*, 147–148; Nikolai Zen'kovich, *Mikhail Gorbachev, zhizn' do Kremlia* (Moscow, 2001), 587.

12. Mikhail Gorbachev, *Memoirs* (New York, 1995), 631; Valentin Varennikov, *Nepovtorimoe* (Moscow, 2001), vol. 6, pt. 3; Valerii Boldin, *Krushnie p'edestala, Shtrikhi k portretu M. S. Gorbacheva* (Moscow, 1995), 15–16.

13. Boldin, *Krushnie p'edestala*, 13–17; *Soiuz mozhno bylo sokhranit'. Belaia kniga. Dokumenty i fakty o politike M. S. Gorbacheva po reformirovaniiu i sokhraneniiu mnogonatsional'nogo gosudarsta*, 2nd ed. (Moscow, 2007), 289–290; Gorbachev, *Memoirs*, 626–630.

14. Boldin, *Krushnie p'edestala*, 182, 263–265, 282, 333–334, 380–381; Stepankov and Lisov, *Kremlevskii zagovor*, 8; Anatolii Cherniaev, *Sovmestnyi iskhod. Dnevnik dvukh ėpokh, 1972–1991 gody* (Moscow, 2008), 972–974; Martin Ebon, *KGB: Death and Rebirth* (Westport, CT, 1994), 3–6.

15. Gorbachev, *Memoirs*, 631–632; Boldin, *Krushenie p'edestala*, 15–17; Varennikov, *Nepovtorimoe*, vol. 6, pt. 3; Dobbs, *Down with Big Brother*, 377–379; Cherniaev, *Sovmestnyi iskhod*, 972–974.

16. Stepankov and Lisov, *Kremlevskii zagovor*, 19.

17. Gates, *From the Shadows*, 424.

18. Ibid., 476–477, 491; Vladimir Kriuchkov, *Lichnoe delo* (Moscow, 2003), 364–475.

19. Boris Yeltsin, *The Struggle for Russia*, trans. Catherine A. Fitzpatrick (New York, 1994), 38–39; Gorbachev, *Memoirs*, 628, 642, 643; *Soiuz mozhno bylo sokhranit'*, 204.

20. Stepankov and Lisov, *Kremlevskii zagovor*, 62, 84–85; *Soiuz mozhno bylo sokhranit'*, 289–290; David Remnick, *Lenin's Tomb: The Last Days of the Soviet Empire* (New York, 1994), 45; Valentin Pavlov, *Avgust iznutri. Gorbachev-putch* (Moscow, 1993), 105–115; Varennikov, *Nepovtorimoe*, vol. 6, pt. 3.

21. Stepankov and Lisov, *Kremlevskii zagovor*, 90; Boldin, *Krushenie p'edestala*, 18–19; Gorbachev, *Memoirs*, 632.

22. Stepankov and Lisov, *Kremlevskii zagovor*, 90–91.

23. Ibid., 107–110; Victoria E. Bonnell, Ann Cooper, and Gregory Fredin, eds., *Russia at the Barricades: Eyewitness Accounts of the August 1991 Coup* (Armonk, NY, 1994), 33–41; *Raspad SSSR: Dokumenty i fakty (1986–1992 gg.)*, vol. 1, *Normativnye akty. Ofitsial'nye soobshcheniia*, ed. S. M. Shakhrai (Moscow, 2009), 827–831; Remnick, *Lenin's Tomb*, 459–460.

24. Gorbachev, *Memoirs*, 633.

25. Beschloss and Talbott, *At the Highest Levels,* 421; Bush and Scowcroft, *A World Transformed,* 526.

CHAPTER 5

1. Boris Yeltsin, *The Struggle for Russia,* trans. Catherine A. Fitzpatrick (New York, 1994), 42–46, 53–54, 57, 61–62, 69, image facing 172; Aleksandr Korzhakov, *Boris El'tsin: ot rassveta do zakata* (Moscow, 1997), 80–84; Victoria E. Bonnell, Ann Cooper, and Gregory Fredin, eds., *Russia at the Barricades: Eyewitness Accounts of the August 1991 Coup* (Armonk, NY, 1994), 170–171, 218–220; Valentin Stepankov and Evgenii Lisov, *Kremlevskii zagovor. Versiia sledstviia* (Moscow, 1992), 110–112; *Krasnoe ili beloe? Drama avgusta-91. Fakty. Gipotezy. Stolknovenie mnenii* (Moscow, 1992), 89–92.

2. Stepankov and Lisov, *Kremlevskii zagovor,* 108, 117–121; *Krasnoe ili beloe,* 95–96; Timothy J. Colton, *Yeltsin: A Life* (New York, 2008), 198.

3. Colton, *Yeltsin,* 198; Evgenii Shaposhnikov, *Vybor. Zapiski glavnokomanduiushchego* (Moscow, 1993), 18–19; Stepankov and Lisov, *Kremlevskii zagovor,* 109, 123.

4. Valerii Boldin, *Krushenie p'edestala. Shtrikhi k portretu M. S. Gorbacheva* (Moscow, 1995), 19–20; Andrei Grachev, *Gorbachev. Chelovek, kotoryi khotel kak luchshe* (Moscow, 2001), 366ff.

5. Bonnell, Cooper, and Fredin, eds., *Russia at the Barricades,* 42–54, 318–321; Stepankov and Lisov, *Kremlevskii zagovor,* 134–135.

6. Stepankov and Lisov, *Kremlevskii zagovor,* 122–123, 133.

7. Ibid., 159–160.

8. Yeltsin, *The Struggle for Russia,* 43–45; Korzhakov, *Boris El'tsin,* 84.

9. *Soiuz mozhno bylo sokhranit'. Belaia kniga. Dokumenty i fakty o politike M. S. Gorbacheva po reformirovaniiu i sokhraneniiu mnogonatsional'nogo gosudarsta,* 2nd ed. (Moscow, 2007), 289; Anatolii Cherniaev, *Sovmestnyi iskhod. Dnevnik dvukh epokh, 1972–1991 gody* (Moscow, 2008), 941; Korzhakov, *Boris El'tsin,* 82; Colton, *Yeltsin,* 147–149, 308–314; Nasir Ghaemi, *A First-Rate Madness: Uncovering the Links Between Leadership and Mental Illness* (New York, 2011).

10. Bonnell, Cooper, and Fredin, eds., *Russia at the Barricades,* 172–175; Yeltsin, *The Struggle for Russia,* 77–78; Colton, *Yeltsin,* 200–201; Aleksandr Rutskoi, *Krovavaia osen'* (Moscow, 1995).

11. Yeltsin, *The Struggle for Russia,* 80, 83; Korzhakov, *Boris El'tsin,* 87–89.

12. Iain Elliot, "On-the-Spot Impressions," in Victoria E. Bonnell, Ann Cooper, and Gregory Fredin, eds., *Russia at the Barricades: Eyewitness Accounts of the August 1991 Coup* (Armonk, NY, 1994), 293–294; Yeltsin, *The Struggle for Russia,* 85–86; *Krasnoe ili beloe,* 99; Bonnell, Cooper, and Fredin, eds., *Russia*

at the Barricades, 95–96; Vadim Medvedev, *V komande Gorbacheva. Vzgliad iznutri* (Moscow, 1994), 196.

13. American Embassy, Moscow to Secretary of State, Washington, August 19, 1991, "Charge's Meeting with RSFSR Foreign Minister: Yeltsin's Next Steps and Letter for President Bush," Bush Presidential Library, Presidential Records, National Security Council, Nicholas Rostow Series: USSR (Coup), no. 2; "Yeltsin's Letter to President Bush," Bush Presidential Library, Presidential Records, National Security Council, Nicholas R. Burns Series, Subject Files: USSR Coup Attempt August 1990 [[sic]], no. 1.

14. Michael R. Beschloss and Strobe Talbott, *At the Highest Levels: The Inside Story of the End of the Cold War* (Boston, 1993), 430–431; Robert M. Gates, *From the Shadows: The Ultimate Insider's Story of Five Presidents and How They Won the Cold War* (New York, 1996), 522; "Reaction to Coup in the Soviet Union," August 19, 1991, White House Travel: Air Force One Channel, C-SPAN Video Library, www.c-spanvideo.org/program/20711-1.

15. Undated letter from Vice President Yanaev to President Bush, Unofficial Translation, Bush Presidential Library, Presidential Records, National Security Council, Nicholas R. Burns Series, Subject Files: USSR Coup Attempt August 1990 [[sic]], no. 1; Memo from Ed A. Hewett, "Meeting between Ambassador Viktor Komplektov and Robert Gates," Bush Presidential-Library, Presidential Records, National Security Council, Nicholas R. Burns Series, Subject Files: USSR Coup Attempt August 1990 [[sic]], no. 1; Gates, *From the Shadows,* 522.

16. Gates, *From the Shadows,* 521–522; Minutes of the Deputies Committee Meeting, August 19, 1991, Bush Presidential Library, Presidential Records, National Security Council, Deputies Committee Files, NSC/DC 300, 301; Beschloss and Talbott, *At the Highest Levels,* 432.

17. Gates, *From the Shadows,* 523; "Statement on the Attempted Coup in the Soviet Union," August 19, 1991, Bush Presidential Library, Public Papers, http://bushlibrary.tamu.edu/research/public_papers.php?id=3316&year=1991&month=8.

18. George Bush and Brent Scowcroft, *A World Transformed* (New York, 1998), 523.

19. Brent Scowcroft, "Memorandum for the President, Subject: Phone Call to President Boris Yeltsin," Bush Presidential Library, Presidential Records, National Security Council, Nicholas R. Burns Series, Subject Files: USSR Coup Attempt, August 1990 [[sic]], no. 2; "Phone Call to Boris Yeltsin: Suggested Talking Points," Bush Presidential Library, Presidential Records, National Security Council, Nicholas R. Burns and Ed A. Hewett Series, USSR Chronological Files: August 1991, no. 1.

20. Bush and Scowcroft, *A World Transformed,* 527–528; "Telecon with President Boris Yeltsin of Republic of Russia, USSR," August 20, 1991, Bush Presidential Library, Memcons and Telcons, http://bushlibrary.tamu.edu

/research/pdfs/memcons_telcons/1991-08-19—Yeltsin.pdf; Beschloss and Talbott, *At the Highest Levels,* 433–434.

21. Yeltsin, *The Struggle for Russia,* 80, 83, 87.

22. Korzhakov, *Boris El'tsin,* 93–94; Theresa Sabonis-Chafee, "Reflections from the Barricades," in Victoria E. Bonnell, Ann Cooper, and Gregory Fredin, eds., *Russia at the Barricades: Eyewitness Accounts of the August 1991 Coup* (Armonk, NY, 1994), 242–245.

CHAPTER 6

1. Alfred Kokh and Petr Aven, "Andrei Kozyrev: nastoiashchii kamikadze," *Forbes* (Russian edition), September 28, 2011, www.forbes.ru/ekonomika /lyudi/74501-andrei-kozyrev-nastoyashchii-kamikadze; American Consul, Strasbourg to Secretary of State, Washington, "Kozyrev in Strasbourg: Stand for Election or Stand Aside," August 22, 1991, Bush Presidential Library, Presidential Records, National Security Council, White House Situation Room Files: USSR Part 4 of 4 Moscow Coup Attempt (1991), no. 5.

2. Andrei Kozyrev, "Stand by Us," *Washington Post,* August 21, 1991.

3. "The President's Press Conference," August 20, 1991, Bush Presidential Library, Public Papers, http://bushlibrary.tamu.edu/research/public_papers. php?id=3317&year=1991&month=8; Michael R. Beschloss and Strobe Talbott, *At the Highest Levels: The Inside Story of the End of the Cold War* (Boston, 1993), 433–434.

4. James A. Baker with Thomas M. DeFrank, *The Politics of Diplomacy: Revolution, War and Peace, 1989–1992* (New York, 1995), 520–521.

5. Memo from McKenney Russell, USIA to Robert Gates, White House, "USIA Media Coverage of Gorbachev Ouster," August 19, 1991; McKenney Russell to Robert Gates, White House, "USIA on Day Two After the Coup," August 21, 1991; McKenney Russell to Robert Gates, White House, "The Coup's Third and Last Day on USIA Media," August 22, 1991, Bush Presidential Library, Presidential Records, National Security Council, Nancy Berg Dyke Series, Subject Files: Soviet Union—Coup—August 1991, Public Diplomacy.

6. Baker, *The Politics of Diplomacy,* 521.

7. Ibid., 160–162.

8. Valentin Stepankov and Evgenii Lisov, *Kremlevskii zagovor. Versiia sledstviia* (Moscow, 1992), 162–168.

9. Evgenii Shaposhnikov, *Vybor. Zapiski glavnokomanduiushchego* (Moscow, 1993), 19, 39.

10. Valerii Kucher, "A Russian Reporter Remembers," in Victoria E. Bonnell, Ann Cooper, and Gregory Fredin, eds., *Russia at the Barricades: Eyewitness Accounts of the August 1991 Coup* (Armonk, NY, 1994), 334; Iain Elliot, "On-the-Spot Impressions," in Victoria E. Bonnell, Ann Cooper, and Gregory Fredin, eds., *Russia at the Barricades: Eyewitness Accounts of*

the August 1991 Coup (Armonk, NY, 1994), 291; Theresa Sabonis-Chafee, "Reflections from the Barricades," in Victoria E. Bonnell, Ann Cooper, and Gregory Fredin, eds., *Russia at the Barricades: Eyewitness Accounts of the August 1991 Coup* (Armonk, NY, 1994), 244–245; Stepankov and Lisov, *Kremlevskii zagovor,* 178.

11. Aleksandr Korzhakov, *Boris El'tsin: ot rassveta do zakata* (Moscow, 1997), 93–94; Michael Hetzer, "Death on the Streets," in Victoria E. Bonnell, Ann Cooper, and Gregory Fredin, eds., *Russia at the Barricades: Eyewitness Accounts of the August 1991 Coup* (Armonk, NY, 1994), 253–254.

12. *Krasnoe ili beloe? Drama avgusta-91. Fakty. Gipotezy. Stolknovenie mnenii* (Moscow, 1992), 113–130; John B. Dunlop, "The August 1991 Coup and Its Impact on Soviet Politics," *Journal of Cold War Studies* 5, no. 1 (2003): 94–127, here 110–111.

13. Stepankov and Lisov, *Kremlevskii zagovor,* 180–184.

14. Ibid., 270–279; Natalia Gevorkian, Natalia Timakova, and Andrei Kolesnikov, *Ot pervogo litsa. Razgovory s Vladimirom Putinym* (Moscow, 2000), chapter "Demokrat"; Masha Gessen, *The Man Without a Face: The Unlikely Rise of Vladimir Putin* (New York, 2013), 108–118.

15. Dunlop, "The August 1991 Coup and Its Impact on Soviet Politics," 111; Stepankov and Lisov, *Kremlevskii zagovor,* 186–187; *Krasnoe ili beloe,* 251.

16. Korzhakov, *Boris El'tsin,* 93–96, 113; Boris Yeltsin, *The Struggle for Russia,* trans. Catherine A. Fitzpatrick (New York, 1994), 93.

17. Beschloss and Talbott, *At the Highest Levels,* 434–435; George Bush and Brent Scowcroft, *A World Transformed* (New York, 1998), 528–530; American Embassy to Secretary of State, "USSR State of Emergency: Situation Report, no. 21, 08:00 [[a.m.]] local, August 21," Bush Presidential Library, Presidential Records, National Security Council, White House Situation Room Files: USSR Part 3 of 4 Moscow Coup Attempt (1991), no. 11.

18. Seymour M. Hersh, "The Wild East," *Atlantic Monthly,* June 1994.

19. "Telecon with President Boris Yeltsin of the Russian Federation," August 21, 1991, Bush Presidential Library, Memcons and Telcons, http://bushlibrary. tamu.edu/research/pdfs/memcons_telcons/1991-08-21--Yeltsin%20[[1]].pdf.

20. Baker, *The Politics of Diplomacy,* 522; Shaposhnikov, *Vybor,* 47–50; "Telecon with President Boris Yeltsin of the Russian Federation," August 21, 1991, Bush Presidential Library, Memcons and Telcons, http://bushlibrary. tamu.edu/research/pdfs/memcons_telcons/1991-08-21--Yeltsin%20[[1]].pdf; "Assorted JAB Notes from Events Related to Attempted Coup in USSR, 8/12–8/22," James A. Baker Papers, box 110, folder 6.

21. Dunlop, "The August 1991 Coup and Its Impact on Soviet Politics," 111; Stepankov and Lisov, *Kremlevskii zagovor,* 186–187; *Krasnoe ili beloe,* 251.

22. Mikhail Gorbachev, *Memoirs* (New York, 1995), 632–640; Anatolii Cherniaev, *Sovmestnyi iskhod. Dnevnik dvukh èpokh, 1972–1991 gody* (Moscow,

2008), 982–983; Stepankov and Lisov, *Kremlevskii zagovor*, 205–207; *Krasnoe i beloe*, 141–142; Dunlop, "The August 1991 Coup and Its Impact on Soviet Politics."

23. Bush and Scowcroft, *A World Transformed*, 531–532; "Telecon with President Mikhail Gorbachev of the USSR," August 21, 2011, Bush Presidential Library, Memcons and Telcons, http://bushlibrary.tamu.edu/research/pdfs /memcons_telcons/1991-08-21—Gorbachev.pdf; Cherniaev, *Sovmestnyi iskhod*, 983; "Exchange with Reporters in Kennebunkport, Maine, on the Attempted Coup in the Soviet Union," August 21, 1991, Bush Presidential Library, Public Papers, http://bushlibrary.tamu.edu/research/public_papers. php?id=3322&year=1991&month=8.

24. Yeltsin, *The Struggle for Russia*, 101; Pavel Palazhchenko, *My Years with Gorbachev and Shevardnadze: The Memoir of a Soviet Interpreter* (University Park, PA, 1997), 311–312; Cherniaev, *Sovmestnyi iskhod*, 983.

25. Stepankov and Lisov, *Kremlevskii zagovor*, 208–210, 213–217, 297.

CHAPTER 7

1. "Press-konferentsiia prezidenta SSSR," *Pravda*, August 23, 1991.

2. "Vozvrashchenie prezidenta SSSR," *Pravda*, August 23, 1991.

3. Anatolii Cherniaev, *Sovmestnyi iskhod. Dnevnik dvukh ėpokh, 1972–1991 gody* (Moscow, 2008), 984; *Lenin's Tomb: The Last Days of the Soviet Empire* (New York, 1994), 494–495; Michael Dobbs, *Down with Big Brother: The Fall of the Soviet Empire* (New York, 1997), 411.

4. *V Politbiuro TsK KPSS po zapisiam Anatoliia Cherniaeva, Vadima Medvedeva, Georgiia Shakhnazarova (1985–1991)* (Moscow, 2000), 497–498; Vadim Medvedev, *V komande Gorbacheva. Vzgliad iznutri* (Moscow, 1994), 199–200; Mikhail Gorbachev, *Memoirs* (New York, 1995), 641.

5. "Press-konferentsiia prezidenta SSSR," *Pravda*, August 23, 1991; *V Politbiuro TsK KPSS*, 497–498.

6. "Rossiiskii trikolor, kak simvol avgusta 1991 g.," Radio Svoboda, August 21, 2009, www.svobodanews.ru/content/article/1804909.html; Boris Yeltsin, *The Struggle for Russia*, trans. Catherine A. Fitzpatrick (New York, 1994), 106–109.

7. *Izvestiia*, August 23, 1991; *Raspad SSSR: Dokumenty i fakty (1986–1992 gg.)*, vol. 1, *Normativnye akty. Ofitsial'nye soobshcheniia*, ed. S. M. Shakhrai (Moscow, 2009), 841–843, 847–849; Medvedev, *V komande Gorbacheva*, 199–200.

8. Yeltsin, *The Struggle for Russia*, 106–109; Korzhakov, *Boris El'tsin*, 115–117; Evgenii Shaposhnikov, *Vybor. Zapiski glavnokomanduiushchego* (Moscow, 1993), 62–65.

9. Yeltsin, *The Struggle for Russia*, 106.

10. "Opros. 'Ulitsa' o M. Gorbacheve," *Argumenty i fakty,* no. 33 (August 23) 1991, 6; Gorbachev, *Memoirs,* 642.

11. Gorbachev, *Memoirs,* 644–645.

12. *V Politbiuro TsK KPSS,* 697–698.

13. Collins to the Secretary of State, "Communist Monuments Coming Down. Lenin May Be Evicted from Mausoleum," August 26, 1991, 2, Bush Presidential Library, Presidential Records, National Security Council, White House Situation Room Files: USSR Part 4 of 4 Moscow Coup Attempt (1991), no. 9.

14. Shaposhnikov, *Vybor,* 63.

15. Korzhakov, *Boris El'tsin,* 116–117, Evgenii Sevostianov, "V avguste 91-go," www.savostyanov.ru/index_6.html; Dobbs, *Down with Big Brother,* 411–417; Yeltsin, *Struggle for Russia,* 100; Remnick, *Lenin's Tomb,* 493–494.

16. "Gorbachev's Speech to Russians: A Major Regrouping of Political Forces," *New York Times,* 6–7; Remnick, *Lenin's Tomb,* 494–495.

17. "Gorbachev's Speech to Russians," 7; Gorbachev, *Memoirs,* 644; Petr Aven and Al'fred Kokh, "El'tsin sluzhil nam!," interview with Gennadii Burbulis, *Forbes* (Russian edition), July 22, 2010, www.forbes.ru/node/53407/print.

18. Aven and Kokh, "El'tsin sluzhil nam!"; Gorbachev, *Memoirs,* 644.

19. Michael R. Beschloss and Strobe Talbott, *At the Highest Levels: The Inside Story of the End of the Cold War* (Boston, 1993), 438.

20. Memorandum of telephone conversation with Boris Yeltsin, August 21, 1991, Bush Presidential Library, Memcons and Telcons, http://bushlibrary .tamu.edu/research/pdfs/memcons_telcons/1991-08-21—Yeltsin%20[2].pdf.

21. American Counsul to the Secretary of State, "Kozyrev in Strasbourg: Stand for Election or Stand Aside," August 21, 1991.

22. *Krasnoe ili beloe? Drama avgusta-91. Fakty, gipotezy, stolknoveniia mnenii* (Moscow, 1992), 116–117.

23. *Raspad SSSR,* 853–856; *V Politbiuro TsK KPSS,* 699–701; Medvedev, *V komande Gorbacheva,* 201–202; Gorbachev, *Memoirs,* 643–645.

24. Cherniaev, *Sovmestnyi iskhod,* 967–968; "TsK KPSS. Ob orientirovke dlia partiinykh komitetov po zakonu RSFSR 'O militsii, 4 iiunia 1991,' RGANI, fond 89, op. 11, no. 90; "Informatsiia o deiatel'nosti partiinykh organizatsii Kompartii RSFSR v usloviiakh deistviia Ukaza Prezidenta RSFSR ot 20 iiulia 1991 g.," RGANI, fond 89, op. 23, no. 8.

25. Valentin Stepankov and Evgenii Lisov, *Kremlevskii zagovor. Versiia sledstviia* (Moscow, 1992), 236–254; "Pugo, Boris Karlovich," http://www. biografija.ru/show_bio.aspx?id=109919.

26. Medvedev, *V komande Gorbacheva,* 198; A. Kutsenko, *Marshaly i admiraly flota Sovetskogo Soiuza* (Kyiv, 2007), 18–21.

27. "Soviet Turmoil. New Suicide: Budget Director," *New York Times,* August 27, 1991; Dobbs, *Down with Big Brother,* 420–421; Stepankov and

Lisov, *Kremlevskii zagovor,* 233–236; *Raspad SSSR,* 85–57; Stephen Kotkin, *Armageddon Averted: The Soviet Collapse, 1970–2000* (Oxford, 2001), 113–117.

CHAPTER 8

1. Fedir Turchenko, *HKChP i proholoshennia nezalezhnosti Ukraïny: pohliad iz Zaporizhzhia* (Zaporizhia, 2011), 108–111.

2. Interview with John Stepanchuk in *Rozpad Radians'koho Soiuzu. Usna istoriia nezalezhnoï Ukraïny 1988–91, pt. 3, http://oralhistory.org.ua/ interview-ua/315/.*

3. Interview with Leonid Kravchuk in *Rozpad Radians'koho Soiuzu. Usna istoriia nezalezhnoï Ukraïny 1988–91,* tape 8, http://oralhistory.org.ua /interview-ua/510; Vasyl' Tuhluk, "Den', shcho zminyv khid istoriï," *Uriadovyi kur'ier,* August 23, 1991.

4. Sergei Rakhmanin, "Boris Sharikov: 'To' chto GKChP provalilsia ia pochuvstvoval, kogda uvidel press-konferentsiiu chlenov komiteta,'" *Zerkalo nedeli,* August 18, 2001.

5. Iurii Shapoval, "Iak HKChP-isty kraïnu z kryzy vyvodyly," *Dzerkalo tyzhnia,* August 19, 2001; Rakhmanin, "Boris Sharikov"; interview with Leonid Kravchuk in *Rozpad Radians'koho Soiuzu. Usna istoriia nezalezhnoï Ukraïny 1988–91,* tape 8, http://oralhistory.org.ua/interview-ua/510; Leonid Kravchuk, *Maiemo te, shcho maiemo. Spohady i rozdumy* (Kyiv, 2002), 94–98; interview with Valentin Varennikov in *Rozpad Radians'koho Soiuzu. Usna istoriia nezalezhnoï Ukraïny 1988–91,* tape 2, http://oralhistory.org.ua /interview-ua/401/.

6. Author's interview with Leonid Kravchuk, Kyiv, September 1, 2011; Kravchuk, *Maiemo te, shcho maiemo,* 99.

7. Dmytro Kyians'kyi, "Akademik. Vitse-prem'ier. Dyplomat," *Dzerkalo tyzhnia,* February 2, 2002; "Ievhen Marchuk: Iakby ia chysto shyzofrenichno zakhotiv zrobyty HKChP," *Ukraïns'ka pravda,* August 12, 2011, http://www .istpravda.com.ua/digest/2011/08/12/51759/view_comments/.

8. Interview with Heorhii Kriuchkov in *Rozpad Radians'koho Soiuzu. Usna istoriia nezalezhnoï Ukraïny 1988–91,* tape 4, http://oralhistory.org .ua/interview-ua/516/; "Iz shifrotelegrammy TsK Kompartii Ukrainy," in *Nezavisimost' Ukrainy: Khronika,* http://usenet.su/showthread.php/222481 -5-5.

9. Interview with Adam Martyniuk, *Rozpad Radians'koho Soiuzu. Usna istoriia nezalezhnoï Ukraïny 1988–91,* tape 4, http://oralhistory.org.ua /interview-ua/603; "Iz vystupleniia Predsedatelia Prezidiuma Verkhovnogo Soveta USSR L. M. Kravchuka po ukrainskomu televideniiu, 19 avgusta 1991 g.," in *Nezavisimost' Ukrainy: Khronika*; US Embassy in Moscow to Secretary of State, August 23, 1991, "Reaction in Ukraine to the Coup in Moscow," 2, Bush Presidential Library, Presidential Records, National Security Council,

White House Situation Room Files: USSR Part 4 of 4 Moscow Coup Attempt (1991), no. 5.

10. Programma *Vremia*, August 19, 1991, www.youtube.com/watch?v =HY5wf-ywETE; Roman Solchanyk, "Kravchuk and the Coup," *Ukrainian Weekly*, September 1, 1991, 2, 10.

11. Turchenko, *HKChP*, 9–54; Serhii Plokhy, *Ukraine and Russia: Representations of the Past* (Toronto, 2008), 165–181. For video clips of the Cossack march of 1990 and the Chervona Ruta music festival of 1991, see "SichCentr 7: Cossack Hogan at Festivals in Zaporozhye," YouTube video posted by SichCentr, July 22, 2009, http://youtu.be/Ex_cFOqEvoQ.

12. US Embassy in Moscow to Secretary of State, August 23, 1991, "Reaction in Ukraine to the Coup in Moscow," 3.

13. Masha Gessen, *The Man Without a Face: The Unlikely Rise of Vladimir Putin* (New York, 2013), 108–118.

14. Interview with Volodymyr Hryniov in *Rozpad Radians'koho Soiuzu. Usna istoriia nezalezhnoï Ukraïny 1988–91*, pt. 3, http://oralhistory.org.ua/ interview-ua/239/; US Embassy in Moscow to Secretary of State, August 23, 1991, "Reaction in Ukraine to the Coup in Moscow," 3.

15. "General Strike Planned by Democratic Groups," *Ukrainian Weekly*, August 25, 1991, 1, 13; Marta Kolomayets, "What the Coup Meant for Ukraine," *Ukrainian Weekly*, August 25, 1991, 1, 10; Solchanyk, "Kravchuk and the Coup," 10.

16. Boris Yeltsin, *The Struggle for Russia*, trans. Catherine A. Fitzpatrick (New York, 1994), 66; interview with Vlodymyr Filenko in *Rozpad Radians'koho Soiuzu. Usna istoriia nezalezhnoï Ukraïny 1988–91*, pt. 4, http://oralhistory.org.ua/interview-ua/438; interview with Ruslan Khasbulatov in *Rozpad Radians'koho Soiuzu. Usna istoriia nezalezhnoï Ukraïny 1988–91*, pts. 1–2; interview with Nikolai Bagrov in *Rozpad Radians'koho Soiuzu. Usna istoriia nezalezhnoï Ukraïny 1988–91*, pt. 3, http://oralhistory.org.ua/interview-ua/372; "Telecon with President Boris Yeltsin of the Russian Federation," August 21, 1991, Bush Presidential Library, Memcons and Telcons, http://bushlibrary.tamu.edu/research/ pdfs/memcons_telcons/1991-08-21--Yeltsin%20[[1]].pdf; Lapychak, "Kravchuk Criticized," 2.

17. Lapychak, "Kravchuk Criticized," 4; Solchanyk, "Kravchuk and the Coup," 10.

18. Evgenii Shaposhnikov, *Vybor. Zapiski glavnokomanduiushchego* (Moscow, 1993), 63–64.

19. "Soveshchanie s rukovoditeliami respublik," *Izvestiia*, August 24, 1991; *Soiuz mozhno bylo sokhranit'. Belaia kniga. Dokumenty i fakty o politike M. S. Gorbacheva po reformirovaniiu i sokhraneniiu mnogonatsional'nogo gosudarsta*, 2nd ed. (Moscow, 2007), 308–309.

20. *Soiuz mozhno bylo sokhranit'*, 309; author's interview with Leonid Kravchuk, September 1, 2011; "Gorbachev's Speech to Russians: A Major Regrouping of Political Forces," *New York Times*, August 21, 1991; Ruslan Kvatsiuk and Oksana Perevoznaia, "Vitol'd Fokin: liudi mogut vyiti na maidan," Gazeta.ua, February 4, 2009, http://www.inosmi.ru/ukraine/20090204/247198.html.

21. Vahtanh Kipiani and Volodomyr Fedoryn, "Shcherbitskii skazal: kakoi durak pridumal slovo perestroika?" *Ukraïns'ka pravda*, September 10, 2011, www.istpravda.com.ua/articles/2011/09/10/53558/view_print; Pylypchuk, "Pid chas HKChP u Kravchuka buly v zapasi shapky z chervonymy zirkamy i tryzubom," Gazeta.ua, August 19, 2011.

22. Solchanyk, "Kravchuk and the Coup"; interview with John Stepanchuk in *Rozpad Radians'koho Soiuzu. Usna istoriia nezalezhnoï Ukraïny 1988–91*, pt. 3, http://oralhistory.org.ua/interview-ua/315; Tuhluk, "Den', shcho zminyv khid istoriï."

23. Solchanyk, "Kravchuk and the Coup"; Chrystyna Lapychak, "Ukraine, Russia Sign Interim Bilateral Pact," *Ukrainian Weekly*, September 1, 1991, 9; Tuhluk, "Den', shcho zminyv khid istoriï"; interview with Volodymyr Yavorivsky in *Rozpad Radians'koho Soiuzu. Usna istoriia nezalezhnoï Ukraïny 1988–91*, pt. 5, http://oralhistory.org.ua/interview-ua/382/.

24. "The Question for Mr. President from Narodna Rada (the 'People's Council')"; George Bush to Ed Hewett (Aboard AF I), August 1, 1991; George Bush to Lukianenko (draft letter, no date), Bush Presidential Library, Presidential Records, National Security Council, Nicholas R. Burns and Ed A. Hewett Series, USSR Chronological Files: August 1991, no. 2.

25. Interview with Levko Lukianenko in *Rozpad Radians'koho Soiuzu. Usna istoriia nezalezhnoï Ukraïny 1988–91*, pt. 4, http://oralhistory.org.ua/interview-ua/541.

26. Interview with Volodymyr Hryniov in *Rozpad Radians'koho Soiuzu. Usna istoriia nezalezhnoï Ukraïny 1988–91*, pt. 3, http://oralhistory.org.ua/interview-ua/239/>; interview with Volodymyr Yavorivsky in *Rozpad Radians'koho Soiuzu. Usna istoriia nezalezhnoï Ukraïny 1988–91*, pt. 5, http://oralhistory.org.ua/interview-ua/382/.

27. Lapychak, "Ukraine, Russia Sign Interim Bilateral Pact," 9; Tuhluk, "Den', shcho zminyv khid istoriï."

28. Interview with Leonid Kravchuk in *Rozpad Radians'koho Soiuzu. Usna istoriia nezalezhnoï Ukraïny 1988–91*, tape 8, http://oralhistory.org.ua/interview-ua/510; Kravchuk, *Maiemo te, shcho maiemo*, 101.

29. Interview with Bohdan Havrylyshyn in *Rozpad Radians'koho Soiuzu. Usna istoriia nezalezhnoï Ukraïny 1988–91*, tape 3, http://oralhistory.org.ua/interview-ua/189; interview with Dmytro Pavlychko, ibid., tape 4, http://oralhistory.org.ua/interview-ua/497/.

30. Akt proholoshennia nezalezhnosti Ukraïny, official website of the Ukrainian Parliament, http://gska2.rada.gov.ua/site/postanova/akt_nz.htm.

31. Kravchuk, *Maiemo te, shcho maiemo,* 102–103; interview with John Stepanchuk in *Rozpad Radians'koho Soiuzu. Usna istoriia nezalezhnoï Ukraïny 1988–91,* pt. 3.

32. Turchenko, *HKChP,* 111–112; Kravchuk, *Maiemo te, shcho maiemo,* 102–104.

CHAPTER 9

1. Vera Kuznetsova, "Ukraina," *Nezavisimaia gazeta,* August 29, 1991.

2. "Soiuz raspadaetsia pod perebranku deputatov," *Izvestiia,* August 28, 1991; S. Chugaev and V. Shcheporkin, "Pravitel'stvo uvoleno, parlament prodolzhaet rabotat'," *Izvestiia,* August 29, 1991; Roman Solchanyk, "Ukraine and Russia: Relations Before and After the Failed Coup," *Ukrainian Weekly,* September 29, 1991, 9.

3. "Gorbachev's Speech to the Russians," *New York Times,* August 24, 1991; Roman Szporluk, *Russia, Ukraine, and the Breakup of the Soviet Union* (Stanford, CA, 2000), 183–228.

4. *Soiuz mozhno bylo sokhranit". Belaia kniga. Dokumenty i fakty o politike M. S. Gorbacheva po reformirovaniiu i sokhraneniiu mnogonatsional"nogo gosudarsta,* 2nd ed. (Moscow, 2007), 310–317.

5. Ibid., 317–319.

6. Jack Matlock, *Autopsy on an Empire: The American Ambassador's Account of the Collapse of the Soviet Union* (New York, 1994), 451.

7. Author's interview with Yurii Shcherbak, Rome, June 19, 2012; Bill Keller, "A Collapsing Empire," *New York Times,* August 27, 1991; Francis X. Clines, "A New Vote Promised. President, in Address to Parliament, Accepts Blame for Coup," *New York Times,* August 27, 1991; Solchanyk, "Ukraine and Russia," 9; *Soiuz mozhno bylo sokhranit',* 314–315.

8. Pavel Voshchanov, "Kak ia ob"iavlial voinu Ukraine," *Novaia gazeta,* October 23, 2003.

9. "Press sekretar prezidenta ofitsial'no zaiavliaet," *Rossiiskaia gazeta,* August 27, 1991; Voshchanov, "Kak ia ob"iavlial voinu Ukraine."

10. L. Barrington, "Russian Speakers in Ukraine and Kazakhstan: 'Nationality,' 'Population' or Neither?" *Post-Soviet Affairs* 17, no. 2 (2001): 129–158; A. M. Khazanov, *After the USSR: Ethnicity, Nationalism and Policies in the Commonwealth of Independent States* (Madison, WI, 1995); N. J. Melvin, "The Russians: Diaspora and the End of Empire," in *Nations Abroad: Diaspora Politics and International Relations in the Former Soviet Union,* ed. C. King and N. Melvin (Boulder, CO, 1998): 27–58; Taras Kuzio, "Russians and Russophones in the Former USSR and Serbs in Yugoslavia: A Comparative

Study of Passivity and Mobilization," *East European Perspectives* 5, no. 13 (June 25, 2003).

11. Solchanyk, "Ukraine and Russia," 9; *Soiuz mozhno bylo sokhranit'*, 315–316.

12. Iu. Afanas'ev, L. Batkin, V. Bibler, E. Bonner, Iu. Burtin, Viach. Ivanov, and L. Timofeev, "Privetstvuem razval 'imperii,'" dated August 28, 1991, in *Nezavisimaia gazeta*, September 3, 1991. Cf. *Soiuz mozhno bylo sokhranit'*, 285–288.

13. Vitalii Portnikov, "Ukraina ne imeet pretenzii k Rosii. Reaktsiia na zaiavlenie press-sekretaria prezidenta RSFSR," *Nezavisimaia gazeta*, August 29, 1991; Solchanyk, "Ukraine and Russia," 9.

14. Voshchanov, "Kak ia ob"iavlial voinu Ukraine"; Vitalii Chervonenko, "Nezavisimost': kak èto bylo" (interview with Yurii Shcherbak), Vovremia.info, August 24, 2007, http://vovremya.info/art/1187882352.html; author's interview with Yurii Shcherbak, Rome, June 19, 2012.

15. S. Tsekora, "Rossiia i Ukraina dogovorilis'," *Izvestiia*, August 29, 1991.

16. Author's interview with Yurii Shcherbak, Rome, June 19, 2012; Nadezhda Kalinina, "Sergei Stankevich: 'net nikakikh osnovanii schitat' putch operetkoi," *Russkii kur'er*, August 14, 2006.

17. Tsekora, "Rossiia i Ukraina dogovorilis'"; Kalinina, "Sergei Stankevich: 'Net nikakikh osnovanii schitat' putch operetkoi"; Solchanyk, "Ukraine and Russia," 11.

18. *Kazakhstanskaia pravda*, August 30, 1991; V. Drozdov, "Kazakhstan i Rossiia: soglasie podtverzhdeno," *Izvestiia*, August 30, 1991.

19. Oleg Moroz, "Za riumkoi kliuchevye voprosy ne reshalis'" (interview with Yegor Gaidar), *Newsland*, May 2, 2011, www.newsland.ru/news/detail/id/690529.

20. Pavel Fel'gengauer, "Novaia forma voenno-ekonomicheskogo soiza '14+1' gde 1 eto Rossiia," *Nezavisimaia gazeta*, August 29, 1991; Liana Minasian, "Tsentr umer. Da zdravstvuet tsentr," *Nezavisimaia gazeta*, August 29, 1991; Aleksandr Gagua, "My pereotsenivaem nashikh partnerov," *Nezavisimaia gazeta*, August 29, 1991; Vasilii Seliunin, "Esli raspad neizbezhen, ego nado khorosho organizovat'," *Izvestiia*, August 29, 1991; O. G. Rumiantsev, "Ne zaboltat' by pobedu," *Izvestiia*, August 30, 1991.

21. I. Litvinova, "Boris El'tsin pribyl v Latviiu. V Rige otkryto pervoe posol'stvo," *Izvestiia*, August 30, 1991; Aleksandr Korzhakov, *Boris El'tsin: ot rassveta do zakata* (Moscow, 1997), 123–124.

22. *Soiuz mozhno bylo sokhranit'*, 315; Vadim Medvedev, *V komande Gorbacheva. Vzgliad iznutri* (Moscow, 1994), 202; Serge Schmemann, "Plea for Survival," *New York Times*, August 29, 1991; *Raspad SSSR: Dokumenty i fakty (1986–1992 gg.)*, vol. 1, *Normativnye akty. Ofitsial'nye soobshcheniia*, ed.

S. M. Shakhrai (Moscow, 2009), 863; Chugaev and Shcheporkin, "Pravitel'stvo uvoleno, parlament prodolzhaet rabotat'," 4.

23. Mikhail Gorbachev, *Memoirs* (New York, 1995), 649–651; Boris Yeltsin, *The Struggle for Russia*, trans. Catherine A. Fitzpatrick (New York, 1994), 108; *Soiuz mozhno bylo sokhranit'*, 317–319.

24. Medvedev, *V komande Gorbacheva*, 205.

25. O. G. Rumiantsev, ed., *Iz istorii sozdaniia Konstitutsii Rossiiskoi Federatsii. Konstitutsionnaia komissiia. Stenogrammy, materialy, dokumenty (1990–1993) v 6-ti tomakh*, vol. 2, *1991* (Moscow, 2008), 814–815; Yeltsin, *The Struggle for Russia*, 109; cf. Gorbachev, *Memoirs*, 647–651.

26. *Raspad SSSR*, 916–920; Yeltsin, *The Struggle for Russia*, 109; "Blitsinterviu. Ter-Petrosian, predsedatel' Verkhovnogo Soveta Armenii," *Argumenty i fakty*, August 29, 1991.

27. *Raspad SSSR*, 920–921; Korzhakov, *Boris El'tsin*, 118–119, 125.

28. Bob Strauss to Secretary of State, "My Meeting with Boris Yeltsin," August 24, 1991, 1–3, Bush Presidential Library, Presidential Records, National Security Council, White House Situation Room Files: USSR Part 4 of 4 Moscow Coup Attempt (1991), no. 6.

CHAPTER 10

1. George Bush and Brent Scowcroft, *A World Transformed* (New York, 1998), 539.

2. Ibid.; Joe Hyams, *Flight of the Avenger: George Bush at War* (New York, 1991); Webster Griffin Tarpley and Anton Chaitkin, *George Bush: An Unauthorized Biography* (Joshua Tree, CA, 2004), 101–114.

3. Anatol Lieven, *The Baltic Revolution: Estonia, Latvia, Lithuania and the Path to Independence* (New Haven, CT, 1994), 82–85, 204–254, 374–384.

4. Author's interview with Nicholas Burns, Harvard University, June 15, 2012.

5. Secstate to Amembassy Bucharest, March 22, 1991, Subject: CSCE: Handling Moldova in CSCE, Bush Presidential Library, Presidential Records, National Security Council, Nicholas R. Burns and Ed A. Hewett Series, Russia Subject Files: 4.3.0—US Relations with Russia, Policy on the Debate over the Union; Nicholas Burns to Ed Hewett, "Response to the Soviet Embassy on the USSR Borders," April 1, 1991, ibid.; George Bush to Mikhail Gorbachev, draft of August 27, 1991, Bush Presidential Library, Presidential Records, National Security Council, Nicholas R. Burns and Ed A. Hewett Series, USSR Chronological Files: August 1991, no. 1.

6. James A. Baker with Thomas M. DeFrank, *The Politics of Diplomacy: Revolution, War and Peace 1989–1992* (New York, 1995), 238; address by Jack Matlock at the Davis Center, Harvard University, October 25, 2011.

7. George H. W. Bush to Mikhail Gorbachev, January 23, 1991, James A. Baker Papers, box 109, folder 9; Jack Matlock, *Autopsy on an Empire: The American Ambassador's Account of the Collapse of the Soviet Union* (New York, 1994), 469–473.

8. Edward W. Walker, *Dissolution: Sovereignty and the Breakup of the Soviet Union* (Lanham, MD, 2003), 55–178; *Raspad SSSR: Dokumenty i fakty (1986–1992 gg.)*, vol. 1, *Normativnye akty. Ofitsial'nye soobshcheniia*, ed. S. M. Shakhrai (Moscow, 2009), 265–635.

9. Author's interview with Thomas Simons, May 13, 2013; George H. W. Bush to Mikhail Gorbachev, January 23, 1991; Robert M. Gates, *From the Shadows: The Ultimate Insider's Story of Five Presidents and How they Won the Cold War* (New York, 1996), 528–529.

10. Bush and Scowcroft, *A World Transformed*, 207, 223; Olgerts Pavlovskis, Chairman of Joint Baltic American National Committee to President Bush, June 13, 1991, Bush Presidential Library, Presidential Records, White House Office of Records Management, Subject Files, General: Economic Summit, London, England, 7/15–17/91; Benjamin L. Cardin and 44 other members of the US Congress to President Bush, July 26, 1991, ibid.; letter from the leadership of the Commission on Security and Cooperation in Europe, signed by Senator Alfonse D'Amato and others, to President Bush, July 26, 1991, ibid.; "Points to Be Made for Meeting with President Boris Yeltsin" [[July 1991]], Bush Presidential Library, Presidential Records, National Security Council, Nicholas R. Burns Series, Subject Files: POTUS Trip to Moscow and Kiev, July 27–August 1, 1991, no. 1; "Points to Be Made for Meeting with Chairman Leonid Kravchuk" [[July 1991]], ibid., no. 3.

11. Bush and Scowcroft, *A World Transformed*, 533–534; Amembasy Moscow, to Secstate, Washington, August 25, 1991, Subject: Baltic Independence Initiative: Letter from Lithuanian President Landsbergis to the President, 1–2, r, Bush Presidential Library, Presidential Records, National Security Council, White House Situation Room Files: USSR Part 4 of 4 Moscow Coup Attempt (1991), no. 7; Amembasy Moscow, to Secstate, Washington, August 26, 1991, Subject: USSR Supreme Soviet Special Session Begins with Endless Procedural Wrangling, ibid., Situation Room Files: USSR Part 4 of 4 Moscow Coup Attempt (1991), no. 9.

12. Slade Gorton to George H. W. Bush, August 23, 1991, Bush Presidential Library, Presidential Records, White House Office of Records Management, Subject Files, General: Russia; Bush and Scowcroft, *A World Transformed*, 538–539.

13. Memorandum of telephone conversation, Bush and Vytautas Landsbergis, August 31, 1991, Bush Presidential Library, Memcons and Telcons, http://bushlibrary.tamu.edu/research/pdfs/memcons_telcons/1991-08-31 —Landsbergis.pdf; Bush and Arnold Ruutel, September 2, 1991, ibid., http://

bushlibrary.tamu.edu/research/pdfs/memcons_telcons/1991-09-02—Ruute l.pdf; Bush and Anatolii Gorbunovs, September 2, 199, ibid., 97804650569 65-text.indd 437 1/7/14 9:39 AM http://bushlibrary.tamu.edu/research/pdfs /memcons_telcons/1991-09-02—Gorbunovs.pdf.; George Bush to Vytautas Landsbergis, August 31, 1991, Bush Presidential Library, Presidential Records, National Security Council, Jane Hall Series, Soviet Union, 1991; Bush and Scowcroft, *A World Transformed*, 539.

14. Bush and Scowcroft, *A World Transformed*, 540; Baker, *The Politics of Diplomacy*, 526.

15. Bush and Scowcroft, *A World Transformed*, 540–541; Michael R. Beschloss and Strobe Talbott, *At the Highest Levels: The Inside Story of the End of the Cold War* (Boston, 1993), 441, 444–445.

16. Bush and Scowcroft, *A World Transformed*, 541–542.

17. Baker, *The Politics of Diplomacy*, 624–636; Bush and Scowcroft, *A World Transformed*, 541–542; Dick Cheney with Liz Cheney, *In My Time: A Personal and Political Memoir* (New York, 2011), 231–232.

18. Bush and Scowcroft, *A World Transformed*, 541–542.

19. Baker, *The Politics of Diplomacy*, 526–527; Gates, *From the Shadows*, 85–96; Mikhail Gorbachev, *Memoirs* (New York, 1995), 661–662; Vladislav M. Zubok, *A Failed Empire: The Soviet Union in the Cold War from Stalin to Gorbachev* (Chapel Hill, NC, 2007), 254–264; Anatoly Adamishin and Richard Schifter, *Human Rights, Perestroika and the End of the Cold War* (Washington, D.C., 2009).

20. Baker, *The Politics of Diplomacy*, 526–529; Boris Pankin, *The Last Hundred Days of the Soviet Union* (London, 1996), 115–122; JAB exchange of notes w/Strauss re: meetings w/Gorbachev/Yeltsin in Moscow 9/11/91, James A. Baker Papers, box 110, folder 7.

21. Pankin, *The Last Hundred Days*, 53, 71, 106; Zubok, *A Failed Empire*, 140; Eric Shiraev and Vladislav Zubok, *Anti-Americanism in Russia: From Stalin to Putin* (New York, 2000).

22. Pankin, *The Last Hundred Days*, 104–105, 113.

23. Baker, *The Politics of Diplomacy*, 526–539.

24. Baker, *The Politics of Diplomacy*, 532–533; Anatolii Cherniaev, *Sovmestnyi iskhod. Dnevnik dvukh épokh, 1972–1991 gody* (Moscow, 2008), 928.

25. Khristina Lew, "Ukrainians Demonstrate Across United States. 5000 rally Across from White House," *Ukrainian Weekly*, September 29, 1991, 1; Marta Kolomayets, "Delegation Representing Free Ukraine Arrives in US. Kravchuk Meets with Bush, Addresses UN Assembly," *Ukrainian Weekly*, October 6, 1991, 1.

26. "Meeting with Leonid Kravchuk, Ukrainian Supreme Soviet Chairman," September 25, 1991, Bush Presidential Library, Memcons and Telcons, http://bushlibrary.tamu.edu/research/pdfs/memcons_telcons

/1991-09-25—Kravchuk.pdf; "Meeting with Soviet Foreign Minister Boris Pankin During the UNGA," September 24, 1991, Bush Presidential Library, Memcons and Telcons, http://bush.tamu.edu/research/pdfs/memcons_telcons/1991-09-24—Pankin.pdf; Bush and Scowcroft, *A World Transformed*, 543; Marta Kolomayets, "Kravchuk Delegation in US Capital Emphasizes Ukraine's Independence," *Ukrainian Weekly*, October 6, 1991, 1; author's interview with Leonid Kravchuk, Kyiv, September 1, 2011; Anatolii Zlenko, *Dyplomatiia i polityka. Ukraïna v protsesi dynamichnykh heopolitychnykh zmin* (Kharkiv, 2003), 239–240.

27. Bush and Scowcroft, *A World Transformed*, 544–545; Telcon with secretary-general of NATO Manfred Woerner, September 27, 1991, Bush Presidential Library, Memcons and Telcons, http://bushlibrary.tamu.edu/research/pdfs/memcons_telcons/1991-09-27—Woerner.pdf.

28. "Address to the Nation on Reducing United States and Soviet Nuclear Weapons," September 27, 1991, Bush Presidential Library, Public Papers, http://bushlibrary.tamu.edu/research/public_papers.php?id=3438&year=1991&month=9; Telcon with Mikhail Gorbachev, president of the USSR, September 27, 1991, Bush Presidential Library, Memcons and Telcons, http://bushlibrary.tamu.edu/research/pdfs/memcons_telcons/1991-09-27—Gorbachev.pdf.

29. Bush and Scowcroft, *A World Transformed*, 544–545; Cherniaev, *Sovmestnyi iskhod*, 990; Pankin, *The Last Hundred Days*, 107; Bush and Scowcroft, *A World Transformed*, 547; "Telecon with Mikhail Gorbachev, President of the Union of Soviet Socialist Republics," October 5, 1991, Bush Presidential Library, Memcons and Telcons, http://bushlibrary.tamu.edu/research/pdfs/memcons_telcons/1991-10-05—Gorbachev.pdf .

30. Gates, *From the Shadows*, 530.

CHAPTER 11

1. Telecon with Boris Yeltsin, President of the Russian Republic," Bush Presidential Library, Memcons and Telcons, http://bushlibrary.tamu.edu/research/pdfs/memcons_telcons/1991-09-25--Yeltsin.pdf; author's interview with Nicholas Burns, Harvard University, June 15, 2012.

2. "Mirotvorcheskaia missiia El'tsina i Nazarbaeva zavershilas'. Podpisano piatistoronnee kommiunike," *Nezavisimaia gazeta*, September 25, 1991; Timothy J. Colton, *Yeltsin: A Life* (New York, 2008), 223; Anatolii Cherniaev, *Sovmestnyi iskhod. Dnevnik dvukh ėpokh, 1972–1991 gody* (Moscow, 2008), 997.

3. Colton, *Yeltsin*, 223; Petr Aven and Al'fred Kokh, "El'tsin sluzhil nam!," interview with Gennadii Burbulis, *Forbes* (Russian edition), July 22, 2010, http://www.forbes.ru/ekonomika/vlast/53407-eltsin-sluzhil-nam.

4. Yegor Gaidar, *Collapse of an Empire: Lessons for Modern Russia* (Washington, D.C., 2007), 228–229.

5. "Silaev protiv Silaeva," *Izvestiia,* September 25, 1991; "Beseda glavnogo redaktora Valentina Logunova s chlenom Gosudarstvennogo Soveta Mikhailom Poltoraninym," *Rossiiskaia gazeta,* September 26, 1991; "Silaev vyshel iz kabineta," *Moskovskie novosti,* September 29, 1991.

6. James A. Baker with Thomas M. deFrank, *The Politics of Diplomacy: Revolution, War and Peace, 1989–1992* (New York, 1995), 538–539; Sergei Stankevich, "Ia dumaiu El'tsin dolzhen prosto vybrat'," *Moskovskie novosti,* September 29, 1991.

7. John Dunlop, *The Rise of Russia and the Fall of the Soviet Empire* (Princeton, NJ, 1995), 261–464; *Soiuz mozhno bylo sokhranit'. Belaia kniga. Dokumenty i fakty o politike M. S. Gorbacheva po reformirovaniiu i sokhraneniiu mnogonatsional'nogo gosudarsta,* 2nd ed. (Moscow, 2007), 328; Aven and Kokh, "El'tsin sluzhil nam!"

8. Yegor Gaidar, *Dni porazhenii i pobed* (Moscow, 1997), 1–259; Vadim Medvedev, *V komande Gorbacheva. Vzgliad iznutri* (Moscow, 1994), 219.

9. Gaidar, *Dni porazhenii i pobed,* 253.

10. Ibid., 256–259, 261–264.

11. Aven and Kokh, "El'tsin sluzhil nam!"

12. Ibid.; Mikhail Gorbachev, *Poniat' perestroiku* (Moscow, 2006), 347.

13. Georgii Shakhnazarov, *Tsena svobody. Reformatsiia Gorbacheva glazami ego pomoshchnika* (Moscow, 1993), 281–282; *Soiuz mozhno bylo sokhranit',* 323–324.

14. Shakhnazarov, *Tsena svobody,* 284–285.

15. *Soiuz mozhno bylo sokhranit',* 327–328; "Prem'er ne soglasilsia s ekonomicheskoi politikoi SSSR," *Kurs,* December 15, 2011, http://www.kurs .ru/15/8946.

16. Cherniaev, *Sovmestnyi iskhod,* 992.

17. *Soiuz mozhno bylo sokhranit',* 323–324, 329.

18. Shakhnazarov, *Tsena svobody,* 287–289; Boris Yeltsin, "Zamechaniia po proektu Soiuznogo dogovora ot 25 oktiabria 1991 g.," Gorbachev Foundation Archive, fond 5, no. 3730.01.

19. Cherniaev, *Sovmestnyi iskhod,* 997; *Soiuz mozhno bylo sokhranit',* 332–333; Medvedev, *V komande Gorbacheva,* 217–218.

20. Cherniaev, *Sovmestnyi iskhod,* 997.

21. Ibid., 997; Boris Pankin, *The Last Hundred Days of the Soviet Union* (London, 1996), 244.

22. "Telecon; with Boris Yeltsin, President of the Republic of Russia," October 8, 1991, Bush Presidential Library, Memcons and Telcons, http://bush library.tamu.edu/research/pdfs/memcons_telcons/1991-10-08—Yeltsin.pdf.

23. Cherniaev, *Sovmestnyi iskhod,* 997, Medvedev, *V komande Gorbacheva,* 218; *Soiuz mozhno bylo sokhranit',* 330–353.

24. *Soiuz mozhno bylo sokhranit'*, 334, 353–354; Edward W. Walker, *Dissolution: Sovereignty and the Breakup of the Soviet Union* (Lanham, MD, 2003), 147; Dunlop, *The Rise of Russia*, 267.

25. Gaidar, *Dni porazhenii i pobed*, 279.

26. Ibid., 278–279; Aven and Kokh, "El'tsin sluzhil nam!"

27. Boris Yeltsin, *The Struggle for Russia*, trans. Catherine A. Fitzpatrick (New York, 1994), 124–126.

28. Aven and Kokh, "El'tsin sluzhil nam!"

29. *Soiuz mozhno bylo sokhranit'*, 353–354.

30. "Telecon with Boris Yeltsin, President of the Republic of Russia," October 25, 1991, Bush Presidential Library, Memcons and Telcons, http://bushlibrary.tamu.edu/research/pdfs/memcons_telcons/1991-10-25—Yeltsin.pdf.

31. Boris El'tsin, "Obrashchenie k narodam Rossii, k S''ezdu narodnykh deputatov Rossiiskoi Federatsii," *Rossiiskaia gazeta*, September 29, 1991.

32. "My boialis' shokovoi terapii, a poluchili shokovuiu khirurgiiu," *Izvestiia*, October 29, 1991; "Samyi populiarnyi prezident nakonets-to gotov k samym nepopuliarnym meram. Gruppu kamikadze vozglavit El'tsin," *Nezavisimaia gazeta*, October 29, 1991; "Rossiiskaia programma reform: reaktsiia v respublikakh neodnoznachna," *Izvestiia*, October 30, 1991.

CHAPTER 12

1. James A. Baker with Thomas M. DeFrank, *The Politics of Diplomacy: Revolution, War and Peace, 1989–1992* (New York, 1995), 515; Gregory Harms and Todd M. Ferry, *The Palestine-Israel Conflict: A Basic Introduction*, 2nd ed. (London, 2008), 141–158; "The Madrid Peace Conference," *Journal of Palestine Studies* 21, no. 2 (Winter 1992): 117–149.

2. "Charter of Paris for a New Europe," www.osce.org/mc/39516; Mary Elise Sarotte, *1989: The Struggle to Create Post–Cold War Europe* (Princeton, NJ, 2009).

3. George Bush and Brent Scowcroft, *A World Transformed* (New York, 1998), 407–410; Baker, *The Politics of Diplomacy*, 286–287, 316–317, 400–410; George Herring, *From Colony to Superpower: U.S. Foreign Relations Since 1776* (New York, 2008), 908–912.

4. Boris Pankin, *The Last Hundred Days of the Soviet Union* (London, 1996), 195–223; Memorandum of Conversation, Meeting with Emir of Bahrain, October 15, 1991, Bush Presidential Library, Memcons and Telcons, http://bushlibrary.tamu.edu/research/pdfs/memcons_telcons/1991-10-15--Isa%20[[2]].pdf; "Talking Points for Syria," September 19, 1991, 1, Bush Presidential Library, Presidential Records, National Security Files, Edmund J. Hull Series, Subject Files.

5. Bush and Scowcroft, *A World Transformed,* 410, 548; Wilson D. Miscamble, *From Roosevelt to Truman: Potsdam, Hiroshima and the Cold War* (Cambridge, 2007), 203–204.

6. Pankin, *The Last Hundred Days,* 230; "The President's Press Conference with President Gorbachev of the Soviet Union in Madrid, Spain," October 29, 1991, Bush Presidential Library, Public Papers, http://bushlibrary.tamu.edu /research/public_papers.php?id=3563&year=1991&month=10.

7. Anatolii Cherniaev, *Sovmestnyi iskhod. Dnevnik dvukh ėpokh, 1972–1991 gody* (Moscow, 2008), 995–996, 1004; Pankin, *The Last Hundred Days,* 230–232.

8. Mikhail Gorbachev, *Memoirs* (New York, 1995), 663; "Telcon with Prime Minister Felipe Gonzalez of Spain," August 19, 1991, Bush Presidential Library, Memcons and Telcons, http://bushlibrary.tamu.edu/research/pdfs/memcons _telcons/1991-08-19—Gonzalez.pdf.

9. Andrew Rosenthal, "Uncertainty on Gorbachev Gives New Twist to Meeting with Bush," *New York Times,* October 28, 1991; T. Kolesnichenko and V. Volkov, "Madridskii marafon," *Pravda,* October 29, 1991; Alan Cowell, "The Middle East Talks: Bush and Gorbachev in Spain: Let the Talks Begin," *New York Times,* October 30, 1991.

10. Luncheon Meeting with President Gorbachev, October 29, 1991, 12:30– 1:15 p.m., Bush Presidential Library, Memcons and Telcons, http://bushlibrary .tamu.edu/research/pdfs/memcons_telcons/1991-10-29--Gorbachev%20[[1]]. pdf; Pankin, *The Last Hundred Days,* 232.

11. Meeting with President Gorbachev of the USSR, October 29, 1991, 1:20– 2:45 p.m., Bush Presidential Library, Memcons and Telcons, http://bushlibrary. tamu.edu/research/pdfs/memcons_telcons/1991-10-29—Gorbachev%20 [2].pdf; Cherniaev, *Sovmestnyi iskhod,* 1004–8, 1012, 1016; *Soiuz mozhno bylo sokhranit'. Belaia kniga. Dokumenty i fakty o politike M. S. Gorbacheva po reformirovaniiu i sokhraneniiu mnogonatsional'nogo gosudarsta,* 2nd ed. (Moscow, 2007), 356–358; Gorbachev, *Memoirs,* 664–665.

12. Cherniaev, *Sovmestnyi iskhod,* 1008–9; Pavel Palazhchenko, *My Years with Gorbachev and Shevardnadze: The Memoir of a Soviet Interpreter* (University Park, PA, 1997), 339–341; Pankin, *The Last Hundred Days,* 234; Pankin, *The Last Hundred Days,* 232.

13. Amembassy Moscow to Secstate Washington DC, Subject: Clarification of Monday's Speech by Yeltsin, October 26, 1991, 1–7, Bush Presidential Library, Presidential Records, National Security Council, White House Situation Room Files: USSR Part 3 of 4 Moscow Coup Attempt (1991), no. 14.

14. Pankin, *The Last Hundred Days,* 224–235.

15. Middle East Peace Conference, 1988–1991, James A. Baker Papers, box 106, folder 7.

16. *Soiuz mozhno bylo sokhranit'*, 358–362; Pankin, *The Last Hundred Days*, 234; Gorbachev, *Memoirs*, 664–665; Cherniaev, *Sovmestnyi iskhod*, 1008–1009; Bush and Scowcroft, *A World Transformed*, 549–550.

17. Cherniaev, *Sovmestnyi iskhod*, 985, 1009–1014; *Soiuz mozhno bylo sokhranit'*, 362–365.

18. Cherniaev, *Sovmestnyi iskhod*, 1012; Palazhchenko, *My Years*, 339–344.

19. Cherniaev, *Sovmestnyi iskhod*, 1014–1016.

20. *Soiuz mozhno bylo sokhranit'*, 367–372; Pankin, *The Last Hundred Days*, 249.

21. Pankin, *The Last Hundred Days*, 236, 248–249; Baker, *The Politics of Diplomacy*, 559; *Soiuz mozhno bylo sokhranit'*, 365–372.

22. Cherniaev, *Sovmestnyi iskhod*, 1017–1018.

23. John B. Dunlop, *Russia Confronts Chechnya: Roots of a Separatist Conflict* (Cambridge, 1998), 1–84.

24. "Vsesoiuznaia perepis' naseleniia 1989 g. Natsional'nyi sostav po respublikam SSSR," *Demoskop Weekly*, http://demoscope.ru/weekly/ssp/sng_nac_89.php.

25. *Chechnia v plamene separatizma*, comp. A. Surkov (Saratov, 1997), 65.

26. Ibid., 62–66; Dunlop, *Russia Confronts Chechnya*, 100–115.

27. Dunlop, *Russia Confronts Chechnya*, 115–117.

28. *Chechnia v plameni separatizma*, 77–80; Dunlop, *Russia Confronts Chechnya*, 115–117, 121.

29. *Chechnia v plameni separatizma*, 73–74, 77.

30. Dunlop, *Russia Confronts Chechnya*, 117–120; *Raspad SSSR: Dokumenty i fakty (1986–1992 gg.)*, vol. 1, *Normativnye akty. Ofitsial"nye soobshcheniia*, ed. S. M. Shakhrai (Moscow, 2009), 965; Cherniaev, *Sovmestnyi iskhod*, 1018; *Chechnia v plameni separatizma*, 79, 81.

31. *Chechnia v plameni separatizma*, 82; Dunlop, *Russia Confronts Chechnya*, 119–120; Voshchanov, "Kak ia ob"iavlial voinu Ukraine."

32. Dunlop, *Russia Confronts Chechnya*, 118–119; Cherniaev, *Sovmestnyi iskhod*, 1018.

33. Cherniaev, *Sovmestnyi iskhod*, 101–198; Gorbachev, *Memoirs*, 688.

34. Georgii Shakhnazarov, *Tsena svobody. Reformatsiia Gorbacheva glazami ego pomoshchnika* (Moscow, 1993), 291–292, 299.

35. Ibid., 287–289, 565–567.

36. Ibid., 565–567; Cherniaev, *Sovmestnyi iskhod*, 1020.

37. Cherniaev, *Sovmestnyi iskhod*, 1021–1023; Vadim Medvedev, *V komande Gorbacheva. Vzgliad iznutri* (Moscow, 1994), 221; *Soiuz mozhno bylo sokhranit'*, 375–382; Pankin, *The Last Hundred Days*, 258; Edward W. Walker, *Dissolution: Sovereignty and the Breakup of the Soviet Union* (Lanham, MD, 2003), 149–150.

38. Palazhchenko, *My Years*, 433.

CHAPTER 13

1. Interview with Stanislaŭ Shushkevich, Davis Center, Harvard University, April 17, 2000; *Soiuz mozhno bylo sokhranit'. Belaia kniga. Dokumenty i fakty o politike M. S. Gorbacheva po reformirovaniiu i sokhraneniiu mnogonatsional'nogo gosudarsta*, 2nd ed. (Moscow, 2007), 384–393; Anatolii Cherniaev, *Sovmestnyi iskhod. Dnevnik dvukh ėpokh, 1972–1991 gody* (Moscow, 2008), 1026–1030.

2. Chrystyna Lapychak, "Parliament Votes to Boycott Union Structures, Passes Law on Ukrainian Citizenship," *Ukrainian Weekly*, October 13, 1991, 1–2.

3. Leonid Kravchuk, *Maiemo te, shcho maiemo. Spohady i rozdumy* (Kyiv, 2002), 110; Valentyn Chemerys, *Prezydent. Roman-ese* (Kyiv, 1994), 277.

4. Georgii Shakhnazarov, *Tsena svobody. Reformatsiia Gorbacheva glazami ego pomoshchnika* (Moscow, 1993), 560–561; Pavel Palazhchenko, *My Years with Gorbachev and Shevardnadze: The Memoir of a Soviet Interpreter* (University Park, PA, 1997), 341; George Bush and Brent Scowcroft, *A World Transformed* (New York, 1998), 550; Andrew Wilson, *Virtual Politics: Faking Democracy in the Post-Soviet World* (New Haven, CT, 2005), 1–32.

5. Palazhchenko, *My Years*, 341; Bush and Scowcroft, *A World Transformed*, 550.

6. Michael R. Beschloss and Strobe Talbott, *At the Highest Levels: The Inside Story of the End of the Cold War* (Boston, 1993), 448; Renee M. Lamis, *Realignment of Pennsylvania Politics since 1960: Two-party Competition in a Battleground State* (University Park, PA, 2009),119ff.

7. Beschloss and Talbott, *At the Highest Levels*, 448–449; Hank Brown to President Bush, September 16, 1991, and draft of Brent Scowcroft's response of December 1991, Bush Presidential Library, Presidential Records, National Security Council, Nicholas R. Burns Series, Chronological Files: December 1991, no. 1; "U.S. Senate Passes Resolution Urging Recognition of Ukraine," *Ukrainian Weekly*, December 1, 1991, 1, 14.

8. "It Would be Prudent, George," *Ukrainian Weekly*, November 24, 1991, 6; Myron B. Kuropas, "Bren and Harry: Two Peas in a Pod," *Ukrainian Weekly*, November 24, 1991, 7; Beschloss and Talbott, *At the Highest Levels*, 447–448.

9. James M. Goldgeier and Michael McFaul, *Power and Purpose: US Policy Toward Russia After the Cold War* (Washington, D.C., 2003), 47.

10. Roman Popadiuk, *The Leadership of George Bush: An Insider's View of the Forty-First President* (College Station, TX, 2009), 155–160.

11. James A. Baker with Thomas M. DeFrank, *The Politics of Diplomacy: Revolution, War and Peace, 1989–1992* (New York, 1995), 560–561; author's interview with Nicholas Burns, Harvard University, June 15, 2012; Jeffrey Smith, "U.S. Officials Split over Response to an Independent Ukraine," *Washington Post*, November 25, 1991.

12. Christopher Cox and other US congressmen to George H. W. Bush, November 26, 1991, 1–6, Bush Presidential Library, Presidential Records, National Security Council, Nicholas R. Burns Series, Chronological Files: December 1991, no. 1.

13. Baker, *The Politics of Diplomacy*, 560–561; "JAB Notes from 11/26/91 Conversation with POTUS (Recognition of Ukraine Independence)," James A. Baker Papers, box 110, folder 9.

14. "Draft Cable to USNATO for Nov 27 NAC," 1–5, Bush Presidential Library, Presidential Records, National Security Council, Nicholas R. Burns Series, Chronological Files: December 1991, no. 3.

15. R. Gordon Hoxie to Robert Gates, November 19, 1991, Bush Presidential Library, Presidential Records, National Security Council, Roman Popadiuk Series, Chronological Files: December 1991; Yaroslav Trofimov, "Vote Brings Wave of Recognition," *Ukrainian Weekly*, December 8, 1991, 3, 6.

16. Marta Kolomayets, "Ukrainian American Leaders Meet with President Bush on the Eve of Ukrainian Referendum," *Ukrainian Weekly*, December 1, 1991, 1, 3, 14; "Rukh Appeals to President Bush," *Ukrainian Weekly*, December 1, 1991, 14; William F. Miller, "Firmly Rooted in Two Lands," Cleveland.com, www.cleveland.com/heritage/index.ssf?/heritage/more/ukraine/ukraine2.html.

17. John R. Yang, "Bush Decides to Accelerate U.S. Recognition of Ukraine," *Washington Post*, November 28, 1991.

18. Ibid.; Baker, *The Politics of Diplomacy*, 561; Bush and Scowcroft, *A World Transformed*, 552; Robert M. Gates, *From the Shadows: The Ultimate Insider's Story of Five Presidents and How They Won the Cold War* (New York, 1996), 531.

19. Cherniaev, *Sovmestnyi iskhod*, 1028–1029.

20. Baker, *The Politics of Diplomacy*, 561; Palazhchenko, *My Years*, 347; Andrei Ostal'skii, "Sovetsko-amerikanskaia razmolvka iz-za ukrainskogo referendum," *Izvestiia*, November 29, 1991; S. Tsikora, "Ukraina: za den'' do vystradannoi voli," *Izvestiia*, November 29, 1991; Cherniaev, *Sovmestnyi iskhod*, 1028–1029.

21. Telcon with President Mikhail Gorbachev of the USSR, November 30, 1991, Bush Presidential Library, Memcons and Telcons, http://bushlibrary.tamu.edu/research/pdfs/memcons_telcons/1991-11-30—Gorbachev.pdf; Bush and Scowcroft, *A World Transformed*, 551–552; Cherniaev, *Sovmestnyi iskhod*, 1029.

22. *V Politbiuro TsK KPSS po zapisiam Anatoliia Cherniaeva, Vadima Medvedeva, Georgiia Shakhnazarova (1985–1991)* (Moscow, 2000), 730; *Raspad SSSR: Dokumenty i fakty (1986–1992 gg.)*, vol. 1, *Normativnye akty. Ofitsial'nye soobshcheniia*, ed. S. M. Shakhrai (Moscow, 2009), 997–998.

23. Cherniaev, *Sovmestnyi iskhod*, 1029.

24. Ibid., 1030.

25. Ibid., 1027–1028.

26. *Soiuz mozhno bylo sokhranit'*, 406, 411–412; Vadim Medvedev, *V komande Gorbacheva. Vzgliad iznutri* (Moscow, 1994), 223.

27. Kravchuk, *Maiemo te, shcho maiemo*, 110–111; Cherniaev, *Sovmestnyi iskhod*, 1027–1028.

CHAPTER 14

1. Leonid Kravchuk, *Maiemo te, shcho maiemo. Spohady i rozdumy* (Kyiv, 2002), 116–117; author's interview with Leonid Kravchuk, Kyiv, September 1, 2011.

2. "Kravchuk Leading, Chornovil Second in Presidential Race," *Ukrainian Weekly*, November 10, 1991, 1, 14; David Marples, "Support Runs High for Independence. Kravchuk Likely to Be Elected," *Ukrainian Weekly*, November 25, 1991, 1–2; Kravchuk, *Maiemo te, shcho maiemo*, 114–115.

3. Georgii Kasianov, *Ukraina 1997–2007. Ocherki noveishei istorii* (Kyiv, 2008), 36–37; information from Yurii Ratomsky, formerly a consultant for the Dnipropetrovsk regional Communist Party committee, December 27, 1991.

4. Interview with Volodymyr Hryniov in *Rozpad Radians'koho Soiuzu. Usna istoriia nezalezhnoï Ukraïny 1988–91*, pt. 3; Kravchuk, *Maiemo te, shcho maiemo*, 114.

5. Viacheslav Chornovil, "Avtobiohrafiia," *Rukh Press* (website), http://rukhpress.com.ua/002005/print.phtml; interview with Viacheslav Chornovil in *Rozpad Radians'koho Soiuzu. Usna istoriia nezalezhnoï Ukraïny 1988–91*, pt. 3, http://oralhistory.org.ua/interview-ua/648/; interview with Levko Lukianenko in *Rozpad Radians'koho Soiuzu. Usna istoriia nezalezhnoï Ukraïny 1988–91*, pt. 4, http://oralhistory.org.ua/interview-ua/541; Chrystyna Lapychak, "In Odessa: One Day on the Trail with Rukh Candidate Viacheslav Chornovil," *Ukrainian Weekly*, November 10, 1991, 1, 9–10.

6. Interview with Viacheslav Chornovil in *Rozpad Radians'koho Soiuzu. Usna istoriia nezalezhnoï Ukraïny 1988–91*, pt. 3, http://oralhistory.org.ua/interview-ua/648/; interview with Dmytro Pavlychko in *Rozpad Radians'koho Soiuzu. Usna istoriia nezalezhnoï Ukraïny 1988–91*, pt. 4; "Ukraine's Presidium Rejects Diaspora Vote on Referendum," *Ukrainian Weekly*, November 24, 1991, 3, http://oralhistory.org.ua/interview-ua/497/.

7. Oksana Zakydalsky, "Larysa Skoryk Speaks at Canadian Friends of Rukh Conference," *Ukrainian Weekly*, October 31, 1991, 1, 11.

8. Marples, "Support Runs High for Independence. Kravchuk Likely to Be Elected"; David Marples, "Kravchuk Leading, Chornovil Second in Presidential Race"; Kravchuk, *Maiemo te, shcho maiemo*, 117–118; Oxana Shevel, "Nationality in Ukraine: Some Rules of Engagement," *East European Politics and Societies* 16, no. 2 (Spring 2002): 386–413.

9. Interview with Mykola Bahrov in *Rozpad Radians'koho Soiuzu. Usna istoriia nezalezhnoï Ukraïny 1988–91*, tape 3, http://oralhistory.org.ua /interview-ua/372; Edward A. Allworth, *The Tatars of Crimea: Return to the Homeland* (Durham, NC, 1998).

10. Marples, "Kravchuk Leading, Chornovil Second in Presidential Race"; cf. interviews with Volodymyr Hryniov and Levko Lukianenko in *Rozpad Radians'koho Soiuzu. Usna istoriia nezalezhnoï Ukraïny 1988– 91*, http://oralhistory.org.ua/interview-ua/239, http://oralhistory.org.ua /interview-ua/541.

11. Zlenko, *Dyplomatiia i polityka*, 66–67; "News Briefs from Ukraine," *Ukrainian Weekly*, December 1, 1991, 2.

12. Interview with Marta Dyczok in *Rozpad Radians'koho Soiuzu. Usna istoriia nezalezhnoï Ukraïny 1988–91*, tape 3, http://oralhistory.org.ua/interview -ua/229/.

13. Kasianov, *Ukraina 1991–2007*, 37; information from Olena Plokhii, who lived in Dnipropetrovsk in the fall of 1991.

14. Anatolii Cherniaev, *Sovmestnyi iskhod. Dnevnik dvukh ėpokh, 1972–1991 gody* (Moscow, 2008), 993–995; "Bush Names Babyn Yar Delegation," *Ukrainian Weekly*, October 6, 1991, 2; Chrystyna Lapychak, "Ukraine Remembers Babyn Yar," *Ukrainian Weekly*, October 13, 1991, 1, 8; interview with Leonid Kravchuk in *Rozpad Radians'koho Soiuzu. Usna istoriia nezalezhnoï Ukraïny 1988–91*, tape 9, http://oralhistory.org.ua/interview-ua/510/.

15. Roman Solchanyk, "Centrifugal Movements in Ukraine and Independence," *Ukrainian Weekly*, November 24, 1991, 8–10; "Minorities Congress Decisively Supports Ukraine's Independence," *Ukrainian Weekly*, November 24, 1991, 1; Dominique Arel, "Language Politics in Independent Ukraine: Towards One or Two Languages?" *Nationalities Papers* 23, no. 3 (1995): 597–622.

16. "News Briefs from Ukraine," *Ukrainian Weekly*, December 1, 1991, 2.

17. Kostiantyn P. Morozov, *Above and Beyond: From Soviet General to Ukrainian State Builder* (Cambridge, MA, 2000), 1–7, 74–75; 133–152.

18. Author's interview with General Kostiantyn Morozov, Kyiv, September 6, 2011; Chrystyna Lapychak, "Deputies Draft Law on Military," *Ukrainian Weekly*, October 27, 1991, 1–2; "Brzezinski Notes Ukraine's Statement," *Ukrainian Weekly*, October 27, 1991, 2; Marples, "Support Runs High for Independence. Kravchuk Likely to Be Elected," *Ukrainian Weekly*, November 25, 1991, 2.

19. Morozov, *Above and Beyond*, 91–152; interview with Kostiantyn Morozov in *Rozpad Radians'koho Soiuzu. Usna istoriia nezalezhnoï Ukraïny 1988–91*, tape 6, http://oralhistory.org.ua/interview-ua/632; author's interview with General Kostiantyn Morozov, Kyiv, September 6, 2011; John Jaworsky, "Ukraine's Armed Forces and Military Policy," *Harvard Ukrainian Studies* 20

(1996): 223–247; Stephen D. Olynyk, "Ukraine as a Military Power," in *Ukraine: The Search for a National Identity*, ed. Sharon L. Wolchik and Volodymyr Zviglyanich (Lanham, MD, 2000), 69–94.

20. Chrystyna Lapychak, "Reflections on an Independent Ukraine," *Ukrainian Weekly*, December 8, 1991, 6.

21. Author's interview with Yurii Shcherbak, Rome, June 19, 2012.

22. Chrystyna Lapychak, "Independence: Over 90 Percent Vote in Referendum: Kravchuk Elected President of Ukraine," *Ukrainian Weekly*, December 8, 1991, 1, 5; Khristina Lew, "Delving into Eastern Ukraine on the Eve of Nationhood," *Ukrainian Weekly*, December 22, 1991, 8–9; Kravchuk, *Maiemo te, shcho maiemo*, 118; interview with Leonid Kravchuk in *Rozpad Radians'koho Soiuzu. Usna istoriia nezalezhnoï Ukraïny 1988–91*, tape 9, http://oralhistory .org.ua/interview-ua/510/.

23. Cherniaev, *Sovmestnyi iskhod*, 1030–1031; *Soiuz mozhno bylo sokhranit'. Belaia kniga. Dokumenty i fakty o politike M. S. Gorbacheva po reformirovaniiu i sokhraneniu mnogonatsional'nogo gosudarsta*, 2nd ed. (Moscow, 2007), 418.

24. George Bush and Brent Scowcroft, *A World Transformed* (New York, 1998), 554; *Soiuz mozhno bylo sokhranit'*, 420.

CHAPTER 15

1. "Telcon with President Boris Yeltsin of the Republic of Russia," November 30, 1991, Bush Presidential Library, Memcons and Telcons, http://bushlibrary. tamu.edu/research/pdfs/memcons_telcons/1991-11-30—Yeltsin.pdf; George Bush and Brent Scowcroft, *A World Transformed* (New York, 1998), 552–553; author's interview with Nicholas Burns, Harvard University, June 15, 2012.

2. Interview with Stanislaŭ Shushkevich, Davis Center, Harvard University, April 17, 2000; Bush and Scowcroft, *A World Transformed*, 552–554.

3. *Soiuz mozhno bylo sokhranit'. Belaia kniga. Dokumenty i fakty o politike M. S. Gorbacheva po reformirovaniiu i sokhraneniu mnogonatsional'nogo gosudarsta*, 2nd ed. (Moscow, 2007), 424.

4. Petr Aven and Al'fred Kokh, "El'tsin sluzhil nam!" interview with Gennadii Burbulis, *Forbes* (Russian edition), July 22, 2010, www.forbes.ru /node/53407/print; David Remnick, *Resurrection: The Struggle for a New Russia* (New York, 1998), 25.

5. Aleksandr Solzhenitsyn, "Kak nam obustroit' Rossiiu?" *Komsomol'skaia pravda*, September 18, 1990; Aleksandr Solzhenitsyn, *Rebuilding Russia: Reflections and Tentative Proposals*, trans. Alexis Klimoff (New York, 1991).

6. Roman Solchanyk, *Ukraine and Russia: The Post-Soviet Transition* (Oxford, 2001), 38; Aven and Kokh, "El'tsin sluzhil nam!"

7. "Newsbriefs," *Ukrainian Weekly*, December 15, 1991; Leonid Kravchuk, *Maiemo te, shcho maiemo. Spohady i rozdumy* (Kyiv, 2002), 128; Valentyn Chemerys, *Prezydent. Roman-ese* (Kyiv, 1994), 245–247, 260–261.

8. Mykhailo Holubets', *Bilovezha ochyma uchasnyka* (Lviv, 1996), 9; "Shushkevich, Stanislav Stanislavovich," in *Kto est' kto v Rossii i blizhnem zarubezh'e. Spravochnik* (Moscow, 1991), 749; Stanislav Shushkevich, "Osval'da ia zapomnil soldafonom," *Izvestiia*, November 21, 2003.

9. David Marples, *Belarus: A Denationalized Nation* (Amsterdam, 1999); Jan Zaprudnik, *Belarus: At a Crossroads in History* (Boulder, CO, 1993).

10. Dmitrii Starostin, "Desiat' let Belovezhskoi pushche," Vesti.ru, December 9, 2001; Stanislav Shushkevich, "Monolog o pushche," *Ogonek*, December 2, 1996.

11. V. V. Semakov, *Belovezhskaia pushcha, 1902–2002* (Minsk, 2002); Peter Duffy, *The Bielski Brothers: The True Story of Three Men Who Defied the Nazis, Built a Village in the Forest, and Saved 1,200 Jews* (New York, 2004).

12. *Katalog fauny Puszczy Białowieskiej* (Warsaw, 2001); Ales' Karliukevich, "Gensek s ruzh'em," *Sovetskaia Belorusiia*, no. 113 (June 21, 2001); Anatolii Cherniaev, Memo for Gorbachev on the organization of Chancellor Kohl's visit to the USSR, June 17, 1991, Gorbachev Foundation Archive, fond 2, no. 8943.1.

13. Mechislav Dmukhovskii, "Belovezhskie tainy," *Sovetskaia Belorussiia. Sobesednik*, December 12, 2003; Leonid Kravchuk, "Shushkevich i El'tsin predstavliali sebia, a ia—voliu naroda," UNIAN, December 5, 2006; Kryzhanivs'kyi, "Tostiv bulo"; Aleksandr Korzhakov, *Boris El'tsin: ot rassveta do zakata* (Moscow, 1997), 127; Viacheslav Kebich, *Iskushenie vlast"iu. Iz zhizni prem"er-ministra* (Minsk, 2008), 190–194.

14. "Kebich, Viacheslav Frantsevich," in *Kto est' kto v Rossii i blizhnem zarubezh'e. Spravochnik* (Moscow, 1991).

15. Mariia Èismont, "Mikhail Babich, byvshii ofitser okhrany Viacheslava Kebicha: V Viskuliakh opasalis' predatel'stva," *Narodnaia volia*, December 12, 2001; *Soiuz mozhno bylo sokhranit'*, 432; Kravchenko, "Belarus' na rasput'eZapiski diplomata i politika," *Narodnaia volia*, nos. 154–157, September 30, 2006.

16. *Soiuz mozhno bylo sokhranit'*, 440; Kravchuk, *Maiemo te, shcho maiemo*, 129–130.

17. Aven and Kokh, "El'tsin sluzhil nam!"; Iurii Zainashev, "Belorusskaia pushcha: chto èto bylo?" *Novye izvestiia*, December 8, 2006; Iurii Shapoval, "Dvi hrudnevi istoriï ne bez morali," *Den'*, December 10, 2004; M. Mikhal'chenko and V. Andrushchenko, *Belovezh'e. L. Kravchuk, 1991–1995* (Kyiv, 1996), 99.

18. Chemerys, *Prezydent*, 268–269; *Soiuz mozhno bylo sokhranit'*, 445–447; Kravchenko, "Belarus' na rasput'e."

19. *Soiuz mozhno bylo sokhranit'*, 433; Kebich, *Iskushenie vlast'iu*, 199–200; Èismont, "Mikhail Babich."

20. Oleg Moroz, "Za riumkoi kliuchevye voprosy ne reshalis'" (interview with Yegor Gaidar), *Newsland*, May 2, 2011, www.newsland.ru/news/detail /id/690529; Kravchenko, "Belarus' na rasput'e."

21. Holubets', *Bilovezha,* 13–14; Kryzhanivs'kyi, "Tostiv bulo"; Kravchenko, "Belarus' na rasput'e."

22. Kravchuk, "Shushkevich i El'tsin predstavliali sebia"; Chemerys, *Prezydent,* 269; Sergei Shakhrai, "Nam udalos' predotvratit' iugoslavskii stsenarii," *Novye izvestiia,* December 8, 2006; Kebich, *Iskushenie vlast'iu,* 201.

23. Gaidar, "Za riumkoi"; Kravchuk, *Maiemo te, shcho maiemo,* 125; interview with Leonid Kravchuk, *Rozpad Radianskoho Soiuzu,* tape 9, http://oralhistory.org.ua/interview-ua/510/; Chemerys, *Prezydent,* 267, 271; Kravchuk, "Shushkevich i El'tsin predstavliali sebia"; Holubets', *Bilovezha,* 13; Kryzhanivs'kyi, "Tostiv bulo."

24. Holubets', *Bilovezha,* 15; Sergei Pashkov, "Sovetskii Soiuz. Poslednie dni," *Vesti nedeli,* December 2, 2001; Igor' Kozhevin, "15 let kazhdyi za sebia," Vesti. ru, December 8, 2006; Stanislav Shushkevich, "Ni po odnomu punktu ne bylo raznoglasii," *Ezhednevnik,* December 9, 2008; *Soiuz mozhno bylo sokhranit',* 435.

25. *Raspad SSSR: Dokumenty i fakty (1986–1992 gg.),* vol. 1, *Normativnye akty. Ofitsial'nye soobshcheniia,* ed. S. M. Shakhrai (Moscow, 2009), 1028–1031.

26. Yegor Gaidar, *Dni porazhenii i pobed* (Moscow, 1996), 148–150; Aven and Kokh, "El'tsin sluzhil nam!"

27. Kebich, *Iskushenie vlast'iu,* 202.

28. Kozhevin, "15 let"; Iakov Alekseichik, "Kholodnyi dekabr' v Viskuliakh," *Sem' dnei,* no. 49 (December 8, 2001).

29. Kravchuk, *Maiemo te, shcho maiemo,* 132.

30. Korzhakov, *Boris Yeltsin,* 128; Holubets', *Bilovezha,* 16; Kravchuk, *Maiemo te, shcho maiemo,* 125; interview with Leonid Kravchuk, *Rozpad Radianskoho Soiuzu,* tape 9, http://oralhistory.org.ua/interview-ua/510.

31. Gaidar, "Za riumkoi"; Kebich, *Iskushenie vlast'iu,* 207–208; "Iz besedy prezidenta Kazakhstana N. Nazarbaeva s redaktorami moskovskikh gazet 15 aprelia 1995 g.," Gorbachev Fund, www.gorby.ru/userfiles/file/iz_besedy_prezidenta_kazakhstana_n.pdf; Christopher Robbins, *Apples Are from Kazakhstan* (New York, 2008), 282–285; Kravchenko, "Belarus' na rasput'e."

32. Kebich, *Iskushenie vlast'iu,* 202–203.

33. Evgenii Shaposhnikov, *Vybor. Zapiski glavnokomanduiushchego* (Moscow, 1993), 125–127.

34. Ibid.; Mikhail Gorbachev, *Memoirs* (New York, 1995), 659; Shakhrai, "Nam udalos'"; Gaidar, "Za riumkoi"; Gaidar, *Dni porazhenii i pobed,* 148–150; "Belovezhskoe ekho," NTV, December 11, 2011.

35. Kravchenko, "Belarus' na rasput'e"; Kebich, *Iskushenie vlast'iu,* 206–207; Chemerys, *Prezydent,* 270.

36. Leonid Kravchuk, "V saune ne parilsia, shampanskogo ne pil," http://bp21.org.by/ru/art/a051207.html; Telcon with President Yeltsin of the Republic of Russia, December 8, 1991, Bush Presidential Library, Memcons

and Telcons, http://bushlibrary.tamu.edu/research/pdfs/memcons_telcons /1991-12-08—Yeltsin.pdf.

37. Shushkevich, "Monolog o pushche"; Kebich, *Iskushenie vlast'iu*, 210–211; Kravchuk, *Maiemo te, shcho maiemo*, 131–132; Gorbachev, *Memoirs*, 659.

38. Michael R. Beschloss and Strobe Talbott, *At the Highest Levels: The Inside Story of the End of the Cold War* (Boston, 1993), 450; Holubets', *Bilovezha*, 17; Chemerys, *Prezydent*, 274; Dmukhovskii, "Belovezhskie tainy"; Anatolii Cherniaev, *Sovmestnyi iskhod. Dnevnik dvukh ėpokh, 1972–1991 gody* (Moscow, 2008), 1034.

39. Chemerys, *Prezydent*, 274.

40. Kravchenko, "Belarus' na rasput'e"; Dmukhovskii, "Belovezhskie tainy."

CHAPTER 16

1. Conor O'Clery, *Moscow, December 25, 1991: The Last Days of the Soviet Union* (New York, 2011), 192–193.

2. Anatolii Cherniaev, *Sovmestnyi iskhod. Dnevnik dvukh ėpokh, 1972–1991 gody* (Moscow, 2008), 1034; *Soiuz mozhno bylo sokhranit'. Belaia kniga. Dokumenty i fakty o politike M. S. Gorbacheva po reformirovaniiu i sokhraneniiu mnogonatsional'nogo gosudarsta*, 2nd ed. (Moscow, 2007), 465; O'Clery, *Moscow*, 192–193; Georgii Shakhnazarov, *Tsena svobody. Reformatsiia Gorbacheva glazami ego pomoshchnika* (Moscow, 1993), 303.

3. Valentyn Chemerys, *Prezydent. Roman-ese* (Kyiv, 1994), 274–275; Leonid Kravchuk, *Maiemo te, shcho maiemo. Spohady i rozdumy* (Kyiv, 2002), 133.

4. *Soiuz mozhno bylo sokhranit'*, 465–466; Andrei Grachev, *Gorbachev. Chelovek, kotoryi khotel kak luchshe* (Moscow, 2001), 401ff.; Michael R. Beschloss and Strobe Talbott, *At the Highest Levels: The Inside Story of the End of the Cold War* (Boston, 1993), 450; O'Clery, *Moscow*, 192.

5. *Soiuz mozhno bylo sokranit'*, 465–469; Cherniaev, *Sovmestnyi iskhod*, 1034; Evgenii Shaposhnikov, *Vybor. Zapiski glavnokomanduiushchego* (Moscow, 1993), 128; "Stanislav Shushkevich: obresti suverennost', no ne raz"ediniat'sia granitsami," *Rossiiskaia gazeta*, December 10, 1991; "Nursultan Nazarbaev: Ia— pragmatik i budu ottalkivat'sia ot sobytii," *Rossiiskaia gazeta*, December 10, 1991.

6. *Soiuz mozhno bylo sokranit'*, 469–470; Beschloss and Talbott, *At the Highest Levels*, 450.

7. Cherniaev, *Sovmestnyi iskhod*, 1035.

8. Author's interview with Nicholas Burns, Harvard University, June 15, 2012; George Bush and Brent Scowcroft, *A World Transformed* (New York, 1998), 556–557.

9. Shaposhnikov, *Vybor*, 128; "Generaly ukhodiat. Pochemu? K kadrovym peremenam v Genshtabe," *Moskovskie novosti*, December 15, 1991; John Dunlop, *The Rise of Russia and the Fall of the Soviet Empire* (Princeton, NJ, 1995), 272–275; *Soiuz mozhno bylo sokhranit'*, 472.

10. "Ratifitsirovano soglashenie o sodruzhestve nezavisimykh gosudarstv. Ukraina," *Izvestiia,* December 11, 1991; Chrystyna Lapychak, "Ukraine Ratifies Amended Agreement on the Commonwealth," *Ukrainian Weekly,* December 15, 1991, 1–2; author's interview with Kostiantyn Morozov, September 6, 2011.

11. "Ratifitsirovano soglashenie o sodruzhestve nezavisimykh gosudarstv. Belorussiia," *Izvestiia,* December 11, 1991; Petr Kravchenko, "Belarus' na rasput'e. Zapiski diplomata i politika," *Narodnaia volia,* nos. 154–157, September 30, 2006; Viacheslav Kebich, *Iskushenie vlast'iu. Iz zhizni prem'er-ministra* (Minsk, 2008), 216–217.

12. *Soiuz mozhno bylo sokhranit',* 472–474.

13. Dunlop, *The Rise of Russia,* 275; "Armiia ne verit soiuznym strukturam," *Rossiiskaia gazeta,* December 13, 1991; Pavel Palazhchenko, *My Years with Gorbachev and Shevardnadze: The Memoir of a Soviet Interpreter* (University Park, PA, 1997), 352.

14. "Vystuplenie Prezidenta RSFSR B. N. El'tsina," *Rossiiskaia gazeta,* December 13, 1991; *Soiuz mozhno bylo sokhranit',* 477–481.

15. Vadim Medvedev, *V komande Gorbacheva. Vzgliad iznutri* (Moscow, 1994), 227; *V Politbiuro TsK KPSS po zapisiam Anatoliia Cherniaeva, Vadima Medvedeva, Georgiia Shakhnazarova (1985–1991)* (Moscow, 2000), 736–739; "M. Gorbachev o situatsii v strane i o sebe," *Izvestiia,* December 12, 1991; Palazhchenko, *My Years,* 352.

16. Nikolai Portugalov, Memo to Mikhail Gorbachev, December, 1991, Gorbachev Foundation Archive, fond 5, no. 10866.1.

17. Cherniaev, *Sovmestnyi iskhod,* 1036; "Gorbachev brosaet vyzov 'Slavianskomu Soiuzu,'" *Izvestiia,* December 10, 1991.

18. James A. Baker with Thomas M. DeFrank, *The Politics of Diplomacy: Revolution, War and Peace, 1989–1992* (New York, 1995), 563.

19. Ibid., 562–564; "Baker Sees Opportunities and Risks as Soviet Republics Grope for Stability," *New York Times,* December 13, 1991; Thomas Friedman, "Baker Presents Steps to Aid Transition by Soviets," *New York Times,* December 13, 1991; John Lewis Gaddis, *George F. Kennan: An American Life* (New York, 2011); Nicholas Thompson, *The Hawk and the Dove: Paul Nitze, George Kennan and the History of the Cold War* (New York, 2009).

20. Baker, *The Politics of Diplomacy,* 535.

21. Proposed agenda for meeting with the president, December 4, 1991, 1:30 p.m.; December 10, Soviet points for meeting with the president, James A. Baker Papers, box 115, folder 8.

22. Congressional Research Service, "CRS Report to the Congress: U.S. Assistance to the Former Soviet Union," March 1, 2007, www.fas.org/sgp/crs /row/RL32866.pdf; Kurt Tarnoff, "CRS Report to Congress. U.S. Assistance to the Former Soviet Union, 1991–2002: A History of Administration and Congressional Action," updated, January 15, 2002, 1–7, www.policyarchive.org

/handle/10207/bitstreams/914.pdf; Olexiy Haran, "Disintegration of the Soviet Union and the U.S. Position on the Independence of Ukraine," discussion paper 95-09, Center for Science and International Affairs, John F. Kennedy School of Government, Harvard University, August 1995, http://belfercenter. ksg.harvard.edu/publication/2933/disintegration_of_the_soviet_union_and _the_us_position_on_the_independence_of_ukraine.html.

23. Friedman, "Baker Presents Steps to Aid Transition," A24.

24. Proposed agenda for meeting with the president, December 13, 1991, 11:00 a.m., James A. Baker Papers, box 115, folder 8; James Baker, "The Politics of Diplomacy," Chapter Files, James A. Baker Papers, box 195, folder 5, ch. 31, 7–8.

25. Baker, *The Politics of Diplomacy*, 564.

26. Ibid.; Celestine Bohlen, "Moscow Misery: The Planes Don't Fly and That's Not All," *New York Times*, December 13, 1991.

27. Beschloss and Talbott, *At the Highest Levels*, xi–xiv, 451–452; John Kohan and Strobe Talbott, "I Want to Stay the Course," *Time*, December 23, 1991.

28. Beschloss and Talbott, *At the Highest Levels*, 452–454; Kohan and Talbott, "I Want to Stay the Course."

29. Beschloss and Talbott, *At the Highest Levels*, 455–456; Baker, *The Politics of Diplomacy*, 565; Cherniaev, *Sovmestnyi iskhod*, 1036–1037; Palazhchenko, *My Years*, 252–254.

30. "Telephone Conversation with President Boris Yeltsin of Russia," December 13, 1991, Bush Presidential Library, Memcons and Telcons, http://bushlibrary.tamu.edu/research/pdfs/memcons_telcons/1991-12-13--Yeltsin. pdf; Bush and Scowcroft, *A World Transformed*, 557.

31. "Telephone Conversation with President Gorbachev of the FSU," December 13, 1991, Bush Presidential Library, Memcons and Telcons, http://bushlibrary.tamu.edu/research/pdfs/memcons_telcons/1991-12-13 --Gorbachev.pdf.

32. Bush and Scowcroft, *A World Transformed*, 556–558.

33. Beschloss and Talbott, *At the Highest Levels*, 455–456; Baker, *The Politics of Diplomacy*, 572.

34. Alfred Kokh and Petr Aven, "Andrei Kozyrev—nastoiashchii kamikadze," *Forbes*, Russian edition, September 28, 2011, www.forbes.ru/ ekonomika/lyudi/74501-andrei-kozyrev-nastoyashchii-kamikadze; Baker, The *Politics of Diplomacy*, 564–567.

35. Baker, *The Politics of Diplomacy*, 567–569; Konstantin Blagodarov, "Ot shedevrov Tsereteli liudi prosto obaldeli," *Komsomol'skaia pravda*, September 4, 2002.

36. "JAB Notes from 12/16/91 Mtg. w/Russian Pres. Yeltsin at the Kremlin, St. Catherine's Hall, Moscow, USSR," James A. Baker Papers, box 176, folder 28; "JAB Notes from 1-on-1 Mtg. w/B. Yeltsin During Which Command and Control of Nuclear Weapons Was Discussed 12/16/91," James A. Baker Papers,

box 110, folder 10; Baker, *The Politics of Diplomacy*, 569–572; Beschloss and Talbott, *At the Highest Levels*, 456–457; Kokh and Aven, "Andrei Kozyrev: nastoiashchii kamikadze"; Palazhchenko, *My Years*, 353.

37. Baker, *The Politics of Diplomacy*, 575–578; Kokh and Aven, "Andrei Kozyrev: nastoiashchii kamikadze."

38. "Telephone Conversation with President Gorbachev of the FSU," December 13, 1991, Bush Presidential Library, Memcons and Telcons, http://bushlibrary.tamu.edu/research/pdfs/memcons_telcons/1991-12-13 --Gorbachev.pdf; Bush and Scowcroft, *A World Transformed*, 556–658.

39. Baker, *The Politics of Diplomacy*, 573–574; Palazhchenko, *My Years*, 355–356.

40. Anatolii Cherniaev, memo, "K besede s Beikerom," December 1991, Gorbachev Foundation Archive, fond 2, no. 19465.1; Cherniaev, *Sovmestnyi iskhod*, 1037.

CHAPTER 17

1. "Vstrecha dvukh prezidentov," *Rossiiskaia gazeta*, December 18, 1991; "Rossiiane podderzhivaiut sozdanie SNG," *Nezavisimaia gazeta*, December 18, 1991.

2. Schedules for December 17, 18, and 19, 1991, James A. Baker Papers, box 110, folder 10.

3. James A. Baker with Thomas M. DeFrank, *The Politics of Diplomacy: Revolution, War and Peace, 1989–1992* (New York, 1995), 578–581.

4. "Nursultan Nazarbaev: Ia pragmatik i budu ottalkivat'sia ot sobytii," *Rossiiskaia gazeta*, December 10, 1991; "Prisiaga Nazarbaeva," *Rossiiskaia gazeta*, December 11, 1991; "Kazakhstan ob"iavil nezavisimost'," *Izvestiia*, December 17, 1991.

5. "JAB Core Points Used During Trip to Moscow, Bishkek, Alma Ata, Minsk and Kiev, 12/15–18/91," James A. Baker Papers, box 110, folder 10; Baker, *The Politics of Diplomacy*, 581, 585–586; "Dzh. Beiker—pervyi gost' nezavisimogo Kazakhstana," *Izvestiia*, December 17, 1991.

6. James Baker, "The Politics of Diplomacy," Chapter Files, James A. Baker Papers, box 195, folder 5, chs. 31, 36.

7. Baker, *The Politics of Diplomacy*, 580–582. Cf. "Zaiavlenie glav gosudarstv Respublika Kazakhstan, Respublika Kyrgyzstan, Respublika Tadzhikistan, Respublika Turkmenistan, Respublika Uzbekistan," *Izvestiia*, December 17, 1991.

8. "Godovshchina dekabr'skikh sobytii proshla spokoino," *Nezavisimaia gazeta*, December 18, 1991.

9. Uak Arken Battaluly, *Materialy genotsida, organizovannogo N. Nazarbaevym protiv Kazakhskogo naroda v dekabre 1986 goda* (Moscow, 2000); Khadzhimurat Kozhanazarov and Aigul Mataeva, "Pravda bessmertna," *Soldat*, March 27, 2003.

10. Baker, *The Politics of Diplomacy*, 538.

11. Bruce Pannier, "Kazakhstan: The Forgotten Famine," Radio Free Europe, December 28, 2007, www.rferl.org/content/article/1079304.html; "Separatizm russkikh regionov v Kazakhstane—vina rukovodstva respubliki," *Nezavisimaia gazeta,* December 11, 1991.

12. "Interv'iu prezidenta Kazakhstana," *Rossiiskaia gazeta,* December 21, 1991.

13. *Soiuz mozhno bylo sokhranit'. Belaia kniga. Dokumenty i fakty o politike M. S. Gorbacheva po reformirovaniiu i sokhraneniiu mnogonatsional'nogo gosudarsta,* 2nd ed. (Moscow, 2007), 486–487.

14. Leonid Levitin, *Uzbekistan na istoricheskom povorote* (Tashkent, 2005), 8–12.

15. "O pis'me v TsK KPSS rabotnikov prokuratury SSSR tt. Gdliana T. Kh. i Ivanova N. V. ot 11 noiabria 1986 goda," RGANI, fond 89, op. 24, no. 18; "TsK KPSS. O khode vypolneniia postanovleniia Politbiuro no. P151/3," RGANI, fond 89, op. 24, no. 19; Anatolii Sobchak, *Khozhdenie vo vlast'. Rasskaz o rozhdenii parlamenta* (Moscow, 1991), chap. 5.

16. "Khlopkovoe delo," YouTube video posted by edglezin, April 1, 2011, www.youtube.com/watch?v=sIKYYY3r_vo; Daniel C. Waugh, *Tamerlane's Heirs: Perspectives on 1991 and Its Aftermath in Central Asia* (Seattle, 2011), 27; "Itogi Ashgabatskoi vstrechi vyzvali vzdokh oblegcheniia v strane," *Izvestiia,* December 14, 1991.

17. Waugh, *Tamerlane's Heirs,* 26–51; "Itogi Ashgabatskoi vstrechi vyzvali vzdokh oblegcheniia v strane," *Izvestiia,* December 14, 1991.

18. "Uchastniki vstrechi v Ashgabate gotovy stat chlenami sodruzhestva. No ravnopravnymi," *Izvestiia,* December 13, 1991.

19. "Put' k sodruzhestvu: Minsk—Ashgabat—Alma-Ata," *Izvestiia,* December 19, 1991; "Istoriia Sovetskogo Soiuza zavershaetsia v stolitse Kazakhstana," *Izvestiia,* December 20, 1991; "Aiaz Mutalibov tozhe v Alma-Ate," *Nezavisimaia gazeta,* December 21, 1991.

20. "Gorbachev predlagaet nazvanie: Sodruzhestvo evropeiskikh i aziatskikh gosudarstv—SEAZ," *Izvestiia,* December 19, 1991; *Soiuz mozhno bylo sokhranit',* 488–492.

21. Anatolii Cherniaev, *Sovmestnyi iskhod. Dnevnik dvukh ėpokh, 1972–1991 gody* (Moscow, 2008), 1037; Mikhail Gorbachev, *Memoirs* (New York, 1995), 660.

22. Boris El'tsin, "My perezhili tragicheskii ėksperiment," *Rossiiskaia gazeta,* December 19, 1991.

23. "Kakie rabochie i predstavitel'nye organy mogut byt' v SNG," *Izvestiia,* December 19, 1991, 2; "Respublika vernet sebe staryi gerb," *Nezavisimaia gazeta,* December 19, 1991.

24. Author's interview with General Kostiantyn Morozov, September 6, 2011; "Oppozitsiia nakalivaet obstanovku. Leonid Kravchuk rukovodit gosudarstvom," *Nezavisimaia gazeta,* December 21, 1991; "Ratifitsirovano soglashenie o sodzruzhestve nezavisimykh gosudarstv. Ukraina," *Izvestiia,*

December 11, 1991; "Sotsiologicheskii opros na aktual'nuiu temu," *Izvestiia*, December 12, 1991.

25. "JAB Notes from 12/18/91 Mtg. w/Ukraine Pres. Kravchuk at Mariinskiy Palace in Kiev, Ukraine," James A. Baker Papers, box 110, folder 10; Baker, *The Politics of Diplomacy*, 581–583.

26. "JAB Notes from 12/18/91 Mtg. w/Supreme Soviet Chairman Shushkevich at the Government Res. Minsk, Belarussia [[*sic*]]," James A. Baker Papers, box 110, folder 10; "Stanislav Shushkevich: obresti suverennost', no ne raz"ediniat'sia granitsami," *Rossiiskaia gazeta*, December 10, 1991; "Belorusskaia delegatsiia ser'eznee drugikh otneslas' k peregovoram," *Nezavisimaia gazeta*, December 28, 1991; "Moldova vstupit v SNG?" *Nezavisimaia gazeta*, December 21, 1991.

27. "Stanet li Belovezhskaia pushcha karabakhskoi," *Rossiiskaia gazeta*, December 21, 1991; Petr Kravchenko, "Belarus' na rasput'e. Zapiski diplomata i politika," *Narodnaia volia*, nos. 154–157, September 30, 2006; Rossiia priznala nezavisimost' Moldovy," *Nezavisimaia gazeta*, December 19, 1991.

28. "Shturmuiut politsiiu," *Nezavisimaia gazeta*, December 10, 1991; "Snova krov' v Dubossarakh," *Izvestiia*, December 14, 1991; "Komitet samooborony Nagorno-Karabakhskoi respubliki," *Izvestiia*, December 20, 1991; "Armeniia ukrepliaet granitsy," ibid., 2; "Nezavisimost' tol'ko togda chego-nibud' stoit, kogda ona umeet sebia zashchishchat'. Novye ukazy prezidenta Armenii," *Nezavisimaia gazeta*, December 21, 1991; "Bezopasnost' ne garantiruetsia," *Rossiiskaia gazeta*, December 21, 1991.

29. Evgenii Shaposhnikov, *Vybor. Zapiski glavnokomanduiushchego* (Moscow, 1993), 129–130.

30. "Istoriia Sovetskogo Soiuza zavershaetsia v stolitse Kazakhstana," *Izvestiia*, December 20, 1991, 1; "Prezident sozdaet armiiu. Chem vse-taki komanduet Leonid Kravchuk?" *Nezavisimaia gazeta*, December 17, 1991; Kostiantyn P. Morozov, *Above and Beyond: From Soviet General to Ukrainian State Builder* (Cambridge, MA, 2000), 183–193; Leonid Kravchuk, *Maiemo te, shcho maiemo. Spohady i rozdumy* (Kyiv, 2002), 145.

31. *Soiuz mozhno bylo sokhranit'*, 493–503; *Raspad SSSR: Dokumenty i fakty (1986–1992 gg.)*, vol. 1, *Normativnye akty. Ofitsial'nye soobshcheniia*, ed. S. M. Shakhrai (Moscow, 2009), 1044–1053; Morozov, *Above and Beyond*, 187–188; Pavel Palazhchenko, *My Years with Gorbachev and Shevardnadze: The Memoir of a Soviet Interpreter* (University Park, PA, 1997), 359–360.

32. *Soiuz mozhno bylo sokhranit'*, 499.

33. Telecon with Nursultan Nazarbayev, Saturday, December 21, 1991, 12:55 EST; Baker, *The Politics of Diplomacy*, 585.

34. "V Alma-Ate rodilos' sodruzhestvo 11 nezavisimykh gosudarstv," *Izvestiia*, December 23, 1991; Cherniaev, *Sovmestnyi iskhod*, 1039.

CHAPTER 18

1. Anatolii Cherniaev, *Sovmestnyi iskhod. Dnevnik dvukh ėpokh, 1972–1991 gody* (Moscow, 2008), 1039; Aleksandr Korzhakov, *Boris El'tsin: ot rassveta do zakata* (Moscow, 1997), 129–130; Conor O'Clery, *Moscow, December 25, 1991: The Last Days of the Soviet Union* (New York, 2011), 207–208.

2. Cherniaev, *Sovmestnyi iskhod*, 1039–1044; O'Clery, *Moscow*, 208.

3. Aleksandr Iakovlev, *Sumerki* (Moscow, 2005), 506–507; Georgii Shakhnazarov, *Tsena svobody. Reformatsiia Gorbacheva glazami ego pomoshchnika* (Moscow, 1993), 307; O'Clery, *Moscow*, 208–219; Boris Yeltsin, *The Struggle for Russia*, trans. Catherine A. Fitzpatrick (New York, 1994), 120–121; Korzhakov, *Yeltsin*, 129–130; Cherniaev, *Sovmestnyi iskhod*, 1040, 1042.

4. Michael Dobbs, *Down with Big Brother: The Fall of the Soviet Empire* (New York, 1997), 447–448; Boris Pankin, *The Last Hundred Days of the Soviet Union* (London, 1996), 86; Yeltsin, *The Struggle for Russia*, 122–123, 305–316; O'Clery, *Moscow*, 211–214; Korzhakov, *El'tsin*, 137–138.

5. Iakovlev, *Sumerki*, 508.

6. Ibid., 507; Memorandum of telephone conversation with President Boris Yeltsin, December 23, 1991, Bush Presidential Library, Memcons and Telcons, http://bushlibrary.tamu.edu/research/pdfs/memcons_telcons/1991-12-23—Yeltsin.pdf.

7. Cherniaev, *Sovmestnyi iskhod*, 1042; O'Clery, *Moscow*, 208, 211–214.

8. O'Clery, *Moscow*, 25–26.

9. Pavel Palazhchenko, *My Years with Gorbachev and Shevardnadze: The Memoir of a Soviet Interpreter* (University Park, PA, 1997), 364–366; "Telecon with Mikhail Gorbachev, President of the Soviet Union," December 25, 1991, Bush Presidential Library, Memcons and Telcons, http://bushlibrary.tamu.edu/research/pdfs/memcons_telcons/1991-12-25—Gorbachev.pdf.

10. Palazhchenko, *My Years*, 365.

11. O'Clery, *Moscow*, 201–205, 218, 226.

12. Ibid., 222, 225; Cherniaev, *Sovmestnyi iskhod*, 1040–1042; "Obrashchenie M. S. Gorbacheva k narodu," December 1991, Gorbachev Foundation Archive, fond 5, no. 10868; Andrei Grachev, "Proekt obrashcheniia Prezidenta SSSR k narodu," December 14, 1991, Gorbachev Foundation Archive, fond 5, no. 10884.1; *Soiuz mozhno bylo sokhranit'. Belaia kniga. Dokumenty i fakty o politike M. S. Gorbacheva po reformirovaniiu i sokhraneniiu mnogonatsional'nogo gosudarsta*, 2nd ed. (Moscow, 2007), 504–507; "Yeltsin po-prezhnemu populiaren. Po krainei mere v Moskve," *Nezavisimaia gazeta*, December 19, 1991.

13. Cherniaev, *Sovmestnyi iskhod*, 1042–1043; Evgenii Shaposhnikov, *Vybor. Zapiski glavnokomanduiushchego* (Moscow, 1993), 136; Mikhail Gorbachev,

Memoirs (New York, 1995), 671–672; *Soiuz mozhno bylo sokhranit'*, 507; Palazhchenko, *My Years,* 366–367; O'Clery, *Moscow,* 231–237.

14. O'Clery, *Moscow,* 236–237, 241–247; Andrei Grachev, *Gorbachev. Chelovek, kotoryi khotel kak luchshe* (Moscow, 2001), 418; Gorbachev, *Memoirs,* 671; Cherniaev, *My Years,* 399; Cherniaev, *Sovmestnyi iskhod,* 1043.

15. Michael R. Beschloss and Strobe Talbott, *At the Highest Levels: The Inside Story of the End of the Cold War* (Boston, 1993), 464.

16. Nick Burns to Dennis Ross and Thomas Niles, December 23, 1991; "Draft Statement on the Resignation of President Gorbachev," Bush Presidential Library, Presidential Records, National Security Council, Nicholas R. Burns Series, Chronological Files: December 1991, no. 1. Cf. "Statement on the Resignation of Mikhail Gorbachev as President of the Soviet Union," December 25, 1991, Bush Presidential Library, Public Papers, http://bushlibrary.tamu.edu/research/public_papers.php?id=3790&year=1991&month=12.

17. Author's interview with Nicholas Burns, Harvard University, June 15, 2012; Beschloss and Talbott, *At the Highest Levels,* 459–460; Nick Burns to Ron McMullen, United States Military Academy, West Point, December 31, 1991, Bush Presidential Library, Presidential Records, National Security Council, Nicholas R. Burns Series, Chronological Files: December 1991, no. 1.

18. "Address on Gorbachev Resignation," December 25, 1991, C-SPAN, http://www.c-spanvideo.org/program/23549-1>; Address to the Nation on the Commonwealth of Independent States," December 25, 1991, Bush Presidential Library, Public Papers, http://bushlibrary.tamu.edu/research/public_papers.php?id=3791&year=1991&month=12.

19. Author's interview with Nicholas Burns, Harvard University, June 15, 2012.

20. Address to the Nation on the Commonwealth of Independent States," December 25, 1991, Bush Presidential Library, Public Papers, http://bushlibrary.tamu.edu/research/public_papers.php?id=3791&year=1991&month=12; From Secstate to all diplomatic and consular posts, "U.S. Policy on Recognition of Former Soviet Republics. Press Guidance," December 28, 1991, Bush Presidential Library, Presidential Records, National Security Council, John A. Gordon Series, Subject Files: Russia, December 1991.

21. "The President's News Conference," December 28, 1991, Bush Presidential Library, Public Papers, http://bushlibrary.tamu.edu/research/public_papers.php?id=3792&year=1991&month=12.

22. James Baker to Mikhail Gorbachev, December 29, 1991, James A. Baker Papers, box 110, folder 10.

23. O'Clery, *Moscow,* 261–262; Cherniaev, *Sovmestnyi iskhod,* 1043–1044; Grachev, *Gorbachev,* 420.

24. Gorbachev, *Memoirs,* 672; Yeltsin, *The Struggle for Russia,* 124.

25. Cherniaev, *Sovmestnyi iskhod,* 1043–1044.

26. Ibid., 1042.

27. Gorbachev, *Memoirs*, 672; Cherniaev, *Sovmestnyi iskhod*, 1042–1043; Grachev, *Gorbachev*, 417–418.

28. O'Clery, *Moscow*, 266–267.

29. Iakovlev, *Sumerki*, 555.

30. Gorbachev, *Memoirs*, 671; Yeltsin, *The Struggle for Russia*, 124; Korzhakov, *El'tsin*, 139.

31. Timothy J. Colton, *Yeltsin: A Life* (New York, 2008), 140–150.

EPILOGUE

1. State of the Union Address, January 28, 1991, CSPAN, http://www.c-spanvideo.org/program/23999-1.

2. Address before a Joint Session of the Congress on the State of the Union, January 28, 1992, Bush Presidential Library, Public Papers, http://bushlibrary.tamu.edu/research/public_papers.php?id=3886&year=1992&month=01.

3. "Bush and Gorbachev Declare End of Cold War," History, A&E Television Networks, History.com, www.history.com/speeches/bush-and-gorbachev-declare-end-of-cold-war#bush-and-gorbachev-declare-end-of-cold-war; Karen Holser, "The First True Post–Cold War Summit," *Baltimore Sun*, July 28, 1991; "Bush Told Gorbachev to Ignore 'Crowing' over Cold War Victory," *Seattle Times*, October 26, 1992.

4. John R. Young, "In State of Union, President Evokes Spirit of Gulf War," *Washington Post*, January 29, 1991.

5. George Bush and Brent Scowcroft, *A World Transformed* (New York, 1998), 559–561; Stephen Kotkin, *Armageddon Averted: The Soviet Collapse, 1970–2000* (Oxford, 2001), 185; Robert M. Gates, *From the Shadows: The Ultimate Insider's Story of Five Presidents and How they Won the Cold War* (New York, 1996), 552.

6. Jack Matlock, *Autopsy on an Empire: The American Ambassador's Account of the Collapse of the Soviet Union* (New York, 1995), 667–672; "The End of the Cold War, the Collapse of Communism, and the Fall of the Soviet Union," part 4 of "The Collapse of the Soviet Union and the End of the Cold War: A Diplomat Looks Back," interview of Jack Matlock by Harry Kreisler, "Conversations with History" series, Institute of International Studies, University of California, Berkeley, February 13, 1997, http://globetrotter.berkeley.edu/conversations/Matlock/matlock-con4.html.

7. George F. Kennan, "Witness to the Fall," *New York Review of Books*, November 1995, 7–10, here 7.

8. Mikhail Gorbachev, *Memoirs* (New York, 1995), 1046.

9. Mark Beissinger, "The Persistent Ambiguity of Empire," *Post-Soviet Affairs* no. 11 (1995); Mark R. Beissinger, "Rethinking Empire in the Wake of

Soviet Collapse," in *Ethnic Politics and Post-Communism: Theories and Practice*, ed. Zoltan Barany and Robert Moser (Ithaca, NY, 2005), 14–44; S. Becker, "Russia and the Concept of Empire," *Ab Imperio*, 2000, nos. 3–4: 329–342; Terry Martin, *The Affirmative Action Empire: Nations and Nationalism in the Soviet Union, 1923–1939* (Ithaca, NY, 2001); Terry Martin, "The Soviet Union as Empire: Salvaging a Dubious Theoretical Category," *Ab Imperio*, 2002, no. 2: 91–105; Jane Burbank and Frederick Cooper, *Empires in World History: Power and Politics of Difference* (Princeton, NJ, 2010), chap. 14; Dominic Lieven, *Empire: The Russian Empire and Its Rivals* (New Haven, CT, 2002), chap. 9; S. M. Plokhy, *Yalta: The Price of Peace* (New York, 2010), chap. 14.

10. Gorbachev, *Memoirs*, 651–657; Evgenii Shaposhnikov, *Vybor. Zapiski glavnokomanduiushchego* (Moscow, 1993), 102.

11. Petr Aven and Al'fred Kokh, "El'tsin sluzhil nam!," interview with Gennadii Burbulis, *Forbes* (Russian edition), July 22, 2010, www.forbes.ru/node/53407/print.

12. Boris Yeltsin, *The Struggle for Russia*, trans. Catherine A. Fitzpatrick (New York, 1994), 116; Gorbachev, *Memoirs*, 658; interview with Valentin Varennikov in *Rozpad Radians'koho Soiuzu. Usna istoriia nezalezhnoï Ukraïny 1988–91*, tape 2, http://oralhistory.org.ua/interview-ua/401/.

13. Francis Fukuyama, "The End of History," *National Interest*, Summer 1989; Francis Fukuyama, *The End of History and the Last Man* (New York, 1992).

14. George Herring, *From Colony to Superpower: U.S. Foreign Relations Since 1776* (New York, 2008), 914; C. J. Chivers, "Russia Will Pursue Democracy, but in Its Own Way, Putin Says," *New York Times*, April 26, 2005.

15. Edward Lucas, *The New Cold War: Putin's Russia and the Threat to the West* (New York, 2009).

16. Craig Unger, *American Armageddon: How the Delusions of Neoconservatives and the Christian Right Triggered the Descent of America—and Still Imperil Our Future* (New York, 2007), 115–117; "Iraq War: 190,000 Lives, $2.2 Trillion," press release, Costs of War Project, Brown University, March 14, 2013, http://news.brown.edu/pressreleases/2013/03/warcosts.

17. George W. Bush, "Commencement Address at the United States Military Academy at West Point, West Point, New York," June 1, 2002, http://www.presidentialrhetoric.com/speeches/06.01.02.html; George W. Bush, "Freedom in Iraq and the Middle East: Address at the 20th Anniversary of the National Endowment for Democracy, Washington, D.C.," November 6, 2003, http://www.presidentialrhetoric.com/speeches/11.06.03.html.

Index